Marriages of Inconvenience
The politics of coalitions in South Africa

EDITED BY
Susan Booysen

First published by the Mapungubwe Institute for Strategic Reflection (MISTRA) in 2021

142 Western Service Road
Woodmead
Johannesburg

Copyright © MISTRA, 2021

ISBN 978-1-920690-26-7

Production and design by Jacana Media, 2021
Cover design: Hothouse Specialist Graphic Designers
Text editor: Tracey Hawthorne
Copy editor: Lara Jacob
Proofreader: Megan Mance
Designer: Ryan Layton
Indexer: Arnia van Vuuren

Set in Stempel Garamond 10.5/15pt

Please cite this publication as follows:
MISTRA. 2021. Booysen, S. (ed.) *Marriages of Inconvenience: The politics of coalitions in South Africa*. Johannesburg: Mapungubwe Institute for Strategic Reflection

All rights reserved. Without limiting the rights under copyright reserved above, no part of this publication may be reproduced, stored in or introduced into a retrieval system, or transmitted, in any form or by any means (electronic, mechanical, photocopying, recording or otherwise), without prior written permission of the copyright holder and/or the publisher.

This book is sold subject to the condition that it shall not, by way of trade or otherwise, be lent, re-sold, hired out or otherwise circulated without the publisher's prior consent in any form of binding or cover other than that in which it is published and without a similar condition being imposed on the subsequent purchaser.

Contents

Preface vii
Acronyms and abbreviations xi
Glossary of terms xiii
Contributors xxi
Introduction – *Susan Booysen with Amuzweni Ngoma* xxv

PART I
APPROACHING POLITICAL COALITIONS IN SOUTH AFRICA: SOUTH AFRICAN PIVOTS, GLOBAL TRENDS, AFRICAN FOUNDATIONS

Chapter 1: The uneven transition from party dominance to coalitions: South Africa's new politics of instability
– *Susan Booysen*............................... 3

Chapter 2: Local government coalitions across South Africa, 2000–16
– *Mcebisi Ndletyana* 29

Chapter 3: The international experience of coalition politics: Democracy, party systems and stability
– *Heidi Brooks*................................ 57

Chapter 4: Electoral systems, party systems and coalitions: Lessons from Southern Africa
– *Khabele Matlosa*........................... 85

PART II
LEARNING FROM AFRICA'S EXPERIENCES: TRENDS AND CASE STUDIES IN GOVERNMENT AND OPPOSITION

Chapter 5: The legacy of multipartyism on political coalitions and rent-seeking in African elections
– *Grant Masterson* 115

Chapter 6: Coalition politics in Kenya: Superficial assemblages and momentary vehicles to attain power
– *Gilbert Khadiagala* 144

Chapter 7: Coalition governments and unrelenting political instability in Lesotho, 2012–20
– *Motlamelle Kapa* 168

Chapter 8: Political parties, alliance politics and the crisis of governance in Malawi
– *Nandini Patel* 193

PART III
ESTABLISHING LEGAL-CONSTITUTIONAL PARAMETERS AND ADMINISTRATIVE REPERCUSSIONS

Chapter 9: The constitutional-legal dimensions of coalition politics and government in South Africa
– *Pierre de Vos* 221

Chapter 10: The impact of coalitions on South Africa's metropolitan administrations
– *Crispian Olver* 253

PART IV
EXPERIMENTING WITH COALITION GOVERNMENTS: CORE CASE STUDIES AND EMERGING CULTURES

Chapter 11: Power, politics and ideology: Understanding councillors' views on the tug of war in the City of Johannesburg
– *Bonolo Makgale* 291

Chapter 12: The Tshwane metropolitan council: Multiparty and multiple coalitions, and imperilled governance
– *Graeme de Bruyn* 318

Chapter 13: Coalitions in Nelson Mandela Bay: Subversions of democracy
– *Mcebisi Ndletyana* 347

Chapter 14: Full cycles and reinventions in coalitions in the Western Cape and Cape Town metro
– *Sanusha Naidu* 381

Chapter 15: Power transition in KwaZulu-Natal: Post-1994 coalitions in action
– *Lukhona Mnguni* 403

PART V
THE WAY FORWARD: MECHANISMS, LESSONS, FUTURES

Chapter 16: Political conditions that facilitate coalition formation and workability
– *Amuzweni Ngoma* 435

Chapter 17: South Africa's zone of coalition government: Conflict in unity
– *Susan Booysen* 461

Notes 484

Index 499

Preface

For all the critique of interparty coalitions, they become inevitable – and essential instruments of governance – when absolute majorities are not realised in an election. Such governments are, in a sense, a product of the people's will in that the electorate asserts a lack of overwhelming confidence in any single contestant in the polls.

Marriages of Inconvenience: The politics of coalitions in South Africa is a research-based volume that collates and interprets lessons that South Africa should take to heart in managing such eventualities. It draws from domestic experiences as well as from case studies on the rest of the African continent and generic instances further afield.

Coalitions in various iterations have been a part of the South African polity since the attainment of democracy in 1994. This started, nationally, with a 'grand coalition' in the form of a Government of National Unity as mandated in the interim constitution. Coalitions have also found expression in some of the country's provinces. After the transition, multiparty governments were sustained at national and provincial levels either as a matter of necessity due to election outcomes or for other political considerations.

At local government level, coalitions have been relatively commonplace in South Africa from the onset of democratically elected municipalities in 2000, with many situations where no single party attained an absolute majority. This gained prominence from 2016 when many metropolitan governments and some large towns became sites of coalition politics. The coalitions have taken a variety of forms, including co-governance arrangements and service-and-supply agreements where minority governments are propped up by other parties on an issue-by-issue basis.

This volume seeks to distil the factors that leverage successful coalitions, along with those that occasion drawbacks. On the whole, it would seem that South Africa is poorly equipped for coalition politics. While instability in coalitions is not unique, this is not an inevitable product of multiparty governance. In many countries, and indeed in some municipalities in South Africa, there is appreciation of the need to govern cooperatively, constructively and in the popular interest when coalitions become inevitable. In some jurisdictions, the culture of coalition politics has become ingrained.

Relevant to all these experiences are critical issues such as electoral and party systems, political culture and the quality of political leadership.

There is recognition of the stabilising effects of coalitions when political parties co-operate and deliver effective governance, through mature consensus-building. But there is also acknowledgement of co-governing arrangements that evince debilitating competition during various phases of the electoral cycle. Some fall apart and get reconstituted. In these instances, governance and service to the public are severely compromised.

Across various chapters of this volume, critical questions on how to stabilise coalition governance in the South African setting are identified. The first pertains to whether there should be post-election workable coalition agreements that are lodged with, and assessed (but not vetoed) by, a competent authority. The second is whether, at local level, the option of a proportional collective executive system – as distinct from an executive mayoralty – should become mandatory when a single party or coalition of parties is unable to attain an absolute majority. Thirdly, strict observance of the laws on the appointment of bureaucrats and on the role of politicians in administrative decisions, including procurement, is even more crucial under coalition government.

There are, however, limits to constitutional and legislative regulation. Interparty goodwill and cooperative and constructive relations cannot be legislated. The maturity of party leaders and citizen activism are both critical in ensuring stability. And so, engendering a culture of stable coalition politics in South Africa may take time and more practical experience; but it is in the nature of party politics that this cannot be attained in a linear fashion and for all time.

The Mapungubwe Institute for Strategic Reflection (MISTRA) hopes that *Marriages of Inconvenience* will help inform the exercise of coalition politics in South Africa. Understanding the determinants of positive and negative experiences, we hope, will nudge parties towards constructive and sustainable coalitions. At the core of this is a commitment to serve the people's economic, social and political interests.

MISTRA wishes to thank the authors and the teams across the publication chain, as well as those who contribute to the Institute's sustenance. May the insights in this volume promote rigorous discourse and prudent coalition practice!

Joel Netshitenzhe
Executive Director

Acronyms and abbreviations

ABC	All Basotho Convention
ACDP	African Christian Democratic Party
AFORD	Alliance for Democracy
Azapo	Azanian People's Organisation
AIC	African Independent Congress
ANC	African National Congress
BNP	Basotho National Party
CCM	Chama Cha Mapinduzi
Cope	Congress of the People
Cosatu	Congress of South African Trade Unions
DA	Democratic Alliance
DC	Democratic Congress
DPP	Democratic Progressive Party
DRC	Democratic Republic of the Congo
EFF	Economic Freedom Fighters
EPRDF	Ethiopian People's Revolutionary Democratic Front
FF+	Freedom Front Plus
FORD	Forum for the Restoration of Democracy
FPTP	first past the post
Frelimo	Frente de Libertação de Moçambique (Front for the Liberation of Mozambique)
GNU	Government of National Unity
ICOSA	Independent Civic Organisation of South Africa
ID	Independent Democrats
IFP	Inkatha Freedom Party
KANU	Kenya African National Union
KOP	Karoo Ontwikkelingsparty
LCD	Lesotho Congress for Democracy
MCA	Metsimaholo Civic Association
MCP	Malawi Congress Party

MDC	Movement for Democratic Change
MEC	member of the executive council
metro	metropolitan municipality
MISTRA	Mapungubwe Institute for Strategic Reflection
MMC	member of mayoral committee
MP	member of parliament
MPLA	Movimento Popular de Libertação de Angola (Popular Movement for the Liberation of Angola)
Nadeco	National Democratic Convention
NARC	National Rainbow Coalition
NFP	National Freedom Party
NNP	New National Party
NP	National Party
Numsa	National Union of Metalworkers of South Africa
PA	Patriotic Alliance
PAC	Pan Africanist Congress
PF	Patriotic Front
PR	proportional representation
Renamo	Resistência Nacional Moçambicana (Mozambican National Resistance)
SACP	South African Communist Party
Sadeco	South African Democratic Congress
SAFTU	South African Federation of Trade Unions
SA Govt	South African Government
SALGA	South African Local Government Association
Scopa	Standing Committee on Public Accounts
SNNPR	Southern Nations, Nationalities and Peoples' Region
SWAPO	South West Africa People's Organisation
TRA	Thabazimbi Residents Association
UDF	United Democratic Front
UDM	United Democratic Movement
ZANU-PF	Zimbabwe African National Union-Patriotic Front

Glossary of terms

In the contexts in which they are used in this book

Absolute majority: One party wins more than half of the total number of valid votes cast in an election, not just of those who voted. In institutions of government it denotes the rule of 50 per cent plus one. See 'simple majority'.

Accountability, horizontal and vertical: Horizontal accountability refers to checks and balances between and among key organs of the executive, judiciary and the legislature, predicated on the principle of separation of powers; vertical accountability denotes the level of responsiveness of the state to citizens' needs and aspirations.

Alliance: When two or more political parties come together, especially in pre-election times, aiming at maximising votes; the parties are likely to share interests and cohere ideologically.

Alternative vote: Electoral system in which voters rank candidates in order of preference: if a candidate receives the first preference votes, s/he is deemed as elected; in the case where no candidate obtains the majority of first preferences, then the first, second, third and other preferences are counted, with the last-placed candidate being eliminated, and their second preferences being reapportioned to others with each count, and this is done until a candidate clears the threshold of 50 per cent of the vote plus one. Also known as 'instant run-off'.

'Big men': Corrupt, autocratic and often totalitarian political operators who unofficially supplant or substitute for their political parties in government.

By-elections: Elections that take place between main elections, to fill an office that has become vacant. In South Africa, by-elections take place at the municipal level in a ward, and between main local elections that are held every five years.

Clientelism: The exchange of goods and services for political support, which usually involves implicit or explicit quid-pro-quo arrangements: the client gives political or financial support to the patron (votes in elections or support in government) in exchange for some special benefit.

Closed party-list PR system: An electoral system in which parties nominate candidates in the form of a list commensurate with the size of the elective seats in the national assembly; the same method applies in replacing MPs. South Africa uses this system at most levels of elections.

Coalition: Concrete cooperative actions between political parties, especially when they collaborate to jointly exercise government power. Coalitions refer predominantly to political parties cooperating in legislative bodies and government, based on the results from a preceding election.

Coalition dominance: When a stable coalition of parties maintains power for a prolonged period.

Confidence-and-supply agreement: A party (or independent members of a legislature) agreeing to support the government in motions of confidence and appropriation or budget votes (supply); they would either vote in favour of a motion, or abstain. It also designates an opposition party agreeing that it will not vote against a minority government.

Consociationalism: Cooperation between different social groups, with guaranteed group representation, on the basis of power-sharing. It is often used in deeply divided societies.

Election: A process in which registered voters vote to choose a political party or a person (or a group of people) to hold public office; see 'referendum'.

First past the post: An electoral system in which voters cast their vote for a candidate of their choice, which had most likely been put forward by a political party; the candidate who receives the most votes wins, irrespective of the vote share. See 'single-member plurality'.

Floor-crossing: When an elected member of a legislature leaves the party on whose ticket s/he had been elected (and does not resign from this legislature) to join another party or to form a new political party.

Formateur: A politician who is appointed to constitute a coalition government.

Fragmented party system: Competitive party politics that comprises more than two (often many) political parties, none of which is able to command an absolute majority in the representative institution.

Government of national/provincial unity: A government inclusive of the main political parties, approximating in many instances a 'grand coalition'; sometimes constituted after a national crisis.

Grand coalition: A government coalition comprising two or more of the largest parties, often of opposing ideologies, in the parliamentary system; see also 'national coalition'.

Horizontal accountability: See 'accountability'.

Hung parliament: A parliament in which no political party (or pre-existing alliance of parties) has enough seats to secure an overall majority.

Incumbency advantage: When an in-office party or official that gains over challengers in elections due to having enjoyed the benefits of easier access to resources or better profiling of achievements through which prospects of re-election were boosted.

Instant run-off: See 'alternative vote'.

Kingmaker (tiebreaker): The political party or person (and sometimes more than one) that holds a deciding vote in which political party will hold the majority in the legislatures of a municipality, province or national government; kingmakers operate when no single party or pre-existing alliance holds an absolute majority. See 'queenmaker'.

Legislative assembly: The legislative or law-making authority of a country, called at the national level the national assembly; the municipal council is the local-level equivalent. In democratic systems, these institutions are constituted by way of elections.

Local government: The third level or local sphere of government. This geographically based administration has limited and localised powers; it is designated a municipality, which in South Africa comprises a council (of elected members) that approves policies and makes by-laws for the municipal area. The council elects a mayor, who is assisted by an executive or mayoral committee made up of councillors. Municipal officials and staff (headed by a municipal manager) implement the work of the municipality.

Metropolitan municipalities: Metropolitan municipalities are single-tier municipalities that govern a conurbation, and differ from the rest of the two-tier local government system consisting of local and district municipalities.

Micro-party: A small political party, typically one focusing on a single issue, or electorally mustering a minimal percentage of support; at national level in South Africa, a party needs 0.25 per cent of the vote to gain one MP.

Mixed member proportional: A mixed electoral system in which voters get two votes: one to decide the representative for their single-seat constituency and one for a political party; this system is used in local government elections in South Africa. In general terms, a proportion (often roughly half) of the elected institution (such as parliament or the municipal council) is elected by plurality majority methods, usually from single-member districts (or wards), while the remainder is constituted by proportional representation lists; these two votes are cast at the same time. Under mixed member proportional, the list proportional representation seats compensate for disproportionality produced by the ward-seat results. See 'parallel system of voting'.

Multiparty pluralism: Multiple political parties exist and contest for power through elections, and most have a fair chance of winning.

Municipal (local) elections: Elections in which candidates and parties contest to become councillors in a municipality.

National coalition: A form of government in which political parties cooperate to form a government; the usual reason for such an arrangement is that no single party has achieved an absolute majority in an election. See also 'grand coalition'.

National elections: Countrywide elections that are held every number of years. In South Africa, national and provincial elections are held jointly every five years, and citizens aged 18 and over are eligible to vote.

National government: The political authority constituted through national elections that controls or governs a nation; it is usually the highest level of government with the most powers.

Outright majority: See 'absolute majority'.

Oversized coalition: A coalition containing more parties than needed to make a majority; see also 'surplus majority coalition'.

Parallel system of voting: In which voters elect representatives through two systems, first a plurality/majority system and second the proportional representation system; the seats a party wins under the first system do not reduce its seats allocated under the second system. See 'mixed member proportional'.

Particracy: A form of government in which political parties more than citizens or individual politicians dominate the political process; accountability is to parties, rather than to the electorate and people generally.

Plurality voting: An electoral system in which voters are allowed to vote for only one candidate, and the candidate who polls more than any other contender is elected, even if s/he does not achieve an absolute majority; the more candidates contesting a constituency seat, the greater the probability that the winning candidate will receive only a minority of the votes cast.

Proportional representation: An electoral system in which seats are allocated to parties based on vote share, and then assigned to party-affiliated candidates on the parties' electoral lists; the system ensures in one vote and vote count that alignment will be achieved between proportion of votes and representatives.

Provincial elections: Elections held concurrently with national elections every five years in South Africa to elect the nine provincial legislatures, held in terms of proportional representation.

Queenmaker: The gender-balanced equivalent of kingmaker; see 'kingmaker'.

Referendum: In which a proposal or issue is subjected to a direct and universal vote in which the entire electorate votes; it may take place at the national or local level. See 'election'.

Rent-seeking: In which, in exchange for enlisting in a coalition that has the potential to be a governing coalition, political parties (and even micro-parties, disproportionate to their size) lobby the main party to transfer public money, wealth or control over government portfolios to them; it is then anticipated that such control will enable parties to leverage favours from the private sector seeking government contracts.

Run-off voting: See 'second ballot'.

Second ballot: An additional or further ballot held to confirm the selection of a candidate, when the preceding ballot (in the same election) did not yield an absolute majority; also known as the two-round system or run-off voting, it is used in the election of both legislative bodies and directly elected presidents.

Simple majority: A majority in which the highest number of votes cast for any one candidate exceeds the number of the second-placed candidate, even if it is not an absolute (outright) majority. The winner in first-past-the-post voting is determined in terms of simple majority; see 'absolute majority', 'first past the post'.

Single-member plurality: The candidate with the most votes is the winner; see 'first past the post'.

Snap election: An election that is called earlier than the fixed-term deadline of the one that had been scheduled, announced often unexpectedly by the party in power with a view to optimising its own prospects.

Supermajority: A majority that requires more than 50 per cent of the vote, or of the members of a legislature that are eligible to vote.

Surplus majority coalition: A coalition containing more parties than needed to make a majority, thus a coalition that includes parties that are not essential to a parliamentary majority; see also 'oversized coalition'.

Two-round system of voting: A run-off in which only the leading candidates contest, due to the requirement in some electoral systems for the winning candidate to receive an absolute majority. See also 'second ballot'.

Vertical accountability: See 'accountability'.

Vote-buying: A two-way process in coalition politics of offering or giving money, goods, services and/or other inducements (e.g., high office) to party leaders who will swing a coalition in a legislative institution in favour of the party making the offers; see also 'clientelism'.

'Wasted vote' thesis: Votes cast for a losing party or candidate, or more broadly a vote that does not help to elect a party or candidate.

Contributors

SUSAN BOOYSEN

Susan Booysen is Professor Emeritus at the University of the Witwatersrand (Wits), and a visiting professor at the Wits School of Governance. She is the author of several books on the ANC, including *Precarious Power* (2021), *Dominance and Decline* (2015) and *The ANC and the Regeneration of Political Power* (2011). *Marriages of Inconvenience* is her fourth edited book. Booysen is Director of Research at the Mapungubwe Institute for Strategic Reflection (MISTRA).

HEIDI BROOKS

Heidi Brooks is a senior researcher at MISTRA, and senior research associate at the Centre for Social Change at the University of Johannesburg. Her research interests lie in democratic theory, and politics and government in South Africa. She is the author of *The African National Congress and Participatory Democracy: From people's power to public policy* (2020).

GRAEME DE BRUYN

Graeme de Bruyn, a Master of Management in Public Policy graduate from the Wits School of Governance, has cross-industry experience in the corporate, government, education and non-profit domains. He is a thought partner, facilitator, programme designer and implementation specialist, using team coaching to bring his practical insights to the management, leadership, organisational and human development sectors.

PIERRE DE VOS

Pierre de Vos is the Claude Leon Foundation Chair in Constitutional Governance in the Department of Public Law at the University of Cape Town. He is the author of more than 80 articles in academic journals and scholarly books on a wide range of constitutional law topics. He is the co-editor of the book *South African Constitutional Law in Context* (2014).

MOTLAMELLE KAPA

Motlamelle Kapa is an Associate Professor of Political Science at the National University of Lesotho. His research interests are coalitions, party systems and elections; traditional leadership, local government and service delivery; and civil society and democratisation; and he has related work in several scholarly publications. He serves on statutory bodies in Lesotho, and briefs international observer missions on parliamentary elections in that country.

GILBERT KHADIAGALA

Gilbert M. Khadiagala is the Jan Smuts Professor of International Relations and Director of the African Centre for the Study of the United States at Wits. He has published widely on Kenyan politics, African international relations and conflict resolution in Africa. He is working on books on South Sudan, leadership in post-conflict Africa and regional integration in Africa.

BONOLO MAKGALE

Bonolo Makgale is the Programme Manager at the Democracy and Civic Engagement Unit at the Centre for Human Rights, University of Pretoria. She has worked in the civil society space for more than 10 years, and is a social justice and human rights activist. She holds a Master's of Management in Public Policy from the Wits School of Governance.

GRANT MASTERSON

Grant Masterson is the Senior Programme Manager: Governance at the Electoral Institute for Sustainable Democracy in Africa (EISA). He has worked in support of African elections across the continent for the past 15 years. His assignments include approximately 30 election observer missions and assessments with the African Union, Southern African Development Community, East African Community and other international bodies. He has edited several volumes, most recently *State Capture in Africa: Old threats, new packaging* (2018).

KHABELE MATLOSA

Khabele Matlosa is the Director of Political Affairs, African Union Commission, Addis Ababa, Ethiopia. He holds a PhD in political economy from the University of the Western Cape. He is a specialist in governance. His latest publication is 'Pondering the culture of violence in Lesotho: A case for demilitarisation' in the *Journal of Contemporary African Studies* (2020).

LUKHONA MNGUNI

Lukhona Mnguni is a lecturer and PhD candidate at the University of KwaZulu-Natal. He holds degrees in community and development studies, and conflict transformation and peace studies. His MSc in Africa and international development is from the University of Edinburgh. He is the author of scholarly articles on South African political parties in relation to elections.

MCEBISI NDLETYANA

Mcebisi Ndletyana is an Associate Professor in the Department of Politics and International Relations at the University of Johannesburg. He holds a PhD in political science from Wits. His latest book is *Anatomy of the ANC in Power: Insights from Port Elizabeth, 1990–2019* (2020). He has edited several books, including two MISTRA publications.

SANUSHA NAIDU

Sanusha Naidu is a policy analyst working as a senior research fellow with the Institute for Global Dialogue at the University of South Africa. Her Master's degree in International Relations is from the University of Staffordshire. Her publications include journal articles on identity politics in South Africa, two edited books on China in Africa, and a special edition of the journal *Politikon* on Africa's engagements with emerging powers.

AMUZWENI NGOMA

Amuzweni Ngoma is a researcher in political economy at MISTRA, and is completing her PhD at Rhodes University. She is the author of 'Political identities of South Africa's professional black middle class' in *The Rise of Africa's Middle Class* (edited by Henning Melber, 2016) and 'Black professionals and the ANC in the 2014 election: Loosening ties?' in *Election 2014* (edited by Collette Schulz-Herzenberg and Roger Southall).

CRISPIAN OLVER

Crispian Olver is a public policy and management expert with extensive experience at senior-management level in local government. He is the author of *How to Steal a City: The battle for the Nelson Mandela Bay* (2017) and *A House Divided: Battle for the Mother City* (2018).

NANDINI PATEL

Nandini Patel is an Associate Professor in political science at the Catholic University of Malawi. With over 30 years of teaching in India and Malawi, Patel's research focuses on democratic institutions and elections. She has conducted multiple studies on Southern Africa, the latest being on the 2019 Malawi elections for the study 'The cost of politics' with Michael Wahman of Michigan State University. She is editing a volume on Malawi's 2019 elections.

Introduction

SUSAN BOOYSEN WITH AMUZWENI NGOMA

POSITIONED IN THE EARLY PHASES of party-political coalition politics and government in South Africa circa 1994–2021, this volume by the Mapungubwe Institute for Strategic Reflection (MISTRA) takes stock, draws lessons and anticipates the future of coalition politics. It considers party-political and governance experiences with coalition politics in South Africa against the background of shifting national balances of power. It sets out to learn from global experiences where party-political alliances and governing coalitions are often the rule, not the exception. It discerns trends and identifies essential driving forces that would help project possible coalition trajectories in South Africa's future. It flags key determinants that could inform future coalition practice, and prepare South Africa for possible continuing turmoil as this form of politics likely becomes the new normal.

The authors hope to contribute to insights into the new politics of instability that is probably to come with South Africa's emerging coalition realities. Much of the detail of the party politics and governance of coalitions has been explored in preceding works (Kadima, 2006; 2013; Schreiber, 2018; Law, 2018), which contributed understandings of how coalitions may unfold in South Africa. The current volume investigates the coalition dynamics anchored in global and particularly African experiences, and positions this in contemporary understandings of the pace and scope of change in the South African party system. It relates broader questions about South Africa's coalition future to the knowledge of early post-colonial South African experiences of coalition formation and maintenance. For this reason, a major part of the text comprises a detailed dissection of the empirical side of how coalition politics has been unfolding across multiple localities in democratic South Africa, especially at the local and provincial levels. This is combined with the volume's dedicated exploration of a set of themes that condition the practice of coalition politics in South Africa – the constitution and the legal framework, the electoral and party system, and the bureaucracy-politician interface. The book captures the 2016 local government elections as a key coalition moment, and examines its tumultuous unfolding trajectory in the context of reviewing democratic South Africa's changing uses of coalition arrangements.

South Africa stands to learn from specific African experiences. The case of Lesotho shows how political culture impacts the exercise of democracy, and how the art of coalition formation has worked for political system goals (such as maintaining elections and multiparty democracy) even as parties seek to outmanoeuvre the electoral system. Malawi reveals collusion between parties and intraparty dynamics that assist in coalition-based succession planning. Kenya shows that opposition parties can unseat a dominant party, even as social cleavage characterises public life and an element of 'big man' politics prevails. This book presents these cases against the crucial backdrop of party and electoral systems in Southern Africa. It further unpacks the trends in forming and sustaining alliances and coalitions internationally (Oyugi, 2006; Meireles, 2016), with a view to cultivating predictive foresights for South African politics.

Informed by research, each chapter weighs up strategic benefits and disadvantages of coalitions. The volume reflects on the dualistic trajectories with which coalitions come – stability and destabilisation, consensus-building and conflict. It recognises the peace-building and stabilisation effects of coalitions when they are formalised into government. It considers the interparty and co-governing arrangements that are intertwined with competition, and which harbour the compulsion to use alliances and coalitions to barter for extended terms, or to circumvent handing power to party-political opponents.

Marriages of Inconvenience: The politics of coalitions in South Africa weighs up these trends, comparing South Africa's experience with the international, while maintaining special emphasis on the pertinent cases of Africa and Southern Africa in particular. It positions this contemporary coalition praxis in the context of the theories and generalisations that the literature delivers. These different dimensions are woven into each of the chapters, and help discern and differentiate the South African rules of the political coalition game.

CONCEPTUAL CONSIDERATIONS

The text of this volume follows the broad parameters that define alliances as they occur in the narratives of cooperation by political parties, with reference to arrangements that are centred on building outright majorities in legislative institutions, with the aim of constituting government. Alliances in the party-political domain aim at maximising votes and mutual interests among parties. Two or more cooperating parties often come together in pre-election times and are likely to cohere ideologically and on some policies. Coalitions concern concrete cooperative actions, especially when political parties collaborate to jointly exercise government power. Coalitions hence refer predominantly to political parties cooperating in legislative bodies and government, based on the results from a preceding election (Kadima, 2006; 2013; Booysen, 2013; 2018). The goals of these political parties range from democratic, accountable governance driven by what is in citizens' best interests and informed by coherence of ideology and policy, to crude accumulation of power, perks and patronage, along with multiple iterations in between. Among their goals is to unseat an entrenched dominant party. Their aims in some instances are brazen party strategy that includes aligning against a common party-political enemy, and using coalition involvement as a tactic to elevate a party or help it leverage access to public and private resources.

Altman's (2000a: 189) well-crafted definition, while referring only to parliamentary parties, assists to focus MISTRA's investigation. A coalition in any legislative institution is a:

> temporal combination of groups or individuals formed to pursue specific objectives through joint action. Specifically, it is a set of parliamentary political parties that agree to pursue a common goal or a common set of goals, pool their resources together in pursuit of this goal, communicate and form … commitments concerning their goals; [and] agree on distribution of payoffs to be received on obtaining their goal.

In this volume, the designation 'original coalition' refers to coalitions that form immediately after elections, while 'interim coalitions' denote changes due to defections from an original coalition, or cases of expansion or reduction in the original coalition. A 'minimal coalition' is a coalition that has the minimum number of coalition partners necessary to secure an outright majority; a 'maximal coalition' (or 'grand coalition' or 'surplus coalition') gathers the largest number that can be united in the coalition formation. This happens, for example, due to ideological convergence or construction of an ideological front against threats, such as those posed by right-wing populists in Germany (see chapter 3).

Reminders of the inherent instability of coalition arrangements are just below the surface of these conceptualisations. Ideological affinity, along with the affect for the leadership of the predominant or main party, the fairness and practicality of the coalition agreement, and proximity to the next election, are among the key factors that will affect the stability of the coalition at stake. As De Swaan (1973: 148) notes, the defection of any one member of a minimal coalition exposes that coalition to the loss of power. In addition, office-seeking coalitions tend to disintegrate more easily than those held together by policy or ideological convergence (Riker, 1962; Sithanen, 2003). Many of the rewards for coalition enlistment can be offered by any party that constructs a majority, be it positions, control of portfolios, prestige of being in government, or prospects for personal or party gain. While the literature poses this dichotomy of coalitions mainly as arrangements of either ideological and policy affinity, or rent-seeking interparty behaviour, this volume argues that these two drivers in the South African context appear in conjunction with each other, albeit in variable configurations, depending on temporality and locality.

The electoral cycle is a certain destabilising factor, given that smaller parties are inclined to withdraw from coalitions as the election approaches. This is to help them assert their own identities to the electorate. The analysis notes Altman's (2000b: 262) explanation of the cyclical nature of coalitions: coalitions are more likely to be constituted directly after an election, and prospects of renewal decrease as the term of governance draws to a close. Withdrawal as elections approach is well recognised. Parties that enter into coalitions but abrogate their manifesto or election promises tend to exit the coalition while there is still sufficient time to make amends with their supporters. Alternatively, parties learn that coalitions hurt their election support and hence prefer to remain in the opposition rather than join a governing coalition.

LEARNING FROM SOUTH AFRICAN, AFRICAN AND OTHER INTERNATIONAL EXPERIENCES

The approach in constructing this volume was to enter into the mix a cross-section of learnings about coalition experiences in South Africa and beyond. Chapter 1 sets out the prevailing party-political foundations of past coalition politics in South Africa. It focuses on the core building blocks of coalition politics – the political parties and associated party systems. It sketches the contours of a period in which a range of the electoral majorities of the African National Congress (ANC) were either declining into minority status, or suffering declines that could bring about minority status. Minority status could nevertheless combine with possible continuous dominance in the sense of remaining the biggest party by an ample margin. These factors depended on opposition parties rising to occupy the space potentially vacated by the ANC, which was not a foregone conclusion. For example, the local by-elections of late 2020 indicated that the ANC might be holding ground, and its dominant-party status might persist, due to its own intraparty fragilities being matched by those of the

Democratic Alliance (DA). The DA as the predominant opposition party suffered intraparty weaknesses that obstructed it from not only rising into the position of coalition leader, but also consolidating and sustaining this position. The host of small and microparties, however, could in turn fill this void. In these conditions of uncertain party-political and coalition futures, it is important to learn from the experiences of coalition formation, maintenance (and dissolution) and impact on governance as manifested in Africa beyond South Africa, and in the global South (Latin America, Asia, Africa and Oceania) and North (including Australia, Canada, most Western European countries, Israel, Japan, New Zealand, Singapore, South Korea, Taiwan and the USA).

The point of departure, based on party-political fundamentals, is that South Africa will increasingly but variably and intermittently enter into interparty coalition arrangements in the years to come, on a trajectory that constitutes a jagged curve.[1] In chapter 2, Mcebisi Ndletyana outlines the inclusive landscape of coalition politics in South Africa at the local government level across multiple electoral experiences. The chapter offers textured illustrations of the prevalence of coalition governments since 2000. South Africa has much to learn from experiences with coalitions internationally. In chapter 3 Heidi Brooks delves into practices across global regions, focusing on sites where coalition governments are the predominant way of political life. The chapter uses a thematic approach to focus attention on trends and possible lessons that emerge from many years of coalition experiences in parts of the world where coalition government is the rule and not the exception. Khabele Matlosa's chapter addresses the interface between electoral and party systems, placing South Africa in the comparative Southern African context. It demonstrates that coalition governments occur across different party systems and electoral systems.

The second part of the book extends the analyses and comparative perspectives, exploring alliances, coalitions and coalition governments in other African countries. Grant Masterson in chapter 5 highlights how multiple countries have both gained and suffered from coalition experiences. Overall, the chapter emphasises the centrality of sound organising practices in whether coalitions will bring stability or ruptures in government. The section is enriched by in-depth explorations through case studies of coalitions and alliance politics in Africa in relation to rent-seeking. The first two Africa-specific case studies, on Kenya, by Gilbert Khadiagala in chapter 6, and on Lesotho, by Motlamelle Kapa in chapter 7, show how coalition arrangements have both stabilised and destabilised governments. The chapters illustrate the complex interfaces between coalitions, social cleavage, electoral system change and military presences in party politics. Both Kenya and Lesotho have a history of needing external intervention and mediation due to conflict ensuing in post-election periods. The third case study, on Malawi, by Nandini Patel in chapter 8, analyses how opposition alliances have helped forge accountability and succession in governance.

Several crucial ingredients to successful coalition politics emerge from the set of domestic South African, broader African and international case studies. The third part of the book draws attention to a selection of these themes that inform coalition practice in the South African context. There is a focus on the all-important role of the legal and constitutional foundations in coalition formation, as analysed by Pierre de Vos in chapter 9. In South Africa such provisions are minimal – the founders of the Constitution had not anticipated the need to specify conditions and mechanisms for coalition formation and government. The chapter pulls together the jurisprudence that supplements the constitutional pointers. In chapter 10, Crispian Olver analyses the extent to which municipal bureaucracies and local politicians clash, collude and cohere. His dissection of this complex interface reveals the vexed character of governance and administration while the council political elephants fight.

The fourth part of the book takes stock of three emblematic metropolitan cases of coalition government in South Africa in the aftermath of the 2016 local government elections and the effects beyond: Johannesburg by Bonolo Makgale in chapter 11, Tshwane by Graeme de Bruyn in chapter 12 and Nelson Mandela Bay by Mcebisi Ndletyana in chapter 13. These coalition governments have become synonymous with political turmoil and governance instability. The three in-progress stories provide author-specific perspectives, and track the unfolding sets of facilitative and obstructive actions. The set of case studies dissects the life-cycles of the vacillating coalitions, which De Bruyn also approaches from the related theoretical perspective. The studies offer invaluable lessons for future coalition practice in South Africa. This part of the book also explores provincial and municipal coalitions in the Western Cape and KwaZulu-Natal. In chapter 14, Sanusha Naidu relates identity politics to evolving coalition practice, and in chapter 15, Lukhona Mnguni unpacks the shifting coalitions of KwaZulu-Natal. The two explorations focus on the now-lapsed provincial coalition governments, the interfaces at the time with national politics and the diversity of ongoing coalitions in municipalities in the two provinces.

The book's final part synthesises core insights. Amuzweni Ngoma in chapter 16 provides an international case-study analysis of a set of key drivers of coalition formation and maintenance. Her analysis highlights the impact of culture, leadership, coalition negotiations and agreements. Chapter 17 by Susan Booysen details essential driving forces, political party mindsets, trends and indicators that are associated with coalition practice. The content is extracted from the international comparatives profiled and the rich collection of South African cases covered in the book, and her categorisations and interpretation of the materials.

This MISTRA volume hence reveals the details of key driving forces shaping coalition formation, maintenance and (potentially) dissolution, as well as the impact of coalitions on public governance. It shows the granularity of trends and indicators that accompany interparty coalition politics and governance. It serves as a roadmap to navigate and track future coalitions.

ANTICIPATING SOUTH AFRICA'S COALITIONS FUTURE

If coalition politics is to become more pronounced in South Africa's political future, it is important to explore the details, contexts and motivations driving it, and what it may entail – and, as far as possible, to anticipate and plan for that future.

It is from these trends and characteristics, and the knowledge of the conditions in which they occur, that South Africa can take valuable lessons on the future shape of the coalition interface between party politics and governance. The rich data, perspectives and interpretations offered in this volume invite readers to use the details, identify unfolding trends and build their own 'coalition castles' – constructs that can make or break developmental governance in South Africa.

REFERENCES

Altman, D. 2000a. 'Coalition formation and survival under multiparty presidential democracies in Latin America: Between the tyranny of the electoral calendar, the irony of ideological polarization, and inertial effects'. Paper presented at the Latin American Studies Association, Miami, Fl.

Altman, D. 2000b. 'The politics of coalition formation and survival in multiparty presidential democracies: The case of Uruguay, 1989–1999', *Party Politics*, 6 (3), 259–283.

Booysen, S. 2013. 'Causes and impact of party alliances on the party system and national cohesion in South Africa', *Journal of African Elections,* 13 (11), 66–92.

Booysen, S. 2018. 'Coalitions and alliances demarcate crossroads in ANC trajectories – ANC electoral conference', *New Agenda: South African Journal of Social and Economic Policy*, 68: 6–10.

De Swaan, A. 1973. 'Coalition Formation and Cabinet Formations: A study of formal theories of coalition formation as applied to nine European parliaments'. PhD thesis, University of Amsterdam.

Kadima, D. (ed.) 2006. *The Politics of Party Coalitions in Africa*. Johannesburg: Electoral Institute for Sustainable Democracy in Africa.

Kadima, D. 2013. 'An introduction to the politics of party alliances and coalitions in socially divided Africa', *Journal of African Elections*, 13 (1), 1–24.

Law, M. 2018. 'Political Party Co-operation and the Building and Sustaining of Coalition'. Research Report. Cape Town: Heinrich Böll Foundation.

Meireles, F. 2016. 'Oversized government coalitions in Latin America', *Brazilian Political Science Review*, 10 (3), http://www.scielo.br/scielo.php?script=sci_arttext&pid=S1981-38212016000300201, accessed 22 January 2020.

Oyugi, W.O. 2006. 'Coalition politics and coalition governments in Africa', *Journal of Contemporary African Studies*, 24 (1), 53–79.

Riker, W.H. 1962. *The Theory of Political Coalitions*. New Haven: Yale University Press.

Schreiber, L. 2018. *Coalition Country: South Africa after the ANC.* Cape Town: Tafelberg.

Sithanen, R. 2003. 'Coalition politics under the tropics: Office seekers, power makers, nation building: A case study of Mauritius'. Paper presented at EISA Roundtable Strengthening Democracy through Coalition Building, http://aceproject.org/ero-en/topics/parties-and-candidates/mauritius.pdf, accessed 2 March 2020.

Part I

Approaching political coalitions in South Africa: South African pivots, global trends, African foundations

THIS SECTION CUTS TO THE CHASE of identifying South Africa's coalition pivot: the state of the African National Congress (ANC), the dominant former liberation movement and since 1994 the governing party, determines overwhelmingly the likelihood of the country steering increasingly towards interparty-coalition dispensations. The ANC circa 2021 is on the verge of either dipping more visibly into the coalitions arena (should its status be confirmed as still dominant but below the 50 per cent threshold) or potentially resurrecting itself out of this danger zone. This section builds on the glossary of concepts and summative theory statements to complement the chapter-specific theoretical frameworks in the rest of the volume. This part of the book positions coalition practice in South Africa historically and geographically. Historically, a coalition culture has been taking shape since the early days of democracy in the 1990s. The variants manifested since 2016 have their roots in these antecedents. South Africa joins much of the global community in this game of instability, disruptive government and coalition contestation that supplements electoral politics in determining who steps into government. South Africa's comparative status in the domains of party system and electoral system help build the platform for this book's analysis of coalition politics in South Africa.

ONE

The uneven transition from party dominance to coalitions
South Africa's new politics of instability

Susan Booysen

COALITIONS IN MULTIPARTY DEMOCRACIES flourish when dominant-party systems decay. When no single party wins an outright electoral majority, interparty cooperation, possible through many different forms of coalitions, becomes inevitable. South Africa's hitherto dominant African National Congress (ANC) was by 2021, in multiple sites of local and some provincial government, hovering on the edge of ceding its outright majorities or had in places already sacrificed this status. At other sites, it vacillated between outright majorities, and the rank of largest party yet without the outright majority, thus intermittently relying on other parties to help achieve a majority. The ANC's internal political vulnerabilities meant that, at the time of compilation of this book, there had not yet been definitive answers as to whether this monolithic liberation movement-turned political party would be able to stabilise at 50+ per cent national support of the electorate or suffer systemic decline.

The corollary of the ANC decline in most of South Africa was escalated prospects for coalition politics – a notoriously unstable form of governance. This signals a new transitional period in South African politics, namely coalition politics, as the new interface between party politics and governance.

Coalitions have been an inextricable but variable part of South Africa's post-1994-election political landscape, although the driving forces and dynamics have been changing. From roughly 1994 to 2016, the predominant dynamic was that of the ascendant ANC using alliances and coalitions as part of its repertoire of subduing and usurping major and minor opposition parties while consolidating power. This since-1994 tradition has helped shape the culture and context of contemporary emerging coalitions in the time of the prolonged (and uneven) decline of the ANC. The new dynamic after 2016 was possibilities for interparty coalitions and coalition governments – and the ANC had to earn its place in these arrangements through negotiations and bartering. At stake were topping up the ANC's 50 per cent in exchange for all or any position and prestige, control over government portfolios, personal financial benefit, policy compromises and service to specific constituent communities.

The fulcrum of coalition activity was centred on, but not limited to, the ANC. The state of opposition politics, and the extent to which opposition parties could fill the vacuums left by ANC losses, was a crucial part of the equation of the future of interparty coalitions, and specifically coalition government in South Africa. The opposition parties themselves were in tenuous positions, hence the strengths they brought to any coalition equation would often be uncertain. It was their weaknesses, and their lack of widespread, compelling appeal to voters, that were instrumental in the ANC being able to maintain its predominant 50+ per cent support levels in many legislative institutions. It was the micro-parties that thrived: just a handful of their votes was the balance that swung coalitions between the ANC and the opposition. Ironically, but probably due to the ANC's liberation-movement credentials, opposition parties that could supersede it did not emerge or grow.[1]

The ANC and its popular electoral strength hence were the pivot around which South Africa's possible coalitions future turned. The once unambiguously dominant liberation movement party was on an uncertain pathway of attempting reinvention and restitution to clear-cut, strong majorities. Early reinvention attempts (laudatory statements and numerous publicly proclaimed intentions) came with contradictory practice (continuous evidence of old and new corrupt government practice and proof of suboptimal organisational ability to enforce resolutions to turn over a new leaf). At various levels of elections – national, provincial and local – the ANC was intermittently shedding support, on occasion to the extent of losing its majority status. In this slipstream there was a cacophony of political initiatives of parties building alliances to displace the ANC, the ANC aligning with parties to stay in power and gain platforms to regain power, and a multitude of opportunistic rent-seeking variations on these themes. It was a time of unpredictable party-political alliances and unstable government that are associated with this interface between party politics and governance.[2]

This chapter explores this new era of instability, which accompanied the increasing manifestation of coalition government in South Africa. The chapter reviews details of the state of the ANC as a still-dominant party operating on the basis of a lessened majority. This builds the analytical foundations of the research in this chapter – the stronger and more dominant the ANC, the less the need and the fewer the prospects for interparty alliances and coalitions. The first part of this chapter makes brief reference to several trends and events, which are then detailed. The next part reviews the ANC and South Africa's experiences with coalitions, and assesses the extent to which these early experiences help contribute to understandings of future coalition practices. This part of the analysis is done through a periodisation and concurrent typology construction of the alliance and coalition experiences. The research draws on the author's monitoring project of party politics in South Africa, and uses data and insights from direct observation and the author's tracking of events.[3] Based on this database of party politics and elections in South Africa, and using an analytically interpretative approach, the chapter identifies trends in alliance and coalition formation.

Table 1.1: Party support across 11 national and local elections, 1994–2019 (%)

Parties with national representation	1994 National	1995/6 Local	1999 National	2000 Local[ii]	2004 National	2006 Local[iii]	2009 National	2011 Local[iv]	2014 National	2016 Local[iv]	2019 National
ANC	62.6	58.0	66.4	59.4	69.9	67.7	65.9	62.9	62.2	54.5	57.50
DA[i]	22.1	21.5	17.0	22.1	12.4	13.9	16.7	24.1	22.2	27.0	20.77
EFF									6.4	8.3	10.79
IFP	10.5	8.7	8.6	9.1	7.0	8.4	4.6	3.6	2.4	4.3	3.38
NFP								2.4	1.6	0.02	0.35
UDM			3.4	2.6	2.3	1.98	0.9	0.6	1.0	0.6	0.45
FF+[v]	2.2	2.7	0.8	0.1	1.0	1.0	0.8	0.4	0.9	0.8	2.38
Cope							7.4	2.2	0.7	0.5	0.27
ACDP	1.2	1.4	0.8	0.4	1.6	1.2	0.8	0.6	0.6	0.4	0.84
AIC									0.5	1.0	0.28
ID					1.7	1.4	0.9				
Agang SA									0.3	0.02	0.08
PAC	1.3	0.7	1.2	1.2	0.7	1.2	0.3	0.4	0.2	0.2	0.19
MF		0.4	0.3	0.3	0.4	0.3	0.3	0.4	0.1	0.04	0.07
Azapo			0.2	0.3	0.3	0.3	0.2	0.2	0.1	0.07	0.07
UCDP			0.8	1.0	0.8	0.8	0.4	0.2	0.1	0.07	
Al Jama-Ah							0.15	0.04	0.14	0.1	0.18
ATM											0.44
Good											0.40

[i] In some instances the Electoral Commission website combines the support for the DP and NP/NNP; the current table does not dissect it; hence, in the first few columns DA+NP/NNP=DA; Stated by the Electoral Commission website to be the percentage for the local government.

[ii] Stated by the Electoral Commission website to be the percentage for the 'Party overall'.

[iii] Percentages on the PR ballot.

[iv] FF+CP.

POLITICAL PARTIES IN SOUTH AFRICA'S NEW EPOCH OF COALITIONS: TRENDS OF TURMOIL AND INSTABILITY

This chapter is premised on South Africa's probable coalitions future, centring on the ANC and the themes of its continuous dominance and revitalisation vis-à-vis possibilities of decline and increasing losses of outright electoral majorities. It is this status of the ANC across South Africa's multiple sites of government that is the core party-political determinant of whether the country will steer towards increasing coalitions in the future or not. Because the core determinant, the ANC as pivot, itself is unstable, South Africa's possible track into a coalitions future is set to be variable too.

The unstable pivot: The state of the ANC as a trigger to coalition formations

Turmoil and instability are two inherent characteristics of both the conceptualisation and the praxis of coalitions and alliances. South Africa's experiences of the disruption of alliances and instability of coalition formations in the period especially since the local government elections of 2016 articulate with much of the international experience. Governing coalitions, or coalition governments, are a frequent phenomenon in world politics, including Africa and Southern Africa. With a few exceptions, coalitions and coalition governments have not guaranteed stability in governance. Coalition government becomes a solution when previously dominant parties lose their preeminent statuses (Brooks, 2004; Booysen, 2015). The unsteadiness in political context is likely to be prolonged, as the still-dominant but declining lead party in South Africa fights for restitution of dominance[4] and opposition parties contest for portions of previous ANC support.

South Africa's coalition epoch is therefore likely to be a time of great instability – not just because interparty governing coalitions are regularly an unstable form of government, but also because the ANC, centrepiece of coalition formation in South Africa, is unstable in its electoral standing. As the ANC's majorities in the national government, several provinces and multiple local government councils became fragile in many cases from 2009 on, coalition experiences proliferated. The early manifestations revealed the types of coalition politics that were likely to unfold and elements of the South Africa-specific coalition culture that took shape.

Should the ANC of the 2020s further undermine its own liberation movement and general democratic and developmental credentials, it will almost inevitably further damage its governing majorities.[5] This will foster coalition governments in the space where social and economic need requires stable government – but such government is far more likely when the government enjoys relatively stable, outright majorities, at the exact time that there are decreasing prospects for it. This means that South Africa needs to learn from local and international experience on how to optimise chances for stability and focus on the essentials of governance, despite being engrossed in a most unstable form of government.

From the 2016 moment when the local government election results drove home the inevitability of high-impact government through coalition arrangements, interparty coalition arrangements became emblematic of ANC efforts to hold onto power, for example, in major metropolitan municipalities. These metropolitan and provincial sites were important to opposition party initiatives as well: they managed to take power from the generally dominant ANC, and establish or consolidate opposition party holds over some provinces or municipalities. The premise of a declining coalitions pivot, the ANC, does not exclude the possibility of the ANC learning from the lessons of sliding majorities and correcting its performance. Its 2016–21 experience included it being forced into minority situations in prominent metropolitan governments. It experienced the effects of destabilised government that resulted from alliances and coalitions with ideologically incompatible parties, bound nevertheless by shared political aspirations and opportunistic rent-seeking.

The South African experience reveals dimensions of a political hegemon that resists ceding its dominance, a party far from succumbing and handing power to coalition partners or opposition parties more generally. Coalitions therefore are an interregnum – they occupy the space between declining power and handing over outright power to opposition parties. While in this space, parties – including the ANC – can rebuild and recover, or go into compromised identities and exacerbated decline.

Fragile opposition parties tipping into the coalition picture

The ANC is on a jagged curve of support decline and growth. It is generally, except for the modest recovery in the 2019 elections, on a line of shedding support. Yet, opposition parties are weak as well. In the prevailing conjuncture, the coalition initiative remains with the ANC – it is the ANC's weaknesses and lapses that determine the presence of coalition opportunities, rather than achievements and initiatives by opposition parties. To date, therefore, it has been these ANC shortfalls that have determined the presence of coalition opportunities.

South Africa's opposition parties are overwhelmingly not internally ideologically coherent, do not have consistently high profiles or clear identities that appeal on a national scale, are not well organised, and structure themselves around the ANC's weaknesses. They construct messages and target their expansion appeals to find resonance with those voters that the ANC is shedding, but become hold-alls that still try to appeal to their existing support bases. They gain what the ANC sheds, and these gains rarely cohere ideologically with the new host. These party migrants could seamlessly depart again to yet another new political home. One of the great weaknesses of party politics in contemporary South Africa is that much of the citizenry is disaffected and alienated from party and electoral politics generally. The fact that large sections of youth in South Africa are not registering to vote, and hence do not participate in numbers in elections (MISTRA, 2019), is but one illustration of the trend. Both the opposition parties and party politics in general in South Africa thus are weak, which means the building blocks for coalitions are also weak.

The opposition's new coalitions that have manifested, both in major metropolitan municipalities and scattered across local municipalities in several provinces, are unstable, in significant part because the parties constituting the coalitions were never coherent. They are not based on bonds that are any deeper than shallow trade-offs that could be offered by any majority alliance. The coalitions are largely based on patronage and rent-seeking[6] – factors that appeal to leaders who trade coalition identities for positions and perks, far more than for ideology, policy and service assurances to communities. In some instances, opposition parties did make policy delivery a condition for coalition buy-in, such as the Economic Freedom Fighters (EFF) in relation to the Democratic Alliance (DA)-led coalitions. The opposition parties were likely to succumb to the lure of offers of control over portfolios (in this instance, in local government) that the bigger parties such as the ANC and the DA made. But even in cases that offered policy and governance gains for the minor coalition partners, party-political profiling as 'able to govern' (control over portfolios would in due course allow them to claim having had experience in governing) and patronage-seeking (to benefit the party or individuals) were important parts of the coalition deals.[7]

In these settings there was ample space for the ANC to counter opposition initiatives and construct governing majorities from within the ranks of the opposition parties. There was some ideological convergence with the EFF, yet when it came to government practice, the ANC followed the more procedural and less extreme options, guided by parliamentary process and constitutionality, albeit far short of the broad human rights approach in the preamble to the constitution. The DA-EFF cooperation survived on modest policy concessions, strategic deployment of EFF members at relevant sites of administration and compromises on budget allocations. A possible ANC-EFF coalition was hovering in the background when, in the run-up to the 2019 election, it appeared that the ANC might not make the outright majority cut nationally and in Gauteng. As the EFF demonstrated in some subsequent municipal coalition negotiations (for example, in Tshwane, in negotiation with the ANC), high-level positions that would elevate it above its electoral standing had a great lure.

The ANC's opposition repertoire
The ANC has a repertoire of dealing with the opposition, enticing them or outmanoeuvring them until they become coalition tools. In post-1994 opposition strongholds, the ANC used cooperation (often

amounting to small coalitions) with and usurpation of opposition parties to gradually subdue them. This was in the ANC's ascendant period of consolidating power, rather than defending or regaining majorities. In a few instances when intra-ANC pressures became unmanageable, the ANC oversaw splits and then gradually pulled individual leaders back into the ANC, in the process weakening and subduing the splitting parties, with the ANC regaining or retaining an electoral edge. This was manifested when the ANC countered the Congress of the People (Cope) in the run-up to the 2009 election.

The ANC has also been in a position of overall national and provincial power to attract parties into its coalition-partners reservoir. It could use this power to divide, rule and conquer – a repertoire followed, for example, with the erstwhile New National Party (NNP), and into the present with the Inkatha Freedom Party (IFP). The ANC also found the scope to enlist in its coalition-construction projects small parties such as the National Freedom Party (NFP), the African Independent Congress (AIC) and the Patriotic Front (PF), and multiple micro-parties. Some of these parties were equally prepared to coalesce with, for example, the DA. There inevitably was some point of convergence on policy or ideology, but the overriding drive was concrete exchanges in the domain of positions, perks and patronage – in a society and economy that are highly reliant on the state as a centre of employment and economic activity.

The small- and micro-party repository

The coalition-partner repository expanded in light of the growth in number of small and micro-parties in South Africa – evident in particular in the national and provincial elections of 2019 (MISTRA, 2019). A total of 48 political parties contested nationally, compared with the 29 of 2014. The provincial figures matched the national trend.

Especially after the 2016 elections, both the ANC and the DA had to negotiate their way into coalition majorities by enlisting the support of a palette of these parties. Some of them were policy-agnostic, and content to be in any coalition that could deliver takings to the leader/s, the party or both. The negotiables included senior positions, especially the mayoralty or deputy mayoralty – some in small towns, others in major metros. The main parties, especially in the stalemate municipalities, often conceded.

These opposition parties were embraced by the bigger parties, the ANC and DA, not as part of a virtuous new form of government, but as a transitional instrument to help the bigger parties buy time, as they outmanoeuvred one another while seeking the opportunity to either return to power, grow in following to gain power, or strike an opportunistic deal that would elevate them into power beyond the scope of their electoral base. This dynamic could change, however, should the ANC establish new electoral credibility, should the ANC split and create a new political force, or should the lead opposition party, the DA, disintegrate and stop being the base from which opposition alliances can cohere.

Coalition governance and democracy in South Africa: Implications of the party mix

Coalition governments are indispensable in a system of democratically elected representation. At the local level in South Africa, coalitions became an indispensable mechanism to constitute governing majorities when elections did not deliver outright majorities. Coalition governance came, nevertheless, with flaws of policy compromise and fused ideological platforms.

Ideological fusion

The coalition-based governing majorities that result from coalition negotiations are interparty constructs rather than mandates derived from an election outcome. To the extent that accountability in democracies with indirect representation through the election of representatives is to political parties, accountability in coalition dispensations is not a farfetched compromise. However, in the mix of parties in coalition governments (and the fact that bargaining and horse-trading are the name of the game), mandates are fused, and citizens do not necessarily get what they had specifically mandated through a party-specific vote. The deals that transpire are driven by the respective party leaderships, both in the particular government structure and in the higher-level party structures that tend to dictate the local coalition frameworks and governance decisions.

South Africa's party-political coalitions were frequently not ideologically coherent, policy driven or internally sociopolitically compatible, as noted above. Yet, in many instances, the political parties forming the coalition were among the South African parties that clustered roughly around a political core, be this centre, centre-left or centre-right. Office-seeking and opportunism, or sharing the payoffs that are associated with holding power, often trumped possible ideological and policy convergence (see Oyugi, 2006): few principled policy bases and little ideological coherence informed coalition politics in South Africa at this time. The prime driver was the quest to be in government – to stay in control, or to exercise control over government resources (possibly but not necessarily to serve constituents). Scoring benefits like insourcing municipal workers or getting specific services for particular groups of constituents were bonuses. In the name of achieving a minimal coalition, parties combined liberalism, religion, nationalism, ethnicity, class and a number of other core party identities. When there was a choice, a party such as the EFF preferred associating with the ANC over the DA, but still, party reward and rent-seeking ruled.

Obfuscated accountability in the games of kingmaking and coalition-crashing

South Africa's relatively recent experience of coalition practice, by global standards, combined with the volatility of the coalitions constructed, meant that by 2020–21 the jury remained out on the electoral repercussions of parties having participated in coalitions. Internationally, parties are known to suffer electoral consequences for cooperating with other parties when there is blame to be shared for poor performance and/or scandals in government (Caramani, 2017). This applies especially to smaller political parties when they are dominated by the dynamics of the bigger partners, as was the case in the British system's 2010 coalition government between the Conservative Party and the Liberal Democrats (Institute for Government, 2012). The Liberals tried to maintain the party's own identity and suffered internal rebellion. Experiences in South Africa's post-2016 coalition period showed that the frequent variations in governing coalitions obfuscated the responsibility for poor and corrupt governance of specific parties.

The practice of alternating and varying coalition partners also meant that the parties in coalitions hardly needed to take account of the rule established internationally: smaller political parties often withdraw from coalitions in the run-up to elections, or develop stronger policy positions, because the electorate punishes small parties that have not been sufficiently visible in coalition governments (Altman, 2000: 260). The bulk of the small parties remained small, irrespective of coalition involvement. Even when small parties stayed in coalitions at one site, their party colleagues at other sites might not have maintained *their* coalition – and party responsibility may have been diluted.

Because of the brinkmanship game in coalitions, alternating kingmaking with coalition-crashing, the smaller parties in South Africa's coalitions have often been disproportionately visible in the pre-election period – elevating and exaggerating their claims to having demonstrated ability to govern, or trading on reputations as reliable rescuers of the main parties. The EFF's withdrawal from the DA cooperative agreement in Johannesburg was one variation on the theme of pre-emptive withdrawal – the move was assertive, rather than a defence against damage.

There were nonetheless diminished chances for the electorate to extract accountability. Even without coalition governments, single parties holding municipal power fared dismally over many decades. The common and sustained trend was that financial probity, efficient management and public accountability was maintained in a fraction of South Africa's municipalities (see, for example, SA Govt, 2020). While coalition government often exacerbated the lack of accountability, it did not invent it. Corruption, mismanagement and dereliction of duty were often the rule rather than the exception, yet it was impossible to dissect which coalition in exactly which period was the main cause of this poor governance. This was evident in two of Gauteng's metropolitan municipalities. In the City of Johannesburg, the neglect of Alexandra township was a political pawn between sequential ANC and DA administrations, and it became a major ANC mobilisation tool in its 2019 national provincial election campaign. The ANC argued that the DA-led administration, in charge of Johannesburg from the 2016 local elections until the ANC displaced it in 2019, had neglected the Alexandra Renewal Project. In Tshwane, the ANC alleged that the DA-led coalition had failed to address the longstanding neglect of a water-supply project for Hammanskraal, while the DA argued that the problem had existed in the antecedent ANC administration. In both metros, both the DA and the ANC could highlight scandals – often of major proportions – that had existed in the time of the alternate coalition administration.

Defacto coalition ungovernability

Coalition governance chaos – coalition-crashing encapsulated in stalemates, walkouts and councillors practising coalition-hopping – also led to municipalities succumbing to ungovernability. The constitution permitted the administrative removal of such coalitions, in certain circumstances, enabled by section 139, such as in the contested case of Tshwane in 2020. In Tshwane's battle of the coalitions, council meetings were repeatedly collapsed and crucial council decisions delayed (see also chapter 12). In other hung councils, stalemate conditions persisted until some councillor was persuaded to defect, or there was a resignation (or death), and a by-election with a new party as victor could resolve matters.

From 1998 to 2018/19, there were around 140 'under administration' municipal interventions (Ledger and Rampedi, 2019: 33–36), besides the multiple cases in which municipalities registered financial distress (Jordaan, 2020), and little effective governance was evident. A large proportion of South Africa's municipalities were therefore in effect ungovernable, due to councillors and officials not doing the tasks for which they had been appointed or elected. Such a background created a culture in which it was a small additional step for gridlocked councils to hold governance to ransom.

PERIODISATION AND TYPOLOGY OF THE ANC'S SEQUENCE OF INTERPARTY COALITIONS

Given the centrality of the party-political standing of the ANC, and the likelihood that past coalition conventions frame future practice, this section concentrates on periodising coalition and alliance practice in South Africa (Booysen, 2014; 2018). The ANC has been only one of many party-political actors, but it has been central to the actions. Five phases are identified for the periodisation component of this analysis.

The uses that the ANC found for party-political alliances and coalitions changed over time. In the early days of South Africa's democracy, coalitions helped the ANC build reconciliation and bring former political foes into the co-governance fold (phase one). The 1994 constitutionally mandated Government of National Unity (GNU) arrangement with the NNP and the IFP illustrated this,[8] but the ANC continued with some form of multiparty government after 1999.

Coalitions also gave the ANC footholds in provincial government where it had not won outright at some stage of the election game, namely in KwaZulu-Natal and the Western Cape. In the Western Cape, this rolled out with the help of floor-crossing (elected representatives changing allegiance in a legislature to a party other than the one on whose ticket the representative had been elected) plus a coalition, but the ANC reign was brief. The arrangements helped the ANC consolidate power over political opponents (phase two). Then came a time of the ANC cresting in electoral support; it had high outright majorities in the bulk of sites of governance. Even at its pinnacle of power in 2004, however, coalitions were in evidence in the ANC repertoire at the local level (and until 2009 in KwaZulu-Natal), foreshadowing future trends.

Interparty competition at the time was low. As Boucek (2012; see also Bogaards and Boucek, 2010) remarks about dominant parties in such conditions, they tend to develop factions and accumulate corruption baggage. The ANC started suffering reputational damage mainly through malfeasance and evidence of poor governance (phase three). The developments triggered a period of the ANC shedding support electorally and being forced into multiple coalitions to help it retain power, especially in high-level metropolitan municipalities (phase four). Coalitions also helped the ANC to regain power at several sites. These were not always sustainable, largely because parties regarded themselves as competitors to the ANC, or the ANC's deficits in credibility made partners fear for damage to their own image (early phase five). There were tentative indications, mainly on the back of municipal by-elections in late 2020 and early 2021, of a fragile and divided ANC doing reasonably well electorally due to the weakness of the opposition, especially the DA. The ANC's residual historical legitimacy also contributed, along with abstention by those who refused to believe that the ANC was self-correcting, and on some refreshed voter belief that the party might contain its rogue and excessively corrupt flank (late phase five).[9]

Hence the ANC used coalitions to (among other things) help it subdue and eclipse its party-political nemeses and bide its time when it got into trouble and lapsed below outright majorities. It used coalitions as a buffer and as a spearhead to change the electoral landscapes before, during and after elections. The scope of these uses is clear from the typology of ANC alliances and coalitions, several of which in different iterations are used by other political parties as well. The ANC is distinguished by the density of its 'fortress' of multiple and diverse alliance-coalition arrangements.

The periodisation intersects with categorising the ANC's coalition and alliance types. A diverse and nuanced set of coalitions and alliances can be identified. They are summarised in Table 1.2. In one of the major turning points leveraged by coalitions in democratic South Africa, coalitions helped the ANC consolidate and secure power in relation to several competing political parties. The GNU of 1994 was a certain type of coalition. Its power-sharing formula helped facilitate the negotiated settlement of 1993–94 (Spitz and Chaskalson, 2000). The prospect and practice of the GNU helped build a transitional consensus in a politically and racially divided country. It also helped establish the legitimacy of elections as a foundation to determine party-political strength. This would help undergird the coalitions of the future.

In another illustration of the power of coalitions, the ANC (in a phase-two manifestation) advanced over the IFP from the 1990s on in KwaZulu-Natal, with the aid of coalition formation (see chapter 15; Booysen, 2018) and co-governance, and while it let migration of the younger generation away from the IFP take its toll. The ANC in KwaZulu-Natal had a longstanding coalition with the IFP. In the course of the coalition and the changing political-security dynamic, it gradually encroached on IFP territory and then eclipsed it. It achieved an outright provincial majority over the IFP in 2009. In the Western Cape, coalition formation with the NNP in 2004 brought the ANC one-term success. In the 1999 provincial election it had won with a plurality of 42 per cent (see chapter 14), but lost provincial control to the NNP and the DP after these two parties formed an alliance (of short duration; see Kadima, 2006: 70; 2013). Coalitions in conjunction with floor-crossing[10] (Booysen, 2006; 2011: 259–289) then helped the ANC gain plurality-based control over the Western Cape for a limited time. By 2004 the ANC had become the biggest party in the province but lacked an absolute majority; the NNP was decaying fast and needed a lifeline. The two parties jointly delivered the outright majority: a coalition and later an amalgamation (absorption of segments of the NNP) were established. In 2005, through floor-crossing, NNP members of the provincial legislature joined the ANC. The ANC became the Western Cape provincial government until 2009, when the DA took over through elections, which it won with a narrow absolute majority.

Although South Africa has experience of coalition government at the national, provincial and local levels, it is at the local level that these experiences have been the most disruptive and caused instability in governance. Coalitions have helped push the ANC out of power, intermittently to date, in several metropolitan municipalities. When the ANC fell below the threshold of 50 per cent support, opposition parties joined forces and displaced the ANC. The displacement was erratic, given the lack of ideological and policy consensus in the new majorities. The ANC regained power in the periods between elections in some of these local-level sites. Its comebacks were achieved both through tactical manoeuvres within existing councils and through winning by-elections, such as those in late 2020 and early 2021. In the division of votes in the 2019 Gauteng provincial elections, the ANC missed a coalition dispensation by decimal points; in the Northern Cape, the ANC revived itself in the run-up to both the 2014 and 2019 provincial elections and retained outright majorities, despite pre-election expectations to the contrary.

The ANC as a multifaceted coalition and alliance in its own right

The ANC also has the status of an amalgam of internal coalitions. The ANC has been practising defacto intra-ANC coalition politics; this constitutes a crucial part of its coalitions-alliances repertoire. First, various manifestations of ANC factions have been cooperating for electoral purposes; together, they help maintain outright ANC electoral majorities nationally and provincially. Second, the ANC is in a close (albeit variable over time) Tripartite Alliance with the Congress of South African Trade Unions (Cosatu) and the South African Communist Party (SACP). Third, and specific to local government, and impacted by the second practice, are the alliances the ANC has with workers and bureaucrats within municipal bureaucracies and workforces. These alliances can make it difficult for an opposition party like the DA to displace the ANC and be successful in government. Fourth, and central to the phenomenon of dissent from the ANC not being channelled into opposition political parties, is the defacto alliance between the ANC and angered, disillusioned civil society and political actors – rather than register discontent through a political party, citizens often choose protest, revolt and electoral withdrawal as a means of political expression (Booysen, 2007; 2021). The ANC also seems to have benefited from significantly lower turnout rates in national elections: it declined from 73.5 per cent in 2014 to 66 per cent in 2019, a drop of 7.5 percentage points: portions of ANC dissent abstained, rather than split or vote for an opposition party, testifying to this defacto alliance. They were angry or disillusioned with the ANC, but still did not transfer their votes to an opposition party. These community actions are not necessarily pro-ANC in sentiment or allegiance, yet the fact that such discontent does not translate into opposition party support means that it legitimises the predominance of the ANC.

Table 1.2: Typology of alliances and coalitions, with special reference to the ANC

Type of formation	Objective or effect	Illustrations – ANC and opposition parties
ALLIANCES and cooperative formations that may lead to formal pre-electoral alliances		
Formal interparty alliances – with electoral participation and potential representation in parliament	Consolidate power, rescue dying parties, build national cohesion	ANC and NNP into ANC
Sub-party and defacto alliances – channelling participation and representation through the mother party	Historical alliances, factional alliances, lead contestation away from electoral arena, take major issues out of party contests or keep contents intra-party	ANC's Tripartite Alliance, governing alliance with SACP and Cosatu; SACP formally in government, over time subsumed into ANC processes
Occasional interparty cooperation – issues, campaigns to restrain dominant party	Restrain governing party, withhold strategic majorities through cooperation agreements	DA, Cope and UDM
COALITIONS inclusive of cooption to help sustain ANC power in government, or gradually help forge mergers		
Governing coalitions – multiparty	National, provincial and local government level, in absence of outright majorities	ANC, NP and IFP in GNU; ANC and NNP in Western Cape; ANC and IFP in KwaZulu-Natal; Range of municipalities with diverse actors, ANC/NFP, ANC/EFF/PA/AIC/IFP/SACP, etc.
Sub-party coalitions, and breakout coalitions of ANC vs ANC	Generate hegemony, focus power	Tripartite Alliance with ANC and SACP (Cosatu members did not take up formal positions in government; SACP contested in Metsimaholo); Fleeting intra-ANC factional alignment with council opposition to oust an ANC faction (eg, Maluti-a-Phofung, Sol Plaatje)
Minority parties into national executive or legislature.	Cooption into government and minor engagement of individuals in government, legitimating ANC and moderating oppositional impacts	Mangosuthu Buthelezi (IFP), continuing senior cabinet member; Mosibudi Mangena (Azapo) as cabinet member; Pieter Mulder (FF+) as deputy minister; Gavin Woods, Mkhuleko Hlengwa (IFP) as Scopa chairpersons; Themba Godi (African People's Convention) as Scopa chairperson; Zanele kaMagwaza-Msibi as deputy minister; Patricia de Lille (Good) as cabinet member

Source: Author's research and conceptualisation, 2020; see also Booysen, 2014.

From split-offs to internal factional alliances

Intra-ANC factions that cast the ANC as the home of all factions often substituted for interparty contestation and in-government coalition formation. These defacto coalitions permeated ANC government across spheres of local, provincial and national government. Factions are common in party politics, but rarely are there factions so hostile and undermining of one another as those in the ANC. The strongest bond between them is the ANC 'brand', which holds huge rent-seeking value and electoral capital due to the substantial extent to what is referred to as 'struggle mythology' (Ranchod, 2013), leadership icons, and the praxis of the 'father state' who 'comes home at night and brings the food' (Booysen, 2013).

The ANC reached the point where it was forced to retain its status as an alliance of factions:[11] after three sequential breakaways (or split-offs), it had become clear that should it suffer another split-off, it would most likely sink below outright-majority levels nationally and in some provinces.[12]

In 1997 the United Democratic Movement (UDM) was formed after Bantu Holomisa's expulsion from the ANC for his revelations of bribes paid to bantustan-fused-into-the-ANC royalty. A decade later, in 2008, Cope split from the ANC after Thabo Mbeki lost the ANC presidency to the corruption-implicated Jacob Zuma at the ANC's 2007 Polokwane elections. Cope was contained to an electoral imprint of 8 per cent of the national vote in 2009, after the ANC conducted an extensive fightback to retain and regain its base. Finally, in mid-2013, the EFF, in effect the youth wing of the ANC, emerged following internal ANC fallout concerning policy and personalities. The EFF's first national electoral imprint was just over 6 per cent. At each breakaway there were expectations of a legitimate and sizable new political force emerging but the ANC apparatus on each occasion succeeded in minimising the party-movement's electoral and representational damages. On all of these breakaway occasions the ANC maintained solid outright majorities. The 2016 local elections, however, revealed a significant denting of the ANC's edge. If the trend had continued, the ANC would have lost its outright majority status in 2019. Instead, the results registered a modest recovery for the party (see Table 1.1).

In another iteration of factional alliances, factional semi-splits occurred in councils across the provinces of Gauteng, Free State, North West, Mpumalanga and the Northern Cape. ANC factions cooperated with opposition parties in these councils to topple a corrupt ANC faction (sometimes a mayor of that faction) that was in charge of the ANC-controlled council (see also Cooper, 2015). These were fleeting voting alliances that constituted defacto brief coalitions. Dissenting ANC councillors supported motions of no confidence against their own party introduced by, for example, the EFF (in Dr J.S. Moroka, Mpumalanga, 2020), the DA (in Lekwa, Mpumalanga, 2020) and the Freedom Front Plus (FF+) (in Mangaung, Free State, 2019). The ANC took action against the rebels who had aligned with opposition parties, for example, by stripping them of their seats.

The local municipality of Maluti-a-Phofung in the Free State was an illustration. The controlling ANC faction had its allegedly corrupt mayor ousted when 16 ANC members (in the 169-seat council) voted with opposition parties. The ANC rebels argued that they had aligned with the DA to bring an end to corruption. The 16 were expelled but 10 of them won seats as independents in 2019, after the 2018–19 period of the municipality having been placed under administration ended (see Makhafola, 2019). A similar process unfolded in the Sol Plaatje municipality, Northern Cape, where 11 ANC councillors worked with opposition parties to oppose the ANC's mayoral candidate. The ANC leadership interpreted the phenomenon in terms of ill-discipline, and blamed divisions on its branches.

The Tripartite Alliance

The Tripartite Alliance (the ANC, the SACP and Cosatu) was an additional manifestation of the ANC inherently being an alliance-coalition construct that strengthened its hold on the broad voting public. Cosatu suffered internal splits amid contestation on the political margins when party politics and trade union matters collided. These growing tensions about, among other things, how trade unions should relate to the ruling party, led to a number of affiliates walking out of Cosatu in 2017 to create the South African Federation of

Trade Unions (SAFTU) under the leadership of Zwelinzima Vavi, who had been serving as Cosatu's general secretary. The National Union of Metalworkers of South Africa (Numsa) was the key union that joined SAFTU. It spawned the Socialist Revolutionary Workers Party in March 2019 and contested the election. It was preceded by another Numsa-related party, the United Front, which contested the 2014 elections, and an Eastern Cape derivative party that contested the 2016 local elections. Neither the United Front nor the Socialist Revolutionary Workers Party could garner enough votes for a single parliamentary seat. These were notable expressions, nevertheless, of a particular type of dissent from the ANC moving, via union formations, into parties that did not threaten the electoral power of the ANC.

The SACP often debated going it alone in elections. The only time it did venture out solo was at the height of the Zuma presidency in the December 2017 local government by-elections in Metsimaholo in the northern Free State. It gained three proportional representation (PR) seats. The phase passed, and by the time of the 2020 by-elections, the SACP was again welcoming the 'resounding ANC victory' in municipal by-elections (SACP, 2020).

This matrix of coalition-alliance actions has worked to safeguard the ANC against losing outright majorities and becoming subject irretrievably to coalition politics.

CONCLUSION

The ANC, as the pivot of coalition politics in South Africa, has used alliances and coalitions both proactively and defensively. On the proactive side have been the arrangements where the party-movement used interparty associations to bolster its share of power and improve its electoral performance. Liaisons with other political parties were leveraged to build joint government and to use this as a platform for ascendance. This was the case when the ANC rose to power in KwaZulu-Natal. The ANC also used the mechanism of floor-crossing in, especially, the 2005–06 period (constitutionally permitted at the time), in combination with its cooperation with the NNP to take power in the Western Cape. Defensively, the ANC has used coalitions to help it to regain power where it had been lost. Illustrations of this category are in the metropolitan-municipal domain, for example the City of Johannesburg. In the domain of alliances, the ANC has worked on labour formations competing with Cosatu not being able to contest effectively. Also as part of its defensive, the ANC has pacified and managed its internal factional fallout in order to prevent further splits.

The proactive defensive dimension is important because it illustrates the extent to which parties, and in this instance the ANC, will use alliances and coalitions as a weapon to outmanoeuvre political opponents. If the ultimate objective is to retain or regain control over representative institutions, it follows that this will be a highly unstable political environment.

The core argument in this chapter has been that coalitions are leveraged when, as in the case of South Africa, the dominant-party system decays. The ANC has been at the helm of South Africa's political system since 1994. Being in power for the ANC is synonymous with having conquered apartheid and the legacies of colonialism. It tends to see other political parties as types of intruders on the party-political terrain. Its repertoire of alliances and coalitions illustrates the wall of defence it has built to contain assaults and regain power where it was lost. Opposition parties and alliances may advance – where their own statuses allow – but are likely to find a network of ANC-directed alliances and coalitions to counter them.

South Africa's experience of coalition governance up to 2021, especially after 2016, has flagged the major problems of instability, alternation of different coalitions in power in the same term of office, and inconsistency in service delivery often triggered by instability in councils. The dynamics of coalition construction has had direct implications for the stability of governance arrangements in the country. Further, governance-related issues have included erosion in democratic accountability; portfolio bartering in exchange for political buy-in, which compromises governance; and corruption related to procurement processes. Councillors are open to better offers from the proponents of alternative coalitions, and instability has been par for the course. A significant part of the instability has resulted from the fact that the party coalition partners have come with their sets of associated bureaucrats: the town and city managers have turned over along with their political principals. Or party-politically associated provincial administrations have taken over city and town administrations, but with little transparency, no direct accountability and uncertain improvement in service delivery.[13]

REFERENCES

Altman, D. 2000. 'The politics of coalition formation and survival in multiparty presidential democracies: The case of Uruguay, 1989–1999', *Party Politics*, 6 (3), 259–283.

amaBhungane. 29 November 2018. 'Firm that won R1bn Joburg fleet contract paid Malema-EFF "slush fund"', *Daily Maverick*, https://www.dailymaverick.co.za/article/2018-11-29-firm-that-won-r1bn-joburg-fleet-contract-paid-malema-eff-slush-fund/, accessed 2 May 2020.

Beardsworth, N. 13 June 2017. 'Why do opposition coalitions succeed or fail?', *African Arguments*, https://africanarguments.org/2017/06/13/why-do-opposition-coalitions-succeed-or-fail/, accessed 12 April 2020.

Bogaards, M. and Boucek, F. 2010. *Dominant Parties and Democracy: Concepts, measures, cases and comparisons*. London: Routledge.

Booysen, S. 2006. 'The will of the parties versus the will of the people? Defections, elections and alliances in South Africa', *Party Politics*, 12 (6), 751–770.

Booysen, S. 2007. 'With the ballot and the brick: The politics of attaining service delivery', *Progress in Development Studies*, 7 (1), 21–32.

Booysen, S. 2011. *The African National Congress and the Regeneration of Political Power*. Johannesburg: Witwatersrand University Press.

Booysen, S. 2013. 'Twenty Years of South African Democracy: Citizen views of human rights, governance and the political system'. Report on focus groups, Freedom House, Washington DC and Johannesburg.

Booysen, S. 2014. 'Causes and impact of party alliances on the party system and national cohesion in South Africa', *Journal of African Elections*, 13 (11), 66–92.

Booysen, S. 2015. *Dominance and Decline*. Johannesburg: Wits University Press.

Booysen, S. 2018. 'Coalitions and alliances demarcate crossroads in ANC trajectories – ANC electoral conference', *New Agenda: South African Journal of Social and Economic Policy*, 68, 6–10.

Booysen, S. 2021. *Precarious Power: Compliance and discontent under Ramaphosa's ANC*. Johannesburg: Wits University Press.

Boucek, F. 2012. *Factional Politics: How dominant parties implode or stabilize*. London: Palgrave MacMillan.

Brooks, H. 2004. 'The dominant-party system: Challenges for South Africa's second decade of democracy', *Journal of African Elections*, 3 (2), 121–153.

Caramani, D. (ed.) 2017. *Comparative Politics* (fourth edition). Oxford: Oxford University Press.

Cooper, I. 2015. 'Zuma, Malema and the provinces: Factional conflict within the African National Congress', *Transformation: Critical Perspectives on Southern Africa,* 87 (1), 151–174.

Electoral Commission of South Africa (IEC). 2019. www.elections.org.za, multiple windows, including the IEC Results Dashboard containing national and all provincial results, accessed multiple dates, 2019–2021.

Hirschman, A. O. 1970. *Exit, Voice, and Loyalty: Responses to decline in firms, organizations, and states*. Boston: Harvard University Press.

Institute for Government. 2012. 'The Coalition: Voters, parties and institutions'. Conference proceedings, University of East Anglia, www.instituteforgovernment.org.uk, accessed 16 December 2020.

Jordaan, N. 2020. 'Sona just a litany of failed promises as municipalities get worse: Outa', TimesLIVE. https://www.timeslive.co.za/politics/2020-02-10-sona-just-a-litany-of-failed-promises-as-municipalities-get-worse-outa/, accessed 7 March 2020.

Kadima, D. 2006. 'Party coalitions in post-apartheid South Africa and their impact on national cohesion and ideological rapprochement', in Kadima, D. (ed.) *The Politics of Party Coalitions in Africa*. Johannesburg: Electoral Institute for Sustainable Democracy in Africa.

Kadima, D. 2013. 'An introduction to the politics of party alliances and coalitions in socially divided Africa', *Journal of African Elections*, 13 (1), 1–24.

Langfield, D. 2014. 'Opposition growth in dominant party systems: Coalitions in South Africa', *Government and Opposition*, 49 (2), 290–312.

Ledger, T. and Rampedi, M. 2019. 'Mind the Gap: Section 139 interventions in theory and in practice'. A PARI report, Public Affairs Research Institute, Johannesburg.

Lindberg, S. I. and Jones, J. 2010. 'Laying a foundation for democracy or undermining it? Dominant parties in Africa's burgeoning democracies', in Bogaards, M. and Boucek, F. (eds.) *Dominant Parties and Democracy: Concepts, measures, cases and comparisons*. London: Routledge, 196–218.

Mac Giollabhuí, S. 2013. 'How things fall apart: Candidate selection and the cohesion of dominant parties in South Africa and Namibia', *Party Politics,* 19 (4), 577–600.

Makhafola, G. 13 September 2019. 'Maluti-a-Phofung has a new mayor, speaker and chief whip', IOL, https://www.iol.co.za/news/politics/maluti-a-phofung-has-a-new-mayor-speaker-and-chief-whip-32904349, accessed 5 March 2020.

Mapungubwe Institute for Strategic Reflection (MISTRA). 2019. Booysen, S.

(ed.), 'Voting Trends 25 Years into Democracy: Analysis of South Africa's 2019 election'. Special report, MISTRA, Johannesburg.

Olver, C. n.d. 'The political economy of rent seeking in South African cities'. PhD proposal, University of the Witwatersrand, Johannesburg.

Oyugi, W. O. 2006. 'Coalition politics and coalition governments in Africa', *Journal of Contemporary African Studies*, 24 (1), 53–79.

Ranchod, R. 2013. *A Kind of Magic: The political marketing of the ANC*. Johannesburg: Jacana Media.

SABCNewsOnline. 9 September 2019. 'ANC in N.Cape facing deep divisions', https://www.sabcnews.com/sabcnews/anc-in-n-cape-facing-deep-divisions/, accessed 5 April 2020.

South African Communist Party (SACP). 12 November 2020. 'SACP in Gauteng welcomes the resounding ANC victory in municipal by-elections', https://www.sacp.org.za/content/sacp-gauteng-welcomes-resounding-anc-victory-municipal-elections, accessed 24 November 2020.

South African Government (SA Govt). 1 July 2020. 'Auditor-General Kimi Makwetu releases municipal audit results', https://www.gov.za/speeches/auditor-general-kimi-makwetu-releases-municipal-audit-results-1-jul-2020-0000, accessed 11 January 2021.

Southall, R. 2005. 'The "Dominant Party Debate" in South Africa', *Africa Spectrum,* 40 (1), 61–82.

Spitz, R. and Chaskalson, M. 2000. *The Politics of Transition: The hidden history of South Africa's negotiated settlement*. London: Hart Publishing.

TWO

Local government coalitions across South Africa, 2000–16

Mcebisi Ndletyana

COALITIONS IN LOCAL GOVERNMENT have been a dominant subject in public discussions since South Africa's local elections of 2016. Yet they are not a novel phenomenon. Coalitions in the country are as old as the new model of local government, introduced in 2000. The 2016 local elections were the fourth set to yield hung councils – those that did not deliver an outright winner. Local government had its highest number of hung councils in 2011. The 2016 local elections, notwithstanding the frenzy generated due to South Africa's several metropolitan municipalities acquiring hung council statuses, produced the lowest number of hung councils.

The year 2016, therefore, simply propelled to public prominence what had been in existence for more than 16 years. Part of the difference, this time around, was that this phenomenon impacted three of the country's most developed metropoles, in the province of Gauteng. With such concentration in this heartland area, the dramatic activities that ensued were bound to be noticed. That these hung councils also included a new political party adept at attracting public attention – the Economic Freedom Fighters (EFF) – added to the media fever (Mbete, 2016).

This chapter provides an overview and a historical account of hung councils and the resultant coalition governments in the period since 2000 in South Africa. Its primary objective is to explain their ebb and flow, marked by an uneven spread, in the sphere of local government. The chapter contends that coalitions are a product primarily of competitive politics occasioned by racial and social fissures and interparty rivalry. Part of the competition stems from the susceptibility of municipalities made up of low-income and indigent residents to the 'big man' syndrome, which tends to engender splits and patron-based parties. These dynamics are illustrated through the use of case studies drawn from different parts of the country at different times. While covering a wide array of municipalities, the chapter directs attention to the minefield of municipal-coalition activities beyond the metropolitan municipalities. (Several chapters in this book, especially chapters 10, 11, 12 and 13, have a dedicated focus on metropolitan coalitions.) The details and concrete actions analysed in this chapter also extend many of the arguments in chapter 1, especially those concerning party dominance, leadership, factionalism and splits, while illustrating in the South African context many of the coalition phenomena and trends at the global level that follow in chapter 3.

FLUCTUATIONS AND PROVINCIAL VARIATIONS

Local government had no fewer than 119 hung councils from 2000 to 2020 (see Table 2.1). From the initial 29 in the 2000 election to the comparable 30 in 2006, their tally fluctuated more in the subsequent two sets of local elections. While most impactful on the balance of power at the local level, the 2016 election yielded the lowest number of hung councils at 27. They were highest in 2011 at 33 (IEC, 2017).

All of South Africa's provinces have had coalition councils, except Mpumalanga. Among the eight provinces that have had coalition councils, the extent of their presence and regularity has been uneven. The Western Cape and KwaZulu-Natal have had coalition councils in

Table 2.1: Coalition councils – Province breakdown, 2000–16 local government elections

Province	Local elections: Number of coalitions per election				Provincial total
	2000	2006	2011	2016	
Eastern Cape	1	1	-	1	3
Free State	-	-	-	1	1
Gauteng	2	-	-	4	6
Limpopo	-	-	-	2	2
KwaZulu-Natal	10	8	19	7	44
Mpumalanga	-	-	-	-	-
Northern Cape	2	-	5	3	10
North West	-	-	-	1	1
Western Cape	14	21	9	8	52
Total	29	30	33	27	119

Source: Author's research and conceptualisation, based on data supplied by the IEC in 2017

every local election. For the first two local elections, the Western Cape had the highest number. That distinction switched to KwaZulu-Natal in 2011, only for the Western Cape, albeit marginally, to reclaim the status in 2016.

The 2011 election also revealed contrasting fluctuations in KwaZulu-Natal and the Western Cape, from the 2006 election. In KwaZulu-Natal the number of hung councils in 2011 went up by more than half, while dropping by roughly the same margin in the Western Cape. After an absence of hung councils in 2006, the Northern Cape re-emerged in 2011 with far more than it had had in 2000. The Free State, North West and Limpopo had hung councils for the first time in 2016. This 2016 election actually produced hung councils in more provinces – eight of out nine – than had been the case up to that time.

Some municipalities had hung council more than once. The Western Cape has the distinction of having four municipalities – Laingsburg, Kannaland, Witzenberg and Prince Albert – that have had hung councils three times. The Laingsburg municipality took it further, to a fourth time. KwaZulu-Natal and the Northern Cape have also had their share of recurrent hung councils, in seven and two municipalities, respectively. The other six provinces have had them only once. Some municipalities, albeit rarely, have had a hung council with only two parties tied, instead of the usual multiple parties. The 2000 local election produced two such councils – Swellendam and Laingsburg in the Western Cape and one, Sentrale Karoo, in the Northern Cape. The Western Cape's Prince Albert municipality followed in 2006.

In the majority of cases, hung councils had a plurality of political parties and organisations (and individuals), ensuring that there would be a kingmaker, or a tiebreaker. The identity of tiebreakers varied, from an established party[1] or a community organisation to an independent candidate. Tiebreakers tended to vary per province, and usually had brief lifespans. KwaZulu-Natal, the Northern Cape and Gauteng tended to have political parties in the role of kingmakers. Some of these parties have been more prominent in certain provinces than others. The National Freedom Party (NFP) and the Minority Front, for instance, featured mostly in KwaZulu-Natal; the African Christian Democratic Party (ACDP) in the Western Cape; the Congress of the People (Cope) predominantly in the Western Cape and the Northern Cape; the Independent Democrats (ID) almost exclusively in the Western Cape; and the EFF largely in KwaZulu-Natal, Gauteng and Limpopo. In a slightly different manner, the Western Cape has seen both political parties and community organisations, to varying degrees, assuming the role of kingmakers. It is the only province that has consistently had community organisations as influential actors in municipal coalitions. While in some provinces community organisations that become tiebreakers tend to have a brief lifespan, rising before one election only to disappear before the next, in the Western Cape a few have endured across elections and played a decisive role in more than one municipality.

THE FLUCTUATIONS, UNEVEN SPREAD AND DIVERGENT ACTORS

While South Africa has been a one party dominant system for most of the post-1994 period (see chapters 1 and 4), it has also been characterised by provincial variations in levels of electoral competition, especially in KwaZulu-Natal and the Western Cape and, to a lesser degree, in the Northern Cape and Gauteng (Booysen, 2011; Schulz-Herzenberg,

2016; Africa, 2016). That said, on closer inspection, it is clear that competition at the local level has not been as intense as provincial comparisons suggested. Parties carved out their own niche areas of electoral support in specific communities that are distinguished by developmental status, language and class. Moreover, the variety of political actors in the coalitions game – some of whom burst onto the political scene, only to disappear with the same suddenness – betrays tensions within existing, old parties. The tensions arise out of power struggles over leadership and the identity of parties. The rest of this chapter uses case-study methodology to unpack these dimensions of coalition politics, as manifested at the non-metro local level in South Africa.

Intraparty rivalry, leadership power struggles and splits

Electoral support for the two main parties in KwaZulu-Natal – the IFP and the ANC – since 1994 initially followed a geographic pattern. The IFP dominated the northern part of the province, and the urban southern part was predominantly ANC. The central part, known as the Midlands, mostly fell to the ANC, with some pockets of IFP support. Unlike the northern part, the southern region has a cosmopolitan identity and was thus disposed towards the universal politics embraced by the ANC. This division of electoral support related to levels of development and the history of each region.

The northern part of KwaZulu-Natal had previously been part of the KwaZulu bantustan. Then a ruling party of the bantustan, the IFP was the only party in the territory. Mangosuthu Buthelezi, the IFP leader and head of the bantustan, had managed to suppress anti-apartheid formations. Buthelezi's government coerced people into joining his party in order to get employment in the public service and, after besmirching others as anti-Zulu, convinced some locals that the IFP was the only party for Zulu speakers (Maré, 1992). Personalities and leadership gradually meshed into the geographic divides. A mark of the distinctiveness of the southern region was the identity of the person that led the re-establishment of the ANC following its unbanning in 1990 – Mosiuoa 'Terror' Lekota. A former Black Consciousness Movement leader who had spent years in Robben Island prison, Lekota is a native Sesotho speaker, but attended secondary school in what was then Natal, where he later started working. Lekota's political identity, in the fairly progressive southern part of the province, trumped his ethnic identity (Sithole, 2013) and he helped establish ANC inroads (see chapter 15).

The emergence of hung councils in KwaZulu-Natal revealed the narrowing of niches that had been occupied by the IFP. The party began to lose grip on municipalities that had previously been its strongholds, leading to hung councils. This process began in the 2006 election and consolidated in 2011. The loss of support was a result of both intraparty rivalry and the ANC's encroachment, in the context of a changing regional security situation. Intraparty rivalry led to splits in 2005 and 2011, culminating in the formation of new parties – the National Democratic Convention (Nadeco) and the NFP, respectively. Ziba Jiyane, then national chairperson of the IFP, led the initial split in August 2005. His departure followed a period of tension between himself and the party's founder and president, Buthelezi. Jiyane had been challenging Buthelezi's autocratic grip on the leadership of the organisation. Even Jiyane's election as national chairperson, in the previous national conference in 2004, had happened in defiance of Buthelezi's wishes. Buthelezi preferred Lionel Mtshali and had instructed Jiyane not to stand. Jiyane went on to trounce Mtshali, winning about 70 per cent of the votes. Stanley Dladla, another candidate who shared Jiyane's platform of introducing internal democracy, also won against Buthelezi's favourite, Zanele kaMagwaza-Msibi. Musa Zondi, Buthelezi's ally at the time, retained his position in the absence from the conference of his rival, a Jiyane ally (News24, 2005).

As preparations for the July 2005 conference got underway, Jiyane's name was touted as a possible challenger to Buthelezi. Buthelezi's supporters denounced Jiyane's reported bid for leadership as an attempt to unseat the leader. In one meeting of the party's national council, around May 2005, Jiyane walked out in protest against accusations that he was undermining Buthelezi's leadership. On his return to the meeting, Buthelezi suggested that Jiyane step down as national chairperson. Jiyane refused, adamant that only the scheduled national conference could decide his fate. His subsequent association with Nadeco, however, suggests that his continued stay in the IFP leadership had become untenable. Nadeco's contest in the 2006 election cost the IFP control of four municipalities: Ndwedwe, uMhlathuze, Mtubatuba and Newcastle. Holding the balance of power between the ANC, on the one hand, and the IFP and its allies, on the other, Nadeco sided with the ANC to form coalition governments in those municipalities.

In the run-up to the 2011 local election, it was kaMagwaza-Msibi's turn to split from the IFP. Previously a beneficiary of Buthelezi's preferential treatment, kaMagwaza-Msibi developed ambitions of her own and rejected the dictates of her former benefactor. As reports of her intention to challenge Buthelezi grew louder, she was told to publicly renounce any plans of challenging the long-serving leader. She refused and her supporters constituted themselves into a faction called Friends of V.Z. Magwaza. Buthelezi instituted a disciplinary hearing against her, which she challenged in court. The disciplinary proceedings, kaMagwaza-Msibi countered, were a ploy to exorcise her from the IFP, thereby protecting Buthelezi from a leadership challenge. She pleaded with the court both to abort the disciplinary process and to order that the party's national conference be held without delay (Sithole, 2011).

The court ruled against kaMagwaza-Msibi – the disciplinary proceedings would continue, raising the likelihood of her expulsion. She quit the IFP and formed the NFP in February 2011. Unlike Nadeco, which by then had been crippled by in-fighting, kaMagwaza-Msibi's NFP had deeper repercussions for the IFP. The tally of IFP-controlled municipalities dwindled to two, a drop from 28 in 2006. Hung councils rose to 19, from eight in 2006. Of the hung councils, the NFP held the balance of power in 18 and was the largest party in one. It sided with the ANC. Splinter parties thus cost the IFP. Splits, however, could not account entirely for the IFP's decline. The proportion of support that the NFP attained in some of the municipalities was notably less compared to the IFP's overall loss. Part of the IFP's electoral losses also went to the ANC, as indicated by the party's sharp rise in some of the municipalities.

From a significant actor and kingmaker in 2011, the NFP became an inconsequential figure in the 2016 election. It suffered the same fate as Nadeco. Months into the 2006 term, Nadeco leaders were pitted against each other. Jiyane suspended the executive, only for them to turn around and suspend him. They denounced him as an autocrat (Khumalo, 2006). Jiyane left the party in December 2007 and re-emerged in 2008 with yet another new and ill-fated party, the South African Democratic Congress (Sadeco). With Sadeco proving unviable, Jiyane went searching for an established party with better prospects. He found that in the DA, in 2011. Jiyane quickly challenged for DA provincial leadership, standing against Sizwe Mchunu, but lost by a slim margin, probably because of an ill-conceived comment: he told a DA meeting in Pinetown, according to journalist Jan-Jan Joubert, 'that he was against equal rights for gay South Africans. That being anti-constitutional, it became an issue against him.'[2] Following this failed leadership bid, Jiyane's interparty tour continued and he joined the ANC. He did not stay long. He switched to the NFP in 2018, only to leave that party too, rejoining the IFP, as he had heard Buthelezi was set to retire (Mthethwa, 2018; Hans, 2019).

Like Nadeco, the NFP proved to be a patron-based party: the party crumbled in the absence of kaMagwaza-Msibi. She fell ill and became less active in the party. This led to instability, with lesser potential successors jostling to fill the vacuum. Others could not accept that, in kaMagwaza-Msibi's absence, as the NFP constitution prescribed, the deputy-president Alex Kekana assumed the powers of the president. But when Kekana exercised those powers, they suspended him, accusing him of attempting to usurp powers he supposedly did not have. The NFP could not fathom electing a president to succeed kaMagwaza-Msibi.

KaMagwaza-Msibi was the party, and without her the NFP was paralysed. It failed to pay registration fees for the 2016 election, registering only at the Nquthu local municipality. Some explained it as an honest lapse occasioned by internal disorganisation; others attributed it to sabotage in collusion with the IFP. Contesting only one municipality, where it won two seats (down from five in 2011), the NFP was virtually wiped off the local political scene in KwaZulu-Natal. This partly explains the substantial reduction in the number of hung councils, compared to the previous election – from 19 to seven (Mngomezulu, 2016).

This leadership and party disintegration dynamic helped the IFP to regain ground in the 2016 election. It wrested back control in nine municipalities that had been under the ANC and/or the NFP after the 2011 election. It did so either through an outright win, or in coalition with the DA and the EFF. This pattern of alliance formation in KwaZulu-Natal was indicative of a general trend among established parties across the country. Other parties – Cope, the ACDP, the FF+, the United Democratic Movement (UDM), the Pan Africanist Congress (PAC) and the ID – also tended to combine voting power in councils, in opposition to the ANC. Conversely, the African Independent Congress (AIC) and the Patriotic Alliance (PA) often voted with the ANC. There have been exceptions, though, and the choice of a partner has not always been clear-cut. Parties have been guided strictly by their own interests.

Splits therefore played a key role in the emergence of local-level coalition governments. Splinter groups took support away from their former party; the proliferation of hung councils in the Northern Cape, Gauteng and Limpopo in 2011 and 2016, to illustrate the wider relevance, resulted from the same phenomenon. Splinter groups from the ANC – Cope and the EFF – became formidable competitors in the municipalities that had been dominated previously by the ANC (Ndletyana, 2010; Mbete, 2016).

Career politicians and factionalism – the triggers for splits

The variety of organisations and individuals that have shaved support off dominant parties, and often emerged as kingmakers in local politics in South Africa, have been spawned by different triggers. The reasons for their emergence range from failure to secure a nomination on the party's election list, to exclusion due to factional affiliation, and expulsion for wrongdoing. Case studies drawn from the Western Cape and Limpopo provide insights into these dynamics.

Nomination onto the party list is coveted in those systems that use party-list proportional representation (PR) as electoral systems, including South Africa. Holding public office is more than an opportunity to provide public service: it also provides a salary. The stakes escalate if a particular politician lacks professional qualifications to secure any other employment. A party can, however, have only a limited number of nominees. Even within that list of nominees, only a certain number, depending on position on the list and the party's electoral performance, will make it into employment as a public representative. It is a highly competitive process, and some employ underhanded tactics to secure a nomination to an electable position. Attendance registers at ANC branch meetings, for instance, have been inflated in order to create a quorum, rival members are misled about the time and venue of branch meetings, and others are denied entry for spurious reasons such as claims of expired membership. In other cases, individuals who have been duly nominated are removed from the list by leaders who insert their own preferred candidates (Ndletyana, 2020).

Individuals react differently to the loss of nomination. Some accept the outcome and remain in the party; others exit to contest elections as independents or form new parties. Sometimes the expulsions are warranted, arising from a breach of party rules, but they are also the result of the purge of rivals. In some instances, expulsions have spurred individuals to launch independent political careers. The way in which individuals leave parties, and then get elected as independents or leaders of community organisations, is a commentary on both the integrity of party processes and voting behaviour in particular communities.

Hung councils in the Western Cape, where community organisations and independents have had a prominent role, are revealing. There are different origins behind these actors, and their new organisations have variable lifespans. Resident organisations that emerged as kingmakers in the southeastern towns of the Western Cape – George, Knysna and Oudtshoorn – were established by former political activists who had been part of the United Democratic Front (UDF), an internal resistance movement that fought against apartheid. An umbrella body that included a number of affiliates, and aligned to the then exiled ANC, the UDF established a strong presence in these small coastal towns. Some of the UDF's activities included centres that provided advisory services to locals, ranging from how to access social services to legal assistance. For largely poor people who lived under an oppressive state, the advisory centres provided a much-needed activist intervention.[3]

Democratisation made these non-profit advisory centres somewhat redundant. Their functions were either no longer needed or were now provided by the democratic state. This change necessitated a rethinking among the activists that staffed them. Either they found new professional paths, or they remained political activists and became career politicians. For those who remained active in the ANC, the governing party, some missed out on public office or appointment into salaried positions. In their ranks were Besel Petros in George, Ricky Aswagen in Knysna and Angeline Lekay in Oudtshoorn. They formed civic organisations in their own communities. Their previous role of providing community service stood them in good stead for electoral politics; they were already prominent and had credibility among locals. It earned them notable numbers of votes in the 2000 elections. Petros's George Community Initiative got three seats; Aswagen's Knysna Community Forum and Lekay's Oudtshoorn Aksie 2000 secured two seats each in their respective hung councils. Their organisations split local votes that would probably have gone to the ANC had they remained in the party.

All three organisations, however, were short-lived. Their lifespans were cut short either by power struggles, or by better prospects of prolonging the political careers of their leaders under established parties. They did not feature in the 2006 elections, but metamorphosed: in that year, the Knysna Community Forum resurfaced as the Oudtshoorn Civic Association; and Petros and Aswagen joined the newly formed ID and were returned as councillors. Already an established and prominent name, Patricia de Lille, the leader of the ID, boosted Petros and Aswagen's standing in their communities and possibly offered much-needed resources for campaigning. For career politicians, the few seats offered by the Knysna Community Forum triggered a fight over leadership in order to leverage election into council, if the organisation won sufficient seats. Those who lost out in the contest simply resurfaced with their own new organisation that assured their nomination.

The case of the Thabazimbi Residents Association (TRA) 10

years later in Limpopo province confirms the disposition of civic associations towards fracturing. Midah Moselane and Mpho Moloko were among the founders of the TRA, and attracted members who had been excluded from the ANC party list: they had been nominated by their ANC branches for the 2016 election, only for their names to be excluded by the party's regional leaders in favour of those leaders' preferred candidates. The TRA registered in the same wards, contesting for the same voters as the ANC. They won two seats, which proved decisive in settling the balance of power in council between the DA, the EFF and the FF+ pact with 11 votes, on the one hand, and the ANC's 10 votes, on the other. Both the DA alliance and the ANC needed the two TRA seats to form a coalition government. The TRA voted with the DA, for which it got the mayoralty.[4] This TRA decision, however, was not unanimous – some had preferred a coalition with the ANC, the party out of which the TRA had been born.

The disagreement led to a schism in the association, which divided into two rival factions, one led by Moselane, the other by Johan Fisher. The latter insisted that their viewpoint enjoyed majority support within the organisation. For defying this majority, Fisher's faction decided that they no longer recognised Moselane as the leader of the TRA. They called a conference, which proceeded to elect new leaders. The newly elected leaders, including Fisher, demanded to occupy the two TRA seats in council. Moselane and her colleague refused to vacate the seats, arguing that they were still the legitimate leaders of the TRA, and denounced the conference that had elected Fisher as a fraud.

The dispute dragged on for two years and was eventually settled in court. Moselane and her colleague lost the court battle (*Thabazimbi Residents Association v Municipality Manager*). They vacated the seats and were replaced by the new TRA leaders. The association kept the mayoralty. Contradictorily, though, they remained in the coalition with the DA alliance, apparently because the ANC would not agree to their demand to retain the mayoralty. The removal of some of the founding leaders of the TRA makes it highly likely that the association may not be returned to council in the next election, which, in turn, implies that the council may return to a majority government.

Populism, charisma and 'big men'

Some breakaway organisations, however, were formed by errant individuals expelled for ill-behaviour. Their erratic behaviour did not stain their popularity in their communities. These are charismatic leaders that capitalise on wedge issues in the community and establish themselves as 'big men'. Besides their personal traits, their electoral popularity stems from societal issues, and coalition politics both relied on and further built these strengths. The Western Cape's eastern and southeastern towns of Beaufort West and Kannaland are instructive of these dynamics.

Only two main political parties in the Western Cape, the DA and the ANC, previously contested the Beaufort West municipality. The ANC won the contest comfortably in 2000 with 61 per cent, giving the organisation eight of the 13 seats in council. The 2006 election saw the entry of a third party, the Independent Civic Organisation of South Africa (ICOSA), formed by Truman Prince. A former member of the ANC, Prince had been expelled from the organisation. Both the municipality where he worked as a city manager and the ANC had suspended him for misusing municipal funds. While serving the suspension he was also found to have solicited sex from underaged prostitutes. This added another infraction against him, for casting the organisation in a bad light. It seemed unlikely that Prince would escape punishment (Kassiem, 2006).

Prince considered the disciplinary processes unwarranted. He felt singled out for unfair treatment. Some of his colleagues in the ANC, Prince felt, had been guilty of the same infractions, but were never dealt with in the same way. Prince resented the treatment because he believed the ANC had won Beaufort West because of him, and that he had been instrumental in the election of the ANC's provincial leaders, Mcebisi Skwatsha and James Ngculu, who were now to expel him. Prince warned Skwatsha that the ANC would lose Beaufort West without him (Prince): 'I told Skwatsha that the day I'm expelled from the party, Skwatsha will have to pack his suitcases … I have won every election I've stood in. Never mind the party, we've won.' The ANC was unrelenting. Ngculu, the party's chairperson, said Prince had a 'bad track record' and 'was a blot on the image of the ANC'

(Kassiem, 2006). At the time Prince also faced charges of assault and public disturbance.

The 2006 election validated Prince's self-estimation. The ANC lost its majority in the Beaufort West council, going down to five seats – the same number of seats won by Prince's ICOSA. The other two parties that won seats were the DA and the ID, with two seats and one seat, respectively. The municipality that the ANC had won comfortably in the previous election was now without a majority party, due to ICOSA having split the vote that hitherto had gone to the ANC. The balance of power rested with the DA's two votes. This put the ANC at a disadvantage, for the DA felt strongly against forming a coalition with the ANC (Zille, 2016); and relations between the ANC and Prince were still strained. However, the DA was uncomfortable associating itself with the controversial figure of Prince, and despite its reluctance to form a coalition with the ANC, the DA could not avoid one. That coalition crumbled. Thereafter, the DA joined forces with Prince's ICOSA – the same leader whose reputation had repulsed them. That coalition, too, dissolved. Prince then led ICOSA into the embrace of his old party, ANC.[5]

Prince's victory revealed much about the man's standing in the community and what influenced local voters' electoral choices. Accusations of misuse of funds and sex with underage girls seemed not to have tainted Prince's image. If they did, the voters did not consider them sufficient to disqualify him from office. Prince had managed to make himself indispensable in local politics. Called reverently by locals *'Beaufort se baas'* (Beaufort's boss), Prince achieved this position through a mixture of populism and patronage. When in trouble or in need, locals approached him for assistance. As a city manager, Prince earned a significant salary and had influence over who got appointed and where municipal funds were spent. He dispensed personal favours to locals and was associated with key developments in the community. As a member of the South African Football Association, he was instrumental in building a local stadium that was envisaged to be a training base for the 2010 Soccer World Cup. He owned a football team, which added to his popularity and esteem. The misuse of public funds, for which he had been suspended, involved payment for bail to get someone out of prison.[6]

In Kannaland, another ICOSA leader, Geoffrey Donson, owes his popularity to a similar posture and circumstances. Also a former ANC member, Donson is a controversial figure whose career has been marked by a number of scandals. Within the 2006 term alone, for instance, Donson was expelled as mayor for abusing municipal funds, and charged and convicted for statutory rape for having a sexual relationship with a 15-year-old girl. He successfully appealed the verdict, getting it reduced to a fine and a suspended sentence. Freed from legal problems, Donson contested a by-election and won. In the following election, of 2011, ICOSA emerged as the largest party with three seats, while the ANC and the DA followed with two each. The same result followed in the 2016 election (Peters, 2010).

Like Prince in Beaufort West, Donson is a 'big man' in Kannaland. Besides holding political office, Donson also runs his own nightclub where he sometimes fills in as a disc jockey, known as DJ Fantastic. Providing entertainment adds to his standing and generates him sufficient income, together with control over public funds, to dispense patronage. Kannaland abounds with stories of Donson instructing officials to use council money to help out residents who have approached him for assistance.[7] Locals may have moral reservations about such misconduct, but for poor people who are often in dire need of help, securing relief at desperate moments oftentimes trumps moral considerations.

Donson and Prince emerged effectively untainted by scandal. The ANC accepted Prince back into the fold in the run-up to the 2011 election, despite having condemned him previously as a blot on their image. In fact, after realising that they could not win outright without him, the ANC decided to dispense with moral considerations and put Prince at the helm of their ticket for the 2011 election. The party won an outright majority. Part of Prince and Donson's appeal derives from the tenor of local politics, which is tinged with racial tension. The predominantly coloured communities suffer general disquiet that policies aimed at racial redress, such as affirmative action and black economic empowerment, discriminate against them in favour of African people. As the author and proponent of such policies, the

ANC is vulnerable to caricature as the party for Africans. It is this sense of exclusion that Prince and Donson exploit, casting themselves as proponents of coloured interests. Their staple of politics is coloured nationalism – in the name of coloureds and for the coloured people.[8]

Many of the municipalities that are prone to have coalitions are marked by their relatively small voting populations. This makes their thresholds for councillor electability easier to meet. A glaring example of this comes from Laingsburg in the 2016 election. A total of 220 votes were enough to get the Karoo Ontwikkelingsparty (KOP) elected to the council. The total number of valid votes cast was 6,157. The KOP got one seat, compared to the three each of the DA and the ANC. The KOP was therefore the kingmaker, and got the mayoralty in return for siding with the DA. This was a typical trade-off, but the subsequent change of the KOP councillor for mayoralty caused controversy. The initial mayor, Aubrey Marthinus, was forced to resign due to embezzlement of funds, making the second candidate on the KOP party list, Johannes Mienies, eligible to fill the post. Mienies had an unusual profile for the coveted position of mayor: he was an unemployed former construction worker who lived with his mother (Jordan, 2018). The ANC complained that Mienies was unfit to be mayor as a consequence of his excessive drinking habits. There was nothing the ANC could do, however; Mienies was the custodian of the KOP seat and the DA needed him to be part of the coalition government.[9]

Rejection of party elites and popular dissatisfaction

Sasolburg exploded into protests in early 2013. The spark was a proposal to merge Metsimaholo, the municipality under which Sasolburg resorts, with Ngwathe, a neighbouring municipality in the northern Free State covering the town of Parys. The two major towns are distinct and hold different meanings for the people of the Free State. Sasolburg, the economic hub, is home to the giant petrochemical company Sasol; Parys is viewed as the centre of provincial political authority due to its being the hometown of then ANC provincial secretary and premier (and subsequently ANC secretary-general) Ace Magashule.

Magashule was considered the most powerful provincial chairperson and premier since democratisation in 1994. A common refrain among locals in the Free State was 'nothing happens in the Free State without Ace'. Pieter-Louis Myburgh (2019) provides a detailed account of how, with a tight grip on both the party and the state, Magashule amassed power through distribution of patronage in the form of appointments and business contracts. This experience and knowledge of Magashule stirred resistance in Sasolburg against the merger, which locals saw as Magashule's way of taking direct control, through proxies in the Ngwathe municipality, over Metsimaholo. Most of the revenue, business contracts and government offices under a merged municipality, locals feared, would relocate to Parys. In the words of one protestor, Sam Mthembu, '[W]e as residents of Metsimaholo do not want to be associated with those thieves' (*Mail & Guardian*, 2013).

In this context the Metsimaholo Community Association emerged to lead the protest. Lucky Malebo, a local notable who had gained prominence as a social critic, took the initiative to set up the organisation. Initially known as the Metsimaholo Residents Association, it attracted interest from a number of politically conscious locals who had become inactive in political organisations. Among them was Sello Hlasa, a former local leader of the Azanian People's Organisation (Azapo), who was then a consultant based in Bloemfontein. Former activists like Hlasa found Malebo's distaste for setting up a proper organisation with structures and a clear leadership hierarchy limiting, however. They increasingly took over the running of the organisation, ultimately renaming it the Metsimaholo Civic Association (MCA).[10]

Sparked by economic concerns, the protest became a rejection of what some local leaders considered an unwelcome intrusion from the outside. This gripe grew as the 2016 election approached. The local ANC choice for mayoral candidate was overlooked: ANC national leaders, at the recommendation of their provincial leaders, announced their own candidate. This infuriated a number of ANC supporters, turning them against the party. In the end, the MCA attracted sympathy from across the political spectrum and throughout the community of Metsimaholo. To thwart Magashule's manoeuvres, the MCA and its supporters decided to contest the election. Presence in council would give them control or sway to implement their plan to assert local influence over decision-making and keep business contracts and major appointments local.

Previously won by the ANC with a total of 26 seats, Metsimaholo did not have an outright winner in the 2016 election. The MCA and the EFF, both ANC offshoots, took some ANC voters, winning two and eight seats, respectively. The ANC remained the largest party with 19 seats, followed by the DA with 12 seats and the FF+ with one. For a 42-seat council, 22 votes were required to form a minimalist coalition government. The three smaller parties (the DA, the EFF and the FF+) had concluded a working arrangement that applied throughout the country. The MCA fell on neither side. It was up to both sides to persuade it to choose between them. To be part of any coalition, the MCA demanded the mayoralty, and on the policy front that both key appointments and tenders for business would go to local recipients. Both groupings were amenable to the MCA demands, but the general membership of the association opposed a coalition with the ANC. Hence, the MCA sided with the smaller parties. Hlasa became mayor and his colleague the chief whip. With the EFF having decided against being part of executive leadership, the DA took the rest of the portfolios in the mayoral committee, along with the speaker position. The EFF got the chairperson positions of the municipal public accounts and the ethics committees.[11]

Within months of inaugurating the coalition, relations soured. The cause, according to Hlasa, was twofold: disagreement over the division of responsibilities and modus operandi of the coalition; and pursuing clashing policy objectives. Hlasa felt the DA's Free State leader, Patricia Kopane, interfered in his mayoral responsibilities and displayed a lack of confidence in his ability. Kopane, also an MP, was a regular presence at Metsimaholo. Hlasa protested, telling Kopane to await his reports and meet with him through the structure they had set up for the coalition. Kopane interpreted Hlasa's reaction as resistance to cooperation. The EFF, meanwhile, invaded a vacant plot of land. Hlasa deemed the invasion illegal and sought a court order that invaders vacate the land or face arrest. They refused to vacate and were arrested. The EFF blamed the arrests on Hlasa.

Before the end of 2016, both the EFF and the DA were pitted against the MCA. Their discontent with Hlasa extended to accusing him of being in cahoots with the ANC and, as a result, having been corrupted. The EFF tried to table a motion of no confidence in Hlasa but it failed due to a technicality. The ANC retaliated with a motion of its own against the speaker, a DA councillor. Seeing the tension in the coalition, the ANC endeared itself to Hlasa. This new alliance raised the possibility that the ANC's motion against the DA speaker might pass. The DA and the EFF boycotted council meetings, which meant some administrative decisions could not be made. This infuriated Hlasa, who instructed officials to deduct the relevant amounts from the salaries of the absentee councillors. Early in 2017, Hlasa held a special council meeting to reshuffle his mayoral committee, and replaced his entire committee with ANC members.

The dismissals hardened attitudes. Both the EFF and the DA continued to boycott council meetings. As the council started working on a budget for the next financial year, the boycott threatened its very continuation. If the budget was not passed by the end of June 2017, the council would be dissolved. But that is exactly what the DA and the EFF had now decided to do – dissolve the Metsimaholo Council. This transpired, as Council failed to pass the 2017/18 budget and was dissolved in July 2017 (Setena, 2017). By-elections were subsequently scheduled for late 2017. When the by-elections came, the parties had fractured even further. The MCA had expelled its former councillors for working with the ANC. Some ANC members contested the by-election under the banner of the South African Communist Party (SACP),[12] alongside two other new entrants, the AIC and Forum 4 Service Delivery. This was a historic event for the SACP. Until then the party had been debating, for more than 10 years, whether or not to contest elections independently (SACP, 2017).

Metsimaholo forced the SACP into a resolution. The local SACP leaders' argument to the SACP's politburo was two-pronged. First, oligarchs had usurped the ANC in the Free State, sidelining ethical leaders for appointment, and the Tripartite Alliance in the province had completely broken down. Second, the ANC had become adversarial towards the South African Municipal Workers Union: before the 2016 elections, the ANC-controlled municipality had fired more than 300 municipal workers over an industrial dispute. After a lengthy protest, the municipality re-employed some but excluded others; to the SACP, this made the ANC leaders a council of 'anti-workers'.[13] The party's politburo gave the go-ahead for its leaders at Metsimaholo to contest the elections independently (Kganyago, 2017).

The November 2017 by-election therefore pitted allies against each other for the first time. The contest raised the possibility of further dividing traditional ANC voters, thereby denying the ANC the chance to regain a majority. As it turned out, the results returned a stalemate that necessitated yet another coalition government. The SACP won three seats and the ANC dropped to 16 seats (from 19). The DA and EFF's combined seats of 19 came in below the requisite 22 for an outright majority. They joined forces with the three newly elected SACP councillors to create a coalition government, and the SACP got the mayoralty.

CONCLUSION

Forming coalition governments is a bargaining process. The South African experience, as illustrated through this set of local case studies, is no different from experiences elsewhere in the world and on the continent (see chapters 3 and 4). Some parties aim to take immediate gains; others defer instant gains for long-term benefits. Each party in these local governments ultimately depends on its number of councillors per council, on the one hand, and the desperation of others, on the other. Some parties have tended to exploit these two factors to the maximum; others have drawn from their authority elsewhere to get the preferred partners to agree to a coalition (as outlined by Herman and Pope, 1973; Kim, 2002; Brams and Kilgour, 2013). This concluding section takes stock of the rules of operation that have emerged from local-level experiences with coalition formation in South Africa since 2016, building on the case studies presented and other cases that illustrate similar operations.

Establishing coalitions at the local level in South Africa has been shown to be an intricate process. The exact intricacy varies, depending on the number of parties with seats and the number of partners required to form a majority. As a starting point, on the rare occasions when the ANC and the IFP (or the ANC and the DA) have been the only two parties with an equal number of seats, forming a coalition has been relatively easy: the choice of a partner was prescribed and the task was clear – to share and rotate the posts. In the instance of a plurality of parties holding seats, the process of negotiations has been more involved.

While the initiative to lead the process has tended to fall on parties with the largest number of seats, choosing coalition partners can be an intricate process of decision-making. The choices are determined by the history of the parties' mutual experiences, what the parties want out of the coalition and whether the dominant party can accede to those conditions. As this chapter's case studies illustrate, once part of a coalition, some partners deviate from agreements and fall into behaviour that undermines the exact coalitions these parties had opted to be part of. Others make decisions, even to the detriment of the municipality, with an eye to influencing national events. Where they have had a choice between the ANC, on the one hand, and the DA or the IFP, on the other, civic organisations and independents have tended to be unpredictable, while established opposition parties – such as the ACDP, the FF+, the UDM and Cope – have tended to vote for one another. The latter point is largely a function of their identity as opposition parties to the ANC, and they have often had to collaborate in the South African parliament to hold the governing party to account. These relations are then replicated in local government.

For most of South Africa's opposition parties going into coalitions, therefore, their choice of coalition partner/s has been informed by their disposition to restrain the power of the dominant party. Some opposition parties have, however, gone with either of the leading parties, as long as their demands are met. For the PA and many other small parties in local councils, it has been about getting posts in the mayoral committee, and whichever party makes that offer gets their vote. In addition, whenever rival parties have approached the PA to change sides in return for an even better post, of mayor or deputy, they have switched with ease. The AIC started off with the aim of using its support as leverage to elicit a policy concession regarding the provincial location of the town of Matatiele from the ANC, but has come to settle for patronage.[14] The AIC has continued to vote for ANC-led coalitions.

The case study research reported in this chapter demonstrates that opposition parties, especially the DA, have not always been consistent in their decision to club together with other opposition parties against the ANC; and some circumstances have made it impossible to avoid a coalition with the ANC. In 2001, for instance, the DA collaborated with the ANC in Kannaland to remove a PAC councillor, Stefan Meyer, who was then mayor. The only PAC mayor in the country at the time, Meyer had been in a coalition with the ANC, but they had had a fallout over Meyer's use of the mayoral discretionary fund.[15] Meyer had initially been in coalition with the DA, but switched to the ANC, using, as do many parties motivating their changes to new alliances, community interest: 'They wanted to exploit certain community issues,' he said, but his 'commitment was to uplift the people. I told them to change their strategy. They did not' (Terreblanche, 2001). The DA and the ANC had four seats each. This time around, they combined against Meyer, whose party had only one seat.

It would not be the first time the DA got into a coalition with the ANC in Kannaland, despite its commitment to the contrary. They were back in coalition again after the 2016 election, after Geoffrey Donson had left the ANC and was the leader of ICOSA. His party was the largest, with three seats, compared to the ANC and the DA, with two each. The ANC and DA formed a coalition government. When asked if the coalition did not violate the DA's stance never to enter into coalition with the ANC, DA provincial leader Masizole Mnqasela explained the contradiction with reference to 'councillors in the municipality doing what's best for the community they represent' (Deklerk, 2018). As for the ANC councillors, they had the approval of neither their colleagues in the local branch nor the provincial leaders; it was purely their own initiative as councillors. And the provincial leaders' appeals to the national office of the party to intervene went unheeded, as if to suggest that it was their local dispute to solve.

Likeness in ideology or history has been another determining factor, along with parties being driven by what is practical or possible. Strange bedfellows have emerged. Consider again the instance of the PAC in Kannaland in 2001. Because of the PAC's history as a liberation movement of Afrocentric ideological orientation, the ANC ought to have been its first choice as coalition partner. Yet these Africanists preferred the proponents of liberalism over fellow African nationalists when it came to the politics of the local municipality. It happened again in 2006 and the setting was the City of Cape Town. The PAC had managed to win one seat, alongside multiple parties like the ANC and the DA. The contest to form a coalition was between these two bigger parties. The PAC's Bennet Joko voted for neither. That is what Joko, according to Helen Zille, had promised the DA he would do: if not a vote for the DA, mayoral candidate Zille's wish was for Joko to abstain (Zille, 2016). Joko was following his party's decision not to vote for the ANC; his abstention gave the DA the majority.

That decision, Joko explained, was preceded by disagreements within the PAC under the leadership of then PAC president, Motsoko Pheko, and his then deputy, Themba Godi. The closeness in ideology and history, Godi had argued, obliged the Africanists to collaborate with fellow African nationalists. Pheko countered that the ANC was not only a rival, but also did not think much of the PAC. Joko himself had experience of the ANC being indifferent to and even contemptuous of the PAC.[16]

It is not uncommon in coalition-making, therefore, for parties to acquire strange partners. The EFF has not only voted for its ideological foe, the DA, but also stands side-by-side with the white right wing, the FF+, in a number of councils. Yet the FF+ wrote to the Electoral Commission seeking to disqualify the EFF from registering for the 2014 national election. The party's fondness for singing liberation songs that were racially insensitive and its policy of nationalisation, argued the FF+, were a threat to racial harmony and the constitutional order (News24, 2013). The FF+ objection failed, and the parties have continued to be at loggerheads on a number of major policy issues, both in parliament and in the public discourse generally. Yet, in a number of councils –Tshwane, Mogale City, Thabazimbi, Metsimaholo – the EFF stands alongside the FF+ in support of the DA.

The EFF's votes are not truly support for the DA, however. Rather, they are an expressed opposition to the ANC, which had rejected its demands in return for a coalition. These included supporting a constitutional amendment to enable expropriation of land without compensation, and nationalisation. The DA does not support those policies either but the EFF has put the DA in power as punishment for the ANC, to magnify its political influence. When the EFF thought it would gain political capital, it abandoned the DA in Nelson Mandela Bay. That decision illuminated the party's role in a debate, taking place at the time in parliament, over the proposed constitutional amendment on land. The EFF explained its attempts to remove the DA-led coalition as punishment for the party's opposition to the proposed amendment. For singling out Nelson Mandela Bay over Tshwane and Johannesburg – where the EFF was also in cahoots with the DA – the party reasoned that its choice was a further attack on white privilege: the DA mayor in Nelson Mandela Bay at the time, Athol Trollip, is white, whereas the two other DA mayors then were both black. In the process, however, the EFF knowingly sacrificed sound leadership in Nelson Mandela Bay. The new individual it helped put into the mayoralty, Mongameli Bobani, already had a reputation for being temperamental and lacking scruples.[17] What mattered for the EFF was a demonstration of power – or 'flexing its muscle' – showing that it could change the power dynamics, regardless of the likely harmful impact in Nelson Mandela Bay.

Individual councillors may exploit the delicacy of coalitions. Their intentions vary between noble objectives of ensuring good governance, and the ignoble aim of securing material gains. In the municipality of Stellenbosch, for instance, councillor Myra Linders would not submit to the DA's party discipline for moral reasons: she objected to some of the motions the party wanted her to vote on, as she found them inimical to the interests of her own constituency.[18] Linders resigned as the party's ward councillor in 2008, precipitating the collapse of the DA-led coalition government. She then stood in the ensuing by-election as an independent and won. Linders next used her sole vote to put a coalition of the ANC and a civic organisation, the Khayamandi Community Alliance, into power. When that coalition also got mired in corruption, she used her swing vote to remove it, and returned the DA-led coalition to power (Williams, 2009). In Mogale City, meanwhile, the DA ascribed its loss of power in 2017 to its own councillors accepting payment to vote for the opposition (Ramphele, 2017). The DA also blamed bribery for its loss of power in Nelson Mandela Bay in 2018: one of its own, Mxolisi Manyathi, abstained from voting on a motion of no confidence against the DA speaker of council, which gave the opposition a majority vote, precipitating the fall of that DA-led coalition government (Ndletyana, 2020).

If not individuals exploiting the desperation of others to make money, parties have manipulated state resources to influence coalition formation. This happened in 2006 in KwaZulu-Natal as the ANC faced off against the IFP. The newly formed Nadeco held the balance of power in three municipalities. After initially voting for the ANC, Nadeco later switched and sided with the IFP. Soon thereafter Ziba Jiyane's business contract with the provincial government was suspended. Jiyane, the founder of Nadeco, was a major shareholder in the bus company Masithembe Bus Service, which had a contract with the provincial government. The Zululand Chamber of Commerce ascribed the suspension to the change of political allegiance in the municipalities where Nadeco was the kingmaker (Mthembu, 2007; Broughton and Mboto, 2007). It was retaliation by the ANC, using its control over the provincial government.

In conclusion, therefore, coalition governments have been a constant presence in local South African politics. Their impact on governance has been mixed. In some rare instances, coalitions have enabled parties to force policy concessions from their partners, with the potential to improve constituents' lives. And independents on occasion have used their swing votes to hold parties accountable for their misconduct. In the main, however, coalitions are prone to instability, which disrupts governance. Their notoriety for instability has, nonetheless, not necessarily prevented their recurrence.

REFERENCES

Africa, C. 2016. 'Status quo entrenched and no surprises in the Western Cape', *Journal of Public Administration*, 51 (3.1), 513–531.

Booysen, S. 2011. *The African National Congress and the Regeneration of Political Power*. Johannesburg: Wits University Press.

Brams, S. J. and Kilgour, D. M. 2013. 'Kingmakers and leaders in coalition formation', *Social Choice and Welfare*, 11 (1), 1–18.

Broughton, T. and Mboto, S. 13 July 2007. 'Jiyane owe debtors', IOL, https://www.iol.co.za/news/politics/jiyane-owe-debtors-361837, accessed 12 January 2021.

Deklerk, A. 24 July 2018. 'ANC and DA live in harmony in small town – much to the dismay of party bigwigs', TimesLIVE, https://www.timeslive.co.za/politics/2018-07-24-anc-and-da-live-in-harmony-in-small-town-much-to-the-dismay-of-party-bigwigs/, accessed 12 January 2021.

Electoral Commission of South Africa (IEC). 2017. Data on hung councils, supplied to the author by the IEC, 9 August 2017.

Hans, B. 3 August 2019. 'Ziba Jiyane rejoins IFP, but sparks war of words ahead of conference', IOL, https://www.iol.co.za/news/politics/ziba-jiyane-rejoins-ifp-but-sparks-war-of-words-ahead-of-conference-30262812, accessed 12 January 2021.

Herman, V. and Pope, J. 1973. 'Minority governments in Western democracies', British *Journal of Political Science*, 3 (2), 191–212.

Jordan, B. 18 March 2018. 'Meet Laingsburg's "mayor by mistake": Coalition politics catapults ex-petrol jockey into power', TimesLIVE, https://www.timeslive.co.za/sunday-times/news/2018-03-17-meet-laingsburgs-mayor-by-mistake/, accessed 12 January 2021.

Kassiem, A. 30 January 2006. 'ANC expels Prince, who scorns hearing', IOL, https://www.iol.co.za/news/politics/anc-expels-prince-who-scorns-hearing-264861, accessed 12 January 2021.

Kganyago, P. 2017. 'Reconfiguration from below: SACP takes responsibility, builds democratic popular power, contests elections in Metsimaholo', *Umrabulo*, 18 (22).

Khumalo, S. 9 August 2006. 'Nadeco president suspended', IOL, https://www.iol.co.za/news/politics/nadeco-president-suspended-288709, accessed 11 January 2021.

Kim, J. 2002. 'When coalition theories meet strange cases: Two coalition governments in Japan, 1993–1994', *Asian Perspective*, 26 (2), 179–208.

Komisa, M. 19 June 2018. 'AIC threatens to pull out of coalition with ANC', SABC News, https://www.sabcnews.com/sabcnews/aic-threatens-to-pull-out-of-coalition-with-anc/, accessed 9 February 2021.

Mail & Guardian. 22 January 2013. 'Municipal merger on hold after violent Sasolburg protests', https://mg.co.za/article/2013-01-22-municipal-merger-on-hold-after-violent-sasolburg-protests/, accessed 12 January 2021.

Maré, G. 1992. *Brothers Born of Warrior Blood*. Johannesburg: Ravan Press.

Mbete, S. 2016. 'Economic Freedom Fighters' debut in the municipal elections', *Journal of Public Administration*, 51 (3.1), 596–614.

Mngomezulu, B. R. 2016. 'Marred in the electoral radar', *Journal of Public Administration*, 51 (3.1), 632–647.

Mthembu, B. 12 July 2007. 'Former Nadeco leader could lose it all', IOL, https://www.iol.co.za/news/politics/former-nadeco-leader-could-lose-it-all-361681, accessed 12 January 2021.

Mthethwa, B. 23 January 2018. 'Serial political party hopper Ziba Jiyane joins NFP', TimesLIVE, https://www.timeslive.co.za/politics/2018-01-23-serial-political-party-hopper-ziba-jiyane-joins-nfp/, accessed 11 January 2021.

Myburgh, P. 2019. *Gangster State: Unravelling Ace Magashule's web of capture*. Cape Town: Penguin Books.

Ndletyana, M. 2010. 'Congress of the People: A promise betrayed?', *Journal of African Elections*, 9 (2), 32–55.

Ndletyana, M. 2020. *Anatomy of the ANC in Power: Insights from Port Elizabeth, 1990–2019*. Cape Town: HSRC Press.

News24. 9 May 2005. 'IFP braces for internal battle', https://www.news24.com/News24/IFP-braces-for-internal-battle-20050509, accessed 11 January 2021.

News24. 22 August 2013. 'FF Plus Versus EFF Constitutional Rights', https://www.news24.com/news24/mynews24/FF-Plus-Versus-EFF-Constitutional-Rights-20130822, accessed 12 January 2021.

Peters, M. 17 January 2010. 'I'll be back, insists disgraced politician', *Saturday Star*.

Ramphele, L. 29 June 2017. 'DA describes losing Mogale City as "politics of the cheque book"', 702, http://www.702.co.za/articles/262393/da-describes-losing-mogale-city-as-politics-of-the-cheque-book, accessed 12 January 2021.

Schulz-Herzenberg, C. 2016. 'Shifting electoral trends, participation and party support', *Journal of Public Administration,* 51 (3.1), 487–512.

Setena, T. 19 July 2017. 'Dissolving of council welcomed by DA', News24, https://www.news24.com/news24/southafrica/local/express-news/dissolving-of-council-welcomed-by-da-20170718, accessed 12 January 2021.

Sithole, J. 2011. 'Inkatha Freedom Party–National Freedom Party dynamics in the KwaZulu-Natal province', *Journal of Public Administration*, 46 (3.1), 1169–1181.

Sithole, J. 2013. 'The African National Congress in Natal, 1990–1995', in *The Road to Democracy in South Africa: Vol 6, Part 1*. Pretoria: Unisa Press.

South African Communist Party (SACP). 2017. 'Declarations and resolutions', 14th National Congress, 10–15 July 2017.

Terreblanche, C. 2 August 2001. 'Opponents oust PAC's only mayor', IOL, https://www.iol.co.za/news/politics/opponents-oust-pacs-only-mayor-69583, accessed 12 January 2021.

Thabazimbi Residents Association v Municipality Manager (Acting): Thabazimbi Local Municipality and Others (4618/2017) [2018] ZALMPPHC 27 (25 May 2018).

Williams, M. 9 December 2009. 'DA bites a big chunk out of the Western Cape', IOL, https://www.iol.co.za/news/politics/da-bites-a-big-chunk-out-of-the-western-cape-467251, accessed 12 January 2021.

Zille, H. 2016. *Not Without a Fight: The autobiography.* Cape Town: Penguin Random House.

THREE

The international experience of coalition politics
Democracy, party systems and stability

Heidi Brooks

IN MANY PARTS OF THE WORLD, the experience of coalition government is a regular phenomenon. Political and government coalitions are seen in various contexts, from previously majoritarian democracies and one-party states, to states with a history of fragmented party systems and power-sharing arrangements. The 'consensus' politics necessitated by political party coalitions, however, can belie the inherently conflictual nature of this type of politics, as well as the variety of democratic experiences engendered by the absence of an electoral majority.

Through a comparative examination of the experience of coalition governments internationally, this chapter examines the conditions in which coalition governments have occurred and their impact on competitive party politics. To complement this volume's section dedicated to the theme of coalitions in Africa (see Part II), it focuses in particular on the experience of coalition government in Western and Eastern Europe, Latin America and Asia. It demonstrates how local and historical context, including the breadth of the ideological spectrum and democratic transition itself, have a bearing on the dynamics of party systems and political stability, and on implications for democratic practice and accountability.

The research draws on a range of literature on coalition politics and democratisation in both established and new democracies. It argues that coalitions have been used for different purposes and with different degrees of success in terms of stabilising democratic party systems and renewing political power. In cases where parties have been able to build stable alliances with ideologically likeminded parties, coalitions have often produced successful experiments in governance through focusing on a set of mutually agreed policies, or have had a democratising effect by accommodating ethnic minorities and developing practices of deliberation and compromise. In other cases, where the party system is especially fragmented, coalitions have prevented the formation of stable party operations, resulting in an increasingly 'polarised pluralism', or undermined the establishment of accountability to citizens by limiting democracy to a compromise among elites.

This chapter begins by introducing the forms of coalition politics experienced internationally, and the frequency and context of coalition formation. With reference to several country examples, it compares the conditions for coalition politics through a comparative examination of party systems, including historical context, democratic transition and cleavages among the electorate. Finally, the chapter reflects on the impact of coalitions on democracy and political stability, considering the extent to which coalitions have either facilitated or undermined consensus and accountability through the cultivation of democratic values and responsiveness to the electorate.

FREQUENCY AND CONDITIONS FOR PARTY COALITIONS

In any system of representative democracy in which three or more parties gain significant parliamentary representation, the possibility exists for coalition government. Bergman et al. (2019), drawing on research undertaken into post-war democracies internationally, note that approximately 'three-quarters of the cabinets in parliamentary systems and more than half of the cabinets in presidential systems' have been coalition governments (Cheibub et al., 2004, as cited in Bergman et al., 2019: 2).

The nature and type of coalition, however, varies. While a majority coalition in government is quite common, in some cases parties opt for minority government with a legislative alliance, ensuring the government of opposition party support on key legislative proposals. In a classic consociational formation, parties may form a grand coalition, as seen in parts of Western Europe, where the government coalition is comprised of the largest parties in the parliamentary system, often two of them. Latin America has experienced rainbow coalitions (as in Chile), in which a multiplicity of different parties come together in a governing alliance, as well as a considerable number of 'oversized' coalitions (as in Brazil), containing more parties than needed to make a majority (Meireles, 2016). Parts of Asia, such as Japan and Malaysia, have experienced periods of coalition dominance, in which a stable coalition of parties has maintained power for a prolonged period. Whatever the formation, parties may enter into various alliances either pre- or post-election, and at the national and/or sub-national level. It is worth noting that the longest-lasting formal coalition in the world is in the People's Republic of China, where, since 1949, the Chinese Communist Party has maintained an official united front of smaller, legally authorised parties, albeit entirely subservient to and inseparable from the Chinese Communist Party. Its context is, of course, that of a defacto one-party state, serving to extend the party's reach and popular legitimacy in the place of pluralist politics (see Wang and Groot, 2018). In representative, multiparty systems, by contrast, the motivations and institutional context for coalition formation are more variable and complex.

Much of the literature on coalition politics focuses on institutional context. Coalitions take place largely in parliamentary systems, an exception being in Latin America (most notably, Brazil, Chile and Uruguay), where coalitions have been used in the context of multiparty presidential systems (Alemán and Tsebelis, 2011: 4). Coalitions are also more likely in a context of proportional representation (PR) and mixed electoral systems (Bellamy, 2012: 457). In contrast, single-member plurality (or first-past-the-post, FPTP) electoral systems lend themselves to majority government.

The choice parties make to enter into a coalition, however, is strategic. Analysis of coalition politics has thus taken place largely within the rational-choice tradition. Müller and Strøm (2004: 4) suggest that there are two factors determining a party's bargaining power in coalition formation: the share of seats resulting from the most recent election; and the party's position relative to other parliamentary parties. In this vein, literature on coalition politics has examined coalitions from two broad approaches: from an opportunistic (or power maximisation) perspective, in which parties enter coalitions to access the fruits of office; and from a policy-based perspective, in which parties enter coalitions to realise ideological or policy goals (Sridharan, 2012: 11–12, 14). Jacoby (2017) adds to this by arguing that parties may also enter into a coalition to 'sterilise' populist or fringe parties – an approach he uses to explain the rationale of grand coalitions in the face of emergent far-right parties in Western Europe.

The party system itself is thus a highly influential factor in the establishment of coalitions (see chapter 4). Both governing coalitions and legislative alliances are more likely in fragmented party systems than in the two-party systems characteristic of the USA and the UK. This focus on institutional context alone, however, risks ignoring the local and contextual factors that impact the formation and functioning of coalitions (Savage, 2016). The dynamics and stability of coalitions are determined by a much broader range of factors.

COMPARING PARTY SYSTEMS: NEW VERSUS ESTABLISHED DEMOCRACIES

At the heart of coalitions are political parties – the fundamental link between the democratic state and citizens. Parties are, as Budge and Keman (1993: 8) point out, what make the democratic state responsive to the population; they are crucial conduits in voicing the popular will. As such, both their organisation and their alliances are crucial to the shape of democracy. It is the party system, moreover, and the relationship between parties, Savage (2016: 503) argues, that provide 'the essential structure of the coalition-bargaining environment'.

With regard to established democracies, there is a vast array of literature on coalition politics and the pattern and maintenance of coalition arrangements (see, for example, Budge and Keman, 1993; Laver and Schofield, 1998; Müller and Strøm, 2000; Moury, 2012). Indeed, much coalition theory itself has emerged largely from the Western European experience (Bergman et al., 2019). In the post-1989 democracies of Eastern Europe, the political institutional framework of the West has been largely replicated. Yet for new democracies, the same theories of coalition formation may not fit so neatly. Here, other contextual determinants, such as 'prior experience, historical factors, and past behaviours' shape the experience of coalition politics (Savage, 2016: 502). This differentiation and the specificities of local conditions and circumstances can indeed be said of the coalition experience everywhere. And while some trends can be identified by region, the party system and trajectory of democracy are shaped by a more nuanced set of factors.

Party system fragmentation

In Eastern Europe, the rapidity of the transition to democracy shaped the party system (Welsh, 1994; Backlund et al., 2019). While both Eastern and Western Europe share the feature of multiple contending parties (and thus propensity for coalitions), the level of party fragmentation and turnover in the former is considerable (Backlund et al., 2019: 73). Comparing new and established democracies, existing data indicate far higher levels of electoral volatility and multipartyism in Latin America and Eastern Europe than in Western Europe. In the first two of these regions, new parties contest elections more frequently and succeed in securing a larger share of the vote than in Western Europe. In the Andean states of Latin America, newly formed political parties acquired 35 per cent of the electoral vote between 1990 and 2002, with a low of 17 per cent in Ecuador and a high of 60 per cent in Peru (Mainwaring et al., 2006: 19). In many cases, this share is not obtained by a united opposition but is rather a case of 'extreme multi-partyism' (Morgenstern et al., 2008: 173–174). It is the number of parties in the electoral arena, their target constituents and the new or prior relationships between parties (or the lack thereof) that determine the possibility, incentives and longevity of party coalitions.

The fragmented parliaments often constitutive of new democracies have therefore lent themselves to the formation of coalitions. In some cases, governing coalitions or legislative alliances have become a norm, if not a necessity. In the new democracies of Eastern and Central Europe, Ibenskas (2015: 747) notes that small parties will form alliances to satisfy the requirements for seats in parliament, while medium-large parties will use alliances for the numerical strength to enter government. States such as Poland and Slovakia, however, have introduced higher legal thresholds for alliances than for individual parties, in the interests of 'consolidating' the party system (Ibenskas, 2015: 745).

Although coalitions have been most common in parliamentary systems, Morgenstern et al. (2008) highlight how Latin America's combination of presidentialism and extreme multipartyism has resulted in the building of legislative alliances between the executive and opposition parties as a means of securing wider support for policies. In these cases, the president's cabinet has included members who are effectively an allied opposition.

A feature of alliances and coalitions in new democracies is also their instability. Although coalitions largely provide greater stability than minority government, the rapidity of many transitions from one-party rule – and the consequent lack of a competitive and institutionalised party system (Ibenskas, 2015; Savage, 2016) – has, in such contexts, resulted in unstable alliances and a high turnover in coalition arrangements. In line with Samuel Huntington's notion of party system institutionalisation, Mainwaring and Scully (1995) suggest that patterns of party competition should exhibit some regularity, or become institutionalised. Savage (2016) points out that if parties' identity or electoral strength is subject to substantial change or fluctuates widely the party system is not institutionalised. In new democracies, such as those in Eastern Europe and Latin America, Pridham (2002: 81) remarks that party systems are 'in a state of some flux' for the first decade: there is no precedent for party interaction, no routinised behaviour (Savage, 2016: 503–504), and parties have not yet constituted themselves as 'unitary actors' (Pridham, 2002: 81) with a consolidated member base (Backlund et al., 2019: 73). As a result, although coalitions may be entered into (in the interests of power maximisation or policy gain), they are frequently short-lived and may not always last into the next election (Ibenskas, 2015: 745).

Economic context, moreover, has an impact on coalition government stability. The transition to democracy in Eastern Europe, for example, took place alongside complete economic transformation from communism to capitalism. Detrimental economic conditions in these states have weakened the stability of multiparty governments, even given the economic variation with the region itself (Backlund et al., 2019: 62). Indeed, Savage (2016) identifies what he refers to as 'incumbency *dis*advantage' – a contrast to the pattern of 'incumbency advantage' observed in established democracies of Western Europe – in which there is a low likelihood of the incumbent retaining political power after an election. Linked to high electoral volatility, corruption, and the inability of incumbent regimes to deliver on policy commitments, this frequent changeover of power has also hindered the development of stable and ongoing coalitions (Savage, 2016: 505–506).

Transitions from one-party rule
Many transitions to democracy have, in one form or another, consisted of a transition from one-party rule to a multiparty, competitive dispensation. With this shift, there has been an inevitable opening-up of the political space to ideological and policy contestation. In religiously or ethnically divided societies, it has provided an important opening

for minority representation. The maturing and institutionalisation of the party system, however, is also influenced by political legacy.

The former socialist states of Eastern Europe are significant in this regard. Backlund et al. (2019: 73) refer to three types of political party in these states: communist successor parties, or 'reform communists', which are the revived parties of the former regime; revitalised historic parties; and newly established parties. The authors note that the presence of established local party structures of communist successor parties gave them somewhat of an advantage over other parties (Backlund et al., 2019: 71). New parties had no existing member base and the high number of new, small parties that contested the early elections resulted in highly fragmented parliaments (Backlund et al., 2019: 73). Prior to the collapse of socialism in Eastern Europe and the Soviet Union, both Poland and the German Democratic Republic were officially governed by united front coalitions of multiple parties or organisations, often under the leadership or control of a single party. Their tight central control by the local Communist Party brought an illusion of a pluralism; it masked the limited support for communism among their populations. Nonetheless, as organisations, these parties were highly successful in penetrating their societies (see, for example, Rueschmeyer, 1991).

Both Ibenskas (2015: 755) and Savage (2016: 501) remark how difficult it has been for communist successor parties to form alliances, especially in the early stages of multipartyism. The stigma of communism and 'distrust' of former ruling parties made the transition for these parties challenging (Savage, 2016: 509). As such, while communist successor parties needed coalitions to legitimise themselves, in the 'hangover' of historic divides, they 'struggled to build alliances and programmatic links' (Savage, 2016: 501). Druckman and Roberts (2007: 10) note, in fact, that in the Czech Republic, Poland and Hungary, 'quite liberal' communist successor parties were punished at the polls. In Eastern Europe, the party system and coalitions have taken time to even begin to form around programmatic alignments, with ideological differentiation on the right–left axis not clearly defined. Post-1989, there is some suggestion that the left has failed to find 'acceptable' ideological ground (Slapsak, 2019).

In Latin America, socioeconomic issues are more identifiable in electoral preference, with a clearer demarcation of left and right in party programmes. Nonetheless, coalitions have sometimes formed around the push for democracy rather than programmatic concerns. In Chile, the coalition government that succeeded General Augusto Pinochet in 1990 emerged out of solidarity in the no-vote referendum on the dictator's continued rule (Siavelis, 2013: 16). While the coalition identified as a centre–left alliance, it failed to reform Chile's socioeconomic structure and instead continued the neoliberal model begun by Pinochet (Sehnbruch and Siavelis, 2013: 3–4).

The dominant-party legacy

In other cases, coalitions have come to characterise the political landscape following periods of party dominance. Since the Indian Congress Party's fall from electoral dominance in the late 1980s, Indian politics has been shaped by coalitions at both the national and regional (state) level. Power-sharing and compromise have become accepted features of the Indian electoral landscape. Despite the establishment of democracy with India's independence from Great Britain in 1947, the dominance of the Congress Party moulded the political landscape and thus the nature of the party system. As a mass movement, the Congress Party itself was somewhat of a grand coalition, housing a broad range of interests. Its opposition from the late 1960s was thus characterised by what Sridharan (2012: 50) describes as a 'broad front anti-Congressism', eventually ripening into a number of religious and state-based parties. The growth of India's party system saw the era of coalition government replaced in 2014 by single-party government under the Bharatiya Janata Party.

Coalition government has also characterised Japan since the end of the Liberal Democratic Party's dominance in 1993. Over the past 20 years, the Liberal Democratic Party's new coalition with the Komeito Party has been out of power for only three years (Nagai and Mizorogi, 2019). Hirose (2012: 242, 264), however, suggests that the party system in Japan, and the alliances that ensued with the end of party dominance, have been far from stable. The end of Liberal Democratic Party dominance was brought about not so much by the emergence of new policy-oriented parties, and thus an institutionalisation of the

Japanese party system, but by breakaways and disintegration within the Liberal Democratic Party itself.

Malaysia, in slight contrast, was ruled, from independence from Britain in 1957 until 2018, not by a single dominant party but by a dominant coalition. Led by the United Malays National Organisation, the Barisan Nasional (National Front) coalition was, in effect, a 'permanent grand coalition' (Wong, 2018: 756) that managed to bring together multiple ethnic identities and 'monopolise the middle ground' of politics (Wong, 2018: 759). However, while in Japan the former dominant party has not been entirely displaced from power, in Malaysia the United Malays National Organisation and Barisan Nasional have been replaced by a new coalition government constituted by their opposition. The end of the Barisan Nasional's dominance is possibly suggestive of an end of ethnic-based coalitions in Malaysia. The emergence of an electorate less swayed by communal anxieties, previously capitalised on by the governing coalition (Saravanamuttu, 2012; Wong, 2018: 755), is indicative of a further factor in the shaping of coalitions: cleavages among the electorate.

Social cleavages and political partisanship

In the democracies of Western Europe, mass political parties have grown out of social cleavages, such as class and religion, that emerged with the move to parliamentary democracy (Backlund et al., 2019: 74). As a result, contemporary political parties in established democracies can often be located on the classic left-right spectrum and, with the exception of some strongly regional or secessionist parties (for example, in Spain), their support bases can be located in socioeconomic and sometimes religious demographics. In new democracies, the process of partisan identification by voters is still evolving: just as party ideologies take time to crystallise in new democracies (Pridham, 2002; Ibenskas, 2015: 744), so, too, have voters themselves often not yet formed partisan attachments to the available parties, and certainly not enduring ones. Yet political partisanship is a measure of the 'rootedness' of parties in society and thus of party institutionalisation (Mainwaring and Scully, 1995; Savage, 2016: 504).

Lack of a clear ideology and policy stance on the part of political parties has itself led to unstable and short-lived coalitions. In Latin America, where many parties focus more clearly on socioeconomic (as opposed to ethno-regional or religious) issues in their appeal to voters, there remains a highly fragmented party system and a tendency for coalitions (quite often, oversized ones), rather than single-party government. Yet in the case of Chile's centre-left coalition government, Concertaçion por la Democracia (Coalition of Parties for Democracy) – the most successful and long-lasting coalition in Latin American history (Siavelis, 2013: 15) – both its left-wing policy agenda and its roots in the Chilean population remained shallow (Luna, 2008, as cited in Siavelis, 2013: 33), a point to which we return later.

In the democracies of Eastern Europe, there has been a delay in the clear formation of attachments to political parties. Backlund et al. (2019: 74) remind us that, in these former socialist states, the first elections in 1990 were primarily '[referendums] on communist rule'. Indeed, for a considerable time, the most salient political cleavage in these countries remained that of support versus opposition for the old regime (Druckman and Roberts, 2007: 9). If we agree that there are unlikely to be more political parties than social cleavages allow for (Wong, 2018: 758), the 'flattening' effect of communism (Druckman and Roberts, 2007: 9) goes some way to explaining the challenges of party formation in this context, and the absence of the political cleavages typical of established democracies. However, while Antoszewski and Kozierska (2019: 349) remark of Poland that there remains a blurring of the distinction between left and right, often linked to the party's origins rather than its contemporary ideology or policies, the increasing salience of economic concerns and cleavages among the electorate of Eastern European states does perhaps render more stable ideological alliances between parties more likely.

It is also notable that in Central and parts of Western and Eastern Europe, politics has been affected by the emergence of parties on the populist right. Indeed, coalition governments and the motivations for coalition formation are increasingly being affected by more 'centrifugal' forces (Pellikaan et al., 2016). In the Netherlands, the growth of the extreme right wing has been particularly notable, not only effecting a decline in the popularity of mainstream parties, but also introducing a diminishing likelihood of the centrist and ideologically aligned coalitions known to the Dutch historically. In Germany, the Christian Democratic Union's grand coalition governments with the Social Democratic Party and the Free Democratic Party, respectively, have, according to Jacoby (2017), been used as a tool for the exclusion of such populist and extremist parties on the political right.

The emergent populist challenge in Western Europe, at both ends of the spectrum, is perhaps a reflection of that electorate's disillusionment with the political centre. An emergent trend in this region is the growth of the extreme left and right. In Italy, Ireland, Spain and Germany, support for the traditional centre-left and centre-right parties is depleting, opening up space for the involvement of more extreme parties that garner support around a small number of 'big issues' (Stephens, 2020). Identity and the uneven effects of globalisation have, in effect, pushed voters increasingly towards the margins and to more radical or extreme parties. In states such as the Netherlands, Germany, Austria and, to a degree, the UK, immigration and the Eurozone crisis have been factors in the growth of the extreme right (c.f. Jacoby, 2017; Pellikaan et al., 2016). The increasing fragmentation of party systems (and 'upending' of the two-party system) in these democracies can, Stephens (2020) suggests, be explained by 'the fracturing of what was once a homogeneous working-class vote'. Italy has similarly seen the emergence of extremist parties on the left and right, around whom the potential for coalition government now revolves, with electoral growth in recent years of both the anti-establishment Movimento 5 Stelle (Five Star Movement) and the far-right Lega.

Since 2015, both Spain and Portugal have seen the notable emergence of firmly left-wing governments. In January 2020, the first coalition government since the return to democracy in Spain was formed between the radical left and social democrats (Stone, 2020). Austerity fatigue and slow recovery from the 2008 financial crisis spurred support for the left in the Iberian countries (Bevins, 2020). Hough and Verge (2009) argue that the wave of decentralisation across Europe from the 1980s onwards has also enabled left coalitions to form first at the sub-state level, thus increasing the chances of national left-left coalitions, as seen most recently in Spain.

Political division, however, can also be shaped by ethno-linguistic fragmentation. In Romania, Slovakia and Bulgaria, ethno-regional parties have formed to represent linguistic minorities within those states (Backlund et al., 2019: 76). In Slovakia, the four-party coalition government in power from 1998 to 2006 – itself a broad alliance of centre-left and centre-right – included the minority Party of the Hungarian Coalition (Pridham, 2002). In Italy and in Spain, ethno-regional parties have contested power at the sub-national level, not necessarily seeking national office (especially given the independence aspirations of Catalonian and Basque separatists in Spain) but to influence policy for their regions and constituents (Tronconi, 2015). In parts of Asia, the partisan identification of the electorate along ethnic or religious lines is also common. Both Malaysia and Sri Lanka are multi-ethnic states whose governing coalitions have relied on a catch-all character (Uyangoda, 2012; Shukri, 2017). Sri Lanka's experience of coalitions in particular has revolved around two competing parties, surrounded by an array of left-wing and ethno-nationalist parties (Uyangoda, 2012: 164). Japan's ethnic homogeneity, in contrast, has produced a dominant conservative-centrist coalition (Hirose, 2012).

COALITIONS AND DEMOCRACY

The sociopolitical dynamics that both shape and transpire from coalition politics are therefore varied. The fragmented character of party systems in many new democracies, and the emergent shift in the ideological breadth of established ones, however, render party coalitions especially relevant to the study of contemporary multipartyism. Local context, the party system, and the motivations and ideological composition of coalition partners nonetheless affect the implications of coalitions for political stability and democracy more generally. The following section considers the comparative impact of party coalitions on representation, accountability and compromise.

A marriage of convenience

Coalitions are strategic. Small parties may utilise them to increase their influence, and larger parties may utilise them to secure power or legislative support. These choices are shaped by the party system, but also by whether a party's motivations are policy driven or office driven. A key question, therefore, concerns the impact of coalitions on democracy. Coalitions necessarily require compromise. As such, they are possibly more likely to involve a departure from a party's own policy commitments than single-party government. For the smaller partner(s) in a coalition, we might ask whether they are likely to become more concerned with access to office than accountability to their constituents. By aggregating political camps and reducing the number of competitors, they also potentially render liberal democracies less competitive.

The answer to these questions, based on international experience, is framed by conditionalities. The electoral context of coalition formation and parties' relative bargaining power are significant (Müller and Strøm, 2000: 4). The ideological breadth of a coalition may also be influential. In Eastern Europe, coalition governments in the 1990s and 2000s have been fairly ideologically broad, with limited programmatic coherence. Ibenskas (2015: 744), reflecting on the context of Central and Eastern Europe, argues that 'parties may be tempted to form opportunistic alliances with ideologically dissimilar partners in order to obtain legislative representation, and dissolve those coalitions after the election'. This would appear to be a classic 'power-maximisation' approach – the rapid dissolution of alliances preventing voters from being able to hold these parties accountable and generating democratic disillusionment and disappointment (Ibenskas, 2015: 744).

Coalitions are often most effective, therefore, when the ideological breadth is not too large. Reflecting on the case of Slovakia, Pridham (2002: 93–95) compares the ideologically disparate left/centre-right coalition from 1994 to 1998 with the more ideologically coherent centre-left/centre-right coalition from 1998 to 2006. Both governments experienced intracoalition frictions, but the latter was able to agree on some basic principles and find areas of commonality on which to deliver. Ibenskas (2015: 744) remarks that 'stable alliances between ideologically close parties … could greatly contribute to the consolidation of democracy by facilitating the formation of a stable party system'. His research on 11 democracies in Central and

Eastern Europe suggests that the tendency for small parties to form alliances with ideologically similar parties reduces 'wastage of votes' and increases 'party-voter congruence'. The merging of ideologically similar parties could be indicative of a consolidating party system. Moreover, despite the large proportion of alliances that collapse before the next election, he also highlights that a history of cooperation between parties increases the likelihood of that coalition forming again (Ibenskas, 2015: 758).

Grand coalitions, as a form of power-sharing union of the largest parties in a democracy, in particular, require sufficient congruence between the parties to govern 'across' the socioeconomic divide (Jacoby, 2017: 332). In states such as Austria, Switzerland, Belgium and the Netherlands, where grand coalitions are common, they have been largely centrist in composition. Ideological proximity to a coalition partner (in a grand coalition or otherwise) might arguably reduce the likelihood of policy compromise. In post-war Germany, for example, Jacoby (2017: 333) notes that a 'renovation logic' – the pursuit of policy goals that would require a constitutional supermajority – dominated coalition formation as the government focused on rebuilding the nation. Post-1990, he argues, this logic has shifted to that of 'sterilisation' of the populist right – a point to which we return.

Parties that have engaged in coalition formation at the sub-national level, as in Spain, have sometimes done so in pursuit of a deliberate strategy that simultaneously rejects coalitions at the national level. The motivation, Renui (2011: 119) argues, are parties' 'intrinsic' policy goals at the regional (sub-state) level, for which office itself is merely instrumental. Spain had historically opted for single-party minority government at the national level, with parliamentary support agreements with opposition parties on select policy issues (Renui, 2011: 116, 120).

Coalition stability

Focus on the motivations that lead to coalition formation, however, risks us overlooking the conditions that enable its maintenance (Martin and Vanberg, 2008). The party system and electoral playing field may shape the likelihood of coalitions emerging, but international experience suggests considerable variation in the duration and maintenance of governing coalitions. Müller and Strøm (2000: 586) observe that interparty conflicts have historically been the second-most-important cause of cabinet termination in Western European coalitions, scheduled elections being the first. The compromise required from coalition politics renders the coalition agreement – that which, in single-party government, would be the party manifesto – critical to the task of government. In the case of post-electoral coalitions, it is all the more important in cementing joint agreement between parties on what their coalition will deliver.

Even in single-party government, issues may arise on which competing factions need to find resolution (Bellamy, 2012: 445). The inherently conflictual nature of politics makes this so, hence the British majoritarian refrain that 'all governments are coalitions' (Paun and Hallifax, 2012: 15). Yet agreement to a coalition requires acceptance by parties that constituent expectations may need to be balanced with policy compromise (Martin and Vanberg, 2008: 503). The degree of compromise required is likely to increase with the ideological distance between the parties. As such, coalition agreements can constrain party behaviour (Moury, 2012; Santana Pereira and Moury, 2018: 94). The formation of a coalition government in Italy following a hung parliament in the 2018 election – the first post-electoral coalition in the country's democratic history – was a marriage of left and far-right that required considerable toning down of policy positions on both sides (Santana Pereira and Moury, 2018: 101). In that case, reconciling policy commitments with compromise proved short-lived. The left coalition partner, the Movimento 5 Stelle, saw decreases in its public popularity in the subsequent months – an electoral indication of constituent discontent with the partnership – while the public popularity of the far-right Lega increased (Santana Pereira and Moury, 2018: 101). Lega's breakaway from the alliance in 2019 resulted in a snap election and a new centre-left coalition between the Movimento 5 Stelle and the centrist Partito Democratico (Democratic Party) (Tondo, 2019). Coalitions may thus be reined in by public opinion as well as by internal instability.

In the case of Slovakia, the four-party coalition from 1998 under the Slovak Democratic Coalition maintained stability by excluding more contentious issues from its governance agenda. Avoidance of the policy areas on which parties clash is only a temporary solution, however, and perhaps indicative of the likely longevity of a coalition arrangement. The unity of the Slovak coalition, Pridham (2002: 95) argues, was ensured only by its solidarity on the goal of integration into the European Union. While this was not enough to hold the coalition together in the longer term, he suggests that agreement on this issue and a common commitment to democracy and the rule of law made for fairly stable and efficient government (Pridham, 2002: 95). It is therefore intuitive that coalitions will prioritise the 'less divisive' issues in their pledges over those on which they disagree (Zubel and Klüver, 2013). 'There are benefits from cooperation that coalition parties want to attain', as Martin and Vanberg (2008: 514) highlight, and 'avoiding conflict raises the level of these benefits substantially'. That said, Timmermans and Moury's (2006: 398–399) research on coalition governments in Belgium and the Netherlands suggests that internal disputes still often arise around issues included in the coalition agreement.

Although the absence of an institutionalised party system in newer democracies might explain some comparative variation in the type and dynamics of coalitions, mechanisms to resolve differences and reach consensus in coalitions have been adopted internationally. Both coalition agreements and a 'coalition committee' or 'council' for the resolution of disputes have become international best practice (Paun and Hallifax, 2012: 15). The practicalities of delivering and fulfilling coalition commitments have been enabled in the UK, Western Europe and Eastern Europe by dedicated dispute resolution and mutual supervision. Reflecting on the case of the Conservative-Liberal Democratic coalition government in the UK between 2010 and 2015, a report by Paun and Hallifax (2012: 7) for the UK Institute for Government remarks that the openness of differences between coalition partners can mean that decision-making processes are more 'formalised and transparent'. In single-party government, meanwhile, internal differences are more likely to be 'swept under the carpet' – and less likely to be highlighted by the media (Pridham, 2002: 95) –

coalitions require that differences be debated. Decision-making may take longer, but is arguably more accountable (Paun and Hallifax, 2012: 15–16).

One of the notable achievements of coalition government in Slovakia in terms of democratic consolidation is believed by Pridham (2002: 93) to be the consultative institutional mechanisms used to resolve policy differences. The mediating personality of political leaders may be important in this regard, as Pridham notes in the Slovak case, but so are political culture and the strength of surrounding institutions. Comparative research by Bergman et al. (2019) into European coalition government suggests that while in Western Europe coalitions emphasise compromise and mutual supervision, Eastern Europe shows more evidence of 'ministerial government' by individuals and parties, and less adherence to the coalition agreement. Moury's (2012: 126, 130) examination of Western Europe suggests that coalition agreements constrain the actions of individual ministers, rendering the transfer of coalition agreements to cabinet decisions more likely. There is, however, variation within established democracies, with greater concentration of power in the prime minister (and less collective control by cabinet) in Germany and Italy than in the Netherlands or Belgium (Moury, 2012: 129), and the lowest level of collective decision-making in Italy. As such, Italian ministers are less likely to be constrained by the coalition agreement than their German, Dutch and Belgian counterparts (Moury, 2012: 131).

Coalitions that have been a feature of fragmented and unstable party systems – as in Eastern Europe and Latin America – have also had an impact on broader political and democratic stability. Maintaining the internal stability of a coalition is perhaps more challenging when the parties cover a wider ideological range. Electoral volatility also renders the future of coalitions uncertain. Neither duration nor rotation of power in its own right is an indicator of democratic strength. However, 'the capacity to use experience and retrospective judgement', as Savage (2016: 502) notes, 'is undermined when actors in the formation process frequently change'. As such, it shines light on the careful balancing of party interests in forming coalitions with the likely response from their wider membership and electorate.

Accountability

An issue related to the management of internal disagreement in coalitions is wider accountability to constituents. The coalition agreement is perhaps what is most likely to confirm or dispel for voters the notion that one or both parties to a coalition may be selling out. Through a published set of commitments, the public can hold parties to account. The plural composition of coalitions can, however, render mechanisms for accountability more challenging. This includes both the vertical accountability of government to the electorate, and the horizontal accountability between government and the wider institutions of state and democracy.

Parliamentary scrutiny and legislative debate can play a role in facilitating both of these. Martin and Vanberg (2004: 15, 16–17, 25) note that it may be the role played by the legislature that enforces a coalition commitment. Its scrutiny can prevent what they refer to as 'ministerial drift' through, for example, mechanisms such as a parliamentary committee system. Given that division can exist within coalition governments as well as between government and opposition, legislatures exert influence on behalf of both. Legislative debate, similarly, is a means of communicating with constituents and accounting for decisions taken (Martin and Vanberg, 2008: 25, 502–503). As such, while the central leadership of a coalition is important for stability, authors have cautioned against policy discussions remaining within the executive to the exclusion of the wider party. Failure to engage with the party activists, they argue, 'will undermine the coalition's stability as well as shutting off an important source of policy ideas' (Paun and Hallifax, 2012: 10).

In Latin America, the weakness and lack of resources at the disposal of legislatures have limited their influence over the executive, while the divided nature of the opposition makes it difficult to challenge the president (Morgenstern et al., 2008: 173, 174). Morgenstern et al. (2008: 171) explain that greater resources at the disposal of executives enable them to build alliances within the legislature, thus limiting the latter's pushback and effectiveness as a check on power. Coalition mechanisms, therefore, by no means suffice in ensuring democratic accountability, horizontally or vertically. The evolution of party politics in Chile, which emerged from the post-dictatorship democratic transition, has been characterised by two large multiparty coalitions (Alemán and Saiegh, 2007: 253). The centre-left five-party coalition, Concertación de Partidos por la Democracia (Coalition of Parties for Democracy), which governed Chile for 20 years from 1990 to 2010, earned the country the reputation of a 'model' democratic transition 'based on multi-party power sharing and consensus' (Siavelis, 2013: 17). Concertaçion utilised extensive mechanisms for coalition management and stability. Yet its very stability belied a disconnect from the electorate. According to Siavelis (2013: 20–21), the elaborate power-sharing arrangements and focus on unity in the governing alliance in effect generated a 'spoils' system, in which power was negotiated and shared between elites to the exclusion of citizens.

In Malaysia, similarly, consociationalism has taken place at the elite level, with limited effects of this unity being felt among 'the masses' (Shukri, 2017: 327). Not unlike Chile's rainbow coalition, in Malaysia this was 'a strategy to bring all parties and communities for closed door negotiations, thus reducing politics to mere administration and elections to being a harmless ritual' (Wong, 2018: 761). The elite concord that took place at the party level in Chile has earned it the description of a partidocracia (particracy): controlled by and accountable to parties rather than the people (Siavelis, 2013: 33). The breadth and duration of Chile's coalition, Sehnbruch and Siavelis (2013: 3) argue, 'led Chileans to believe that elite politicians were engaged in a process of government by negotiation and horse trading rather than true representative democracy and that citizen input mattered little'. Alongside the failure to challenge the severe inequality in Chilean society, Concertaçion's coalitional strength was also eventually its downfall (Siavelis, 2013: 18).[1]

Traditions of consensus and accommodation

Political scientist Richard Bellamy suggests that the very notion of compromise – inherent to coalition politics – can be viewed either positively or negatively. The latter sees compromise as 'inherently unprincipled and undemocratic', the former as part and parcel of a pluralist, democratic society (Bellamy, 2012: 442, 445): 'To accept democracy,' Bellamy argues, 'is to accept compromise.' As such, while representative democracy sees politics as adversarial, there are developmental benefits that can derive from compromise through the process of deliberation (Gutmann and Thompson, 2004). From Bellamy's (2012: 445, 447) perspective, then, the deliberation demanded of coalition politics 'can cultivate agreement and compromise in a positive way': rather than involving merely 'shallow compromise', it may involve 'deep compromise', which is a process of reasoning and accommodation.

It is thus possible to see how coalitions, in some contexts, serve to foster not only a politics of compromise, but a deeper set of values about democratic accommodation. Just as coalitions may involve more formal and transparent processes of decision-making than single-party government (Paun and Hallifax, 2012), so too can they put democratic values to the test and open the democratic space to traditionally excluded voices. Sridharan's (2012: 55) research on India shows that coalition governments, following the end of Congress Party dominance, while unstable, were important in generating incentives for a new accommodation of India's Muslim minority and other historically marginalised groups. In a state long used to party dominance, he argues that coalitions, particularly at the federal level, forced 'compromise and accommodation with a range of larger and smaller coalition partners and external supporting parties'.

In Sri Lanka, not dissimilarly, the switch to a proportional representation (PR) electoral system provided greater impetus for coalitions. In contrast to the winner-takes-all principle of the single-member plurality system, the proportional distribution of seats to votes in a PR system opened up access to the state for small and ethnic minority parties (Uyangoda, 2012: 229). The very precarity of coalitions, and the reliance on their partners for support, may mean that they have to respond to popular bottom-up demands or take into account niche (minority) concerns. The end of national coalition government in India, with the advent of the single-party government of the Hindu-nationalist Bharatiya Janata Party since 2014 has, in fact, raised concerns of a dangerous ethnic majoritarianism and the exclusion of religious minority representation (Adeney, 2015).

Bellamy (2012: 465) concedes that deeply divided societies may not be able to form a 'democratic community' in which deep compromise can be achieved. Where there does exist a 'democratic community', however, he sees consensus politics as not needing to involve the trade-off between accommodation and accountability assumed in coalition politics. Political elites can, instead, play an important role in the transference and embedding of democratic values. When the rules of the game are accepted, democracy can begin to consolidate. This has led, in some cases, to a greater culture of consensus politics but, in others, to a form of elite pact in which compromise takes place to the exclusion of democratic participation.

Whatever the process of consensus-building achieved during coalition government, however, Pridham (2002: 79) remarks that the closer parties come to the next election, the more they come to see themselves, once again, as competitors.[2] He thus considers how far coalitions can 'contribute to democratic consolidation through evolving elite behaviour' (Pridham, 2002: 76). Where elite acceptance of democratic values is itself in a formative stage, this can impact either positively or negatively on 'mass attitudes' (Bellamy, 2012: 79). Grand coalitions are perhaps a test of elites' capacity for compromise and consensus formation, yet they can also have the effect of narrowing (not broadening) democratic debate. As the major parties dominate the political playing field, they are forced to compromise by moving further to the centre (Jacoby, 2017; Santana Pereira and Moury, 2018). In Germany, Jacoby (2017: 341, 344) suggests that the Christian Democratic Union–Social Democratic Party coalition succeeded in doing this by controlling and narrowing to a very limited range of views the policy agenda on the Eurozone crisis.

When grand coalitions are used as a response to insurgent challenges from extremist parties, however, their utility in this regard can backfire by, in turn, stimulating populist or fringe reaction (Jacoby, 2017). The tendency for centrism to 'spark the growth of extremism' means that, when employed as a strategy to 'close ranks' against extremist parties (as in Germany and Austria), it may be exacerbating the very problem it seeks to remove (Jacoby, 2017: 330) – an outcome realised in both states. The 2017 federal elections in Germany saw the far-right

Alternative für Deutschland (Alternative for Germany) elevated to the third largest party in the German parliament, and it made marked gains in the 2017 state elections in eastern Germany (Connolly, 2019). In Austria, despite splits within its leading populist-right Freedom Party, Mudde (2019) suggests this should by no means be seen as the demise of the far-right influence in Austrian politics.

LESSONS FROM INTERNATIONAL EXPERIENCE FOR AFRICA

The relatively recent transition to multiparty democracy on the African continent and the prevalence of ethnic and religious cleavages in many states render lessons from international experience especially relevant. As with the international cases discussed here, local political context and history in African states play an important role in shaping the nature and longevity of coalitions. There, nonetheless, remain useful lessons from comparative experience. The formation of coalitions in multi-ethnic states, as cases in Asia and Eastern Europe suggest, can provide means for marginalised or minority groups to attain political influence, and may be significant for Africa in overcoming the dangers of ethnic polarisation. The cultivating of compromise and consensus politics may have both stabilising and democratising benefits for democracies where political power has been closely associated with ethnic majoritarianism. Communal pacts may, however, serve to exclude certain groups or deepen existing ethno-regional cleavages, perhaps taking parties further away from more clearly programmatic or ideological agendas.

The experience of new democracies internationally also provides examples of states where the dominant or one-party legacy has impacted on the forging of competitive party systems. Much as in Africa, as the next two chapters suggest, this history has also increased the likelihood of coalition formation, given the difficulties for newcomer parties in establishing organisational structures and consolidating networks of support. This is reinforced by the presence of often long-serving former liberation movements. Opposition alliances in these contexts may be narrowly opportunistic or lack ideological coherence, with implications for longevity and voter confidence, and may be exacerbated by the nature of politics in Africa as a zero-sum game. As such, party system institutionalisation, as elsewhere in the globe, will be an ongoing factor in the likelihood of coalition formation and in the potential of coalitions to foster, not undermine, political accountability and stability. Much will also depend, however, on the embedding of values of accommodation and consensus among the African political elites themselves, highlighting the centrality of their role in young democracies for the transference of democratic values.

CONCLUSION

This chapter showed that coalitions internationally are a mixed variety, and that factors relating to local context and prior experience shape their impact on political stability and the dynamics of multiparty democracy. Through a comparison of coalition arrangements in several regions, this chapter has shown that coalitions have been used for different purposes and with different degrees of success in terms of stabilising democratic party systems and renewing political power. It has done this largely through a comparison of new and established democracies, and the nature of their political history and party systems as determinants of coalition formation.

Stable alliances of ideologically likeminded parties can, and have, produced some successful experiments in governance through focusing on areas of commonality. Coalitions with greater programmatic diversity have nonetheless sometimes had a democratising effect by accommodating previously excluded groups, and developing the traditions of deliberation and compromise required of consensus politics. The consensus formation involved in coalitions can generate important values of accommodation and the appreciation of difference. Coalitions are, however, shaped by their broader context. As such, historic experience, societal cleavages and the institutionalisation of the party system have a bearing on the intersection of coalitions and political stability.

Internationally, societies with party systems that remain highly fragmented have experienced cycles of unstable coalition government, with a knock-on effect on future government formation. Many such societies are likely to experience coalitions for a long time to come, and so the motivations of coalition partners are particularly important to their success. In established democracies, the increasing fragmentation of the party landscape and growing popularity of fringe parties render the composition and dynamics of future coalitions far less certain. Either way, the links between political parties and the electorate, and the practice of ongoing accountability, will be synonymous with their democratising potential. Valuable mechanisms for the maintenance of coalitions – to generate stability and resolve disputes – can enable stable and effective government. They can also, however, confine the process of consensus-building to elites, excluding broader society from the act of democratic compromise.

On the African continent (the subject of chapters 4 and 5), several of the issues affecting new democracies internationally may well have resonance. Many parts of Africa are characterised by the ethnic and religious diversity that has shaped party cleavages in parts of Asia and Eastern Europe. The experience of transition from one-party rule and the dominance of former liberation movements also render the challenges of party system institutionalisation relevant to African democracies. Challenges to long-time incumbents may only be viable through opposition coalitions with broad-based appeal and collaborative programmes. Any coalition that comes to power, moreover, will need to grow its roots among, and constantly account to, the electorate to avoid a lapse of coalition politics into elite bargaining.

REFERENCES

Adeney, K. 2015. 'A move to majoritarian nationalism? Challenges of representation in South Asia', *Representation*, 50 (1), 7–21.

Alemán, E. and Saiegh, S. M. 2007. 'Legislative preferences, political parties, and coalition unity in Chile', *Comparative Politics*, 39 (3), 253–272.

Alemán, E. and Tsebelis, G. 2011. 'Political parties and government coalitions in the Americas', *Journal of Politics in Latin America*, 3 (1), 3–28.

Antoszewski, A. and Kozierska, J. 2019. 'Poland: Weak coalitions and small party suicide in government', in Bergman, T., Ilonszki, G. and Müller, W. (eds.) *Coalition Governance in Central Eastern Europe.* Oxford: Oxford University Press.

Backlund, A., Ecker, A. and Meyer, T. M. 2019. 'The economic and political context of coalition politics in Central Eastern Europe', in Bergman, T., Ilonszki, G. and Müller, W. (eds.) *Coalition Governance in Central Eastern Europe.* Oxford: Oxford University Press.

Bellamy, R. 2012. 'Democracy, compromise and the representation paradox: Coalition government and political integrity', *Government and Opposition*, 47 (3), 441–465.

Bergman, T., Ilonszki, G. and Müller, W. 2019. *Coalition Governance in Central Eastern Europe.* Oxford: Oxford University Press.

Bevins, V. 14 February 2020: 'The left takes center stage in Spain', *Intelligencer*, https://nymag.com/intelligencer/2020/02/the-left-coalition-government-in-spain.html, accessed 26 April 2020.

Budge, I. and Keman, H. 1993. *Parties and Democracy: Coalition formation and government functioning in twenty states.* Oxford: Oxford University Press.

Connolly, K. 27 October 2019. 'Far-right AfD surges to second place in German state election', *The Guardian*, https://www.theguardian.com/world/2019/oct/27/far-right-afd-surges-to-second-place-in-german-state-elections, accessed 10 April 2020.

Druckman, J. N. and Roberts, A. 2007. 'Communist successor parties and coalition formation in Eastern Europe', *Legislative Studies Quarterly,* 32 (1), 5–31.

Gutmann, A. and Thomson, D. 2004. *Why Deliberative Democracy?* Princeton: Princeton University Press.

Hirose, T. 2012. 'Coalition politics in Japan', in Sridharan, E. (ed.) *Coalition Politics and Democratic Consolidation in Asia.* New Delhi: Oxford University Press.

Hough, D. and Verge, T. 2009. 'A sheep in wolf's clothing or a gift from heaven? Left-left coalitions in comparative perspective', *Regional and Federal Studies*, 19 (1), 37–55.

Ibenskas, R. 2015. 'Understanding pre-electoral coalitions in Central and

Eastern Europe', *British Journal of Political Science*, 46, 743–761.

Jacoby, W. 2017. 'Grand coalitions and democratic dysfunction: Two warnings from Central Europe', *Government and Opposition,* 52 (2), 329–355.

Laver, M. and Schofield, N. 1998. *Multiparty Government: The politics of coalition in Europe.* Ann Arbor: University of Michigan Press.

Mainwaring, S. and Scully, T. R. 1995. 'Introduction: Party systems in Latin America', in Mainwaring, S. and Scully, T. R. (eds.) *Building Democratic Institutions: Party systems in Latin America.* Stanford: Stanford University Press.

Mainwaring. S., Bejarano, A. M. and Leongómez, E. P. 2006. *The Crisis of Democratic Representation in the Andes.* Stanford: Stanford University Press.

Martin, L. W. and Vanberg, G. 2004. 'Policing the bargain: Coalition government and parliamentary scrutiny', *American Journal of Political Science,* 48 (1), 13–27.

Martin, L. W. and Vanberg, G. 2008. 'Coalition government and political communication', *Political Research Quarterly,* 61 (3), 502–516.

Meireles, F. 2016. 'Oversized government coalitions in Latin America', *Brazilian Political Science Review*, 10 (3), 1–31.

Morgenstern, S., Negri, J. J. and Pérez-Liñán, A. 2008. 'Parliamentary opposition in non-parliamentary regimes: Latin America', *The Journal of Legislative Studies,* 14 (1/2), 160–189.

Moury, C. 2012. *Coalition Government and Party Mandate: How coalition agreements constrain ministerial action.* Abingdon: Routledge.

Mudde, C. 2 October 2019. 'The new Austrian government will brand itself as moderate – but don't believe it', *The Guardian,* https://www.theguardian.com/commentisfree/2019/oct/02/the-new-austrian-government-will-brand-itself-as-moderate-but-dont-believe-it, accessed 2 May 2020.

Müller, W. C. and Strøm, K. 2000. *Coalition Governments in Western Europe.* Oxford: Oxford University Press.

Nagai, O. and Mizorogi, T. 6 October 2019. 'Japan's ruling coalition outshines other developed democracies', *Nikkei Asian Review,* https://asia.nikkei.com/Politics/Japan-s-ruling-coalition-outshines-other-developed-democracies, accessed 2 May 2020.

Paun, A. and Hallifax, S. 2012. *A Game of Two Halves: How coalition governments renew in mid-term and last the full term.* London: Institute for Government.

Pellikaan, H., De Lange, S. L. and Van der Meer, T. W. G. 2016. 'The centre does not hold: Coalition politics and party system change in the Netherlands, 2002–12', *Government and Opposition,* 53 (2), 231–255.

Pridham, G. 2002. 'Coalition behaviour in new democracies of Central and Eastern Europe: The case of Slovakia', *The Journal of Communist Studies and Transition Politics,* 18 (2), 75–102.

Renui, J. M. 2011. '"Spain is different": Explaining minority governments by diverging party goals', in Andeweg, A. W. (ed.) *Puzzles of Government Formation: Coalition theory and deviant cases.* Abingdon: Routledge.

Rueschmeyer, M. 1991. 'Participation and control in a state socialist society: The German Democratic Republic', *East Central Europe*, 18 (1), 23–53.

Santana Pereira, J. and Moury, C. 2018. 'Planning the "government of change": The 2018 Italian coalition agreement in comparative perspective', *Italian Political Science*, 13 (2), 92–103.

Saravanmuttu, J. 2012. 'Twin coalition politics in Malaysia since 2008: A path dependent framing and analysis', *Contemporary Southeast Asia*, 34 (1), 101–127.

Savage, L. 2016. 'Party system institutionalization and government formation in new democracies', *World Politics*, 68 (3), 499–537.

Sehnbruch, K. and Siavelis, P. M. 2013. 'Political and economic life under the rainbow', in Sehnbruch, K. and Siavelis, P. M. (eds.) *Democratic Chile: The politics and policies of a historic coalition, 1990–2010*. Boulder: Lynne Rienner Publishers.

Shukri, S. F. 2017. 'The role of ethnic politics in promoting democratic governance: A case study of Malaysia', *Intellectual Discourse*, 25 (2), 321–339.

Siavelis, P. M. 2013. 'From a necessary to a permanent coalition', in Sehnbruch, K. and Siavelis, P. M. (eds.) *Democratic Chile: The politics and policies of a historic coalition, 1990–2010*. Boulder: Lynne Rienner Publishers.

Slapsak. S. 9 November 2019. 'What happened to the left in Eastern Europe after 1989? And what is its future?', *Al Jazeera,* https://www.aljazeera.com/indepth/opinion/happened-left-eastern-europe-1989-191107212736021.html, accessed 4 May 2020.

Sridharan, E. 2012. 'Coalitions and democratic deepening in India', in Sridharan, E. (ed.) *Coalition Politics and Democratic Consolidation in Asia.* New Delhi: Oxford University Press.

Stephens, P. 13 February 2020. 'Europe must embrace a new way of politics: The two-party system that prevailed for so long has been upended', *Financial Times*, https://on.ft.com/38pydBb, accessed 4 March 2020.

Stone, J. 7 January 2020. 'Spain gets new left-wing coalition government after socialist leader wins vote', *The Independent*, https://www.independent.co.uk/news/world/europe/spain-parliament-election-pedro-sanchez-left-wing-coalition-latest-a9273756.html, accessed 29 April 2020.

Timmermans, A. and Moury, C. 2006. 'Coalition governance in Belgium and the Netherlands: Rising government stability against all electoral odds', *Acta Politica*, 41, 389–407.

Tondo, L. 5 September 2019. 'Italy's new coalition sworn in as doubts cast over longevity', *The Guardian*, https://www.theguardian.com/world/2019/sep/05/italys-coalition-enemies-open-way-matteo-salvini-returna, accessed 2 May 2020.

Tronconi, F. 2015. 'Ethno-regionalist parties in regional government: Multilevel coalitional strategies in Italy and Spain', *Government and Opposition,* 50 (4), 578–606.

Uyangoda, J. 2012. 'The dynamics of coalition politics and democracy in Sri Lanka', in Sridharan, E. (ed.) *Coalition Politics and Democratic Consolidation in Asia.* New Delhi: Oxford University Press.

Wang, R. and Groot, G. 2018. 'Who represents? Xi Jinping's grand united front work, legitimation, participation and consultative democracy', *Journal of Contemporary China*, 27 (112), 569–583.

Watson, K. 26 October 2020. 'Jubilation as Chile votes to rewrite constitution', *BBC News,* https://www.bbc.com/news/world-latin-america-54687090, accessed 29 October 2020.

Welsh, A. 1994. 'Political transition processes in Central and Eastern Europe', *Comparative Politics*, 26 (4), 379–394.

Wong, C. 2018. 'The rise, resilience and demise of Malaysia's dominant coalition', *The Round Table*, 107 (6), 755–769.

Zubel, R. and Klüver, H. 2013. 'Legislative pledges and coalition government', *Party Politics,* 21 (4), 603–614.

FOUR

Electoral systems, party systems and coalitions
Lessons from Southern Africa

KHABELE MATLOSA

ELECTORAL SYSTEMS AND PARTY SYSTEMS are mutually reinforcing and can either advance democratisation or shield autocratisation. Southern Africa is home to multiple cross-cutting iterations, which reveal complex interfaces with multiparty elections and coalition politics. Party coalitions in the region come in various forms, in particular electoral alliances, majority/minority coalition governments, grand coalitions, governments of national unity and legislative coalitions.

Electoral systems underpin the democratic essence of elections. Most electoral systems in Southern Africa are a relic of colonialism, requiring reform for local adaptation. The region is home to three families of electoral systems: plurality/majority, proportional representation (PR) and mixed systems. *Party systems* that have shaped contemporary politics in the region include multiparty systems, dominant-party systems and one case of a no-party system. There are currently no cases of one-party and two-party systems – the former is notorious for anchoring autocratisation. As elsewhere on the continent, the majority of countries in Southern Africa experienced authoritarianism of both the one-party and military varieties between the 1960s and 1980s. Furthermore, the autocratic apartheid system was institutionalised in South Africa and Namibia.

Since their independence in 1966 and 1968, respectively, Botswana and Mauritius have stood out as the trailblazers of democratisation in Southern Africa. External factors such as the end of the Cold War and internal factors like popular struggles played an important role in propelling the democratic transitions in the region during the 1980s. These transitions brought multiparty elections to the centre of contestation for state power. The early transitions in the region included the demise of apartheid in Namibia (1989) and South Africa (1994), the termination of the main thrusts of civil wars in Mozambique (1992) and Angola (1994), the end of one-party rule in Madagascar (1989), Zambia (1991), Seychelles (1991), Tanzania (1992) and Malawi (1993), and the collapse of military rule in Lesotho (1993). While celebrating the reintroduction of multiparty elections in the region, caution nevertheless needs to be exercised, as elections are a double-edged sword. They can shield autocracy, as is the case in Eswatini and Zimbabwe, the same way that they promote democracy. It is this ostensibly contradictory nature of elections that drove Cheeseman and Klaas (2018: 1) to observe that 'the greatest political paradox of our time is this: there are more elections than ever before, and yet the world is becoming less democratic'.[1]

The next section introduces the key concepts that inform the interface between and among electoral systems, party systems and coalitions. This is followed by a discussion on the confluence of electoral systems and party systems in Southern Africa. Then I investigate how coalitions impact the five core values of electoral systems, namely those of representation, accountability, participation, inclusiveness and political stability, distilling the lessons learnt.

INTERFACE BETWEEN AND AMONG ELECTORAL SYSTEMS, PARTY SYSTEMS AND COALITIONS

Lindberg (2006: 1) reminds us that 'while there are many views on what democracy is – or ought to be – a common denominator among modern democracies is elections'. An election is a process whereby a people belonging to a particular territorial state (the electorate), under the authority of a single institutional state, choose their leaders (at various levels of government) periodically to manage their national affairs as an expression of popular sovereignty (Matlosa, 2004: 22). An election constitutes the heartbeat of representative democracy.

On their own, however, elections do not guarantee democracy, nor are they synonymous with it (Cowen and Laakso, 2002). Such a perception amounts to what Karl (1986) terms 'the fallacy of electoralism' – the perception that the mere holding of regular elections, irrespective of their quality, qualifies a country as a democracy. It is this notion that exposes elections as a double-edged sword. It is capable of advancing democratisation under favourable conditions, yet it is also capable of shielding autocratisation in an inclement political climate. Concerns about the adverse effects of elections, and electoral authoritarianism, are articulated by Schedler (2002; 2006) when he addresses elections in the context of the 'menu of manipulation'. Elections are agents of democratisation, but they are also the tools of manipulation aimed at anchoring authoritarianism, he argues.

Do elections promote democratisation or autocratisation?

> 'Elections make democratisation more likely if … they serve to make *repression* "expensive" and counterproductive, and spur the opposition to unify and mobilise; *and if* they make a policy of *tolerating* the opposition seem to the rulers as if it will make their rule more legitimate, *but* in fact trigger defections of state actors to the opposition and create self-fulfilling expectations about the continuation of competitive politics' (Lindberg, 2009: 87; emphasis in the original).

'Elections make *autocratisation* more likely if ... they serve to make repression "cheap", easy to target at the opposition leaders, or even unnecessary; *and if* they make it possible for the regime to control *toleration* of the opposition, to split the opposition, and to use elections as a vehicle for patronage; or if elections simply make *toleration* too costly for the incumbents' (Lindberg, 2009: 87; emphasis in the original).

Elections have no meaning outside electoral systems. An electoral system refers to an institutional arrangement for translating votes cast by the electorate into seats in representative institutions at various levels of government (national, provincial, district, municipal). Reynolds (1999: 89) observes that an electoral system is a critical institution that shapes and influences the rules for political competition over state power in that this single institution determines 'what parties look like, who is represented in parliament, and ultimately who governs'. The nature and workings of an electoral system are defined by five key variables (Reynolds et al., 2005: 5), which jointly deliver much of the shape of the political system.

1. The method of designing or demarcating electoral divisions or constituencies (i.e., the nature of the delimitation process)
2. The voting procedure used (voting for parties, individuals or both)
3. The mathematical formula that is used to calculate election results and translate valid votes cast into parliamentary seats (i.e., statistical formula and thresholds)
4. The ballot structure and voting procedure (whether the voter makes a single choice or multiple choices expressing a series of preferences)
5. The nature of district magnitude (how many representatives to the legislature that district elects)

Political parties are organised groups of people that are formed with the sole purpose of articulating and aggregating the interests of the group, contesting control of state power and government, and directing a country's development process in line with their ideological orientation and policy frameworks (Matlosa, 2007: 20). Reilly (2008: 3) argues that 'political parties have long been recognized as essential components of representative democracy. Indeed, it is difficult to imagine how governance of modern states could be accomplished without meaningful political parties.' In the African context, political parties in their current incarnation are a fairly recent phenomenon, dating to the era of decolonisation. As Salih (2003: 2) observes, they 'emerged to prepare the political elite to assume power when their countries were poised to gain independence'.

Parties operate within the framework of the particular party system in each country. Salih and Nordlund (2008: 43) define party systems as the networks of internal and external relationships that characterise the existence and functioning of parties. For Kadima (2014: 3), a party system refers to 'the way in which various parties interact at a particular level of political competition and/or cooperation'. A party system conditions the intraparty governance dynamics as well as the interparty relations. A party system can be described with reference to three factors: the number of political parties competing for power, the size of parties as reflected by their votes and parliamentary seats, and the type of relationships between and among parties (in and outside of parliament). The way parties are governed internally and the manner in which they relate to one another during and between elections have the net effect of solidifying or denuding their institutionalisation.

The nature of interparty relations, in combination with and often as a result of their relative electoral strengths, influence whether or not parties enter into coalitions before, during or after elections and/or referendums. Coalitions are 'party-to-party partnerships' aimed at 'aggregating interests and reaching a middle ground' (Salih and Nordlund, 2008: 60) in contesting elections/referendums, passing specific legislation, influencing parliamentary debates and/or forming a government. A coalition denotes a temporary pact or partnership between two or more political parties for the purposes of gaining more influence or power than they would otherwise have as individual parties (NDI/Oslo Center, 2015: 13).

It is within this context that party coalitions have been constructed, deconstructed and reconstructed over time, conditioned by, among other things, the electoral system, the party system and regime types. Coalition building in the Southern Africa region remains generally work in progress.

THE CONFLUENCE OF ELECTORAL SYSTEMS AND PARTY SYSTEMS: A COMPARATIVE ANALYSIS

The confluence of electoral systems and party systems and their effects on party coalitions are captured by Harris and Reilly (1998: 191–192) when they observe that 'in translating the votes in a general election into seats in the legislature, the choice of electoral system can effectively determine who is elected and which party gains power. Even with exactly the same number of votes for parties, one system might lead to a coalition government and another to a single party assuming power.'

Party systems
Globally, there are five types of party systems, distinguishable by the number of parties and their effectiveness vis-à-vis competition over, and control of, state power.

1. The *one-party system* comprises one single party that monopolises state power, in accordance with stipulation in the national constitution (de-jure one-party system) or wherein a single dominant ruling party exists in the context of other parties, and practically makes it well-nigh impossible for the other parties to function and contest state power (defacto one-party system). The one-party system marked Southern Africa's political landscape between the 1960s and 1980s. For instance, Zambia was a typical de-jure one-party system from 1972 to 1990, while Lesotho was a defacto one-party system between 1970 and 1986. The one-party system was swept away in the onset of the democratisation wave of the early 1990s.

2. The *two-party system* exists in situations where a multiplicity of political parties exist, but only two parties or alliances/coalitions of parties on opposite sides of the political divide have a real chance of winning state power. This system does not exist in Southern Africa.

3. The *dominant-party system* exists where, despite a multiplicity of parties, one party or one coalition is so dominant that it wins multiparty elections regularly over a long period of time (over three successive elections, according to Sartori, 1976), with slim prospects for being dethroned in the foreseeable future. The largest number of countries in Southern Africa (10 in total) are classified as having dominant-party

systems (Table 4.1). Botswana is the longest-enduring dominant-party system in the region, since independence in 1966.

4. The *multiparty system* (as used conceptually in this volume) exists where a multiplicity of parties operate and have the capability to effectively contest elections, on their own or through alliances, with more or less equal prospects of winning control of the levers of state power, in their own right or through coalitions. Four countries in Southern Africa are characterised as multiparty systems (Table 4.1).

5. The *no-party system* exists where political parties by law are not allowed to operate and elections are conducted on individual merit. Only one country in Southern Africa, Eswatini, operates this party system. Eswatini is an absolute monarchy; its political system is anchored in a dynastic autocracy in which political parties have no role.

Electoral systems

The dominant influence for adoption of particular electoral systems in Southern Africa has been the overbearing colonial and neocolonial linkages between Southern African countries and former colonial powers. The majority of countries in the region adopted the political institutions of their former colonial masters as part of the political settlement of the decolonisation struggles. Most of these states were under British colonial rule, and on independence they adopted largely the Westminster constitutional frameworks and political arrangements that go with it.

Plurality/majority systems

Plurality/majority systems are premised on 'the principle that a candidate(s) or party with a plurality of votes (i.e., more than any other) or a majority of votes (i.e., 50 per cent plus one – an absolute majority) is/are declared winners' (Reynolds et al., 2005: 180). Under this system a country is divided into different, albeit relatively equal, electoral zones known as constituencies, from which contestants have to emerge in order to occupy their seats in the legislature. The winner of an election is the candidate 'who gains the most votes, but not necessarily an absolute majority of the votes. Voters choose their favoured candidate by placing a tick or a cross on the ballot paper, and the winner is simply the candidate who gains a plurality of votes' (Reilly, 2001: 15).

This system is used for the election of their legislatures by eight countries in Southern Africa, as depicted in Table 4.1. Botswana and Eswatini operate the winner-takes-all plurality, first-past-the-post (FPTP) system, and the president in the former is selected in parliament, while the prime minister in the latter is appointed by the absolute monarch. Zambia uses the FPTP system along similar lines, where both MPs and the president are elected on a simple plurality of votes, allowing room for minority government, with serious implications for legitimacy of rule. In Madagascar, Tanzania and Zimbabwe, MPs are elected on the basis of FPTP, while the president is elected on the basis of the majoritarian two-round system requiring 50 per cent plus one of the national vote, and a possible run-off if no one garners the required vote tally in the first round of voting.

Mauritius operates the FPTP, modified in such a way that it allows for a block vote and compensates losers. The prime minister is appointed by the president following elections on the basis of the power configuration in the national assembly. Of the 70 members of the national assembly, 62 are elected through a block vote. The country is divided into 20 constituencies and each returns three MPs, while the Island of Rodrigues elects two MPs (EISA, 2019). In early 2000, the Mauritian government commissioned a review of the system. The review was undertaken under the leadership of Justice Albie Sachs of South Africa. The Sachs report, made public in 2001, proposed reform of the electoral model towards the mixed member proportional system (Matlosa, 2004; Kasenally, 2009: 280). Despite the establishment of a parliamentary select committee to consider the Sachs report and its recommendations, there was no consensus, and the report has been gathering dust on the shelves of parliament.

Malawi used to operate a simple plurality system (a pure FPTP) whereby even the president could be elected on the basis of a national vote of less than 50 per cent. This leads to a minority government with implications for legitimacy and stability. In 2020 the country introduced the majoritarian variant to its winner-takes-all system. The High Court of Malawi issued a historic judgment in February 2020, in a case that challenged the results of the presidential election of 21 May 2019. The court annulled the results and ordered a fresh poll within 150 days. The judgment pronounced:

> (I)n view of our determination that the majority to be attained by a candidate to the office of President is a minimum of fifty percent (50 per cent) plus one vote of the total valid votes cast during the presidential election, for purposes of the fresh elections to be held and herein and all future elections, Parliament must within 21 days from the date hereof, including Sundays, Saturdays and Public holidays, make appropriate provisions for the holding of presidential run-off elections in the event that no single candidate secures the

Table 4.1: Typology of electoral systems and party systems in Southern Africa

Country	Electoral system	Party system
Angola	Proportional representation (PR)	Dominant
Botswana	Plurality[i]	Dominant
Democratic Republic of the Congo (DRC)	PR	Dominant
Eswatini	Plurality	No-party
Lesotho	Mixed Member Proportional[ii]	Multiparty
Malawi	Plurality/Majority[iii]	Multiparty
Mauritius	Plurality	Multiparty
Madagascar	Plurality/Majority	Multiparty
Mozambique	PR	Dominant
Namibia	PR	Dominant
Seychelles	Mixed	Dominant
South Africa	PR	Dominant
Tanzania	Plurality/Majority	Dominant
Zambia	Plurality	Dominant
Zimbabwe	Plurality/Majority	Dominant

[i] Plurality system: The type of first-past-the-post (FPTP) system where a simple plurality of votes determines the winner(s) of elections.
[ii] Mixed Member Proportional system: Some members are elected in FPTP constituency elections and the rest by PR.
[iii] Plurality/Majority system: An FPTP system in which the plurality component is applied for the election of MPs, while the majoritarian system kicks in for the election of the president in the form of the two-round system that requires the winner to attain 50% +1 votes.

Sources: Matlosa, 2003; 2004: 27; 2007: 37–41; Salih and Nordlund, 2008: 43–51; Erdmann and Basedau, 2013: 35.

constitutional majority under section 80(2) of the Constitution (*Saulos Klause Chilima & Lazarus McCarthy Chakwera v Arthur Peter Mutharika & the Electoral Commission*).

In 2006, Patel and this author were commissioned by the Malawi Electoral Commission to evaluate Malawi's electoral system and recommend appropriate reforms. Our report made three key recommendations: for presidential elections, a 50 per cent plus one formula and provision for run-off (two-round system); for parliamentary elections, a combination of the mixed member proportional system, ensuring a larger proportion of parliamentary seats occupied through the FPTP system and a relatively smaller proportion of seats occupied through a PR compensatory component; and for local government elections, the maintenance of FPTP (Matlosa and Patel, 2006: 53). While the last recommendation was for the maintenance of the status quo, the first recommendation has been implemented 14 years down the line.

The FPTP system has anchored Eswatini's no-party dynastic autocratisation, shielded by the façade of regular (s)elections. This electoral system has also solidified dominant-party systems in Tanzania, Botswana and Zimbabwe, where the political hegemony of the ruling Chama Cha Mapinduzi (CCM), the Botswana Democratic Party and the Zimbabwe African National Union-Patriotic Front (ZANU-PF), respectively, has remained entrenched since their independence in 1963, 1966 and 1980, respectively. Madagascar and Malawi have exhibited characteristics of party fragmentation, reinforced and reproduced over time by the FPTP system (Lembani, 2014). The two countries share a history of one-party systems, and in the case of Madagascar even military rule (1972–76). Part of the fragmentation therefore is owing to the embryonic nature of the multiparty system itself. Given the regularity with which politicians change allegiances and alliances over time, it was not surprising that in an in-depth analysis of party fragmentation and politics of the belly and personality cult in the country, Malawi was caricatured as 'a democracy of chameleons': politicians change colour day and night on the basis of the age-old maxim that in politics there are no permanent friends and enemies

(Englund, 2001: 14). In Malawi, fusion and fission of political parties are two sides of the same coalition coin.

Mauritius is the longest enduring multiparty system in Southern Africa. It is also one of the countries where coalitions are institutionalised (Oyugi, 2006; Kadima and Kasenally, 2006). During the 1991 elections, the Mauritian Socialist Movement became the governing coalition. It was replaced in the 1995 elections by the coalition involving the Mauritian Labour Party and the Mouvement Militant Mauricien (Mauritian Militant Movement). The 2000 elections were won by the coalition comprising the Mouvement Militant Mauricien and the Mauritian Socialist Movement, while the 2005 elections were won by the Social Alliance coalition. This brief historical account demonstrates how unpredictable election outcomes are in Mauritius. The Mauritian experience proves the relative utility, to the advance of democratisation, of the notion as the central plank of electoral governance, of procedural certainty and substantive uncertainty (Mozaffar and Schedler, 2002) – that while electoral rules and regulations must be predictable and known ahead of the process, election results should not be known and determined before the actual process.

Proportional representation systems
Proportional representation (PR) electoral systems essentially balance a party's share of the national votes and a concomitant share of its legislative seats. Each party's political track record in terms of national votes should be reflected in the composition of a parliament. Harris and Reilly (1998: 195) aptly observe that 'for many new democracies, particularly those that face deep divisions, the inclusion of all significant groups in the parliament can be an important condition for democratic consolidation'. Outcomes based on consensus-building and power-sharing usually include a PR system. It is, evidently, the most inclusive and broadly representative of all electoral systems in use globally. It is widely considered to be useful, especially in post-conflict settings, in advancing recovery, reconstruction, reconciliation, constructive management of diversity, social harmony and nation-building.

This system is in use in five countries in Southern Africa (Table 4.1). One interesting common feature of these countries is that they are either post-conflict (Angola, Mozambique, Namibia and South Africa) or are still engulfed in protracted violent conflict (Democratic Republic of the Congo, DRC). This is an indicator that the adoption of the closed party-list, PR electoral system[2] in these countries was informed primarily by the quest for peace, which is the conditio sine qua non for nation-building, reconciliation, social harmony, post-conflict recovery, reconstruction and development. The PR systems in Angola and South Africa have no thresholds.[3] In Mozambique there was a threshold of 5 per cent in force for the 1994, 1999 and 2004 elections; it was removed ahead of the 2009 elections (Kadima and Matsimbe, 2006; Mulhovo, 2018). In the DRC, the PR system has a threshold of 1 per cent for the national assembly and 3 per cent for provincial elections.[4] In Angola, Mozambique and Namibia, the PR systems operate alongside the two-round system for the election of the president. The DRC used the PR system together with the two-round system during its 2006 elections only; the constitution was subsequently changed to allow for one single round, hence the 2011 and 2018 elections were held under a single presidential round system. The democratic transitions in these countries are relatively new. The transitions in Namibia (1989) and South Africa (1994) are traceable to the demise of the minority-based apartheid system in these countries, and the introduction of majority rule and representative democracy. Besides Namibia and South Africa sharing a comparable apartheid past, their post-apartheid political evolution bears twin-like resemblance. The other twins are Mozambique and Angola, whose transitions date back to the 1990 Rome Agreement and the 1994 Lusaka Protocol, respectively. Emerging from brutal and intransigent Portuguese colonialism, these two countries have traversed a similar post-colonial journey of civil war, peace, one-party rule and transition to a multiparty system. They are now stable dominant-party systems. However, Mozambique's stability has been threatened since 5 October 2017 by the terrorist insurgency in its Cabo Delgado province of the Al Sunnah wa Jama'ah Islamist movement, which exploits pre-existing structural faultlines deriving from socioeconomic grievances.[5]

Conversely, peace has been elusive in the war-torn DRC, where protracted violence has continued raging in the eastern part of the country. The mediation brokered by South Africa in the early 2000s resulted in an all-inclusive agreement that was endorsed by the parties in April 2003. This was followed by a transitional government of national unity between 2002 and 2006 (Kadima and Tshiyoyo, 2009). The transitional government included all warring parties, a bicameral parliament, a referendum, a new constitution and the establishment of various democratic institutions, including an electoral management body, and transitional elections in 2006. Subsequently, the country relapsed into civil war. It is not surprising, therefore, that politics in the DRC is highly militarised.

Angola, Mozambique, Namibia, South Africa and Zimbabwe, unlike other countries in the region, experienced armed struggle as a key instrument in attaining liberation and freedom from settler colonialism. The former liberation movements assumed state power following protracted wars. These movements turned themselves into political parties. Their political hegemony over society has been overwhelming and therefore undergirds the dominant-party system that is so engrained in these countries (Booysen, 2011; Bauer and Taylor, 2011; Southall, 2013; Bereketeab, 2018). Movimento Popular de Libertação de Angola) (MPLA, the Popular Movement for the Liberation of Angola) and Frente de Libertação de Moçambique (Frelimo, the Front for the Liberation of Mozambique) continue to dominate the political landscapes in Angola and Mozambique, respectively. The South West Africa People's Organisation (SWAPO) and the ANC dominate politics in Namibia and South Africa, respectively. In both countries, however, the electoral dominance of these former liberation movements is declining (Booysen, 2011; Southall, 2013; Schreiber, 2018), even if in some instances on a jagged curve.

Following a transition to multiparty politics in 2003, the DRC held its transitional election in 2006, which was marred by political violence (Kadima and Tshiyoyo, 2009). The country has held subsequent elections, in 2011 and 2016, which were tainted with blood. The DRC has been a dominant-party system, with Joseph Kabila's People's Party for Reconstruction and Democracy having exercised political hegemony over a long time. In 2018, for the first time in the post-Mobutu era, the DRC experienced a peaceful transfer of power through elections when Felix Tshisekedi of the Union for Democracy and Social Progress replaced Kabila at the helm of state.

Mixed systems
Mixed systems involve a combination of the plurality/majority and PR systems in which the results of the election process are interlinked (mixed member proportional) or processed separately (mixed member parallel) in determining representation in the legislature. Through this hybridity, a deliberate attempt is made 'to combine the positive attributes of the plurality/majority (or other) and the PR electoral systems. In a mixed system, there are two electoral systems using either an integrated formula (mixed member proportional system) or using different formulae running alongside each other (parallel system). The votes are cast by the same voters and contribute to the election of representatives under both systems' (Reynolds et al., 2005: 91).

Two countries in Southern Africa have adopted mixed systems (see Table 4.1), and a Constitutional Court ruling in 2020 potentially opened the way for South Africa to move in this direction too.[6] Seychelles operates the parallel system, in which 25 MPs are elected on the basis of the FPTP system and nine are elected on the basis of PR. Lesotho operates the mixed member proportional system, in which 80 members of the national assembly are elected on the basis of FPTP and 40 in terms of PR.

While elections in Seychelles have been relatively peaceful, elections in Lesotho (as in Malawi) are considered war by other means, largely because of the country's socioeconomic underdevelopment wherein the political elite, lacking recourse for a decent livelihood in the minuscule private sector, eye the state as a lucrative site for fast wealth accumulation by fair or foul means. Shale (2017: 45) attributes this election-related instability to what he terms the 'politics of poverty'. Contestation over state power, therefore, becomes a fierce do-or-die affair. This observation suggests that there is also value in investigating the political economy of electoral systems, party systems and coalition politics in Southern Africa. In the Lesotho case, the fierce war over state power has been compounded by the deepening fragmentation of the country's party system, which has been accentuated by coalition governance since the 2012 general elections.

Seychelles experienced the one-party system between 1977 and 1991, in the iron grip of the Seychelles People's Progressive Front. It transitioned to a multiparty system in the early 1990s. During the 1992 elections the Seychelles People's Progressive Front retained its hold on state power through a multiparty election. It has won all subsequent elections, including those of 1993, 1998, 2001 (presidential), 2002 (national assembly), 2006 (presidential) and 2007 (national assembly). In 2009, the party changed its name to Parti Lepep (the People's Party). The new Parti Lepep won elections in 2011 and 2015. Thus, Seychelles appears to have a dominant-party system. However, the outcome of the elections held in October 2020 threw a spanner in the works of the dominant-party system when Wavel Ramkalawan, leader of the opposition Seychelles Democratic Alliance, dislodged Danny Faure, leader of the Parti Lepep (Al Jazeera, 2020).

Since the 1993 transition to democracy in Lesotho, various political parties have been at the helm of state power: the Basutoland Congress Party, from 1993 to 1998; the Lesotho Congress for Democracy (LCD, a breakaway group from the Basutoland Congress Party), from 1998 to 2012, exhibiting a tendency towards a dominant-party system; a coalition government led by the All Basotho Convention (ABC, a splinter group from the LCD), involving the LCD and the Basotho National Party (BNP, itself a splinter group from the Basutoland Congress Party), from 2012 to 2015 (see Deleglise, 2018); a coalition government led by the Democratic Congress (DC) from 2015 to 2017 that involved six other parties and splinter groups from parties; from 2017 to 2020 there was again a multiparty coalition, this time comprising four main parties; and a grand coalition between the ABC and the DC, in which the ABC led, from May 2020. Lesotho's party system, therefore, is highly fragmented, anchored in strong personality cults, and marked by intraparty and interparty conflicts that have witnessed the country holding three snap elections in the space of six years, in 2012, 2015 and 2017. In Lesotho, party coalitions live side by side with party collusions and political collisions.

THE IMPACT OF COALITIONS ON ELECTORAL SYSTEMS: LESSONS LEARNT

The literature identifies five types of party coalitions.

1. *Electoral alliances*, which Kadima (2014: 2) defines as 'the coming together of at least two political parties prior to an election in order to maximise their votes'. This trend has been pronounced in Mauritius, Mozambique and Malawi. It is likely to be further entrenched in Malawi, following the 2020 introduction of the 50 per cent plus one national vote tally required to win the presidency and the two-round system for this election. In the run-up to the mid-2020 presidential election, the Malawi Congress Party (MCP) entered into a coalition with the United Transformation Movement, together with seven smaller parties, known as the Tonse alliance, to lock horns with a coalition comprising the ruling Democratic Progressive Party (DPP) and the United Democratic Front (UDF).[7 8]

2. *Coalition governments* occur when no single political party is able to win a clear majority of parliamentary seats in order to form government on its own (NDI/Oslo Center, 2015: 15). This was the case in Lesotho during its snap elections in 2012, 2015 and 2017, as well as local government elections at several sites in South Africa, including, in 2016, major metropolitan councils.

3. *Grand coalitions* occur when a country's main political parties – those that are typically the main competitors for control of government – unite in a coalition government. This was the case in Lesotho in mid-2020 involving the ABC and the DC, with support from a number of smaller parties.

4. *Governments of national unity* emerge typically in post-conflict situations, often as part of the outcomes of peace agreements tasked mainly with 'overseeing the development of a new constitution and other fundamental reforms' (NDI/Oslo Center, 2015: 17). This was the case in South Africa between 1994 and 1997, with its Government of National Unity (GNU) involving the African National Congress (ANC), the New National Party (NNP) and the Inkatha Freedom Party (IFP) (Booysen, 2014: 72; Jolobe, 2018: 76). The DRC also experienced a government of national unity during its transitional

Table 4.2: Types of electoral systems and representation in Southern Africa

Electoral system	Constituency representation	Party representation
Single-member plurality	Maintains traditional link between representative and constituents. Representatives often elected on a minority of total votes ('wasted vote' thesis).	Distortion of votes/seats ratio. Minor parties disadvantaged unless support is regionally concentrated. Discourages multiplication of parties; tendency towards two-party system; one-party system; dominant-party system.
Single-member majority (a) Alternative vote (b) Second ballot	Both maintain traditional link between representative and constituents. In both cases, representatives are usually elected by majority.	Distortion of votes/seats ratio. 'Wasted vote' thesis does not apply; small parties survive even if unsuccessful. Tendency towards multiparty system.
Proportional representation (a) Party list (b) Single transferable vote	Individual representatives usually owe election more to party than to voters. Representatives forced to compete for first preference votes.	Approximate congruence between vote shares and seat allocations. Minor parties usually gain fair representation; easy entry for new parties. Tendency towards multiparty systems.
Mixed plurality/proportional representation/mixed member proportionality	Maintains traditional link between representative and constituents.	Approximates congruence between vote shares and seat allocation. Minor parties usually gain fair representation.

Source: Jackson and Jackson, 1997, as cited in Matlosa, 2004: 25.

government of 2002–06. It involved government, opposition and civil society organisations and some military formations. Zimbabwe's government of national unity between 2008 and 2013 involved a power-sharing arrangement between ZANU-PF and the Movement for Democratic Change (MDC) (Matlosa and Shale, 2013: 15–17).

5. *Legislative coalitions* involve a political pact of at least two parties with the aim 'to pursue specific legislative goals without a division of cabinet/executive responsibilities' (NDI/Oslo Center, 2015: 18). For Jolobe (2018: 76), legislative party coalitions 'support parties represented in cabinet during the parliamentary or legislative processes of voting and debates'. While electoral alliances are common in the region, they tend to collapse after elections, weakening prospects

Table 4.3: Public mistrust in political parties in Southern Africa

Country	Electoral system	Mistrust in ruling party (%)	Mistrust in opposition parties (%)
Botswana	Plurality	45	58
Lesotho	Mixed	50	76
Madagascar	Plurality/Majority	67	62
Malawi	Plurality/Majority	65	55
Mauritius	Plurality	69	70
Mozambique	Proportional	38	51
Namibia	Proportional	40	62
South Africa	Proportional	60	70
Tanzania	Plurality/Majority	34	57
Zambia	Plurality	44	60
Zimbabwe	Plurality/Majority	39	59

Source: Afrobarometer, 2020.

for legislative coalitions. But in Mozambique a legislative coalition has been manifested in the form of the Democratic Union and the Resistência Nacional Moçambicana (Renamo, the Mozambican National Resistance)-Elections Union, whose main purpose was to challenge Frelimo's dominance both in elections and in parliament (Mulhovo, 2018; Kadima and Matsimbe, 2006).

Electoral systems are designed, therefore, to translate principles of elections and electoral values into practical politics, to help give effect to democracy and democratic governance. The practices of coalitions, however, also affect the values that characterise electoral systems. Hence, in the following subsections, I address two questions: How do party coalitions impact the core values of electoral systems, and what are the lessons learnt? The content is organised around the values of representation, accountability, participation, inclusivity and stability.

Representation

One of the virtues of an electoral system is that it facilitates the broad representation of key political forces individually or in organised form through political parties (see Table 4.2). Proportional systems promote fairly equitable distribution of legislative seats, more so than plurality/majority systems. The PR system in South Africa facilitates a fair representation of key political forces in the legislature, particularly

Table 4.4. Voter turnout in elections in Southern Africa: Comparison over time

Country	Electoral system	Turnout in 1990s or in transitional elections (%)	Turnout in latest election up to 2019 (%)
Angola	Proportional	86.91 (1992)	76.13 (2017)
Botswana	Plurality	76.55 (1994)	83.51 (2019)
DRC	Proportional	70.29 (2006)	45.40 (2018)
Eswatini	Plurality	60.39 (1998)	44.62 (2018)
Lesotho	Mixed	72.28 (1993)	46.37 (2017)
Madagascar	Plurality/Majority	60.00 (1993)	40.00 (2019)
Malawi	Plurality/Majority	80.03 (1994)	71.28 (2019)
Mauritius	Plurality	79.69 (1995)	77.01 (2019)
Mozambique	Proportional	87.89 (1994)	51.41 (2019)
Namibia	Proportional	97.04 (1989)	60.38 (2019)
Seychelles	Mixed	86.52 (1993)	87.61 (2016)
South Africa	Proportional	86.87 (1994)	66.05 (2019)
Tanzania	Plurality/Majority	76.51 (1995)	62.68 (2015)
Zambia	Plurality	44.44 (1991)	56.03 (2016)
Zimbabwe	Plurality/Majority	30.81 (1995)	83.10 (2018)

Sources: IDEA, 2020; IFES, 2019.

given that it does not use a threshold. The current mixed member proportional system in Lesotho has broadened representation in parliament, in much the same way that it has fostered proliferation of parties and post-election coalitions. In both South Africa (2002–09) and Lesotho, floor-crossing of MPs in the legislature tended to distort representation, undermine the respective electoral models and accentuate fragmentation of the party systems.

The gradual introduction of floor-crossing in South Africa in 2002 and 2003 (abolished in 2009) led to the proliferation of parties (17 parties were established through floor-crossing) and tended to subvert the representational mandate of MPs (Faull, 2007). According to Mamabolo, 'The impact of floor-crossing was to distort proportionality, negating the proportions occasioned by voter choice. In a sense, floor-crossing was almost the antithesis to the objectives of the proportional representation system.'[9]

While in South Africa floor-crossing in the national assembly was outlawed by constitutional amendment in January 2009, in Malawi, floor-crossing is supposed to be followed by by-elections, but in practice this has not been happening.[10] In Lesotho, a governance reform process was underway in 2020 that considered proposals to introduce a party law to regulate the functioning of political parties, regulate floor-crossing in parliament, limit the tenure of the prime minister to two terms, and introduce a threshold for parties to gain parliamentary seats. The perennial problem of floor-crossing in parliaments in Southern Africa (notably in Lesotho and Malawi; see chapters 7 and 8) has been undermining representation. A case can be made for outlawing it altogether, or at least requiring by-elections once a constituency-based MP crosses the floor.

The first lesson is that party coalitions facilitate broad representation of key political parties in the apparatuses of the state, especially the legislature and the executive. But floor-crossing in parliament tends to distort the electoral system and accentuate fragmentation of the party system.

Accountability

The electoral system must also ensure accountability of elected officials to the electors – voters must be able to hold their representatives accountable. The literature points to the strength of the FPTP electoral system when it comes to accountability of MPs to the voters. But evidence shows that citizens are unhappy about the responsiveness of political parties to their livelihood demands across the board, irrespective of the type of electoral and party system in place. Due to poor accountability of politicians to citizens, public mistrust in parties rises (see Table 4.3). The details about trust in political parties in Southern Africa show the extent to which distrust is manifested, irrespective of the electoral system that applies. Party coalitions may compound both the horizontal and vertical accountability[11] crisis of regimes in Southern Africa, thereby worsening the public trust deficit of parties.

The second lesson is that in democratic settings, state-society relations are anchored in accountability, which is a predictor for state responsiveness. Where accountability is weak or dysfunctional, citizens lose trust in political parties. Public trust in political parties is dwindling in contemporary politics, an ominous warning that the era of political parties may be on the decline. Parties are in crisis and

Table 4.5. Women in Southern Africa's national assemblies: An indicator of inclusiveness

Country	Electoral system	Election year	Total seats	Women in national assembly (number)	Women in national assembly (%)
Angola	Proportional	2017	220	65	30
Botswana	Plurality	2019	65	7	10.8
DRC	Proportional	2019	500	64	12.8
Eswatini	Plurality	2018	73	7	9.6
Lesotho	Mixed	2017	120	28	23.3
Madagascar	Plurality/Majority	2019	151	27	17.9
Malawi	Plurality/Majority	2019	192	44	22.9
Mauritius	Plurality	2019	70	14	20
Mozambique	Proportional	2019	250	106	42.4
Namibia	Proportional	2019	104	46	44.2
Seychelles	Mixed	2020	35	8	22.9
South Africa	Proportional	2019	400	184	46.6
Tanzania	Plurality/Majority	2020	393	141	36.7
Zambia	Plurality	2016	167	28	16.8
Zimbabwe	Plurality/Majority	2018	270	86	31.9

Source: Inter-Parliamentary Union.

they need to be redeemed (Magolowondo, 2018). Although data are still inconclusive, there is a likelihood that party coalitions may deepen mistrust in parties and compound the crisis of parties.

Participation

The electoral systems ought to ensure meaningful citizen participation during elections. PR systems are more participatory than plurality systems. This is because, by their very nature, FPTP systems disenfranchise voters in that they lead to considerable vote wastage. Party coalitions have the potential to accentuate low participation of voters in elections, more so given declining public trust in parties (Table 4.3) and the fact that elites often dominate coalition-formation actions. Table 4.4 illustrates a trend of generally declining voter turnout (with some exceptions, like Zambia and Zimbabwe), which could be worsened by volatile coalition politics.

The third lesson is that effective and meaningful citizen participation during and between elections is the hallmark of democratisation. But elections often work for elites, while they fail to put bread on the table for ordinary citizens. Poverty, hunger, inequality, unemployment and disease drive discontent, which in turn fosters a loss of public faith in elections, hence plummeting voter turnout in the region. Appropriate policy interventions are required, therefore, to stem the tide of declining citizen participation in elections, especially among the youth. Party coalitions ought to advance citizen participation. Lesotho, for instance, registered an impressive voter turnout (72 per cent) in the 1993 transitional election (following military rule), which ushered in the current multiparty democracy. However, with the onset of coalition politics and the recurrent collapse of coalition governments, the voter turnout has declined considerably – to 50 per cent in 2012, and 46 per cent in 2015 and 2017, respectively (IDEA, 2020).

Inclusiveness

Electoral systems are expected to facilitate the inclusion of marginalised and vulnerable social groups in society, especially women and youth who constitute generally more than 50 per cent and over 70 per cent of populations, respectively. Proportional systems tend to be more conducive to women's political inclusion, compared with plurality systems (Table 4.5). However, evidence also shows that even plurality/majority systems can promote gender equality if they combine with voluntary and legislated gender quotas, as in Tanzania.

The fourth lesson is that the electoral systems and party systems ought to ensure inclusiveness of marginalised and vulnerable social groups, especially women and youth. Evidence points to Southern Africa's mixed performance of inclusiveness in respect of women's participation and representation in national assemblies. Although there are exceptions, PR systems tend to deliver better inclusivity. Party coalitions appear not to have any specific impact on this indicator. Parties need to invest in gender quotas within their own internal governance structures, as well as in terms of nomination of election candidates and representatives in the legislatures. Inclusiveness requires transformative leadership and vibrant citizen engagement.

Stability

Electoral systems should help ensure sustainable political stability and durable peace in a country. By and large, the stability of a country, especially its governance, is dependent on the legitimacy of the government. As to which electoral system is capable of best ensuring political legitimacy, stability and peace, the record is mixed in Southern Africa. Botswana and Mauritius have remained stable (despite a range of interparty and electoral tensions) for decades with their FPTP electoral systems, while Malawi and Zimbabwe, using the same electoral model, have been politically unstable. With their PR systems, Namibia and South Africa have enjoyed stability and durable peace. In contrast, the DRC, with the same system, continues to be ravaged by war, and Mozambique has experienced electoral violence, a trend that has been compounded by the insurgency of the Al Sunnah wa Jama'ah movement since 2017. With its mixed-member proportional system, Lesotho remains a conflict-ridden society, while Seychelles with its mixed-member parallel system is a peaceful tourist paradise.

The fifth lesson is that states in Southern Africa are still grappling with issues of nation-building that require political stability and durable peace. They are socioculturally diverse societies. They often face the triple burden of underdevelopment, legacies of autocracy and of protracted violent conflict. These challenges have been compounded by state responses to COVID-19, which have included states of emergencies, which have severely restricted rights and freedoms of citizens. Political instability in the region manifests vividly through electoral violence. Irrespective of the electoral systems and party systems in place, party coalitions tend to exacerbate political instability and may compromise nation-building, peace-building, post-conflict recovery, and reconstruction and development priorities. This is, in part, due to the tendency for coalitions to trigger intraparty tensions and interparty conflicts. They also destabilise the state system, with the frequent incidences of collapse of governments that may impair legitimacy of rule. This is worsened in cases where the electoral model allows for floor-crossing in parliament.

While this is a prominent pattern, it is nevertheless not the only one. There are instances where coalition governments (Malawi), or a government of national (and provincial) unity (South Africa), have helped some Southern African countries to navigate the challenging pathways of political transition and allowed former belligerents and adversaries to learn to work together, thus contributing to peace and nation-building.

CONCLUSION

This chapter has investigated the interface between and among electoral systems, party systems and party coalitions in Southern Africa. It highlights the impact of party coalitions on the core values of the electoral systems, namely representation, accountability, participation, inclusiveness and stability. Three key conclusions emerge from the discussion.

First, when it comes to coalitions, there is a mutually reinforcing relationship between electoral systems and party systems, and both can promote democratisation in much the same way as they can shield autocracy. This, in part, explains how and why elections in their particular settings of electoral systems are a double-edged sword.

Second, party systems co-exist with a variety of electoral systems, and vice-versa. Consequently, in country contexts, a particular party system may appear in combination with several types of electoral systems; there is no necessary one-on-one pairing of party and electoral systems. Interparty coalition governments occur across the different electoral systems.

Finally, when assessed against the five key values of the electoral systems, party coalitions have a positive correlation with some (e.g., representation), a negative correlation with others (e.g., stability) and a neutral or variable correlation with yet other values (e.g., inclusiveness).

REFERENCES

Afrobarometer. 2020. Afrobarometer Survey, 2016/18, Round 7, http://www.afrobarometer.org, accessed 2 August 2020.

Al Jazeera. 25 October 2020. 'Seychelles opposition candidate wins presidential election', https://www.aljazeera.com/news/2020/10/25/seychelles-opposition-candidate-wins-presidential-election, accessed 2 February 2021.

Bauer, G. and Taylor, S. 2011. *Politics in Southern Africa*, 2nd edition. London: Lynne Rienner Publishers.

Bereketeab, R. (ed.) 2018. *National Liberation Movements as Government in Africa*. London: Routledge.

Booysen, S. 2011. *The African National Congress and the Regeneration of Political Power*. Johannesburg: Wits University Press.

Booysen, S. 2014. 'Causes and impact of party alliances and coalitions on the party system and national cohesion in South Africa', *Journal of African Elections,* 13 (1), 66–92.

Cheeseman, N. and Klaas, B. 2018. *How to Rig an Election*. New Haven: Yale University Press.

Cowen, M. and Laakso, L. 2002. 'Elections and election studies in Africa', in Cowen, M. and Laakso, L. (eds.) *Multi-party Elections in Africa*. New York: Palgrave, 1–26.

Deleglise, D. 2018. 'The rise and fall of Lesotho's coalition governments', in Ngubane, S. (ed.) *Complexities of Coalition Politics in Southern Africa,* Monograph Series, No. 1, Accord, Cape Town, 9–46.

Erdmann, G. and Basedau, M. 2013. 'An overview of African party systems', in Doorenspleet, R. and Nijzink, L. (eds.) *One-Party Dominance in African Democracies*. London: Lynne Rienner Publishers, 25–48.

Electoral Institute for Sustainable Democracy in Africa (EISA). 2019. *African Democracy Encyclopaedia Project,* https://www.eisa.org.za/wep/wepindex.htm, accessed 10 May 2020.

Englund, E. (ed.) 2001. *A Democracy of Chameleons: Politics and culture,* Blantyre: Christian Literature Association of Malawi.

Faull, J. 2007. 'South Africa's use of floor-crossing, coalitions and alliances for entrenching electoral democracy'. Conference Paper, Independent Electoral Commission on Reflections on the State of Electoral Democracy in South Africa, 8–10 October, Johannesburg.

Harris, P. and Reilly, B. (eds.) 1998. *Democracy in Deep-Rooted Conflict: Options for negotiators*. IDEA Handbook Series. Stockholm, Sweden.

International Foundation for Electoral Systems (IFES). 2019. *Elections Guide*. Washington D.C.: Democracy Assistance and Elections News.

International Institute for Democracy and Electoral Assistance (IDEA). 2020. *Voter Turnout Database*. Stockholm, Sweden.

Inter-Parliamentary Union. IPU Global Data on National Parliaments, https://data.ipu.org/, accessed 2 November 2020.

Jolobe, Z. 2018. 'The politics of dominance and survival: Coalition politics in South Africa 1994–2018', *Complexities of Coalition Politics in Southern Africa*. Africa Dialogue, Accord.

Kadima, D. 2014. 'An introduction to the politics of party alliances and coalitions in socially divided Africa', *Journal of African Elections,* 13 (1), 1–24.

Kadima, D. and Kasenally, R. 2006. 'The formation, collapse and revival of political party coalitions in Mauritius: Ethnic logic and calculation at play', in Kadima, D. (ed.) *The Politics of Party Coalitions in Africa*. Johannesburg: EISA, 73–110.

Kadima, D. and Matsimbe, Z. 2006. 'RENAMO Uniao Electoral: Understanding the longevity and challenges of an opposition party coalition in Mozambique', in Kadima, D. (ed.) *The Politics of Party Coalitions in Africa*. Johannesburg: EISA, 149–178.

Kadima, D. and Tshiyoyo, D. 2009. 'Democratic Republic of Congo', in Kadima, D. and Booysen, S. (eds.) *Compendium of Elections in Southern Africa, 1989–2009*. Johannesburg: EISA, 91–146.

Karl, T. 1986. 'Imposing consent? Electoralism versus democratisation in El Salvador', in Drake, P. and Silva, E. (eds.) *Elections and Democratisation in Latin America, 1980–1985*. San Diego: Centre for Iberian and Latin American Studies.

Kasenally, R. 2009. 'Mauritius', in Kadima, D. and Booysen, S. (eds.) *Compendium of Elections in Southern Africa, 1989–2009*. Johannesburg: EISA, 269–306.

Lembani, S. 2014. 'Alliances, coalitions and the weakening of the party system in Malawi', *Journal of African Elections*, 13 (1), 115–149.

Lindberg, S. 2006. *Democracy and Elections in Africa*. Baltimore: Johns Hopkins University Press.

Lindberg, S. 2009. 'Democratisation by elections: A mixed record', *Journal of Democracy,* 20 (3), 86–92.

Magolowondo, A. 2018. 'Strengthening democratic institutions in Africa: The special role of political parties', *African Journal of Democracy and Governance*, 5 (3), 183–200.

Matlosa, K. 2003. 'Survey of Electoral Systems and Reform Imperatives in the SADC Region'. EISA Occasional Paper No. 12.

Matlosa, K. 2004. 'Electoral systems, constitutionalism and conflict management in Southern Africa', *African Journal on Conflict Resolution*, 4 (2), 11–53.

Matlosa, K. 2007. 'Political Parties in Southern Africa: The state of parties and their role in democratization'. IDEA Research Report, Stockholm.

Matlosa, K. and Patel, N. 2006. 'Towards Electoral System Reform in Malawi'.

Report for the Malawi Electoral Commission, July.

Matlosa, K. and Shale, V. 2013. 'The pains of democratization: The uneasy interface between elections and power-sharing arrangements in Africa', *Africa Review*, 5 (1), 1–23.

Mozaffar, S. and Schedler, A. 2002. 'The comparative study of electoral governance: Introduction', *International Political Science Review*, 23 (1), 5–27.

Mulhovo, H. 2018. 'The intricacies and pitfalls of the politics of coalition in Mozambique', in Ngubane, S. (ed.) *Complexities of Coalition Politics in Southern Africa*, Monograph Series No. 1, African Centre for the Constructive Resolution of Disputes, Durban, 47–72.

National Democratic Institute and Oslo Center for Peace and Human Rights (NDI/Oslo Center). 2015. 'Coalitions: A guide for political parties'. Mimeo, Washington D.C.

Oyugi, W. 2006. 'Coalition politics and coalition governance in Africa', *Journal of Contemporary African Studies*, 24 (1), 53–79.

Reilly, B. 2001. *Democracy in Divided Societies: Electoral engineering for conflict management.* New York: Cambridge University Press.

Reilly, B. 2008. 'Introduction', in Reilly, B. and Nordlund, P. (eds.) *Political Parties in Conflict-Prone Societies: Regulation, engineering and democratic development.* Tokyo: United Nations Press, 3–24.

Reynolds, A. 1999. Electoral Systems and Democratization in Southern Africa. Oxford: Oxford University Press.

Reynolds, A., Reilly, B. and Ellis, A. (eds.) 2005. *Electoral System Design: The new international IDEA handbook*. Stockholm: IDEA.

Salih, M. 2003. 'Introduction: The evolution of African political parties', in Salih, M. (ed.) *African Political Parties: Evolution, institutionalisation and governance*. London: Pluto Press, 1–33.

Salih, M. and Nordlund, P. 2008. *Political Parties in Africa: Challenges for sustained multiparty democracy.* Africa Regional Report. Stockholm: International IDEA.

Sartori, G. 1976. *Parties and Party Systems: A framework for analysis.* Cambridge: Cambridge University Press.

Saulos Klause Chilima & Lazarus McCarthy Chakwera v Arthur Peter Mutharika & the Electoral Commission, High Court of Malawi, Lilongwe, 3 February 2020.

Schedler, A. 2002. 'Elections without democracy: The menu of manipulation', *Journal of Democracy*, 13 (2), 36–50.

Schedler, A. 2006. 'The logic of electoral authoritarianism', in Schedler, A. (ed.) *Electoral Authoritarianism: The dynamics of unfree competition.* London: Lynne Rienner Publishers, 1–26.

Schreiber, L. 2018. *Coalition Country: South Africa after the ANC*. Cape Town: Tafelberg.

Shale, V. 2017. 'Political parties and political instability in Lesotho', in

Thabane, M. (ed.) *Towards an Anatomy of Persistent Political Instability in Lesotho, 1966–2016.* Roma: National University of Lesotho, 23–46.

Southall, R. 2013. *Liberation Movements in Power: Party and state in Southern Africa.* Pietermaritzburg: University of KwaZulu-Natal Press.

Part II

Learning from Africa's experiences: Trends and case studies in government and opposition

AFRICA'S DIVERSE, INTRICATE EXPERIENCES with alliance and coalition politics provide much of the canvas on which the relatively new South African praxis unfolds. Coalition formations have been evident in government at multiple sites where erstwhile party dominance has declined, outright majorities for single parties have receded, and no clear-cut alternative, strong parties have emerged. Vacillating electoral majorities, and instability through fluctuating alliances and coalitions, have become the new political reality. Party politics and the strategy of constructing legislative or executive majorities dominate this political play. This section illustrates the substantial extent to which patronage and the rent-seeking behaviour of political parties, along with strategic positioning, trump ideological coherence and policy-seeking as driving forces for coalition formation and operation.

FIVE

The legacy of multipartyism on political coalitions and rent-seeking in African elections

Grant Masterson

While multipartyism is not new in Africa, the continent's experience of multipartyism was limited during the era of largely one-party states, creating a perception that multiparty political formations, and particularly political alliances and coalitions, have not featured in African election and governance contexts for as long as they have prevailed in other regions in the world. Coalitions and political alliances are, in fact, a common feature of political association across the African continent. In the multiparty era, the number and frequency of political party coalitions, alliances and cooperative agreements have increased, along with the number of political parties.

The perception that Africa's history of multiparty coalition-making is limited is not necessarily justified: there are several key features of coalitions in the African political context that make the exploration of political party coalitions in Africa an exciting and fast-developing field.

It is simultaneously a Janus-faced phenomenon in Africa. This chapter demonstrates why alliances and coalitions are not only effective but structurally encouraged in African democracies. It also explores why these arrangements are often volatile and unstable, regardless of the sound reasons underlying their formation. The chapter uses a series of small case studies to illustrate coalition trends that cut across the continent.

Clearly, any chapter that sets out to provide a snapshot of coalitions across Africa is both ambitious and extremely limited in its ability to explore the deeper nuance of each country context and the rich history behind coalition formations. This chapter therefore does not attempt detailed descriptions of existing coalitions, leaving this task to other sections of this volume, which explore informative case studies in greater depth. This chapter pays close attention to the interconnections between elections and coalition-building. First, it explores the structural considerations that have shaped African coalitions. Second, it examines common types of coalitions, with examples. And, third, it reflects on the relationship between coalition governments and rent-seeking behaviour.

The legacy of colonial institutions and systems, particularly divide-and-rule tactics, bequeathed a convoluted set of tribal, ethnic and religious identities to post-colonial states – identities that have often been exploited to the benefit of Africa's new political elites in many forms, one of the most disingenuous being elite coalition-building. This chapter highlights the fraught conditions in which many elections are conducted, particularly the winner-takes-all dynamic that reduces elections to a zero-sum game. It explores the features of rent-seeking as a key factor in motivating parties to enter into these arrangements, why winning coalitions often start out with elevated expectations of cleaner government, and how these expectations have historically disappointed in many contexts.

THE IMPACT OF COLONIALLY INHERITED ELECTORAL SYSTEMS ON COALITION POLITICS

Inherited and adapted electoral systems, power structures and histories of African states have historically served to entrench one-party-state rule, even beyond the reintroduction of multiparty politics in many African countries. This has created specific challenges and structural weakness in opposition parties in these systems, and shaped coalition politics as a pragmatic response to these challenges. Conversely, the likelihood of further success of dominant parties has often made the option of coalition and alliance politics attractive to fringe parties, whose votes are necessary to shore up support for these dominant parties once they enter a period of decline. This underlines one of the key features of most coalitions: parties enter into these agreements with the purpose of improving their chances of accessing political power.

The legacy of colonial structures endures stubbornly in political systems long after the fall of colonial rule in many parts of Africa (Rodney, 1973; Mazrui, 1994; Alemazung, 2010). Africa's dominant colonial powers, Britain and France, bequeathed African states two distinct forms of political governance during the fall of colonial rule. Over time, the distinction between the Francophone presidential system and the British parliamentary structures have blurred into insignificance. In present-day Africa, most African states are dominated by the executive branch of government, even in states that inherited strong legislative institutions from the colonial powers (Mizuno and Okazawa, 2009; Lodge, 2017).

The legacy of centralised rule has had two key consequences for coalition formation in Africa. The first has been the hindering of opportunities for opposition coalitions to form, due to the consolidation of single-party systems. However, for their short-term political survival, some opposition political parties and politicians have allowed themselves to be absorbed by the ruling party to continue pursuing political goals within the space allowed. One of the long-term implications of this history has been the awkward and often stilted reintroduction of opposition political parties into the political sphere after absences of decades, often led by leaders more familiar to

Table 5.1: Botswana 2014 and 2019 election results vs seats in parliament

Political party	Votes		Percentage votes (%)		Number of seats won		Percentage of elected seats (%)	
	2014	2019	2014	2019	2014	2019	2014	2019
Botswana Democratic Party (BDP)	320,657	406,561	46.5	52.7	37	38	64.9	66.7
Umbrella for Democratic Change (UDC)	207,113	277,121	30.0	35.9	17	15	29.8	26.3
Botswana Congress Party (BCP, joins UDC in 2017)	140,998	-	20.4	-	3	-	5.3	-
Alliance for Progressives (AP, a splinter off a component of the UDC)	-	39,561	-	5.1	-	1	-	1.8
Botswana Patriotic Front (BPF; Ian Khama joins)	-	34,028	-	4.4	-	3	-	5.3
Independents	21,484	12,734	3.1	1.7	0	0	0	0
Total	690,252	778,181	100		57	57	100	

Source: EISA.

an electorate for their historical ties to the ruling party. This saddles opposition parties with the baggage of the ruling party, making them less attractive to voters seeking alternatives, while at the same time undercutting their messaging by casting the parties as disgruntled offshoots of the dominant party.

The second and more enduring consequence has been the crippling of the ability of national legislatures to constrain the power of the executive and hold it to account. This has meant that in executive-dominated electoral systems, particularly those in which the presidential ballot is separate from the legislative-assembly ballots, opposition party alliances in the pre-election period have limited utility to overcome the incumbency advantages enjoyed by the majority candidate. For opposition coalitions, the goal of eroding the dominance of a ruling party is frustrated by the centralisation of power within the executive. Under successive regimes in Zimbabwe from 2000 to 2015, for example, the power of the executive was increased to the point that even with a strong showing in national assembly elections, opposition coalition parties remained sidelined and largely powerless in the country's political governance structures (Van Cranenburgh, 2008; Simpson and Hawkins, 2018).

When unpacking the poor performance of opposition parties in elections since the 1990s, many explanations have focused on the systematic and entrenched benefits enjoyed by the ruling parties, including to set the rules of engagement, determine advantageous timeframes for elections, and enjoy access to state resources such as state media broadcasters, financial support and pairing state projects with party interests. While the number of party names on a ballot paper may have increased with the advent of multipartyism, opposition political parties initially made very little impact on the political composition of government. In the words of Kura (2008), 'African democracies could be labelled as illiberal civilian autocracies'. Political power has remained highly concentrated in dominant ruling parties, with opposition parties not only faring poorly at the polls, but often unwittingly aiding dominant ruling parties to bolster their flagging fortunes by publicly depicting other opposition parties in an unfavourable light. Perhaps the most brazen example of this has been in Botswana, where the Botswana Democratic Party has ruled since 1960, and more recently adopted the slogan 'There is still no alternative'.

This highlights one of the major obstacles faced by opposition parties in overcoming the incumbency advantage. An Afrobarometer survey of 36 African countries indicated that by 2015 a significant majority of African citizens preferred multipartyism over other forms of governance, but that fewer respondents trusted opposition politicians than ruling party politicians (35 vs 46 per cent) (Afrobarometer, 2017). Lekalake (2017) notes of this finding that:

> There's a much more lopsided distribution of power and resources for opposition parties in countries with dominant governing parties than for those in competitive party systems.

This, coupled with a lack of governance experience, makes it difficult for opposition parties to be seen as credible alternatives.

While opposition parties attempt to erode dominant-party support and bolster their own performance, they also face offensives on their own support base from other opposition parties. Dominant ruling parties throughout Africa like to claim that all opposition parties work together to 'overthrow' the ruling party, but outside of legal and legitimate political alliances and coalitions, this is rarely the case. Growing opposition parties in Africa have often had greater success at consolidating their support by eroding the support of other opposition parties rather than mounting a meaningful challenge against the entrenched support for dominant parties. This phenomenon is particularly pronounced in first-past-the-post (FPTP) electoral systems, where opposition candidates 'split' the vote between themselves, allowing a ruling-party candidate to win a seat with a mediocre demonstration of support. To continue drawing on the Botswana example, its 2014 election results indicated that popular support (taken as total aggregated support across all constituencies) for the ruling Botswana Democratic Party was below 50 per cent (this changed in 2019), but due to opposition parties splitting the vote between their candidates, the Botswana Democratic Party was still able to return 37 MPs to parliament, out of the 63 seats, giving it a majority of the seats needed to form a new government (Table 5.1). Although the Umbrella for Democratic Change successfully brought together three of the largest opposition political parties under one banner, the Botswana Congress Party, by remaining outside of the Umbrella for Democratic Change, effectively played spoiler in key wards in central and eastern Botswana, enabling the Botswana Democratic Party to hold onto these key seats in these regions. In both 2014 and 2019 the Botswana Democratic Party's seat tally was further bolstered by an additional six seats appointed by the president, who is constitutionally permitted to appoint six distinguished citizens as MPs.

Opposition parties have responded to these challenges in many different ways. In terms of results at the ballot box, the most effective opposition strategy for overcoming the incumbency advantage of entrenched ruling parties has been through some form of electoral alliance, merger or coalition agreement. In the case of Botswana's 2014 and 2019 results, members of the Umbrella for Democratic Change and the Botswana Congress Party, and later also the Alliance for Progressives and the Botswana Patriotic Front, to an extent, were able to clearly see a path to unseating the ruling party from power through some form of alliance, merger or coalition arrangement. It was problematic, however, that there were several of these alliances competing against one another. Election results of this nature are often the catalyst for new discussions between political formations about new arrangements, such as consolidating the support two parties enjoy and leveraging greater cumulative political power as a result. The Umbrella for Democratic Change experience demonstrates, however, that effective political coalitions, when they have the right credentials in place, can overcome inherent voter distrust of opposition politicians by combining the reputations and efforts of several opposition parties under a single banner.

TYPES OF COALITIONS IN AFRICA

Shale (2007) names three main types of political alliances/coalitions that feature in African states: the front, the electoral alliance, and the unity or merger. This section also explores the distinction between deliberate coalition agreements, and political opportunism as a motivation for coalition formation. The analysis cites examples of each of these four types of coalitions to illustrate their application in practical terms.

Political fronts

Fronts are political coalitions that contest an election on behalf of a collective of partners, whose participation in the front is to support and encourage support of the collective fronting entity. This type of electoral coalition occurs when the partners within an alliance share a common vision, purpose and objectives, and do not want their individual entities to contest and therefore fragment the overarching cause to which they jointly subscribe. Fronts are often associated with ideological positions, as the purpose of a front is primarily to consolidate resistance to an opposing or alternative ideology. In the African context this has included armed struggles against colonialism and apartheid.

Examples of political fronts include the African National Congress in South Africa, whose alliance partners the South African Communist Party and the Congress of South African Trade Unions do not typically contest elections, but rather negotiate within the Tripartite Alliance, for example around a policy platform, and receive positions in ANC governments. Another example is the Tigray People's Liberation Front, which led a group of Ethiopian allies to victory over the Mengistu Haile Mariam communist regime. Although the Tigray People's Liberation Front was largely responsible for successfully overthrowing the Mengistu regime, the Front would not vie for power itself, preferring to cooperate with its other liberation partners through the Ethiopian People's Revolutionary Democratic Front (EPRDF). The EPRDF was committed to preventing the resurgence of the communist regime, and to securing Ethiopia's sovereign borders, particularly the shared borders between Ethiopia and Somalia, and Ethiopia and Eritrea.

Fronts are often more effective as pre-electoral tactics than they are post election, when coordination and cooperation need to be strengthened in order to deliver on promises made to the electorate and leverage the gains of the election through exercising power. Fronts defer much of the effort of coordination and power-sharing among alliance partners until such time as the effectiveness of the front based on electoral results can be measured. This does not mean that all negotiations occur in the post-election period, since fronts often need to agree on which party's candidates will stand for election in specific wards (or how they will be positioned on party lists for proportional representation). The degree to which these negotiations are effectively executed can be a key determinant of the success of the front. Fronts often occur among parties whose leaders and candidates have been unable to find sufficient common ground to build a more concrete form of unity prior to an election, but recognise that without cooperation their collective efforts will result in the individual parties nullifying one another to a significant extent.

The Movement for Democratic Change-Alliance (MDC-Alliance)

that formed prior to the 2018 elections in Zimbabwe is an informative example of a front. The MDC-Alliance included seven political parties, most of which were splinters from the original MDC, which had periodically challenged the ruling Zimbabwe African National Union-Patriotic Front (ZANU-PF) since 2000, but had experienced serial splits that fragmented its electoral challenges. The splits inadvertently assisted ZANU-PF to retain power through the lack of unity among opposition parties. The 2018 elections were viewed, nevertheless, as a unique opportunity for an opposition front to supplant ZANU-PF, as for the first time since independence Robert Mugabe was not a candidate on the ballot. Despite the heightened anticipation of change at the ballot box, the opposition divisions remained pronounced, heightened by disagreements between senior leaders of the participating parties as to the preferred candidate to lead the alliance. The MDC's long-time leader, Morgan Tsvangirai, died just months before the elections. With minimal time to pursue more substantive negotiations or coalition arrangements, the seven parties agreed to coordinate their activities under the banner of the MDC-Alliance. In this way, it defused one of the acrimonious disputes between the splinter groups that claimed ownership of the naming rights of the MDC (three of the coalition partners claimed the MDC nomenclature as their own, adding by hyphen the name of the group leader, e.g., MDC-Tsvangirai).

While the front was successful in realigning seven of the largest opposition parties under a common banner to challenge the ruling party's dominance, a lack of coordination hampered the MDC-Alliance's efforts. MDC-Alliance organising secretary Amos Chibaya, in an interview during the pre-election assessment mission to the 2018 elections of the Electoral Institute for Sustainable Democracy in Africa, admitted that the MDC-Alliance had not managed to properly coordinate its strategic deployment of candidates to maximise the strength of its electoral offering. He went on to explain that the terms of the MDC-Alliance agreement between the parties, which assigned specific constituencies to specific alliance partners based on proportional considerations, had at times weakened the challenge to the ruling party. He explained that the agreement did not always consider the popularity of candidates based on their historical track records, hence popular constituency candidates were removed from the ballot to enable an alliance partner to field a weaker candidate in the name of proportionality. In some instances this resulted in the stronger candidates opting out of the MDC-Alliance to run in their constituencies as independent candidates, effectively nullifying the advantages of the front.

The results of the 2018 Zimbabwe elections therefore were mixed for the MDC-Alliance. Although the consolidation of support behind the MDC-Alliance presidential candidate, Nelson Chamisa, saw him win 44.3 per cent of the national vote, he did not match the 50.8 per cent of the national vote that ZANU-PF's Emmerson Mnangagwa achieved. The effect of the deficient coordination of the front was even more pronounced at the national assembly level of the election, conducted in terms of the FPTP electoral system: despite the MDC-Alliance's strong showing in the presidential elections, it secured only 89 of the 270 seats, trailing significantly behind ZANU-PF's 179 seats (Zimbabwe Electoral Commission, 2019). In the post-election period, the three MDC parties concluded formal agreements that would formalise the MDC-Alliance into a merger.

Electoral alliances or pacts

This type of political coalition is most useful when opposition fragmentation is hurting the opposition's chances at overturning a dominant majority through splitting the vote (Oyugi, 2006). It typically ascribes to a common set of fundamental values or principles which otherwise allow parties to continue to pursue their own objectives (Karume, 2002; Shale, 2007). In this way, political parties are not asked to abandon their individual identity or go through the often challenging task of merging with other parties into common structures. Rather, political parties within an electoral pact can campaign in their own capacity but encourage their supporters to vote for the collective entity in an election.

Electoral pacts are one of the quickest forms of alliance to establish. Depending on the laws of a country, it is sometimes not even necessary to register them as a legal entity; parties simply campaign under the banner of a common purpose. They are typically best suited to opposition groupings, as they rely primarily on a common opponent to focus the minds and efforts of alliance members. The type of electoral system will require more coordination (such as in the case of Lesotho with its mixed electoral system), or less in cases of proportional representation. Pacts therefore offer less value in terms of coordination and pooling of resources than other forms of coalitions/alliances (described below) but require fewer resources to establish and work effectively when coordination is neither desirable nor possible.

An example of an informal electoral pact occurred during Tanzania's 2020 national elections when the opposition Chadema party (its support based largely on the mainland) called on its supporters in Zanzibar (a semi-autonomous region with separate elections for Zanzibar's house of representatives) to cast their ballots for the opposition Alliance for Change and Transparency–Wazalendo party. This saw Chadema opting not to contest constituencies where Alliance for Change and Transparency–Wazalendo candidates were considered strong; and, similarly, Alliance for Change and Transparency–Wazalendo deferred to Chadema candidates in Chadema strongholds, to avoid splitting the vote. As with many such electoral pacts, the primary focus of these two parties was on challenging the hegemony of the dominant Chama Cha Mapinduzi (CCM) party, and the intent of this informal electoral pact was to reduce the potential for diluting or splitting opposition votes in favour of CCM candidates.

This adhoc electoral pact had a limited effect; there was no evidence that Chadema or Alliance for Change and Transparency–Wazalendo voters heeded the calls at the October 2020 polls. The election results were disappointing for both parties, not bringing the two opposition parties anywhere close to defeating the CCM.

Political party mergers

A merger of two or more political parties is the process whereby all amalgamating entities give up their individual identities and assume a new or rebranded identity. This process includes the merging of political structures and the integration of staff from the merging entities into a single unified structure that directs all political activity within the merged party. It is fairly common for successful pre-election coalitions to formalise their pre-election pacts into mergers in the post-election period, as the benefits of cooperation have been measured at the ballot box and, if significant, are likely to persuade the partners in the electoral pact that continuing cooperation will ensure similar returns in future. Mergers also assist the process of coordinating the exercise of power in the state, by removing the individual and sometimes asynchronous decision-making structures of different parties and rationalising decision-making within a single structure.

Tanzania's CCM was formed at the union of Tanganyika and Zanzibar in 1977. The merger, between the two ruling parties at the time, the Tanganyika African National Union and Zanzibar's Afro-Shirazi Party, rationalised the political governance structures in the new union of Tanzania, ensuring that the CCM has ruled both mainland Tanzania and Zanzibar since the merger. The Tanganyika African National Union and Afro-Shirazi Party had ruled the mainland and Zanzibar, respectively, since independence in 1961, and the merger, pursued deliberately by then Tanganyika African National Union president Julius Nyerere, was viewed as a shoring-up of support in Zanzibar against potential secession from the union. The CCM merger was successful in coordinating the exercise of political power, particularly in Zanzibar, which elects its own president and national assembly, as well as contributing to the union's national assembly and voting for the union presidency (Masterson, 2009). The CCM merger facilitated closer cooperation between the united republics and Zanzibari presidents, and the two national assemblies. However, the merger also created challenges, the most profound of which has been the CCM's determination to prevent Zanzibar's government changing hands, despite several extremely closely contested elections, including those of 2005, 2010 and 2015. In the event that the CCM were to lose power in Zanzibar, as a result of the merger, this would create a situation in the semi-autonomous islands of twin centres of power in governing Zanzibar, which the merger was designed to prevent in the first place.

Despite the historical significance of the merger, the CCM has struggled to fully maximise the coordination and synergy a merger is meant to facilitate. The CCM's Zanzibar structures are viewed at times as less active and not organised as well as their counterparts on the mainland. In addition, and despite around 50 years of union, many Zanzibaris (including CCM members) view themselves as 'other' than mainlanders. Tensions have also flared at times over perceived exploitation of Zanzibar's resources by the union government, while union MPs have publicly complained about the disproportionate representation of Zanzibar in the union, while also having the benefit of its own government. While the merger between the Tanganyika African National Union and Afro-Shirazi Party has delivered a long, unbroken series of election victories for the CCM, in other respects the merger has failed to achieve the level of political unity between Zanzibar and the mainland that Nyerere had hoped for.

Opportunistic alliances

Analysis of coalitions and alliances often assumes that the collaboration between parties is deliberate and directed towards intentional objectives. Often, however, such decisions are spontaneous and temporal reactions to political circumstances. These opportunistic alliances fail to merge their support bases due to potential incoherence, or collapse within a relatively short space of time, and as such they are less likely to lead to impacts beyond a temporary alignment of interests. Opportunistic alliances, particularly successful ones, can have significant and long-lasting political and governance repercussions. Opportunistic coalitions are most typically associated with election results that produce hung legislative bodies, or, in the case of presidential elections, second-round elections. Opportunistic alliances form when the election results suggest that the alignment of interests between two (or more) political parties or candidates will likely lead to a numerical majority result. These alliances are opportunistic due to the pivoting that happens by candidates who had previously contested against one another, but now align their interests to achieve a majority result following an election. To illustrate, the 2020 alliance between Malawi's Saulos Chilima-led United Transformation Movement and Lazarus Chakwera's Malawi Congress Party was driven purely by the electoral results (paradoxically nullified)[1] which suggested that an alliance between the two parties would overturn the ruling majority of

President Peter Mutharika's Democratic Progressive Party.

What marks the United Transformation Movement-Malawi Congress Party experience as opportunistic was their initial refusal to acknowledge the impact a split vote was likely to have on their individual party performances in relation to the Democratic Progressive Party. When the annulled results from 2019 all but confirmed what both parties had previously denied – that their split vote would have handed the election to the Democratic Progressive Party's incumbent, Dr Mutharika – the two leaders were incentivised to put aside their personal ambitions and work together towards a common objective. A key change to the electoral framework, which changed the simple majority to a 50 per cent plus one vote system for presidential candidates, helped to bring the two leaders together.

Not all opportunistic coalitions share these features. In some instances, coalitions are used by political leaders as a means through which to leverage their influence for a preferential role within a more successful party. This type of opportunism occurred ahead of Nigeria's 2019 elections, when the ruling party and major opposition parties both announced pre-election alliances with multiple smaller parties. In July 2018, the largest opposition party, the People's Democratic Party, announced the formation of a super-alliance that, in its own words, was going to overturn the majority of the ruling All Progressives Congress. It heralded the unification of some 38 political parties in the alliance. Not to be outdone, the All Progressives Congress announced later that month that its own coalition of some 20 political parties was poised to retain and even extend the electoral majority it enjoyed. While the numbers sound impressive, the actual support bases of many of the parties brought into the People's Democratic Party and All Progressives Congress alliances were so negligible as to make almost no difference to the electoral landscape.[2]

While the complex heterogeneity of Nigeria's politics makes the coalitions of multiple ethnically representative parties 'good politics' (Page, 2018), the political impact of these coalitions on the overall outcomes of the polls was often dismissed. The motivations behind the alliances were primarily not about increasing vote share. Lining up behind the major parties were the actions of '… many smaller parties, most of whom are "mom-and-pop" operations' (Page, 2018). Others described the members of the coalitions as 'briefcase parties', lacking considerable weight (Tella, 2018). Page (2018) described many of these 'opportunistic' parties as

> [possessing] little more than their acronyms, subsisting day-to-day by selling endorsements or renting themselves out to defeated [All Progressives Congress] or primary [People's Democratic Party] candidates seeking a second chance to run in the general election. Some are used by ambitious politicians to build up sufficient voting strength to be co-opted by one of the major parties.

This type of opportunistic association was primarily about a show of strength by the main parties, in exchange for position and prestige for the smaller parties. One of the interesting features of Nigeria's 2019 elections, as a result of these alliances, was the consolidation of political power behind the All Progressives Congress and the People's Democratic Party. The third largest political party by results, the All Progressives Grand Alliance secured a mere nine of the 360 seats in the house of representatives. Results of this nature solidify the consolidation of power in mega-coalitions, although in Nigeria, few political formations seem to endure.

THE ROLE OF COMPLEX COALITIONS IN MAINTAINING AND UNSEATING LONG-TERM INCUMBENTS' AGENDAS

Thus far, this chapter has focused on exploring the value for political parties to contest elections as alliances or coalitions. With the two biggest threats to dominant parties historically having been breakaway splits from within the party, and the formation of strong opposition coalitions to contest the dominance of the incumbent parties, these dominant parties have developed strategies to nullify the efficacy and success of these coalitions. One of the prevalent responses to emerging opposition alliances has been in the immediate electoral domain to invalidate or otherwise prevent the announcement of results in elections where these alliances or coalitions performed better than expected.

In 2005, the EPRDF, Ethiopia's incumbent and previously dominant party, entered the elections promising evidence of enhanced democratic freedoms for its citizens under Prime Minister Meles Zenawi. Zenawi was attempting to cast himself in the international community as the great reformer. The EPRDF, itself a coalition of multiple ethnic political parties, expected to face no meaningful challenge to its electoral dominance, thanks to a fractured opposition and its own track record of dominance. However, early results announced by the National Election Board of Ethiopia showed that two opposition alliances, the Coalition for Unity and Democracy and the United Ethiopian Democratic Forces, had taken all the seats in Addis Ababa, the capital city, and had won 185 of the 200 seats announced at that point. With 547 seats in the Ethiopian house of representatives, this represented a massive improvement on the 12 seats these two coalitions had previously mustered. It caught the EPRDF off guard.

Ethiopia's multi-ethnic character necessitated coalitions and alliances between the many ethnically based political parties that contested democratic elections in that country. The EPRDF is itself an alliance between parties representing majority ethnicities in Ethiopia, as this is the only way to secure the necessary number of seats under Ethiopia's federal system. A key ally within the EPRDF has always been the Tigray People's Liberation Front. The majority of the leadership of Ethiopia's Armed forces are Tigrayan, making the Tigray People's Liberation Front alliance with the other members of the EPRDF key to securing the loyalty of the armed forces.

The Coalition for Unity and Democracy was similarly composed of four opposition parties with strong representation in four of Ethiopia's nine federal states, and in both the self-governing administrations in Addis Ababa and Dire Dawa. These four parties drew support from Amhara, Oromia and the Southern Nations, Nationalities and Peoples' Region (SNNPR), Addis Ababa and Dire Dawa. The Coalition for Unity and Democracy coalition leveraged the prominence of several of its senior leaders (most notably as former ministers under the government of Mengistu Haile Mariam), as well as the ethnic loyalties of their voter base. The SNNPR state in particular is a composite of over 40 linguistic groups and more than 15 ethnic tribes. It is also Ethiopia's most rural state, with less than 10 per cent of its population living in urban areas. The four members of the Coalition for Unity and Democracy shared the common objective of a political dispensation based primarily on ideology rather than identity. Paradoxically, its support was drawn predominantly from ethnic communities with stronger sympathies towards the old regime, particularly groups feeling excluded under the new Tigray-dominated EPRDF.

According to the preliminary announcements by Ethiopia's National Election Board, the Coalition for Unity and Democracy had won all 21 seats in Addis Ababa and 89 seats out of the 200 announced to that point. This angered supporters of the EPRDF, who recognised the designated front man of the Coalition as the leader of the All Ethiopian Unity Party, engineer Hailu Shawul, a former member of the Mengistu Haile Mariam Derg regime. The EPRDF, supported by the Tigray, had previously overthrown this regime. The possibility of a revival of the regime, which was responsible for millions of deaths under Mengistu Haile Mariam, was unacceptable to many EPRDF officials.

The EPRDF responded by announcing its own calculations, pre-empting the National Election Board's announcements and declaring that, despite the early lead the opposition coalitions had secured in the elections, the EPRDF had won 317 of the 547 seats and was the rightfully elected governing party. The prime minister then enacted a state of emergency before the results were announced, banning public gatherings and unleashing the state security forces to maintain order. Opposition claims that the vote counting was being rigged were effectively muted when the National Election Board suspended the count for more than a week. The final results of the 2005 polls were released more than a month later than required by law, and of the 547 seats, the National Election Board of Ethiopia announced final results for only 307, with the EPRDF winning 139, the Coalition for Unity and Democracy 93 and the United Ethiopian Democratic Forces 42. The National Election Board annulled many of the remaining seats due to irregularities, ordering re-runs in several regions. Opposition parties, including the Coalition for Unity and Democracy and the United Ethiopian Democratic Forces, opted to boycott these re-run elections, claiming victory in the elections and refuting the final results which saw the EPRDF sweep the remaining seats and secure a 327-seat majority in the house. International observers, including from the European Union, criticised the delays and annulments of the results (European Union, 2005).

As a postscript to this, the contested 2005 elections marked the end of Ethiopia's brief shift towards a more open political environment, as the EPRDF would in the next two years unleash a battery of new legislation outlawing opposition parties, hamstringing funding of political activities, decimating a burgeoning civil society in Ethiopia, and entrenching a near monopoly for itself in the national assembly that persisted until recent reforms were introduced by current prime minister Abiy Ahmed.[3] Although improving significantly on their performance, the Coalition for Unity and Democracy and the United Ethiopian Democratic Forces alliances were unprepared at the time for the asymmetrical use of state power by the EPRDF to frustrate their efforts at the ballot box, and in spite of what would in other circumstances have been considered successful coalition tactics, neither alliance was permitted by the EPRDF (given the latter's monopoly on state power) to enjoy the rewards of their most successful showing at the polls.

The nature of Ethiopia's sociopolitical structure is such that no single ethnic group is able to gain the seats necessary to form a majority government. This has meant that even the ruling EPRDF relies on regional ethnic alliances to bolster its support. As Ethiopia potentially moves back towards more open and competitive elections in 2020–21, newly formed (and old, but revived) political parties scramble to negotiate their way into complex electoral alliances with parties from other regions, and cobble together support for their collective formations. Almost all of Ethiopia's federal states are ethnically homogeneous or include a dominant ethnicity (the exception being SNNPR, which is a collection of disparate ethnic identities and languages with little in common except geographic proximity). This has meant that any party serious about winning a majority of seats in the house of representatives has to ensure that it allies with parties bringing seats from other states to the house of representatives. As the EPRDF found out in 2005, predicting the outcomes of such alliances in such a fragmented political system can be extremely difficult, hence its retreat from reforms back into autocratic centralism.

EXPLORING THE RELATIONSHIP BETWEEN RENT-SEEKING AND POLITICAL COALITION FORMATION

The pursuit of power is often assumed to be an end in itself, but more often than not, power and the ability to wield it are secondary considerations to the pursuit of the financial benefits that derive from its use. Grand corruption, kleptocracy and fraud have stripped billions from economies in developing countries in the post-colonial era, including in Africa. It has had severe societal, political and institutional impacts in these states. Coalitions and alliances in many instances have created the platforms from which such rent-seeking access to state resources could be leveraged.

Rent-seeking in this chapter refers to the portion of costs paid over to renters in excess of the inherent value of the product or service being secured (Fischer, 2004). The concept denotes actions in which the politically connected make easy money by virtue of their closeness to government: they get government and private sector contracts, mining rights and favourable policies simply because they are close to those in government (see, for example, Gumede, 2015). The prevalence and severity of rent-seeking behaviour in African states is rarely disputed (Abegaz, 2013), nor is there doubt about the role of political elites in benefiting from and facilitating rent-seeking behaviours, particularly with respect to state contracts and tenders. Still, tangible evidence of the phenomenon is hard to come by. Accordingly, much of the available research on rent-seeking focuses on the perceptions of interest groups such as citizens or business lobbies (Transparency International, 2019).

Much of the analysis of the impact of rent-seeking on African countries is based, therefore, on observing the supposed effects of rent-seeking within the state and society (see Pring and Vrushi, 2019). Some of these proxy indicators include state fragility (Mbaku and

Paul, 1989; Asongu and Kodila-Tedika, 2016), public institutional weakness (Coolidge and Rose-Ackerman, 1997), perception indexes (Corruption Perception Index, 2019), and separating ubiquitous rents from harmful rents (Zuniga, 2017). Given the centrality of political leadership in these proxies, there is surprisingly little available research into the role that political formations, particularly political coalitions, play in combating, encouraging or facilitating rent-seeking behaviours, including in the African context.

A causal relationship

Evidence from the literature suggests that a causal relationship exists between the prevalence of rent-seeking behaviours in a state and the nature of its impact on political governance. Theorists have long argued over the merits of different political governance systems and their roles in constraining or encouraging rent-seeking behaviours (Mohtadi, 2003; Hayakawa and Venieris, 2017). However, while there are strong opinions on what type of political system is more or less conducive to rent-seeking, an analysis of African states with coalition governments suggests that there is little reason to believe coalitions have any effect on the prevalence or absence of rent-seeking in a country.

In a 2019 analysis of corruption-perception trends, Mauritius and Rwanda appear on the list of least corrupt countries in the index, while at the other end of the spectrum, Nigeria, Kenya, Mauritania and the Democratic Republic of the Congo (DRC) appear among the most corrupt countries (Ojekunle, 2019). While these countries share several features, for the purposes of this chapter it is important that both these sets of countries are currently ruled by political coalitions. Mauritius and Rwanda are consistently ranked near the top of most governance rankings and indexes, while the other group of countries trend much lower (Mo Ibrahim Foundation, 2019). The rest of this section considers the interface between rent-seeking and coalition governance in a case study from each of these two sets of countries – Mauritius as one of the least prone to rent-seeking, and Kenya as one of the countries most prone to it.

Mauritius

Mauritius has long been regarded as one of Africa's least corrupt societies. The political system is also associated with regular alternation of power, frequently requiring near-majority parties forming coalitions with smaller parties to secure the numerical majority required to form a government. The Mouvement Militant Mauricien (Mauritian Militant Movement) required the support of the Parti Mauricien Social Démocrate (Mauritian Social Democratic Party) to secure a majority in the 1976 elections, before winning the 1982 elections outright, bolstered by political alliances with the Mauritian Socialist Party and the Rodrigues People's Organisation. A split within the Mouvement Militant Mauricien in 1983 saw the emergence of a new party, the Militant Socialist Movement, which would supplant the Mouvement Militant Mauricien and its allies in fresh elections precipitated by the split. The Militant Socialist Movement formed a ruling coalition with the Labour Party and the Mauritian Social Democrat Party, and held power until 1995. However, the Mouvement Militant Mauricien and the Militant Socialist Movement would join forces in support of cutting ties with the British monarchy in 1990, before the Mouvement Militant Mauricien and the Labour Party formed a coalition prior to the 1995 elections and successfully ended 12 years of Militant Socialist Movement dominance. Subsequent elections have seen the internal balance of power shift between the Mouvement Militant Mauricien, the Militant Socialist Movement and the Labour Party, with the three entering into short-term political alliances and coalitions for specific election periods.

By the standards of African ruling parties, the history of ruling coalitions in Mauritius can be considered extremely volatile. Despite this political volatility, Mauritius consistently ranks as one of the best performing states on most indexes that rank corruption measures. However, attributing this success to the unusual nature of Mauritian politics, particularly the interconnectedness between the big three political parties and their ever-shifting network of alliances and coalitions, is not compelling. Some have argued that although Mauritius has benefited from pro-citizen policies and the relatively similar ideological positions of the three broadly socialist parties that have dominated its politics, the notion that this is due to the coalition structures themselves is rejected by Mauritian scholars. Kasenally[4] notes that: '… Mauritian exceptionalism is not only an overrated notion, it has in fact been the source of complacency and inaction among the island's political leaders.'

Kasenally dismissed as coincidence the notion that Mauritius's relative stability and historically excellent track record on corruption were at least partly attributable to the nature of its coalition politics, putting it 'down to luck'. She pointed out how, since her 2011 article that highlighted the island's complacency (Kasenally, 2011), Mauritius has been rocked by several public grand-corruption scandals that have involved the highest political figures in the country.

Prominent scandals have included former prime minister Navin Ramgoolam in 2015 being arrested on money-laundering charges after the discovery of US$23.3 million in foreign currency at his official residence.[5] In the same year, then technology minister and subsequent prime minister Pravind Jugnauth resigned after being charged with a conflict of interest in government procurement contracts (England, 2015). He was acquitted of the charges and within a month appointed to the Ministry of Finance and Economic Development. In 2018, President Ameena Gurib-Fakim was forced to resign after a scandal involving the use of a credit card belonging to a London-based NGO, Planet Earth Institute, after suspicious links between the president and Angolan businessman Alvaro Sobrinho raised questions about how the latter had managed to establish himself in Mauritius's tightly regulated financial sector.

Despite these scandals, the relative amounts, as well as the accountability demonstrated in at least some cases, underscore the ongoing institutional resilience in Mauritius (Allison, 2018). The scandals were significant in a country not used to such high-profile corruption cases, but Mauritius remained low in measures of widespread rent-seeking behaviours. In the Transparency International Global Corruption Barometer survey for 2019, less than 6 per cent of Mauritians reported that they paid bribes to police (Transparency International, 2019). However, Mauritian citizens in the same survey also reported a steep loss of trust in political leaders, while trust in institutions, the judiciary and other groups remained stable. Mauritians have clearly lost confidence that their political leaders are prepared to hold one another to account, despite the transparency and accountability wrought by the coalition nature of the country's politics. Declining trust in political parties and leaders, despite the coalition arrangement, therefore undermines the argument that coalitions help explain Mauritius's historical track record on corruption.

Kenya

At the other end of the spectrum, Kenya has consistently ranked among the most corrupt countries in Africa. In the same perceptions index that ranked Mauritius the sixth-best in Africa on corruption, Kenya was ranked in the bottom 20. Kenya, similar to Mauritius, is a country familiar with political coalitions, shifting alliances and temporal political arrangements. However, the two countries have diverged significantly in terms of their corruption trajectories. Since 2013, Kenya has been ruled by the Jubilee Party, a coalition of forces centred around the president, Uhuru Kenyatta, and the vice president, William Ruto.

An opportunistic alliance (Kadima and Owuor, 2014; see also chapter 6), the two men faced charges in the International Criminal Court over post-election incitement to violence (allegedly against one another's ethnic groups) after the 2007 election violence that displaced hundreds of thousands and saw ethnic murders across much of the country. In a defensive counterpunch, the two accused joined forces to contest the 2013 elections as allies, in the hope that presidential immunity could deflect the charges facing them in The Hague. Bankrolled by the Kenyatta family fortune (Nzioka and Namunane, 2014; Odidi, 2014), and uniting their ethnic groups behind a narrative that described the two as victims of International Criminal Court persecution and anti-Africa sentiment, the Jubilee Party was initially a pre-election alliance for the 2013 elections between 11 political parties, which formalised the alliance into a merger after its election victory.

Initial expectations that the Jubilee Party would improve the endemic rent-seeking culture that existed in Kenya were high (see Iraki, 2009). Kenyatta's election as president came on the back of a comparatively clean image regarding corruption, and his rhetoric during campaigning as well as during his early speeches put cleaning up the graft within Kenya's government as one of his top priorities. However, at a point well into the Kenyatta and Jubilee Party coalition's second term in office, frustration with the levels of rent-seeking and corruption in Kenya were at historical highs.

The year 2018 was one of scandals, with many public and state entities and senior Jubilee Party officials implicated in big corruption scandals. Kenyatta was forced onto the defensive to justify his party's record on anti-corruption. In 2018 alone, the list of scandals uncovered included one involving the National Youth Service worth about US$82 million; a scam at the National Cereals and Produce Board, involving appointed Jubilee Party officials, to the tune of around US$18 million; a Kenya Railways fraud scheme involving more than 50 officials, to the value of approximately US$2 million; a scandal at the Kenya Power Corporation involving the fraudulent awarding of contracts for defective and substandard power transformers (which included interference in the selection of service providers in 525 cases) worth about US$4 million; a land scandal in Ruaraka involving approximately US$14 million in payments to Jubilee Party officials in charge of the project; the arrest of multiple officials at Kenya Pipeline Company for abuse of office; and a fictitious-payments scheme uncovered at the National Health Insurance Fund (Keter, 2019).

Kenyatta in his personal capacity remained above these scandals, but Kenyan opposition critics, media and civil society were increasingly critical of his apparent soft approach to dealing with graft allegations involving Jubilee Party officials. Kenyatta deflected accountability at times for his lacklustre anti-corruption record, accusing the Kenyan judiciary and anti-corruption institutions of 'sluggish' efforts to tackle the issue (Miriri, 2016). Key among the criticisms levelled at Kenyatta were his apparent unwillingness at times to deal with allegations that involved his vice president, William Ruto. During the Jubilee Party's first term, 2013–17, the president and the vice president cooperated, particularly as they faced down the threat of the International Criminal Court. This demanded unity within the Jubilee Party coalition, which, opponents of the party allege, provided space for Ruto and other senior members of the coalition to pursue enrichment schemes with impunity. During his second term as president, Kenyatta's relationship with Ruto appears to have soured, and the president became more eager to see the corruption charges investigated (Gaitho, 2020; Mwaura, 2020). Whether or not this latter-day pivot on the part of Kenyatta has anything to do with a newfound desire to follow through on his initial promises to clean up Kenya's rent-seeking culture, or is motivated by strategic considerations as new coalitions and alliances emerge, is not within this chapter's scope of enquiry. It is clear, however, that the Jubilee Party coalition's performance on corruption ranks among the weakest in Kenya's post-colonial history.

CONCLUSION

While Africa's history includes long periods of one-party-state rule, this term is often misleading when the composition of the ruling party is dissected, as several states' one-party systems produced co-opted alliances enforced through legislative and constitutional stipulations. Even during the period when one-party states were historically prevalent, in the 1970s and 1980s, several ruling political formations were the product of coalitions and alliances.

The reintroduction of competitive multiparty politics in the early 1990s opened new fronts for political coalitions among opposition parties, a feature that has become particularly attractive as a viable means of disrupting the status quo and overturning electoral majorities. Given the ethnic, social and historical diversity of many African states, the possibility that coalitions and alliances will become less prevalent in the future seems highly improbable. Far more likely, given the many heterogeneous societies within which multiparty elections take place today, coalitions, both ruling and opposition alliances, are likely to increase in prevalence and relevance in shaping the political governance of African states.

REFERENCES

Abegaz, B. 2013. 'Political parties in business: Rent seekers, developmentalists, or both?', *Journal of Development Studies*, 49 (11), 1467–1483.

Afrobarometer. 20 March 2017. 'Highlights of Round 6 survey findings from 36 countries'. http://afrobarometer.org/sites/default/files/summary_results/ab_r6_afrobarometer_global_release_highlights8.pdf, accessed 13 May 2020.

Alemazung, J. A. 2010. 'Post-colonial colonialism: An analysis of international factors and actors marring African socio-economic and political development', *The Journal of Pan African Studies,* 3 (10), 62–84.

Allison, S. 21 March 2018. 'Trouble in paradise as Mauritius tackles corruption scandal', *ISS Today*, Institute for Security Studies.

Asongu, S. and Kodila-Tedika, O. 2016. 'State fragility, rent-seeking and lobbying: Evidence from African data', *International Journal of Social Economics,* 43 (10), 1016–1030.

Coolidge, J. and Rose-Ackerman, S. 1997. 'High-level rent-seeking and corruption in African regimes: Theory and cases', Policy Research Working Paper Series 1780, The World Bank.

Corruption Perception Index. 2019. Transparency International, https://www.transparency.org/en/cpi, accessed 24 May 2020.

Electoral Institute for Sustainable Democracy in Africa (EISA). African Democracy Encyclopaedia Project, https://www.eisa.org.za/wep/bot2014results.htm, accessed 24 May 2020.

England, A. 23 September 2015. 'Uncertainty lingers as scandal rocks Mauritian politics', *Financial Times*, https://www.ft.com/content/c691cddc-532c-11e5-b029-b9d50a74fd14, accessed 27 May 2020.

European Union. 2005. Ethiopia Legislative Elections 2005. European Union Election Observation Mission, http://www.eods.eu/library/FR%20ETHIOPIA%202005_en.pdf, accessed 13 May 2020.

Fischer, P. 2004. *Rent-seeking, Institutions and Reforms in Africa: Theory and empirical evidence for Tanzania.* University of Konstanz, Germany.

Gaitho, M. 26 May 2020. 'Going after Ruto will not solve Kenya's ills', Daily Nation, https://www.nation.co.ke/oped/opinion/going-after-Ruto-will-not-solve-Kenyas-ills-/440808-5563832-al5coy/index.html, accessed 27 May 2020.

Gumede, W. 10 September 2015. 'Rent-seeking is gobbling up our economy', *Mail & Guardian*, https://mg.co.za/article/2015-09-10-rent-seeking-is-gobbling-up-our-economy/, accessed 20 November 2020.

Hayakawa, H. and Venieris, Y. 2017. 'The invisible hand of rent-seeking: Capitalism, democracy and budget deficits', *Journal of Reviews on Global Economics,* 6, 380–394.

Iraki, X. 20 January 2009. 'Welcome to Kenya: The land of the rent seekers',

Standard Media, https://www.standardmedia.co.ke/article/1144004419/welcome-to-kenya-the-land-of-rent-seekers, accessed 23 April 2020.

Kadima, D. and Owuor, F. 2014. 'Kenya's decade of experiments with political party alliances and coalitions: Motivations, impact and prospects', *Journal of African Elections*, 13 (1), 150–180.

Karume, S. 2002. 'Factional intrigues and alliance politics', *Journal of African Elections*, 2 (1), 1–13.

Kasenally, R. 2011. 'Mauritius: The not so perfect democracy', *Journal of African Elections*, 10 (1), 33–47.

Keter, G. 1 January 2019. 'Big scandals that rocked Jubilee in 2018', *The Star*, https://www.the-star.co.ke/news/2019-01-01-big-scandals-that-rocked-jubilee-in-2018/, accessed 27 May 2020.

Kura, S. 2008. 'African ruling political parties and the making of "authoritarian democracies": Extending the frontiers of social justice in Nigeria', *African Journal on Conflict Resolution*, 2, https://www.accord.org.za/ajcr-issues/african-ruling-political-parties-and-the-making-of-authoritarian-democracies/, accessed 4 May 2020.

Lekalake, R. 2017. 'Why opposition parties in southern Africa struggle to win power', *The Conversation*, https://theconversation.com/why-opposition-parties-in-southern-africa-struggle-to-win-power-72889, accessed 5 May 2020.

Lodge, T. 2017. 'First generation constitutions in Africa', in Masterson, G. and Meirotti, M. (eds.) *Checks and Balances: African constitutions and democracy in the 21st century.* EISA, https://www.eisa.org.za/pdf/symp2015bk.pdf, accessed 20 April 2020.

Masterson, G. 2009. 'Tanzania and Zanzibar', in Kadima, D. and Booysen, S. (eds.) *Compendium of Elections in Southern Africa 1989–2009: 20 years of multiparty democracy.* Johannesburg: EISA.

Mazrui, A. 1994. 'Recolonization or self-colonization? Decaying parts of Africa need benign colonization', inMazrui, A. M and Mutunga, W. M. (eds.), *Debating the African Condition: Governance and leadership.* Lawrenceville, N.J.: Africa World Press.

Mbaku, J. and Paul, C. 1989. 'Political instability in Africa: A rent-seeking approach', *Public Choice*, 63, 63–72.

Miriri, D. 18 October 2016. 'Kenya's Kenyatta blames agencies for sluggish anti-corruption fight', Reuters News Service, https://www.reuters.com/article/us-kenya-corruption/kenyas-kenyatta-blames-agencies-for-sluggish-anti-corruption-fight-idUSKCN12I1R6, accessed 27 May 2020.

Mizuno, N. and Okazawa, R. 2009. 'Colonial experience and postcolonial underdevelopment in Africa', *Public Choice,* 141 (3/4), 405–419.

Mo Ibrahim Foundation. 2019. Ibrahim Index of African Governance. https://mo.ibrahim.foundation/iiag, accessed 27 May 2020.

Mohtadi, H. 2003. 'Democracy, rent-seeking, public spending and growth',

EconPapers. University of Minnesota, 1–12.

Mwaura, W. 18 May 2020. 'A marriage of inconvenience: Kenya's president turns on his deputy', *Mail & Guardian*, https://mg.co.za/africa/2020-05-18-a-marriage-of-inconvenience-kenyas-president-turns-on-his-deputy/, accessed 27 May 2020.

Nzioka, P. and Namunane, B. 20 February 2014. 'Political families own half of private wealth', *Daily Nation*, https://mobile.nation.co.ke/news/Kenyans-Wealth-Families-Politicians/-/1950946/2215578/-/format/xhtml/-/krwmhtz/-/index.html, accessed 23 April 2020.

Odidi, B. 29 September 2014. 'Who owns Kenya?' *This is Africa: African Identities*, https://thisisafrica.me/african-identities/owns-kenya/, accessed 23 April 2020.

Ojekunle, A. 2 April 2019. 'These are the 20 most corrupt countries in Africa right now', *Business Insider*, https://www.pulse.ng/bi/politics/these-are-the-20-most-corrupt-countries-in-africa-right-now/vd2fc2k, accessed 27 May 2020.

Oyugi, W. 2006. 'Coalition politics and coalition governments in Africa', *Journal of African Contemporary Studies*, 24 (1), 53–79.

Page, M. 12 July 2018. 'In Nigerian politics, there are no permanent friends and no permanent enemies', *Quartz Daily Brief*, https://qz.com/africa/1326945/nigeria-buhari-sees-apc-party-split-to-pdp-coalition/, accessed 23 May 2020.

Pring, C. and Vrushi, J. (eds.) 2019. 'Global Corruption Barometer Africa 2019: Citizens' views and experiences of corruption', Transparency International, https://afrobarometer.org/sites/default/files/publications/Publications%20conjointes/partenaires/ab_r7_global_corruption_barometer_report.pdf, accessed 22 April 2020.

Rodney, W. 1973. *How Europe Underdeveloped Africa*. London: Bogle-L'Ouverture Publications.

Shale, V. 2007. 'Opposition party alliances and elections in Botswana, Lesotho and Zambia', *Journal of African Elections*, 6 (1), 91–117.

Simpson, M. and Hawkins, T. 2018. *The Primacy of Regime Survival: State fragility and economic destruction in Zimbabwe*. London: Palgrave Macmillan.

Tella, K. 13 July 2018. 'Nigerian political parties form grand coalitions ahead of 2019 polls', *The African Courier*, https://www.theafricancourier.de/africa/nigerian-political-parties-form-grand-coalitions-ahead-of-2019-polls/, accessed 23 May 2020.

Transparency International. 2019. Global Corruption Barometer – Africa, https://www.transparency.org/en/gcb/africa/africa-2019, accessed 27 May 2020.

Van Cranenburgh, O. 2008. 'Big men rule: Presidential power, regime type and democracy in 30 African countries', *Democratization*, 15 (5), 952–973.

Zimbabwe Electoral Commission. 2019. Zimbabwe 2018 Harmonised Elections Report, https://www.eisa.org.za/pdf/zim2018zec.pdf, accessed 22 May 2020.
Zuniga, N. 2017. 'Harmful rents and rent-seeking'. Anti-Corruption Resource Centre. Transparency International.

SIX

Coalition politics in Kenya
Superficial assemblages and momentary vehicles to attain power

GILBERT KHADIAGALA

KENYA IS ONE OF AFRICA's deeply divided countries, where ethnic and regional fragmentation has stymied the organisation of competitive politics for many years. The onset of multiparty pluralism in the early 1990s brought a host of coalitions in Kenyan politics amid the triumphalism of Africa's second liberation. Coalitions at the national level, for the most part, have attempted to tame the fissiparous ethnic cleavages that have characterised Kenya since independence. While coalitions among ethnic-based political parties have dominated politics, since the mid-2000s, coalition governments have also become common. This chapter suggests that although coalitions between political parties for the purpose of governance are inevitable elite bargains in deeply divided polities such as Kenya, they reflect the narrowness of ethnic-centred political participation. Coalitions in Kenya have often promised to reduce ethnic fragmentation and consolidate national unity (Horowitz, 1985; Reilly, 2001; Kuperman, 2015), but they have, in effect, prevented the evolution of solid political parties that would transcend ethnic politics. Strong personalities with only tenuous social bases disproportionately fund and control Kenya's political parties. This means that as assemblages of elites without any meaningful popular base, Kenyan coalitions invariably mirror the weaknesses of political parties. Furthermore, the fragmentation of ethnic political coalitions has been deepened by the first-past-the-post (FPTP) electoral system that Kenya has maintained since independence. In a centralised presidential system such as Kenya's, political elites prefer FPTP because it consolidates ethnic blocs in the struggles for power.

This chapter addresses these themes by analysing key moments in Kenya's coalition-making. It starts with a brief discussion of coalitions in the early 1960s, followed by an analysis of the political bargains that followed the inauguration of competitive politics in the 1990s. These sections examine the decade-old attempts by various coalitions to defeat the then dominant party, the Kenya African National Union (KANU), leading to the elections of 2002. Second, the analysis focuses on two coalitions that emerged after the defeat of KANU, including the Government of National Unity (GNU) established after the electoral violence of 2007–08. Third, I probe the state of political alliances since the 2013 and 2017 elections, and the ongoing turbulence in the ruling Jubilee Alliance. I conclude with a brief assessment of future trajectories. Given the complexity of political parties and coalitions, the details in Table 6.1 offer comparative perspectives on the major parties, their leaders and their ethnicity, and whether they ever attained power. The chapter uses secondary source data from existing scholarship and media accounts. These data have been periodised to provide a chronological and comprehensive narrative of the history of coalition politics in Kenya. These sources are supplemented by personal observations and reflections.

Table 6.1: Political parties and coalitions in Kenya, 1963–2020

Years	Parties	Leaders	Ethnicity	Party or coalition?	Did it gain power?
1963–66	Kenya African National Union (KANU)	Jomo Kenyatta and Jaramogi Oginga Odinga	Kikuyu and Luo	Party	Yes, 1963–1978 under Kenyatta
	Kenya African Democratic Union (KADU)	Ronald Ngala and Masinde Muliro	Giriama and Luhya	Party	No
1966–71	Kenya's People's Union (KPU)	Jaramogi Oginga Odinga	Luo	Party	No
1978–91	Kenya African National Union (KANU)	Daniel Arap Moi	Kalenjin	Party	Yes, following Kenyatta's death in 1978
1991–97	Kenya African National Union (KANU)	Daniel Arap Moi	Kalenjin	Party	Yes
	Forum for the Restoration of Democracy (FORD)	Masinde Muliro	Luhya	Party	No
	FORD-Asili	Kenneth Matiba	Kikuyu	Party	No
1997–2002	Kenya African National Union (KANU)	Daniel Arap Moi	Kalenjin	Party	Yes
	FORD-Asili	Kenneth Matiba	Kikuyu	Party	No
	National Development Party (NDP)	Raila Odinga	Luo	Party	No
2002–05	Kenya African National Union (KANU)	Uhuru Kenyatta	Kikuyu	Party	No
	National Rainbow Coalition (NARC)	Mwai Kibaki and Raila Odinga	Kikuyu and Luo	Coalition	Yes
2005–08	Party of National Unity (PNU)	Mwai Kibaki	Kikuyu	Coalition	Yes
	Orange Democratic Movement (ODM)	Raila Odinga	Luo	Coalition	No
2008–13	Government of National Unity (GNU)	Mwai Kibaki and Raila Odinga	Kikuyu and Luo	Coalition	Yes, negotiated by Kofi Annan
2013–20	Jubilee Party	Uhuru Kenyatta and William Ruto	Kikuyu and Kalenjin	Coalition	Yes
	National Super Alliance	Raila Odinga	Luo	Coalition	No

Source: Author's compilation, applying data in this chapter.

ETHNICITY AND COALITION-BUILDING, 1963–91

Kenyan nationalism entailed the search for unity among political elites led primarily by the two largest ethnic groups – the Kikuyu under Jomo Kenyatta and the Luo led by Jaramogi Oginga Odinga. Organised as KANU, these leaders jointly spearheaded the negotiations for independence and nationhood. However, on the eve of independence in 1963, minor ethnic groups, particularly the Kalenjin, Luhya, Kamba and others from the coast region, formed an alliance called the Kenya African Democratic Union to challenge what they perceived as the hegemony of the Kikuyu and the Luo. While Kenya African Democratic Union leaders strongly advocated for a decentralised system of government that would distribute resources to all ethnic groups, KANU favoured a centralised state that would help consolidate power and forge a coherent nation (Nyangira, 1986; Hornsby, 2012). Subsequently, KANU proceeded to build a heavily centralised presidential system (Nyong'o, 1989: 229–251).

Towards the mid-1960s, KANU's centralist impulses triumphed, leading to the dissolution of the Kenya African Democratic Union and the beginning of Kenyatta's entrenchment of a one-party state. At the same time, ideological and personality differences between Kenyatta and Odinga surfaced to shatter the short-lived Kikuyu-Luo political coalition. Marginalised from power, Odinga created his own political party, the Kenya People's Union (KPU), composed of his Luo supporters. Thereafter, the Kenyatta state used draconian measures to proscribe the KPU and detained its leaders. On Kenyatta's death in 1978, Daniel Arap Moi, a Kalenjin from the Rift Valley, became president. Moi perfected the repressive institutions that Kenyatta had bequeathed, making KANU the only legal party in 1982 (Atieno-Odhiambo, 1987).

The rapid disintegration of the nationalist coalition was largely a result of the fluidity of ethnic bargains that were to dominate post-colonial politics as political leaders sought power and resources. Leys (1975) argues that 'tribalism' or ethnicity is, at heart, a class project, since the new middle class, wearing ethnic garb, could only consolidate power by exclusionary strategies of mobilising narrow regional and ethnic interests. To stabilise rule, these politicians also resorted to patronage, rewarding pliable constituencies while punishing recalcitrant ones (Kitching, 1980). Thus, throughout the Kenyatta and Moi eras, KANU became a repressive patronage machine that dispensed economic benefits to its core ethnic constituencies, the Kikuyu and Kalenjin, respectively. It is also for this reason that, during Kenyatta's rule, the Luo and other groups out of power felt economically marginalised; under Moi, the Kikuyu joined the marginalised groups (Throup and Hornsby, 1998).

COALITIONS IN THE FORMATIVE PHASE OF COMPETITIVE POLITICS, 1991–97

The ethnic political coalitions that characterised Kenya's political landscape for 30 years coalesced around the objectives of stability and nation-building through the centralisation of power. But as the country descended into a one-party state under Moi's KANU, the Kalenjin effectively became the dominant and monolithic ruling coalition, sowing the seeds of instability and political protests (Ajulu, 2002). Due to relentless domestic and international pressure on the KANU government, Moi was forced to rescind the constitutional ban on parties in December 1991, starting the slow path towards multiparty competitive politics and new coalitions (Widner, 1992; Barkan, 1998). Although these coalitions were built on existing regional and ethnic faultlines, there were efforts by political leaders to construct broad-based ethnic coalitions that would lend a national image to the anti-KANU front. Following wide consultations, opposition parties and civic leaders created the Forum for the Restoration of Democracy (FORD), a multi-ethnic power bloc to contest KANU. According to Ndegwa (1997: 609), FORD 'articulated a unitary nationalist vision, with a liberal conception of citizenship, and offered majority rule institutions as appropriate to structure public affairs in post-single-party Kenya'.

But hopes for a united coalition against KANU soon vanished in the lead-up to the 1992 elections, a victim of the polarising and centrifugal forces of ethnicity. As before, leaders from the Kikuyu and the Luo ethnic groups began to mobilise along ethnic lines in the new scramble for power. As Throup and Hornsby (1998: 94) observe, rather than creating a stable coalition front, FORD became a victim of leadership squabbles:

> Almost from its registration, FORD suffered from endemic factionalism. Its leaders were divided not only by their different views of party policy but by ethnicity and generation. These divisions quickly developed into a network of rival alliances, which soon became bickering factions, jostling for the party's presidential nomination. Once these divisions became apparent to the public, the great emotional response to multiparty democracy and the tremendous popular enthusiasm created by FORD's registration would be replaced by disillusionment with politicians and the political process amid the failed hopes that had been aroused.

Two major factions emerged from FORD: FORD Kenya, an alliance of Luo and Luhya, led by Odinga; and FORD–Asili (in Swahili, 'authentic'), a predominantly Kikuyu faction led by Kenneth Matiba, a prominent entrepreneur. Although civil society organisations advocated for a united opposition that could straddle the ethnic divides, the ethnic fragmentation of FORD was unstoppable. FORD Kenya, for instance, witnessed mass defections as professionals saw the increasing 'ethnicisation' of the party by its Luo leader. A similar trend characterised FORD–Asili, which became associated largely with wealthy Kikuyu elites from central Kenya. Worsening the fortunes of the opposition was a new Kikuyu party, the Democratic Party led by Mwai Kibaki, a former vice president in Moi's government (Asingo, 2003; Ndegwa, 1998).

Unlike in the early 1960s when Kikuyu and Luo leaders coalesced under KANU, now they went their separate ways by creating their own parties. As in the 1960s, however, Moi rallied minority ethnic groups that were fearful of dominance by the Kikuyu and the Luo, just as the Kenya African Democratic Union had done before. Moi also adroitly used the might of state power to unleash electoral violence on opposition strongholds in the Rift Valley, and Western and Coast provinces. In this regard, Moi supporters declared parts of the Rift Valley 'KANU zones', where opposition parties were not allowed to campaign (Klopp, 2001; Omolo, 2002).

The combination of opposition splintering and government violence contributed to the electoral outcome when in the December 1992 elections Moi won with 36 per cent of the vote and the three opposition parties got a combined 62 per cent. Moi also benefited from a change in the law that had mandated that a winning presidential candidate needed to obtain at least 25 per cent of the votes cast in five of the eight provinces, even if the candidate did not obtain a majority of the popular vote.

Basking in its electoral victory, KANU sought to regain its legitimacy. Throup and Hornsby (1998: 533) note:

> For KANU the worst was over as the opposition had been faced and defeated at its time of maximum support and unity. Nonetheless, care was required. With new, unstable political parties, and ethnicity as a driving force, there was no guarantee that some event or individual might not initiate a new alliance or drive 'KANU tribes' into the hands of the enemy. It was essential to demonstrate that there was no alternative to KANU. KANU's strategy was therefore one of containment and attrition, not consensus, focusing on bringing marginal Districts back into the fold.

As opposition parties struggled with the realities of a semi-competitive political environment, civil society re-emerged to campaign for constitutional reforms that would contribute to levelling the political playing field. Through violent mass campaigns in the mid-1990s, civic actors forced opposition parties and the government to enact limited reforms in parliament before the 1997 elections. These reforms included the formation of an electoral commission with representatives from major opposition parties; the abolition of laws preventing freedom of political expression and association; and the registration of all unregistered political parties (Harbeson, 1998; Mutua, 2008).

For opposition parties, however, these reforms were too few and came too late to make a significant difference to the electoral outcome. Just as in the 1992 elections, KANU resorted to ethnic mobilisation and electoral violence to win the elections. Moreover, as Peters (2001: 32) notes, opposition parties were facing severe internal challenges to being effective competitors:

> All the three main parties were at different stages of disintegration and thus paralyzed at the core. Ever since the 1992 elections, due to the personal ambitions of various party leaders and ethno-political differences between the Luo and Kikuyu, the political parties had been preoccupied with internal leadership quarrels. Even as the 1997 elections drew closer, they proved neither capable of settling these quarrels nor agreeing on a common and single presidential candidate, the only realistic approach to unseat Moi.

Despite winning the 1997 elections with 41 per cent of the vote, KANU managed only a very narrow majority in parliament, making it difficult for it to govern without support from one of the opposition parties. Although the Democratic Party leader, Kibaki, called for a rejection of the presidential results, none of the opposition parties supported this move. Matiba's FORD-Asili boycotted the election, but this did not affect the voter turnout, which was close to 65 per cent. The momentous factor occasioned by the 1997 election was the change in the political landscape of opposition parties. In the Luo region, a new party, the National Development Party led by Raila Odinga (the son of Jaramogi Oginga Odinga), won almost all the parliamentary seats. In the central region of the Kikuyu, Kibaki's Democratic Party became the most important party, replacing Matiba's FORD–Asili. Kibaki also won nearly twice the number of parliamentary seats of those of the National Development Party (Cowen and Kanyinga, 2000).

FORGING A WINNING COALITION, 1997–2002

Coalition-building across ethnic political parties in the initial phase of pluralism was stymied by the zero-sum nature of political parties, the internecine disputes within and across these parties, and the structural advantages that KANU continued to exercise through the control of state power. Pluralism promised competitive politics, but the political parties that arrived reflected the widespread pattern of 'big man' politics, the absence of internal democracy, and a lack of organisation (Wanyande, 2003; Elischer, 2008; Khadiagala, 2010). After the 1997 constitutional reforms, new political parties arose seeking a national outlook, but they remained urban and marginal. Paradoxically, after the legalisation of parties, KANU remained one of the few parties with a national outlook because of previous years of mobilisation. Ndegwa (1998: 194) captures the dismal state of parties in Kenya after the 1997 elections, suggesting that both KANU and the opposition shared 'fundamental conceptions of leadership and of the relationship between the state and its citizens: a patriarchal, patronizing, elitist, and, ultimately, disempowering attitude toward the citizenry'.

However, while KANU had won two elections (1992 and 1997), it was ill-prepared for the battles around Moi's succession, as he was serving his final term in office. The jostling for the succession presented new opportunities for political parties to enter into coalitions that were to dramatically alter the course of Kenyan politics. At this moment, political parties woke up to the necessity of alliances across ethnic and regional lines, in a marked departure from the previous ethnic enclaves.

Moi was the first leader to invite Odinga's National Development Party into government, in March 2002, because of the latter's strength in Luoland. The merger of KANU and the National Development Party into the New KANU created a formidable coalition, uniting the Luo and the Kalenjin (Kagwanja, 2003).

The new coalition, in turn, ignited parallel initiatives by many other political parties to form similar coalitions. The most significant of these was the National Alliance for Change, created in January 2002 under the leadership of Kibaki's Democratic Party, with the incorporation of 13 political parties from Western, Nairobi and Eastern provinces. The

National Alliance for Change subsequently changed its name to the National Alliance Party of Kenya. As the voters prepared for the 2002 elections, the Kenyan political landscape was divided into the terrain of two grand coalitions: The New KANU, led by the Luo and the Kalenjin; and the National Alliance Party of Kenya, led by the Kikuyu and a cross-section of minor ethnic groups (Mutua, 2008; Kagwanja, 2009). The stability of the New KANU alliance was, however, shattered in July 2002 when Moi unilaterally chose Uhuru Kenyatta (the son of the first president, Jomo Kenyatta) as his preferred successor, rather than Odinga. Moi calculated that the young Kenyatta was more important in bringing the Kikuyu vote solidly to the New KANU than Odinga's Luo votes. Marginalised from the New KANU, Odinga and his supporters joined the National Alliance Party of Kenya, culminating in the formation of the National Rainbow Coalition (NARC), with Kibaki as the presidential candidate. Kibaki and Odinga agreed on a pre-election power-sharing arrangement that would govern the relationship after the December 2002 elections. NARC was the first coalition since the early 1960s in which prominent Kikuyu and Luo leaders created an organisation that downplayed ethnic differences. The Kikuyu and the Luo are the largest ethnic groups, making this an exceptional coalition (the Moi coalition was between the Luo and the Kalenjin). This new Kikuyo-Luo coalition enabled Kibaki to win the December 2002 elections with 62 per cent of the vote, ending KANU's rule (Steeves, 2006).

THE COLLAPSE OF THE NARC ALLIANCE, 2003–07

NARC's victory stemmed from the grievances that had accumulated in 24 years of KANU rule, particularly economic mismanagement, nepotism and the spectre of a collapsed state. In NARC, the citizens saw the potential for new forms of organising politics, away from the prevailing narratives of ethnicity and regionalism. Having created a winning coalition that demonstrated the power of collective mobilisation, Kibaki and Odinga faced the formidable test of sustaining the momentum. As was the case with the previous coalitions, however, NARC collapsed in acrimony amid the resurgence of ethnic mobilisation over fundamental national concerns. These differences resulted in the post-election violence of 2007–08, sparking external mediation to force a power-sharing agreement. This further underscores the fact that coalitions in Kenya do not produce stability because they are elite vehicles for gaining power.

In less than a year after the elections, the coalition collapsed, following Odinga's complaints about marginalisation by the Kikuyu in the NARC government. In accusing Kibaki of dependence on his ethnic cohorts from Central province, Odinga also pointed to Kibaki's failure to implement the pre-election power-sharing agreement. Consequently, Odinga pulled out of NARC and the cabinet, paralysing the government and forcing Kibaki to seek new alliance partners, including KANU leaders. Furthermore, the Odinga group accused Kibaki of corruption, economic mismanagement and continued marginalisation of non-Kikuyu regions. More critically, NARC's collapse developed into a battle that crystallised around the constitutional reforms that had started in the late 1990s (Anderson, 2003; Barkan, 2004).

Civil society actors had campaigned for constitutional reforms since the mid-1990s. In the last few years of the KANU regime, Moi had relented and created a national constitutional review commission that presented its findings to the Kibaki administration. However, as various organs, including parliament, debated the proposed reforms in preparation for a national referendum, there were intense conflicts on some of the provisions, particularly the powers of the executive branch. The Kibaki government leaned more towards the continuation of a strong presidency, while the Odinga faction favoured a parliamentary system of government with limited presidential powers (Mutua, 2008; Miguna, 2012). The recriminations over the constitution set the stage for a constitutional referendum in November 2005, characterised by ethnic polarisation. On the eve of the referendum, Odinga rallied a new movement, the Orange Democratic Movement, to oppose the draft constitution, while parties allied to Kibaki's new coalition, the Party of National Unity, turned out to vote for the draft constitution. In a highly divisive vote, the opposition won by 57 per cent, handing Kibaki a crushing defeat (Elischer, 2008). According to Mutua (2008:

229), political analysts blamed Kibaki's humiliating loss 'on a number of factors, including his hands-off style, corruption scandals, power struggles within NARC, a protest against perceived Kikuyu hegemony, and the government's failure to formulate an inclusive and consultative constitutional review process'.

The alliances crafted during the referendum marked the return, in earnest, of the divisive ethnic alliances that had characterised postcolonial politics. When NARC had frayed, key Kikuyu and Luo leaders had retreated into their ethnic and regional strongholds. It was against this background that Kenya faced one of the most divisive periods in its history, as the Orange Democratic Movement and the Party of National Unity battled for votes in the December 2007 elections. The Orange Democratic Movement's campaign platform focused on the importance of devolved governance, a clean government, and equitable resource distribution, while the Party of National Unity campaigned on the Kibaki government's record of reviving the economy (Wanyama, 2010). At the end of the elections, the Orange Democratic Movement was emboldened by the gains it had made in winning 99 parliamentary seats against the Party of National Unity's 43 (out of 210), but it claimed that the government had colluded with the electoral commission to deny the presidential victory to Odinga.

Following the declaration of Kibaki's victory, Kenya in 2007–08 descended into a wave of violence that left more than 1,000 dead and 600,000 displaced (Gibson and Long, 2009; Branch and Cheeseman, 2009). Ndii (2016) blamed the collapse of NARC on Kibaki:

> Kibaki tore up the political covenant [with Odinga], tribalized the government and went back to the post-independence doctrine of wealth above all else. The Kibaki administration's belligerence and political thuggery brought the country to the brink of civil war. Ironically, Kibaki ended up with exactly the same cohabitation in his second term that he had refused to honour in the first place.

With the Party of National Unity and the Orange Democratic Movement unable to end the violence, the international community intervened in a mediation initiative (Kanyinga, 2011). These efforts led to the appointment by the African Union of the Panel of Eminent Personalities, chaired by Kofi Annan. Within a 40-day period, the mediators produced a power-sharing government. Following an amendment to the constitution, parliament enacted the National Accord and Reconciliation Act that established a coalition government, the Government of National Unity (GNU), at the end of February 2008. It consisted of the president, vice president, prime minister, two deputy prime ministers and a cabinet of 40 members appointed from both the Party of National Unity and the Orange Democratic Movement. Odinga became the prime minister, while Kibaki remained president (Lindemayer and Kaye, 2009).

COALITION-BUILDING IN THE AFTERMATH OF ELECTORAL VIOLENCE, 2008–13

Pressure from the Annan mediation team had prodded the Kenyan players into a coalition government. The GNU coalition partners had barely worked together before, and continued to be suspicious of one another. As the first experiment in power-sharing, the GNU gave the leaders the opportunity to govern collectively while minimising their continued differences. The dilemma, however, was whether the GNU would provide the momentum to unlock the logjam on national reconciliation and constitutional reforms before the 2013 elections, or degenerate into paralysis.

The GNU was criticised by both Kibaki and Odinga, because it was a compromise they had had to accept to escape more conflicts. Odinga bickered about a power-sharing arrangement that did not give him substantive power or resources. As one of his close confidantes, Miguna (2012: 271–272), wrote:

> More than a year since the National Accord had been signed, it was obvious to observers that President Kibaki and his Party of National Unity cohorts had no intention of adhering to the power-sharing agreement. Kibaki had placed one road block after another in Raila's path. The President continued to make

all important decisions without any regard to the provisions of the National Accord that compelled him to consult the Prime Minister … Raila was finding it impossible to exercise any of the supervisory or coordinating responsibilities that the Accord granted him. GNU ministers and senior civil servants affiliated to the party openly disregarded and defied the Prime Minister.

Kibaki's allies, on the other hand, grudgingly accepted the GNU, acknowledging that it was a painful but necessary step in attempts at national reconciliation.

Despite these differences, the GNU established a host of commissions to address longstanding questions of ethnicity, inequalities and regional imbalances that had obstructed national cohesion. In addition, through international pressures, the government established a commission of inquiry to investigate the circumstances that had led to the 2007 post-election violence. Equally vital, the GNU restarted the process of constitutional reforms that had stalled since the 2005 referendum. During the constitutional negotiations, both sides quibbled over many key constitutional issues, especially the devolution of power, the powers of the executive branch, and resource-sharing mechanisms between the central government and decentralised bodies. Following a period of horse-trading, however, the coalition partners arrived at a compromise that culminated in the August 2010 constitution that citizens approved through a referendum. Among its key provisions were a bill of rights, devolution of power and resources to decentralised county governments, and safeguards to prevent ethnic conflicts (Kanyinga and Long, 2012). Odinga lost the campaign to introduce a parliamentary system of government that would have strengthened the power of parliament at the expense of the executive. As a result, the strong presidency continues to be a cause of disagreement between the county and central governments (Cheeseman et al., 2016).

Although the 2010 constitution was a major milestone for the Kibaki-Odinga coalition government, two major events overshadowed this achievement. First was the split within the Orange Democratic Movement that saw the departure of William Ruto, a former Odinga ally from Rift Valley. Ruto had contributed significantly to the Orange

Democratic Movement's success among the Kalenjin voters, and had expected Odinga to choose him as one of the party's deputy prime ministers in the GNU, rather than be placed in an ordinary ministerial position. After his resignation, Ruto formed the United Republican Party in January 2012 to advance his political ambitions. Second, the indictment by the International Criminal Court of six Kenyan leaders, including Kenyatta and Ruto, for their leading roles in the 2007 electoral violence reverberated throughout Kenya. The commission that investigated the events of 2007–08 had proposed the establishment of a local tribunal to try the suspects, but a deeply divided parliament failed to agree on its establishment. Consequently, the International Criminal Court took on the task of trying the suspected perpetrators (Mueller, 2014).

The International Criminal Court became a further convulsive force in Kenya's fractious coalition government, contributing to the birth of the Jubilee Alliance comprising Ruto's United Republican Party and Kenyatta's The National Alliance, which Kenyatta had created in May 2012. Both Kenyatta and Ruto presented the Jubilee Alliance as a way to heal the wounds inflicted during the 2007–08 electoral violence, and pleaded for forgiveness and reconciliation. At about the same time, the two leaders made their preliminary appearances together at the International Criminal Court in The Hague, in a move that brought sympathy from ethnic loyalists. As Kabukuru (2013: 31) observed:

> Both Kenyatta and Ruto have managed to not only make the ICC [International Criminal Court] an election campaign tool, but they have also swayed the majority of the public to their side. The two men have turned the ICC into a blessing and reinvented their political careers. They have used every available opportunity to score political points and effectively turn their ICC debacle into a sympathy-seeking platform.

With the establishment of the Kikuyu-Kalenjin coalition, Odinga created a new alliance, the Coalition for Reform and Development, composed of mainly leaders from Western, Eastern and Coast provinces, to prepare for the 2013 elections. During the election campaign, Western countries leaned heavily towards the Coalition for Reform and Development, claiming that the international community would not accept the indicted Jubilee leaders (Wrong, 2013). But this support for the Coalition for Reform and Development backfired, as it galvanised huge voter turnouts in Jubilee strongholds, particularly among the youth, who mobilised through social media and depicted the Jubilee coalition as marking a generational change in Kenyan politics. Under Kenya's FPTP electoral system, Kenyatta and Ruto won both the popular presidential vote as well as the largest number of parliamentarians. The decisive win of Jubilee with solid margins in the Kikuyu and Kalenjin areas reaffirmed the seismic electoral shift arising from the intervention of the International Criminal Court. As Wolf (2013: 169) pointed out, 'Western interference had the opposite effect of its intention – helping Jubilee both to mobilise its existing support base more energetically and to win over a limited but critical number of additional voters.'

THE JUBILEE COALITION IN POWER: THE HONEYMOON PHASE, 2013–17

The Jubilee Alliance leaders described themselves as the digital generation, to differentiate them from the GNU coalition leaders, who were much older. More importantly, the new coalition solidified the Kalenjin and Kikuyu ethnic blocs, reducing the ability of other ethnic groups to be competitive in future elections. Some Kenyan analysts depicted this phenomenon as the 'tyranny of numbers' in which the numerical superiority of the Kikuyu and the Kalenjin could not be defeated by any combination of opposition coalitions (Ngunyi, 2013; Githuku, 2013; Nderitu, 2018). After the 2013 elections, Kenyatta and Ruto hinted that the Jubilee Alliance would guarantee that in future elections power would rotate among the coalition partners. According to this scenario, after Kenyatta completes his two presidential terms in 2022, Ruto, the current deputy president, will assume the presidency for 10 years, before a new set of leaders emerges from the two communities. Jittery about the prospects of never gaining power, opposition parties warned that proposals for a permanent coalition of Kalenjin and

Kikuyu would signal profound instability, marginalisation, and a reversal of the gains from the constitutional reforms.

Unlike the problems that confronted the GNU governing coalition, the Jubilee leaders agreed to share major positions in the cabinet and government. This power-sharing arrangement extended to all layers of government, in which Kikuyu and Kalenjin obtained most of the senior positions to the exclusion of other ethnic groups. This exclusionary governance was reminiscent of the era of the one-party state when purges in the civil service of ethnic groups from opposition regions deepened cronyism, corruption and patronage. In addition to undermining professionalism, these purges also weakened the integrity and independence of critical government institutions such as the Electoral Commission, the National Treasury and the security services (Khadiagala, 2019: 56–57). Under the Jubilee coalition, the patronage networks that were built on massive corruption at the centre resurfaced, particularly as Jubilee elites sought resources to reward their large numbers of supporters. In the first years of the Jubilee coalition government, Ruto, in particular, was accused of involvement in widespread grand-corruption schemes to build constituencies that would be critical for his future campaigns (Herbling, 2018; Niba, 2020).

Alongside the prevalence of patterns and practices that had prevailed under the KANU government, the Jubilee coalition started the gradual process of recentralisation of power. Although the 2010 constitution had created decentralised institutions with resources devolved to county governments led by governors, acute conflicts arose between the central government and counties on the distribution of these resources. Pitting the governors against the central government, these resource conflicts involved the governors seeking to wrest fiscal power from the central government. By the end of Jubilee's first term, these conflicts remained a major source of county grievances and seemed to be impeding decentralisation (Cheeseman et al., 2016).

THE JUBILEE COALITION IN POWER: THE END OF THE DREAM? (2017–20)

The division of state institutions between factions of the Jubilee Alliance enabled the coalition to retain a sense of cohesion and common purpose. With the opposition parties consigned to the periphery, Kenyatta and Ruto formally dissolved their previous parties (The National Alliance and the United Republican Party) into a unified Jubilee Party in March 2016. Many observers hailed the merger, which also included a number of other minor parties, as the first step in the building of large national political parties based on identifiable ideologies and policies. But the party constitution gave sweeping powers to its leader, Kenyatta, with 'overall authority over the other officials and members of the party' (Langat, 2020). In the aftermath of the 2017 elections, these powers became a source of contention between Kenyatta and Ruto.

Although comfortable in their majorities, the Jubilee partners did not encourage credible and transparent electioneering processes in the lead-up to the August 2017 elections, which they claimed to have won by 54 per cent. The Supreme Court subsequently nullified the results, charging that the elections were characterised by the manipulation of the voting and counting processes. Although most observers hailed the nullification as the maturation of judicial independence in Kenya, the opposition boycotted the re-run of the elections in October 2017, calling for the overhaul of the electoral body before new elections (Nyabola, 2017).

After Jubilee's contested victory, violence broke out in opposition regions between security forces and protestors, ushering in renewed fears of escalation into full-blown civil war. Odinga's supporters threatened secession to redress political and economic marginalisation. Proponents of secession complained of the control of the presidency by the Kikuyu and the Kalenjin since independence, the perennial rigging of elections, socioeconomic marginalisation and extrajudicial killings (Burke, 2017; Mbaku, 2018). In an act of brinkmanship, Odinga rallied his supporters in Nairobi in February 2018 to inaugurate himself as 'the people's president'.

Amid a fresh cycle of violence, Kenyatta and Odinga met secretly in

March 2018 and agreed on a political truce. The two leaders negotiated secretly without consulting their followers, underscoring the personalisation of political alliances. As part of the truce, both sides set up a reconciliation body, the Building Bridges Initiative, to work out long-term measures to reduce ethnic tensions and foster reconciliation. From the outset, the Kenyatta-Odinga rapprochement appeared to be a temporary truce that would lower the political temperature and enable Odinga to save face after the tumultuous events sparked by the 2017 elections. In the two years following its establishment, however, Kenyatta and Odinga transformed the Building Bridges Initiative into a state-funded constitutional review commission to collect countrywide opinions on issues including ethnic antagonism, corruption and power devolution. In November 2019, the Building Bridges Initiative task force released a preliminary report with recommendations: the introduction of the position of prime minister in an effort to dilute presidential power, bigger budgets for the 47 counties to implement development schemes, a leaner and more representative cabinet, and privatisation of government services as a solution to rampant corruption (BBI Task Force, 2019).

Although critics charged that the Building Bridges Initiative recommendations merely regurgitated issues that previous government commissions had treated comprehensively (Gathara, 2019; Ghai, 2020), throughout 2020 the task force met as a constitution-making body to propose substantial amendments to refine its recommendations. In October 2020, the task force unveiled its new constitutional provisions, approved by the country through a referendum in April 2021. Except for a few changes, the proposed constitution mirrors some of the core power-sharing elements contained in the 2008 Kibaki-Odinga GNU. The key provision is the expansion of the executive branch to comprise a president, a deputy president, a prime minister and two deputy prime ministers to 'promote greater inclusivity, and mitigate the drawbacks of the winner-take-all electoral formula' (Mukami, 2020). Under this proposal, the president chooses a prime minister from the largest political party in parliament. The task force also proposed the retention of the current FPTP electoral system, including provisions where the people directly elect the president, who must obtain 50 per cent plus one of all votes cast, and 25 per cent in a majority of the country's 47 counties (Adamba, 2020).

President Kenyatta and his new partner Odinga touted the new constitutional proposals as the panacea for peace that would end political and election-related violence. The biggest loser in the Building Bridges Initiative process was Ruto, because Kenyatta used his vast powers in the Jubilee Party and the COVID-19 crisis to orchestrate the removal of Ruto's supporters from the Jubilee Party and the government (Gaitho, 2020). At the end of 2020, in anticipation of Kenyatta's support for Odinga to succeed him in the presidential elections of 2022, Ruto started to look for a new political party that would enable him to compete in those elections.

The new Kenyatta-Odinga partnership signalled the rearrangement of political loyalties in Kenya in predictable directions. As the latest iteration in political coalitions, it exhibits the instabilities of personality- and ethnic-based coalitions: founded on a handshake between the two leaders who ostensibly represent their ethnic groups, the coalition is set to essentially remain hostage to the idiosyncrasies and vicissitudes of the two leaders. In the words of Gaitho (2020), on the ever-changing coalitions in Kenya:

> The Uhuru-Ruto bromance faded after their [2017] electoral victory and with that the rationale for Jubilee to stick together as the latter's 2022 vehicle. In the meantime, Mr Kenyatta and Mr Odinga banded together, but there is little evidence that they have any higher goals beyond stopping Mr Ruto's ascent. The rapid creation and demolition of special purpose political vehicles has been the bane of Kenya.

In Kenya, coalitions are momentary vehicles to attain power rather than mechanisms for building enduring institutions of participation, accountability and legitimacy. If, as seems likely, the Jubilee Party collapses in the face of the acrimony between its leaders, it will be a cautionary tale about suspect sturdiness of coalitions in the absence of strong political parties.

CONCLUSION

Kenya has struggled to find functional political coalitions because of the persistence of weak political parties founded on strong personalities who often do not countenance internal democracy or solid organisational platforms. As opportunistic machines that seek power, most of these parties still have a long way to go in building constituencies beyond their narrow ethnic or regional domains.

Thus, the narrowness of political parties in their support bases mirrors the inability of the state to create common symbols of nationhood and belonging. In such a context, too, it is difficult for parties to create alliances or coalitions that are durable and can articulate programmes and policies that have national reach and resonance. The experiences of party coalitions and coalition governments reveal that in the absence of institutionalised and principled political parties, coalitions will remain brittle. There is *an urgent need for the growth of political parties as public institutions with broad-based membership and programmes,* but the existing elite- and ethnic-driven parties have no stake in such national encompassing political coalitions because they thrive on the persistence of ethnicity.

REFERENCES

Adamba, M. 21 October 2020. 'BBI Report: The arguments for and against', *The Standard*.

Ajulu, R. 2002. 'Politicised ethnicity, competitive politics, and conflict in Kenya: A historical perspective', *African Studies*, 61 (2), 251–268.

Anderson, D. 2003. 'Briefing: Kenya's elections 2002: The dawning of a new era?', *African Affairs*, 102 (407), 331–342.

Asingo, P. 2003. 'The political economy of transition in Kenya', in Oyugi, W., Wanyande, P. and Odhiambo-Mbai, C. (eds.) *The Politics of Transition from KANU to NARC*. Nairobi: Heinrich Böll Foundation.

Atieno-Odhiambo, E. S. 1987. 'The ideology of order and Kenyan politics', in Schatzberg, M. (ed.) *The Political Economy of Kenya*. Boulder, Col.: Praeger Publishers, 177–201.

Barkan, J. 1998. 'Toward a new constitutional framework in Kenya', *Africa Today*, 45 (2), 213–226.

Barkan. J. 2004. 'Kenya after Moi', *Foreign Affairs*, 83 (1), 87–100.

Branch, D. and Cheeseman, N. 2009. 'Democratization, sequencing, and state failure in Africa: Lessons from Kenya', *African Affairs,* 1089 (403), 1–26.

Building Bridges Initiative (BBI) Task Force. 2019. 'Building Bridges to a United Kenya: From a nation of blood ties to a nation of ideals'. A Report of the Presidential Task Force on Building Bridges to Unity. Nairobi.

Burke, J. 27 October 2017. 'Kenya election: Government accused of "genocide" against ethnic minorities', *The Guardian.*

Cheeseman, N., Lynch, G. and Willis, J. 2016. 'Decentralization in Kenya: The governance of governors', *Journal of Modern African Studies*, 54 (1), 1–35.

Cowen, M. and Kanyinga, K. 2000. 'The 1997 elections in Kenya: The politics of community and locality', in Cowen, M. and Laakso, L. (eds.) *The Politics of Multiparty Elections in Africa.* Oxford: James Currey.

Elischer, S. 2008. *Ethnic Coalitions of Convenience and Commitment: Political parties and party systems in Kenya*. Hamburg: German Institute of Global and Area Studies.

Gaitho, M. 22 April 2020. 'Now is not the time for political survival duels, but our survival', *Daily Nation.*

Gathara, P. 30 November 2019. 'Kenya's BBI Report is the political elite's attempt to rewrite history', *Al Jazeera.*

Ghai, J. C. 6 January 2020. 'Why BBI will not solve Kenya's problems', *Democracy in Africa.*

Gibson, C. and Long, J. 2009. 'The presidential and parliamentary elections in Kenya, December 2007', *Electoral Studies,* 28 (3), 497–502.

Githuku, N. 2013. 'Votes that Bind: Ethnic politics and the tyranny of numbers'. Institute of African Studies, Columbia University, New York.

Harbeson, J. 1998. 'Political crisis and renewal in Kenya: Prospects for democratic consolidation', *Africa Today,* 45 (2), 161–183.

Herbling, D. 22 August 2018. 'Kenya deputy leader seen as the most corrupt in survey', *Bloomberg News.*

Hornsby, C. 2012. Kenya: A history since independence. London: I. B. Taurus.

Horowitz, D. L. 1985. *Ethnic Groups in Conflict.* Berkeley: University of California Press.

Kabukuru, W. 8 January 2013. 'The ICC's long shadow over impending elections', *New African.*

Kagwanja, P. 2003. 'Facing Mount Kenya or facing Mecca? The Mungiki, ethnic violence and the politics of Moi succession in Kenya, 1987–2002', *African Affairs,* 102 (406), 25–49.

Kagwanja, P. 2009. 'Courting genocide: Populism, ethno-nationalism, and the informalization of violence in Kenya's 2008 elections', *Journal of Contemporary African Studies,* 27 (3), 365–387.

Kanyinga, K. 2011. 'Stopping a conflagration: The response of Kenyan civil society to the post-2007 election violence'. *Politikon*, 38 (1), 85 –109.

Kanyinga, K. and Long, J. 2012. 'The political economy of reforms in Kenya: The post-2007 election violence and a new constitution', *African Studies*

Review, 55 (1), 31–51.

Khadiagala, G. 2010. 'Political movements and coalition politics in Kenya: Entrenching ethnicity', *South African Journal of International Affairs*, 17 (1), 65–84.

Khadiagala, G. 2019. 'Persistent ethnic polarization in Kenya', in Carothers, T. and O'Donohue, A. (eds.) *Democracies Divided: The global challenge of political polarization.* Washington D. C.: The Brookings Press, 38–64.

Kitching, G. 1980. *Class and Economic Change in Kenya: The making of an African petite-bourgeoisie.* New Haven: Yale University Press.

Klopp, J. M. 2001. 'Ethnic clashes and the winning of elections: The case of Kenya's electoral despotism', *Canadian Journal of African Studies,* 35 (3), 473–517.

Kuperman, A. 2015. 'Designing constitutions to reduce domestic conflict', in Kuperman, A (ed.) *Constitutions and Conflict Management in Africa: Preventing civil war through institutional design.* Philadelphia: University of Pennsylvania Press, 1–26.

Langat, P. 22 April 2020. 'Ruto faces dilemma in renewed battle for grip on Jubilee Party', *Daily Nation*.

Leys, C. 1975. *Underdevelopment in Kenya: The political economy of neo-colonialism.* Berkeley: University of California Press.

Lindemayer, E. and Kaye, J. 2009. *A Choice for Peace? The story of forty-one days of mediation in Kenya.* New York: International Peace Institute.

Miguna, M. 2012. *Peeling Back the Mask: A quest for justice in Kenya.* Nairobi: Gilgamesh Africa.

Mueller, S. 2014. 'Kenya and the International Criminal Court (ICC): Politics, the election and the law', *Journal of Eastern African Studies,* 8 (9), 25–42.

Mukami, L. 21 October 2020. 'Kenya BBI Report: The key changes to Kenya's political system', *Daily Nation*.

Mutua, M. 2008. *Kenya's Quest for Democracy: Taming leviathan.* Boulder: Lynne Rienner.

Mbaku, J. M. 2018. *Foresight Africa Viewpoint. Elections in Africa in 2018: Lessons from Kenya's 2017 electoral experiences.* Washington D.C.: Brookings Institution.

Ndegwa, S. 1997. 'Citizenship and ethnicity: An examination of two transition moments in Kenyan politics', *American Political Science Review,* 91 (3), 599–611.

Ndegwa, S. 1998. 'The incomplete transition: The constitutional and electoral context in Kenya', *Africa Today,* 45 (2), 193–211.

Nderitu, A. W. 2018. *Kenya, Bridging Ethnic Divides: A commissioner's experience on cohesion and integration.* Nairobi: Mdahalo Publishing.

Ndii, D. 31 March 2016. 'Kenya is a cruel marriage', *Daily Nation*.

Ngunyi, M. 15 February 2013. 'The tyranny of numbers in Kenya's elections', *The Standard*.

Niba, W. 20 February 2020. 'William Ruto's presidential bid in peril after multi-billion arms procurement linked to his office', *Daily Nation*.

Nyabola, N. 2 September 2017. 'Why did Kenya's Supreme Court annul the elections?', *Al Jazeera*.

Nyangira, N. 1986. 'Ethnicity, class, and politics in Kenya', in Schatzberg, M. (ed.) *The Political Economy of Kenya*. New York: Praeger, 15–32.

Nyong'o, P. A. 1989. 'The disintegration of the nationalist coalition and the rise of presidential authoritarianism', *African Affairs*, 88 (351), 229–251.

Omolo, K. 2002. 'Political ethnicity in the democratisation process in Kenya', *African Studies*, 61 (2), 209–221.

Peters, R-M. 2001. 'Civil society and the election year 1997 in Kenya', in Grignon, F., Rutten, M. and Mazrui, A. (eds.) *Out For the Count: The 1997 general elections and prospects for democracy in Kenya*. Kampala: Fountain Publishers, 29–49.

Reilly, B. 2001. *Democracy in Divided Societies: Electoral engineering for conflict management*. London: Cambridge University Press.

Steeves, J. 2006. 'Presidential succession in Kenya: The transition from Moi to Kibaki', *Commonwealth and Comparative Politics*, 44 (2), 211–233.

Throup, D. and Hornsby, C. 1998. Multi-Party *Politics in Kenya: The Kenyatta and Moi states and the triumph of the system in the 1992 elections*. London: James Currey.

Wanyama, F. 2010. 'Voting without institutionalized political parties: Primaries, manifestos and the 2007 general elections in Kenya', in Kanyinga, K. and Okello, D. (eds.) *Tensions and Reversals in Democratic Transitions: The Kenya 2007 general elections*. Nairobi: Society for International Development, 61–100.

Wanyande, P. 2003. 'The politics of alliance building in Kenya: The search for opposition unity', in Oyugi, W., Wanyande, P. and Odhiambo-Mbai, C. (eds.) *The Politics of Transition from KANU to NARC*. Nairobi: Heinrich Böll Foundation.

Widner, J. 1992. T*he Rise of a Party-State in Kenya: From 'Harambee!' to 'Nyayo!'* Berkeley, C.A.: University of California Press.

Wolf, T. 2013. 'International justice versus public opinion: The ICC and ethnic polarization in the 2013 Kenya elections', *Journal of African Elections,* 12 (1), 143–177.

Wrong, M. 12 March 2013. 'Indictee for President!', *The New York Times*.

SEVEN

Coalition governments and unrelenting political instability in Lesotho, 2012–20

Motlamelle Kapa

Lesotho held three parliamentary elections, in 2012, 2015 and 2017, in which no party emerged an outright winner, thus forcing parties to form coalition governments. All three coalition governments collapsed before the end of their respective five-year constitutional terms. Why and how did this happen? Adopting a qualitative approach and using secondary sources, this chapter answers this question by reflecting on the recurrent trends in these coalitions. The core theme that emerges has implications for political stability.

Two further trends are discernible. First, there has been a vicious circle of conflicts between and within coalition partners that has caused the collapse of coalition governments within three years of the five-year parliamentary term, leading to snap elections, which in turn have produced hung parliaments and further rounds of conflicts and unstable coalition governments. Second is the use of politicised and polarised security institutions by politicians to fight political battles to stay in power and access state-generated rents within the context of the weak economic base of the country in which the state is the main source of economic survival and accumulation for the elite.

BACKGROUND TO THE COALITION PHENOMENON IN LESOTHO POLITICS

Lesotho has a history of post-election conflict caused by the refusal of losers in electoral contests to accept the outcome. The worst conflict was that of 1998, which took the country to the brink of civil war. Had South Africa and Botswana not intervened militarily, under the auspices of the Southern African Development Community (SADC), civil war might have erupted (Makoa, 2014: 103; Kapa, 2009: 4).

In response to the conflict, Lesotho instituted far-reaching but inconclusive constitutional and electoral reforms. The reforms led to the introduction in 2002 of the mixed-member proportional electoral system, replacing the first-past-the-post (FPTP) model, which tended to exclude some parties from parliament, even when they had a reasonable support base among the citizens (Kapa, 2009: 1). This is because the key principle in seat allocation under the FPTP is plurality of votes, rather than proportionality of votes to seats. To illustrate, in the 1993 polls, the winning Basutoland Congress Party achieved 74.7 per cent but swept all 65 parliamentary seats, leaving 25.3 per cent of the voters without representation by their political party of choice. In 1998, the Lesotho Congress for Democracy (LCD) received 60.7 per cent of the total votes but amassed 79 seats in the (now enlarged) parliament, while other parties had no parliamentary representation (Kapa, 2008: 346).

Following the implementation of the constitutional and electoral reforms in 2002, the new mixed-member proportional system was used and produced the outcome reflective of its spirit. For the first time, 10 parties got parliamentary representation, reflective of the principle of proportionality between party seats and votes. Unlike in all previous post-election periods, all parties accepted the outcome. The LCD won 79 FPTP seats and did not receive any proportional representation (PR) seats. The Lesotho People's Congress got five seats (FPTP and four

PR). All other parties shared the remaining 39 PR seats: the Basotho National Party (BNP) got 21; the National Independent Party got five; the Basutoland African Congress got three; the Basutoland Congress Party got three; and the Lesotho Workers Party, Marematlou Freedom Party, Popular Front for Democracy and National Progressive Party secured one seat each (see Matlosa, 2008: 29).

ALLIANCES AND COALITIONS IN LESOTHO: CONCEPTUAL CONSIDERATIONS

Lesotho has experienced both pre- and post-election political party collaboration since 2007. The emerging coalition studies literature in Africa regards collaborative arrangements formed before elections as alliances and those after as coalitions (see, for example, Kadima, 2014; Booysen, 2014; Kapa and Shale, 2014). Kadima (2014: 2) defines an alliance as 'the coming together of at least two political parties prior to an election in order to maximise their votes', while a coalition refers to 'the agreement of a minimum of two political parties to work together in parliament and/or in government on the basis of the election outcome'. This distinction also informs this chapter.

While the literature points to several motivations for coalition formation in different contexts, office-seeking and policy-seeking motives are dominant. The former refers to a situation where parties are aware that 'neither or none of them can win an election and govern on its own', thereby spurring them to get into coalition formation for purposes of sharing power and attendant material resources (Oyugi, 2006: 54). Riker (cited in Volden and Carrubba, 2004: 521) in his classical analysis identifies office-seeking as a political arrangement in which parties 'join governments in order to divide up the benefits of controlling the executive'. Parties also form coalitions not necessarily to be in government but to be in parliament in order to influence policy in their favour (Newton and Van Deth, 2005: 234).

Several types of coalitions are differentiated, and all have had application in Lesotho. Legislative coalitions consist of political parties that support ruling parties during legislative processes of voting and debates (Heywood, 2007: 288). An executive or cabinet coalition is a 'formal agreement between two or more parties that involves a cross-party distribution of ministerial portfolios' and is motivated by the need to ensure majority control of parliament (Heywood, 2007: 288). Cabinet coalitions emerge as a result of elections that produce hung parliaments. Cabinet coalitions have a challenge regarding the number of constitutive parties and the number of seats they bring into the arrangement. There is a need for individual parties to maximise gains of political spoils, on the one hand, and accumulate adequate seats for survival of the coalition itself, on the other. This dilemma produces coalitions based on the principle of the minimal winning coalition – the idea that a coalition must include only the parties needed to obtain a working majority 'since the spoils of office are fixed' (Geys et al., 2006: 958). As Geys et al. argue, the advantage of a minimal winning coalition is to reduce costs and time, given that the time to reach decisions tends to increase along with the number of parties involved.

There are also cases where parties form surplus majority or oversized coalitions. According to Volden and Carrubba (2004: 521), oversized or surplus majority coalitions are made up of parties that are not essential to a parliamentary majority. These are formed when three conditions exist: when the number and diversity of parties in the legislative chamber is large, when bills are hard to pass, and when legislation is costly or not clearly beneficial to coalition members (Volden and Carrubba, 2004: 522). The last type is a grand, or national, coalition, comprising all major parties, and tends to be formed only in times of national crises (Heywood, 2007: 88).

Lesotho has had multiple electoral alliances, and cabinet and legislative coalitions since it adopted the mixed member proportional electoral system. Lesotho's parties have been characterised by deep-seated rifts, with no realistic prospects for collaboration until facilitated by the constitutional and electoral reforms following the 1998 polls. The mixed member proportional system helped bring this change. After the 2012 elections, which produced the first hung parliament, the BNP, the LCP and the All Basotho Convention (ABC) hurriedly stitched together the country's first cabinet coalition. This was a typical minimal winning coalition with a majority of 61 out of the 120 seats. It was supported, at the beginning, by six other micro-parties that had a total of 10 seats, which in effect gave it the semblance of a legislative coalition ('Nyane, 2016: 183).

The 2015 elections again produced no outright winner, forcing the second coalition, this time between the Democratic Congress (DC) and six other parties (the LCD, the Popular Front for Democracy, the National Independent Party, the Marematlou Freedom Party, the Basutoland Congress Party and the Lesotho People's Congress) with a combined 65 parliamentary majority. The arrangement drifted from the minimal winning coalition logic in that the DC, the LCD and the Popular Front for Democracy could have formed a cabinet with their 61 seats. The choice of coalition partners related to both the desire to have a parliamentary majority, and ephemeral interparty opportunistic friendships and hostilities, established towards the end of the ABC-led coalition.

In the run-up to the 2017 elections, the DC and the ABC formed electoral alliances with other parties to maximise their electoral gains. The DC pact included the LCD and the Popular Front for Democracy. Under the arrangement, the DC and LCD did not field competing candidates in the constituencies where each of them had demonstrated relative strength in the 2015 elections. If one of them had been strong in a constituency, they fielded one common candidate in that constituency and encouraged their supporters to vote for this candidate. They also agreed not to field opposing candidates in the constituency where the leader of the Popular Front for Democracy stood, and all the supporters of the three parties were encouraged to vote for him (EISA, 2017: 19–20). The ABC, the BNP, the Alliance of Democrats and the Reformed Congress of Lesotho had a different arrangement. They agreed to contest elections separately, but form a cabinet coalition after elections (EISA, 2017: 21).

After the elections, which produced the fourth hung parliament, the ABC, the BNP, the Alliance of Democrats and the Reformed Congress of Lesotho formed the fourth cabinet coalition, with a parliamentary majority of 63 seats. The Lesotho system allows floor-crossing in parliament, and four DC members took this step, two to the Alliance of Democrats and two to the ABC. The defections increased the majority of the coalition to 67. However, the coalition collapsed after

Table 7.1: Lesotho's coalition governments, 2012–20

Period/Years	Sequence	Coalition partners
June 2012 to February 2015	First coalition	All Basotho Convention (ABC), Lesotho Congress for Democracy (LCD) & Basotho National Party (BNP)
April 2015 to May 2017	Second coalition	Democratic Congress (DC), Lesotho Congress for Democracy (LCD), Popular Front for Democracy (PFD), Marematlou Freedom Party (MFP), Basutoland Congress Party (BCP), National Independent Party (NIP) & Lesotho People's Congress (LPC)
August 2017 to May 2020	Third coalition	All Basotho Convention (ABC), Alliance of Democrats (AD), Basotho National Party (BNP) & Reformed Congress of Lesotho (RCL)
May 2020 to date (late 2020)	Fourth coalition (agreement was between ABC and DC but the two parties were allowed to bring in other parties, as reflected at right)	All Basotho Convention (ABC) (Basotho National Party & Reformed Congress of Lesotho), Democratic Congress (DC) (Movement for Economic Change & Popular Front for Democracy)

Source: Author's review based on the details in this chapter.

about three years due to conflicts within the ABC. This precipitated the formation of a grand coalition between one faction of the ABC with 33 seats (another faction with 18 seats joined later) and the DC. Other smaller parties joined under each of these big parties, resulting in an 87-seat-strong coalition (details of these coalitions are discussed below; an overview of the sequence of coalitions is shown in Table 7.1).

THE GENESIS OF POLITICAL PARTIES' COLLABORATION IN LESOTHO: PRE-2007 ELECTION ALLIANCES

This section sketches the beginnings of the collaboration of political parties in Lesotho in the run-up to the pre-2007 parliamentary elections. It highlights the composition of these groupings, their effect on the newly introduced mixed member proportional electoral system and political stability, the mediation efforts by internal and external actors, and the outcome thereof. Having realised the shortcomings in the country's electoral laws, Lesotho politicians formed electoral alliances that manipulated the mixed member proportional system by allowing them to access seats under the PR component, and turned the system into 'mixed member parallel' (as opposed to 'proportional'), beneficial to bigger parties while unfair to smaller ones. This led to conflict between the opposition parties and the government over allocation of the PR seats.

Lesotho has held nine parliamentary elections since the formation of modern political parties in the 1950s. Five of these (in 1965, 1970, 1993, 1998 and 2002) did not attract any form of cooperation among political parties. Instead, parties maintained acrimonious relations because of the country's weak economic base, with each seeking to access state-generated economic opportunities through state power. Matlosa (2017) rightly attributes the recurrent political instability in Lesotho to the underdeveloped and weak economy, with limited natural resources, leaving the state as the main avenue for economic survival and accumulation for the elite, who also use the military in their struggle for power.

However, following constitutional and electoral reforms, which introduced the mixed-member proportional electoral system in 2002, the past four elections (in 2007, 2012, 2015 and 2017) have seen Lesotho's political parties working together. In the run-up to the 2007 polls, nine parties formed alliances. These alliances were prompted by the new mixed-member proportional system (which embraces a proportionality principle that is not a feature of FPTP). Leaders of political parties saw the opportunity, through the PR component of the system, to secure additional seats in parliament (Kapa, 2008: 349). The outcome of the elections reflected the true spirit of the mixed member proportional system, but not the ambitions of the LCD. The LCD preferred the mixed-member parallel model, which would allow it to access the PR seats, and during its conference decided that the leadership should form alliances that would ensure access to the PR seats (see Kapa, 2017: 271). But it was not only the LCD that had this ambition; other parties also went ahead and formed pre-election alliances (see below). They 'manipulated the poorly drafted rules of the mixed electoral system' to maximise their gains in that 'supporters of the bigger parties were sensitised to use the PR ballot to vote for the smaller decoy parties and use the constituency ballot to vote for bigger parties' ('Nyane, 2016: 4). These parties submitted their PR lists containing the joint names of their respective memberships to the Electoral Commission. The LCD–National Independent Party alliance secured 21 PR seats, and the ABC/Lesotho Workers Party won 10 PR seats. In its allocation of seats, the Electoral Commission treated these alliances as separate entities from the parties forming them. The National Independent Party and the Lesotho Workers Party alliances thus got their own seats, separate from the LCD and the ABC (see Kapa, 2009).

In this way, parties undermined the spirit of the mixed-member proportional system and turned it into the mixed-member parallel system, which, just like the FPTP model, denied smaller parties parliamentary representation as assured through the mixed-member proportional system.

The difference between the two variants is captured by Gallagher (cited in Kapa, 2008: 247):

> The list seats are awarded to parties purely on the basis of their list votes, without taking any account of what happened in the constituencies. This benefits larger parties, which retain the over-representation they typically achieve in the constituencies, and offers less comfort for smaller ones than a compensatory system would do.

The application of the model in Lesotho had the outcome therefore of over-rewarding the bigger parties and punishing the smaller ones when it came to parliamentary representation. The final allocation of the PR seats is reflected in Table 7.2.

The smaller parties felt cheated by this arrangement. One of these parties, the Marematlou Freedom Party, took the Electoral Commission and the government to the High Court, seeking a reallocation of the PR seats, based on the spirit of the proportionality of the mixed system, as originally intended when Lesotho adopted it. The court ruled that the Marematlou Freedom Party had no locus standi (right to bring an action) in the case, and that the court itself had no jurisdiction over the case. It was a protracted case that did not solve the dispute. External mediation efforts by the Southern African Development Community were futile. The ruling LCD refused to cooperate with the regional body on the matter (Kapa, 2009: 6–7).

The result was general political instability marked by nationwide stayaway protest actions called by the opposition, combining with efforts by the country's civil society to mediate. The outcome of the mediation was the reform in 2011 of the electoral law, especially concerning electoral alliances and how the PR seats should be allocated (Kapa, 2017: 281).

FORMATION, SURVIVAL AND STABILITY OF THE FIRST COALITION GOVERNMENT, 2012–14

The 2012 polls produced Lesotho's first hung parliament and the first executive coalition. The coalition faced political and security crises that were caused by a power struggle between the prime minister and his deputy, leading to the collapse of the government and a snap election in 2015. The government encountered several challenges, and collapsed before the end of its five-year constitutional term. The first challenge was the coalition agreement itself. According to Sejanamane (2016: 289), the agreement allowed the coalition partners to implement a 'semi-feudal' arrangement in which they 'shared government ministries' rather than keeping the government as one entity under the overall authority of the prime minister. Sejanamane (2016: 289) observes that these parties had agreed to divide the government into three parts, with each party controlling the ministries allocated to it and also having exclusive rights to appoint senior staff in these ministries. He also observes that the coalition agreement, which was 'a political arrangement', was 'elevated to a legal document', leading the deputy prime minister to challenge the constitutional powers of the prime minister on the basis that those powers were not consistent

Table 7.2: Consolidated Lesotho election results, 2007–17

Party/Alliance	Total party votes		Party seats			
			FPTP		PR	
	2007	2012	2007	2012	2007	2012
All Basotho Convention (ABC)	0	138,917	17	26	0	4
Alliance of Congress Parties (ACP)	20,263	-	0	-	1	-
Basotho Batho Democratic Party (BBDP)	8,474	2,440	0	0	1	1
Basotho Congress Party (BCP)	9,823	2,531	0	0	1	1
Basotho Democratic National Party (BDNP)	8,783	3,433	0	0	1	1
Basotho National Party (BNP)	29,965	23,788	0	0	3	5
Democratic Congress (DC)	-	218,366	-	41	-	7
Lesotho Congress for Democracy (LCD)	0	121,076	62	12	0	14
Lesotho People's Congress (LPC)	-	5,021	-	0	-	1
Lesotho Workers Party (LWP)	107,463	2,408	0	0	10	1
Marematlou Freedom Party (MFP)	9,129	3,300	0	0	1	1
National Independent Party (NIP)	229,602	6,880	0	0	21	2
Popular Front for Democracy (PFD)	15,477	11,166	0	1	1	2
New Lesotho Freedom Party (NLFP)	3,984	-	0	-	0	-
Others	-	12,400	-	0	-	0
Total	442,963	551,726	80	80	40	40

Table continues on facing page

with the coalition agreement. Although Sejanamane's observation is accurate, the parties probably had limited time to draft the coalition agreement, given that they had just two weeks after elections to form a government, in terms of the country's national constitution.

Another challenge was the loss of parliamentary majority when two of the ABC MPs, for Koro-Koro (Thabiso Litšiba) and Stadium Area (Mophato Monyake), crossed the floor in May 2014. Litšiba had been hoping to be appointed to the cabinet, and when this did not happen, he defected to the opposition DC; Monyake was not happy to

Table 7.2: Consolidated Lesotho election results, 2007–17 (cont.)

Party/Alliance	Total party seats (FPTP + PR)		% of party votes	
	2007	2012	2007	2012
All Basotho Convention (ABC)	17	30	0.0	25.2
Alliance of Congress Parties (ACP)	2	-	4.57	-
Basotho Batho Democratic Party (BBDP)	1	1	1.91	0.44
Basotho Congress Party (BCP)	1	1	2.22	0.46
Basotho Democratic National Party (BDNP)	1	1	1.98	0.62
Basotho National Party (BNP)	3	5	6.76	4.31
Democratic Congress (DC)	-	48	-	39.6
Lesotho Congress for Democracy (LCD)	62	26	0.0	21.9
Lesotho People's Congress (LPC)	-	1	-	0.91
Lesotho Workers Party (LWP)	10	1	24.26	0.44
Maremaltou Freedom Party (MFP)	1	1	2.06	0.60
National Independent Party (NIP)	21	2	51.83	1.25
Popular Front for Democracy (PFD)	1	3	3.49	2.02
New Lesotho Freedom Party (NLFP)	0	-	0.90	-
Others	-	0	-	2.00
Total	120	120	100	100

Table continues overleaf

have been fired from his ministerial position (Letsie, 2015: 92). These defections exposed the coalition to the threat common to minimal winning coalitions: it reduced the parliamentary majority from 61 to 59 seats. The problems of the coalition emanated from within the ABC as a party, rather than from other coalition partners, a development that the proponents of the minimal winning coalition may not have anticipated.

The third challenge was the deep polarisation and instability within and between state institutions due to politicisation – 'the substitution of political criteria for merit-based criteria in the selection, retention,

Table 7.2: Consolidated Lesotho election results, 2007–17 (cont.)

Party/Alliance	Total party votes		Party seats			
			FPTP		PR	
	2015	2017	2015	2017	2015	2017
All Basotho Convention (ABC)	215,022	235,729	40	47	6	1
Alliance of Democrats (AD)	-	42,686	-	1	-	8
Basutoland Congress Party (BCP)	2,721	3,458	0	0	1	1
Basotho National Party (BNP)	31,508	23,541	1	0	6	5
Democratic Congress (DC)	218,573	150,172	37	26	10	4
Democratic Party of Lesotho (DPL)	-	2,801	-		-	1
Lesotho Congress for Democracy (LCD)	56,467	52,052	2	1	10	10
Lesotho People's Congress (LPC)	1,951	2,364	0	0	1	0
Movement for Economic Change (MEC)	-	29,420	-	1	-	5
Marematlou Freedom Party (MP)	3,413	2,761	0	0	1	1
National Independent Party (NIP)	5,404	6,375	0	0	1	1
Popular Front for Democracy (PFC)	9,829	13,200	0	1	2	2
Reformed Congress of Lesotho (RCL)	6,731	4,037	0	0	2	1
Others	12,353	13,096	0		0	
Total	563,972	581,692	80	*77	40	40

Table continues on facing page

promotion, rewards, and disciplining of members of public service' (Peters and Pierre, 2004: 2). The process of politicisation was a product of what was about to become a one-party-dominant system under the LCD (from 1998 to 2002), and did not stop even after the party underwent five splits due to internal power struggles. Figure 7.1 depicts these splinter parties and the years of their formation.

The LCD's dominance led to heavy politicisation of the public service through its appointing and promoting of its loyalists into strategic positions in the public service, military, police and judiciary. The appointments and promotions were not based on any merit-based processes, but rather on political affiliation to the party. The

Table 7.2: Consolidated Lesotho election results, 2007–17 (cont.)

Party/Alliance	Total party seats (FPTP + PR)		% of party votes	
	2015	2017	2015	2017
All Basotho Convention (ABC)	46	48	38.13	40.52
Alliance of Democrats (AD)	-	9	-	7.34
Basutoland Congress Party (BCP)	1	1	0.48	0.59
Basotho National Party (BNP)	7	5	5.59	4.05
Democratic Congress (DC)	47	30	38.78	25.82
Democratic Party of Lesotho (DPL)	-		-	
Lesotho Congress for Democracy (LCD)	12	11	10.01	8.95
Lesotho People's Congress (LPC)	1	0	0.35	0.41
Movement for Economic Change (MEC)	-	6	-	5.06
Marematlou Freedom Party (MP)	1	1	0.61	0.47
National Independent Party (NIP)	1	1	0.96	1.10
Popular Front for Democracy (PFC)	2	3	1.74	2.27
Reformed Congress of Lesotho (RCL)	2	1	1.19	0.69
Others	0		2.19	2.65
Total	120	*117	100	100

* The number of FPTP and total seats (FPTP+PR) does not add up to the actual totals of 80 and 120 because of failed elections in three constituencies (Teyateyaneng, Hololo and Thupa-kubu) due to the death of candidates before elections; the elections in these constituencies were won by the ABC, which had a total of 51 seats.

Source: Adapted from EISA website.

constitutional and legal framework of Lesotho empowers the prime minister to (alone and/or through mandatory advice to the king, without any process of transparent and competitive recruitment) appoint the heads of key state institutions (Rakolobe and Kapa, 2018)

CRACKS IN THE CABINET COALITION AND THE MILITARY'S 2014 INTRUSION

The process of politicisation deepened under the coalition governments, with each incoming government seeking to replace public servants appointed by its predecessor (see Rakolobe, 2019: 8). The 2012 coalition government inherited highly politicised public institutions, leading to mutual distrust between the officials (who owe allegiance to the regime that appointed them) and the incoming political masters; massive attempted (and in some cases successful) removals of these officials; unprecedented polarisation and instability between and within public institutions, especially the army and the police, as well as the political system as a whole; and ultimately open confrontation between the prime minister (also the leader of the leading party in the coalition, the ABC) and the deputy prime minister (also the leader of the second party, the LCD) (Kapa, 2019: 60).

Public disagreements between the prime minister and his deputy exposed widening cracks in the coalition, leading to the LCD forming an alternative coalition with the DC in June 2014, and planning to pass a motion of no confidence in the prime minister and the government. The prime minister reacted by invoking constitutional clauses to advise the king to prorogue parliament in order to avert the impending no-confidence motion.

The threats to the survival of the coalition government reached a climax when, on 29 August 2014, the prime minister attempted to remove from office the commander of the Lesotho Defence Force, Lieutenant-General Tlali Kamoli, and replace him with Brigadier Maaparankoe Mahao. Kamoli defied the prime minister, arguing that the prime minister had been ill-advised; he refused to leave office. The deputy prime minister vetoed the decision and announced on national television and radio that the commander had not been dismissed, arguing that the prime minister had not consulted him when taking the decision to dismiss Kamoli (Kapa, 2019: 64). The deputy prime minister was backed by his party's newfound ally, the DC.

The position of both the deputy prime minister and the DC arguably emboldened Kamoli and those close to him in the army to

Figure 7.1. Parties that broke away from the LCD

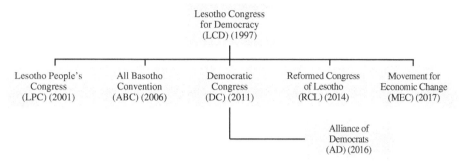

Source: Author's conceptualisation based on details in this chapter.

carry out military raids, on the night of 30 August 2014, against the Lesotho Mounted Police Service headquarters and some of its stations in Maseru, on the grounds that the Mounted Police Service was planning to arm some members of the ABC to attack members of the LCD and the DC. The army also raided the official residence of the prime minister, and the residences of the leader of the BNP and Mahao (Sejanamane, 2016: 293). The raids led to the killing of a police sub-inspector, Mokheseng Ramahloko (while on duty at the headquarters); and the flight to South Africa of (among others) the prime minister and the BNP leader, the commissioner of police, the newly appointed Lesotho Defence Force commander Maaparankoe Mahao, all of whom returned, under South African security detail, following mediation by the Southern African Development Community (Kapa, 2019: 65).

The intrusion of the military into politics had far-reaching consequences. It added a security dimension to a political crisis and ended prospects for a political settlement of the conflict between the prime minister and his deputy. The power struggle between these two shifted the crises 'from the political sphere into the security sphere, and could not be resolved easily in the political sphere' (Sejanamane, 2016: 292). Sejanamane further shows that there were two centres of power, both in the government (prime minister and deputy prime minister) and in the army (Kamoli and Mahao). The military raids intensified political instability and deepened polarisation between the army and the police service, paralysing the latter for some days. According to Ntaote (2014), the then acting commissioner of police, Masupha Masupha, described the police as 'psychologically traumatised' due to fearing 'ambush while on duty'.

Ultimately, the Southern African Development Community mandated the then South African deputy president, Cyril Ramaphosa, to mediate in the crisis. The key outcomes of the mediation were the Maseru Facilitation Declaration 2014, signed by all political leaders and committing to, among other things, holding an early election, in February 2015; and the Maseru Security Accord 2014, signed by three security bosses, the 'two commanders' of the Lesotho Defence Force, Kamoli and Mahao, and the commissioner of police, Khothatso Tšooana, to proceed on special leave of absence outside Lesotho until after the elections (Sejanamane, 2016: 295).

The main challenges of Lesotho's cabinet coalition, which led to its collapse (and the subsequent 2015 poll) were the power struggle between the prime minister and his deputy. The pre-2015 election period attracted attention from the Southern African Development Community and other external actors, due to the high levels of instability and the military appropriating political space (Booysen, 2015). The Electoral Commission was under pressure to deliver successful elections within a short time, and ultimately coped, for there were no serious complaints about the process. The media were as polarised as the nation along political party lines in reporting electoral processes. Political parties campaigned in a tense and volatile environment (Kapa, 2019: 66). Due to the general atmosphere of insecurity and Prime Minister Thomas Thabane's concerns about the partisan stance of the military, Ramaphosa and his mediation team resolved to confine military personnel to barracks and allowed only helicopter pilots to deliver election material to places difficult to reach (Sejanamane, 2016: 295).

THE SECOND COALITION, THE POST-2015-POLL GOVERNMENT AND THE UNRELENTING SECURITY CRISIS

The 2015 electoral outcome again produced no outright winner, forcing the second coalition, this time between the DC and LCD with five other micro-parties (the Basutoland Congress Party, the National Independent Party, the Marematlou Freedom Party, the Popular Front for Democracy and the Lesotho People's Congress) that had achieved one seat each. The inclusion of the four small parties in the coalition (when the DC, LCD and Popular Front for Democracy had 61 seats, sufficient to form a government) was a safeguard against a loss of majority through defections, as had happened after the 2012 elections when the cabinet coalition ran into trouble. Such action could again precipitate the collapse of government.

The elections resolved the legitimacy crises of the post-2012 government, but not the recurring security crises. According to Matlosa (2017: 179), the Southern African Development Community did not address the security crises, opting instead for the easier option of a snap election, and ignoring the deep-rooted structural and institutional factors that had triggered the crises. The decision to call snap elections postponed the crises, which recurred under the new government. Sejanamane (2016: 295) describes the 2015 polls as having taken place in a 'security vacuum' in which foreign forces secured the prime minister 'to protect him from his own military', and indicates that this 'was hardly a sign of a political crisis; it was clearly a security issue that would persist beyond the elections'. The government failed to resolve the security crises because it allowed the politically partisan military under Lieutenant-General Kamoli to perpetrate violence against those who opposed it. As Sejanamane (2017: 4) describes it, the regime was 'a front for the military which ruled'. The country was probably saved from any ensuing security crises by the collapse of the coalition, due to internal power struggles within the DC as the main party in the coalition.

Immediately after assuming office in March 2015, the coalition government reversed key public service appointments made by its predecessor, in the process also perpetuating the politicisation and reinforcing the instability of the public service and the political system. It took the following actions: it demoted Lieutenant-General Mahao to his old rank of brigadier and removed him from the position of commander of the Lesotho Defence Force on the grounds that both his promotion and his appointment were illegal; it reinstated Kamoli as the commander of the Lesotho Defence Force, arguing that his removal had been illegal; it dismissed the commissioner of police, Khothatso Tšooana; and it purged all principal secretaries and district administrators appointed by the predecessor government, and replaced them with its own loyalists (Rakolobe, 2019: 9).

The government also allowed Kamoli to be vengeful with his perceived enemies in the army. About 60 Lesotho Defence Force members whom Kamoli's command suspected of being loyal to Mahao were detained, tortured and court-martialled for alleged mutiny. Elements of the Lesotho Defence Force ambushed and assassinated Mahao in June 2015 (Sejanamane, 2016: 299). This assassination forced the government to solicit assistance from the Southern African Development Community to establish a commission of inquiry to investigate the circumstances surrounding it and make appropriate recommendations. The commission recommended that the government of Lesotho remove Kamoli as Lesotho Defence Force commander, suspend all Lesotho Defence Force members implicated in cases of murder, facilitate the return of all exiled Basotho, and provide security for political leaders in exile. It took substantial pressure, internal and external, for the government to act on these recommendations (Sejanamane, 2016: 299). After much pressure on government, Kamoli was removed in December 2016 and charged with various offences, including for the murders of Mahao and sub-inspector Mokheseng of the Lesotho Mounted Police Service.

The coalition government did not finish its term due to internal conflict within the DC, rather than any interparty conflicts, as was the case with the 2012 coalition. Mosisili, who had been a leader of the DC for 18 years, was scheduled to retire. Mosisili's deputy in the party, Monyane Moleleki, would ordinarily have been the successor but was not Mosisili's choice. This triggered a protracted power struggle and division of the DC into two factions. One, composed of the majority of the national executive committee and the youth league of the party, sided with Moleleki; the other, which included the women's league committee, supported Mosisili (Matlosa, 2017: 154).

The bitter factional leadership contest peaked when on 10 November 2016 the pro-Moleleki DC national executive committee sought to withdraw the party from the coalition government, citing the failure of the government to unite the politically polarised nation, along with nepotism, corruption and deteriorating relations with development partners. Mosisili challenged this resolution, arguing that the national executive committee had no powers, in terms of the party's constitution, to withdraw the party from the coalition government. The national executive committee suspended him for his stance, but he retaliated by also suspending the 10 members of the national executive committee, including Moleleki. Mosisili sued the national executive committee for suspending him and won the case, leading to Moleleki and his supporters in the national executive committee forming a new party, the Alliance of Democrats, and crossing the floor in parliament (Matlosa, 2017: 156). With the support of the ABC, the BNP and the Reformed Congress of Lesotho, Moleleki's Alliance of Democrats successfully pushed through parliament an unprecedented motion of no confidence against Prime Minister Mosisili and the government on 1 March 2017 (*The Post*, 2017). In response, Mosisili used his constitutional powers to advise King Letsie III to dissolve parliament and call an election – the third in a five-year period. Being a constitutional monarch, the king accepted the advice, effectively ending the life of parliament and getting the country to prepare for elections on 3 June 2017 (Ntsukunyane, 2017).

THE 2017 POLLS AND POST-POLL GOVERNMENT REINVENTING INSTABILITY

The volatility and instability of coalition government did not subside after the 2017 election. The results of the election produced yet another hung parliament (see Table 7.2). The results also reflect the performances of new parties, the Movement for Economic Change and Democratic Party of Lesotho. Many others also emerged in the run-up to the elections, but registered insignificant performances.

The post-2017 election coalition of the ABC, the BNP, the Alliance of Democrats and the Reformed Congress of Lesotho was threatened from the onset by persistent security crises and internal conflicts within the ABC, which led to the coalition's collapse on 11 May 2020. Security crises abated with time, as heads of security agencies steered away from party politics and left politicians to deal with their own political problems. This left ABC intraparty conflicts as the sole factor threatening the survival of the coalition government – until it led to the collapse of the government. I highlight the effects of these two factors on the stability of the government below.

Security crises became entrenched. The key indicators of these crises were polarisation, instability and indiscipline in the army, such that even after Kamoli left office, his successor, Lieutenant-General Khoantle Motšomotšo, was assassinated in his office, allegedly by Brigadier Bulane Sechele and Colonel Tefo Hashatsi, allegedly for selling them out to the police by agreeing to cooperate with the police in handing over members of the army who had criminal cases, reversing the position that had been taken by Kamoli (Muzofa, 2017). Sechele and Hashatsi were also immediately shot dead, allegedly by Motšomotšo's bodyguards. Other implicated members of the Lesotho Defence Force were, at the time of writing, still in custody pending finalisation of their cases.

The ABC had an internal conflict caused by the election of Professor Nqosa Mahao as the deputy leader during the party's elective conference of February 2019. The party was divided into two factions, one supporting Mahao and the other the party leader, Thomas Thabane, and those close to him. The Thabane faction rejected Mahao's candidacy, alleging that he did not qualify for nomination based on the party's constitution. The matter was settled by the Court of Appeal, which ruled that Mahao was eligible for elections (*Korokoro Constituency Committee vs Executive Committee of the ABC*).

The rift between the two factions persisted, widened and became manifest in four ways. First, the pro-Mahao faction of the ABC MPs voted with the opposition over the government's new regulations prohibiting wool and mohair farmers from exporting their produce, forcing them to sell locally to a Chinese businessman at prices lower than they were getting before (Phakela, 2019). The move exposed the fragility and instability of the government.

Second, the ABC national executive committee (dominated by supporters of Mahao) and the opposition supported the commissioner of police in his move to have the prime minister and his wife appear before the courts to answer a charge of murder of the prime minister's second wife. The Lesotho Mounted Police Service commissioner and his deputy had been pushing for the two to appear before the courts of law. In response, the prime minister attempted to suspend the commissioner from his position, but he lost the court case in which the commissioner challenged the move (Kabi, 2020: 4).

Third, the Mahao-led faction of the ABC, with the DC, the BNP and the Popular Front for Democracy, condemned the prime minister and called on him to leave office for destabilising security forces by attempting to fire the commissioner of police and planning to fire the commander of the army for refusing to help remove the commissioner of police from office (Kabi, 2020). The prime minister had attempted for the second time to suspend the commissioner of police on 17 April 2020. The latter sought a court order to block this suspension until the case was heard in court. Thus, the army was seen surrounding the Lesotho Mounted Police Service headquarters and stations in Maseru on 18 April 2020, but withdrew the same day (Kabi, 2020: 4). The security forces appeared united in resisting the prime minister's interference in their daily operations. They succeeded in steering away from the faction fights of the ABC.

Last, the ABC national executive committee and DC formed a new grand coalition and submitted an agreement to that effect to parliament on 11 May 2020, supported by other parties (Rapapa and Letsoasa, 2020; ABC and DC, 2020). The agreement excluded the LCD and the Alliance of Democrats, both of which preferred a government of national unity to the grand coalition.

The arrangement forced the Thabane-led government to resign – and the new coalition of the ABC and the DC to take over. The ABC co-opted the BNP and the Reformed Congress of Lesotho, while the

DC invited the Movement for Economic Change and the Popular Front for Democracy.

Dr Moeketsi Majoro (MP for the ABC) and Mathibeli Mokhothu (leader of the DC) took over as prime minister and deputy prime minister, respectively, in terms of their agreement. The parties shared ministerial positions in proportion to their share of parliamentary seats. The ABC gave ministerial positions to the leaders of the BNP and the Reformed Congress of Lesotho, and a deputy minister post to the deputy leader of the BNP. The DC shared two of its ministerial posts with the leaders of the Popular Front for Democracy and the Movement for Economic Change. The rest of the parties in parliament at the time pledged legislative support to the coalition, giving it a majority of 87 seats and making it less fragile than its predecessors. The coalition assured the six coalescing parties access to state resources, both at the time and during the then forthcoming election campaign period, factors that could enhance their electoral performance come the 2022 election.

The prime minister was not ready to leave office before 31 July 2020, as per his own statement, and could arguably have advised the king to dissolve parliament due to the pressure he found himself under. But parliament passed the Ninth Amendment to the Constitution Act, 2020, which bars the prime minister from advising the king to dissolve parliament unless he obtains the majority support of the MPs. Previously the prime minister had two options when a vote of no confidence was passed on his government: resign from his office within three days after the passing of the vote, or advise the king to dissolve parliament. The Ninth Amendment to the Constitution Act gives the prime minister one option only: resign from the office of prime minister. It also led to a change of government without an election and stabilised parliament for its five-year term.

CONCLUSION

This chapter has shown that throughout the periods of the three coalition governments, common trends which adversely affected the political stability of Lesotho are discernible. Perennial interparty and intraparty conflicts have led to party splits and parliamentary floor-crossing, resulting in the collapse of governments and early elections. The elections have in turn produced hung parliaments, forcing unstable coalition governments amid political and security crises. In addition, politicisation and polarisation of security institutions have been exacerbated through all coalition periods, intensifying political instability and aiding the collapse of the past two governments. Politicians have used politicised security institutions to fight their political battles in a quest to stay in power and have access to economic benefits, within the context of the weak economic base of the country, in which the state is the main source of accumulation.

The general national consensus is that the way out of recurrent political and security crises is comprehensive constitutional and institutional reforms that have the potential to professionalise politicised public institutions (including the army and the police), and promote and protect long-term political stability, national unity and reconciliation (Government of the Kingdom of Lesotho, n.d). However, it remains to be seen if the reforms will indeed produce these outcomes, or whether politicians will once again find a way to circumvent new attempts at regulation and stabilisation.

REFERENCES

All Basotho Convention (ABC) and Democratic Congress (DC). 2020. 'The Coalition Agreement for Restoration of rule of law, Implementation of National Reforms Programme and Stimulation of Economic Growth'. Maseru.

Booysen, S. 2014. 'Causes and impact of party alliances on the party system and national cohesion in South Africa', *Journal of African Elections,* 13 (1), 66–92.

Booysen, S. 2015. 'Lesotho's parliamentary elections of May 2015', *Electoral Studies,* 40, 430–433.

Electoral Institute for Sustainable Democracy in Africa (EISA). 2017.

'National Assembly Elections, 3 June'. EISA Election Observer Mission Report No. 56, EISA, Johannesburg.

Geys, B., Heyndels, B. and Vermeir, J. 2006. 'Explaining the formation of minimal coalitions: Anti-system parties and anti-pact rules', *European Journal of Political Research*, 45 (1), 957–984.

Government of the Kingdom of Lesotho (n.d). *The Lesotho We Want: Dialogue and reforms for national transformation: Vision, overview and roadmap*, Maseru.

Heywood, A. 2007. *Politics*. Houndsmill: Palgrave Macmillan.

Kabi, P. 23–29 April 2020. 'Army chief defied orders to arrest me: Molibeli', *Lesotho Times*.

Kabi, P. 25 April 2020. 'Political parties attack Thabane over army deployment', *Lesotho Times*, https://lestimes.com/political-parties-attack-thabane-over-army-deployment/, accessed 15 May 2020.

Kadima, D. 2014. 'An introduction the politics of party alliances and coalitions in socially divided Africa', *Journal of African Elections*, 13 (1), 1–24.

Kapa, M. A. 2008. 'The politics of coalition formation and democracy in Lesotho', *Politikon: South African Journal of Political Studies,* 35 (3), 339–356.

Kapa, M. A. 2009. 'The case of Lesotho's mixed member proportional system', *Africa Insight*, 39 (3), 1–10.

Kapa, M. A. 2017. 'The role of civil society in conflict situation in Sub-Saharan Africa: A case study of Lesotho', in Berhanu, K. and Chimanikiri, D. P. (eds.) *The Roles of Civil Society in Conflict Management and Peace Building in Eastern and Southern Africa*. Addis Ababa: Organisation for Social Science Research in Eastern and Southern Africa.

Kapa, M. A. 2019. 'Lesotho 2015 polls and political stability: Challenges and prospects for the future', in Rupiya, M. R., Teffo, L., Gutto, S. and Grey, R. (eds.) *The Challenges of Political Succession & Elections in Africa*. Pretoria: UNISA Press.

Kapa, M. A. and Shale, V. 2014. 'Alliances, coalitions and political system in Lesotho: 2007–2012', *Journal of African Elections,* 13 (1), 93–114.

Koro-koro Constituency Committee vs Executive Committee of the ABC, Co f A (CIV) No. 10 of 2019. https://lesotholii.org/courtnames/court-of-appeal/2019, accessed 20 April 2020.

Letsie, T. W. 2015. 'Lesotho's February 2015 elections: A prescription that never cured the sickness', *Journal of African Elections*, 14 (2), 81–109.

Makoa, F. K. 2014. 'Beyond the electoral triumphalism. Reflections on Lesotho's coalition government and challenges'. *Strategic Review for Southern Africa*, 36 (1), 100–110.

Matlosa, K. 2008. 'The 2007 general election in Lesotho: Managing the post-election conflict', *Journal of African Elections*, 7 (1), 20–49.

Matlosa, K. 2017. 'Understanding political crises of Lesotho's post-2015 elections', in Thabane, M. (ed.) *Towards Anatomy of Persistent Political Instability in Lesotho, 1966–2016*. Roma: National University of Lesotho, 130–159.

Newton, K. and Van Deth, C. J. 2005. *Foundations of Comparative Politics*. Cambridge: Cambridge University Press.

Ntsukunyane, L. 10 March 2017. 'King backed himself into a corner', *Lesotho Times*, http://lestimes.com/king-backed-himself-into-a-corner/, accessed 28 April 2020.

Ntaote, B. 16 November 2014. 'Police still traumatised by army raid', *Sunday Express*, https://sundayexpress.co.ls/police-still-traumatised-by-army-raid/, accessed 29 April 2020.

Muzofa, N. 5 September 2017. 'Motšomotšo shot dead', *Lesotho Times*, http://lestimes.com/motsomotso-shot-dead/, accessed 29 April 2020.

'Nyane, H. 2016. 'Formation of a government in Lesotho in the case of hung parliament', *Law, Democracy and Development*, 20, https://www.ajol/index.php/ldd/issue/view/14538.online, accessed 28 April 2020.

Oyugi, O. W. 2006. 'Coalition politics and coalition governments in Africa', *Journal of Contemporary African Studies*, 24 (1), 53–79.

Phakela, M. 2019. 'Government appeals against wool and mohair ruling', *Lesotho Times*, http://lestimes.com/govt-appeals-against-wool-and-mohair-ruling/, accessed 29 April 2020.

Peters, B. G. and Pierre, J. 2004. 'Politicization of the civil service: concepts, causes, consequences', in Peters, B. G. and Pierre, J. (eds.), *Politicization of the Civil Service in Comparative Perspective: The quest for control*. London: Routledge, 1–14.

Rakolobe, M. 2019. 'Politicised public service and corruption in Lesotho', *Strategic Review for Southern Africa*, 41 (1), https://www.thepost.co.ls/local-news/mosisili-loses-confidence-vote/, accessed 28 April 2020.

Rakolobe, M. and Kapa, M. A. 2018. 'Politicised public service, coalition politics and instability in Lesotho', *Journal of Public Policy in Africa*, 6 (1), 40–50.

Rapapa, T. and Letsoasa, M. 2020. 'Configuration of ABC/DC coalition'. Letter to the Speaker of the National Assembly of Lesotho (Rapapa on behalf of the ABC; Letsoasa on behalf of the DC).

Sejanamane, M. 2016. 'Lesotho's 2015 elections in the context of security vacuum', *African Security Review*, 25 (3), 288–305.

Sejanamane, M. 2017. *Struggle Against Impunity in Lesotho*. Morija: Morija Printing Works.

The Post, 3 March 2017. 'Mosisili loses confidence vote', https://www.thepost.co.ls/local-news/mosisili-loses-confidence-vote/, accessed 28 April 2020.

Volden, C. and Carrubba, C. J. 2004. 'The formation of oversized coalitions in parliamentary democracies', *American Journal of Political Science*, 48 (3), 521–537.

EIGHT

Political parties, alliance politics and the crisis of governance in Malawi

NANDINI PATEL

THE FORMATION AND OPERATION of party alliances have had a far-reaching impact on governance in Malawi. Party alliances have been used as a vehicle to subvert or circumvent the constitution and violate the rule of law, actions that have been driven by purely personal political agendas. The point is evident in issues like the attempt to extend the presidential-term limit, and crucial amendments to the constitution, including the repeal of the section on the senate, and the repeal of the provision on the recall of elected MPs by constituents for reasons such as non-performance. These amendments were carried out by incumbents, with the help of opposition party alliance partners.

From the time that Malawi embarked on multiparty politics in 1994 to the present there has been only one instance, in 2009, that a single party could win a majority in the legislature. Even then, the achievement was countered by the fact that the party that won the presidency did not garner numbers in parliament. This necessitated parties in parliament to align. There have been serial pre- and post-electoral alliances, for the presidency and the national assembly. These alliances have not been based on ideology or broad consensus; instead, they have been constructed by the party leader and the inner circles of party influence. Alliances to enjoy the spoils of office have also been formed, without regard for policies or national development.

Along with Malawi's practice of the presidential system of government, the principle focus of pre-electoral alliances in Malawi has been on the presidency, with a lesser focus on parliament. The executive has been able to govern without legislative support. Because the president is directly elected for a fixed term of office, s/he will be able to form the government and stay in power (even if s/he loses support in the ranks of the MPs) unless impeached. In this context, the executive has resorted to collusive ways of inducting opposition leaders and members into government, in particular those who enter parliament through interparty alliances. Lack of legislation requiring the parties to stipulate the timeframe, objectives and other details of alliance frameworks has rendered alliances a matter of personal operational space of the party leaders.

Malawi's presidency is based on the electoral system of first-past-the-post (FPTP), which has resulted in the president winning, for example, with less than 40 per cent of the votes. Correcting this, the Constitutional Court[1] ruling on the May 2019 presidential election effected a majoritarian electoral system that replaced the plurality system and was applied in the presidential election of 2 July 2020. Given that parties operate on strong regional support bases, the new electoral system would in future require stronger and cross-cutting support bases.

This chapter focuses on the interface between party politics and the alliance-coalition practice in Malawi. After background and specific conceptual considerations, the chapter presents a descriptive analysis of Malawi's political parties' formation, and the party system that has evolved. It pinpoints the weak institutionalisation of parties, a factor that impinges on alliance formation. Party alliance types have materialised in phases. These are identified, followed by an analysis of triggers in Malawi politics that precipitate alliances. In the final section, the chapter illustrates how political alliances have impacted governance in subverting the constitution and impinging on the rule of law.

THE CONTEXT AND TRIGGERS OF PARTY FRAGMENTATION AND 'COLLUSIVE' ALLIANCES

Malawi has a presidential system of government with a fixed term of office for the president (Patel and Tostensen, 2006). Both the president and parliament are directly elected by the people for fixed terms, and both have their separate mandates given to them by the people. Therefore, parliament cannot end the tenure of a president (except by impeachment), and the president cannot dissolve parliament. As such, the Malawi government does not face the same threats to stability that are faced by coalition governments in parliamentary or semi-parliamentary systems, in which two or more parties join to form coalitions for power-sharing. However, the political realities and electoral outcomes in Malawi compel parties to unite and form alliances before and/or after elections.

Political parties aligning, fragmenting and realigning has been an integral part of Malawi's multiparty democratic process. The party system in Malawi after the transition in 1993 emerged with three political parties with their roots entrenched in the three regions of Malawi – the Malawi Congress Party (MCP) in the Centre, the United Democratic Front (UDF) in the South, and the Alliance for Democracy (AFORD) in the North. The southern region had the higher population numbers, which meant the UDF could win the presidency. But in the legislature, the MCP and AFORD gained more seats. Regionalism betokened ethnicity, and these identities played a pivotal role in party building, instead of ideologies pursuing national developmental goals and objectives. The voting behaviour led to the observation that 'Malawi seemed to be moving in a dangerous direction, for where ethnicity is the most salient issue consolidating political constituencies, large-scale violence is the inevitable result' (Kaspin, 1995: 597). In the past 25 years Malawi has not experienced large-scale violence, but there has been sporadic violence after elections. In the run-up to and after the 2019 tripartite elections (when the president, the national assembly and local councillors were elected on the same day) the violence was more intense and prolonged.

In the three parliamentary and presidential elections (held concurrently on three occasions) between 1994 and 2004, the party that won the presidency, the UDF, did not secure the majority of seats in the legislature. Hence, while the UDF won the executive, the opposition parties secured more seats in parliament. This required the UDF to seek the support of the smaller opposition party, AFORD, to get government business to unfold smoothly. The major opposition party, the MCP, also sought the support of AFORD, for purposes of a stronghold in the house and to keep the executive in check.

CONCEPTUAL FRAMEWORK WITH APPLICATION TO MALAWI

Party coalitions and alliances, two interlinked concepts, have been well researched from diverse global perspectives. However, most studies have been conducted on parliamentary systems in which coalitions are common and often necessary to prevent governments from failing when votes of no confidence are carried. Scholars have argued that the presidential system is not conducive to coalitions because '[p]residentialism is ineluctably problematic as it operates according to the rule of a "winner-takes-all" arrangement that tends to make democratic politics a zero-sum game, with all the potential for conflict' (Linz, 1990: 56). Because presidential governments do not require parliamentary confidence, interparty coalitions are not institutionally necessary. Linz's definition of presidentialism also implies that presidentialism is a system that does not facilitate political cooperation and cohesion.

There may, however, be exceptions to Linz's argument. For instance, in the case of Latin America's presidential democracies, the presidents use cabinet appointments to form and manage government coalitions in the absence of majority legislative support. When the president's party lacks a majority in the legislature, presidents tend to include other parties in their cabinets to form government coalitions and strengthen their bases of support. The sharing of executive powers among the coalition parties facilitates the legislative process. However, extending the coalition base too broadly poses challenges in these presidential democracies. Altman (2000: 260) argues that building a coalition in democracies that use the presidential system serves the same objectives as in parliamentary democracies, namely,

> [i]t increases the ability of the executive to get its program through the legislature and the ability of the parties to legislate solutions to pressing national problems. It is also important for some reasons unique to presidential systems. Because presidents without a legislative majority do not fall, several outcomes become more likely: (a) divided government or stalemate; (b) constitutional crisis; (c) attempts at circumvention of the legislature; (d) impeachment, which can be a traumatic experience; and (e) regime instability.

These outcomes are not strange in the context of African presidential systems. In the case of Malawi, the circumvention of the legislature and constitutional crisis have particular resonance. Such subversive moves were undertaken by parties that came together in a range of alliances and coalitions that amounted to collusive arrangements.

The term 'alliance' has been applied widely by parties in Malawi. Alliances conventionally designate cooperation between political parties that do not aim immediately at constituting a government, whereas coalitions point to interparty cooperation with a view to constituting a government (Kadima, 2014). However, in the case of Malawi, with its convoluted processes of political parties regularly changing their alliances (Lembani, 2014), especially with a view to reconstituting government, it is often impossible to designate the political practice as pointing to either an alliance or a coalition.

PATTERNS OF POLITICAL PARTY CONFIGURATION IN MALAWI

Malawi has undergone many phases of political party formation and fragmentation since 1993, when the 30 years of single-party MCP rule was broken. This section pursues a periodisation of the major developments that collectively inform the evolution of political parties and the party system in Malawi – the key actors in the continuously changing alliances and coalitions that are synonymous with contemporary Malawian politics. It takes stock of the major events and election results that shaped the political parties, before the analysis turns to the details of the alliances and coalitions among the parties.

From stable to fragmented party system: 1994–2004

In 1994 the MCP was relegated to the status of being the opposition party. The UDF-led government came to power and was faced with a strong opposition party in the legislature. The balance between the parties, however, remained fluid to some degree, not least due to the practice of floor-crossing. In the first 10 years of post-MCP rule, the scenario of the opposition having higher numbers in the national assembly fed into an iterative practice of breaching (by technical circumvention) section 65 of the constitution that disallows floor-crossing by elected MPs – the MPs found surreptitious ways to overcome the legal and technical limits to floor-crossing. Beyond parliament, the UDF's non-adherence to democratic norms in its internal affairs (like regular party conventions and elections) also led to an increase in the number of independent candidates contesting parliamentary seats. The three main parties – the UDF, the MCP and AFORD – fragmented over the issue of the UDF president's bid to have the presidential term extended.

Parties fragmenting owing to presidential term-limit extension bid: 2004

The attempt to extend the presidential term (rendering it open-ended) left the UDF, the MCP and AFORD fragmented. The president of AFORD, Chakufwa Chihana, supported Bakili Muluzi's open-term

Table 8.1: Party strength in parliament, 1994–2004

Political party	Number of seats per election		
	1994	1999	2004
United Democratic Front (UDF)	85	93	49
Malawi Congress Party (MCP)	56	66	58
Alliance for Democracy (AFORD)	36	29	6
National Democratic Alliance (NDA)	n/a	n/a	8
Republican Party (RP)	n/a	n/a	15
People's Progressive Movement (PPM)	n/a	n/a	8
Movement for Genuine Democratic Change (Mgode)	n/a	n/a	3
People's Transformation Party (Petra)	n/a	n/a	1
Independents	n/a	4	39
Total seats	177	192	192

Source: Malawi Electoral Commission results in Malawi Government Gazettes, 1994–2004.

bid, as did the MCP. Members of AFORD who did not support the open-term agenda formed a new party called the Movement for Genuine Democratic Change. The president of the MCP, John Tembo, supported Muluzi's open-term bid, but there were members in the MCP who were against the term extension and they formed a new party, the Republican Party.

The UDF lost several senior members to other parties. The presidential contest in 2004 was between the UDF, with Bingu Mutharika as the presidential candidate, and the MCP, with Tembo and a collective of new parties that emerged as the Mgwirizano (Unity) coalition[2] and that included new parties and an MCP breakaway. The UDF won the presidency. The parliamentary contest was between the main parties, the UDF and the MCP, and the new parties and independent candidates.

Ruling party with a majority – a new chapter in party history: 2009
The situation changed in 2009, when the Democratic Progressive Party (DPP), which had broken from the UDF in 2005, won the

Table 8.2: Party strength in parliament, 2009–19

Political party	Number of seats per election		
	2009	2014	2019
Democratic Progressive Party (DDP)	114	51	62
Malawi Congress Party (MCP)	26	48	55
Independents	32	52	55
United Democratic Front (UDF)	17	14	10
People's Party (PP)	n/a	26	5
United Transformation Movement (UTM)	n/a	n/a	4
Alliance for Democracy (AFORD)	1	1	1
Chipani cha Pfuko	n/a	1	0
Maravi People's Party	1	n/a	n/a
Malawi Forum for Unity and Development (MUD)	1	0	n/a
Total*	192	193	192

* One seat not filled in 2009 and 2019

Source: Malawi Electoral Commission.

parliamentary elections with a sweeping majority of 114 seats out of 193. The win should have eased the acrimony between the executive and legislative arms of government, but the opposite happened. In her 2009 post-election speech, the vice president had said, 'Let me underscore the sentiments expressed by the State President that the DPP-led government will in no way take advantage of its majority seats in parliament to abuse its powers or to question the legitimate separation of powers that builds the backbone of any democratic system' (as quoted in Ott and Kanyongolo, 2009: 12). However, these good intentions were soon abandoned as the DPP government proceeded to tamper with the process of selection of the leader of the opposition in parliament by insisting that the person must be elected by all the parties in parliament (including the party in the majority). This meant, in effect, that the DPP wanted full control of parliament. The DPP also proceeded to appoint all the heads of the parliamentary committees, including the critical ones for oversight – the public appointments committee, the public accounts committee, and the budget and finance committee.

The positive economic policies of 2005–09 were followed by a degeneration into bad governance. Inappropriate policies were then implemented, leading to fiscal deficit, growing inflation and depletion of international gross reserves due to an overvalued exchange rate. There were signs of withdrawal of donor support. Suspecting such a move by donors, Mutharika announced his 'zero deficit' budget plan. The post-2009 period became one of economic upheaval. President Mutharika's zero-deficit policy brought devastating consequences for the people, with fuel and forex crises. Democratic governance too received a setback with the passing of legislation that threatened freedom of assembly and demonstration, and academic freedom, and the suppression of autonomy for local governing bodies.

Table 8.2 shows that parties that emerged out of fragmentation of a bigger party, like the National Democratic Alliance faction, disintegrated and disappeared, and members of the Mgwirizano coalition that had won 27 seats in 2004 failed to win even one seat in 2009. New parties like the People's Party and the United Transformation Movement emerged out of fragmentation of the DPP due to undemocratic ways of leadership succession. The DPP declined from 114 seats in 2009 to 62 in 2019. The party weaknesses also kept the number of independents in parliament constantly high.

Fragmentations of the DPP: 2010 and ongoing

The fragmentation of the DPP began in 2010, shortly after the undemocratic leadership succession approach of the president, who had wanted to appoint his brother, Arthur Peter Mutharika (known as Peter Mutharika), as the party president. This drove the vice president, Joyce Banda, to form a new party, the People's Party, while she was occupying office on the DPP ticket. A constitutional coup was attempted by members of the inner circle of the DPP who wanted to stop Banda from taking over the office of the president after the sitting president, Bingu Wa Mutharika, died in 2012 of cardiac arrest. The party's inner circle wanted Peter Mutharika to take over the presidency. The constitutional coup attempt failed, the constitution was upheld, and Banda became the new president of Malawi. The People's Party became a defacto ruling party and MPs flocked to join it, just as they had in the case of the DPP in 2005.

The DPP won the 2014 elections with Peter Mutharika as president and Saulos Chilima as vice president. Four years down the line, party leadership succession issues resurfaced and the DPP faced another round of fragmentation, with Chilima forming a new party, the United Transformation Movement. He did this while he was in office as the vice president on the DPP ticket, following in the footsteps of Banda. This practice of forming a party while in an elected office representing another party became an unabated trend.

Thus, lack of intraparty democracy and not following a succession plan for leadership contributed to the fragmentation of the parties that have been in government since the start of multiparty politics in Malawi, namely the UDF and the DPP. Party weaknesses helped reinforce floor-crossing and the rise of independent candidates as regular features of Malawi politics.

PARTY ALLIANCES, DISINTEGRATION AND RE-ALLIANCES: 1994–2019

Relentless instability and reinvention of party-political alliances and coalitions in Malawi stand out as key features of this country's political and government landscape (Table 8.3). Against the background of political party strength mediated by election results, presented above, the current section assesses how the alliances and coalitions materialised, and explores the dynamics around their unsustainability.

AFORD moving from government to opposition: 1994–99

In Malawi's first year of the multiparty government in 1994, there were three shifts in party alliances, from opposition alliance to government alliance, and back to opposition alliance. In the 1994 elections, the president of the UDF was the alliance candidate of the UDF and four other parties: the United Front for Multiparty Democracy, the Malawi National Democratic Party, the Congress for the Second Republic and the Malawi Democratic Union. The agenda in the run-up to the election was almost entirely focused on bringing about a change from

Table 8.3: Malawi's governing coalitions, 1994–2020

Period/years	Sequence	Coalition partners
May to September 1994	First coalition	Malawi Congress Party (MCP) & Alliance for Democracy (AFORD)
September 1994 to 1995	Second coalition	United Democratic Front (UDF) & Alliance for Democracy (AFORD)
2004 to 2009	Third coalition	United Democratic Front (UDF) & Alliance for Democracy (AFORD)
2014 to 2019	Fourth coalition	Democratic Progressive Party (DPP) & United Democratic Front (UDF)
2019 and continuing	Fifth coalition	Malawi Congress Party (MCP) & United Transformation Movement (Tonse alliance)

Source: Author's research and conceptualisation, 2020.

the one-party system to a multiparty system, and having a common electoral candidate who was likely to enable a win against the MCP candidate, Dr Hastings Banda, the former president who had ruled for almost 30 years under the system of single-party rule.

After its electoral victory, Bakili Muluzi, the president of the UDF and the largest party in the alliance, formed a 25-member cabinet, including members of the Malawi National Democratic Party and the United Front for Multiparty Democracy. He kept three posts unfilled in the hope that AFORD would also join the government. However, AFORD did not join the government at that time. In the national assembly, the UDF as the single largest party was followed by the MCP and AFORD (Table 8.1).

The opposition parties, the MCP and AFORD, were not in any formal alliance but worked together in the first session of the national assembly, from May to September 1994. Their joint power ensured that the speaker was from AFORD and both deputy speakers from the MCP. All seven operative committees of parliament had a large representation from the opposition and were even chaired by opposition members. The opposition actively deliberated in the house, but they also resorted to frequent walkouts and boycotts that blocked government activities. This created a hostile environment. The UDF felt compelled to move towards a stronger alliance before the next session of parliament to enable government business to proceed and to have the new democratic constitution of Malawi adopted by the house. Adopting the formula of a minimum winning coalition, the UDF pursued an alliance with AFORD.

The UDF-AFORD alliance indeed helped the UDF-led government to function smoothly, as it faced a less confrontational parliament. However, this alliance was short-lived – less than a year. The AFORD party president, Chihana, resigned from the second vice presidency, a position that had been created by a constitutional amendment to accommodate AFORD. However, the six MPs of AFORD who had defected along with the president to the UDF chose to stay on in government and did not follow their president in returning to their party. It was unclear why the AFORD president decided to leave the alliance, as the alliance had not been based on any publicised framework of agreement. Some politicians reckoned the party president had secured too little in the power-sharing stakes; others believed that AFORD could not work with the UDF, given the party's corrupt and unprofessional modes of operation. The UDF survived the first term with the help of the six AFORD MPs who decided to continue working with the UDF in the government until the end of the first term. These MPs had crossed the floor, and as per the constitution should have had their seats vacated, but stayed on as MPs in violation of the law. These AFORD MPs had crossed therefore when they first moved to the UDF but retained their MP statuses. The UDF and AFORD next formed an informal but short-lived alliance. As this alliance ended, AFORD reverted to being in the opposition. Yet, the six MPs remained with the UDF and their seats were not declared vacant by the speaker, as should have happened had the law been enforced.

Internal factions arose in both the MCP and AFORD as a result of their alliance relations. Nonetheless, for the 1999 elections, the MCP and AFORD formed an electoral alliance for the presidential race, with the MCP's candidate as the presidential candidate and AFORD's president as the running mate. For the parliamentary seats, the two parties contested separately. The MCP won 66 seats, whereas AFORD won 29. The UDF contested on its own and won the presidency.

A new coalition in the electoral race: 2004

The fragmentation of the opposition meant that the ruling party alliance – the UDF and AFORD – might win the election even if their electoral support was dwindling (Gloppen et al., 2006). To prevent this from happening, civil society organisations, primarily organisations from different Christian denominations, initiated a process of dialogue and negotiation among opposition parties with the objective of forming a grand election coalition and fielding a joint presidential candidate. As the talks progressed, seven political parties, mostly new and small ones, signed up for the coalition. This coalition became known as Mgwirizano. The president of the Republican Party, Gwanda Chakuamba, led the coalition as its presidential candidate, together with the People's Progressive Movement president, Aleke Banda, as his running mate; senior politicians who broke away from the MCP and the UDF found a new political niche in Mgwirizano. The largest opposition party, the MCP, chose not to join the coalition and contested on its own.

The coalition won 27 parliamentary seats. It disintegrated after the electoral defeat.

The UDF and MCP pre-electoral alliance: Arch enemies become friends: 2009

The 2009 pre-electoral alliance of the UDF and the MCP, hatched at the last minute by the two party leaders, focused only on the presidency of Malawi. Bakili Muluzi attempted a political comeback in 2009, claiming his eligibility to stand again for president based on section 83(3) of the constitution, which states that the president, the first vice president and the second vice president may serve a maximum of two consecutive terms, but leaves open the possibility of non-consecutive terms. Muluzi argued that he was eligible to stand, as the constitution does not bar a person from standing after a break following two consecutive terms. The matter went to court and, after a drawn-out process, the court ruled that presidents are only eligible to serve a 'maximum of two five-year terms', which effectively meant that Muluzi, now the UDF presidential candidate, could not stand in the 2009 election or future elections.

Given this failed comeback attempt, and with the singular agenda of defeating Bingu Mutharika, Muluzi decided that the UDF would enter into an alliance with the MCP. The UDF-MCP electoral alliance was arrived at by a collusive arrangement by the two party presidents. The UDF under Muluzi fielded a candidate to be the running mate to the MCP presidential candidate, John Tembo, instead of nominating a presidential candidate of its own.

The message in their rallies was consistent with their common agenda: 'a desperate electoral alliance resolved to remove Mutharika at all costs. Hitherto, they had cooperated informally as opposition parties in the legislature. This had not generated much mutual trust between them' (Chinsinga, 2009). These inconsistencies reflected poorly on the performance of the two parties for the parliamentary seats – the UDF was reduced to 17 in 2009 from its 49 in 2004, and the MCP to 26 from 58. The DPP, in contrast, scooped 114 seats, and the president won with a comfortable majority. The DPP government became more aggressive and intolerant, and overall governance experienced a setback.

Post-electoral DPP-UDF alliance: From collusion to constitutionalism? 2014 and 2019

In the run-up to the 2014 elections, there were good options available for forming strong pre-electoral alliances among the presidential candidates of four major contesting parties – the MCP, the UDF, the DPP and the People's Party. An alliance would have given a sure 50 per cent plus one vote, and a strong foothold. Instead, the parties chose to run separately. The winner, the DPP, won with a bare 36.4 per cent of the national vote. In an alliance, 'one party would have to accept the vice presidential office, which carries no particular powers or prerogatives, and the holder of that office may be consigned to a purely symbolic role' (Svasand, 2014), and none of these parties wanted to settle for this option. An additional factor was that the People's Party president, Joyce Banda, had already been president for two years (2012–14); it would have been difficult for her to accede to being a deputy presidential running mate instead of being in the presidential stakes.

After the 2014 election, the UDF as a party was in the opposition in parliament. Nevertheless, the UDF's president was given a post of cabinet minister in the DPP government. This was a personal arrangement between the two party presidents, arrived at without broader consultation. The MPs of the UDF were confused as to whether they belonged to a ruling coalition or were part of the opposition. This kind of co-optation of a leader from another party was a repetition of 1994, when the AFORD president was inducted into the UDF government as the second vice president.

After being in this informal alliance from 2014 to 2019, the DPP might have been expected to form an electoral alliance with UDF going into the 2019 elections. However, President Peter Mutharika opted for a running mate from within the DPP, thus leaving out the UDF as alliance partner. Through this act, Malawi's political history was being rewritten.

Peter Mutharika won 39 per cent of the presidential vote for the DDP, followed by the MCP's Lazarus Chakwera at 35 per cent; vice president Saulos Chilima of the United Transformation Movement achieved 20 per cent. Chakwera and Chilima, however, challenged the results in the Constitutional Court, arguing that the Malawi Electoral Commission had helped Mutharika rig the polls. In early 2020 the Constitutional Court of Malawi nullified the poll results, citing wide-ranging irregularities, and ordered fresh elections within 150 days.

Electoral alliances for the presidential rerun of 2020

For the fresh 2020 elections of the president, the DDP (the incumbent) announced its re-alliance with the UDF. The opposition MCP, and the new entrant, the United Transformation Movement, which had split off the DPP, announced an electoral alliance called the Tonse coalition. Several smaller parties, such as AFORD, the People's Party and the People's Transformation Party, joined the alliance.

The two main opposition parties, the MCP and the United Transformation Movement, formed their re-alliance without first clarifying the alliance leadership. While voting on the amendment to section 80(2) of the constitution after the Constitutional Court ruling that proposed a majoritarian system for the election of the president, the MCP and the United Transformation Movement were on the side of a yes vote, while the People's Party voted no. The yes vote was 93, against 80 no votes, 18 absentees and one abstention. This victory was a first for the MCP and the United Transformation Movement as an alliance. It remains to be seen whether these alliances are sustained and contribute towards the consolidation of democracy and constitutionalism.

TRIGGERS OF INSTABILITY, FRAGMENTATION AND COLLUSION

One of the key issues informing interparty relationships in Malawi included section 65 of the constitution,[3] concerning floor-crossing, especially in the 2005–08 period. Within a year after the 2004 elections, president Bingu Mutharika had fallen out with former president Bakili Muluzi and abandoned the UDF, the party that had sponsored him for the presidency. He formed his own party, the Democratic Progressive Party (DPP), and continued on that ticket. Mutharika did not seek a fresh mandate after forming the new party; he continued to complete his presidential term with the support of MPs poached from other parties. These MPs had crossed the floor and survived as MPs because their seats were not declared vacant as required by law.

Other key issues were the attempted impeachment of the president, the exposure of 'Cashgate',[4] the constitutional coup attempt in 2012 following the death of President Mutharika (and the counter-action to stop Vice President Banda from assuming the presidency), and the rejection of electoral reforms bills by parliament (in 2017 and 2018). A brief consideration of these issues sheds light on the dynamics of alliances and coalitions in Malawi.

Floor-crossing as a trigger of co-optation and shifting coalitions
If the saga of the presidential term extension took much time and attention in the early 2000s, the issue of floor-crossing dominated the political scene in subsequent years. The opposition alliance of the UDF and the MCP, and the Mgwirizano coalition in parliament, were keen to see the anti-defection law, encapsulated in section 65 of

the constitution on the role of the speaker, applied to MPs who had crossed the floor, or who had been poached by another party in the course of their term of election. The DPP-led executive was equally determined to thwart the implementation of the law. Despite a High Court ruling in 2007 that upheld section 65, it was not implemented up to the time of the Supreme Court ruling of 2018.

The case of President Mutharika completing a term with the support of MPs poached from opposition parties (who had crossed the floor to the DPP), as well as independent MPs, illustrates the role of floor-crossing in creating instability in the legislature, as well as elevated potential for shifting coalitions and power change between elections. Constitutionally, the speaker is vested with the power to declare the relevant seat vacant if an MP crosses the floor. However, the speaker could not apply the law on defection because of an amendment to this section in 2001, during President Muluzi's tenure, where political expediency ruled. The scope of the section was extended beyond political parties to include 'any association or organisation political in nature'. Mutharika used this amended version and invoked his referral powers by asking the court to interpret the constitutional validity of section 65.

He contended that there was a contradiction between section 65, which prohibits floor-crossing, and section 32, which guarantees freedom of association. He wanted section 65 deleted from the constitution. A drawn-out legal process followed, with an injunction obtained in October 2005. The injunction was served[5] on behalf of 41 MPs who had crossed the floor to the DPP, to stop the speaker from taking action against the floor-crossing MPs. The injunction made it impossible for the speaker to process petitions presented to him to declare vacant seats for legislators deemed to have crossed the floor. The speaker could only invoke section 65 after all injunctions obtained by legislators on both sides of the political divide had been withdrawn.

Legal processes continued. In June 2007 judgment was delivered (Chilenga, 2008). The High Court ruled in favour of upholding the anti-floor-crossing section 65, validating its application to all MPs who had crossed the floor from one party to another.[6] However, there was too little time to invoke section 65 and lift all the injunctions before the end of the prevailing electoral term in May 2009.

The speaker lamented the fact that, as long as the issue of section 65 remained unsettled, history would repeat itself (Chimango, 2012), with serial instability in the legislature and an associated inability to fulfil legislative functions. The number of sittings of Malawi's national assembly between 2004 and 2009 justified the speaker's concern. 'Parliament only met for a total of 30 weeks during the entire term. In some fiscal years, of 2006/2007 and 2008/2009, Parliament met only once and otherwise stood virtually suspended' (IPI, 2009). The meetings occurred only during the budget sessions, which were tense and acrimonious. The MCP-UDF opposition was firm on not allowing any debate on the budget until section 65 had been implemented (and floor-crossing had been eliminated), either sequentially or concurrently with the budget. However, the executive insisted on passing the budget first, before discussing any other issue, thus creating an impasse.

Floor-crossing was not the only issue demonstrating disrespect for electoral mandates and disregard for the legislative function of the national assembly of Malawi. A motion was filed to impeach the president, citing seven grounds as just cause. Fearing a possible impeachment move, the 2008 budget session was split into two segments in a cynical ploy to nominally satisfy the minimum constitutional requirement of at least two sittings in a year, after which the president immediately prorogued parliament, not allowing for any other action.

Electoral reforms

Malawi's electoral reform process has been ongoing, and some important administrative reforms have been undertaken since the 2014 so-called tripartite elections. Two critical reform issues were embodied in the recommendations submitted by the special Law Commission (2017) to the minister of justice and constitutional affairs: the introduction of a majoritarian electoral system requiring the winner to obtain 50 per cent plus one vote; and a change in the appointment of the electoral commissioners to advance neutrality and efficiency. The reform on the electoral system was required to curb floor-crossing and instil political stability by normalising executive-legislative relations; and it was crucial for the reform on the electoral commission to be implemented before the 2019 polls to ensure efficiency and win public confidence, which was at its lowest ebb after the 2014 elections.

The poor management of the 2014 tripartite elections and public frustration with the challenges faced during the 2014 process were a call to expedite the reform process but the Law Commission's recommendations did not receive the urgency they deserved. The cabinet diluted some of the recommendations but finally did table them before parliament. The deliberations on these reforms in parliament revealed neither commitment nor seriousness to pass the reforms. There was an opportunity for the MCP-PP opposition to align and cooperate to get the reforms through, but it did not happen. There was, in fact, a lack of political will across the political spectrum for these reforms to be effected.

The post-2019 elections scenario reflects the importance of the reforms for political stability. The Constitutional Court ruling (*Chilima & Chakwera VS Mutharika & EC*) on the presidential results of 2019 directed that:

> (i)n view of our determination that the majority to be attained by a candidate to the office of the President is a minimum of fifty per cent (50%) plus one vote of the total valid votes cast during the presidential elections, for the purposes of the fresh elections to be held herein and all future presidential elections, parliament must, within 21 days from the date hereof, make appropriate provisions for the holding of Presidential run-off elections in the event no single candidate secures the Constitutional majority under Section 80(2) of the Constitution.

It took the Constitutional Court until 2020 to enforce the application of the 50 per cent plus one rule for the rerun of Malawi's presidential elections.

THE IMPACT OF ALLIANCES ON CONSTITUTIONALISM AND GOVERNANCE

Malawi's alliances and coalitions had significant implications for the establishment and confirmation of constitutionalism and for democratic governance.

Circumventing the constitution and affecting governance

Several major constitutional amendments were pursued for which the ruling party needed the support of the opposition. These were the repeal of the provision to recall elected MPs by their constituents, the suspension of the establishment of the senate, the repeal of the sections on the senate from the constitution, and the attempt to extend the presidential-term limit.

The constitution of Malawi, adopted in 1994, was an interim one-year constitution, which was to be passed and permanently adopted by an elected parliament. A conference was convened by the parliamentary constitutional committee to examine the interim constitution and propose amendments where necessary. In May 1995, parliament voted to adopt the constitution with two amendments. The amendments were controversial, and the issues continue to surface in discussions on governance. One amendment was the repeal of section 64 of the interim constitution, which provided for the recall of elected MPs by constituencies.

The second concerned the constitutional section on the upper house of legislature, the senate. The amendment sought the suspension of the establishment of the senate until the end of May 1999.

When the new constitution was adopted in 1995, a bicameral legislature consisting of a national assembly and a senate was envisaged and provided for. However, the constitution provided that the senate would only take effect at a subsequent date, May 1999, at the end of the first term of the government elected in 1994. During that interim period, the constitution provided that the national assembly would operate as parliament. Events in later years demonstrated that there was a strong motivation to cut the section on the senate from the constitution.

With AFORD joining the UDF in government through an alliance-coalition, the adoption of the constitution with the controversial amendments became easy. In turn, AFORD secured seven ministerial positions and the second vice presidency, an office specially created through a constitutional amendment (section 80(5)) to accommodate the president of AFORD in the executive government at this level.

The following term of office of the UDF government, from 1999, introduced another set of controversial constitutional amendments, which were pursued with new attempts at party alliances. The national assembly was specially convened for a week to table bills concerning the repeal of the constitutional section on senate and extension of the presidential-term limit. As per the time limit provided by the amendment of 1995 for the establishment of the senate (it was not to be established before the end of May 1999), there was pressure to constitute the senate by May 1999. It became apparent that the UDF government had no intention to constitute the body, and was planning ways to prevent the possibility of having an upper house. It claimed to be doing this due to cost, saying the country could not afford it. The UDF, however, was not keen to have another chamber of parliament which could give more capacity and role to the legislative arm of government. Although the UDF got more seats in the 1999 elections than it had before, it did not have a majority and needed an alliance with one of the two opposition parties, the MCP or AFORD.

The MCP was going through leadership tussles, and the UDF took advantage of the situation by forming a loose alliance with one of the MCP factions to get the required numbers to pass the amendment. In January 2001 the bill repealing the sections of the constitution dealing with the senate was passed by 139 assenting out of 192 votes, giving the two-thirds majority of the house. Civil society, opposition political parties AFORD and a faction of the MCP, and many other stakeholders, held strongly opposing sentiments on the abolition of the senate. Those who wanted the senate saw it as a body created by the constitution with well defined roles and functions. Others opposing it saw it as an additional strain on the resources and perhaps a reason for a delay in the work of government.

Some have argued that the abolition of the senate was

unconstitutional. Section 45(8) of the constitution is relied on as a primary basis for this argument (Chigawa, 2008). The section provides that '(u)nder no circumstance shall it be possible to suspend this Constitution or any part thereof or dissolve any of its organs, save as is consistent with the provisions of this Constitution'. The repeal of the sections on the senate was in direct contravention of the section that guaranteed security of the constitution and all organs within it.

Attempts to extend the presidential-term limit through undemocratic alliances

Soon after taking office following the 1999 elections, President Muluzi was tasked with getting the constitution amended to extend the presidential-term limit. This agenda gathered momentum with the president of AFORD and the president of the MCP supporting the bid. The MCP faction, led by the party president, Tembo, along with most of the AFORD MPs, formed an informal pro-government legislative coalition and voted in support of the amendment, which would amount to extending Muluzi's presidential tenure beyond two terms. The opposition parties fragmented due to the leaders supporting the 'open term' bill. The bill was introduced as a private member's bill by an opposition member from AFORD in July 2002. With 95 of parliament's 192 seats, the UDF needed the support of an additional 33 opposition MPs to obtain a two-thirds majority of 128 votes. There were allegations of cash transactions to buy opposition support. A total of 29 opposition MPs and one independent eventually voted for the amendment (see ISS, 2002). The bill was narrowly defeated by three votes.

The extension bid on the presidential term was pursued further after this defeat. The UDF pursued the agenda with some modifications: instead of an 'open term' bill, it was to be a 'third term' bill, and would allow the president to serve for the previously allowed two terms, plus an additional one. The bill was to be introduced in October 2002 as a government bill, giving it more weight, instead of a private bill. To bolster government strength on the pending vote, President Muluzi announced the formation of a government of national unity. It included five members of the opposition AFORD being added to a new cabinet, and party president Chihana reappointed as the second vice president. They replaced the UDF ministers who had opposed the president's project for term extension. However, with the groundswell against the term extension and strong opposition to it by civil society and donors, the bill was dropped at the last minute.

The constitution of Malawi thus triumphed. However, it left the three parties fragmented. Members of AFORD who did not support the open-term and third-term agendas formed a new party called the Movement for Genuine Democratic Change, and the MCP faction that was against the term extension formed a new party, the Republican Party. The UDF lost several of its senior members to other parties.

CONCLUSION

While Malawi has a democratic constitution, adopted by a deliberative process, the spirit of constitutionalism – a commitment to abide by the principles of the constitution – is yet to evolve. The tendency to set aside the constitution and rule with impunity, as has been evident in the regular violation of the section on floor-crossing, and amending the constitution to suit narrow political gains, demonstrates the low level of constitutionalist orientations in practising politics in Malawi.

Political parties' disregard of intraparty democratic norms and practices resulted in senior members leaving their parties, forming a new party or joining another party. Such disregard has been seen in, for example, not holding regular conventions, and not ensuring fair competition for key party-political positions. Party structures to practise recruitment, resource mobilisation and management, and transparency and accountability have also remained weak and fragile. Hence, while political parties are at the centre of alliance and coalition politics in Malawi, they have remained underdeveloped in many respects.

Party alliances have often been based on personal decisions by party leadership, rather than collective decisions. A semblance of interparty trust, dialogue and cooperation are necessary to reach consensus on the fundamental rules and structures regulating political competition and governance, and the policies on which a high degree of stability is desirable. Malawi's history of political party alliances shows that adhoc and short-sighted alliance formation has weakened parties. Two of the three stable parties of the past, AFORD and the UDF, have already faced such weakening.

Three reasons related to alliance and coalition formation in Malawian politics, and how these processes affect intraparty democracy, stand out as causal factors. First, there has been non-adherence to intraparty democracy to ensure fair chances in leadership succession. Second, the formation of pre-electoral alliances happens as a matter of convenience in power-sharing rather than on grounds of common political ideology and shared understanding of policy goals. And, third, the lack of inclusivity and collective participation of party members in alliance formation and implementation has damaged party credibility. Even more important than these party dynamics is that intraparty and interparty relations, and the incessant and vacillating formation of alliances and coalitions, has had a damaging, obstructive impact on governance in Malawi. Frequently, the preoccupation with attaining and retaining state power through elite collusion has left little time for the substantive matters of government.

REFERENCES

Altman D. 2000. 'Politics of coalition formation and survival in multiparty presidential democracies: Uruguay 1989–1999', *Party Politics*, 6 (3), 259–283.

Chigawa, M. 2008. 'The senate as the 2nd chamber of parliament in Malawi – Its relevance, composition and power'. Paper presented at the *Malawi Law Journal* launch conference, 16–17 July 2008.

Chilenga, M. 2008. 'Dikastocracy: Is it undermining democracy in Malawi? Towards consolidation of Malawi's democracy'. Occasional Papers Series No. 11, Konrad Adenauer Stiftung, Lilongwe.

Chilima & Chakwera VS Mutharika & EC. Final Judgment, draft. In the High Court of Malawi, Constitutional Reference No. 1 of 2019.

Chimango, L. J. 2012. 'Section 65 of the Malawian constitution: the role of the Speaker, 2005–2009', *Malawi Law Journal*, 6 (2), 121–142.

Chinsinga, B. 2009. 'Malawi's political landscape', in *Democracy in Progress: Malawi's 2009 parliamentary and presidential elections*. Zomba: Kachere Series.

Gloppen, S., Kanyongolo, E., Khembo, N., Patel, N., Rakner, L. et al. 2006.

'The Institutional Context of the 2004 General Elections in Malawi'. Research report, Chr. Michelsen Institute, Bergen.

Institute for Policy Interaction (IPI) Malawi. 2009. 'Parliamentary Observation Reports 2005–2008'. Report of parliamentary sessions in Malawi, with technical support from IDASA (SA), funded by The International Research & Consulting Centre, Switzerland.

Institute for Security Studies (ISS). 2002. 'Situation Report: Malawi: The slippery slide towards autocracy?', https://issafrica.org/research/situation-reports/situation-report-malawi-the-slippery-slide-towards-autocracy-chris-marol, accessed 20 May 2020.

Kadima, D. 2014. 'An introduction to the politics of party alliances and coalitions in socially divided Africa', *Journal of African Elections,* 13 (1), 1–24.

Kaspin, D. 1995. 'The politics of ethnicity in Malawi's democratic transition', *Journal of Modern African Studies,* 33 (4), 595–620.

Law Commission. March 2017. *Law Commission Report No. 32.* Report on the Review of the Electoral Laws. Lilongwe: Government Printers.

Lembani, S. S. 2014. 'Survival of minority governments in Malawi: Coalitions or collusions? Actors, approaches and consequences for party system and state governability', in *Malawi before the 2014 Tripartite Elections: Actors, issues, prospects and pitfalls: An analytical stocktaking.* Blantyre: Friedrich Ebert Stiftung, Botswana, and Institute for Policy Interaction.

Linz, J. 1990. 'The perils of presidentialism', *Journal of Democracy,* 1 (1), 51–69.

Malawi Electoral Commission, www.mec.org.mw, accessed 2 May 2020.

Ott, M. and Kanyongolo, F. E. 2009. *Democracy in Progress: Malawi's 2009 parliamentary and presidential elections.* Zomba: Kachere Series.

Patel, N. and Tostensen, A. 2006. 'Parliament executive relations in Malawi 1994–2004'. CMI working papers, WP 2006: 10.

Svasand, L. 2014. 'Political parties: Fragmentation and consolidation, change and stability', in Patel, N. and Wahman, M. (eds.) *The Malawi 2014 Tripartite Elections: Is democracy maturing*? Lilongwe: National Initiative for Civic Education and Institute for Policy Interaction.

Part III

Establishing legal-constitutional parameters and administrative repercussions

POLITICAL PARTIES AND THEIR COALITIONS are affected by the scope of constitutional and legislative prescription and control. The Constitution of the Republic of South Africa clearly underestimated the post-1996 prospects of coalition government: it hardly envisaged that beyond the conciliatory notion of a government of national unity at the foundational stage of South Africa's democracy there would be a need to constitutionally manage these coalition formations. Ordinary legislation and accumulating jurisprudence have had to fill the gap. Equally, coalition practice in South Africa is focused on the party-political interface, and the right of majority parties (or coalition formations) to ring in their administrations of choice. This is conducive to instability and ineffectiveness at best, and breakdown at worst. Sound governance and political accountability for poor governance are often neglected. The chapters in this section have a dedicated focus on two of the core dimensions of coalition politics in South Africa – the constitutional-legal and the political-administrative interfaces with coalition praxis.

NINE

The constitutional-legal dimensions of coalition politics and government in South Africa

PIERRE DE VOS

THE SOUTH AFRICAN CONSTITUTION does not contain specific provisions regulating the formation and functioning of coalition governments in the national, provincial and local spheres of government. Neither does ordinary legislation contain such specific regulatory provisions. However, the constitution establishes a hybrid version of the system of parliamentary government,[1] which applies at the national, provincial and – with slight variations – local government level, and the choice of this system has important consequences for how coalition governments are formed and how they operate (Dodd, 2015: 4).

In a system of parliamentary government, executive power resides in the head of the executive and their cabinet (at the national level) or executive committee (at other levels). The cabinet or executive committee is usually appointed by the head of the executive from the members of the legislature. The cabinet or executive committee is held accountable to and can be removed by the parliament, provincial legislature or municipal council. While the head of the executive and their cabinet or executive committee retain the confidence of the legislature, they wield considerable power (Dodd, 2015: 4).

Where support for the executive by the legislature is in doubt or vulnerable to sudden shifts in loyalty by legislators of different political parties, government tends to be less stable and less able to wield its power decisively. Because the head of the executive can be removed from office by the relevant elected legislative body, the system of parliamentary government impacts directly on how coalition governments are formed and how stable they are (Cheibub et al., 2004: 566). It has been claimed that 'the parliamentary system will give a country strong and efficient government only [in cases where] the majority consists of a single party' (Lowell, 2013: 70; Dodd, 2015: 7). While this overstates the case, parliamentary systems in which no party enjoys a legislative majority do tend to be more unstable and less long lasting than systems in which the head of the executive is separately elected (Dodd, 2015: 11).

In this chapter I explore this issue with reference to the South African version of parliamentary government, at a time when the electoral dominance of the governing party appears to be on the wane and the likelihood of no one party obtaining an absolute majority in the various legislative bodies at the national, provincial and especially local government level is increasing (Götz et al., 2016). As the life of the government in a parliamentary system of government is literally dependent on the will of the majority of elected representatives – but perhaps, to some extent, also on the will of the political party leaders (Dodd, 2015: 5) – a situation where no party obtains a majority of seats in the relevant legislature potentially leads to a more unstable government than in systems in which the head of the executive is directly elected by the electorate. This is because in hung legislatures more than one party will have to work together to elect the head of the executive, to pass legislation, and to ensure its long-term ability to govern effectively, and to survive. This suggests that the stability of the government will formally depend on the whims of the elected representatives of political parties in a legislative body, although, in fact, it is more likely to depend on political party leaders who, for various reasons discussed in this chapter, retain considerable control over the conduct of their elected representatives. The situation in South Africa has, however, been clouded by two Constitutional Court judgments, which have the potential to weaken the grip of party leaders on their elected representatives in various legislative bodies, thus injecting a further element of uncertainty into the mix. This is because it can no longer be taken for granted that all the elected representatives of a party will always follow the instructions of party bosses on when to support legislative initiatives, or, more importantly, when to support a vote of no confidence in any of the incumbents.

I conclude that the current constitutional and legal architecture regulating the establishment and functioning of government in the national, provincial and local spheres in South Africa, read with the relevant Constitutional Court judgments, leave coalition or minority governments vulnerable, as they are at the mercy of the whims of elected representatives and political party leaders and, to a lesser extent, of the ambition and even the greed of individual elected representatives.[2] Taking the system of parliamentary government as a given (because it is unlikely that changes to the constitution could be effected), it is unclear – from a constitutional and legislative perspective – how much could be done to prevent this kind of instability in minority and coalition governments. I suggest, from a constitutional and legal perspective, that imposing an additional legal precondition for political parties to be entitled to form a coalition or minority government may reduce the problem at the local government level, at least, where this can be done without amending the constitution.

I now discuss the formal legal rules – contained in the Constitution and, to a lesser extent, in ordinary legislation – that establish the governance architecture within which coalition governments are formed and maintained. I then consider other constitutional and legal provisions and court judgments that may influence the functioning of various aspects of legislative government, and describe the impact these have on the formation and stable functioning of coalition governments.

PARLIAMENTARY GOVERNMENT AND ITS IMPACT ON COALITIONS IN SOUTH AFRICA

The constitutional and legislative framework that determines how coalition governments can be formed and how they may operate in the national and provincial spheres in South Africa differs from the constitutional and legislative framework applicable to local government. The national and provincial spheres are regulated largely by the relevant provisions in the South African constitution, while local government is regulated by ordinary legislation. While there are many similarities between the two systems (national and provincial versus local), there are also small but significant differences, which necessitate a separate discussion of the constitutional and legislative provisions applicable to the former and the latter.

Parliamentary government and coalitions at the national and provincial level

The South African constitution formally establishes the national assembly at the national level, and the provincial legislatures at the provincial level, as the directly elected legislatures in which political parties are represented by party representatives is proportional to the percentage of support they garnered at the ballot box (section 46(1) and section 105(1)).[3] The percentage of seats garnered by each party in the national assembly and in each provincial legislature has a profound impact on the identity of the president and premiers and their respective executives. This is because the national assembly elects both the speaker and the president from among its members 'at its first sitting after its election, and whenever necessary to fill a vacancy' (section 86(1) and section 52(1)), while provincial legislatures similarly elect the premiers of their provinces and the provincial speaker from among its members (section 128(1) and section 111(1)). When elected president, a person ceases to be a member of the national assembly (section 87). The president retains the right to attend and speak in the national assembly, subject to its rules and orders, but may not vote (section 54). The same is not true for people elected as premiers or mayors, who remain members of their respective legislative bodies. In terms of item 6 in schedule 3 of the constitution, these elections for president and premier are conducted by secret ballot. This means that if one party wins more than 50 per cent of the seats in the national assembly, that party's candidate is likely to be elected speaker of the national assembly, while the leader of that party (or another candidate nominated by the majority party) is likely to be elected president of the country. Similarly, when a party wins more than 50 per cent of the seats in a provincial legislature, that party's candidate for speaker is likely to be elected speaker of that legislature, while its candidate for premier is likely to be elected premier of that province. This power to elect the speaker is a significant power, as the speaker is the administrative head of the legislature (De Vos and Freedman, 2014: 133), and the rules bestow important powers on the speaker to control proceedings in the legislature and, if needed, to cast the deciding vote when there is a tie (*United Democratic Movement v Speaker of the National Assembly and Others*, 2017: para 86). While speakers are required to be impartial, and must make all decisions in a rational manner, in practice, control of the speakership provides a distinct advantage to the political party of which the speaker is a member, as speakers sometimes use their discretion to favour their party.[4]

The power to elect the president is even more significant, because the president is the head of state and the head of the national executive (section 83(a)), which means that the executive authority of the Republic is vested in him or her (section 85(1)). The president also has the power in terms of the constitution to appoint and dismiss the deputy president and ministers, and assign their powers and functions (section 91(2)). Similarly, the power to elect a premier is significant, as the executive authority of the province is vested in the premier (section 125(1)), which means this person has the power to appoint and dismiss the members of the executive council (MECs), and assign their powers and functions (section 132(2)). A party that wins an outright majority of seats in a legislature would be able to use its majority to take full control of both the legislature and the executive. This is likely to lead to a stable government that will be able to govern effectively, or at least as effectively as could be expected, given the quality of the party's representatives in the legislature and the executive, besides the nature of the party's policies.

However, if no party wins more than 50 per cent of the seats in the national assembly or in a particular provincial legislature, the election of the speaker and the president or premier will require support from the elected representatives of two or more parties. After an election, or after a vacancy occurs in the office of the president or a premier, the election of a new president or premier becomes a pressing concern. This is because the legislature has only 30 days to elect a new president or premier. If the national assembly fails to elect a new president within 30 days after the vacancy has occurred, the acting president must dissolve the national assembly (section 50(2)(b)), after which new elections for the national assembly would have to be held within 90 days (section 49(2)). Similar provisions apply to a failure of a provincial legislature to elect a premier within 30 days after a vacancy occurs in that office (section 109(2)(b) and section 108(2)). It is important to note that these provisions apply both to a situation where the legislature fails to elect the president or a premier within 30 days following an election, and when this failure occurs after the president or a premier resigns or is removed from office by the legislature. Where no party wins a majority of seats in the relevant legislature, the first order of business for each of the parties in the legislature would therefore be to try and reach an agreement with other parties in order to obtain majority support to secure the election of a chosen candidate as speaker and as president or premier, as the case may be.

After the election of a speaker, president or premier, the head of the executive will form a new government by appointing ministers or MECs. But this is not the end of the matter. Section 102(1) of the constitution allows the national assembly to pass a vote of no confidence in the cabinet, excluding the president, with a vote supported by a majority of its members (currently, that would be 201 MPs). If that happens, the cabinet (which includes the deputy president) is dissolved and the president is then required to 'reconstitute the cabinet'. This provision could be used to force the president to remove some cabinet ministers and replace them with others, with the implied threat that if he or she does not do so, the national assembly would remove the president from office in terms of section 102(2) of the constitution (Butler, 2013: 4). This section empowers the national assembly to remove the president from office by passing a vote of no confidence in the president with a vote supported by a majority of 201 of its members.

This provision lies at the heart of the system of 'parliamentary government'. It signals that the government serves at the pleasure of the legislature (in this case, the national assembly).[5] Identical provisions provide for the removal of the provincial cabinet or premier by a vote of no confidence (section 141). The constitution similarly provides for the removal of the speaker in the national assembly and in provincial legislatures by a vote of no confidence supported by a majority of members of the legislature (section 52(4) and section 111(4)). These provisions are not applicable only to minority or coalition governments, as a party with an outright majority in the legislature may utilise them to remove the president, premier or speaker in which the majority party no longer has confidence (Butler, 2013: 4). However, the constitution's provisions for a vote of no confidence will become more important when no party obtains a majority of the seats in a legislature – especially where there is no formal arrangement to cooperate or support the coalition of minority government between parties who voted for the incumbent president or premier. This is because parties that wish to unseat the government could rely on this provision to remove the executive if they can manage to engineer a switch of allegiance by one or more smaller parties that voted for the incumbent.

Parliamentary government and coalitions at the local level

The constitution and other enabling legislation deal differently with governance at the local government level. In terms of section 151(2) of the constitution, both the executive and legislative authority of a municipality is vested in its municipal council. Section 160(1)(a) of the constitution confirms that the municipal council 'makes decisions concerning the exercise of all the powers and the performance of all the functions of the municipality'. However, section 160(1)(b) and (c) allow the municipal council to elect a chairperson and an 'executive committee and other committees, subject to national legislation'. The Local Government: Municipal Structures Act 117 of 1998[6] is the national legislation that was adopted to regulate this. Section 7 of the

Act allows for the establishment of different types of municipalities, and for present purposes much depends on what type of municipality is established (De Visser, 2009). In terms of this section the three most important systems for municipal government are:

The *collective executive system*, which allows for the exercise of executive authority through an executive committee, in which the executive leadership of the municipality is collectively vested (section 7(a)). This system provides for executive-arm power-sharing between parties proportional to the number of seats each party obtains in the municipal council election (section 43(2)).

The *mayoral executive system*, which allows for the exercise of executive authority through an executive mayor, in whom the executive leadership of the municipality is vested and who is assisted by a mayoral committee (section 7(b)). This system is a majoritarian system in which the municipal council is required to elect a mayor from among its members (section 55(1)), and the executive mayor must then appoint a mayoral committee from among the councillors to assist the executive mayor (if the municipal council has more than nine members (section 60(1)(a)).

The *plenary executive system*, which limits the exercise of executive authority to the municipal council itself (section 7(c)(c). This system is used only for very small municipalities.

For the purposes of studying coalition government, the focus here is on the mayoral executive system of government.[7] This system is similar to the system that applies at the national and provincial levels. Whether the system is a mayoral executive system or not, the first order of business at the first sitting of the council after its election, or after a vacancy occurs, is the election of a speaker from among the councillors (section 36(2)). The candidate who eventually receives the absolute majority of votes cast will be elected speaker (item 7, schedule 3). The speaker is designated the chairperson of the municipal council (section 36 (1) and (2)). The speaker may be removed from office by passing a resolution with a majority vote (section 40). As is the case with the speaker of the national assembly and of provincial legislatures, the speaker of a municipal council has considerable power – especially when no party holds a majority in that council – as he or she convenes and presides over meetings of the municipal council (section 37), decides on the timing of votes (including votes of no confidence), and can influence proceedings with procedural rulings.

In a mayoral executive system, the municipal council, after electing the speaker, must elect an executive mayor with an absolute majority of the votes cast in the council within 14 days after the council's election (section 55(1)). When a vacancy occurs in the office of the executive mayor, a new election of the mayor must be held 'when necessary' (section 55(2)). The Local Government: Municipal Structures Act does not prescribe a specific period within which such a vacancy must be filled – which differs from the filling of a vacancy of a president or premier. The Act is also silent on what happens if the council fails to elect a speaker or an executive mayor at the first sitting after a local government election (which, as noted, must occur within 14 days after the council election) or if these positions are not filled within a reasonable period after a vacancy occurs. Section 24 of the Act merely states that the term of office of a municipal council is five years. The absence of a legal obligation requiring the election of a new speaker or mayor within a limited time period after the vacancy occurred, and the absence of any requirement that a new council election be held if the council fails to elect a speaker or mayor within a prescribed period, present potential difficulties, as it may incentivise parties whose preferred candidate is not likely to be elected as speaker or mayor to delay the election of a new speaker or mayor (*Democratic Alliance and Others v Premier for the Province of Gauteng and Others*, 2020: paras 7–12). This may lead to a situation in which a municipal council remains without a municipal government for many weeks or even months.

In terms of item 6 of schedule 3 of the Local Government: Municipal Structures Act, a vote for speaker or executive mayor must be conducted by secret ballot. The position of mayor is pivotal in an executive mayoral system because where a municipal council has more than nine members, the executive mayor is empowered to appoint a mayoral committee from among the councillors to assist the executive mayor, and may delegate specific responsibilities to each member of the committee, and may also dismiss a member of the mayoral committee (section 60(1)). The mayoral committee consists of the deputy executive mayor (if any) and as many councillors as may be necessary for effective and efficient government, 'provided that no more than 20 per cent of the councillors or 10 councillors, whichever is the least, are appointed' (section 60(2)). The executive mayor's powers must be 'exercised and performed by the executive mayor together with the other members of the mayoral committee' (section 60(3)).

The executive mayor system is similar to the hybrid parliamentary government system that applies in the national and provincial sphere, as described above. The speaker and executive mayor therefore also need to retain the confidence of a majority of members of the municipal council. This is because the speaker (section 40) and the executive mayor (section 58) can be removed from office when the council passes a vote of no confidence in either. A simple majority of votes (not an absolute majority of members of the council) is needed for the vote to pass. These provisions are not only applicable to minority or coalition governments, as a party with an outright majority in the legislature may utilise them to remove the executive mayor or speaker from office if they lose the political support of their party's council members. However, politically it is more likely that a speaker or executive mayor will be voted out of office when no party enjoys an absolute majority on a council.

A further legal consideration that may impact on the stability of a coalition government at the local government level is the provisions in section 139(1)(c) of the constitution, which allow a provincial executive to dissolve a municipal council within that province and appoint an administrator. This is ultimately likely to lead to a fresh election within 90 days of the dissolution of the government. Section 139(1)(c) of the South African Constitution provides as follows:

> When a municipality cannot or does not fulfil an executive obligation in terms of the Constitution or legislation, the relevant provincial executive may intervene by taking any appropriate steps to ensure fulfilment of that obligation,

including: (c) Dissolving the Municipal Council and appointing an administrator until a newly elected Municipal Council has been declared, if exceptional circumstances warrant such a step.

The result of the dissolution decision is that the municipal council is immediately dissolved and an administrator takes over the functions of the council until fresh elections are held, which must occur within three months after the dissolution of the council (*Democratic Alliance and Others v Premier for the Province of Gauteng and Others*, 2020: para 9; *Mnquma Local Municipality and Another v Premier of the Eastern Cape and Others*, 2009: para 81). The appointment of an administrator is a stop-gap option that is meant to pave the way for a fresh election. However, as the Gauteng High Court noted, there is no guarantee that this move will resolve the impasse. Accordingly, the court warned that

> … an election as a result of the dissolution decision may in fact result in many of the same councillors returning to their positions again, resulting in a hung Municipal Council. There is no guarantee that a fresh election will resolve the relevant obligation. It is an option more reliant on hope than certainty and as such cannot, objectively, be viewed as capable of resolving the problem at hand (*Democratic Alliance and Others v Premier for the Province of Gauteng and Others*, 2020: para 89).

Problems may arise when one party governs the province and another party or coalition of parties govern the municipality, especially when those parties who wish to unseat the coalition government act in a way aimed at triggering the application of section 139 of the constitution. This is well illustrated by the High Court judgment in *Democratic Alliance and Others v Premier for the Province of Gauteng and Others*, which dealt with an attempt by the Gauteng government to invoke section 139(1)(c) to dissolve the Tshwane municipal council. At the time the DA governed the city as a minority government, as no party had won a majority of seats in the local government election of 2016. The ANC, which governs the province, attempted on more than one occasion to dislodge the DA from government. As a result, a situation arose where the Tshwane municipal council found itself without a mayor, a mayoral committee or a municipal manager. The municipal council failed for months to elect a new mayor (Seleka, 2020; De Vos, 2020). The High Court ascribed this state of affairs to the inability of the municipal council 'to convene and run council meetings to transact and take necessary decisions in line with its responsibilities' and blamed the ANC and the EFF, which had staged disruptions and walkouts, 'thus depriving the Municipal Council of the necessary quorum' (*Democratic Alliance and Others v Premier for the Province of Gauteng and Others*, 2020: paras 7–8). Although the court did not make a finding on the motive of the ANC and EFF councillors, it did find that the dissolution of the city council was invalid because there was another, less drastic, way to solve the problem, namely for all councillors to attend council meetings and elect a new mayor. It thus ordered all councillors from the ANC and the EFF to attend and remain in attendance at all meetings of the City of Tshwane Metropolitan Municipality Council, unless they had a lawful reason to be absent (as they were required to do by the relevant code of conduct) (*Democratic Alliance and Others v Premier for the Province of Gauteng and Others*, 2020: para 109). The judgment highlights the power of political parties and their elected representatives to destabilise fragile coalition or minority governments. It also highlights the power of the courts to rectify perceived abuses.[8] It is not clear that the order made by the High Court in this case will ultimately address the political dysfunction in the Tshwane council. This raises question about what the limits of the law are in fixing essential political dysfunction (De Vos, 2020).

Irrespective, section 139(1)(c) of the constitution adds a further legal mechanism to resolve an impasse that may arise when a hung council is unable to elect a speaker or a mayor, or when a minority or coalition government is so weak or unstable that the municipal government is unable to fulfil its basic governance obligations. As discussed in more detail below, there is also a danger that the provision could be abused, when one party governs the province and another party or coalition of parties governs the municipality.

THE ROLE OF POLITICAL PARTIES IN FORMING AND MAINTAINING COALITION GOVERNMENTS

It is only possible to understand how the hybrid form of parliamentary government functions in practice by considering the role played by political parties and their leaders in the formation and maintenance of the executive authority. Political party leaders (whether national, provincial or regional) are often the hidden hand behind the actions of individual elected representatives, who normally adhere to strict party discipline. Decisions on who to support in an election as speaker, president, premier or executive mayor are therefore not necessarily taken exclusively by the elected representatives of a party, but are likely to be heavily influenced by the relevant party leaders (Southall, 2005: 71). Almost invariably the president – although not an MP after their election as president – is the leader of the governing party. Similarly, the national executive committee of the ANC has a decisive role in deciding the party's candidate for premier (and executive mayor). While this may be attributed partly to political culture, several constitutional and legal provisions enhance the power of political parties and their leaders vis-à-vis that party's elected representatives when deciding on candidates for president, premier and executive mayor.

First, the electoral system used at both the national and the provincial level, and to a slightly lesser extent at the local government level, enhances the power of party bosses vis-à-vis elected party representatives. Currently, in the national and provincial sphere, no person can serve in the national or any of the provincial legislatures without being a member of a political party and without having been chosen or selected by that political party to represent the interests of the political party in the respective legislatures.[9] This is because at the national and provincial level, political parties – and not individual candidates – contest elections, and voters cast their votes for the political party of their choice (*Ramakatsa v Magashule*, 2012: para 66). To get elected, candidates must be placed sufficiently high on the party's relevant electoral list, which is done according to criteria and in terms of a process determined by that political party (De Vos, 2015: 41). To be re-elected, an elected representative is incentivised to act in a manner that will ensure that they retain a spot high up on the party's relevant electoral list. It must be noted that this system is meant to change, as the Constitutional Court held in June 2020 that the electoral system at the national and provincial level should be changed to allow independent candidates unaffiliated to a political party to stand for election to the national assembly and provincial legislatures (*New Nation Movement NPC and Others v President of the Republic of South Africa and Others,* 2020). The Constitutional Court gave parliament 24 months to amend the electoral system to allow for this, which means a new system must be adopted by June 2022. However, it is unclear at the time of writing what this system will entail and how it will impact on the power of political parties.

Given that party leaders retain influence over who appears on the party's electoral list and how high up they appear, representatives are unlikely to act in a manner that would defy the instructions of party bosses, unless intraparty considerations incentivise them to do so (Lodge and Scheidegger, 2006: 30–31). At the local government level, the mixed electoral system provides that 50 per cent of councillors are elected as ward councillors in terms of a plurality electoral system, with each winning candidate representing a ward, while 50 per cent are elected from a closed list on a proportional representation (PR) basis (section 22, Local Government: Municipal Structures Act). This means that a person could be elected to a municipal council via the ward councillor route without being a member of a political party. Ward councillors also do not have to worry about appearing sufficiently high up on their parties' relevant electoral lists. In practice, however, the hold of political parties over councillors remains strong, because party leaders in the national, provincial or regional sphere have a considerable say in who the party's ward councillor candidate will be.[10] This activates the same dynamic as described above regarding the accountability of elected representatives to party structures vis-à-vis accountability to the electorate.

Second, all elected representatives who were elected on a political party ticket to an elective body in the national, provincial or local government sphere must retain their membership of the party on whose ticket they were elected in order to remain in the relevant legislature.

In the national and provincial spheres, a member of the legislature loses membership of a provincial legislature if he or she 'ceases to be a member of the party that nominated that person as a member of the legislature' (section 47(3) and section 106(3)). At the local government level, a councillor who was elected from a party list 'and ceases to be a member of the relevant party' automatically loses their seat in the municipal council (section 27(c) of the Local Government: Municipal Structures Act), while a ward councillor who was nominated by a party as a candidate in the ward election and ceases to be a member of that party also loses their seat automatically (section 27(f)(i)).[11] In the latter case, a by-election must be held in that ward and the councillor who lost their seat because of a loss or forfeiture of party membership, may stand in that election as an independent candidate (Russon, 2011: 76). The hold of political parties over ward councillors is thus somewhat weakened, as independent candidates who previously represented a political party as a councillor have in the past successfully defended that ward seat in a by-election (Russon, 2011: 85–86).

Nevertheless, the threat of expulsion from a political party remains a powerful weapon in the hands of political party bosses to keep elected representatives in check. This power is somewhat curtailed by the fact that political parties are constitutionally required to adhere to their own constitutions. These constitutions and rules of political parties must also be consistent with the constitution, which is the supreme law of the country (*Ramakatsa v Magashule*, 2012: para 72). This means elected representatives may be able to block their expulsion by challenging it in court for not having followed the procedures prescribed by its constitution. This is illustrated by the case of the former mayor of Cape Town, Patricia de Lille, who challenged the ruling by the DA that she had ceased to be a member of the party; she won the case (*De Lille v Democratic Alliance and Others*, 2018). This tactic, however, requires deep pockets and can postpone but not prevent the inevitable, as De Lille's ultimate agreement to leave the party illustrates.

Third, strict party discipline is imposed on elected representatives through the adoption of specific party policies and provisions in party constitutions which formalise the 'deployment' of party candidates for certain important executive positions. As the Constitutional Court remarked in *United Democratic Movement v Speaker of the National Assembly and Others* (2017), a governing party has a great influence on, or dictates, who gets appointed or elected as senior office-bearers in parliament. (The same is true for the election of office bearers at the provincial and local government level.) The Court further suggested that it 'would be quite surprising if the senior office bearers in Parliament were not appointed or elected with a significant input by the president and other senior party officials' (*United Democratic Movement v Speaker of the National Assembly and Others*, 2017: para 76). A perusal of the policies and the constitutions of the two main political parties underscores this. For example, at the ANC's 52nd National Conference in 2007, the conference imposed specific deployment rules to regulate who the party's candidates for president and premierships should be. The rules instructed that, at the provincial government level, the provincial executive committee of the ANC in the respective provinces 'should recommend a pool of names of not more than three cadres in order of priority who should be considered for Premiership', after which the national executive committee of the ANC would 'make a final decision based on the pool of names submitted by the [provincial executive committee]'. At the national government level, the conference agreed that 'the ANC President shall be the candidate of the movement for President of the Republic' (ANC 52nd National Conference, 2007). Section 5.4 of the ANC constitution also requires all ANC members who hold elective office in any sphere of government at the national, provincial or local level 'to be members of the appropriate caucus, to function within its rules and to abide by its decisions under the general provisions of this Constitution and the constitutional structures of the ANC'. Similarly, section 2.5.4.7 of the DA constitution of 2018 states, 'Any member, including a public representative, is guilty of misconduct if he or she unreasonably fails to comply with or rejects decisions of the official formations of the Party', while section 9.3.5 of the constitution states, 'Members [of a legislative caucus] must at all times adhere to and support decisions of the relevant caucus and must not differ publicly from any decision once it has been taken except when it has been decided by the caucus that a member may on a question of conscience exercise a free vote.' These provisions in political party constitutions give party leaders a powerful tool to keep individual elected representatives in check and to enforce party discipline. However, the grip of party leaders does not entail absolute control over elected representatives, especially when a party is riven by factional disputes. For example, in August 2020 a number of ANC councillors supported a vote of no confidence in Mangaung mayor Olly Mlamleli, thus ousting her from office (McCain, 2020; see also chapter 1).

The factors discussed above all bolster the power of political parties and their leaders vis-à-vis their elected representatives in national, provincial and municipal legislatures. This suggests that where the leaders of various political parties come to an agreement on forming a coalition, or on another arrangement to establish a minority government, the major factor that may lead to instability and inefficiency of a coalition government would be the behaviour and attitude of party leaders. In this view, the instability of some coalition governments should be blamed on the sometimes opportunistic cooperation between parties whose ideologies and programmes differ fundamentally, on the political immaturity of party leaders, and on the concomitant jostling for power and access to positions and other resources, which – at the local government level at least – often leads to the removal of speakers and executive mayors. But Constitutional Court jurisprudence in 2017 established two important principles which may weaken the hold of party leaders over their elected representatives.

LEGAL AND OTHER FACTORS THAT WEAKEN PARTY CONTROL OVER ELECTED REPRESENTATIVES

If, as argued above, parties are normally able to enforce strict party discipline on their elected representatives in part because of the vagaries of the current electoral system, the provision for the dismissal of representatives by expelling them from the party, and party constitutions that enforce caucus discipline, this would mean that the strength and stability of coalition governments depend to a large extent on the behaviour of extra-legislative party leaders who are guided by political (and perhaps also financial) incentives (Mtyala 2011; Nicholson and Coetzee, 2014). This argument needs modifications in two distinct respects.

First, in two judgments handed down in 2017, both dealing with the rules governing the removal from office of a sitting president, the Constitutional Court pushed back against the notion that because members of the national assembly assume office through nomination by political parties, MPs can be expected at all times to pursue the interests of their respective political parties. While these judgments dealt with the MPs elected to the national assembly, the principle also applies to party representatives elected to provincial legislatures and, to a large extent, municipal councils. In *Economic Freedom Fighters and Others v Speaker of the National Assembly and Another* (2017), the court had to decide whether the rules of the national assembly provided an appropriate procedure to be followed when considering removal (impeachment) of the president in terms of section 89 of the constitution. As section 89 only allows for impeachment of the president on the limited grounds that the president is guilty of a serious violation of the constitution or the law or serious misconduct, or because of an inability to perform the functions of office, the court held that the rules required a factual inquiry to be held on whether any of these grounds existed before the national assembly as a whole was permitted to make a political call on whether to support the president's impeachment (*Economic Freedom Fighters and Others v Speaker of the National Assembly and Another*, 2017: para 176).

In doing so, the majority of the court provided a radically different vision of the relationship between elected representatives and party leaders than the one described in the previous section. The court noted that the national assembly is elected 'to represent the people and to ensure government by the people under the Constitution', that 'the interests served and advanced by the exercise of its powers must be the collective interests of the people it represents', and that the powers of the national assembly 'must primarily be exercised to promote only the people's interests and the institutional objectives' of the national assembly (*Economic Freedom Fighters and Others v Speaker of the National Assembly and Another,* 2017: para 141). In a pivotal passage, the Constitutional Court argued that

> [t]he fact that members of the Assembly assume office through nomination by political parties ought to have a limited influence on how they exercise the institutional power of the Assembly. Where the interests of the political parties are inconsistent with the Assembly's objectives, members must exercise the Assembly's power for the achievement of the Assembly's objectives. For example, members may not frustrate the realisation of ensuring a government by the people if its attainment would harm their political party. If they were to do so, they would be using the institutional power of the Assembly for a purpose other than the one for which the power was conferred. This would be inconsistent with the Constitution (*Economic Freedom Fighters and Others v Speaker of the National Assembly and Another*, 2017: para 144).

This judgment suggests that while elected representatives would normally be subject to party discipline to support the policies and programmes of the party, this would not be permitted if this is not believed to be in the interest of the public. The Constitutional Court judgment seems to impose an obligation on MPs in certain situations to follow the dictates of personal conscience, as guided by the provisions of the South African Constitution. This point was driven home by the Constitutional Court in *United Democratic Movement v Speaker of the National Assembly and Others* (2017), a case in which the court was asked to declare that the speaker of the national assembly was permitted to order that a vote of no confidence in the president be held via secret ballot. Holding that the constitution did permit the speaker to do so, the court pointed out that the constitution required MPs to swear or affirm faithfulness to the Republic and obedience to the constitution and law, not to their political parties. Thus, when a conflict arises 'between upholding constitutional values and party loyalty, their irrevocable undertaking to in effect serve the people and do only what is in their best interests must prevail' (*United Democratic Movement v Speaker of the National Assembly and Others*, 2017: para 79). The court argued, idealistically, that because the electoral commission publishes the electoral lists of each political party before every election, voters would be aware 'which candidates are on that party's list and whether they can trust them'. Thus, according to the court, the loyalty of elected representatives to constitutional values should trump party loyalty because that is what voters voted for and what the constitution demands. For all the reasons set out in the previous section, in practice, it would be difficult for an individual MP (or elected representative in the provincial or local sphere) to follow their conscience against the strict instruction of party leaders – unless factional battles have weakened the party leadership and its authority to the extent that elected representatives believe that no action would be taken against them for defying the party line. It is therefore unclear what effect, if any, this judgment would have on the behaviour of individual elected representatives in times of high political drama, especially in cases where they are called on to vote for the party's candidate for speaker, president, premier or executive mayor, or where they are called on to vote for the removal of any incumbent. But given the increased judicialisation of politics – the tendency to revert to courts to resolve fundamentally political disputes (Le Roux and Davis, 2019: 5) – the likelihood that questions about the passing of votes of no confidence will end up in the court is not insignificant. When this happens, those challenging the removal from office will be able to rely on these passages in cases where the removal was demonstrably orchestrated for a nefarious or corrupt purpose or for some other reason not in line with the values of the constitution.

Second, in theory, the power of party leaders vis-à-vis elected representatives has been weakened by the ruling of the Constitutional Court in *United Democratic Movement v Speaker of the National Assembly and Others* (2017) allowing speakers to order voting by secret ballot when considering a no-confidence motion in a speaker, president, premier or executive mayor. Recall that a secret ballot is already required for the election of all these posts, but the constitution and, in the case of municipal councils, legislation, are silent about whether the speaker is permitted to allow a vote of no confidence to be conducted by secret ballot. Providing for a secret ballot would, in theory, allow individual elected representatives to vote for the candidate of their choice, and thus weaken party discipline and make the outcome of elections – especially in hung legislatures – less predictable. On the other hand, where voting occurs by secret ballot it becomes difficult for political parties to hold individual elected representatives accountable. This may lead to legislators voting for impermissible reasons, most notably because the representative was persuaded to vote by offering him or her a position or a monetary incentive (which is widely known as a bribe). In dealing with this question in *United Democratic Movement v Speaker of the National Assembly and Others* (2017: para 60), the Constitutional Court struck a delicate balance, holding that nothing in the constitution prevented the speaker of the national assembly from scheduling a secret vote when a motion of no confidence is tabled in the national assembly, but that this would not always be required. The Constitutional Court decided the case at a time when various opposition parties were attempting to hold former president Jacob Zuma accountable for various alleged and proven misdeeds. Although the court dealt specifically with the question of whether the speaker of the national assembly was permitted to hold a secret ballot in a vote of no confidence against the president in terms of section 102(2) of the constitution, the principles established also apply in the provincial and local spheres.

It is important to note that this judgment on the secret ballot is directly linked to the duty of the legislature to hold the president and the executive accountable, and did not speak directly to a situation where the vote of no confidence is conducted purely in an attempt to replace one governing coalition with another. Admittedly, it might sometimes be difficult to determine whether the ballot was conducted for the former or the latter reason, but if one studies the judgment carefully, it becomes clear that a secret ballot would be more appropriate in the former situation than in the latter. In the context of this case, dealing with attempts to remove former president Zuma from office, the Constitutional Court stated that a vote of no confidence was a powerful tool to hold the president accountable for his failure to carry out his constitutional obligations.[12] A vote of no confidence can be viewed as a last resort to which legislators would turn 'should regular mechanisms prove or appear to be ineffective' and when 'the people's representatives have, in a manner of speaking, virtually given up on the President or Cabinet' (*United Democratic Movement v Speaker of the National Assembly and Others*, 2017: para 46). The Constitutional Court linked the vote of no confidence to the duty of elected representatives to put country before party in cases where the head of the government is acting against the interests of 'the people'. This is, of course, not the only possible reason why political parties would support a vote of no confidence, especially in a hung legislature in which support for a coalition or minority government is fluid, and such a vote could topple a government and pave the way for a new coalition to take control of the government. The danger here is that individual elected representatives could be persuaded to support a vote of no confidence conducted by secret ballot for reasons that have nothing to do with their conscience or with holding the executive accountable. In the United Democratic Movement case the Constitutional Court signalled an awareness of this potential problem, and warned that a secret ballot would not always be appropriate. The court warned that secrecy could diminish the individual accountability of elected representatives, and that a secret vote could undermine the requirement for elected representatives to act in an open and transparent manner. In many cases the electorate would be entitled 'to know how their representatives carry out even some of their most sensitive obligations, such as passing a motion of no confidence', and the speaker is obliged to take this into account when 'considering whether voting is to be by secret or open ballot' (*United Democratic Movement v Speaker of the National Assembly and Others*, 2017: para 80).

There is always a danger that an MP, provincial legislator or council member could be bribed or otherwise persuaded to support such a vote, and this should be taken into account by any speaker when considering whether to allow a secret ballot or not. The Court warned in United Democratic Movement that the speaker should not discount the possibility that dishonest legislators would be swayed by bribes or 'other illegitimate methods of gaining undeserved majorities'. It warned that this 'possibility must not be lightly or naively taken out of the equation as a necessarily far removed and negligible possibility when the stakes are too high' (*United Democratic Movement v*

Speaker of the National Assembly and Others, 2017: para 81). In short, while a secret ballot may be required in cases in which the president, premier or mayor is genuinely being held accountable, the speaker should not allow a secret ballot in a vote of no confidence if there is a real possibility that this will turn the voting process into 'a fear- or money-inspired sham' (*United Democratic Movement v Speaker of the National Assembly and Others,* 2017: para 82). It is not clear how a speaker would know that a specific vote of no confidence falls into the one or other category. The judgment invests speakers with a considerable responsibility, which is made even more difficult by the fact that speakers remain members of their respective political parties and may be pressured to make a decision that would favour their own party. On the other hand, speakers run the risk that their decision would be challenged in a court and overturned. Thus far, it appears that speakers have dealt with this conundrum by interpreting the Constitutional Court judgment not as *permitting* a vote by secret ballot, but *requiring* it.

Though debate is unfolding on this issue at the time of writing, all votes of no confidence conducted after the handing down of this judgment have been conducted by secret ballot. If speakers routinely decide to conduct votes of no confidence by secret ballot, it will render the outcome of votes of no confidence more unpredictable, and may potentially lead to less stable coalition governments. In legislatures when no one party enjoys an absolute majority or in which it enjoys a minimal majority, the danger is that no-confidence votes conducted by secret ballot may lead to pocketbook politics[13] and could increase practices of vote buying. If this happens, minority or coalition governments are less likely to be stable and well functioning.

COALITION AND CONFIDENCE-AND-SUPPLY AGREEMENTS

Due to the manner in which the parliamentary system of government is regulated by the constitution and other legislation, the only sine qua non for the establishment of a government at the national, provincial or local level is the election of a president, premier or executive mayor by the majority of members of a particular legislature. Where no party obtains a majority of seats in a particular legislature, this necessitates the formation of a minority or coalition government, whose stability will depend largely on the willingness and ability of the legislators of the relevant political parties (and the respective leaderships of those parties) to work together, and on how committed the legislators of smaller parties (and the leadership of those parties) involved in the coalition or minority governments are to the arrangement that led to the election of the president, premier or executive mayor. When a speaker decides that legislators vote by secret ballot on a no-confidence motion in the president, premier or executive mayor, there is also a possibility that individual legislators from parties that support the government would be persuaded by financial or other incentives to support a vote of no confidence. It is unlikely that the legislature will tamper with South Africa's current system of parliamentary government, as it would require major rewriting of parts of the constitution (at least to amend the governance system at the national and provincial level), and the adoption of amendments by at least two-thirds of the members of the national assembly. This means that the formation of government at all three levels of government will continue to hinge on the election of the president and premiers, and, to some extent at least, executive mayors, and that the stability of these governments will continue to be at the mercy of the legislators and leadership of the parties represented in a legislature.

Little can be done to address the potential problems that arise from secret-ballot, no-confidence votes, as the Constitutional Court judgment on the matter can be undone only through constitutional amendment.[14] On the face of it, a more promising avenue for change could be to impose additional requirements (over and above securing the election of a preferred candidate as president, premier or executive mayor) for the formation of a coalition or minority government. Would it be possible to require that parties enter into formal coalition agreements, or confidence-and-supply agreements,[15] as a precondition for forming a government? This question is pertinent, as formal coalition agreements help to secure both intraparty and interparty commitment to the stability of the coalition or minority governments (Moury, 2011: 388). These kinds of agreements can be viewed as contracts through which parties commit themselves to cooperate in such a 'way that when they go through unpleasant situations, party leaders have a mechanism by which they can resist temptation or intra-party pressure to renege on their commitments' (Müller and Strøm, 2008: 165). As it is usually easier to get party regulars to approve concessions to coalition partners when they are included in a package deal, a coalition agreement may also reduce the potential destabilising impact of small 'kingmaker' parties (Müller and Strøm, 2008). Two types of agreements are of interest here. At one end of the spectrum, there is the formal coalition, in which the parties that form the coalition agree on a shared policy agenda, set out in a formal partnership agreement that includes how many and which executive posts would be held by which party (Hazell and Paun, 2009: 6). Such an agreement could include procedural safeguards, creating formal mechanisms to facilitate interparty consultation between coalition partners and resolve disputes between them (Hazell and Paun, 2009). Alternatively, the leading party could enter into a confidence-and-supply agreement with smaller parties. Such an agreement would ensure the support of smaller parties on crucial votes in exchange for policy or other concessions, an arrangement that can help preserve the identity of smaller parties (Hazell and Paun, 2009).

Neither the South African constitution nor legislation currently regulates coalition agreements, or such confidence-and-supply agreements. The constitution or ordinary legislation also does not impose any obligations on political parties to reach such agreements as a precondition for the establishment of governing coalitions or functional minority governments. There are also no firmly established political conventions in South Africa that require political parties to enter into coalition agreements as a prerequisite for the forming of coalition or minority governments. The relevant provisions of the constitution and other legislation currently focus exclusively on discrete events – the election or removal of speaker and president, premier or executive mayor – and leave the actual functioning of the government that is formed after such an election up to the parties. I would argue that this laissez-faire approach, combined with other political factors beyond the scope of this chapter, have had a major impact on the stability of such governments in the local government sphere. Imposing a two-step process for the formation of a government could reduce instability of such governments. The first step would be that the relevant legislature elects the head of the executive (president, premier or executive mayor), as is currently required. The second step would require the aspiring government to demonstrate that it is likely to enjoy a working majority to pass important legislation and to function as a government, by submitting a formal coalition agreement reached between the parties that will constitute the coalition, or – where a minority government is formed – by submitting a confidence-and-supply agreement reached between the parties that support the election of the head of the executive. The institution or individual(s) to whom such agreement is to be submitted and the power of veto is here left open for further reflection. This, however, should be as simple as possible to prevent undue complications and should be handled in the political terrain (e.g. the speaker rather than the judiciary).

However, any legislation imposing additional requirements for the formation of a government in the national and provincial sphere will be unconstitutional and invalid. This is because it would amount to an indirect amendment of the constitutional procedures regulating the formation of a government. An indirect amendment of the constitution without following the prescribed procedure for constitutional amendment would be unconstitutional and invalid. At the national and provincial level, any change would require a constitutional amendment. Although such an amendment would be less drastic than the amendment of the provisions that establish a parliamentary system of government, and would have a slightly better chance of being adopted, it remains a long shot. At the local government level, ordinary legislation regulates the formation of the municipal government, and it would therefore be far easier to adopt additional requirements for the formation of a government.[16]

CONCLUSION

South Africa opted for a slightly amended or hybrid version of a parliamentary system of government at the national, provincial and local level, instead of a system with a directly elected head of the executive, or a presidential system. The fundamental difference between the two systems is that under a presidential system the government cannot be replaced, even if a majority of the legislature so wishes. Because the government can be replaced in a legislative system of government if the majority of members of the legislature cease to support it, the position of the executive potentially becomes precarious when one party does not obtain a majority of seats in the legislature (Cheibub et al., 2004: 566). On the other hand, as the literature suggests, a parliamentary system generates more incentives for parties to form coalitions (Mainwaring, 1990; Huang, 1997: 138). This is more likely to happen when the policy differences between the dominant party, and some other parties that together constitute a legislative majority, are small. Where these differences are small, the dominant party would be able to make necessary policy concessions to the other parties and offer them enough incentives to hold the coalition together (Austen-Smith and Banks, 1988; Cheibub et al., 2004: 566).

In the hybrid parliamentary system operating in South Africa, however, when no party obtains an absolute majority in the legislature, parties will be forced to work together – whether formally or informally – to ensure the election of the head of the executive, which is a precondition for the formation of a government. This may lead to more unstable government. However, the parliamentary system of government is entrenched in the constitution, which can be amended only with the support of two-thirds of the members of the national assembly, as well as by six of the nine provincial delegations to the National Council of Provinces (Constitution of the Republic of South Africa, section 74(3)), and it is unlikely that such proposed amendments would garner the requisite majority in the national assembly.

In the absence of such a radical overhaul of the system of government, other smaller changes could be effected for the benefit of more stable and efficient coalition government. The existing electoral system, strict party discipline, and provisions that require an elected representative to retain membership of the party on whose ticket they were elected to remain a member of the relevant legislative body, all tilt power away from individual elected representatives towards party leaders. Simultaneously, the 2017 Constitutional Court pushback, rhetorically at least, asserts the power of individual elected representatives to act according to their conscience and according to the dictates of the constitution in service of the electorate. It is unclear, however, to what extent these developments may have an influence on the stability of coalition governments or on their effectiveness.

Ensuring strong party control over elected representatives might look more promising. This is because in this system, party leaders enforcing strict discipline may help to stabilise a coalition by preventing rogue elected representatives from selling their vote to opposition parties trying to topple the government. But, as the Tshwane example illustrated, party leaders desperately trying to topple the incumbent coalition government and take power could become part of the problem if they cannot muster a majority but use their power of disruption (in the form of non-attendance of council meetings) to indirectly collapse the government.

The pessimistic conclusion is that the problem with coalition government in South Africa has thus far been political, not legal or constitutional. Where parties that work together have large policy differences, or where those parties are not animated primarily by their stated ideological commitments but rather by the urge to acquire government power and the access to resources and patronage that this presents, the normal ideological glue that may hold coalitions together is absent. Given this dynamic, imposing an additional legal requirement on parties that seek to form a governing coalition or enter into a confidence-and-supply arrangement to submit a formal coalition or confidence-and-supply agreement, might go some way to reduce the instability of a government when no party won an outright majority of seats in the legislature.

REFERENCES

ANC 52nd National Conference. 20 December 2007. 'Resolutions', https://www.numsa.org.za/article/ancs-52nd-national-conference-resolutions-2008-08-04/, accessed 2 November 2020.

Austen-Smith, D. and Banks, J. 1988. 'Elections, coalitions, and legislative outcomes', *American Political Science Review*, 82 (2), 405–422.

Butler, A. 2013. 'The state of the South African presidency', *Journal of the Helen Suzman Foundation*, 71, 4–9.

Cheibub, J. A., Przeworski, A. and Saiegh, S. M. 2004. 'Government coalitions and legislative success under presidentialism and parliamentarism', *British Journal of Political Science*, 34 (4), 565–587.

Constitution of the African National Congress, 2017, https://www.anc1912.org.za/constitution-anc, accessed 12 November 2020.

Constitution of the Republic of South Africa, Act No. 108 of 1996.

De Lille v Democratic Alliance and Others (7882/18) [2018] ZAWCHC 81; [2018] 3 All SA 684 (WCC) (27 June 2018).

Democratic Alliance and Others v Premier for the Province of Gauteng and Others (18577/2020) [2020] ZAGPPHC 119; [2020] 2 All SA 793 (GP) (29 April 2020).

Democratic Alliance v Speaker of the National Assembly and Others (CCT 143/15; CCT 171/15) [2016] ZACC 11; 2016 (5) BCLR 618 (CC); 2016 (3) SA 580 (CC) (31 March 2016).

Democratic Alliance Federal Constitution (2020), https://cdn.da.org.za/wp-content/uploads/2020/11/09091807/DA-Constitution-As-Adopted-on-31-October-2020-final.pdf, accessed 12 November 2020.

De Visser, J. 2009. 'Developmental local government in South Africa: Institutional fault lines', *Commonwealth Journal of Local Governance*, 13 (2), 7–25.

De Vos, P. 2015. 'It's my party (and I'll do what I want to)?: Internal party democracy and Section 19 of the South African Constitution', *South African Journal on Human Rights*, 31 (1), 30–55.

De Vos, P. 28 October 2020. 'Will a recent SCA judgment help to fix the political dysfunction in Tshwane?', *Constitutionally Speaking*, https://constitutionallyspeaking.co.za/will-a-recent-sca-judgment-help-to-fix-the-political-dysfunction-in-tshwane, accessed 9 November 2020.

De Vos, P. and Freedman, W. 2014. *South African Constitutional Law in Context*. Oxford: Oxford University Press.

Dodd, L. 2015. *Coalitions in Parliamentary Government*. Princeton, N. J.: Princeton University Press.

Economic Freedom Fighters and Others v Speaker of the National Assembly and Another (CCT76/17) [2017] ZACC 47; 2018 (3) BCLR 259 (CC); 2018 (2) SA 571 (CC) (29 December 2017).

Economic Freedom Fighters v Speaker of the National Assembly and Others; Democratic Alliance v Speaker of the National Assembly and Others (CCT 143/15; CCT 171/15) [2016] ZACC 11; 2016 (5) BCLR 618 (CC); 2016 (3) SA 580 (CC) (31 March 2016).

Gerber, J. 27 August 2018. 'DA axes Nelson Mandela Bay councillor after speaker's ousting', *News24*, https://www.news24.com/news24/southafrica/news/da-axes-nelson-mandela-bay-councillor-after-speakers-ousting-20180827, accessed 5 June 2020.

Götz, G., Khanyile, S. and Katumba, S. 14 December 2016. 'Voting patterns in the 2016 local government elections', Gauteng City Region Observatory, https://www.gcro.ac.za/outputs/map-of-the-month/detail/voting-patterns-in-the-2016-local-government-elections/, accessed on 9 November 2020.

Hazell, R. and Paun, A. (eds.) 2009. *Making Minority Government Work: Hung parliaments and the challenge for Westminster and Whitehall*. Institute for Government, https://www.instituteforgovernment.org.uk/sites/default/files/publications/Making%20minority%20government%20work.pdf, accessed 12 November 2020.

Huang, T. 1997. 'Party systems in Taiwan and South Korea', in Diamond, L., Plattner, M. F., Chu, Y. and Tien, H. (eds.) *Consolidating the Third Wave Democracies: Themes and perspectives*. Baltimore, Md.: Johns Hopkins University Press, 135–159.

Le Roux, M. and Davis, D. 2019. *Lawfare: Judging politics in South Africa*. Johannesburg: Jonathan Ball Publishers.

Lodge, T. and Scheidegger, U. 2006. 'Political parties and democratic governance in South Africa', https://eisa.org/pdf/rr25.pdf, accessed 3 November 2020.

Lowell, A. L. 2013. *The Governments of France, Italy and Germany*. Boston: Harvard University Press.

Mainwaring, S. 1990. 'Presidentialism in Latin America', *Latin American Research Review*, 25 (1), 157–179.

Majola v The President (48541/2010) [2012] ZAGPJHC 236 (30 October 2012).

McCain, N. 8 August 2020. 'Mangaung mayor ousted in motion of no confidence', *News24*, https://www.news24.com/news24/SouthAfrica/News/mangaung-mayor-ousted-in-motion-of-no-confidence-20200808, accessed on 18 November 2020.

Mnquma Local Municipality and Another v Premier of the Eastern Cape and Others (231/2009) [2009] ZAECBHC 14 (5 August 2009).

Moury, C. 2011. 'Coalition agreement and party mandate: How coalition agreements constrain the ministers', *Party Politics*, 17 (3), 385–404.

Mtyala, Q. 30 November 2011. 'Security for DA man after ANC bribery claims', *IOL*, https://www.iol.co.za/news/south-africa/western-cape/

security-for-da-man-after-anc-bribery-claims-1189481, accessed 17 November 2020.

Müller, W. C. and Strøm, K. 2008. 'Coalition agreements and cabinet governance', in Strøm, K., Müller, W. C. and Bergman, T. (eds.) *Cabinets and Coalition Bargaining: The democratic life cycle in Western Europe*. Oxford: Oxford University Press.

New Nation Movement NPC and Others v President of the Republic of South Africa and Others (CCT110/19) [2020] ZACC 11; 2020 (8) BCLR 950 (CC); 2020 (6) SA 257 (CC) (11 June 2020).

Nicholson, Z. and Coetzee, C. 7 May 2014. 'ANC accused of trying to bribe DA man', *IOL*, https://www.iol.co.za/capetimes/news/anc-accused-of-trying-to-bribe-da-man-1684803, accessed 18 November 2020.

Nyakombi, M. 14 November 2016. 'ANC members tire of waiting for imposed ward councillors to resign', *GroundUp*, https://www.groundup.org.za/article/anc-members-tired-waiting-imposed-ward-councilors-resign/, accessed 9 November 2020.

Premier for the Province of Gauteng and Others v Democratic Alliance and Others (394/2020) [2020] ZASCA 136 (27 October 2020).

Ramakatsa v Magashule (CCT 109/12) [2012] ZACC 31; 2013 (2) BCLR 202 (CC) (18 December 2012).

Russon, R. D. 2011. 'Ten years of democratic local government elections in South Africa: Is the tide turning?', *Journal of African Elections*, 10 (1), 74–98.

Seleka, N. 27 February 2020. 'Still no mayor for Tshwane after EFF and ANC walk out of council meeting', *News24*, https://www.news24.com/news24/SouthAfrica/News/still-no-mayor-for-tshwane-after-eff-and-anc-walk-out-of-council-meeting-20200227, accessed 9 November 2020.

Southall, R. 2005. 'The "Dominant Party Debate" in South Africa', *Africa Spectrum*, 40 (1), 61–82.

The Citizen. 2017. 'DA alleges opposition councillor was bribed to betray them', https://citizen.co.za/news/south-africa/1538389/da-alleges-one-councillors-bribed-betray/, accessed 2 November 2020.

Tlouamma and Others v Mbethe, Speaker of the National Assembly of the Parliament of the Republic of South Africa and Another (A 3236/15) [2015] ZAWCHC 140; 2016 (1) SA 534 (WCC); [2016] 1 All SA 235 (WCC); 2016 (2) BCLR 242 (WCC) (7 October 2015).

Toxopeüs, M. 18 July 2019. 'Municipalities (I): Evaluating executive authority in municipalities', Politicsweb, https://www.politicsweb.co.za/opinion/municipalities-i-evaluating-executive-authority-in, accessed 8 June 2020.

United Democratic Movement v Speaker of the National Assembly and Others (CCT89/17) [2017] ZACC 21; 2017 (8) BCLR 1061 (CC); 2017 (5) SA 300 (CC) (22 June 2017).

Wolf, L. 2014. 'The right to stand as an independent candidate in national and provincial elections: *Majola v The President'*, *South African Journal of Human Rights*, 30 (1), 159–182.

TEN

The impact of coalitions on South Africa's metropolitan administrations

Crispian Olver

South Africa's eight metropolitan municipalities differ substantially from the remaining 256 municipalities in terms of their sheer size, resources and economic activity. They are home to 39.9 per cent of the population, generate 55.9 per cent of the national GDP, and spend 59.3 per cent of local government revenues (Stats SA, 2016; Arndt et al., 2018; National Treasury, 2020).[1] The scale and economic importance of such massive conurbations require unique governance arrangements, which emphasise long-range vision and planning, innovation, and the management of complex systems, in addition to the bread-and-butter local government issues of utility services, land-use planning and community services. In recognition of their unique needs, metropolitan areas are governed by integrated single-tier municipalities, while the rest of the country is governed by a two-tier system of local and district municipalities.[2]

On the interface between politics and municipal administration, Max Weber, one the founders of modern sociology, argued that for modern bureaucracy to be effective, it had to be separated from both politics and the personal interests of its incumbents. Instead, it had to be constituted according to objective rules, with each office having a clearly defined sphere of competence arranged in a hierarchical manner under a rigorous system of discipline and control. Above all, a bureaucracy had to be meritocratic, its personnel selected and appointed on the basis of competence, with promotion according to performance, not political connections (Weber, 1978: 331). Weber commented that the involvement of political parties in appointments to the bureaucracy could lead to disastrous outcomes, and saw the relationship between bureaucracies and political parties as inherently fraught. He argued for a clear separation between the spheres of politics and administration (Weber, 1978: 395).

Subsequent authors have questioned the empirical basis of the distinction (Evans, 1995; Svara, 1999; Peters, 2001; Alford et al., 2017). The Weberian tradition has been criticised for presenting the challenges faced by managers as a set of binary choices, when it is more akin to a blurred zone that requires skilful navigation. Svara (1999) talks about the mutual interdependence and interconnections between politicians and senior administrators. Alford describes the relationship with politicians as characterised by 'interdependency, extensive interaction, distinct but overlapping roles', with 'political supremacy and administrative subordination coexisting with reciprocity of influence' (Alford et al., 2017: 755). According to Alford, most public-sector managers view the dividing line as blurred, a zone of interaction within which a range of practices and behaviours take place. There may be merit to both Alford's and Weber's versions. For instance, Peters (2001) has suggested that the line of separation between politics and administration is a device, a 'useful fiction' that can structure the debate and legitimate certain actions. Evans (1995: 32) argues that bureaucracies must be both autonomous and embedded, combining the meritocratic aspects of Weberian bureaucracy with institutional channels that allow for constant social renegotiation and engagement about goals and policies.

This chapter explores these themes in relation to South African local government, in which a Weberian administrative model sits uncomfortably alongside robust political involvement in municipal administration. Certainly, the South African legislative framework for local government makes a clear separation between the role of the municipal manager[3] as head of the administration and municipal accounting officer, and the executive mayor or executive committee that oversees, reviews and sets policy, and makes recommendations to council.[4] The terminology ('executive committee', 'executive mayor') is confusing, as it implies a power to put plans or actions into effect, when in law this is limited to a supervisory or oversight function. The legal ambiguity may be partly to blame for the persistent problems in the way in which the administrative and so-called executive structures interrelate, and beyond them, for the way in which the political domain as a whole – the councillors in council and the leaders of political parties represented in council – interrelate with officials within the municipal administration.

Coalitions in local government have tended to accentuate problems in the political-administrative interface, even though there have been some remarkably stable coalitions, which have been able to insulate the administration from political infighting and build performing administrations. Others have had a more deleterious impact than pre-existing single-party-dominant systems. This chapter reviews the impact of coalition government on the administration in metropolitan municipalities, concentrating on the post-2016 period. It draws on primary research undertaken by the author in three metropolitan municipalities (Johannesburg, Tshwane and Nelson Mandela Bay), complemented by the work of other authors who have been exploring the terrain of local public administration.

THE RELATIONSHIP BETWEEN POLITICS AND ADMINISTRATION IN LOCAL GOVERNMENT

This political-administrative interface has vexed democratic local government almost from the inception of the current system in 2000. For instance, in a comprehensive review of the new local government system undertaken in 2009,[5] tensions between politicians and municipal administrations were found to be widespread, with insufficient separation of powers between political parties and councillors, and in turn between councillors and the municipal administration. Political factionalism and polarisation were found to have contributed to the deterioration of municipal functionality. This was ascribed to battles over access to state resources, which had led to a 'culture of patronage and nepotism' and rendered the formal municipal accountability system 'ineffective and inaccessible to many citizens' (De Visser and Steytler, 2009: 99).

Such tensions have not been restricted to local government. In its thoroughly researched and consulted diagnostic report, the National Planning Commission listed tensions in the political administrative interface as contributing to the uneven performance of the public service as a whole, and bemoaned the level of political influence over the day-to-day operations of the public service (NPC, 2011: 24). A rich body of South African literature has sought to explain the extent of political influence over public administration (Von Holdt, 2010; Netshitenzhe, 2012; Chipkin, 2013; Beresford, 2015; Chipkin and Swilling, 2020). In the context of the political transition, the state has been viewed as the focal point for new classes seeking access to state resources, linked to the rise of patronage-based party politics (Von Holdt et al., 2011; Netshitenzhe, 2012; Beresford, 2015). Others have described the process of transformation of the state as a deliberate effort to bring the state under political control, in which loyalty and adherence to party policy were more important than impartiality and autonomy (Chipkin, 2016: 19). As part of this project, political discretion was introduced into the recruitment process and even the design of posts, and in the absence of entrance examinations or performance-related career advancement, the administrative autonomy of the state was reduced.

The extent of political interference has been confirmed by municipal managers, who have cited numerous instances of political pressure in the appointment of staff and the awarding of contracts, sometimes backed by threats to life and family members if they did not comply. The Institute of Municipal Managers' annual conference observed that conflict between mayors, municipal managers and speakers was an accepted part of their working conditions (SALGA, 2017). Successive auditor-general reports into the state of municipal finances have commented on the extent to which political infighting at the council level and interference in municipal administrations have weakened oversight and resulted in a lack of consequences for poor financial management. According to the auditor-general, the role of political leadership is critical – their inaction, or inconsistent action, creates a culture of no consequences: 'The leadership sets the tone at the top at municipalities. If the municipality's leaders are unethical; have a disregard for governance, compliance and control; and are not committed to transparency and accountability, it will filter through to the lower levels of the municipality' (Auditor-General of South Africa, 2019).

The appointment of 'politically aligned' senior management in municipalities is a widespread practice, but as a South African Cities Network survey[6] of the built environment in cities found, politically connected senior officials can at times be useful, linking administrative projects to political support and imperatives. However, they are also vulnerable to conflicts that may arise between them and political players. This becomes particularly problematic at junior levels, in instances where political intervention is sought to address minor administrative matters and disciplinary issues. In addition, successful working relationships between councillors and administrations become heavily dependent on the personalities involved. As noted by the South African Cities Network, 'Personality clashes between MMCs [members of mayoral committees] and officials or mayors and officials can derail projects, as can difficult management styles, and some may be interested in the abuse of the state for their own ends. This is a significant threat to built environment projects and spatial transformation' (Foster, 2019: 19).

THE IMPACT OF COALITION POLITICS

Electoral outcomes have interacted with what appears to be an already vexed interface between politics and administration in different ways. The South African local government electoral system combines ward-based representation with a proportional representation (PR) system that ensures parties are represented in council in proportion to the total number of votes they receive.[7] This has accentuated the role that political parties play in municipal affairs and, compared to first-past-the-post (FPTP) systems, has also resulted in more frequent instances where there is no outright majority for any party.

Coalition governments have been a feature of South African local government since the system was introduced in 2000. Municipal managers have noted that conflicts between political and administrative spheres were accentuated in coalition governments where political tensions were hardwired into the ruling coalition (SALGA, 2017: 21). The South African Cities Network survey commented that '(c)oalition based executives are inherently unstable, and minority coalitions are particularly unstable, with executives particularly sensitive to political wind changes… Senior management instability also leads to uncertainty and low morale amongst mid-ranking officials, driving out those with transferrable skills' (Foster, 2019: 3).

However, other coalitions have proven successful in managing the affairs of their local constituencies. For instance, a survey by Good Governance Africa found that of the 20 best performing municipalities in the country, five were governed by multiparty coalitions. They ascribed this to improved levels of oversight of those administrations. Coalition partners supposedly had a collective interest in preventing the abuse of office by other partners, and the increased oversight, coupled with the consequences of the coalition slipping up, helped to limit abuse and improve government performance (Good Governance Africa, 2019).

The positive effects of coalitions on governance in some municipalities initially appeared to accord with the metropolitan experience. Until the 2016 local government elections, the only example of coalition government in metropolitan areas had been in

Cape Town (2006–11), in which the Democratic Alliance (DA), with 43 per cent of the seats in the council, had assembled a coalition with smaller parties to hold a narrow majority. During this period, the city manager and a large proportion of the senior managers who had been appointed under the previous African National Congress (ANC) administration were replaced. Nevertheless, the current city manager in Cape Town, Lungelo Mbandazayo, who worked in Cape Town at the time, noted that while the then mayor, Helen Zille, micromanaged the administration, she achieved results. 'Helen always gets things done. She is not the person to just refer you to someone else. She will always follow up. She does not leave you in the lurch. If you want something done, she will follow up until she gets what she wants. I didn't have a problem with that' (Olver, 2019: 81). The DA promoted Cape Town as a good-governance model and used it to build its electoral base, going on to win an outright majority of 61 per cent in the 2011 local government elections.

METRO COALITIONS POST-2016

Disruptive political developments in the metros[8] were to impact negatively on metro administrations, sometimes dramatically. The events highlighted the difficulties faced by coalition governments.

In the 2016 local government elections dramatic changes occurred, with four previously ANC-run metropolitan municipalities falling under coalition governments. The DA obtained 46.71 per cent in Nelson Mandela Bay, 43.15 per cent in Tshwane and 38.41 per cent in Johannesburg, enabling it to pull together multiparty coalitions with the support of other smaller parties, including a confidence-and-supply agreement with the Economic Freedom Fighters (EFF). The ANC narrowly missed a majority in Ekurhuleni and retained control through a coalition with smaller parties (Table 10.1).

The coalition in Ekurhuleni was to prove remarkably stable, headed by the outspoken ANC mayor Mzwandile Masina, who remains an advocate of the ANC's so-called 'radical economic transformation' faction. The ANC needed only one party to pull together a majority coalition, but entered a formal coalition with the African Independent

Table 10.1: Comparative results in four metros in the 2016 local government elections

Metro	Votes per party (ward plus PR) (%)			
	DA (%)	ANC (%)	EFF (%)	Other (%)
Ekurhuleni	34.15	48.64	11.23	5.98
Johannesburg	38.41	44.50	11.09	6.00
Nelson Mandela Bay	46.71	40.92	5.12	7.25
Tshwane	43.15	41.25	11.63	3.97

Source: IEC, 2020.

Congress (AIC), the Pan Africanist Congress (PAC), the Patriotic Alliance (PA) and the Independent Ratepayers Association of South Africa.[9] There have been some disagreements between the ANC and coalition members over the treatment of officials implicated in financial irregularities, but the coalition has remained intact.

The nature of the DA-led metro coalitions post-2016 took a particular form, as these were minority coalitions without a voting majority in council. The EFF initially supported the DA-led coalitions on a confidence-and-supply basis, in which they did not accept positions within the mayoral committees, and instead supported the election of the mayor, the approval of the budget, and other matters on an issue-by-issue basis. There was no formal coalition agreement between the EFF and the DA, which led to some difficulties for the administration in responding to subsequent divisions.

The EFF held the balance of power in Johannesburg and Tshwane, and neither the DA nor the ANC could muster sufficient votes to control council without their support. In Johannesburg, the mayor, Herman Mashaba, had a more collaborative relationship with the EFF, partly because the EFF had been given considerable influence over appointments, procurement and policy decisions in the metro. However, Mashaba resigned as mayor in October 2019 due to a divisive battle within the DA, providing an opportunity for the ANC to persuade the smaller parties in the council to side with them and form a new coalition government.

In Tshwane, the DA's first mayor, Solly Msimanga, had a turbulent history and was replaced in February 2019 with Stevens Mokgalapa, whose tenure was similarly troubled. As relations with the EFF soured, the DA's engagement with the EFF became increasingly fractious, to the extent that the mayor could no longer secure meetings with the EFF.

In Nelson Mandela Bay, the DA could potentially rule with smaller parties alone, excluding the EFF, but when the United Democratic Movement (UDM) deputy mayor, Mongameli Bobani, was removed in April 2017 over allegations of corruption, the coalition did not have sufficient votes in council to muster a majority. The trigger came in August 2018, when the EFF vowed to remove DA mayor Athol Trollip to punish the DA over its land policy. The DA's coalition partners switched sides, collaborated with the ANC to remove the DA from power, and installed a new coalition with Bobani as mayor. After a disastrous tenure during which new allegations of corruption surfaced, Bobani was removed in December 2019, and an interim ANC mayor installed. Bobani succumbed to COVID-19 in November 2020. On the day of his funeral a warrant for his arrest was issued by the Hawks, along with warrants for nine prominent ANC leaders and officials, over their alleged involvement in fraud relating to the city's Integrated Public Transport System. The following month the ANC lost control of the municipality to a DA-led coalition, with DA provincial leader Nqaba Bhanga elected mayor.

MANAGEMENT INSTABILITY UNDER COALITION GOVERNMENTS

There was significant administrative upheaval following the 2016 elections, with new city managers appointed in three of the four coalition-run metros. The South African Cities Network survey of senior management in metros following the elections noted that in cities led by coalitions, senior officials felt inadequately protected from their MMCs and the mayor. In two instances, this was attributed to weak city managers who avoided conflict and were focused on their own survival (Foster, 2019: 5).

Despite changing its municipal manager, Ekurhuleni's management team appeared to stabilise. Subsequently, nevertheless, the chief financial officer, the executive director for transport and the chief operating officer were suspended over alleged financial misconduct, with coalition partners raising concerns that the action taken by the municipality had been too lenient (Madia, 2019).

In Johannesburg, there were considerable changes in management following the elections. Many senior management contracts were due for renewal, and in the process very few of the previous incumbents were reappointed. The incoming mayor, Herman Mashaba, openly claimed that the senior management were loyal to the previous ANC regime, were implicated in corruption and were trying to undermine his administration.[10] Disciplinary cases were instituted against a number of managers, sometimes on spurious charges,[11] and, together with expiring contracts and some resignations, this led to changes in the posts of city manager, chief operating officer, chief financial officer, head of legal services, head of the Johannesburg Metropolitan Police Department, executive director for human settlements, executive director for planning and executive director for transport, as well as the chief executive officers of the Johannesburg Roads Agency, Pikitup, and Johannesburg Water and City Power, among others. A DA MMC at the time was critical of the wholesale changes, saying that '(h)e [the mayor] has gutted the administration, pulled much more power into this office than [the former ANC mayor] Parks [Tau]. Officials are now scared to sit on procurement panels, they are scared about any bending of rules to get things done'.[12] However, the removal of managers seemed to come unstuck when it came to finding suitable replacements that were acceptable to coalition partners. As the former MMC explained, the leverage given to the EFF over appointments resulted in poorly qualified staff being appointed.[13]

In Tshwane, the city manager took up the post six months after the election, by which time the organogram had been changed.[14] The city manager was able to fill the new posts, but commented that he was under pressure to appoint specific people in certain positions, which was the source of much friction between the city manager and the executive mayor. According to Mosola, he (Mosola) simply refused to appoint staff that he considered unfit for the position.[15]

Nelson Mandela Bay initially retained the city manager, who had been appointed some nine months previously and had not made wholesale changes to the administration. But after the DA had been removed from the coalition, one of Bobani's first moves was to suspend the city manager over allegations of corruption and improper advice to council. National Treasury noted the suspension 'of a very capable city manager' (Mashoeshoe and Mokgabodi, 2019). At the time of writing, some 18 months later, the case had still not been finalised, even though Bobani was no longer the mayor. In addition, other key senior executive positions had not been filled, including those of chief financial officer and head of corporate services. Furthermore, the Integrated Public Transport System was being run by an acting head 'whose skills and experience in how the [Integrated Public Transport System] works is very questionable' (Mashoeshoe and Mokgabodi, 2019: 3). The city manager, Johan Mettler, also noted that in Nelson Mandela Bay certain executive director positions were filled by persons he did not consider suitable for the position, but given that he had, by that stage, been suspended, he was powerless to do anything.

The extent of the turbulence in metropolitan administrations is demonstrated by comparing the average tenure for municipal managers. In local government as a whole, they last an average of three and a half years (Foster, 2019: 19), while in metros the average tenure is 15 months (Auditor-General of South Africa, 2019: 16). As the auditor-general noted in making this finding, stability in key leadership positions correlates closely with both financial and overall performance (Auditor-General of South Africa, 2019: 16). The South African Cities Network study also found that the effect on lower levels, particularly mid-ranking officials, was profound, resulting in uncertainty and low morale, and driving out those with transferrable skills (Foster, 2019: 3).

POLITICAL INTERFERENCE AND GOVERNANCE ISSUES

Political interference in the administrative affairs of the metros, which was already a feature of the pre-2016 system, continued under metro coalitions.

Previous studies have documented extensive political interference in the Ekurhuleni metro administration, for instance, in the housing delivery process (Marutlulle and Ijeoma, 2015) and in supply chain management (Legodi, 2017). Since the 2016 coalition, Ekurhuleni's governance and institutional arrangements appear to have been stable, and it has managed to improve its key performance areas[16] for governance from 76 per cent in 2015/16 to 82 per cent in 2017/18 (Bell and Baloyi, 2019: 15). However, the auditor-general commented that the level of assurance provided by senior management, internal audit, the audit committee and the municipal public accounts committee had regressed during the 2017/18 financial year (Bell and Baloyi, 2019).

In Johannesburg, there have been reports of political interference in the affairs of the administration under both ANC (Comrie, 2018; 2019) and DA rule (Mailovich, 2018; Phillips, 2018; Brümmer and Reddy, 2019). During Mashaba's term, the chief executive officer of the Johannesburg Roads Agency resigned over the mayor's failure to stop interference by the Johannesburg Roads Agency board chair in supply-chain matters (Phillips, 2018). The stability of Mashaba's administration seemed to depend on certain coalition partners being granted access to areas of influence and patronage, namely the Johannesburg Roads Agency, in the case of the IFP and the EFF (Phillips, 2018), and various appointments, insourcing arrangements and tenders, in the case of the EFF (Reddy, Brümmer and amaBhungane, 2018; Brümmer and Reddy, 2019). The consultations required by coalition politics also caused administrative decision-making to slow down. The executive director in charge of the transport department found that everything took twice as long to arrange: 'It's a nightmare. I have reduced my targets, not because I do not have the skills in my department, just because of how long it takes to get a decision. And it is affecting our credibility,' explained Seftel.[17] National Treasury assessed the state of governance in Johannesburg during the 2018/19 financial year as fragile, and noted that while council continued to meet and conduct its business, the progress with decisions from the municipal public accounts committee had been poor (Voigt, 2019).

In Tshwane, the city manager found that MMCs and other councillors had already formed relationships with the administration and were used to giving direct instructions to them. The city manager took a hard line on the relationship between executive directors and MMCs. He insisted that if any MMC or councillor wanted to give an instruction to any of his staff, it must be in writing and brought to the city manager's attention. Drawing such a definitive line was not popular, because it shut down opportunities for 'any opportunistic behaviour': 'I had to make it absolutely clear that I was the boss, and that I was the only person who could give instructions to the administration. In fact, I took disciplinary action against a number of managers for transgressing this instruction,' said Mosola.[18] The former city manager commented that heads of departments preferred the previously blurred lines of accountability, in which they could get instructions from both the city manager and the MMC, as the gap this created allowed for gaming the system and corrupt transactions to take place. In his efforts to hold the line between the administration and politics, the city manager felt that he never had support, either from managers or from politicians.[19]

In the context of fractious coalition politics in Tshwane, decision-making became unduly delayed. The arrangement with the EFF meant that on most strategic issues the DA had to consult at a senior level with the EFF to reach a decision. Only then could the matter be passed on to the city manager for implementation. For the officials, this created a potentially chaotic situation that was difficult to manage. Every process became extended because of the consultation that was needed with different political parties, and what would normally take one week to achieve was pushed out to four weeks. This forced a level of micro-management on the city manager that was almost impossible to sustain.[20]

As the DA's relationship with the EFF imploded in Tshwane, the city manager became the effective interlocutor between the parties, forcing him to broker agreements between them. As a result, the city manager became involved in the politics of the city, and he felt that he had crossed the line that should exist between politics and administration. He was forced to play this role for a two-year period, before he himself fell out with the council leadership and left the city in August 2019. 'The management of the city under these circumstances was very difficult,' said Mosola.[21] National Treasury commented on the situation in the metro, noting that the lack of a clear majority and differences in party policies were risks that affected the city's institutional stability (Maja, 2019).

Even in the previously stable Nelson Mandela Bay coalition, problems arose after April 2017 because it was difficult for the administration to predict whether items would pass council. In the circumstances, planning became impossible, as the officials had to constantly take account of new contingencies or initiatives demanded by coalition partners.[22] The city manager, Johan Mettler, found that the coalition arrangements and pressure on delivery had created the space for certain politicians to bypass the normal lines of accountability. The relationship between city managers and their subordinates was already somewhat confused, with executive directors who are meant to report to the city manager having direct engagement with their MMCs. Mettler found that certain MMCs now took to issuing direct instructions to their executive directors without going through the city manager: 'Suddenly everyone in the municipality had become an expert on something. I found that there were parallel operations running in finance and electricity. This resulted in accountability for delivery becoming really confused, and it tested the relationships in the municipality like never before'.[23]

In Nelson Mandela Bay, the officials found themselves also being drawn into coalition politics. Even if the mayor supported an item, he still had to consult his caucus and his coalition partners, and in many instances would come back to the administration with a compromise formulation, which the city manager then had to implement. The city manager found that he had to try and anticipate these compromises to be prepared for what ensued. Frequently he had to engage with MMCs and coalition partners informally, outside the formal channels of communication, to solicit their views on matters.[24] The consequence of the extended consultation processes was that there was less time to act once decisions were made, while the volume of work, especially having to deal with additional considerations from council, increased. As a result, the entire system became stressed, and this was felt throughout the organisation.[25] This led National Treasury to conclude that '(t)here have been many worrying signs of the loss of many of the past governance and financial gains in Nelson Mandela Bay over the last 3 months, upon entry of the new coalition government' (Mashoeshoe and Mokgabodi, 2019: 3). The extent of the political fallout between the coalition partners in Nelson Mandela Bay was even observed by the normally sanguine auditor-general, in noting that the political infighting negatively influenced their assessment of the assurance provided by council, the mayor and senior management (Auditor-General of South Africa, 2019: 17).

At the same time, municipal managers and section 56 managers[26] are not merely passive bystanders, and they themselves have an impact on the political sphere that can affect the balance of power between coalition partners. Municipal managers strongly influence what information councillors from different parties receive, and shape the policy alternatives that are presented. Officials can delay or redirect decision-making processes and can set the terms for debates in ways that clarify, obfuscate or distort issues. At times, municipal managers are required to give legal advice on highly political matters, which can tip decision-making in favour of one or other party. Officials have also been active or passive collaborators in directing resources from municipalities to political parties, and some stakeholders, such as organised labour, are active participants in municipal politics in their own right, supporting particular coalition partners.[27] While political interference is often presented as a one-way, top-down phenomenon, it frequently cuts both ways.

Policy uncertainty
Other than in Ekurhuleni, a high degree of policy uncertainty accompanied the changes in coalitions, particularly when this affected long-range planning instruments that were used to inform operational

decisions. For instance, there appeared to be an incoherent stance on core development planning concerns, such as social and spatial integration, densification and mixed-income settlements. This may reflect the inevitable learning curve that new political leadership needs to undergo. In Nelson Mandela Bay, this had been assuaged by a sound working relationship between the city manager and the DA mayor, Athol Trollip, but relations with the subsequent coalition under Bobani deteriorated.[28] In Johannesburg and Tshwane, in particular, the DA appeared to be unable to have consensual discussions on policy issues within its coalition, and technocrats who had to deal with these issues ended up being caught in the middle.[29] In Johannesburg there was resistance to the carefully constructed spatial development strategy, especially insofar as it related to the Corridors of Freedom,[30] which was seen as the previous administration's legacy, and with which the mayor did not wish to be associated. The officials had to find ways to broach the same issues using different language. For instance, the officials obtained traction with the concept of 'transit-orientated development corridors'. While the corridors were in the interests of some property developers, there were inherent conflicts between the DA's pro-market approach, which protected the interests of middle-class residents and large developers, and the EFF's approach to land invasions and land expropriation without compensation. The planning executive director found an inability to rise above narrow party considerations, and described the confused approach to spatial planning as 'fake it as you go', as opposed to real consensus around spatial-planning objectives.[31]

In Tshwane, similarly, policy dissonance was most marked over land. It was not possible to get any council decision on land or development, particularly if it involved council land. Any references to land had to be taken out of council decisions. For two years no city-owned land could be made available to developers, and the city was only able to offer long-term leases to developers. This had a massive impact on the development of the city, not least because the city was unable to raise revenue, which it sorely needed, or to make use of other tools normally at its disposal to drive development. As the city manager noted, 'The fallout went to the extent of stopping projects even after they had been approved by council. The overall impact was that the city was unable to fulfil its obligations, and to provide the services that it was meant to.'[32]

This confused approach to policy extended to other catalytic projects, such as the bus rapid transport systems, Rea Vaya in Johannesburg and Are Yeng in Tshwane. In Johannesburg there was a high degree of emphasis on performance targets, such as fixing potholes and traffic lights, but complex integration projects such as Rea Vaya did not feature on the agenda.[33] National Treasury noted that Johannesburg was underspending on the public transport network grant, which funded the Rea Vaya system, due to delays in awarding contracts for key components of the system (Voigt, 2019: 18). Even in Ekurhuleni, 'implementation challenges' were noted with regard to the Integrated Rapid Public Transport Network (Bell and Baloyi, 2019: 4), although this had more to do with supply chain issues than policy alignment.

Similar findings emerged from the South African Cities Network study, which found that instability in both the politics and the administrations threatened the long-term strategic vision for spatial transformation and the ability to land spatially transformative built-environment projects. This was particularly evident when it came to allocating budgets to spatial transformation projects and spending those budgets (Foster, 2019: 18).

The impact on the budget process

The most difficult problems arose in terms of preparing and adopting budgets, and in containing the fiscal fallout from unaffordable compromises. While Ekurhuleni, with its stronger coalition structure, did not appear to experience difficulties in passing the budget, this was a problem in the three metros under DA-led coalitions, as in the case of budget adjustments. These coalitions did not have sufficient votes in council to muster a majority, and it was difficult to predict whether items would pass council. The EFF held the swing vote in each council, and insisted on certain measures to get their budgets passed.

In Johannesburg, the EFF insisted on insourcing all previously outsourced personnel contracts. Mayor Mashaba's view was that all previous contracts implemented by the ANC were corrupt, so he had no problem with abandoning existing outsourcing contracts. As a consequence, Johannesburg placed approximately 10,000 additional staff on the payroll.[34] The rushed and politically driven insourcing affected service delivery. For instance, the guards at the Rea Vaya stations did not get communications facilities or a back-up centre, and were unable to effectively safeguard stations and passengers. The Westbury station was vandalised during protests when the security staff ran away.[35] Executive directors in Johannesburg also complained that undue delays in signing off the budget were impacting on their performance. The executive director for transport commented that '(a)ll my performance indicators are down; in fact, my performance is the poorest it has ever been. Part of the reason is that the city manager spent six months before he signed the budget. Everything was set up, but the city manager went back and forth, and refused to sign.'[36]

In Tshwane, the 2019/20 budget adjustments were never approved, which meant that there was no budget for some urgent items that needed funding.[37] The compromises reached as part of securing approval for the budget were sometimes unaffordable. For example, an additional 1,500 security guards were insourced at a cost of approximately R1.2 billion per annum, in a city already in financial distress. The city manager advised the executive mayor and council in writing against this measure. The metro already had an excessively high personnel budget, with some 28,000 staff with an overall low level of productivity. The former city manager complained that '(i)t would take 10 people to do a job that one person could do. By my calculation there were 13,000 excess staff [inherited from previous administrations], and we had to find a way to cut numbers. This was a critically important issue that needed attention, but it was not possible to have this sort of discussion with the politicians.'[38]

In Nelson Mandela Bay, the city manager reported that the 2017/18 budget became 'a free-for-all', with every councillor wanting spending items added for their wards. The multiple amendments pushed out timelines and caused the municipality to miss its deadlines for submitting the draft budget. The final budget was only submitted in June, almost at the start of the financial year.[39] In addition, the EFF used its leverage with the already fractured coalition to push for insourcing, and approximately 500 workers were insourced, without following proper procedures. The auditor-general subsequently flagged this as a material irregularity, which council had to rescind. The city manager obtained a legal opinion and tried to insist on proper procedures for the initial batch of workers. By April 2017, the coalition was already fractured and the EFF pushed for a further 100 workers. It then became a free-for-all, and no procedures or requirements were followed. In the 2018/19 financial year irregular expenditure went up by R1.2 billion.[40]

Unsurprisingly, these impacts on budgets and financial management have shown up in the metros' financial sustainability and audit reports.

The impact on financial sustainability and audit

The 2017/18 financial year was the first full financial year under the new coalition governments. For that year Johannesburg, Tshwane and Ekurhuleni submitted financial statements with 'material misstatements' in significant areas, and it was only their subsequent correction that allowed these metros to escape a qualified audit finding.[41] Nelson Mandela Bay had a qualified audit finding for the seventh year in a row. With respect to irregular expenditure, the top three amounts incurred in the 2017/18 year (out of all eight metros) were for Nelson Mandela Bay (R2,712 million), Tshwane (R1,684 million) and Johannesburg (R707 million). However, it must be noted that all eight metros were found to have material irregularities regarding their supply chain management processes. In terms of financial health and cash positions, Tshwane was rated worst (liabilities exceeded assets, requiring intervention), Johannesburg and Nelson Mandela Bay were rated 'of concern', while the other five metros were rated as being financially sustainable. While the metros under coalition governments appeared to be faring the worst, the auditor-general noted an aggregate decline in all the drivers of internal control across the metros, reflected in regression in the audit outcomes of metros and their inability to move towards a clean audit status (Auditor-General of South Africa, 2019: 15).

The financial health of a municipality can be assessed using the cash coverage index (Table 10.2), which measures the length of time, in months, that a municipality can manage to pay for its day-to-day

Table 10.2: Cash coverage index in selected metropolitan municipalities

Metro	Cash coverage index (months)			
Financial year	2014/15	2015/16	2016/17	2017/18
Ekurhuleni	3.6	3.5	2.3	1.4
Johannesburg	1.5	1.3	0.8	0.6
Tshwane	0.3	0.5	1	1
Nelson Mandela Bay	2.1	2.2	2.2	3.6

Source: National Treasury, 2020.

expenses using just its cash reserves. An index above three months is good, an index below one month is seriously concerning, and an index between one and three months is average but with some concern.

The cash coverage data indicate that both Ekurhuleni and Nelson Mandela Bay have remained financially healthy, although the decline in cash coverage in Ekurhuleni raised concern. Tshwane was in a poor financial position before 2016 and remained so after 2016; its cash coverage rose only slightly to one month, which remains critically below the three months it should be at. Johannesburg showed a marked deterioration since the 2016 elections – its cash coverage fell below one month in 2016/17 and 2017/18.

Another measure of financial health is the extent to which municipalities are able to spend their capital budget, which usually includes large infrastructure projects, and is a good measure of their ability to plan, implement and spend responsibly, and hence of their overall capacity (Table 10.3). Municipalities should be able to spend at least 95 per cent of their capital budgets. Between 85 per cent and 95 per cent spending is a concern, while below 85 per cent is extremely worrying.

In terms of capital spending, both Ekurhuleni and Nelson Mandela Bay have shown improvements since the 2016 elections, while Johannesburg deteriorated in 2016/17, followed by a recovery in 2017/18. Tshwane showed marked deterioration in both years.

National Treasury's own assessment of the financial health of the metros during the 2018/19 financial year provides additional insights into these aggregate indicators. Ekurhuleni was noted to be financially

Table 10.3: Underspending of capital budget in selected metropolitan municipalities

Metro	Underspending (%)			
Financial year	2014/15	2015/16	2016/17	2017/18
Ekurhuleni	-19.5	-11.9	-8.0	-10.6
Johannesburg	-17.5	-4.9	-22.6	-6.8
Tshwane	-6.2	-0.7	-29.3	-18.2
Nelson Mandela Bay	-7.0	-14.1	-7.8	-1.6

Source: National Treasury, 2020.

viable; however, cash was reducing at a high rate due to operating deficits (Bell and Baloyi, 2019). In Johannesburg, it was noted that the city's deteriorating financial position threatened its longer-term financial sustainability. This was driven by a decrease in cash and cash equivalents of R856 million, outstanding creditors of R13 billion, a decrease in the consumer collection rate[42] to 90.7 per cent, and an increase in electricity losses to 23.3 per cent (Voigt, 2019). Tshwane was already under a financial recovery plan, and while the city had cash in the bank, this was not sufficient to cover its liabilities and its fixed monthly costs (also known as cost coverage). The delay in collecting revenue (more than 30 days) was adding to the fragility of its finances (Maja, 2019: 19). Nelson Mandela Bay's financial position was noted to be stabilising, but there was an increase in outstanding debtors, reflected by an 86 per cent collection rate, well below the average for metropolitan municipalities (Mashoeshoe and Mokgabodi, 2019: 5).

The impact on corruption

Corruption has been previously documented in metropolitan municipalities falling under ANC rule, but the laxity in financial controls, unstable political environment and short-term nature of many of the political interests combined to create a fertile environment in which corruption could flourish under coalitions. As the Tshwane city manager commented, 'Everyone was in it for themselves. The DA and EFF politicians and the officials were all trying to eat. Because the centre did not hold, the conditions for corruption mushroomed.'[43]

As noted earlier, corruption had been documented in the Ekurhuleni metro prior to 2016 relating to housing delivery (Marutlulle and Ijeoma, 2015), supply chain management (Legodi, 2017) and the 2010 World Cup (Madia, 2019), and subsequent to 2016 there had been financial irregularities reported in relation to the finance and transport divisions (Madia, 2019). It does not appear that there is a higher incidence of corruption, and based on the governance indicators, the incidence of corruption has probably fallen.

In Tshwane, there were prominent instances of corruption under the previous ANC administration. The ANC had pushed through a costly outsourcing of its electricity metering and revenue collection to an underqualified company, PEU Capital Partners, without competitive tendering. The 10-year contract value was estimated at R27 billion, and, according to the newly appointed mayor (at the time), Solly Msimanga, the city was losing more than R630 million annually (Poplak, 2017). There were allegations of political corruption in other areas as well – security tenders, the rollout of smart meters, the free wifi-hotspot rollout and the bus rapid transit system, and the Tshwane metro police deputy chief was alleged to be at the centre of a large tender-fraud system (De Waal, 2011). Following the 2016 elections, concerns were raised regarding a contract with engineering company GladAfrica to project manage Tshwane's entire capital budget valued at R12 billion. The lack of a competitive appointment process[44] and excessive fees paid on the GladAfrica contract raised serious concerns. After defending the contract for some months, the city manager eventually agreed the contract was irregular, based on findings by the auditor-general, who red-flagged some R317 million paid to GladAfrica.

In Nelson Mandela Bay prior to 2016 there had been prominent instances of corruption relating to the bus rapid transit system, various supply chain contracts and the housing delivery process, linked to the regional ANC patronage machine, which have been extensively documented (Olver, 2017). After 2016, allegations of corruption surfaced implicating the (second coalition) mayor, Mongameli Bobani, in relation to public health contracts. The officials involved in the contract were implicated in terms of a forensic report and found guilty of fraud. As the city manager noted,

> A toxic mix of short-term political gains predominated at the expense of long-term service delivery. The tendency to do corrupt deals increased. There already was some low-level corruption taking place, but during this period councillors were able to give instructions directly, especially from the different factions. Even though the ANC were not in the coalition, the regional executive started once again giving direct instructions into the administration… Coalition partners had to look after each other's interests, especially in the light of the lawlessness that the second coalition in the [Nelson Mandela Bay municipality] ushered in.[45]

There were allegations of corruption under the previous ANC administration in Johannesburg, relating to a conflict of interest of former MMC for finance (and subsequent ANC mayor) Geoff Makhubo, and his involvement with Regiments Capital, which managed aspects of the city's finances. The new DA mayor for Johannesburg, Herman Mashaba, prominently led an anti-corruption campaign. The city's group forensic and investigation services announced in 2019 that it had completed over 100 forensic investigations into serious criminal cases from the previous administration which had been reported to the Hawks (City of Johannesburg, 2019). Despite Mashaba's allegations and much-vaunted clean-up operation, the period of the DA-led coalition has not been without its own scandals. In January 2018 Mashaba suspended his MMC for finance over allegations of nepotism (Nicolson, 2018). There were allegations by metro officials that the EFF was given control over key appointment processes in the city of Johannesburg as well as patronage over tenders. This was described as a quid pro quo for the EFF working with Mashaba's DA-led administration (Reddy, Brümmer and amaBhungane, 2018). For instance, an investigation exposed corruption in a 2017 tender for Johannesburg's fleet-management services with a value of R1.26 billion (Brümmer and Reddy, 2019). There is no evidence that the DA itself benefited from these contracts, but the investigations appeared to confirm that resources were being diverted to particular coalition partners to hold the coalition together.

The Gauteng City Region Observatory Quality of Life survey[46] provides some insight into the long-term trends in aggregate levels of corruption in each of the Gauteng-based metros (Figure 10.1). Respondents were asked whether they had ever been asked to pay a bribe to a government official, traffic cop, policeman or other public servant. While the responses are not specific to local government, they do provide insight into the overall level of public-sector corruption experienced by residents in each of the metros.

While the incidence of corruption appears to be increasing overall in Gauteng (reflected in the rise of the percentage of people who have been asked for a bribe), this increase is accentuated in Tshwane, while the other metros track the overall Gauteng trend fairly closely. Given the often piecemeal and sometimes anecdotal nature of corruption allegations, it is difficult to draw definitive conclusions regarding whether corruption levels in metropolitan administrations have changed significantly before and after 2016, but there is enough evidence to conclude that the conditions have been created for corruption to persist.

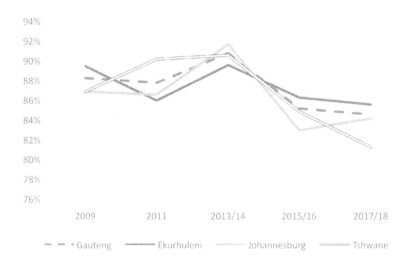

Figure 10.1: Respondents who have not been asked to pay a bribe, by metropolitan area and for Gauteng overall (percentage)

Source: De Kadt et al., 2019.

The impact on service delivery

Service delivery in the metros has been affected in various ways. Ekurhuleni increased its built-environment performance targets[47] from 71 per cent in 2016/17 to 73 per cent in 2017/18; water losses decreased from 30.6 per cent to 28.5 per cent, and electricity losses from 13.4 per cent to 11.7 per cent (Bell and Baloyi, 2019: 14). In Johannesburg, the city reported a performance of 56 per cent against service delivery indicators for 2017/18; electricity losses increased from 20.2 per cent in 2016/17 to 23.3 per cent in 2017/18 but water losses declined from 26.8 to 25.5 per cent (Voigt, 2019: 4). In Tshwane only two out of 13 service delivery and budget improvement targets were achieved in 2017/18.[48] The biggest challenges related to water provision (water losses increased from 23 per cent in 2016/17 to 28 per cent in 2017/18) and land invasions, with a mushrooming of informal settlements stretching the city's ability to meet service-delivery targets (Maja, 2019: 19). In Nelson Mandela Bay it was noted that the city's service delivery performance was deteriorating, with only 52 per cent of service delivery targets met in 2017/18, down from 81 per cent in

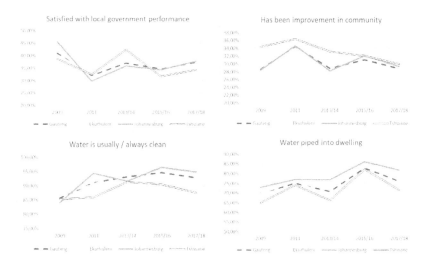

Figure 10.2: Trends in local government service provision and citizen satisfaction

Source: De Kadt et al., 2019.

2016/17 (Mashoeshoe and Mokgabodi, 2019: 5). Reasons cited were an upsurge in invasions of private and public land, illegal occupation of completed and unallocated houses, and disjointed planning between the city and human-settlements department. Water losses jumped from 36 per cent in 2016/17 to 41 per cent in 2017/18, well above the norm of 15–30 per cent for metros (Mashoeshoe and Mokgabodi, 2019: 6).

The Gauteng City Region Observatory Quality of Life survey allows for comparison between the Gauteng-based metros over time, with the survey results for 2017/18 providing insights into the situation in each metro a year after the 2016 local government elections (Figure 10.2).

The survey results provide a mixed picture. There was some improvement in citizen satisfaction before and after the 2016 elections in all the metros, although the overall results were low. On the other hand, respondents indicated a decline in assessments of community improvement and condition of water services across all the metros. Comparisons between the metros across all the indicators indicate that Tshwane was underperforming and Ekurhuleni better performing, compared to their peers and Gauteng as a whole. These trends confirm the assessments by National Treasury noted above.

SUMMARY OF THE IMPACTS ON ADMINISTRATION

The changes that have taken place in metros run by coalition governments need to be understood against the broader background of local government in South Africa. Regardless of whether municipalities are run by coalitions or majority parties, the interface between municipal administration and council politics is vexed – political instability in council has a deleterious effect on administrative performance, and political interference in administrative appointments and procurement is one of the primary drivers of corruption in local government. The inherent instability of municipal coalitions, and the trade-offs that are required to keep coalition partners together, have combined to accentuate their impact on municipal administrations. This has been particularly difficult in the context of coalitions involving partners with diametrically opposed ideological or policy positions.

In the three metros run by such coalitions, political instability and policy misalignment have fed into management instability, with a high turnover of key management positions. Officials have found themselves pulled into playing political-brokering roles as coalitions fell apart, and lines of accountability within the administration have been subverted (although political interference has also been extensively documented under previous ANC administrations). The added requirements for consultation have created delays in administrative processing, and substantially slowed down municipal performance. This has been particularly evident with respect to the budget-approval process, and is also reflected in declining service delivery performance and deteriorating financial viability. At the same time, unauthorised expenditure has increased substantially in three of the four metros under coalition governments.

For municipal administrations, coalition governments are undoubtedly harder to manage, although this is not insurmountable. Municipal administrations seek stability and predictability; they are slow-moving bureaucracies that need time to gear up different policy orientations. Such stability is normally found in a majority dispensation or a coalition whose politics are fundamentally stable. The difficulty arises when there is no political stability and the administration is unable to anticipate change.

POSSIBLE REMEDIES

Various suggestions have been put forward to ameliorate the dysfunction in the political/administrative interface. The role played by political leadership in relation to the administration is instrumental. For instance, the auditor-general has spelled out practical steps that leaders can take to improve accountability (Auditor-General of South Africa, 2019: 7):

- Set the tone from the top through ethical leadership, good governance and accountability.
- Capacitate and stabilise the municipal administration, and keep it free from political interference.

- Enable and insist on robust financial and performance-management processes and controls, as well as regular, credible reporting to enable all levels of leadership to perform their monitoring and oversight function.
- Ensure consistent, appropriate and swift consequences for transgressions and irregularities.

These suggestions are well made, and much will be achieved if they are adopted by political leaders in local government, but the auditor-general has been making these points each year with little traction.

The South African Cities Network report focused its recommendations on the practical steps that officials in the built environment could follow to improve performance relating to their projects (Foster, 2019: 15):

- Cultivate allies in the administration and among politicians for particular projects.
- Find political cover from the mayor or other politicians.
- Be flexible and willing to repackage projects to provide a politically acceptable mix of projects.
- Stay above politics but be aware of political dynamics so that pitfalls can be avoided and common ground found.
- Find the right messenger, particularly for conveying contentious issues.
- Build a case around financing projects and lock in the budgets.

While this advice is germane to all metros, it could as easily be read as an officials' guide on how to survive coalition politics. It should be noted that seeking cover from political office bearers could prove to be a risky strategy if party officials become involved and exploit the situation.

With respect to issues that are specific to coalitions, the managers interviewed as part of the research for this chapter made some useful suggestions. There are practical steps that parties can take to make coalitions more predictable. For instance, a formal coalition agreement, even if the agreement with the partner was only on a confidence-and-supply basis, would assist to clarify the terms of the relationship, not just for the political parties involved, but, crucially, for the managers who are required to interpret and implement coalition decisions.[49] The foundation of a coalition should be a mutually agreed framework that sets out some commonly agreed principles on how the parties should agree or disagree on matters. While coalition agreements certainly can help, it was also noted that without an underlying level of trust and commitment, they are insufficient to hold a coalition together.

Party caucuses play an important role in mandating the political stance adopted by political leaders. Similarly, regular coalition caucuses can assist to hammer out policy differences and provide a guide to the mayoral committee members. Of course, ideology also matters: coalitions are going to be easier to manage if they are based on certain common principles and policy positions. For the DA and the EFF, for example, this is particularly difficult, as they occupy opposite ends of a spectrum of policy options.

The executive mayor model has been raised as problematic by some managers, pointing out that the composition of the mayoral committee under an executive mayor does not have to be proportional to the parties in council. This works for majority governments, but coalition and minority governments may be better suited to the executive committee system that is widely followed in KwaZulu-Natal. The suggestion has been made that the trigger for the executive mayor system should be a majority of 50 per cent plus one. Alternatively, following an election, the largest party could have a window period during which it may attempt to form a government, failing which the default executive committee arrangement kicks in.

Other managers felt that the problem was not, in fact, a legal one, but rather one created by political parties who assume powers that they do not have in law. As Mosola explained, 'We need to make it clear that executive mayors and MMCs can get into serious trouble with the law for transgressing it. The city manager is obliged to explain this to them. Executive mayors just grab these powers and bully the administration into submission'.[50] Mettler clarified this in a conversation he had with his executive mayor when he said that 'the how is mine, the what is yours'.[51] As the head of the administration, the city manager is the only person who should give instructions to the administration. Politicians cannot assume to take executive powers; the law does not permit them to do so. The operative word for politicians is 'oversee', whereas the terms used in legislation for city managers and executive directors is 'manage' or 'execute'. In this respect, the executive mayor model creates some difficulties, as it gives the mayor the notion that they are actually in charge of implementation.

Good faith, professionalism and respect for each other's roles are fundamental in the relationship between the city manager and the executive mayor, but it must also extend to the broader political and administrative environments to make coalitions work. As was pointed out by Mettler, this cannot be legislated, but must be voluntarily embraced by the parties: 'The administration must be allowed to present facts and, if necessary, bad news, and not be accused of having an agenda in doing so.'[52] The Institute of Municipal Managers similarly concluded that role clarity and an open relationship between the mayor and the municipal manager are critical to effective governance. The Institute's conference report noted that '(t)rust is central to good governance. As the interface between the political and administrative spheres in local government, municipal managers need a trust relationship with all political parties to function effectively' (SALGA, 2017). This requires a balance between political leadership and administrative management, an agreement on common goals, and an understanding by both sides of where to draw the line between effecting a political mandate and implementing administrative imperatives. Alford et al. (2017: 755) suggested that such understandings be encoded in public service bargains or compacts entered into between politicians and public servants around mutually agreed values, objectives and ways of working. Given the renewed focus on social compacts in the South African context, this could well be a practice that could have traction in local government.

The relationship of trust between politicians and officials must be founded on a respect for the roles and responsibilities of the different functionaries [officials and politicians]. As municipal managers have emphasised, these roles are already clearly set out in legislation. Reinforcing lines of accountability is important for the smooth running of the administration. In this regard, the political neutrality of the municipal manager is crucial. This theme was taken up by the National Planning Commission when it urged that '(i)t is critical for public servants to forge a collective professional identity and loyalty to the values of the Constitution rather than any political party' (NPC, 2011: 24). Municipal managers have similarly urged that their orientation should be politically neutral. Given that legislation prescribes that a municipal manager's contract cannot extend beyond a year after any local government election, the incoming governing party has the option to retain or change the incumbent. In the interest of continuity and political non-interference, an appointment should be made on purely technical grounds to ensure political neutrality. The managers also noted that in the current climate of deep and divisive distrust within local government, however, it was difficult if not impossible for a municipal manager to maintain trust relations with all political parties (SALGA, 2017: 24).

The other solution that has been raised by municipal managers relates to their permanent appointment. The local government system before 1994 treated town clerks and other local government managers as permanent staff, which gave them a measure of autonomy and insulated them from political interference. The introduction, after 2000, of maximum terms of five years was meant to accelerate transformation in the system but it also opened it up to abuse. The Institute of Municipal Managers noted that '(i)ncompetent and abusive leadership are serious issues that need discussion and resolution. Autocracy, dictatorship and even physical abuse are realities in some municipalities' (SALGA, 2017). They also worried that when abuse was reported to Cooperative Governance and Traditional Affairs and the provincial MEC for local government, matters were not followed up, there were no consequences, and managers consequently felt that government was not protecting them. As a result, competent managers left the system at a high rate. The South African Local Government Association (SALGA) conference concluded that '(t)he Local Government system needs to be reviewed, with an emphasis on professionalising the municipal manager environment to provide legal and other protection against, inter alia, the contravention of labour regulations and discourage political interference' (SALGA, 2017: 25).

CONCLUSION

At the beginning of this chapter I noted that some authors have found that the normal functioning of government requires public managers to engage with politics in various ways. This has been borne out by the South African local government experience. The former city manager for Johannesburg captured this point when he stated that 'while the job of a municipal manager is not political, it does require interacting with all political parties equally and having the conviction to act in the best interest of a sustainable municipality' (SALGA, 2017: 24). While South African municipal managers have agreed that they should accept deployment in a political environment as a reality, this did not mean that they had to accept the deployment of incompetent people without the skills for the job at hand (SALGA, 2017: 26). Clearly, managers' engagement in the political domain involves working in a zone with a high degree of ambiguity, but this may well be necessary, given the demands of the situation. As Alford et al. noted, while politicians are meant to deal with external policy actors, in practice this role is shared with senior officials (Alford et al., 2017: 757).

The traditional view of the relationship between the political and administrative spheres is that these domains must be separated by a clear dividing line, and that measures are required to sterilise the bureaucracy from political interference in administrative decisions. The legislative framework in South Africa reinforces the Weberian distinction, and it is imperative that both political parties and officials respect and reinforce the autonomy of bureaucracy and protect its institutional integrity. But this is only the starting point for sound relationships between political and administrative spheres. In reality, the dividing line between the domains is blurred, and managers are required to engage with politics in various ways. The interface is better conceptualised as a privileged zone of interaction within which a range of practices and behaviours take place. In the absence of clear guidelines about how to navigate the zone, informal rules predominate, and even these are fluid and open to interpretation. There are positive examples of informal rules that have been developed based on mutual support and interdependence, distinct but complementary roles, and reciprocity of influence. In their most advanced form, these informal rules can constitute a compact between politicians and public servants around mutually agreed values, objectives and ways of working. Given the accentuation of political-administrative interactions in municipal coalition governments, such compacts could form an essential basis for successful coalition governments in the future.

REFERENCES

Alford, J., Hartley, J., Yates, S. and Hughes, O. 2017. 'Into the purple zone: Deconstructing the politics/administration distinction', *The American Review of Public Administration*, 47 (7): 752–763.

Arndt, C., Davies R. and Thurlow, J. 2018. 'Urbanization, Structural Transformation and Rural-Urban Linkages in South Africa'. *Urbanisation Review, City Support Programme*, National Treasury, Pretoria.

Auditor-General of South Africa. 2019. 'MFMA 2017/18 Consolidated General Report on the Local Government Audit Outcomes'. Audit report, http://www.agsa.co.za/Portals/0/Reports/MFMA/201516/GR/1.%20 2015-16%20MFMA%20-%20Consol%20GR%20-%20Complete%20 Document.pdf, accessed 2 March 2020.

Bell, K. and Baloyi, K. 2019. 'City of Ekurhuleni Metro (EKU). 4–5 February 2019. Budget and Performance Review'. 2018/19 Mid-Year Budget and Performance Assessment, National Treasury, Pretoria.

Beresford, A. 2015. 'Power, patronage, and gatekeeper politics in South Africa', *African Affairs*, 114 (455), 226–248, https://doi.org/10.1093/afraf/adu083, accessed 1 April 2020.

Brümmer, S. and Reddy, M. 19 September 2019. 'Tender comrades, part one: Trailing the Juju tractor', *Daily Maverick*, https://www.dailymaverick.co.za/article/2019-09-19-tender-comrades-part-1-trailing-the-juju-tractor/, accessed 20 September 2019.

Chipkin, I. 2013. 'Whither the state? Corruption, institutions and state-building in South Africa', *Politikon*, 40 (2), 211–231, https://doi.org/10.10 80/02589346.2013.798457, accessed 2 April 2020.

Chipkin, I. 2016. 'The State, Capture and Revolution in Contemporary South Africa'. PARI Working Paper, Public Affairs Research Institute, Johannesburg.

Chipkin, I. and Swilling, M. 2020. *Shadow State: The politics of state capture*. Johannesburg: Wits University Press.

City of Johannesburg. 2019. 'Mashaba meets head of the Hawks over serious corruption uncovered in Joburg', press statement, https://www.joburg.org.za/media_/Pages/Media/Media%20Statements/2019%20Media%20 Statements/2019%20January/Mashaba-meets-Head-of-the-Hawks-overseriouscorruption-uncovered-in-Joburg.aspx, accessed 2 June 2020.

Comrie, S. 6 December 2018. 'Geoff Makhubo, Jo'burg ANC leader, scored millions from city contract', *Daily Maverick*, https://www.dailymaverick.co.za/article/2018-12-06-geoff-makhubo-joburg-anc-leader-scored-millions-from-city-contract/, accessed 5 May 2020.

Comrie, S. 13 August 2019. 'How state capture inc funded the ANC', *Daily Maverick*, https://www.dailymaverick.co.za/article/2019-08-13-how-state-capture-inc-funded-the-anc/, accessed 2 December 2019.

De Kadt, J., Ballard, R., Cheruiyot, K., Culwick, C., Hamann, C., et al. 2019. 'Insights from GCRO'S Quality of Life V Survey (2017/18)'. Survey findings, Gauteng City Region Observatory, Johannesburg.

De Visser, J. and Steytler, N. 2009. 'State of Local Government in South Africa: Overview Report'. Working documents, National State of Local Government Assessments, Department of Cooperative Governance and Traditional Affairs Pretoria.

De Waal, M. 19 October 2011. 'Barry Bateman; the Newsman vs Tshwane Corrupt Ltd', *Daily Maverick*, https://www.dailymaverick.co.za/article/2011-10-19-barry-bateman-the-newsman-vs-tshwane-corrupt-ltd/, accessed 2 May 2019.

Electoral Commission (IEC). 2020. Municipal Election Results 2016, http://www.elections.org.za/content/Elections/Municipal-elections-results/, accessed 12 May 2020.

Evans, P. 1995. *Embedded Autonomy: States and industrial transformation*. Princeton, N. J.: Princeton University Press.

Foster, K. 2019. 'Cities Political Administrative Interface in the Built Environment'. Research report, Built Environment Integration Task Team, South African Cities Network, http://www.sacities.net/images/BEITT_POLITICAL_ADMINISTRATIVE_INTERFACE_RESEARCH_REPORT_FINAL.pdf, accessed 10 May 2020.

Good Governance Africa. 2019. 'Government Performance Index 2019', https://gga.org/wp-content/uploads/2019/04/GGA-GPI-2019-FINAL-25-April-2019.pdf, accessed 3 May 2020.

Legodi, L. 2017. 'Governance Challenges in Combating Supply Chain Management Corruption in Ekurhuleni Metropolitan Municipality'. Master's thesis, University of the Witwatersrand, Johannesburg.

Madia, T. 21 February 2019. 'ANC, Ekurhuleni coalition partner at odds over council COO's future', *News24*, https://www.news24.com/SouthAfrica/News/anc-ekurhuleni-coalition-partner-at-odds-over-council-coos-future-20190221, accessed 2 March 2019.

Mailovich, C. 4 May 2018. 'Graft alleged as City of Johannesburg agencies skip AGMs', *Business Day*, https://www.businesslive.co.za/bd/national/2018-05-04-graft-alleged-as-city-of-johannesburg-agencies-skip-agms/, accessed 5 May 2018.

Maja, J. 2019. 'City of Tshwane, 28 and 29 January 2019. Budget and Performance Review'. 2018/19 Mid-Year Budget and Performance Assessment, National Treasury, Pretoria.

Marutlulle, N. and Ijeoma, E. 2015. 'Obstacles to housing delivery in Ekurhuleni Metropolitan Municipality: A critical review of output and input', *Africa's Public Service Delivery and Performance Review*, https://doi.org/10.4102/apsdpr.v3i4.101, accessed 10 May 2016.

Mashoeshoe, M. and Mokgabodi, B. 2019. 'Nelson Mandela Bay (NMA) 07 and 08 February 2019. Budget and Performance Review'. 2018/19 Mid-Year Budget and Performance Assessment, National Treasury, Pretoria.

National Treasury. 2020. 'Municipal Money South Africa'. Interactive financial data, https://municipalmoney.gov.za/, accessed 12 May 2020.

Netshitenzhe, J. 15 June 2012. 'Competing identities of a national liberation movement and the challenges of incumbency', *ANC Today*, http://www.anc.org.za/docs/anctoday/2012/at23.htm#art2, accessed 17 July 2019.

Nicolson, G. 15 January 2018. 'Herman Mashaba sacks Joburg finance MMC for nepotism', *Daily Maverick*, https://www.dailymaverick.co.za/article/2018-01-15-newsflash-herman-mashaba-sacks-joburg-finance-mmc-for-nepotism/, accessed 1 March 2018.

National Planning Commission (NPC). 2011. 'Diagnostic Overview'. Assessment report, National Development Plan Source Documents, National Planning Commission, The Presidency, Pretoria.

Olver, C. 2017. *How to Steal a City: The battle For Nelson Mandela Bay*. Cape Town: Jonathan Ball.

Olver, C. 2019. *A House Divided: The feud that took Cape Town to the brink*. Cape Town: Jonathan Ball.

Peters, B. 2001. *The Politics of Bureaucracy*. London: Routledge.

Phillips, S. 25 May 2018. 'Flashing red lights about tenders and governance while head of the Johannesburg Roads Agency', *Daily Maverick*, https://www.dailymaverick.co.za/article/2018-05-25-flashing-red-lights-about-tenders-and-governance-while-head-of-the-johannesburg-roads-agency/, accessed 30 May 2018.

Poplak, R. 18 May 2017. 'City budget: The great unholy Tshwane alliance brings us Pretoria on the Rhine', *Daily Maverick*, https://www.dailymaverick.co.za/article/2017-05-18-trainspotter-city-budget-the-great-unholy-tshwane-alliance-brings-us-pretoria-on-the-rhine/, accessed 20 May 2017.

Reddy, M., Brümmer, S. and amaBhungane. 29 November 2018. 'Firm that won R1bn Joburg fleet contract paid Malema-EFF "slush fund"', *Daily Maverick*, https://www.dailymaverick.co.za/article/2018-11-29-firm-that-won-r1bn-joburg-fleet-contract-paid-malema-eff-slush-fund/, accessed 2 December 2018.

South African Local Government Association (SALGA). 2017. 'Report of the 11th National Municipal Managers Forum 31 August to 1 September

2017, George, Western Cape'. Minutes, SALGA, Pretoria.

Statistics South Africa (Stats SA). 2016. 'Community Survey 2016'. Statistical release P0301, Statistics South Africa, Pretoria.

Svara, J. 1999. 'The politics-administration dichotomy model as aberration', *Public Administration Review*, 58 (1): 51–58.

Voigt, W. 2019. 'City of Johannesburg, 31 January 2019 to 01 February 2019. Budget and Performance Review'. 2018/19 Mid-Year Budget and Performance Assessment, National Treasury, Pretoria.

Von Holdt, K. 2010. 'Nationalism, bureaucracy and the developmental state: The South African case', *South African Review of Sociology*, 41 (1), 4–27. https://doi.org/10.1080/21528581003676010, accessed 2 March 2020.

Von Holdt, K., Langa, M., Molapo, S., Mogapi, N., Ngubeni, K., et al. 2011. 'Insurgent Citizenship, Collective Violence and the Struggle for a Place in the New South Africa'. Centre for the Study of Violence and Reconciliation, University of the Witwatersrand, Johannesburg.

Weber, M. 1978. *Economy and Society: An outline of interpretive sociology*. Berkeley, C. A.: University of California Press.

De Vos, P. 28 October 2020. 'Will a recent SCA judgment help to fix the political dysfunction in Tshwane?', *Constitutionally Speaking*, https://constitutionallyspeaking.co.za/will-a-recent-sca-judgment-help-to-fix-the-political-dysfunction-in-tshwane, accessed 9 November 2020.

Part IV

*Experimenting with coalition governments:
Core case studies and emerging cultures*

Anchored in Part I, which sets out the range of democratic South Africa's coalition government experiences, the in-depth case studies of South Africa's post-2016 local governments in this section reveals the dynamics that dominate the field. The metropolitan case studies of coalition practice in South Africa reveal the contours of the metropolitan cliff-hangers in which governance comes second, dwarfed by interparty war by means of coalition politics. The studies show the party politics and political strategies that characterise the new coalition politics in South Africa. The section explores, furthermore, how coalition politics in two of South Africa's provinces, KwaZulu-Natal and the Western Cape, in the earlier decades of democracy helped position interparty coalitions firmly in the culture of conquest by coalition.

ELEVEN

Power, politics and ideology
Understanding councillors' views on the tug of war in the City of Johannesburg

Bonolo Makgale

The 2016 South African local government elections were a game-changer in the City of Johannesburg. Once considered impossible, coalition politics became a serious consideration, if not the only game in town, in the aftermath of the 2016 poll. For the city, coalition politics immediately raised a host of questions around policymaking, the power-brokering influence of the Economic Freedom Fighters (EFF) and service delivery. After 21 years of uninterrupted African National Congress (ANC) hegemony locally, Johannesburg's political landscape changed with the coming of a Democratic Alliance (DA)-led coalition to govern the city. Neither the ANC nor the DA nor the EFF was able to garner the requisite majority to take over single-party control of the municipality.

This change signalled a new administrative phenomenon of the Johannesburg municipality, one in which coalition politics were at play in a previously ANC-dominated jurisdiction. This shift resulted from the growing dissatisfaction with service delivery and corruption in the municipality, which diluted the electoral support that the ANC previously held, and transferred this shifting vote to the DA and the EFF, the two major opposition political parties, and an assemblage of small parties.

The ANC's post-liberation electoral dominance was threatened with the trend of ANC misgovernance and allegations of corruption, especially with regard to 'state capture' at national level. While racial segregation was abolished in its structural sense, institutionally it persisted and presented as a threat to society. There was also a further widening of the gap between the rich and the poor under the watch of an ANC government. In positioning this chapter, the next section explores questions about the quality of democracy, procedurally and substantively, as the major causal factor in election results, and the consequent resort to coalition governance. At the same time that citizens of the City of Johannesburg grappled with their choices for municipal governance, a hung council arose and an interparty tug of war ensued. As the parties and their coalitions fought it out, democratic governance and citizen interest came second.

Thus, in the face of what can only be termed an 'open sesame' moment for opposition parties, coalition government was constituted in the wake of the 2016 local government elections. This coalition was spearheaded by the main opposition party, the DA, along with a number of smaller opposition parties, in order to take advantage of the ANC's decline in electoral support. The EFF was not part of the coalition, and opted rather to operate as a collaborator in policy issues, in a confidence-and-supply arrangement.[1] After three years, and roughly two years before the end of its term, amid altered political conditions, especially at national level, the alliance buckled, and the ANC paired with the EFF to assume power.

This chapter examines the nature, rationale and success of coalition politics in the City of Johannesburg, with a focus, first, on the stability or otherwise of the 2016 DA-led coalition and, second, on the ANC's late-2019 coalition with the EFF and its impact on local governance. To understand coalitions, Kadima (2014: 2) points out that it is necessary to investigate their inception, durability and demise, as well as the factors that influence these factors. This chapter chooses durability of coalitions as its central focus. It takes the absence of willingness by political parties to compromise as an indication of competitive power play. As a step towards understanding the nature of the coalition, the analysis focuses on the rationale behind these formations: were they done with the aim of bringing greater administrative and political cohesion and effective governance, or as attempts to gain or regain executive power in the interest of parties and individual leaders? The chapter asserts that the challenges befalling coalition governments are often related to ideological, identity and policy divergences, as the semi-structured interviews with party representatives reveal. These policy and ideological factors do not stand in isolation, but serve to position the parties in relation to their constituencies and help determine future electoral appeal.

Data were gathered, first, through semi-structured interviews with councillors, municipal officials and a party official.[2] A total of 10 participants were interviewed for the study: seven councillors (with an emphasis on DA councillors, to get an understanding of the character of the then governing coalition), two City of Johannesburg officials and one senior official of the ANC.[3] The interviewees came from both large and small parties within the coalition. The second part of the study is supported by a project of monitoring unfolding Johannesburg council developments. To this end, a senior ANC official was interviewed.

The interviews shed light on how the coalition navigated governance challenges in the city, and how the EFF agenda, combined with the ANC's determination to return to power after having lost outright Johannesburg municipal power in 2016, ultimately led to the collapse of the DA-led coalition. The chapter analyses the tipping point that saw the ANC resume control of the city. This became possible due to the weaknesses and fragilities of the DA coalition. This chapter's primary focus is on unpacking the formation and maintenance of that DA-led coalition. The data reveals the ideological rifts, and identity and policy divergences that ultimately led to the collapse of the DA coalition, and the reinstatement of the ANC as the administrator for South Africa's economic hub (Mailovich, 2019).

Following the resumption of ANC control over the Johannesburg municipality, allegations of corruption emerged involving both the antecedent DA administration and the renewed ANC administration.

During the COVID-19 pandemic, the City of Johannesburg was associated with systemic corrupt practices, including tender fraud for personal protective equipment (Cox, 2020). Furthermore, in late 2020 the Zondo Commission of Enquiry into state capture heard evidence of the new, post-DA coalition ANC mayor, Geoff Makhubo, having benefited personally and on behalf of the ANC from contracts awarded when he was the city's MMC for finance, before the DA took over.

2016 ELECTORAL OUTCOMES IN THE CITY OF JOHANNESBURG

The 2016 election result delivered a hung council – not one of the three biggest parties, the ANC (44.6 per cent), the DA (38.4 per cent) and the EFF (11.1 per cent), was able to garner the requisite 50 per cent majority to take control of the municipality (Table 11.1). While the ANC secured 121 out of 270 seats, the DA spearheaded a coalition with the Inkatha Freedom Party (IFP), the African Christian Democratic Party (ACDP), the United Democratic Movement (UDM), the Congress of the People (Cope), the Freedom Front Plus (FF+) and the Al Jama-Ah party, amassing a total of 115 council seats. Choosing not to officially partner with any side, the EFF with its 30 seats elected to play a (conditional) supporting role to the DA-led coalition. The results demonstrated the considerable decline of the ANC's support between 2006 and 2016 – a loss of approximately 20 percentage points. In the same period, the DA's support rose by roughly 11 percentage points (Table 11.2).

FAILURE TO COMPROMISE: THE DRIVING FORCE OF THE JOHANNESBURG COALITIONS

Coalition governments are a difficult political art to master, as they invariably involve having to compromise on a wide variety of issues with other coalition members, including on legislative policy and reforms (Moury and Timmermans, 2013: 17). A middle ground often has to be forged, involving the advancement of the parties' goals, while at the same time creating an administrative and political climate of stability to govern.

Table 11.1: Johannesburg 2016 local election results and corresponding seat allocations

Political party	Percentage support	Ward and PR seats		Total seats
		2017	2015	
African National Congress (ANC)	44.55	84	37	121
Democratic Alliance (DA)	38.37	51	53	104
Economic Freedom Fighters (EFF)	11.09	0	30	30
Inkatha Freedom Party (IFP)	1.72	0	5	5
African Independent Congress (AIC)	1.50	0	4	2
Freedom Front+ (FF+)	0.34	0	1	1
African Christian Democratic Party (ACDP)	0.30	0	1	1
Al Jama-ah	0.27	0	1	1
United Democratic Movement (UDM)	0.26	0	1	1
Congress of the People (Cope)	0.18	0	1	1
Patriotic Alliance (PA)	0.15	0	1	1
Total	100	135	135	270

Note: The Pan Africanist Congress (0.13%) and African People's Convention (0.11%) were the next two parties in line, just missing a PR seat. Eighteen parties that contested the Johannesburg race did not win any seats. The Bolsheviks Party of South Africa (57 votes) and the United Front of Civics (49 votes) were the two worst performers, both ending on 0.00 per cent of the Johannesburg vote.

Source: Booysen (2016), based on IEC Results Summary.

Ideological differences and the concomitant failure or unwillingness to reconcile them often count as factors that lead to the collapse of coalitions. I found this to have been the case in the Johannesburg municipality. Councillors in the coalition spearheaded by the DA noted that the challenge with the coalition was that parties were often obliged to compromise on core principles – and this strained both the individual parties and the relations between them. In the discussions that follow, concerning rationale for coalition formation, it is assessed how the DA and other coalition parties formed the coalition in order to remove the ANC from power. This rationale bound the parties superficially, but the shared purpose did not translate into a deeper bond that could sustain the coalition.

The EFF assumed a strategic queenmaker status, opting not to officially join the coalition, but rather to use its ability to swing municipal power between the DA-led coalition and the ANC, for its own party-political advantage. For the EFF, despite failing to secure a majority in any municipality in 2016, the election results presented an unparalleled opportunity. With just 11 per cent of total votes in the city, the EFF emerged from the elections as the uncompromising queenmaker, allowing it to select and, where possible, then alternate the party (DA or ANC) it would anoint as the victor in Johannesburg. This contributed to a situation that resulted in the collapse of the DA-led coalition government, and the ANC establishing its own coalition government in the City of Johannesburg a few years later.

These developments in the City of Johannesburg presented evidence in support of Kadima's (2014: 1) contention that post-election coalitions become increasingly prevalent as contemporary African politics develop. Likewise, as political dynamics change, it is common for parties to vacillate between losses and gains in electoral support.

SUCCESSES AND CHALLENGES OF COALITION FORMATION IN THE CITY OF JOHANNESBURG: INSIGHTS FROM THE LITERATURE

Theories of coalition governance help shed light on the Johannesburg municipality's coalition governments since 2016. Kadima (2014) defines coalitions as an association of at least two political parties, working together in parliament (or another legislative institution) or government, based on election outcomes. According to Kapa and Shale (2014), the inherent feature of a coalition is a collaboration of two or more parties – and, in their most basic form, coalitions aim to reduce the dominance of another party. Oyugi (2006) further emphasises that a coalition is 'a process of organizing parties collectively in pursuit of a common goal'. The rationale behind the formation of a coalition government is oftentimes to gain control of the executive. This is commonly referred to as classical coalition governance, that is, a function of political expediency premised on achieving a majority (Oyugi, 2006).

Table 11.2: Comparative Johannesburg local election results, 2006–16: Main parties

Political party	Local election					
	2006		2011		2016	
	Total votes (PR)	Party's proportion (%)	Total votes (Ward + PR)	Party's proportion (%)	Total votes (Ward + PR)	Party's proportion (%)
African National Congress (ANC)	433,051	62.74	1,272,354	58.56	1,121,948	44.64
Democratic Alliance (DA)	187,116	27.11	752,304	34.62	966,192	38.44
Economic Freedom Fighters (EFF)[i]	-	-	-	-	279,192	11.09
Inkatha Freedom Party (IFP)	23,460	3.37	35,490	1.63	43,320	1.72
Registered	1,739,292		2,010,121		2,239,966	
Voted	703,195		1,107,068		1,287,755	

[i] The 2016 elections were the EFF's first local government election; the party was founded in July 2013.

Source: Booysen (2016), based on IEC Results Summary.

The reality is that coalitions are often conceived for opportunistic reasons, rather than in collective interest (Oyugi, 2006). In the case of Johannesburg, opportunism would be understood in the context of the desire to occupy office. This is in line with the prevailing trend in African politics to use coalitions as a tool to hold office, as argued by Kadima (2014). He cites the example of the Mauritian coalition history of 1991, which revealed a tendency to engage in 'a marriage of convenience' (Kadima 2014). Likewise, the Mgwirizano coalition formed in 2004 in Malawi was an instance of political unseating, wherein the goal was to remove the prevailing United Democratic Front from power, with no real political alignment between the coalescing parties. This contrasts with ideological convergence or policy-seeking theories, which propose that coalitions focus on achieving policy goals (Burge and Laver, 1986).

COALITION RATIONALE AND CHARACTER IN THE CITY OF JOHANNESBURG, 2016–19

The question arises therefore whether the Johannesburg coalitions were formed with the aim of bringing greater administrative and political cohesion, or to exert control over the municipality. This section explores the multiple levels and dimension of clashes, and the absence of compromise and a shared coalition identity, beyond the power-seeking imperative that permeated the Johannesburg coalitions. The emphasis in this instance is on the period 2016–19.

In the case of the Johannesburg municipality prior to the 2016 election result, no negotiations concerning the formation of a coalition had been attempted, or been necessary to reach an outright majority, among political parties. It was only after the Electoral Commission (IEC, 2016) announced the results that the parties convened to negotiate forming a coalition.

The main rationale of taking power from the ANC

The majority of the councillors interviewed argued that the formation of the 2016 coalition government in the City of Johannesburg was about taking power from the ANC and maximising the DA-led coalition's control over the municipality, as opposed to a policy rationale. Both councillors (from several parties) and senior officials argued that the preceding ANC-led government had tended to abuse power, and that the ANC had a longstanding reputation of corruption and financial irregularities during its executive tenure over the municipality. The reasons behind the 2016 project of coalition formation were to counteract the corruption allegations surrounding the ANC and then South African president, Jacob Zuma (Booysen, 2016), as well as complaints of service delivery inefficiencies, and the related desire to unseat the incumbent party, the ANC. When councillors were asked about the rationale behind the coalition government formation, two of them said:

> With regard to the City of Johannesburg ... we agreed on taking power away from the ANC because they do not listen to the

people, and whether you are in power or not we should have a common goal. We agreed to surrender some of our policies for the purpose of unseating the ANC. This coalition is about power; we were tired of the ANC and wanted to provide [for the] basic needs of our constituencies.

The rationale for the coming together of the DA and other minority parties was therefore to unseat the ANC. It was an instance of office-seeking with the concomitant hope that majority power would give them access to advance their intended policies as articulated in their election manifestos. One of the smaller party-political fish in the coalition pond confirmed the essential coalition intention, emphasising that 'we wanted to take power from the ANC'. A minority party councillor noted that the smaller parties in the Johannesburg council associated with the DA coalition initiative shared the goal of taking power from the ANC.

Several councillors' interview responses confirmed how power-seeking dominated policy-seeking. Out of seven councillors, five averred that parties in the coalition were more concerned about power than policy. Some also argued it was about tenders and state contracts. The answers also revealed nuances in the balance between power-centric and policy-centric agendas.

Enforcing power fused with securing policy

Noting that the power and policy theories are not necessarily mutually exclusive, two of the councillors interviewed stated that coalition politics in Johannesburg was about both securing power and enforcing policy. This could be said with regard to both the successive coalition governments that held forth between 2016 and 2021. When asked about the tension between power and policy within the DA-led coalition, for example, two DA councillors remarked:

In the City of Johannesburg, it is a bit of both power and policy. We wanted to take power from the ANC. But we have shared policies. The DA is pro-poor, same with the EFF, the IFP and the ACDP. It is all because of the history of this country. This coalition is about power … but I think it is also about policy alignment and principle, because if it wasn't, we would have struggled to work together.

Coalition councillors from the other parties had contradictory interpretations of the coalition driving forces. Some saw this DA-led coalition as 'stillborn'. A councillor from one of the larger parties noted that the coalition had merely been an act of siding with the 'lesser devil'. The DA had expectations of using its electoral dominance to influence the EFF into joining forces with them in a coalition. However, this did not happen, especially owing to the fact that the EFF was clear from the outset that its act of cooperation was a 'marriage of convenience' to destabilise the ANC. The party's cooperation with the coalition did not amount to support of most of the DA's policies, because the EFF found them to be anti-black. The DA interviews also suggested that they thought that, given their experience with coalitions in the Western Cape, they would be able to exercise influence over the EFF in a cooperative formation with the party.

Unable to put into effect its intended legislative promises due to a failure to consistently secure the EFF's swing vote, and unable to reconcile with the EFF's policies, the DA failed to signal to its voters that it was taking the electorate's concerns seriously (Klüver and Spoon, 2016: 1). The DA's approach to the coalition highlighted a lack of policy preparedness, which became glaring given that there was no comprehensive coalition agreement to codify the basic policy principles that the members would adopt. The research also established that the DA-led Johannesburg municipality did not formulate new policies – councillor interviewees noted that the City was implementing several of the ANC policies.

When councillors were asked what inherent qualities differentiated Johannesburg's 2016 coalition government from the preceding administration, a minority party councillor responded that they did not believe that the policies of the ANC and the DA were substantially different from each other. An interviewee observed that '(o)ne [party] will speak about transformation and the other will speak about diversity. They both focus on the semantics. They are different sides, but they are the same coin.' On policy provisions another interviewee said: 'The housing policy of the government led by the DA is the same [as] that of the ANC.' One minority party councillor commented that the two successive governments were implementing similar policies, with little effort and resources being directed towards the persistent housing delivery issue, for example. Furthermore, the allegations of maladministration became a metaphorical political football tossed between the ANC and the DA. The agenda hence became one that was less concerned with policy than with managing power dynamics.

Prioritising service delivery and surmounting corruption
At its onset, coalition governance temporarily allowed for a semblance of good governance in the City of Johannesburg. DA councillors were quick to assert that coalition politics under the DA had resulted in better service delivery than in the preceding ANC period. They argued this case with reference to less funds being lost due to corruption, and more funds being channelled into the provision of services. Councillors remarked that the centrepiece of the coalition deal was the election of an executive mayor whose decision-making power was restricted to collective consensus. This was the DA assertion, but councillors from some of the smaller parties had contradictory positions. They noted delays in service delivery due to policy differences and availability of resources. The DA also contradicted itself because, on the one hand, the councillors in these interviews argued that they did not have enough resources and hence were being sabotaged or prevented from implementing coalition policy and other decisions; yet, on the other hand, they claimed they had addressed service delivery. Nonetheless, the DA councillors believed they were faring much better than the preceding ANC government.

Speaking on what they saw as rampant corruption during the ANC-led government, and service delivery by the DA-led coalition, a councillor from a coalition majority political party described the situation thus:

> I was actually in the city council in the previous [ANC] government between 2009 and 2013. I think the major difference between then and now is that the vast majority of money is directed towards service delivery and the business in government. Statistics have uncovered that R18 billion was skimmed out of finances over the last decade. So, [that was] R18 billion of corruption. What needs to be done with this [DA-led] government is make sure that corruption is not tolerated.

A councillor from the majority political party in the 2016–19 coalition (the DA) stated that coalition government presented the idea of shared power, and losing power, in favour of democracy: the democratic expression was in the electorate using the vote to remove the ANC from power, while the ANC's loss of power paved the way for democracy in power-sharing. Commenting on this, a councillor stated that 'this would get to focus people's minds on doing what they should be doing as a government, and the idea [that] sharing power, in turn, makes politics more fluid'. Coalition politics, it was argued, allowed more space for parties to identify and appoint officials on the basis of merit as opposed to overwhelmingly on party allegiance. The sense of most of this set of interviewees was that the impact of this system of merit-based appointments was to create a new system of shared decision-making, which promoted accountability among the parties and allowed for minimisation of corrupt practices. Most councillors interviewed, predominantly from the DA, agreed that the DA-led coalition had managed to combat corruption and was prioritising good governance.

The clash of policy and ideology
DA policy, which is essentially free market-oriented, was presented as the antithesis of the EFF's hardline, socialist-oriented policies, while the ANC was in between these two categories. Hence, and as Booysen (2016: 543) argues, the co-governance arrangement between the DA and the EFF required that the DA would 'negotiate continuously with its ideological nemesis in order to [try and] find consensus'. Commenting on the ongoing ideological compromises, a councillor from the DA said:

> The whole free market system which allows for social security, that is, a free market system aligned with democracy, has been the most successful system in the increase of wealth when you compare it to the alternative. That is our [DA] ideology. I said to my constituency that our party needs to be more vocal about this, because we represent the most successful ideologies in the world in human history. The EFF examples are Zimbabwe and Venezuela, where people are living in poverty at the moment; even in Cuba. So what do they have to offer people?

The DA councillor interviewee argued that the ANC was in the middle, and that '(t)hey don't know whether they are ... socialist or ... free market; they have an emotional attachment towards socialism because it helped them achieve liberation, but it does not really work'. When there is an ideological clash, the interviewee continued, '[I]t's between the EFF and the DA, mainly concerning the issue of land rights' and specifically on the DA's free market approach to land. This DA councillor lauded the party's own position, stating that a party's land reform strategy should be informed not by achieving quantitative land targets, but by its support of a thriving commercial-agricultural sector.

Housing proved to be a major concern for the City of Johannesburg, with a huge backlog of houses to be provided (Manomano, Tanga and Tanyi, 2016). Despite the DA vowing to provide comprehensive housing delivery and the EFF provoking mass land grabs and occupations, the different ideologies underpinning how housing delivery would be effected elicited a deadlock that ultimately hampered delivery. The DA in the context of the Johannesburg municipality assumed the main policy issue amounted to inequality in service delivery, citing in its housing policy that 'the complexity of human settlements in South Africa makes it imperative to make progress on all fronts using all available instruments',[4] accordingly promising comprehensive service delivery in effecting human settlement delivery in the country, according to a DA councillor interviewee.

Most of the DA-dominated group of councillors interviewed concurred that differing ideologies between parties was the main cause of disagreements in the Johannesburg municipality, with the DA and the EFF frequently clashing on the land debate. This smaller party interviewee stressed the need for compromise:

> If we are in a coalition, we have agreed that we must surrender who we are for the purposes of this. In multiparty politics, you have different parties with different ideologies, but they are gathering on a common goal. That is how the City of Johannesburg coalition politics was formed … by different political parties in order to topple the ANC and look at the common goal.

Kadima (2014) references coalitions as beacons of change in historically divided societies, such as South Africa, noting, however, that they will struggle to succeed where divisiveness on policy issues impedes responsiveness by coalition members. This applied to the DA-EFF relationship. The EFF had various non-negotiable policies based on the seven cardinal pillars that guided its activities concerning land expropriation, as quoted by an EFF councillor (EFF, 2014). The EFF would not compromise on these, and this led some councillors in the interviews to regard them as 'chaos causers' and 'obstructers of progress'.

Interparty and intraparty clashes subsuming service delivery

DA coalition energy that was intended to be focused on meeting policy commitments was redirected away from service delivery towards quelling party clashes between coalition members, and these were largely clashes with the EFF. A councillor noted that '… it was not mentioned expressly, but going through all these stages and fighting to reach consensus would inevitably delay service delivery…' Policy advancement requires deliberation and consensus on a common policy purpose and determination to achieve the policy goals. Yet, at this stage the DA-led coalition was driven by office-seeking and office retention, operating without a coordinated plan as to how to respond to the policy and service issues within the municipality.

None of the councillors interviewed mentioned the electorate nor emphasised the need to improve service delivery. This was compounded by the fact that the coalition did not have sufficient faith in the then mayor, Herman Mashaba. The policy and trust deficit brought to light the inherent personality politics within the coalition. The councillors contended that Mashaba was more of a businessman than a 'statesman'. In the meantime, the electorate was expecting the DA-led government, having pledged comprehensive service delivery, to show itself to be different from the ANC government, which, councillors noted, had let down the electorate.

THE DESTABILISING ROLE OF THE EFF AS QUEENMAKER

Where there is more than one political party or coalition vying for power, one can identify the common party whose sway will ultimately decide the winning party (Brams and Kilgour, 2009: 1). The position of queenmaker, held by the EFF in the council of the City of Johannesburg, underpinned the eventual demise of the DA-led coalition. This role is critical to understanding the EFF's influence on the balance of power in South Africa's coalition politics. The strategic political game the EFF played not only pushed the ANC from power, but subsequently collapsed the DA's coalition hold over the city. That collapse in turn ushered in an ANC-led coalition in 2019–20.

The EFF has long prized its role as queenmaker of party politics, even remarking confidently on the eve of the May 2019 national and provincial elections that no party would win an outright majority – and would hence have to depend on the EFF to build a majority. Realising at the time that the party could acquire queenmaker status, the EFF operated strategically, as highlighted in an interview statement by an EFF councillor:

> I can tell you why the EFF chose the way that they played. The City of Johannesburg's budget is bigger than any [other] municipality in this country; as a matter of fact, it is bigger than many provincial budgets in this country. If utilised correctly and efficiently, it could make a huge difference in the lives of

Johannesburg residents. The ANC has been looting the coffers of Johannesburg. Then we asked ourselves, 'Who is the better devil? Is it the one who has been milking the coffers of the city or the one who is so obsessed with power?' And the decision was to vote against corruption first. One of our cardinal pillars is anti-corruption and that is why we didn't vote with the ANC. It was strategic.

In one way or another, most interviewees, both councillors and officials, accused the EFF of playing politics, being disruptive or abusing its power in the City of Johannesburg. The EFF's exercise of power was identified virtually across the board as hampering the effectiveness of coalition governance. This was on the assumption, however, that the EFF should behave like a standard coalition partner, which it was not.

The EFF viewed its own strategic and policy stances as a matter of principle. It emerged from the interviews that the EFF had clear intentions to push its own party policies and hence deliberately impede the progress of the DA-led coalition. Coalition politics could often force parties to compromise on their policies, noted one councillor. In contrast, an EFF councillor asserted that such compromises could not be made by the EFF: 'We have to stick to those [core principles], even if it means bringing the coalition down.' Members of the coalition government criticised the EFF for this principle-driven behaviour in the City of Johannesburg's coalition government, and for the disruptive role it played in the national assembly. The resentment of the EFF's use of its deciding vote in the Johannesburg council is reflected in this DA interviewee's words on the EFF, referring to the range of metropolitan councils where DA coalitions were in power:

> Sometimes I feel they abuse their power, because the truth is, even though we have different policies and ideologies, there are times where you should allow other organisations to make their own input and take their own decisions based on their own policies that could assist the municipalities going forward.

An EFF councillor dismissed the characterisation of the party as queenmaker, preferring the designation of 'principled political actor': 'We are not "queenmakers". Like I said, it's a matter of principle. It's about who agrees with us at the end of the day; it's about advocating for our people's manifesto.' Irrespective of the semantics, the effect of the EFF's actions testify to its influence on the rise and fall of coalitions in Johannesburg. Its influence also created a divisive governance style that led to stagnation in the provision of services, besides the direct party-political fallout and clashes. The EFF vacillated, at the one level according to ideology and community interest, but at another according to a much-maligned game of power play and material benefits.

Another councillor noted that the EFF exhibited unhealthy power behaviours, manifested mostly in its decision not to join the coalition as a conventional partner, but rather to work with the coalition on an issue-by-issue basis, so as to retain its continuous bargaining power through the swing vote. Expounding further, the councillor stated:

> The EFF knows and understands governing processes. For a young party it is powerful. I would have preferred if they were part of [the] coalition. Then we can engage, because we can all learn from them … they have a significant role to play in the politics of this city. But … it is the way they do things that troubles me.

The EFF used its strategic queenmaker role to hold the ANC to ransom and make it accountable for alleged corruption and maladministration. Within African politics there are many examples where parties joined forces under the slogan 'the enemy of my enemy is my friend' (Sridharan, 2008: 16; Africa Dialogue, 2018). The EFF interviewee seemed uncomfortable to accept this but all other councillors saw the power issue expressed by the EFF. An EFF councillor noted that they had no illusions about the DA (they were fully aware of the party's political underpinnings), but had committed to support the DA on policy issues where it benefited the EFF's electorate and could improve governance of the city.

This was particularly evident when Mayor Mashaba attempted

to privatise Pikitup, the municipality's waste management service provider. The EFF rejected this development and threatened to use its influence to remove the mayor from power (Mdaka, 2016). This was evidence of the EFF's role as queenmaker. The EFF's constitution and documents note that the party's intention is to 'capture political and state power through whatever revolutionary means possible to transform the economy for the benefit of all, in particular Africans' (EFF, 2017: 4). An EFF councillor proudly noted the party's cardinal pillars, which are reflected in its policy document, the first being 'land expropriation without compensation for equal redistribution and use' (EFF, 2017: 4). The EFF councillor conceded that they were fully aware that the DA would oppose their policies, considering that the DA remained a 'white party' that prioritised its constituents living in the elite suburbs of Johannesburg, but that they had joined forces with the DA nonetheless in order to defeat the ANC.

ANC REGAINS POLITICAL CONTROL OF JOHANNESBURG

There was considerable evidence that the ANC was prepared to use various elements of its massive leverage, including its control of provincial and national government, to make it difficult for the DA coalition in Johannesburg to survive. A DA councillor argued, for example, that the national government had made numerous attempts to sabotage the DA's efforts in housing provision at the municipal level. The DA argued that the ANC kept a tight grip on funding in ways that would frustrate the coalition's effectiveness. A few of the DA councillors observed that the city was not receiving sufficient funds from the Gauteng provincial government. The political tension between the ANC and the DA was seen to have triggered either a reduction in funding, or insufficient increases in resources required for service delivery, and in particular for housing.

According to councillors, before the DA-led coalition government took over, the Gauteng provincial government used to increase the local government grant to Johannesburg beyond what was given by the national government. It was not in the ANC's interest, however, to see Mashaba succeed, they argued. It is alleged that the Johannesburg municipality did not get an adequate operating budget, despite existing parameters and stipulations as to how such funds should be allocated. The local government equitable share formula review prescribes these parameters, which have, as a primary objective, the provision of funds to 'enable municipalities to provide basic services to poor households'. This objective is derived from section 214(2)(d) of the constitution, which highlights 'the need to ensure that the provinces and municipalities are able to provide basic services and perform the functions expected of them'. In response to the ANC's deemed failure to abide by these prescriptions, a DA councillor claimed that the ANC was deliberately frustrating the budget-approval process under the guise that the DA coalition was 'anti-poor'.

Such allegations were exacerbated by another pivotal and frequently divisive coalition matter – budget allocation and approval. It was a key tension in coalition governance. The tension mostly concerned budget priority and allocation, and subsequent service delivery. Reaching consensus on budget approvals proceeded at a slow pace and had a resultant lag effect on service delivery. One DA councillor confirmed: 'That is the matter we fight about most in the coalition: … service delivery and where the bulk of the budget should be channelled.'

On the side of the ANC, no sooner had the DA-led coalition assumed control of the Johannesburg municipality in 2016 than the ANC began to allege that the DA was mismanaging municipal funds and thus was failing to effect service delivery. The ANC claimed that the DA was abusing state resources to achieve party-political ends, alleging that the mayor, Mashaba, had been forcing local government employees to issue politically slanted media statements. ANC spokesperson Jolidee Matongo argued in a statement that Mashaba had been 'using the metro's communication resources' and 'bending the rules of engagement between government and political party in the institution' (ANA, 2016).

Meanwhile, frustration was mounting over delays in service delivery. Minority parties, having experienced challenges with the DA, including ideological ones, opted to forge a new arrangement with the ANC, hoping for refreshed cooperative governance (Pieterse, 2019).

A councillor from one of the smaller parties argued that the DA's Johannesburg coalition was a 'difficult animal to manage':

> From a coalition perspective, it is difficult to manage different ideologies because you sit with multiple parties. My party is apolitical; it is just that we have biblical principles. You sit with the DA, Cope, [the] IFP and the FF+ around the table. The AIC [African Independent Congress] and the EFF vote [with us, on occasion] but they are not sitting with us around the table, yet they have voting powers. Now you sit with all these parties and they each have their own ideologies and objectives, and it is a very difficult animal to manage. What you have to manage is the relationship as a collective.

In addition to interparty conflicts, the lack of a clear system of power-sharing, though to a lesser extent, was a reason for some of the minority parties to abandon the DA-led coalition. A councillor from a smaller political party said the particular party was open to negotiations on coalition policies, and to compromise, where reasonably needed. Should the coalition's policies severely compromise its voters' interests, however, they would be prepared to withdraw from the coalition governance arrangements. The concession from a small party councillor was that coalition politics tended to cause political parties to surrender individual party policies in favour of those of the coalition. Policies, ideologies and constituency interests thus emerged as the parties' bottom lines when they took stock of what caused the breakdown of the DA's Johannesburg coalition – even if opposition to the ANC and its corruption had been the initial coalition glue.

Prospects of better ideological alignment within party coalitions in the city seemed to exist between the ANC and the EFF. However, an ANC senior official interviewed said that the ANC may simply not be ready to accept that its policies share similarities with those of the EFF, despite the obvious convergence. He argued that, aside from the personality politics between the ANC and Julius Malema, the differences between the two parties were not as stark as they are often made out to be. On these grounds he reckoned that an ANC-led coalition would have a better chance of success than the DA-led coalition. In an attempt to strengthen its position in preparation for the scheduled 2021 local elections, the ANC sought to woo minority parties into formally joining in a coalition (Hlatshaneni, 2019).

TIPPING POINTS TOWARDS THE COLLAPSE OF THE DA-LED COALITION

Throughout the duration of the DA-led coalition, a series of tipping points began to manifest. The drawback of an office-seeking coalition, as noted by Law (2018), is that they are more volatile and prone to infighting due to the fact that ideological convergence is not a primary concern during formation. This is supported by worldwide data that suggest that this kind of coalition is susceptible to breakdown as it lacks common policy foundations and ideological underpinnings (Law, 2018: 7). In such settings there is a greater chance for destructive personality clashes and individualistic party ambitions.

The lack of a formal coalition agreement and consensus regarding the coalition guiding policy (on the assumption that such an agreement would have been adhered to) was a final tipping point that triggered the demise of the DA-led Johannesburg coalition. The presence of such an agreement may have forced coalition members to collaborate and compromise on party ideals for the sake of service delivery. Instead of developing core coalition policy, however, the DA-led coalition had focused on establishing a power alliance capable of unseating the ANC.

Councillors pointed out that though there was no formal coalition agreement, there was a dispute-resolution mechanism for cases of conflict and disputes. In practice, however, it appeared ineffectual, failing to bring interparty agreement and cohesion. A senior official opined that because of consistent deadlocks, there were growing indications that voters were becoming alienated from Mashaba's leadership; he was seen to be favouring the policies of the coalition at the expense of those of the DA. This emerged also around the Alexandra shutdown (see *Mail & Guardian*, 2019), when the ANC and communities that supported it tested the waters in the run-up to the national and provincial elections of mid-2019.⁵ Mashaba had pledged to build temporary structures to replace those demolished by the Red Ants.⁶ The structures never materialised, as was narrated by one councillor from one of the big parties: the DA maintained that erecting temporary structures would amount to a form of land grab. Mashaba's position to rebuild houses thus contrasted with the DA's housing stance, and the DA did not approve, confirmed one of the councillors.

This policy compromise between Herman Mashaba, considered to be centre-right, and the left-wing EFF caucus was unexpected. In and beyond the coalition, Mashaba was lauded as a skilled negotiator whose expertise was enough to sway even the toughest opponents (the EFF) in his favour. One of the councillors interviewed elaborated: 'He is skilled at negotiation' and 'from time to time managed to persuade [the ANC and the EFF] to work together'. The interviewee held the equal belief that Mashaba did seem to prioritise the coalition over the DA, and for this reason he was often called the mayor of the city/coalition, and not a DA party leader.

The Maimane and Mashaba resignations: The death knell for the DA-led coalition

Most often, when a coalition is being formed, it is done by one domineering political party known as the 'formateur' (Law, 2018: 15). In this case, that role was assumed by the DA as the main opposition party to the ANC. Hence, the DA's status as being by far the strongest among the opposition parties meant that it would not only act as formateur, but also as coalition leader, and ultimately hold senior positions within the governance structure. It was therefore a DA-dominant coalition, which at times left the lesser coalition partners feeling resentful. A senior official from a small party struggled with calling this a DA-led coalition government, preferring to designate it a 'multiparty government' because the former definition gave the DA too much power.

On the resignation in October 2019 of both DA national leader Mmusi Maimane and Johannesburg mayor Herman Mashaba from the DA and their respective leadership positions, a destabilising ripple effect ensued. Mashaba's resignation came at a time when the coalition had reached a peak of vulnerability, and rumours of the municipality being broke had begun to negatively affect the coalition's credibility (Nicolson, 2019). Maimane cited among his reasons for stepping down that the DA had failed to restructure its mandate in a manner that appealed to the majority of black voters (Al Jazeera, 2019); Mashaba argued that he could not continue in a party that pretended that race did not matter. Having been elected the first black DA leader in 2015, Maimane had been a central bargaining asset in a historically white-liberal party. Mashaba, with his ability (up to a point) of appeasing and working with the EFF, had been indispensable to the operation of the DA-led coalition. Without these two leaders, DA coalition politics in Johannesburg changed character and collapsed.

Before Mashaba's resignation, a few councillors were of the opinion that he was not going to last in his position because the DA did not approve of him on occasion, choosing the coalition over the party's positions. A senior official's analysis of Mashaba was that '(p)olitically the DA does not really agree with him. If it was up to them, they would've removed him as mayor because [things] which he allows to happen in the City of Johannesburg, and programmes which he leads in implementation, are not found in the manifesto of the DA'. More fundamentally, Mashaba's ability to govern Johannesburg was constantly questioned, because he was seen to be, after all, a businessman with no political experience.

The scene was set, therefore, for the ANC, which had been waiting in the wings to return to power in the City of Johannesburg. This happened in early December 2019. In a tense council vote, the ANC's Geoff Makhubo (also regional chairperson of the ANC in Johannesburg) received 137 of the votes cast (out of the total of 270 potential council votes), followed by the DA's Funzela Ngobeni with 101, and the EFF's Musa Novela with 30 votes. With less than two years before the next set of local government elections, Makhubo realised that it would be a complex task to lead this next Johannesburg coalition government, saying, 'We approach the coalition in a manner that doesn't have a big-brother/small-brother syndrome. While we are the largest party, we recognise that being large is not a sufficient condition to govern' (Mailovich, 2020).[7]

CONCLUSION

In retrospect, one can say that there were certain red flags to be seen well before the formation of the first Johannesburg coalition government, the DA-led version of 2016. They signalled its eventual demise. The constant back and forth between the DA and the EFF confirmed that the two parties' ideological divergence was ruling supreme, and that policy confluence was not materialising either.

The information presented in this chapter shed light through the voices of councillors and officials on how the DA-led coalition's rationale to maximise control over the Johannesburg municipality played out. It followed years of inadequate service delivery at the hands of the ANC. Deeming itself capable of effecting the will of the electorate, and of changing municipal government with a view to improving service delivery to the people, the DA-led coalition was assembled. This would later prove to cause problems, as the lack of the essential glue of coalition agreement and core coalition policy led to calamitous ideological clashes within the coalition. The DA was decidedly not well prepared for the interplay of political ideologies and perhaps was driven by the illusion that somehow it might be able to win over the EFF and use its electoral power to determine how the city was to be governed. Furthermore, the lack of preparedness of the coalition political parties was exposed as they, too, seem not to have expected the extent of the ANC's loss of popular support that was manifested in 2016. Due to the ANC's historical domination of local government elections in Johannesburg between 2000 and 2011 (see Natalini, 2010), opposition parties appeared less prepared for what resulted in 2016. Without forewarning of the 2016 turnaround, it had not been possible for the parties to have pre-formulated a comprehensive contingency policy.

The examination of the role of the EFF as the queenmaker revealed the party's ability to sway votes on an issue-by-issue basis, which resulted in often unpredictable power outcomes, which were to the detriment of the DA. Playing queenmaker was a party aim that was made apparent repeatedly, and should have eliminated any delusions the DA may have held of swaying the EFF in its direction.

The details of this analysis demonstrate the problems that befall coalition governments that are formed despite their ideological, identity and policy divergence. Equally, it shows how ephemeral coalitions may turn out to be when ideologically diverse parties unite against an external force or threat, which in 2016 was the ANC. Subsequent developments showed how service delivery to citizens fell victim to coalition squabbles. While being consumed in the dichotomies of the power dynamics within and outside of the coalition, the DA, either knowingly or unknowingly, compromised effective local governance in the Johannesburg municipality. It is evident that unless alliances are better coordinated ideologically, and in terms of power objectives, endemic power struggles will result.

REFERENCES

Africa Dialogue. 2018. 'Complexities of Coalition Politics in Africa', Monograph Series No. 1/2018, https://media.africaportal.org/documents/ACCORD-Monograph-2018-1.pdf, accessed 28 October 2020.

African News Agency (ANA). 10 October 2016. 'ANC accuses Mashaba of forcing metro officials to spread DA message', *Polity*, https://www.polity.org.za/print-version/anc-acuses-mashaba-of-forcing-metro-officials-to-spread-da-message-2016-10-10, accessed 1 February 2021.

Al Jazeera. 2019. 'South Africa's Mmusi Maimane quits as Democratic Alliance leader', https://www.aljazeera.com/news/2019/10/south-africa-mmusi-maimane-quits-democratic-alliance-leader-191023153508820.html, accessed 22 May 2020.

Amashabalala, M. and Madisa, K. 29 November 2020. 'ANC wants its mayor to face a new probe'. *Sunday Times*.

Brams, S. J. and Kilgour, D. M. 2009. *Kingmakers and Leaders in Coalition Formation*. New York: New York University Press.

Booysen, S. 2016. 'Edging out the African National Congress in the City of Johannesburg: A case of collective punishment', *Journal of Public Administration*, 51 (3.1), 532–548.

Booysen, S. (ed.) 2019. 'Voting Trends 25 Years into Democracy: Analysis of South Africa's 2019 election'. Special report, MISTRA, Johannesburg.

Burge, I. and Laver, M. 1986. 'Office seeking and policy pursuit in coalition theory', *Legislative Studies Quarterly*, 11 (4), 485–506.

Cox, A. 2 October 2020. 'City of Joburg claims it was investigating R80m PPE tender fraud before story broke', *IOL*, https://www.iol.co.za/the-star/news/city-of-joburg-claims-it-was-investigating-r80m-ppe-tender-fraud-before-story-broke-b2b3fa5c-dadd-4f02-a216-94b5fb9d198c, accessed 1 February 2021.

Economic Freedom Fighters (EFF). 2014. '7 Cardinal pillars of the EFF', https://tuteconomicfreedomfighters.wordpress.com/2014/04/15/7-cardinal-pillars-of-the-eff/, accessed 3 May 2020.

Economic Freedom Fighters (EFF). 2017. 'Constitution: Code of Conduct and Revolutionary Discipline', http://www.myvotecounts.org.za/wp-content/uploads/2019/04/EFF-Constitution-x-Code-of-Conduct-Secretary-General-2017.pdf, accessed 22 May 2020.

Electoral Commission of South Africa (IEC). 2019. 'Results summary', http://www.elections.org.za/content/LGEPublicReports/402/Detailed%20Results/GP/JHB.pdf, accessed 23 May 2020.

Electoral Commission of South Africa (IEC). 2016. 'Municipal elections report', file:///C:/Users/User/Downloads/2016%20Municipal%20Elections%20Report%20(2).pdf, accessed 1 May 2020.

Hlatshaneni, S. 22 October 2019. 'ANC woos EFF to seize Johannesburg', *The Citizen*, https://citizen.co.za/news/south-africa/politics/2194094-anc-woos-eff-to-seize-johannesburg/, accessed 1 May 2020.

Kadima, D. 2014. 'An introduction to the politics of party alliances and coalitions in socially divided South Africa', *Journal of African Elections,* 13 (1), 1–24.

Kapa, M. and Shale, V. 2014. 'Alliances, coalitions and the political system in Lesotho 2007–2012', *Journal of African Elections*, 13 (1), 93–114.

Klüver, H. and Spoon, J. 2016. 'Who responds? Voters, parties and issue attention', *British Journal of Political Science,* 46 (3), 633–654.

Law, M. 2018. 'Political party co-operation and the building and sustaining of coalitions'. Background paper, Political Party Co-operation and the Building and Sustaining of Coalitions in South Africa Initiative, https://za.boell.org/sites/default/files/background_paper_-_7_may_symposium_-_political_party_cooperation_and_the_building_and_sustaining_of_coalitions.pdf, accessed 1 May 2020.

Mail & Guardian. 13 May 2019. 'Development of Alex has been arrested, inquiry hears', https://mg.co.za/article/2019-05-13-the-development-of-alex-has-been-arrested-inquiry-hears/, accessed 1 May 2020.

Mailovich, C. 4 December 2019. 'ANC retakes Jhb as DA coalition collapses', *Business Day*, https://www.businesslive.co.za/bd/national/2019-12-04-anc-regains-control-of-city-of-johannesburg/, accessed 1 February 2021.

Mailovich, C. 19 March 2020. 'Profile: New Joburg mayor Geoff Makhubo faces tough challenge', *Financial Mail,* https://www.businesslive.co.za/fm/fm-fox/2020-03-19-profile-new-joburg-mayor-geoff-makhubo-faces-tough-challenge/, accessed 16 May 2020.

Makgale, B. 2020. 'Coalition Politics and Urban Governance in Johannesburg's Housing Policy'. Master's thesis, Wits School of Governance, University of the Witwatersrand.

Manomano, T., Tanga, P. T. and Tanyi, P. 2016. 'Housing problems and programs in South Africa: A literature review', *Journal of Sociology and Social Anthropology*, 7 (2), 111–117.

Mdaka, Y. 1 September 2016. 'EFF threatens to remove Mashaba if Pikitup is privatized', *Destinyman*, https://www.destinyman.com/2016/09/01/eff-threatens-remove-mashaba-pikitup-privatised, accessed 7 April 2020.

Moury, C. and Timmermans, A. 2013. 'Inter-party conflict management in coalition governments: Analysing the role of coalition agreements in Belgium, Germany, Italy and the Netherlands', *Politics and Governance*, 1 (2), 117–131.

Natalini, L. 26 June 2010. 'The role of political parties at the local government level: A reflection on South Africa at the time of the policy process of review on decentralisation', *AISA Policy Brief*, https://media.africaportal.org/documents/No-26.-The-Role-of-Political-Parties-at-the-local-government-level.pdf, accessed 1 May 2020.

Nicolson, G. 2019. 'Mashaba resigns: "I cannot reconcile myself with a group who believe that race is irrelevant"', *Daily Maverick*, https://www.dailymaverick.co.za/article/2019-10-21-mashaba-resigns-i-cannot-reconcile-myself-with-a-group-who-believe-that-race-is-irrelevant/, accessed 1 May 2020.

Oyugi, W. O. 2006. 'Coalition politics and coalition governments in Africa', *Journal of Contemporary African Studies*, 24 (1), 53–79.

Pieterse, M. 10 December 2019. 'What's needed to fix collapsing coalitions in South Africa's cities?', *The Conversation,* https://theconversation.com/whats-needed-to-fix-collapsing-coalitions-in-south-africas-cities-128526, accessed 30 April 2020.

Sridharan, E. 23 September 2008. *Coalition politics in India: Types, duration, theory and comparison,* Working Paper, Institute for South Asian Studies, https://www.files.ethz.ch/isn/132602/ISAS_working%20paper_50.pdf, accessed 1 May 2020.

TWELVE

The Tshwane metropolitan council

Multiparty and multiple coalitions, and imperilled governance

GRAEME DE BRUYN

'... the importance of serving in a municipal council is that party political affiliation and agendas are eschewed for the greater good of communities'
– Judge President Dunstan Mlambo,
Gauteng High Court, 2020[1]

THE AUGUST 2016 MUNICIPAL ELECTIONS were disruptive, reshaping the political space in South Africa. Among other things, it halted the electoral and governing hold of the African National Congress (ANC) on the metropolitan municipalities of South Africa. There were far-reaching implications for local and, in particular, metropolitan governance in South Africa, and the City of Tshwane offered an example of how governance may have been adversely affected. As the High Court judgment on the Tshwane council dissolution affirmed, the yardstick for coalition governing lies in serving the common interests of residents. The Tshwane political coalitions could help prioritise service delivery to all residents (*Democratic Alliance and Others v Premier for the Province of Gauteng and Others*, 2020: para 33). However, the evidence from Tshwane gave reason to perceive coalition politics and the coalition council as unresponsive to voters' preferences, with residents limited in holding the coalition governments to account for their actions.

In this context, this chapter traces the determinants, functioning and demise of the various political alliances and coalitions that constituted the local government in Tshwane from 2016 to 2020. Using the coalition life-cycle analytical approach, and extending the available model, the analysis highlights the ingrained instability that characterises political alliances and coalitions. Its investigation sheds light on the extent to and manners in which coalition operations can adversely affect governance. It confirms the importance of leadership skill and electoral prospects in the sustainability of coalitions. The chapter also dissects the range of the varied cooperative arrangements that applied between political parties in the case of Tshwane. These have been branded, for example, as 'governing across divisions' (Pieterse, 2019), representing 'the true government of maturing democracy' (Sebake, 2020), agreement 'between parties adjacent on the political spectrum' (Gottschalk, 2019), and 'no one get[ting] who they voted for' (BizNews, 2016). These depictions indicate reasons to dissect the factors that influenced coalition politics at the time in Tshwane, and to consider the place of coalition politics in local government in South Africa. In line with much of the literature, the chapter acknowledges the interplay of national and local politics in the operation of the Tshwane coalition, and considers additional factors such as intraparty politics, political leadership and temporary shifts, such as pending elections that affected renegotiations and coalition stability.

Coalitions in the Tshwane council were manifestations of multi-coalitions and multiple coalitions, with specific reference to the conduct of the ANC, the Democratic Alliance (DA) and the Economic Freedom Fighters (EFF). The DA-led council had a formal coalition agreement with smaller parties, except for the EFF, with which it had a non-binding service-and-supply agreement to guide its cooperation. Intraparty politics and the operationalisation of coalition politics amounted to various interparty pacts (or alliances) and formal coalitions – this chapter will use the generic phrase 'coalitions' to designate this palette of interparty engagements. Much of the time the shared objective in pursuing these coalitions was to 'maximise power or advance party policy objectives' (Law, 2018: 6). When explaining coalition formation, its outcomes and patterns, the implications and costs of political coalitions are approached usefully through the intersection of governance, the role of the political leadership, and the 'private beliefs and decision-making of individuals' (Chan and Leung, 2008: 625). Finally, the complex interplay of interparty and intraparty politics during 2016–20 drives coalition formation – and dissolution.

From the governance perspective, Tshwane (Pretoria) has substantial administrative and political significance to South Africa. It is not just one of the biggest metropolitan councils in the country (and the largest municipality in terms of landmass), but is the administrative seat of government, and Gauteng home to the national government's seat of power, the Union Buildings. It is divided into seven regions, with 107 geographically allocated wards. It has 214 elected councillors, made up of 107 ward and 107 proportionally elected councillors (see Table 12.1). This chapter explores how and why the first phase of the 'cooperation relationship' (EFF, 2020) between the DA and the EFF was established and then collapsed. It reflects on the evolving impasse of a dissolved municipal council, absent executive leadership, and the continued litigation and counter-litigation that escalated to interventions at the level of provincial and national government.

The next section provides background on coalition-building by outlining the origins of political coalitions in the Tshwane metropolitan municipality. This is followed by the application of a life-cycle approach to illuminate coalition patterns and dynamics, and the analysis details the multiple Tshwane coalitions. This is followed by a discussion on political leadership and its causal impact during coalition formation.

THE GENESIS OF POLITICAL COALITIONS IN TSHWANE

The 2016 municipal election outcomes in Tshwane brought to the fore the realities of the change wrought by political coalitions. A shift in power was registered in the Tshwane municipality (among others), and the ANC lost its majority control of South Africa's capital. The election result catalysed weeks of power-sharing negotiations on the structuring of governing agreements. Law (2018: 3) concluded that

> ... after 22 years of almost complete electoral dominance by the African National Congress (ANC), signs began to emerge that their grip on power was starting to wane, and a more competitive multi-party structure was beginning to emerge.

There was a fundamental change in the ANC's previous above 60 per cent electoral support, which had prevailed since the first round of post-1994 local government elections of 1995 (Mokgosi et al., 2017: 39). This decline was accompanied by a deteriorating economy and rising unemployment, as well as a more contested political system (Scheurkogel, 2018: 143). There was unanimity among the main opposition parties at the time to unseat the dominant ANC (Mkhabela, 2016: 7). This contributed to a new political environment in which coalition politics entered the political mainstream.

The election results brought about a hung council in the City of Tshwane, as neither the ANC (the pre-election incumbent that now had 41.2 per cent or 89 seats) nor the DA (with 43.1 per cent or 93 seats) attained a sufficient majority to govern the council without the EFF (with 11.7 per cent of the municipal votes). The ANC was displaced by the DA, which effected co-governing arrangements with the EFF, the Freedom Front Plus (FF+), the Congress of the People (COPE) and the African Christian Democratic Party (ACDP), and assumed power in Tshwane. Table 12.1 shows the electoral performance of the political parties and the 2016 seat allocation in the council.

At the start of the 2016 wave of new coalitions, the DA's then leader, Mmusi Maimane, in hopeful tones, elaborated on political coalitions in terms that showed expectations to improve governance:

> While coalitions are complex and difficult to manage, we are optimistic that we can form governments that are united by the one galvanising force which is the delivery of better services and in so doing move South Africa forward again (BusinessTech, 2016).

Formulations and definitional orientations matter, and can enhance or limit the understanding of coalition governments, as the rest of the analysis of coalition politics in Tshwane will demonstrate. Terms such as 'alliance' and 'coalition' signify interparty cooperation, but each has its own unique operating mechanisms and processes (Kadima, 2014: 2). The 'alliance' between the DA and EFF, and the 'coalition' between the DA and its other partners in Tshwane, 2016–17, were temporary, and their formation a necessity to form a coalitional municipal council, due to its status as a hung council. Political parties' expressed expectations of political coalitions also illuminate the varying interpretations. For instance, the ACDP portrayed the post-2016 era as one of multiparty government, involving cooperation, while the participating parties retain their respective identities (Dludla, 2016). The spectrum of descriptions of political coalitions articulates with the range of governance mechanisms and practices.

Contending coalition descriptions are regularly discussed without sufficient consideration of the exact aspects that are being examined, and whether it is the dynamics, mechanisms, types and/or stages involved in coalitions that are being considered. Terms such as 'multiparty governance', 'coalitions' and 'party alliances', though interrelated, are used in divergent ways.

POLITICAL COALITION LIFE-CYCLE ANALYSIS

The intricacies and disruptive shifts of the multi-coalitions and multiple coalitions, and the subsequent fate of the Tshwane coalitions, may be understood, in terms of the framework put forward by Müller and Miller (2005: 2), as a 'systematically linked' and dynamic life-cycle of

Table 12.1: Tshwane council 2016 – Party performance and seat allocation

Political party	Votes (%)	Ward seats	Proportional representation (PR) seats	Total seat allocation
Democratic Alliance (DA)	43.15	39	54	93
African National Congress (ANC)	41.25	68	21	89
Economic Freedom Fighters (EFF)	11.63	0	25	25
Freedom Front Plus (FF+)	1.99	0	4	4
African Christian Democratic Party (ACDP)	0.49	0	1	1
Congress of the People (Cope)	0.24	0	1	1
Pan Africanist Congress of Azania (PAC)	0.17	0	1	1
Total	98.92	107	107	214

Source: IEC, various; Tshwane Annual Report, 2017/2018 (2019).

'intraparty politics', coalition government formation and the governing of agreements. For current purposes, coalitions are conceptualised as post-election cooperation between at least two political parties (Booysen, 2018: 67). Coalition formation in Tshwane was also formal and informal, temporary, encompassing a range of interests for the attainment of a singular or broader objective, and can be characterised by collusive, predatory (compulsion to have power over opponents) or rent-seeking imperatives (Leftwich, 2010: 105; DLP, 2012: 6). One of the lessons of the Tshwane coalition government was that 'political pettiness' (Pieterse, 2019) and party interests led to instability and derailed the Tshwane coalition and the council's ability to 'conduct its business and serve its residents' (North Gauteng High Court, 2020: 4).

Müller et al. (2019: 9) offer a life-cycle approach to coalitions. They describe behaviour and patterns of coalition formation that are useful for the interpretation of the Tshwane coalitions. Mapping the features and levels of complexity of a life-cycle of political 'coalitionary behaviour' offers insights into the range of inputs and their impacts on the interrelated dimensions of political coalitions. This chapter uses a modification of the coalition life-cycle thinking of Müller et al. (2019), as illustrated in Figure 12.1 – the adapted schematic framework of the stages of political coalitions and the interrelated contextual factors that affect the stages. Whereas the original model used a four-phase process of coalition formation, the adaptation incorporates the developments of the Tshwane coalition journeys. The adapted coalition life-cycle approach provides for an analysis of the complexities within the different stages of coalition politics in Tshwane.

Figure 12.1 incorporates dimensions such as conflict and governance of both the interparty relations and the council's mandate to serve residents (e1). Along the life-cycle, the stages are those of formation, governance interspersed with conflict, renegotiations, and termination or exits from the coalition(s). In his study of the politics of party alliances and coalitions, Kadima (2014) posited that the institutional setting, the political party regime, ideologies and the type of electoral system (party lists, proportional representation (PR), first-past-the-post (FPTP) and individual councillors at ward level) give rise to different types of coalition partner calculations among political parties. Accordingly, during the unfolding period of multi-coalitions

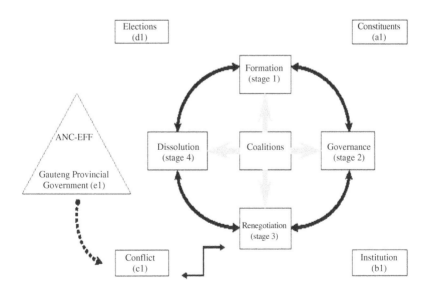

Figure 12.1. Coalition life-cycle: Tshwane multi-coalitions

Source: Adapted from Müller et al. (2019).

in Tshwane, allegiances of some of the represented parties shifted to the ANC, and renegotiations followed. Given the causal impact and the interrelationship between them, the four stages are discussed in tandem, while the major influences are drawn into the analysis.

Formation and governance

By way of the application of the coalition life-cycle approach (Müller et al., 2019) to the Tshwane coalitions (Figure 12.1, stage 1), the multiparty nature of these coalitions, competing delivery preferences, parties coveting the same strategic positions in council (mayor and mayoral committee), and all aiming to use their performances to optimise post-2016 electoral prospects (in a next cycle of elections) epitomised conflicting expectations. These competing claims precipitated coalition instability and stalemates (illustrated further down, in the analysis in relation to the rationale for the fracturing of the coalition between the DA and the EFF). At the formation of the Tshwane coalitions there were formalised agreements between some of the parties, but not with the EFF. The EFF was not formally part of the Tshwane coalition; it was therefore neither bound by agreements, nor compelled to vote for coalition proposals or in the interests of sustaining the coalition (Schreiber, 2018). At its formation, the Tshwane coalition could therefore be described as a minority government with a tenuous confidence-and-supply arrangement with the EFF.

In August 2017, the DA experienced difficulties with managing coalition agreements, and, by November 2019, the then interim leader of the party, John Steenhuisen, acknowledged that 'forming governments in Tshwane with the EFF was a mistake' (Polity, 2019). There were multiple attempts to oust the first DA-led council mayor. The challenges with coalition governance were further exposed when the EFF, which had been in a voting pact with the DA, voted against the 2019/20 budget (Nkanjeni, 2019). The lack of formalised conventions of partnering and/or an agreed-to development agenda between the coalition parties were significant stumbling blocks. Had such documents been present, a more definitive evaluation of the DA-led coalition would have been possible.

Constituents, governance and mounting conflict

Constituents (Figure 12.1, a1) are a primary component of the operational environment of political coalition-building. The life-cycle model positions constituents as voters – as municipal stakeholders who have a direct or indirect concern with governance in the city – on the assumption that coalition formation will be tailored to the preferences of the electorate (see Figure 12.1). In the case of the EFF, the party defined its constituents as party supporters, and the party guarded against possible repercussions that coalition compromises could hold for the relationship with its constituents. It closely guarded its brand of politics, especially where the national-level party leaders would be unable to justify deployed councillors' coalition-based decisions.

For a coalition to be stable, these constituents' interests and preferences are supposed to be an integral part of building coalitions – but they were not at the time of the formation and operation of the DA-led coalition (unless one counts the indirect EFF leadership's interpretation of representing interests on behalf of select constituents). They later became a defacto component, in helping to mount opposition to the DA-led coalition, and contributed to its subsequent collapse. Moafrika Mabogwana articulated his party's role as an opposition, asserting that 'we are in the council to represent our constituency' (The Clement Manyathela Show, 2020). Mabogwana noted that the EFF would protest and do 'everything in its power' to satisfy the expectations of its constituency, even protest against its coalition partner. Another constituent, the South African Chamber of Commerce and Industry, added its voice to the coalition-building discussions (Polity, 2016):

> We would like to encourage the parties that are in negotiations in the hung metros ... to speed up the process so that service delivery is not negatively affected. As the voters have spoken, it is important for political parties to elevate the interests of South Africa and its communities above narrow sectional or political considerations.

As evidence, whereas the initial DA mayoral candidate was voted for by the electorate (being the candidate who led the party into the local election of 2016), the subsequent mayor was determined by party-specific considerations, rather than what Hobolt and Karp (2010: 303) describe as founded on citizen (constituent) choice of candidate integrity, alignment with electorate interests, experience or capabilities.

Conflict and renegotiations

The 2016 DA-led multiparty political coalition ejected the ANC from its position of dominance in Tshwane, this change being the common goal of the majority of the alliance of political parties in the council, and more so of the DA and the EFF. With the unstable and loosely constructed governing arrangement between the DA and the EFF (Figure 12.1, stage 2), the EFF changed its position. Its initial position was limited to issue-by-issue voting support to the DA. By 19 May 2019, the DA confirmed that power-sharing renegotiations – bargaining (Figure 12.1, stage 3) – had been initiated with the EFF. The EFF was demanding more control of the municipal council. During this phase of the life-cycle, the DA-led coalition was beset by institutional disruptions (among others, no signed-off operational budget, inability to effect senior staff appointments, and stalled negotiations with labour unions). The EFF-initiated renegotiations and contests for the removal of the most senior members of the mayoral-executive leadership disrupted the already tenuous stability of the 2016 coalition. In November 2019, Mbuyiseni Ndlozi indicated important factors in coalition conflict and collapse: the DA had had its chances, and its dealings with the coalition partners were hostile, and council decisions were made in isolation; and the EFF renegotiation position was premised on the party being afforded a 'chance to govern on our own in one city' (SABC News, 2019).

A critical event that exacerbated the interparty conflict between the DA and the EFF occurred on 6 December 2019, when the motion of no confidence in the second DA-led coalition mayor, Stevens Mokgalapa, carried. Mokgalapa had commenced his mayoralty in March 2019 and his removal from office was met with both protest and celebratory song. The DA, the EFF and the ANC each occupied different sides of the council chambers. Drawing on the research on coalition government intrapolitics and conflict by Müller and Miller (2005: 7), it is clear that the December 2019 events were instrumental in collapsing the 'governance and stability' of the Tshwane council. The events demonstrated that the DA and EFF agenda of preventing ANC overall control in the Tshwane council, which had been the main focus at the beginning of this coalition, was exhausted. It sealed the fate of these two parties' council cooperation. The DA councillors interrupted efforts to resume council proceedings after an acting EFF speaker tried to continue with the council agenda. The DA leadership reverted to the courts for adjudication.

Dissolution and new coalitions

The DA-led multiparty administration's functioning became constrained by the EFF's 'absence from council and a lack of cooperation' (eNCA, 2017). This prompted the DA mayor at the time to register the possibility of walking away from the agreement entered into with the EFF. It was a protracted period of dissolution. Court actions were filed. The positional bargaining and instability in the Tshwane council and municipality led to multi-level stalemates. These stalemates were between the ANC and the DA-led council, the DA and the EFF, the ANC Gauteng and the DA. As the bottom line, this led to the termination of the DA-led alliance with the EFF, and to common purpose coalitions among the Gauteng provincial government and the ANC and the EFF (Figure 12.1, e1). This new partnership followed without constituents (Figure 12.1, a1) having had any recourse to elections (figure 12.1, d1). The developments unfolded within the same 2016–21 electoral term. The next section elaborates on the process of dissolution and reconstitution (of new alliances), using the frame of multi-coalitions and multiple coalitions.

THE POST-2018 EMERGENT COALITIONS

Political coalitions in Tshwane have been distinguished by their character as multi-coalitions and multiple coalitions. This perspective is used to outline the developments from the initial DA-led coalition to the establishment of two independently formed alliances (Figure 12.1, e1). In line with the modified life-cycle of coalition model (Figure 12.1), the incumbent DA-led coalition of 2016 was disrupted by intracoalition conflict, and these disruptions preceded and pre-empted the official breakdown of the DA-EFF coalition. What emerged were simultaneous but interrelated actions of common purpose (or 'coalitions') between the Tshwane ANC and the ANC provincial government, and the ANC and the EFF.

The political coalitions in Tshwane have gone through cycles of negotiation, establishment, collapse and newly structured alliances, and could be considered as a 'tale of two halves'. The first part of coalition-building, in 2016, occurred between the DA, the EFF, Cope, the ACDP and the FF+. The second part, which was a nascent multiple-level coalition and occurred outside of the DA-led coalition, appeared first from mid-2019 to March 2020. It comprised, initially, what resembled an attempt at coalition governing between the EFF and the ANC.

The ANC and EFF coalition

The EFF party structures held an internal review after the May 2019 general elections and, among other things, consolidated aspects of the party's stance on coalition arrangements in Tshwane. The EFF was in favour of political parties returning to negotiations to discuss how to share power at the local level. The EFF-DA renegotiations were confirmed in July 2019 by the DA's James Selfe (then federal executive chair). Selfe pointed out the EFF's demands for a formalised coalition, and for 'putting up its own mayor' in Tshwane. The DA rejected the ultimatum, even at the risk of losing power in Tshwane (Nkanjeni, 2019).

EFF leader Julius Malema announced that the party would no longer be voting with the DA. As part of its revised coalition position (Figure 12.1, stage 3), the EFF outlined its intent: it had joined the coalition in 2016 and withdrawn in 2019 as part of its effort to gain experience to govern. The EFF's Tshwane caucus's March 2020 response emphasised that the party's ultimate prize was governing the council and expanding its electoral base. The EFF's bargaining for the formalisation of its Tshwane coalition with the DA, in which it campaigned for the mayorship and positions on the mayoral committee, led to a stalemate and then the collapse (dissolution) of the coalition.

The reality was that neither the DA nor the EFF had an outright majority in Tshwane. The EFF with its 11 per cent of the votes could only remove the DA and its remaining partners from the Tshwane council with the support of the ANC's electoral votes (illustrated in Table 12.1). With the EFF's 2016 stance of not forming coalitions with the ANC still hovering, it was an unexpected shift by the EFF to form an alliance with the ANC. The ANC's Tshwane regional chair remarked (Madisa, 2019):

> The ANC has decided to put the interests of our people first and we have taken a position to work with either of the parties – DA, EFF and other small parties – that put the interests of our people first.

The EFF reneged on its voting-support agreement with the DA and seemed to switch allegiance to the ANC, three years after entering the cooperative arrangement with the DA. The EFF's new position was also based on the narrative of the DA's escalating governance failures, non-delivery of services, errant political leaders, nepotism in staffing appointments, and supply-chain corruption (North Gauteng High Court, 2020). The Gauteng ANC's provincial secretary unexpectedly announced that the party was in 'talks with all other parties in Tshwane to forge a coalition government' (Sokutu, 2020). As Sokutu summarised, notwithstanding this statement of engaging all political parties, the ANC intentionally excluded discussions with the DA. The ANC/EFF-coalition talks were premised on the ANC's plans to reposition itself for the next round of local government elections (Figure 12.1, e1). These 2019 renegotiations between the ANC and the EFF were notable for the ANC's apparent willingness to cede strategic municipal positions to the EFF.

In her study of coalition formation at the Dutch municipal level, Wieldraaijer (2015) argued that coalitions can be explained on the basis of 'electoral volatility' and the role of dominant parties (in Tshwane's case, the ANC). As noted previously, the formation of the DA-EFF alliance was generally understood as aimed at the attainment of both parties' opening goal of unseating the ANC. The subsequent goal for the DA and the EFF was to improve their electoral competitiveness (Mokgosi et al., 2017: 49) in future local government elections. Thus, the EFF explained the end of the DA-EFF coalition (2016–19) by noting that, despite exhaustive efforts to assist the DA in governing, the DA had failed to, among other things, formalise and regularise informal settlements, as agreed to by a resolution and an allocated budget. A resurgent ANC's behaviour contributed to the malfunction of the DA-led coalition. At the 2016 formation of the DA-EFF pact, it was predicted that such a 'coalition' was doomed to fail because of the parties' mismatched ideologies. As Mokgosi et al. (2017: 42) observed, the voting agreement between the DA and the EFF 'had little to do with ideological convergence' and similarly little with proximity to power 'as per theories of size and ideology'.[2]

Similarly, when the ANC in August 2016 engaged in coalition discussions to structure an ANC-EFF coalition, the EFF's rejection of these advances was seen as congruent to the EFF's political stance of being anti-ANC and aware of voters' (constituents') discontent with pre-2016 ANC governing in Tshwane. How then does one explain the developments around the post-2018 ANC-EFF coalition discussions?

Two factors pertaining to the EFF's internal review of the performance of the Tshwane arrangement are to be noted. It is likely that the EFF factored in the reality of its 2016 election promises, which might realistically only materialise after the next round of elections. In addition, and drawing on Falco-Gimeno and Fernandez-Vazquez (2020: 3), the EFF placed a premium on advancing its ideological reputation with voters. In analysing the EFF, Mbete (2015: 36) emphasised the value the EFF places on 'political performance and populist political style'. On this basis, the post-2018 alliance discussions indicate the EFF's aim of governing a metropolitan city as a political priority. The initial unseating of the ANC by the DA-EFF coalition was just a prelude to the EFF's goal to govern. This goal did not change, only the EFF's coalition partner. These efforts were derailed by failed litigation in the Supreme Court of Appeal (2020).[3]

Alliance of the Gauteng provincial executive with the Tshwane ANC and the EFF

The provincial government of Gauteng is led by the ANC, with the City of Tshwane under the jurisdiction of the province through the Gauteng Department of Cooperative Governance and Traditional Affairs. More fundamentally, the Tshwane region is one of the Gauteng ANC's strategic political areas. The Gauteng provincial government seemed to facilitate the Tshwane ANC's regional political interest to reclaim the Tshwane council. Among the indicators was the March 2020 statement by the ANC Tshwane chairperson, Kgosi Maepa, that 'we don't want a coalition government. We want a decisive victory because the ANC is the only organisation with a plan' (Jacaranda FM, 2020).

Part of placing Tshwane under administration would involve holding by-elections in Tshwane within 90 days of the council's dissolution. The Gauteng government MEC reporting to the National Council of Provinces liaised with the Electoral Commission to keep it in the loop (NCOP, 2020: 11). Prior to the dissolution of the council, the MEC's intervention entailed meetings with the administrative and political leadership of Tshwane, and direct engagements with the speaker of council, to stabilise Tshwane council politics. When these efforts failed to bring the desired outcomes, the Gauteng provincial government invoked the dissolution of the Tshwane DA-led council and the appointment of an administrator to manage the affairs of the council. The provincial government's intervention was triggered on 'account of unacceptable, unjustifiable and unreasonable walkouts and disruptions by councillors during council meetings' (NCOP, 2020: 11), which impacted on the council and municipality's functioning. As the North Gauteng High Court (2020) argued, this state of affairs disrupted 'council's ability to conduct its business' by 'continued disorders of council meetings by ANC and EFF councillors staging walkouts'.[4] Through the invocation of section 139(1)(c) of the constitution, the ANC's and EFF's objective of destabilising the DA-led coalition was accomplished.

With the dissolution completed and by-elections as the next step, the ANC Gauteng chair (and premier) stated that 'the ANC doesn't want power at all costs in Tshwane', noting that 'we have exposed the complete collapse of governance and administration led by the Democratic Alliance' (Zulu and Ntshidi, 2020). This is important, as the ANC Gauteng secretary Jacob Khawe had informed the party's regional congress delegates on 10 February 2020 that 'the party was hard at work to woo the support of the EFF in wrestling for the political control of Tshwane and to forge a coalition government' (Sokutu, 2020).

This politically coordinated orchestration of events spearheaded by the Tshwane ANC region testifies to the existence of a defacto and adhoc coalition, evident in the convergence of interests between the ANC-controlled Gauteng executive, the ANC and the EFF. It would seem that the Gauteng executive's placing Tshwane under administration was premised on neither its stated objective of stabilising the council nor of addressing issues of 'governance and accountability' (North Gauteng High Court, 2020: 7). The Gauteng provincial government's intervention is distinguished as an adhoc coalition formation that would be a foundation for ANC and EFF interests to be pursued.

The new alliance signalled the multiple levels of interests in the governing of Tshwane. The provincial interventions enabled the trumping of the DA as the ANC's political opposition. Dissolving the council was one route, and this required the full involvement of the Gauteng executive and also national government structures. The Gauteng provincial government and the national government (in the body of the National Council of Provinces and national minister) as conflicted intermediaries constituted themselves as a coalition of interest, more akin to an 'unprincipled coalition' (Kadima, 2014: 8).

The timeline of the provincial government's interventions in Tshwane illustrates the sequence of the alliance-shifting events (Table 12.2). In particular, there was synchronicity of the Gauteng ANC announcing its campaign to reclaim Tshwane simultaneously with the MEC accelerating steps to eject the DA. Furthermore, as the High Court outlined, on 4 March 2020, the MEC enquired from the Tshwane council speaker whether the dissolution directives were presented to the council, granting the Speaker three days to respond (North Gauteng High Court, 2020: 10). Tellingly, despite the three-day response period, which was communicated on 4 March 2020, the day of the MEC enquiry, the Gauteng executive council took the dissolution decision. This decision was confirmed with the premier and MEC media briefing announcing the resolution on 5 March 2020 (North Gauteng High Court, 2020: paras 26–28). This dissolution intervention is further foregrounded by the DA court action that blocked the removal of the mayor and the speaker in December 2019.[5]

Eventually, the DA took the council dissolution decision to the Gauteng High Court, which ruled, in April 2020, that the ANC Gauteng executive's dissolution order was 'invalid' and was 'set aside'. All councillors in the DA-led coalition municipality were ordered to attend all meetings. The Gauteng executive (through the MEC) responded with an appeal to the Supreme Court of Appeal, which, amid the COVID-19 pandemic, extended the presence of the administrator. On 27 October 2020, the Supreme Court of Appeal dismissed the appeal of the Gauteng premier, and the MEC for Cooperative Governance and Traditional Affairs, ending the term of the appointed administrator. The Gauteng High Court ruled that dissolving of the council would end up with new elections, which would likely result in the same councillors returning in their positions, and likely manifest in another hung council. As the court averred, there was no guarantee that elections would resolve the problem at hand (Supreme Court of Appeal, 2020).[6]

Regardless of the different logics behind these actions, the net effect was that the City of Tshwane was under administration, with a dissolved council, bereft of political and executive leadership (with no city manager, no speaker and no mayor), and with democratic legitimacy a fatality.

Core aspects of the Supreme Court of Appeal and High Court judgments, with relevance to governance and coalitions, included the Supreme Court of Appeal's position that 'a municipality must be governed by its elected municipal council' and the councillors of the EFF and ANC must 'attend and remain in attendance at all meetings of the City of Tshwane Metropolitan Municipality Council unless they have a lawful reason to be absent'.[7] A new mayor, Randall Williams of the DA, was elected on 30 October 2020, and a new mayoral committee was to lead the council to the 2021 local government elections.

Table 12.2: Timeline of Tshwane alliance switching to the Gauteng provincial executive alliance

Date	Triggering event
16 January 2020	Council meeting: motion of no confidence in the mayor, speaker, acting speaker and chair of chairs; meeting loses its quorum after ANC and EFF councillors walk out.
23 January 2020	MEC for Human Settlements, Urban Planning, Cooperative Governance and Traditional Affairs issues a media statement suspending the speaker as a member of council.
12 February 2020	MEC initiates investigation into the conduct of the speaker.
4 March 2020	MEC enquires whether the speaker served the section 139(1)(a) directives to council.
5 March 2020	Gauteng Premier announces the dissolution and administration of the municipal council.
9 March 2020	National Minister of Cooperative Governance and Traditional Affairs approves dissolution.
10 March 2020	DA and the City of Tshwane are presented with the notice to dissolve the municipal council.
29 April 2020	High Court judgment and order in DA High Court challenge of the dissolution and administration of the municipal council declared invalid and set aside.
27 October 2020	Supreme Court of Appeal dismisses appeal of Premier of Gauteng, executive council for the province and MEC for Cooperative Governance and Traditional Affairs.

Sources: North Gauteng High Court, 2020: 9-10; NCOP, 2020: 11.

GOVERNANCE IN THE TIME OF COALITIONS IN TSHWANE

How governance unfolded in the time of the politics of coalitions is a matter that is not adequately emphasised (Mokgosi et al., 2017: 53; see also chapter 10). This section details the performance of the DA-led coalition municipality on the benchmark of governance, conceived as sound administration, service delivery and economic development. Consistent with findings by multiple scholars (including Mpangalasane, 2020; Nyoka, 2020), this chapter argues that the service delivery mandate was not a primary concern for political parties seeking coalitions. De Visser and Steytler (2016: 3) define governance inclusively as the provision of citizen-directed deliverables, and the factors also include political infighting, conflict at senior-management level, and councillor and human resource management. Regarding governance in Tshwane, Mbete asserts that all of the parties were complicit, having helped to preside over a political situation that had regressed beyond weakening service delivery (quoted in Nyoka, 2020). While considering service delivery in the informal areas in the time of Tshwane coalition government, multiple sources, including the North Gauteng High Court in Pretoria, Gauteng MEC Lebogang Maile (2020), the Tshwane metropolitan's internal reports, and research by Mpangalasane (2020), affirm deficits in service delivery, and the coalition council's 'failure to respond to the concerns of residents (Mkhabela, 2016: 24).

Maile (2020) framed this as a 'collapse of governance, service delivery and institutional stability'. Failures were evident, especially if service delivery incorporates municipal accountability, transparency, responsiveness, and effective and inclusive service delivery through following the rule of law (De Visser and Steytler, 2016; Mpangalasane, 2020). The Gauteng Department of Cooperative Governance and Traditional Affairs, through Maile, averred that the City of Tshwane had been jeopardised by poor governance from the inception of the post-election coalition government (NCOP, 2020: 11). Between 2016 and 2020, Tshwane had witnessed intraparty politicking, evident in blame-shifting and mudslinging, and what the ACDP and Cope termed a lack of consequence management (NCOP, 2020: 18). During the National Council of Provinces' dissolution inspection, all represented political parties in the then DA-led council offered their accounts of governance in Tshwane. The DA concurred that 'the reason behind the vacancies is because of a failure of the ANC and EFF councillors who have continually collapsed', or simply had not been attending, meetings of the council since December 2019 (NCOP, 2020: 18). The FF+ concurred on the issue of council meeting walkouts (NCOP, 2020: 17). The ANC argued that the dysfunctionality in Tshwane's council was evident in the corrupt award of a multibillion-rand tender, the negative findings by the auditor-general, the appointment of unqualified personnel and inquorate meetings. The ANC further cited the 'absence of the Mayor; of the City Manager; MMCs and adjustment budget' (NCOP, 2020: 15). The EFF submitted that the speaker was 'suppressing democratic practices' (NCOP, 2020: 17). However, the High Court identified and lambasted the ANC and the EFF for their role in Tshwane's administrative and governance challenges (North Gauteng High Court, 2020: 24, para 72).[8]

In a review of the 2017/18 period, the municipality's performance on accountability and corporate governance was described as a 'mixed bag of fortunes' with noteworthy progress (Tshwane Annual Report, 2017/18, 2019: 17). The City's biannual customer satisfaction survey in 2018 reflected Tshwane's residents' satisfaction at 57 per cent, and that of businesses at 50 per cent, with the overall satisfaction rate reported as 59 per cent (City of Tshwane Resident Satisfaction Survey, 2018).

Political fragmentation and obstruction aside, there were gains during the DA-led administration. These contrasted with the misgivings and implosion of the coalition council, driven by large-scale corruption, and political and administrative instability. While the post-2016 assessment of the National Council of Provinces referred to the council's 'serious governance challenges and widespread corruption' (NCOP, 2020: 11), this situation predated the 2016 coalition-led municipality. The 2011/12 auditor-general report of Gauteng municipalities found that the

> City of Tshwane had material findings in … material amendments to the financial statements, usefulness and reliability of service delivery reporting and an upward trend on unauthorised, irregular as well as fruitless and wasteful expenditure as a result of non-compliance with laws and regulations (Auditor-General, 2013).

Contrary to the ANC's argument that poor governance was the preserve of the DA and the DA-led coalition, its own record indicated that there were senior management and governance issues in the ANC-led council. For example, for the installation of a multi-year electricity meter system estimated at R27 billion, the High Court found that the contract had been 'irregular and unconstitutional' (North Gauteng High Court, 2016: para 49). In addition, in 2014, the City's chief financial officer, Andile Dyakala, was suspended for tender fraud. Part of what the 2016 coalition council had had to manage was the legacy of a cash-strapped City with insufficient provisions to address the city's service delivery backlogs (Msimanga, 2017). Governance unfolded amid budget deficits and administrative instability present during the pre- and post-coalition governments in the City. Financial sustainability for the audit years 2014/15 and 2015/16, illustrated in the auditor-general's findings, were unqualified audit opinions, with unauthorised expenditure in 2015/16 at R2.03 billion (Tshwane Mayoral Committee Report, 2018: 40).

During the DA-led coalition period, especially 2017–18, there was some progress in terms of investments, job creation as well as in capital and operational projects in the expanded public-works programme (Tshwane Annual Report, 2017/2018, 2019). However, the auditor-general's audit outcomes for 2018–19 concluded that 'instability in political or administrative leadership', like Tshwane's situation, correlated with an inability to improve financial audit outcomes (Makwetu, 2020). Tshwane's irregular expenditure amounted to R2.9 billion, and its municipal entity, the Housing Company of Tshwane, had an audit assessment stating 'unqualified with findings' (Auditor-General of South Africa, 2019).[9]

Governing came to a complete deadlock with the disbanded council meeting of 16 January 2020, which was to consider the motions of no confidence in the mayor, the speaker and the acting speaker, and the chair of chairs (North Gauteng High Court, 2020: para 23). Nonetheless, these actions and non-actions resulted in compromised governance that severely affected the 'stability in the City' (Nyoka, 2020).

COALITION GOVERNING AND POLITICAL LEADERSHIP

The behaviour, decision-making and preferences of political actors (elected representatives) are one of the variables consequential to the efficiency and stability of coalition governing (Chan and Leung, 2007: 171). As Teles (2013: 23, 25) emphasised, political leaders are important for good governance, as they need to be responsive, and guide and influence the creation of 'rival strategies based on citizens' preferences'. While political coalitions are more complex than merely a function of individual political actors, leading a coalition includes managing intracoalition conflict. Thus, coalition leaders' roles and personalities influence the initiation, sustainability and termination of alliances (Kadima, 2014: 8). This flags the requirement for both individual and collective political leadership; it is not merely a leader's attributes that are important, but also the 'way they perform their role' (Teles, 2013: 32–34). The political disposition of coalition leaders is critical, particularly how they perceive their roles and one another's motives, as coalitions are inherently about cooperation and bargaining.

In Tshwane, the constantly changing agenda for the coalition government, and the jockeying for roles on the mayoral committee, in development projects and for senior appointments, created what Vercesi (2016: 174) posited as the 'difficulty of formulating final decisions' in a coalition council. Divergent positions emanate from the preferences of factions, individuals and party leaders. At the individual level, Teles's (2013: 23) research on the 'exercise of leadership' offers a critical reference point, particularly in relation to 'governing as a way to improve coordination and providing strategic leadership'. In this vein, Solly Msimanga, the first of the Tshwane DA-coalition mayors, in his first state of the city address, declared that it was crucial to 'identify the key service delivery challenges that transcended ideologies and united those parties dedicated to improving the lives of the people of our city' (Msimanga, 2017). Msimanga's political leadership of the coalition-led municipality was first tailored around his executive mayor role, which entailed oversight of the governance and mandate of the council, and acting as leader of the multiparty coalition-cooperation project. After the August 2018 motion of no confidence in Msimanga, he reiterated that 'we need to work with the EFF, as it will be delusional to think that we can do this without the EFF' (Polity, 2018).

Msimanga's political leadership of 'persuasion and bargaining' (Teles, 2013: 23), and his inattention to the cohesiveness of coalition partners, are said to have been important components in the failure of the DA-led coalition. Msimanga would be judged to have incompletely harnessed the opportunities to mobilise residents around a coalition platform that steered citizens' receptiveness to the coalition agenda. He was seen to have had fewer engagements with the EFF over the latter phase of the coalition. The DA's Gauteng chief whip, Mike Moriarty, disclosed that his Tshwane DA colleagues ascribed the collapse of the DA-led Tshwane coalition to this (The Clement Manyathela Show, 2020).

In March 2019, Stevens Mokgalapa was elected as the DA's second Tshwane coalition mayor; he resigned in February 2020, after having been discredited. His misbehaviour affected the credibility of the DA and weakened the stability of party and personal coalitions (Nyhan, 2009: 7). Collectively, Msimanga's departure and Mokgalapa's tenure created upheaval and shifts in coalition cohesion. Their incumbencies were marked by failure to optimise their roles as coalition leaders. The ideological rift between the DA and the EFF was wide, and there were limited efforts to establish common ground. Even early on in the coalition, however, the EFF leader pointed out that the two parties 'would never agree on ideological issues' (BusinessTech, 2016). This was not just an expression of ideological distancing; it set the EFF's oppositional tone for its time of cooperating with the DA in the governance of Tshwane.

Much of the malfunctioning of the Tshwane coalition government was a question, therefore, of a political leadership that had a sufficient grasp of the intricacies of the institutional and legislative terrain of municipalities, but miscalculated the extent to which coalition politics are 'leader-centred'. In November 2019, the EFF's Mbuyiseni Ndlozi noted the significance of the DA's 'inadequacy of leadership' and poor performance in establishing a sense of inclusion and building consensus (SABC News, 2019). Moriarty acknowledged, too, that the Tshwane DA leadership's arrogance and poor management of the relations between councillors and coalition leaders were detrimental, contributed to the termination of the DA-EFF pact, and helped foster broad discontent in the council (The Clement Manyathela Show, 2020).

For the former DA mayor of Johannesburg, Herman Mashaba, Msimanga's leadership of Tshwane was controversy-ridden. Mashaba (despite his own controversies) likened Msimanga, his political peer and colleague to a failed mayor (Beaumont, 2020: 131). A slightly moderated view would be that Msimanga's initial progress in the governance of the city was countered by agitation for his resignation due to allegations of corruption and the appointment of an underqualified chief of staff – against the background of a complex arrangement of a minority government coalition with an unstable confidence-and-supply arrangement with the EFF.

CONCLUSION

This chapter documented the context of multi-coalitions and multiple coalitions post-2016 in Tshwane through the lens of the coalition life-cycle framework. The analysis brought out the difficulties of institutionalising political coalitions, with special reference to Tshwane. Core to this chapter is that the scepticism about political coalitions centres on their being seen as overly adversarial, seemingly unprincipled and often enacting a flagrant disregard of constituents' interests. The analysis reflects that the poor performance of Tshwane's political parties in a coalition context that can be ascribed only in part to inexperience or ideological preferences.

Political parties are prone to 'change coalition partners' (Falco-Gimeno and Fernandez-Vazquez, 2020: 5) and maximise their own payoff (Chan and Leung, 2007: 171), whether mid-term or during subsequent elections. The prevalence of vested interests also requires that citizens guard against destabilisation through wilful disruptions by elected representatives, imprudent deployment of the provincial government apparatus, and governing through unjustified litigation.

In the case of coalition governance in Tshwane, none of the political parties can claim innocence. Individual (personal) and party political aspirations reigned supreme, and by implication compromised decision making on the very governance issues that led to the intervention of the courts. The analysis shed light on the conditionalities to and political prerogatives in coalitions that mark each of the phases in a coalition life-cycle.

REFERENCES

Auditor-General of South Africa. 2013. 'General report on the audit outcomes of local government: Gauteng', https://www.agsa.co.za/Portals/0/MFMA2011-12Extracts/MFMA_2011-12_provincial_reports/AGSA_MFMA_GAUTENG_2011_12.pdf, accessed 5 May 2020.

Auditor-General of South Africa. 2019. 'Consolidated General Report on the local government audit outcomes, Municipal Finance Management Act, 2017–18', https://www.agsa.co.za/Reporting/MFMAReports/2017-2018MFMA.aspx, accessed 1 June 2020.

Beaumont, M. 2020. *The Accidental Mayor: Herman Mashaba and the battle for Johannesburg*. Johannesburg: Penguin Random House.

BizNews. 17 August 2016. 'No coalition, but DA to eject ANC in Jhb, Tshwane with "tacit" EFF support', www.biznews.com/leadership/2016/08/17/no-coalition-but-da-to-eject-ANC-in-Jhb-tshwane-with-tacit-EFF-support/amp, accessed 23 October 2020.

Booysen, S. 2018. 'Coalitions and alliances demarcate crossroads in ANC trajectories', *New Agenda*, 68, 6–10.

BusinessTech. 17 August 2016. 'DA announces coalitions with smaller parties', https://businesstech.co.za/news/government/133536/da-announces-coalitions-with-smaller-parties/, accessed 27 May 2020.

Chan, C. and Leung, H. 2007. *Rule-based stability criteria for coalition formation under uncertainty.* Proceedings of the 9th Conference on Enterprise Information Systems, AIDSS, Madeira, Portugal, 171–177.

Chan, C. and Leung, H. 2008. 'International stability of coalitions in belief-based non-transferable utility games'. Proceedings of the 21st International FLAIRS Conference, Association for the Advancement of Artificial Intelligence, Florida.

City of Tshwane Resident Satisfaction Survey. 2018. www.tshwane.gov.za/sites/residents/Services/Pages/Customer-Satisfaction-Survey, accessed 2 March 2020.

Democratic Alliance and Others v Premier for the Province of Gauteng and Others (18577/2020) [2020] ZAGPPHC 119; [2020] 2 All SA 793 (GP) (29 April 2020), http://www.saflii.org/za/cases/ZAGPPHC/2020/119.html, accessed 4 January 2021.

Developmental Leadership Program (DLP), 2012. 'Coalitions in the politics of development: Findings, insights and guidance from the DLP coalitions workshop'. Research and policy workshop report, Sydney, 15–16 February 2012. www.dlprog.org/ftp/, accessed 4 July 2020.

De Visser, J. and Steytler, N. 2016. 'Confronting the state of local government: The 2013 Constitutional Court decisions', *Constitutional Court Review,* 1–23, http://repository.uwc.ac.za/bitstream/handle/10566/4029/de-Visser_Confronting-the-state_2016.

pdf?sequence=1&isAllowed=y, accessed 17 June 2020.
Dludla, S. 2016. 'DA bringing about "new era in SA politics"', *IOL*, https://www.iol.co.za/news/politics/da-bringing-about-new-era-in-sa-politics-2058243, accessed 5 June 2020.
Economic Freedom Fighters (EFF). 2020. 'Practice note and heads of argument'. Constitutional Court of South Africa. CC case no.: 82/2020-91/2020 (17 July 2020).
Electoral Commission (IEC). www.elections.org.za, accessed on multiple dates 2020.
eNCA. 1 September 2017. 'DA threatens to walk away from coalition', https://www.enca.com/south-africa/da-threatens-to-walk-away-from-coalition, accessed 12 June 2020.
Falco-Gimeno, A. and Fernandez-Vazquez, P. 2020. 'Choices that matter: Coalition formation and parties' ideological reputations', in *Political Science Research and Methods,* 8 (2), 285–300.
Gottschalk, K. 20 December 2019. 'Mutual hatred a big reason coalitions fail in SA', *IOL*, www.iol.co.za/news/opinion/mutual-hatred-a-big-reason-coalitions-fail-in-sa-39547294, accessed 25 October 2020.
Hobolt, S. B. and Karp, J. A. 2010. 'Voters and coalition governments', Electoral Studies, 29, 299–307.
Jacaranda FM. 5 March 2020. 'ANC eyes "decisive victory" in Tshwane by-elections', https://www.jacarandafm.com/news/news/anc-eyes-decisive-victory-tshwane-elections, accessed 2 July 2020.
Kadima, D. 2014. 'An introduction to the politics of party alliances and coalitions in socially divided Africa', *Journal of African Elections,* 13 (1), 1–24.
Law, M. 2018. 'When foes become friends and friends become foes: Party political co-operation and the building and sustaining of coalitions'. Background paper, Political Party Cooperation and the Building and Sustaining of Coalitions Symposium, Heinrich Böll Foundation, https://za.boell.org/sites/default/files/background_paper_-_7_may_symposium_-_political_party_cooperation_and_the_building_and_sustaining_of_coalitions.pdf, accessed 25 May 2020.
Leftwich, A. 2010. 'Beyond institutions: Rethinking the role of leaders, elites and coalitions in the institutional formation of developmental states and strategies', *Forum for Development Studies,* 37 (1), 93–111.
Madisa, K. 4 July 2019. 'ANC willing to work with DA in Tshwane for good of the people', *Sowetan Live*, https://www.sowetanlive.co.za/news/2019-07-04-anc-willing-to-work-with-da-in-tshwane-for-good-of-the-people/, accessed 3 May 2020.
Maile, L. 11 March 2020. 'If coalitions are our new normal, then we need to get better at it fast', *Pretoria News,* http://www.iol.co.za/pretoria-news/opinion/if-coalitions-are-our-new-normal-then-we-need-to-get-better-

at-it-fast-44595930, accessed 25 October 2020.

Makwetu, K. 1 July 2020. Auditor-General media statements, https://www.gov.za/speeches/auditor-general-kimi-makwetu-releases-municipal-audit-results-1-jul-2020-0000, accessed 2 July 2020.

Masipa, T. S. 2017. 'The rise of multi-partyism in South Africa's political spectrum: The age of coalition and multi-party governance'. The 2nd Annual International Conference on Public Administration and Development Alternatives, 26–28 July 2017, Botswana, https://bit.ly/311SsUH, accessed 14 May 2020.

Mbete, S. 2015. 'The Economic Freedom Fighters: South Africa's turn towards populism?', *Journal of African Elections*, https://www.eisa.org.za/pdf/JAE14.1Mbete.pdf, accessed 1 June 2020.

Mkhabela, H. 2016. 'South African local elections 2016: From one party dominance to effective plural democracy', Études de l'Ifri, www.ifri.org, accessed 18 May 2020.

Mokgosi, K., Shai, K. and Ogunnubi. O. 2017. 'Local government coalition in Gauteng province of South Africa: Challenges and opportunities', *Journal of Conflict and Social Transformation*, 6 (1), 37–57.

Mpangalasane, C. 2020. 'The impact of coalition government on service delivery: City of Tshwane metropolitan'. Master's thesis, North West University.

Msimanga, S. 6 April 2017. State of the City Address 2017, Tshwane, http://www.tshwane.gov.za/sites/about_tshwane/CityManagement/Pages/City-of-Tshwane-Speeches.aspx, accessed 21 May 2020.

Müller, W. C. and Miller, B. 2005. 'Coalition government and intra-party politics'. Paper, European Consortium for Political Research, University of Granada, 14–19 April, https://ecpr.eu>Filestore>PaperProposal, accessed 25 May 2020.

Müller, W. C., Bergman, T. and Ilonszki, G. 2019. 'Extending the coalition life-cycle approach to Central Eastern Europe: An introduction', https://books.google.co.za/books?id=C6rDDwAAQBAJ&pg=PA1&source=gbs_toc_r, accessed 30 May 2020.

National Council of Provinces (NCOP). 2020. 'Report of the select committee on Cooperative Governance and Traditional Affairs', 9-26. No 34/2020, 18 March 2020, https://pmg.org.za/tabled-committee-report/4110/, accessed 8 June 2020.

Nkanjeni, N. 5 July 2019. 'ANC's Kgosi Maepa says the party condemns the pair's inability to work things out', *Sowetan*, https://www.sowetanlive.co.za/news/south-africa/2019-07-05-anc-unimpressed-with-eff-withdrawing-from-da-coalition-in-tshwane, accessed 12 June 2020.

North Gauteng High Court. 2016. *Afrisake NPC and Others v The City of Tshwane.* Case No: 74192/2003. *Metropolitan Municipality and Others* (74192/2003). [2016] ZAGPPHC 641 (22 July 2016).

North Gauteng High Court. 2020. *Democratic Alliance and Others v Premier for the Province of Gauteng and Others*. Case No: 18577/2020.

Nyhan, B. 2009. 'Strategic outrage: The politics of presidential scandal'. D.Phil dissertation, Duke University.

Nyoka, N. 18 May 2020. 'Battle for control of the City of Tshwane is back on', *New Frame*, https://www.newframe.com/battle-for-control-of-the-city-of-tshwane-is-back-on/, accessed 1 June 2020.

Pieterse, M. 2019. 'What's needed to fix collapsing coalitions in South Africa's cities', www.wits.ac.za/news/latest-news/opinion/2020/2020-01/whats-needed-to-fix-collapsing-coalitions-in-south-africas-cities.html, accessed 1 November 2020.

Polity. 8 August 2016. 'SACCI: IEC local government results in South Africa', https://www.polity.org.za/print-version/sacci-iec-local-government-results-in-south-africa-2016-08-08, accessed 22 June 2020.

Polity. 31 August 2018. 'Msimanga to reach out to EFF after motions of no confidence fails', https://www.polity.org.za/article/msimanga-to-reach-out-to-eff-after-motions-of-no-confidence-fails-2018-08-31), accessed 21 July 2020.

Polity. 29 November 2019. 'DA doesn't close the door on working with the EFF to retain control of Joburg – Steenhuisen', https://www.polity.org.za/article/da-hasnt-closed-the-door-on-working-with-eff-to-retain-control-of-joburg-steenhuisen-2019-11-20, accessed 28 October 2020.

SABC News. 26 November 2019. 'Dr Mbuyiseni Ndlozi discusses EFF's mayoral candidate for city of Joburg', https://m.youtube.com/watch?v=uYgqJWkKbHY, accessed 22 June 2020.

Schreiber, L. 21 September 2018. 'Taking stock of South Africa's fragile coalitions', News24, https://www.news24.com/amp/news24/columnists/guestcolumn/taking-stock-of-south-africas-fragile-coalitions-20180921, accessed 8 July 2020.

Scheurkogel, I. S. 2018. 'Is the African National Congress stuck in transition? A case study: City of Tshwane, South Africa', *International Journal of Innovative Research and Advanced Studies*, 5 (8).

Sebake, B. 5 March 2020. 'A maturing democracy and coalition governance: SA politics at a crossroads', *News24*, www.news24.com/amp/news24/columnists/guestcolumn/opinion-a-maturing-democracy-and-coalition-governance-sa-politics-at-a-crossroads-20200210, accessed 17 October 2020.

Sokutu, B. 10 February 2020. 'ANC in talks with parties to form coalition for Tshwane', *The Citizen,* https://citizen.co.za/news/south-africa/politics/2239479/anc-in-talks-with-parties-to-form-coalition-for-tshwane/, accessed 21 May 2020.

Supreme Court of Appeal, 27 October 2020. Media summary. www.saflii.org/za/cases/ZASCA/2020/136media.pdf, 30 October 2020.

Teles, F. 2013. 'The distinctiveness of democratic political leadership', *Political Studies Review*, 13 (2), 22–36.

The Clement Manyatela Show. 2020. 'What's happening in the City of Tshwane?' The Best of Eusebius McKaiser, *Radio 702*, https://omny.fm/shows/mid-morning-show-702/what-is-going-on-in-the-city-of-tshwane', accessed 18 June 2020.

Tshwane Mayoral Committee Report. 20 March 2018, http://www.tshwane.gov.za/sites/Council/Lists/Council%20Calendar/Attachments/50/05.6%20Part%20IIIB%20Council%2029%2003%202018.pdf, accessed 27 June 2020.

Tshwane Annual Report, 2017/2018. 31 January 2019. Special council meetings, https://bit.ly/3hL9HiR, accessed 14 June 2020.

Vercesi, M. 2016. 'Coalition politics and inter-party conflict management: A theoretical framework', *Politics & Policy,* 44 (2), 168–219, https://onlinelibrary.wiley.com/doi/abs/10.1111/polp.12154, accessed 2 November 2020.

Wieldraaijer, J. 2015. 'Explaining coalition types: An analysis of government formation at the Dutch local level', Master's thesis, Leiden University.

Zulu, S. and Ntshidi, E. 16 February 2020. '"We want service delivery in that city," says Makhura about troubled Tshwane', *Eyewitness News*, https://ewn.co.za/2020/02/16/we-want-service-delivery-in-that-city-says-makhura-about-troubled-tshwane, accessed 18 May 2020.

THIRTEEN

Coalitions in Nelson Mandela Bay
Subversions of democracy

Mcebisi Ndletyana

After 21 years of majoritarian government, Nelson Mandela Bay inaugurated a coalition government on 18 August 2016. Local elections had not yielded an outright winner. Seats were shared among nine political parties. For a council with a total of 120 seats, 61 seats were required to form the city government. The Democratic Alliance (DA), which had the largest number of seats at 57, managed to weave together a coalition. That coalition only lasted until August 2018. It was replaced by another coalition, dominated by the African National Congress (ANC), with a mayor, Mongameli Bobani, from the United Democratic Movement (UDM). Just over a year later, in December 2019, the second coalition fell. Thereafter, and almost for the entire year of 2020, Nelson Mandela Bay was governed by a loose coalition dubbed 'the black caucus', without a mayor.

The alternation of the Nelson Mandela Bay coalitions epitomised instability. This chapter examines the causes of the instability and its consequent impact on municipal performance. It covers the period between August 2016 and early 2021, a timespan of just over four years, during which Nelson Mandela Bay was governed by three coalitions.

Table 13.1: Nelson Mandela Bay 2016 election results and seat allocation

Political party	Valid votes received	Votes percentage (%)	Council seats
Democratic Alliance (DA)	355,471	46.71	57
African National Congress (ANC)	311,416	40.92	50
Economic Freedom Fighters (EFF)	38,951	5.12	6
United Democratic Movement (UDM)	14,569	1.91	2
African Independent Congress (AIC)	7,222	0.95	1
United Front (UF)	7,181	0.94	1
Congress of the People (Cope)	5,587	0.73	1
African Christian Democratic Party (ACDP)	2,712	0.36	1
Patriotic Alliance (PA)	2,040	0.27	1

Source: IEC, various; Tshwane Annual Report, 2017/2018 (2019).

The chapter focuses on each of the three. While broadly driven by similar considerations, these coalitions illuminate different dynamics. The conclusion draws out what the respective dynamics reveal about coalition governments in Nelson Mandela Bay.

The instability of the three coalitions, the chapter contends, derives, first, from both the nature and the conduct of the coalition. In one instance, there was a formal coalition agreement, and, in another, none. Where there was an agreement, partners failed to adhere to the terms. Personal interests of individual leaders, the second factor, took precedence over collective objectives. This was even more pronounced in the instance where a coalition agreement was nonexistent. In the latter instance, the coalition was driven purely by financial gain for both individuals and party. Crippling factionalism worsened impropriety. Third, political parties were unable to subdue interparty rivalry to common interests. Rivalry at the national level soured their approach to disputes in Nelson Mandela Bay. One party did not even put stock on how its decisions impacted on local governance, but handled local issues in a way that buttressed its bargaining position at the national level.

CONSIDERATIONS FEEDING INTO THE FORMATION OF NELSON MANDELA BAY'S COALITIONS

Coalition formation is a bargaining process. Political parties enter into coalitions for various reasons, and have preferences for partners. Some seek policy gains, while some enter into a coalition to secure patronage for their leaders (or members). Interparty rivalry and positioning for a next round of elections often reign supreme; or it can be factional contests and party-political leadership at the local site of governance, or at higher levels, that will impact the formation and sustainability of the particular coalition.

This range of factors, and multiple variations on these themes, had an impact on the series of coalitions that formed in the Nelson Mandela Bay metropolitan municipality from 2016 to 2021. This chapter narrates and analyses how these themes unfolded (and alternated) to dominate and direct the tumultuous tale of coalition politics in Nelson Mandela Bay.

Ideological parameters and bargaining for policy: 2016

Policy similarities make for an attractive partner, offering a higher degree of cooperation and, consequently, stability. But parties do not always get their preferred partners. In such instances, parties are forced into coalition with less preferred partners. Oftentimes this entails compromises, especially if parties have pronounced policy differences, and/or are offering patronage to leaders to take positions in government or to their members in the bureaucracy (Laver et al., 1987; Brams and Kilgour, 2013).

While not yielding an outright winner, the 2016 election results promised a manageable process of coalition formation. Of the nine parties that secured seats on the Nelson Mandela Bay council, only two got substantial numbers – the DA with 57 and the ANC with 50. The numerical advantage handed the two parties the initiative to lead the coalition-making process. A coalition of two of the largest parties would have been easiest to conclude and was likely to be stable. Instead of multiple partners, each would have just had one partner with whom to deliberate. It would have limited the scope of issues for deliberation and shortened decision-making processes. That coalition was improbable from the onset. The DA and the ANC are ideological adversaries, and have radically divergent histories and different constituencies. Liberalism holds sway within the historically white DA, while the predominantly African ANC embraces centre-left policies. Notwithstanding these differences, the two parties' election manifestos exhibited little ideological slant. Elections were generally contested over practical problems of service delivery and the misconduct of leaders.[1]

From the side of the ANC, it was the DA's resistance to racial redress and its general association with racism that obstructed the possibility of a coalition. Under former DA leader Tony Leon, the party had fashioned itself as a fierce opponent of racial redress, thereby extending its appeal to white conservative voters. Leon's successor, Helen Zille, diversified the leadership of the party, but she was as opposed to racial redress as her predecessor. Incidents of racism in the party in Nelson Mandela Bay, such as councillor Stanford Slabbert circulating a racist email to party colleagues, exacerbated the party's image on race. The DA was similarly eager to dissociate itself from the ANC. It promised a different government to the ANC's, whose corruption had made headlines from the early 2000s, and presented itself as an alternative (Zille, 2016). The DA approached the 2016 coalition talks with the objective of taking over from the ANC and distinguishing itself as an alternative. If a coalition was to form, therefore, it was to be led by not the two biggest parties, but by either the DA or the ANC, together with the smaller parties.

The DA had an edge over the ANC to form a coalition. Of the seven smaller political parties, three – the UDM, the African Christian Democratic Party (ACDP) and the Congress of the People (Cope) – were favourably disposed towards the DA; and one, the African Independent Congress (AIC), could swing either way. The three parties were united in their local campaign against ANC corruption, and had a history of collaboration nationally to hold then president Jacob Zuma accountable for abusing state resources to improve his Nkandla homestead (Jafta, 2017).[2] Combined, the three parties held four seats, which would give the DA a controlling majority of 61 votes. The undecided AIC, based in Matatiele, is an issue-based party that was spawned by a grievance in Matatiele over the redrawing of provincial boundaries in 2005 (Makhafola, 2017).[3]

The AIC hardly campaigned in the 2016 Nelson Mandela Bay elections. Its plan was to use whatever support it gathered as a bargaining chip with the ANC government in the provincial demarcation of the town of Matatiele. But the AIC managed to garner a surprisingly notable number of votes in other parts of the country, including in Nelson Mandela Bay. The general consensus, however, was that the party had benefited from partial similarity with the ANC, both in logo and in name, and the fact that it was placed next to the ANC on the ballot paper.[4] Since the AIC's 2005 formation, the ANC had never sought AIC support. For the first time in 2016, the AIC was in a position to bargain with the ANC. In addition to Nelson Mandela Bay, the ANC sought its support in the metro of Ekurhuleni in Gauteng, where the ANC had also fallen short of an outright majority. Reports at the time suggested that the ANC had become amenable to considering the AIC's longstanding gripe (Makhafola, 2017). The AIC's support for the ANC, however, was not guaranteed: it depended on what offer the ANC made. Were the offer not persuasive, the AIC would be open to persuasion by the DA. This would increase the majority of the DA-led coalition by two votes.

The other three smaller parties – the EFF, the Patriotic Alliance (PA) and the United Front – were potential coalition partners to the ANC. Both the EFF and the United Front were offshoots of the ANC-led liberation movement, and broadly shared the same ideological tradition. The PA's founder, Gayton McKenzie, was a strong defender of then ANC president, Jacob Zuma, as he came under accusations of abuse of state resources and for enabling state capture. McKenzie even wrote a book, *Kill Zuma – By Any Means Necessary* (2017), in which he portrayed Zuma as a victim of failed assassination attempts by established financial interests. Zuma could persuade McKenzie to support the ANC in Nelson Mandela Bay. Ideologically though, the PA presented a problem to the ANC. It is an ethno-nationalist party, committed to advancing the interests of coloured people (Kuse, 2016). This was not an intractable problem for the ANC, however: the party could claim, with some evidence, that it had always attended to the needs of coloured communities, and would do more to dissuade perceptions of marginalisation.

When it came to the actual coalition negotiations, however, it was tough going for the ANC. The EFF made demands the ANC could not meet. These included nationalisation of mines, expropriation of land without compensation, immediate provision of free education, and the removal of Jacob Zuma as president (see Mbete, 2016). Meeting the EFF's demands would not simply require compromises on the part of the ANC, but would mean capitulation. It would entail a drastic change of policies on land and the economy, as well as the fall of national government. The EFF, although extremely small compared to the ANC, would come out the major winner, while the ANC would be reduced to following the EFF's lead. That was untenable for the ANC. A further complication for the ANC forming a majority coalition was animosity between the leaders of the PA and the EFF, McKenzie and Julius Malema. They even traded insults publicly: McKenzie called Malema a thief, and Malema denounced McKenzie as a thug (News24, 2014). The EFF would not vote for a coalition government that included the PA.

THE ORIGINAL 2016 DA COALITION

The DA succeeded in forming a coalition government. Coalition partners entered into a contract, which was, however, soon undermined by the pursuit of personal interests and the failure of party leaders at the national level to rein in their wayward local leaders. National leaders of the UDM and DA seemed indebted to their truant local leaders, especially Mongameli Bobani, but also Athol Trollip, to a point of sacrificing the effectiveness of the coalition government. Interparty contracts meant little amid the pursuit of personal aggrandisement.

The coalition agreement: Not a guarantee for a stable coalition
The coalition agreement was concluded between the parties' national leaders on 16 August 2016. In addition to the DA, the signatories were the ACDP, Cope, the FF+ and the UDM. The 'co-governance

agreement', as they called it, applied across the country, in each municipality where the partners were represented. Partners committed themselves to promoting commonly held general principles, such as the eradication of poverty, non-racialism and inclusiveness, and the separation of powers. Beyond these broad principles, the coalition undertook, among other things, to adopt a zero-tolerance attitude to corruption, and to select a 'fit for purpose' executive management team. They also undertook to stamp out allocation of jobs related to the public works programmes that were apportioned along political lines, and ban the use of blue-light security motorcades for government executives (Co-governance Agreement, 2016).[5]

While partners generally shared common principles, the coalition agreement also sought to achieve coherence in how the coalition would function. No partner, it stated, would introduce anything new in council without canvassing it among other partners, nor criticise another publicly. A platform for regular interactions, a political management committee, was set up in council to ensure consensus on governance and to address whatever disputes might arise. If a dispute could not be settled at the level of the political management committee, it would be elevated to senior leaders to resolve. The idea was to put as much effort as possible into resolving disputes, rather than disagreeing publicly, which risked breaking the coalition.

The Nelson Mandela Bay coalition government was, accordingly, set up on 18 August 2016. Each of the partners was included, with the DA's Athol Trollip taking up the mayoralty, and his party filling most positions on the mayoral committee and in council. The UDM's Mongameli Bobani, whose party had two seats, got the deputy mayor position and was also responsible for the portfolio of public health. The other two partners, the ACDP and the Cope, got one representative each on the mayoral committee. With the government formed, the DA-led coalition was set to govern, guided by the co-governance agreement. The mere presence of the agreement was not a guarantee that the coalition would proceed efficiently, however. Its efficiency would also hinge on compliance with the agreement and the ability of the partners to invoke the dispute-resolution mechanism effectively as and when necessary.

The major challenge for the coalition, observed the political editor of a local newspaper, was likely to be a personality clash between the mayor and his deputy:

> It is an unlikely alliance, a marriage between two vastly different men. Both strong and commanding, but worlds apart in terms of their personalities. While Trollip comes across as firm, steady and resolute, Bobani is more spirited, boisterous and somewhat unpredictable (De Kock, 2016).

The problem was more than a personality clash. Trollip and Bobani also differed on governance issues. Unlike the DA, Bobani did not believe, for instance, that the municipality should suspend and prosecute officials and companies that were suspected of having looted funds intended for the installation of a public transportation system in the metro. Asked how they planned to overcome their differences, Trollip quipped: 'the art of politics and the art of coalition governance is to find out where those differences are so that we can co-operate' (De Kock, 2016). It remained to be seen if this indeed was possible.

Self-interest trumps collective agreement and national leaders intervene

Within months of being inaugurated, it emerged that it may be impossible for the DA and the UDM to work together. An issue over which they had disagreed in the past – dismissal of corrupt staff – resurfaced, and Bobani would not accede to Trollip's authority as mayor. Bobani wanted Mod Ndoyana reinstated as executive director in the municipality. The previous mayor, Danny Jordaan, had fired Ndoyana following a disciplinary process that found him guilty of six charges (out of 10 levelled against him), including fraud and dishonesty. Bobani not only wanted Ndoyana reinstated, but also wished to appoint his political adviser, Nombeko Nkomane, as executive director in his own portfolio of public health (De Kock and Mngxitama-Diko, 2017). Bobani's insistence on the appointments was an attempt to impose direct influence, if not hold, over management. This went against the governance prescript against politicians interfering in management.

Trollip opposed both attempts, which soured relations with his deputy.

Unable to get his way, Bobani vowed to withdraw his party's votes from the coalition. The coalition was left vulnerable to a vote of no confidence. Without the two UDM votes, it was only assured of 59 votes – 57 from the DA, one from Cope and another from the ACDP, and this fell below the 61-vote majority. The first sign of attempts to dissolve the coalition was the UDM boycotting the council meeting of 26 January 2017. That denied the coalition of a majority to pass its motions. The ANC latched onto the rift as an opportunity to oust the DA coalition. 'We will start negotiating with the other parties. Politics is about power and we will take advantage of any disagreements in the marriage between the DA and those other parties,' said Gift Ngqondi, the party's regional spokesperson (De Kock, 2017a). A series of attempts to oust the coalition followed. The first, planned for the Council meeting on 1 February 2017, never materialised. The party did not table it due to insufficient numbers on its side. Other opposition parties – the EFF, the PA and the United Front – refused to support the ANC (De Kock and Mngxitama-Diko, 2017).

From February 2017 onwards, the two UDM councillors voted with the opposition. Bobani's own personal interests drove the rift. It had nothing to do with policy and ideological issues. To this end, the UDM in Nelson Mandela Bay no longer felt bound by the coalition agreement. National leaders interceded to resolve the impasse. Revelations of Bobani's misconduct around April 2017 complicated the resolution of the stalemate. Officials in Bobani's portfolio, public health, came under investigation for making irregular payments; there was suspicion they had done so on Bobani's instruction. Bobani slated the probe as 'harassment of black officials' and one of Trollip's ways of bullying him (Butler, 2017). For the DA, Bobani was the cause of the stalemate. James Selfe, DA federal chair at the time, described Bobani as 'destructive' and thus not 'compatible for a good working relationship' (De Kock and Capa, 2017a). Trollip wrote to Bantu Holomisa, the UDM's leader, advising him to propose someone else to replace Bobani in the mayoral committee by the end of business on 16 May 2017. If Holomisa failed to do so, Trollip undertook not only to fire Bobani, but also to replace him with someone of his own choosing.[6] Holomisa ignored the ultimatum. 'Just because you differ in opinions about procedures, you can't expel a person for that,' Holomisa reasoned (Mngxitama-Diko, 2017). Trollip fired Bobani as head of public health. Bobani remained deputy mayor, for that was an elected position requiring a council vote to remove him. The DA aimed to have Bobani removed at the next council meeting.

Escalating disputes and coalition stalemate

Bobani's removal as deputy mayor would eliminate prospects for saving the coalition. This jeopardised not only the coalition in Nelson Mandela Bay, but the one in Johannesburg as well. For this reason, the partners resolved on 22 May 2017 to have one last attempt at resolving the problem. The DA halted its plans to table a motion to remove Bobani as deputy mayor. They set up a three-person team[7] to investigate and recommend a remedy. Though committing to one more attempt, it was clear that attitudes had hardened. In order to increase prospects of the last-ditch effort succeeding, Holomisa insisted that the DA should reverse its decision to fire Bobani. Selfe rejected the idea and maintained that Bobani's dismissal remained (Isaac, 2017).

While the panel sat, Bobani continued with his oppositional stance towards the coalition. He not only voted against the coalition, but also brought along a crowd to taunt Trollip. One of them, Nontobeko Speelman, in response to enquiring journalists, repeated Bobani's favourite line of attack: 'We don't want Trollip as mayor – he is dishonest and runs the city like a farm' (De Kock et al., 2017). A number of items that the coalition had hoped to pass could not be passed due to Bobani voting with the opposition. For Trollip, the incident proved that the DA had to act against Bobani. Even Holomisa, 'who has a blind spot to Councillor Bobani', noted Trollip, 'should be convinced by the day's events' (De Kock et al., 2017). But Holomisa remarked that the incident be referred to the three-person committee. 'We cannot always jump when Mayor Trollip calls us,' he retorted (De Kock et al., 2017).

When the three-person panel eventually released its report on 26 May 2017, it was not helpful either. The panel was mandated not to apportion blame, but simply to uncover and report facts. Even the factual findings were not definitive. The panel relied largely on unsubstantiated reports and did not do an investigation of its own. Essentially, rather than seeking to resolve the matter, the panel sought to appease both parties to the point of issuing unreasonable reprimands for the sake of appearing impartial. Three findings illustrate the stalemate. On the exchange of accusations – Bobani is 'uncontrollable', 'irrational' and 'undermines the coalition'; and Trollip 'does not consult properly' – the panel found that it was 'not possible to decide who is truly at fault. The evidence indicates acts of departure from the Agreement by both parties, especially as the disputes escalated'. As for the initial cause of the disputes – appointments – the report refuted that Bobani's insistence on appointing his political advisor was nepotism, as this 'refers to an official unfairly advantaging family members in appointment. This is not the case in the suggested appointments' (Alberts et al., 2017). However, the report went on to state:

> The law insists that the best person for the position must be offered the job, taking into account equity laws. The coalition agreement states that there will be no cadre appointment which is commonly understood to be unfairly advantaging party members.

In reference to the incidents that took place at the council meeting the day after the coalition decided to set up the panel to investigate, the report found Bobani and Trollip equally blameworthy: Trollip for expressing disapproval of Bobani's behaviour in the media, which 'added fuel to the fire'; and Bobani for 'organising a public demonstration' that undermined the decision not to escalate matters (Alberts et al., 2017). Instead of paving the way for a remedy, therefore, the findings of the panel complicated the problem. Having identified Bobani as the primary cause of the chasm in the coalition, the DA did not accept that Trollip was equally culpable. Rather, it insisted on Bobani's removal as deputy mayor. Holomisa was equally adamant that if anyone had to go, it should be both men, for the panel had found both guilty (Herald Reporter, 2017). He dismissed Trollip's allegation of corruption against Bobani, saying Trollip was not an honest broker. Holomisa added that Bobani had allegations of corruption against

Trollip that required investigating.⁸ The stalemate persisted and it did not seem likely that it would be broken.

Bobani's disruptive behaviour reflected more than just a problem of temperament. It was also enabled by intraparty personal loyalty. Holomisa would not bring himself to sanction Bobani. He seemed to value him more than he did a stable coalition. Bobani had been with Holomisa from the inception of the UDM in 1997, and was probably the only leader of that cohort still left in the party. And throughout its 24-year existence in the city, the UDM had not known any leader but Bobani. Hence the party was built around Bobani. It was a patron-based party, making Bobani indispensable in order for the party to retain its presence in Nelson Mandela Bay.

Besides internal party dynamics, the UDM and the DA also disagreed on the distribution of power within the coalition. Holomisa believed that Bobani deserved as much say in the running of the coalition as Trollip himself, while the latter considered himself the ultimate authority. Even though the coalition agreement suggested a level of equality among the partners, the principle became contestable in practice.

THE COALITION IN FLUX: NASCENT BLACK CAUCUS COALITION COUNTERED BY A SMALL KINGMAKER PARTY, 2017

Meanwhile, Bobani had effectively become part of the opposition; and the opposition to the DA had grouped itself into the so-called black caucus. With only 59 votes, the DA needed two more votes to carry its motion to remove Bobani as deputy mayor. Only the PA offered its support to the DA. This was unexpected. The PA's Marlon Daniels, according to *The Herald*, 'was a staunch critic of the DA' (Makunga, 2017). Daniels reasoned that the PA 'cannot and will not sit and watch the other opposition mobilising and uniting around race to make decisions on the fate of the citizens' (De Kock, 2017b). This was while the PA itself had been formed on the basis of racial mobilisation of coloureds and was unambiguous about fighting for coloured interests only. Daniels clearly sought to trade his vote for the deputy mayor position, as well as the portfolio of public safety and security. Yet it remained unclear if the motion would pass: Daniels' support had lifted the DA coalition to a tie with the black caucus at 60 votes each.

On 25 August 2017, Daniels tabled the motion of no confidence in the deputy mayor. The opposition sought to thwart its passage by walking out of the chamber in order to deny the meeting a quorum. Their execution of the plan, however, was untidy: instead of simply walking out, they made a show of it, singing and dancing as they exited. The opposition probably anticipating this, and while most were still in the chamber, the speaker, a DA official, called for voting on the motion. The motion had its quorum in terms of number of councillors present in the chamber and it passed. The opposition challenged the motion, saying the meeting did not have a quorum. The 60 votes that came from the DA coalition supporting the motion, the speaker reasoned, constituted the majority of those in the chamber at the time. Bobani threatened to challenge the decision, but, for the time being, his expulsion as deputy mayor stood (De Kock and Capa, 2017b).

A coalition of 60 councillors out of 120 was precarious. It could only pass motions that were unrelated to financial matters and by-laws, with the support of the speaker, who had a casting vote in the instance of a tie. On any matter relating to finance and by-laws, the coalition would need to get one more vote from the opposition, as the speaker was not allowed to cast a tie-breaker on such issues (NMB Municipality, 2007). Besides getting occasional support from some opposition parties, it also meant that coalition partners themselves always had to vote in unison. Neither was guaranteed. The coalition was on the brink of collapsing, something they had intended to avert by entering into a contract. Ultimately, the contract meant nothing to Bobani's UDM.

Conflicting and transient interests: Sources of reprieve and demise
The EFF temporarily sustained the DA coalition's precarious hold on power. As soon as the EFF developed new interests outside the metro, however, it turned against the coalition, sacrificing proper governance in Nelson Mandela Bay in the hope of making gains at the national level. The national leadership of the EFF had scant interest in the

performance of the Nelson Mandela Bay municipality. The metro was important to the EFF only to the extent that it enabled the party to pursue national prominence, regardless of the adverse implications to the municipality.

The EFF's support for the DA coalition stemmed from its opposition to the ANC's returning to power. This denied the opposition coalition (the black caucus) a majority. Throughout 2017, the opposition was unable to pass a vote of no confidence in the coalition due to the EFF's support for the DA coalition. The DA's dependence on the EFF, in turn, meant the party had to make significant comprises. One was the absorption onto the fulltime municipal staff of the previously outsourced security personnel of roughly 460. This went against the DA's belief of limiting state employment. Another compromise entailed expenditure on road infrastructure in preparation for an international sporting activity, the Ironman 70.3 World Championships of September 2018. The triathlon event was expected to attract 4,500 athletes and 12,000 visitors from around the world. It would boost the local economy, but required municipal expenditure (Parfitt, 2018).

Part of the preparation involved upgrading a 40-kilometre stretch of road around the seaside area, estimated to cost R200 million. The coalition government proposed that council redirect a sum of R13 million, which had initially been set aside for resurfacing roads throughout the city, including townships, towards the fund. The opposition, including the EFF, protested that money that had been designated for use in the township areas would go towards tarring a road in a predominantly suburban area (Capa, 2017). The coalition's proposal was unlikely to pass, and plans were revised. Instead of upgrading the entire route, they focused only on the parts that really required upgrading. The revised plan reduced expenditure drastically to R25 million, and little was taken from the R13-million allocation.

The DA's concessions to the EFF demonstrated reciprocity. Each got what it wanted from the other. But the DA needed the EFF more, and sought to cement the relationship by offering EFF leaders more financial benefits and positions of influence in council. The EFF's Yoliswa Yako was voted chair of the municipal public accounts committee, replacing a councillor from the ACDP, a coalition partner.

Other opposition parties abstained from voting, and insinuated betrayal on the part of the EFF. 'It is known that this was a promised arrangement,' said the ANC's Andile Lungisa, which happened in exchange for voting with the DA. Yako retorted that '(t)hese are bitter politicians who are not getting the attention they need and would [indicate] any kind of progress [as] being an arrangement' (Capa and Parfitt, 2018).

Lungisa's attack on Yako was disingenuous. The ANC was similarly inconsistent in its council voting decisions. While seeking to oust the DA-led coalition, the ANC also at times voted with the DA coalition, especially on expenditure and budgetary matters. It supported the DA coalition to pass the 2017/18 budget and approve expenditure of a special allocation from the Treasury. Some of its allies also voted for the budget, but none approved the expenditure of the allocation, due to disagreement over some of the expenditure items. The ANC supported the expenditure on securing agreement from the DA that some funds would be used for buying vacant land for housing construction. This was an easy condition for the DA to meet; it had already decided that most of the money would be used for infrastructure, and demolition and reconstruction of houses that had irreparable cracks. All this was to take place in the townships, the traditional support base of the ANC. This made it difficult for the ANC to vote against the expenditure, and still claim to advocate for the poor (Ndletyana, 2020a).

Small parties bargaining and vacillating

Divergent interests within the opposition therefore enabled the DA coalition to remain in power. As long as the coalition met their interests, the EFF and the PA (and later the AIC) were willing to support it. It was all about bargaining. The threat only came when the coalition could not meet their demands. That happened towards the end of 2017. The PA's Daniels was unhappy that the coalition was reluctant to appoint him deputy mayor. Daniels complained that he had been promised the position as a reward for providing the vote to remove Bobani. Instead, he was only given the public health portfolio, where he replaced Bobani. Daniels quit in protest and led a motion of no confidence in the coalition in November 2017. It was defeated with the support of the EFF.

Similarly to the PA, the EFF too then changed its stance towards the DA-led coalition, resolving to vote for a motion of no confidence. Malema explained the change of stance as punishment of the DA for refusing to support a motion, tabled in parliament, for expropriation of land without compensation. The shift in position had nothing to do with Trollip or governance issues in the metro. Malema used the metro to shine a spotlight on a national matter the EFF was heralding in parliament. Because of his white complexion, Trollip made for an easy populist target. The EFF continued to support black DA mayors in Johannesburg and Tshwane. Ousting Trollip was akin to 'cutting the throat of whiteness', Malema said (News24, 2018).

The motion was set for tabling in the council meeting of 30 March 2018. With the EFF leading the charge, it seemed set to pass. The night before the meeting, however, the balance of power suddenly changed. The PA, yet again, struck a deal with the DA. This was the same party that had been in a coalition with the DA in August 2017 only to quit three months later, and which had then tabled a motion of no confidence in the coalition government. Trollip promised Daniels the deputy mayor position and another portfolio in the mayoral committee. Daniels wanted public safety and security, but Trollip refused and offered him the transport portfolio instead, which Daniels eventually accepted (De Kock and Capa, 2018). The offer of the deputy mayor position to Daniels seemed sincere this time around. On the day of the council meeting, it emerged that the AIC would also vote with the DA, as punishment for the ANC for continuing to ignore its demand for Matatiele to be transferred back into KwaZulu-Natal.

As the meeting got underway, the DA coalition had a guaranteed majority of 61 votes. They never got to vote, though. The order of the agenda became a subject of dispute. The EFF wanted the speaker position, instead of the mayoralty, to be voted on first, but the speaker refused, saying the agenda had already been set and could not be changed. Demanding that they start with the speaker was a strategic move on the part of the EFF, which wanted to have its own speaker just in case the subsequent vote on the mayor was a tie and a deciding vote was required. The DA was alert to the ploy. Neither would budge. The meeting descended into chaos, marked by 'insults, threats and scuffles' (Capa and Nkosi, 2018a).

The second attempt, on 10 April 2018, ended similarly chaotically.

As in the previous meeting, the DA entered with an assured 61-vote majority. This had sapped the EFF's zeal to table the motion, and they got into bickering over who was qualified to pay tribute to the late Winnie Mandela. The speaker was forced to adjourn the meeting (De Kock and Nkosi, 2018). It was the second council meeting that ended in disorder due to a stalemate over a vote of no confidence. The EFF was not deterred, however, and a month later, on 10 May 2018, it tabled another motion. But the party rescinded the motion on the day as it realised it lacked a majority: two ANC councillors, Andile Lungisa and Bongo Nombiba, were in prison following criminal convictions (Capa and Nkosi, 2018b).

Governance through theatrics and collapsing council meetings

For the greater part of 2018, therefore, the opposition was preoccupied with bringing down the DA-led coalition government. This became the sole reason for attending council meetings. When it appeared that they would not succeed, they would then seek to collapse the meeting. This meant that other items on the agenda were unlikely to be passed. The coalition government had to develop creative strategies to get motions passed, especially where they had a majority, before the opposition walked out. They exploited the opposition's penchant for theatrics. Instead of simply walking out, they would shuffle towards the door, singing, as if to taunt the coalition. While this was unfolding, the speaker would table the motions and quickly have them passed.

At other times, one or two opposition parties would break ranks with allies to vote with the coalition government on matters of interest to their constituencies. They did not want to be blamed for a total breakdown of government, which would have harmed their constituencies. The ANC, for instance, agreed to return to the chamber on 30 March 2018, after its earlier attempts to vote out the coalition had come to a chaotic halt. They returned specifically to vote on critical items, for example, expenditure on the Ironman Championship, permanent employment of security personnel, hiring of more plumbers to deal with the problem of water leaks, and expenditure on public lighting. It was brinkmanship: employ antics as long as there was a reasonable chance of success, but avoid causing a total breakdown.

THE ANC'S GAME PLAN: TAKING BACK POWER AND POSITIONING FOR 2021

Unlike most of the smaller parties, and as the second largest party in the council, the ANC was playing a long-term game. The size of its electoral support made it possible for the party to return to government. It did not want to conduct itself in a way that would jeopardise its prospects of re-election. Conversely, leaders of small opposition parties were less concerned with future elections. The EFF seemed not to care to improve electoral fortunes locally, but was more interested in national prominence. For the PA's Daniels, it was all about financial benefits; he would do or say anything, even contradicting himself from one day to another, as long as he got what he wanted.

Around mid-2018, however, the ANC followed the EFF's cue and adopted a zero-sum-game approach. The party rejected the 2018/19 budget, voting against it four times. The budgetary allocations, the ANC's Rory Riordan reasoned, did not follow the customary 80:20 ratio in favour of capital expenditure in the townships. Instead, most of the funds, according to Riordan, were allocated to support services, and this would later be used in the suburbs. City manager Johann Mettler and acting chief financial officer Jackson Ngcelwana disputed Riordan's claims. Mettler explained that funds allocated to support services were used to implement major projects earmarked for that year, and did not go towards unrelated or undefined items. Failure to pass the budget meant that council could be dissolved – and the opposition's repeated rejection of the budget seemed aimed precisely towards that end. Differences within the opposition, however, once again saved the coalition. Despite the continuation of the Matatiele stalemate, the AIC voted with the coalition government on 12 June 2018 to pass the budget (Ndletyana, 2020a).

The ANC's shift towards zero-sum tactics was prompted by the financial difficulties it was suffering following its loss of power in the metro. Political office had afforded access to patronage. '*Asinamali* [we don't have money],' Mbulelo Gidane, then regional treasurer, told an enquiring journalist in July 2018, and explained, 'Once you're not in the office of government, no business people listen to you and it's very difficult to go to province and ask for money' (Ndletyana, 2020a: 295). The party could not host commemorative events nor turn on the lights at the office. Both the operations and the visibility of the party were in jeopardy. There was a sense of urgency, bordering on desperation, to return to office, reclaim access to patronage and salvage its financial problems. Thus the ANC endeavoured to bring down the coalition government at all costs. Repeated rejection of the budget was part of that plan. It wanted to change power rather than wait for the scheduled 2021 local elections.

The AIC again thwarted the ANC's plans – it helped the coalition government pass the budget. This showed the vulnerability of the DA's marginal coalition. It was wholly at the mercy of other parties, which had shifting interests. Many of its coalition partners were not dependable, supporting the party as and when it suited them. The PA proved adept at the bargaining game; it exploited not only the vulnerability of the coalition, but also the desperation of the ANC to return to office. With 60 votes on each side, the DA coalition could also not garner sufficient votes to elect Marlon Daniels deputy mayor, as it had promised. The ANC-led opposition also needed Daniels' vote to get the 61 votes they needed to collapse the coalition. Daniels offered them his vote in return for the deputy mayor position but the EFF would not agree; cold relations between the PA and the EFF had not thawed. Since the ANC could not offer what the EFF considered a credible ANC candidate, the EFF favoured the UDM's Mongameli Bobani for mayor instead. Daniels remained with the DA and vowed to vote against the motion scheduled for 27 August 2018. The two blocs went into the council meeting evenly poised at 60 votes each (Ndletyana, 2020a).

As the proceedings got underway, it became apparent that it was not only the rival parties that sought to benefit from the delicate balance of power in the metro. Individuals within parties also sought to exploit the situation for self-gain. DA councillor Mxolisi Manyathi abstained on the motion of no confidence in the speaker, Jonathan Lawack. His abstention gave the ANC and its allies the majority of 60 against the coalition's 59 votes. The ANC's Buyelwa Mafaya was elected the new speaker, and went on to preside over the election of a new mayor: the

UDM's Bobani. Manyathi ascribed his defiance of his own party to racism in the DA, claiming that black councillors were disrespected in the party. His complicity in bringing down the DA coalition was a vengeful act. An account from within the DA was that Manyathi, one of the accused in a trial on charges of fraud (and about whom the DA had already had discussions whether he should be suspended, even before his trial concluded), wanted to profit from his membership of the party before his expulsion. Rumours were that Manyathi was paid by the ANC to defy his own party (Ndletyana, 2020a).

Political parties and their individual councillors were intent on gaining something out of the coalition. For Manyathi, it would have been financial gain, while the EFF gained limelight at the national level. Each party was pursuing its own interest. As an opposition party on the rise, the DA considered Nelson Mandela Bay critical to maintaining its electoral growth. The party was determined to perform well as further proof that it was a viable alternative to the ANC. For the DA, Nelson Mandela Bay was not about making immediate gains, but about governing properly in a way that would yield long-term benefits.

THE ANC-DOMINATED COALITION: RENT-SEEKING BY ANY MEANS NECESSARY

The ANC-dominated coalition from late 2018 onwards was the opposite of its DA predecessor. Whereas the DA-led coalition had seen its tenure as an opportunity to endear itself to the broader electorate through proper governance, its successor had no such intention. The ANC-dominated coalition utilised its return to power to relieve itself of financial strain, at both the individual and the organisational level. It was resolute and quick in execution, without any concern for appearance of impropriety or damage to the integrity of government and its institutions. It would take its instinct for self-preservation, not regret for disgraceful conduct and siphoning of municipal resources, to halt the downward spiral.

Bobani was not the ideal candidate for mayor, but the UDM had the two crucial votes the allies needed to maintain a majority. His coalition partners were indifferent to Bobani's penchant for misdemeanour, as long as they got to sit in government and share in the spoils. There was no agreement over the objectives of the new coalition government or its modus operandi. It paved the way for Bobani to do as he pleased. Bobani's election as mayor foretold the conduct and governance that would follow at city hall. His clash with Trollip revealed an uncontrollable personality, a man bent on getting his way. Propriety was not Bobani's main concern. He insisted on returning to office Mod Ndoyana, who had been suspended for corruption.

Bobani's first order of business was to summon a list of tenders that the municipality was due to advertise and managerial positions that were to be filled. Executive managers refused on the grounds that, as city manager Johann Mettler explained, 'It is illegal to interfere in this manner in the procurement process of the metro' (Ndletyana, 2020a: 298–299). Bobani was already displeased with Mettler for having blocked his misdeeds earlier and now, for resisting the mayor's impropriety, Mettler was targeted for removal. Bobani suspended Mettler on 27 September 2018 on dubious grounds. He alleged, for instance, that Mettler had concluded an irregular contract with a media company, Mohlaleng Media, and improperly appointed Vuyo Zitumane as executive director. Soon thereafter, council's municipal public accounts committee ruled that the appointment had been procedural, and an investigation instigated by council also cleared Mettler of impropriety in the Mohlaleng contract.

Mettler's suspension had been vindictive, and was intended to open a way to appoint a city manager that politicians could control for nefarious ends. Bobani replaced Mettler with Nolwandle Gqiba as acting city manager. Barely a month later, on 16 October 2018, Gqiba quit, citing 'family reasons'. Noxolo Nqwazi was given the job, but was fired unceremoniously within weeks: she got the news on a Sunday afternoon from a journalist. Nqwazi said she had had no idea of her pending dismissal, but Bobani insisted (falsely) that she knew and 'did not have a problem at all'. At a subsequent council meeting Bobani would not reveal his real reasons for dismissing her. Next, Peter Nielson was appointed, irregularly, as acting city manager. Nielson did not have the requisite academic qualifications, and anyway only a chief financial officer and executive directors could be appointed into an acting city manager post. Nielson was a director in the department of infrastructure and engineering, which fell under Lungisa's portfolio. When his qualifications were questioned at a council meeting, Lungisa defended Nielsen, describing him as the 'most competent senior manager' (Ndletyana, 2020a: 301).

Bobani's election wrought instability in the administration of the municipality. Within less than four months of being elected mayor, Bobani had fired not only the city manager, but also three acting city managers, in quick succession. They were all replaced due to refusal to comply with political instructions. It is not unthinkable that the third appointee, Peter Nielson, would also be approached to execute improper actions. The new year of 2019 brought continued mayhem in city management, and by November Bobani had appointed four more acting city managers, one of whom, Nobuntu Mpongwana, a deputy director, was even less qualified than Nielson. Mpongwana was appointed shortly after having returned to work on winning a case against her dismissal for approving payment to a company without a proper contract. Within a week or so of acting in that position, Mpongwana went on sick leave and appointed Mvuleni Mapu in her place. Mapu was one of several employees that Bobani had brought back to work – they had been suspended while the municipality pursued disciplinary actions against them for alleged corruption. Soon after his appointment, Mapu instructed the law firm that had been assigned to pursue the disciplinary actions (including his own) to halt the proceedings (Kimberley, 2019a).

The mayor had an interest in the matter of suspended officials. Some of them worked in the public health portfolio,[9] which Bobani had previously headed, and he was implicated in the alleged corruption. The same applied regarding an ongoing legal trial involving Andrea Wessels, one of many people accused of defrauding the municipality of funds intended for the installation of a public transportation system. Wessels was challenging an order authorising the public prosecutor to seize her house as the proceeds of crime. In his attempt to aid Wessels' case, Bobani instructed the municipality's chief accountant, Karel Kramer, to write a false affidavit saying that payments to Wessels did not come from the public transport system grant, but from the municipality's own funds. This would have apparently made it difficult for the prosecutor to seize the property. Responding to Kramer's admission that Bobani had pressurised him, Bobani denied ever doing so (Kimberley, 2019b).[10] Bobani was an implicated party in the public transport system-related fraud and was seemingly helping out a fellow accomplice.

Although he brought only two votes into the coalition, Bobani was putting the mayoralty to maximum use towards his own interests. He never consulted with the coalition partners, for instance, on the appointment of acting city managers or returning the suspended officials to work. At one point, ANC and EFF councillors in the municipal public accounts committee did not convene their meeting because they doubted the legality of the acting city manager, Mpongwana, who was part of the proceedings. Their resolutions would be declared null and void, they feared. Coalition partners, especially the ANC, also benefited from the impropriety that thrived in Bobani's tenure. In late 2018, the ANC's Lungisa, in charge of the portfolio on infrastructure and engineering, got his department to issue a contract worth more than R21 million to clean drains. When officials would not sign off on it, on account of it being irregular, Lungisa got council to pass a resolution for the issuing of the tender. The deal was supposedly meant for small businesses, but there was hardly any proof of work done, some were never paid, others were paid multiple times, and approximately R5 million of the money could not be accounted for (Ndletyana, 2020a). Because of his fervent support for the irregular tender, it could not be discounted that Lungisa, or those close him, had benefited. The deal got the attention of the auditor-general's office. When the auditors started investigating, they received death threats and fled the municipality. They relocated to East London, continuing their investigation from there (Kimberley, 2020).

Bobani was thus not the only beneficiary in the coalition. This was affirmed by other coalition partners' repeated protection of Bobani against motions of no confidence, and the lengths to which the ANC-speaker, Buyelwa Mafaya, was willing to go to protect the mayor. When the number of ANC councillors dropped by one, as one of them went to prison in July 2019, the speaker put council in recess for six weeks until by-elections were held. Council had never been placed in recess on account of preparing for by-elections: Mafaya was protecting Bobani and herself against motions of no confidence.

In the meantime, the municipality showed aggravated signs of dysfunctionality. Filth was strewn across the city. 'The main function of a municipality is to remove refuse in communities ... If the municipality cannot ... that municipality is non-existent,' fumed the ANC premier of the province, Oscar Mabuyane, following a visit to Port Elizabeth in August 2019 (Capa, 2019). Two months earlier, Treasury had written to the metro enquiring about progress on recovering stolen funds and holding the culprits accountable. The response was unsatisfactory, suggesting either ignorance or indifference. In October 2019, Treasury issued an ultimatum, threatening to recall the R3 billion it had granted the municipality if it did not get conclusive answers in 14 days.

Only the ailing administration and a possible financial collapse of the municipality prompted the coalition partners to turn against Bobani. The unseemly state of affairs did not augur well for a party such as the ANC, which hoped to improve its electoral fortunes in 2021. In early October 2019, the ANC approached Bobani to resign, but he refused. Now referring to him as 'deranged' and 'insane', the ANC vowed to push him out (Kimberley and Nkosi, 2019a).

What followed in the next month or so revealed how low Nelson Mandela Bay politics had sunk. It had become enmeshed with criminality, and councillors were willing to resort to strong-arm tactics to protect their positions. A special council meeting scheduled for 17 October 2019 was cancelled in dubious circumstances. The speaker had been forced to convene that meeting through a petition signed by 117 councillors, including from the ANC. Speaker Mafaya said falsely that the police had informed her that councillors were likely to come under attack and that their safety could not be guaranteed. Liziwe Ntshinga, the provincial commissioner of police, disputed ever having issued a security threat. Mafaya had simply fabricated a security threat in order to prevent a council sitting (Sain, 2019).

Still determined to oust Bobani, councillors petitioned the speaker to convene another special meeting. It was scheduled for 4 November

2019, but was cancelled on the morning of the day when ANC and AIC councillors withdrew their signatures from the petition they had submitted to the speaker. They cited threats of violence they had received if they went ahead with voting. It was said the source of the threatening messages could not be traced, but the AIC's Tshonono Buyeye got his threatening message that morning after informing the meeting of whips that he intended to vote against Bobani (Nkosi and Kimberley, 2019). This pointed to the likelihood that the messages came from one of the councillors present in that meeting of whips.

With the council seemingly unable to oust Bobani, the provincial government became determined to intervene. Two months earlier it had mooted two options in the absence of Bobani being voted out: dissolution of the council or an administrative takeover. Local politicians were not keen on dissolving the council, preferring a takeover. Dissolution would spell an end to their employment as councillors, and there was no guarantee that the party would win back the metro in a general by-election. An administrative takeover became the preferred option (Nkosi, 2019).

The motion for Bobani's removal was back on the agenda for a council meeting scheduled for 5 December 2019. Two days before the meeting, it seemed it might suffer the same fate as previous ones, when councillors received a second agenda without the motion. The acting city manager noted that the agenda had been changed on the instruction of the speaker, but Mafaya denied knowledge of the revised agenda and committed to the original one. The motion was finally tabled. More than 110 councillors voted in favour, bringing an end to Bobani's infamous mayoralty and a second coalition that had lasted just more than a year (Kimberley and Nkosi, 2019b).

Factionalism deepens the morass

Bobani's removal from the mayoralty did not, however, restore stability in the running of the metro. For almost the whole of the following year, 2020, the metro failed to elect a new mayor, and management remained marred by instability. Remedial attempts were met with determined resistance, mainly from those who wielded power in council. A new mayor was likely to displace them. Refusal to elect a new mayor was effectively a way of protecting their positions, which entailed defying party instructions to restore normalcy in council. The defiance was partly aided by factionalism, especially within the dominant partner in the coalition, the ANC.

With Bobani booted out of office, the UDM's two votes became neutral. Hence, neither power bloc could garner a majority to elect a new mayor, and the two leading parties – the DA and the ANC – were forced to consider cooperating. The ANC, however, could not agree on this. ANC regional leaders led the initiative, while some councillors, led by Andile Lungisa, opposed it. Lungisa even took to following one of the regional leaders, Luvuyo Nqakula, to see whom he was meeting. At some point he was followed to the house of Nqaba Bhanga, the DA leader in council, and photographs of the cars that were parked outside were taken.[11] On his way home, Nqakula's car was accosted and he was warned against 'conniving with the enemy'. The police did not take these threats lightly. There were genuine concerns that some of the ANC councillors who supported cooperation with the DA, such as Mike Koenaite and Ncediso Captain, could be physically harmed, or even killed.[12] The police took to accompanying Bhanga to site visits.

Faced with the likelihood of the two leading parties cooperating to elect a new mayor, the speaker refused to convene council sittings. Mafaya was likely to lose her position with the advent of a new mayor. Equally determined to change the leadership in council, the DA alliance decided to petition Mafaya for a special council meeting. As it was signed by a majority of 62 councillors, Mafaya could not shrug off the petition and agreed to a meeting on 19 March 2020.[13] The special meeting was held as planned but never completed its business. One of the signatories to the petition had resigned his seat just before the meeting, and another withdrew his signature. With the number of petitioners reduced to 60, Mafaya ruled that the petition no longer enjoyed majority support and thus suspended the council meeting. This reasoning was flawed, as courts would later rule (Ndletyana, 2020b): 60 councillors constituted a majority in a now-reduced council size of 119 councillors. But Mafaya had no interest in procedural accuracy; she was simply intent on blocking the vote that would likely have ejected her and her colleagues out of leadership positions in council.

However, Mafaya could not suspend council meetings indefinitely. Her faction then resolved to woo back its old ally, Bobani, in an attempt to increase its numbers. In return for his party's two votes, Bobani demanded that the black caucus vote to rescind the December 2019 resolution that had removed him as mayor. Unsurprisingly, ANC regional leaders, together with some likeminded councillors in the caucus, opposed any alliance with Bobani. Mafaya nonetheless tabled the motion to reinstate Bobani at the council meeting of 29 June 2020.[14] This was derailed by a technicality when DA councillors pointed out that the removal of a mayor could not be rescinded by a vote – a new mayor had to be *elected*. The objection prevailed.

Mafaya's determination to cling to power went beyond protecting her income. The benefits of incumbency extended to influence over awarding tenders. The acting mayor, Tshonono Buyeye, was now mimicking his predecessor. He unilaterally, without council approval, removed the acting city manager, Noxolo Nqwazi;[15] and Mafaya, the speaker, manipulated proceedings in council to fake a majority support for the appointment of a new acting city manager, Mvuleni Mapu. Mapu was not only a notorious figure, but his appointment was in defiance of party instructions: both regional and provincial leaders had instructed the ANC caucus, just the day before the council meeting, to retain Nqwazi as acting city manager, and not vote for Mapu.[16]

Nqwazi was the casualty of rent-seeking manoeuvres. She refused to rescind a decision offering a tender to Steven Dondolo for the distribution of fuel to municipal vehicles. Lungisa and his allies had an alternative, preferred service provider in mind. But Nqwazi refused to manipulate the process in favour of Lungisa's preference. When instructions and death threats failed to force her to resign, Buyeye decided to adopt powers he did not have by removing Nqwazi from the acting position. In December 2019, council resolved that only it could hire and fire a city manager and executive directors. Employing twisted logic, Buyeye and the ANC chief whip, Lutho Suka,[17] justified the infraction as compliance with the law, in that a person could not act in a position beyond 90 days.

Fractures within the ANC, therefore, prevented the election of a new mayor for almost the whole of 2020, thereby prolonging mismanagement in the municipality. Lungisa's faction not only defied regional party leaders, but also ignored directives from provincial leaders. They acted as they pleased, pursuing their own factional interests without any sanction. For a party that prided itself on imposing party discipline, this defiance suggested that the dissident councillors did not think they would be punished. And when sanction was eventually delivered, it was more symbolic than proportionate to the infraction: of the councillors who had defied the provincial instruction not to vote for Mapu as acting city manager, only Lungisa was subjected to disciplinary action. For Lungisa, this was yet another infraction: for almost two years, he had refused to comply with the provincial executive committee's instruction to resign from the mayoral committee, an instruction that had followed his criminal conviction for assault on another councillor.

It is not clear what had suddenly emboldened the ANC's provincial executive committee to summon Lungisa for a disciplinary hearing. He had defied them for almost two years. Now, appearing in front of the disciplinary committee, Lungisa offered to comply with the longstanding instruction to resign as an MMC, and the committee promptly accepted. The matter ended there. He was not sanctioned for his defiance of almost two years, nor for the recent breach of party discipline (voting for Mapu). The punishment was lenient, suggesting unwillingness on the part of the provincial executive committee to act decisively against Lungisa. His accomplices in the ANC caucus were left unpunished. And they persisted with their defiance. Their ally, acting mayor Buyeye, swiftly appointed the disgraced former mayor, Bobani, onto the mayoral committee to replace Lungisa, against the wishes of party leaders in both the region and the province. Bobani, however, did not occupy this position for long. In November 2020 this kingmaker and kingpin of the Nelson Mandela Bay coalitions succumbed to COVID-19-related complications.

Factionalism within the ANC had prevented it from acting in unison in the collective interests of the party. Even the threat of the municipality suffering financial collapse would not get ANC councillors to cooperate. Treasury had withheld financial grants and demanded, among other things, that council elect a new mayor. Both the acting mayor and the speaker, supported by Lungisa's faction in the ANC caucus, had resisted Treasury's instruction. They even appealed a court judgment ordering the speaker to convene a council meeting to elect a new mayor: Buyeye contended that there was no reason to elect a new mayor, as he was capable of acting in that role. For refusing an instruction to convene a meeting and using municipal funds to challenge the court, Mafaya has not been sanctioned by the party. This suggests that she enjoys protection from some groupings at the party's provincial headquarters.

RETURN OF A BRUISED AND FRAGILE DA COALITION

It was only on 4 December 2020 that Nelson Mandela Bay was able to elect a new mayor, the DA's Nqaba Bhanga. He was elected with the support of both old allies that were part of the DA's initial coalition, as well as the United Front and the AIC. The election was marred by the antics that had come to characterise the proceedings of council. While the meeting, which had been ordered by a court, was going on, municipal guards stormed it and snatched the speaker, Mafaya, out of the chamber. The intention was to abort the meeting, preventing it from electing a new mayor. The DA and its allies, however, insisted that the meeting continued. They dismissed the speaker's removal as a staged kidnapping, and called on the acting city manager, Mandla George, to resume proceedings as a presiding officer. Though permitted by law, George was reluctant, citing threats to his family and himself. Instead, he authorised and oversaw the election of one of the councillors, the PA's Marlon Daniels, to assume the role of speaker and oversee the election of the mayor. George fled the meeting promptly thereafter (Nkosi and Kimberly, 2020).

The ANC subsequently challenged the legality of the election. Its objection centred around the election of Daniels as speaker, saying it was not procedural. The MEC for local government, Xolile Nqatha, agreed with the ANC, and declared Nqaba Bhanga's election as mayor null and void. Bhanga and his allies insisted that not only had procedures been followed, but that the move had been made necessary by Mafaya's absconding from the meeting (Dayimani, 2020a). And Mafaya's failure to institute charges of kidnapping, as she had promised, added credence to the conclusion that she had staged her own kidnapping, possibly with the support of Andile Lungisa, who was lurking outside the chamber as the antics played out inside. Lungisa, who was on parole following a three-month stint in prison, had expressed opposition to the election of a new mayor on the day he came out of prison (Dayimani, 2020b). At the time of writing, George had since undertaken to approach the court to rule on the legality of Bhanga's election. In the meantime, Bhanga continued as mayor.

CONCLUSION

The experience of Nelson Mandela Bay affirms the fragility of coalitions. Yet coalitions are not fated to collapse. Their fate is determined by a number of factors. These include political context and party identity; the margin of the majority; the size and character of the parties involved; whether they see themselves as a regional or national party, and the personalities in leadership positions. In Nelson Mandela Bay, the confluence of these factors made the repeated breakdowns inevitable.

Political context and party identity impeded the formation of what would likely have been a stable coalition between the DA and the ANC. Their varying and divergent identities, however, would not allow for a rapprochement. Unable to form a coalition, the two leading parties went for likeminded parties. These were parties with somewhat similar policies and past experiences of collaboration. For the DA, however, these coalition partners behaved in ways that limited prospects for a coalition that carried a minimal majority: one or two partners could bring the coalition down. Hence, the DA was desperate to placate partners, a situation that some parties exploited for short-term, material gains. Patron-based and small parties – the UDM, the PA, the AIC and the United Front – proved particularly adept at exploiting the fragility of coalitions. Patron-based parties are not guided by principles or ideology, nor are they subject to members who may disagree and hold them accountable. Instead, they are guided by the personal whims of their leaders, which makes for an uneasy relationship if such leaders are unscrupulous. Small patron-based parties have doubtful chances of re-election and this predisposes them towards seeking immediate material benefits. This leads either to a collapse of the coalition, as other partners disapprove of the resultant impropriety, or tolerance of misdemeanour, as partners seek to keep the coalition intact at all costs.

It does not follow that bigger parties are necessarily prone to good government. Bigger parties stand a fair chance of getting a majority in a following election, and it may be assumed that they would not govern in a way that damages such electoral prospects. However, internal party dynamics can intervene. Unlike the DA, the ANC was incoherent in its responses: it was riddled with factions that pursued contradictory interests, leading to counterproductive behaviour. Factions showed that they can be as parasitic as small-sized patron-based parties. They are not interested in the good of the whole party; their own interest is what counts. Because they are fighting another faction, they are insecure about their future in the party and therefore embezzle funds to guarantee some financial security. This limits the prospects of the party's improving its electoral fortunes.

How a party sees itself also has a bearing on how it behaves in the coalition context – does the party see itself as a regional or a national party? Election into a coalition at a metro does not necessarily mean a party will prioritise that locality. If it considers itself a national party, such as the EFF, then local interests assume a secondary role. Local interests prevail to the extent that they generate national headlines: the EFF forced policy concessions from the DA because it gave them national prominence. That victory somewhat affirmed the party's overall orientation as a champion of the downtrodden, while also benefiting locals. The local benefit, however, was simply coincidental, not the primary objective.

Finally, the current state of politics in the metro could very well be replicated in a following election. It is doubtful that either of the two leading parties will get an outright majority in the next local election. The DA acquitted itself well during its tenure, but the party's conservative turn at the national level, marked also by the exodus of prominent black leaders, is unlikely to win it new voters, especially African voters. It is possible that the newly formed Abantu Integrity Movement, led by Mkhuseli 'Khusta' Jack, may become a notable actor that significantly changes the balance of power in the metro (Ncokazi, 2020). A former leader of the UDF, ANC member and co-founder of Cope, Jack is a highly prominent and respected personality in Nelson Mandela Bay. The Abantu Integrity Movement is likely to offer an attractive alternative to disillusioned voters, especially those who have historically voted for the ANC. Other small parties that have embroiled themselves in notoriety may disappear as their supporters punish them. This assures a certain degree of plurality of parties, but still does not guarantee that the 2021 election will yield a majority party to form a stable local government. Depending on which parties emerge out of the 2021 election as largest, tumultuous coalition politics is likely to persist.

REFERENCES

Alberts, A., Cassim, F. and Downs, J. 26 May 2017. 'Investigation into matters relating to the dispute between the Mayor and Deputy Mayor of NMBMM'. Report by the ACDP, COPE and FF Plus on a dispute in the coalition, http://udm.org.za/nmbmm/, accessed 2 August 2020.

Brams, S. J. and Kilgour, D. M. 2013. 'Kingmakers and leaders in coalition formation', *Social Choice and Welfare,* 11 (1), 1–18.

Butler, L. 24 April 2017. 'Bobani attacks Trollip's style', *The Herald.*

Capa, S. 25 August 2017. 'Bay risks losing Ironman champs without funds', *The Herald.*

Capa, S. 28 August 2019. 'A trucking disgrace', *The Herald.*

Capa, S., and Nkosi, N. 31 March 2018 (2018a). 'Day of insults, threats', *The Herald.*

Capa, S. and Nkosi, N. 11 May 2018 (2018b). 'Attempts to unseat Trollip drag on', *The Herald.*

Capa, S. and Parfitt, O. 26 January 2018. 'EFF councillor elected to public accounts chair', *The Herald.*

Co-Governance Agreement Between the African Christian Democratic Party ('ACDP'), the Congress of the People ('COPE'), the Democratic Alliance ('DA'), the Freedom Front Plus ('FF+') and the United Democratic Movement ('UDM'), 16 August 2016.

Dayimani, M. 8 December 2020 (2020a). 'Bhanga rejects MEC's letter which declared his election as NMB mayor unlawful', https://www.news24.com/

news24/southafrica/news/bhanga-rejects-mecs-letter-which-declared-his-election-as-nmb-mayor-unlawful-20201208, accessed on 16 December 2020.

Dayimani, M. 5 December 2020 (2020b). 'Lungisa denies causing chaos in NMB council, as new mayor Nqaba Bhanga vows to root out corruption', https://www.news24.com/news24/southafrica/news/lungisa-denies-causing-chaos-in-nmb-council-as-new-mayor-nqaba-bhanga-vows-to-root-out-corruption-20201205, accessed on 16 December 2020.

De Kock, R. 5 September 2016. 'Dawn of a new alliance', *The Herald*.

De Kock, R. 20 June 2017 (2017a). 'Trollip in move to woo new partner', *The Herald*.

De Kock, R. 28 January 2017 (2017b). 'What now, Mr Bobani?' *The Herald*.

De Kock, R. and Capa, S. 27 April 2017 (2017a). 'Zitumane's bombshell claims', *The Herald*.

De Kock, R. and Capa, S. 25 August 2017 (2017b). 'Bobani booted out', *The Herald*.

De Kock, R. and Capa, S. 29 March 2018. 'How PA sealed late-night deal', *The Herald*.

De Kock, R. and Kimberley, M. 21 November 2018. 'City sought to halt all cases started by Mettler', *The Herald*.

De Kock, R. and Mngxitama-Diko, A. 1 February 2017. 'ANC plan to unseat Trollip falls flat', *The Herald*.

De Kock, R., Mngxitama-Diko, A. and Capa, S. 24 May 2017. 'Peace deal teeters', *The Herald*.

De Kock, R. and Nkosi, N. 10 April 2018. 'Athol Trollip vote council meeting "permanently adjourned"', *The Herald*.

Electoral Commission of South Africa (IEC), www.elections.org.za, accessed 17 October 2016.

Eyewitness News, 26 March 2019. 'Distinguishing your AIC from ANC: AIC on how election ballot paper was drawn up', https://ewn.co.za/2019/03/27/distinguishing-your-aic-from-anc-iec-on-how-elections-ballot-paper-was-drawn-up, accessed 2 April 2020.

Herald Reporter, 29 May 2017. 'Bay coalition future in doubt, says Holomisa', *The Herald*.

Isaac, J. 23 May 2017. 'Coalition leaders sort out differences', *The Herald*.

Jafta, J. 5 September 2017. Constitutional Court Judgment, Case CCT 76/17.

Kimberley, K. 8 July 2019 (2019a). 'AFU hits back at Bobani accountant', *The Herald*.

Kimberley, M. 23 October 2019 (2019b). 'Battle to get IPTS graft update from Hawks', *The Herald*.

Kimberley, M. 20 January 2020. 'AG digs up fresh dirt on drain-cleaning project', *The Herald*.

Kimberley, M. and Nkosi, N. 3 October 2019 (2019a). 'Bobani must go', *The

Herald.

Kimberley, M. and Nkosi, N. 5 December 2019 (2019b). 'Mongameli Bobani voted out as Nelson Mandela Bay mayor', *The Herald*.

Kuse, K. M. 1 June 2016. 'Not politics that grabbed crowd, but speaker's life experience', *The Herald*.

Laver, M., Rallings, C. and Thrasher, M. 1987. 'Coalition theory and local government: Coalition payoffs in Britain', *British Journal of Political Science*, 17 (4), 501–509.

Mngxitama-Diko, A. 18 May 2017. 'Fate of Bay leaders at stake', *The Herald*.

Makhafola, G. 7 February 2017. 'AIC awaits report ANC's report on Matatiele', www.iol.co.za, accessed 24 March 2020.

Makunga, N. 21 June 2017. 'Can't afford mindless strife', *The Herald*.

Mbete, S. 2016. 'Economic Freedom Fighters' debut in the municipal elections', *Journal of Public Administration,* 51 (3.1), 596–614.

Ncokazi, Z. 10 November 2020. 'Mkhuseli Jack reveals Abantu Integrity Movement as new party', *The Herald*.

Ndletyana, M. 2020a. *Anatomy of ANC in Power: Insights from Port Elizabeth 1990–2019.* Cape Town: HSRC Press.

Ndletyana, M. 11 September 2020 (2020b). 'Who will vote for a party that brought ruin upon the Bay?', *The Herald*.

Nelson Mandela Bay Metropolitan Municipality (NMB Municipality). 6 September 2007. Rules of Order.

News24. 24 April 2014. 'Malema responds to Gayton McKenzie's open letter', https://www.news24.com/you/Archive/malema-responds-to-gayton-mckenzies-open-letter-20170728, accessed 26 March 2019.

News24. 4 March 2018. 'We are cutting the throat of whiteness – Julius Malema', https://www.politicsweb.co.za/news-and-analysis/we-are-cutting-the-throat-of-whiteness--julius-mal, accessed 20 March 2018.

Nkosi, N. 15 November 2019. 'ANC won't back move to dissolve council', www.heraldlive.co.za, accessed 16 December 2020.

Nkosi, N. and Kimberley, M. 5 November 2019. 'Threats derail council meeting', *The Herald*.

Nkosi, N. and Kimberley, M. 4 December 2020. 'DA's Nqaba Bhanga elected Nelson Mandela Bay mayor', *The Herald*.

Parfitt, O. 13 January 2018. 'R175m off Ironman budget', *The Herald*.

Sain, R. 17 October 2019. 'SAPS rubbishes claim that NMB council meeting cancelled on policy advice', *IOL*, https://www.iol.co.za/news/politics/saps-rubbishes-claim-that-nmb-council-meeting-cancelled-on-police-advice-35173130, accessed 21 January 2021.

Zille, H. 2016. *Not Without a Fight.* Cape Town: Penguin Books.

FOURTEEN

Full cycles and reinventions in coalitions in the Western Cape and Cape Town metro

SANUSHA NAIDU

The political dynamics in the Cape Town metro and Western Cape generally highlight a party-political narrative that challenges the hegemonic identity of African National Congress (ANC) electoral dominance applicable to much of the country. The Western Cape thus holds a coalition dynamic that diverges from the norm. The conventional precedent that has characterised South Africa's democratic environment has been ANC-centric, whereby the liberation movement-turned political party has generally been the most favoured choice among the electorate, particularly for the working class, marginalised and dispossessed. To this end, the logic is that the majority of voters will rationally vote for the ANC.

This is not the case in the Western Cape. Electoral dynamics and party-political support are both tested there, and also draw attention to the undercurrents of coalition-building in the province. In investigating these trends, this chapter reflects on what type of coalition arrangements have materialised, and determines what conditions and factors have shaped the Western Cape's coalition formations. The analysis refers to the processes of forming a majority presence in the legislative institution through entering into pre- and post-electoral agreements or a consociational form of compact or power-sharing – processes that have been linked to perceptions of protecting the interests and securities of minority groups.[1]

Through this lens, the chapter examines the dynamics of coalition politics in the province. It links contemporary dynamics to the founding conditions of 1994 and considers the political undercurrents in the Western Cape. It weighs up the extent to which these factors have influenced party-political support from 1994 to the present. It assesses the push-and-pull factors that have shaped the behaviour, identity and ideological leanings of political parties in their electoral and coalition footprints in the Cape Town metro and the province generally.

The first section provides an overview of the emergence and dissolution of waves of coalition arrangements as they have evolved in the province since 1994. This will include the National Party (NP)/New National Party (NNP) as the first provincial government; the rising dominance of the Democratic Party (DP), which in turn morphed into the Democratic Alliance (DA); the power-sharing agreement of the DP/DA-NNP; the return of the NNP-ANC partnership; and the formation of the DA-ID (Independent Democrats) alliance. This section also considers some of the coalition arrangements that have emerged, particularly after the 2016 local government elections, in the peripheral areas of the province.

Section two examines the strategic choices and decisions that have influenced contestation of political power and interparty coalitions in the Western Cape. The analysis considers the granular nature of identity politics, the choices made by political parties in coalition partnerships, and the extent to which the debate on racialised voting blocs (such as 'the coloured vote') is a prevailing factor in understanding the unfolding nature of coalition frameworks in the provincial landscape.

CYCLES OF COALITION FORMATION AND DISSOLUTION

The Western Cape has been host at provincial and local government levels to multiple cycles of party political alliances and coalitions. These formations have been part of government, and have both helped and helped destroy multiple political parties in the close to three decades of multiparty democracy in South Africa.

The NP attaching itself to coalitions

The erstwhile NP/NNP epitomised the use of coalitions as vehicles for political survival and opportunity. It adopted coalition vehicles to survive in the years after South Africa's transition to democracy. In the process of working for survival, beyond an internal transition that helped it gain votes among the coloured working class, it first attached itself to the DP and then to the ANC. Its overarching battle was to remain relevant as a political actor. On the cusp of the country's first democratic election in 1994, the identity of the NP had already shifted from being the dominant power as the architect of apartheid, to being a joint participant in change. It had reoriented itself in favour of a negotiated political transition. It then moved into the mandated power-sharing arrangement with the ANC in a post-apartheid government of national unity (GNU) (Booysen, 2011: 290–291).

The negotiated settlement, and significantly the component of the 'sunset clause', was a critical tenet for the NP's positioning among a strategic voting constituency in the bureaucracy of the state. Mangcu (2003: 106) notes that the clause promoted 'the idea ... that the new government would guarantee security of job tenure for civil servants and security officials for five years into the new democracy'. Such an assurance enabled the NP to gesture to its electoral constituency, including minority groups employed in the civil service, that it was still able to protect them, acting as a vanguard of their interests by assuaging fears that a majoritarian-led black government would impinge on their material status in a post-apartheid society. It also meant that the electoral base of the NP, comprising a broad cross-section of minority groups, provided the party with electoral traction. It assisted the NP to obtain 20 per cent of the national vote in the 1994 elections. This helped affirm the NP as a partner in the GNU.

The GNU coalition-partner status pointed to the way the NP sought to maintain both its relevance at the national level and its identity-related positioning at the provincial level. The Western Cape provided the backdrop to this political identity: the NP won an outright provincial majority of 53.2 per cent of the votes cast in 1994. This victory provoked mixed reactions, and led to questions of whether the NP was using identity politics of race to help shape voter behaviour in the province.

The NP's engagement in the GNU was the first test of its electoral identity in coalition frameworks. The GNU set the parameters for how the party defined its relationship with the ANC at the national level, while conducting its pushback campaign against the ruling party in the province. By using adversarial election campaigning in the province, the NP aroused the anxiety of the ANC being unable to govern, plunging the country into chaos, creating economic uncertainty and leaving the country in a state of instability and lack of prosperity (Africa, 2015: 127). It argued that a majoritarian black-led government would compromise the socioeconomic rights of minorities (Africa, 2010: 11–12). The provincial results meant that campaigns such as 'Stop the Comrades' [the ANC] '[were] more successful … given the concerns about violence and the pre-existing belief that the ANC would be most likely to start it, [and] the NP's campaign messages about the ANC's involvement in boycotts, strikes, arson and other acts of violence fell on fertile ground' (Africa, 2010: 13).

The unravelling of the NP, the rise of the DP and the NNP-DP power-sharing agreement

The success of the NP in the Western Cape, however, could not sustain the party at the national level. By the time the permanent constitution of 1996 was adopted, the NP was experiencing internal fragmentation. Part of the dilemma for the NP was the backlash of its traditional support base of white voters, who accused the party of compromising its identity by what they felt as 'selling out' to the ANC. The NP had to contend with this section of its voter base, made up of middle- and working-class white voters that constituted the mainstay of its support, migrating to a new political home, the DP. To safeguard the interests of its traditional constituency, the NP exited the GNU and redefined itself as solely an opposition party (see Booysen, 2011). The latter also saw the NP reinvent itself as the NNP, which included a leadership change, with F.W. de Klerk stepping down and Marthinus van Schalkwyk taking over (Schulz-Herzenberg, 2005). The exit from the GNU exposed the party's structural weaknesses. The dominance of the ANC in the GNU, and the fact that the GNU was a temporary framework, signalled that the arrangement contradicted the NP's attempt to be a robust opposition party, as its supporters desired. At a minimum, there was a lack of consensus among its membership regarding the party entering into and participating in the GNU coalition arrangement (Jolobe, 2018: 87). The fact that the GNU was not intended to be a permanent arrangement also reduced its usefulness to the NP.

In the Western Cape the party still held traction through the 1996 local government elections, though in the period 1997–98, it experienced its support in by-elections swinging towards the DP (Booysen, 2011: 296). Recognising the inherent flaws underlining the NNP, the DP saw the NNP's exit from the GNU as an opportunity to take advantage of the NNP's imminent demise (Welsh, 1999: 91). The NNP weakened, and this enticed the party to enter a cooperation agreement[2] with the DP in 1997, focused on ensuring that it retained political stature in view of the 2000 local government elections. Part of the engagement saw the NNP and the DP work together in the provincial legislature, as well as the DP being invited onto the province's executive.

In the period before the 1999 elections, Tony Leon took over as DP leader from Zach de Beer. Leon steered the DP into building its electoral footprint and opposition voice. According to Welsh (1999: 91), by the 'beginning of March 1996', the DP held a 'series of meetings' that aimed at fashioning 'a new approach' for its electioneering. The rationale was to get a realignment of the opposition landscape, and position the DP to lead the charge as a vibrant alternative to the ANC. Party strategists gauged that a two-pronged strategy was required in order to capture the political terrain hitherto occupied by the NP-NNP. The first part required an assessment of where the NNP fit within the overall framework. For the DP, the NNP did not constitute a coherent political centre that could warrant a strategic discussion around the kind of democratic liberalism that the DP was envisaging. The DP leadership reckoned the NNP was amorphous, and hence the better option would be to expedite the NNP's demise (Welsh, 1999: 93). The DP would then capture the space left behind by the NNP, and consolidate its positioning as an alternative to the ANC. The second part was to use the space left by the NNP and realign the dynamics of opposition politics by proposing a cooperative framework of engagement that would see opposition parties come together under a broad collective arrangement (Welsh, 1999: 93). The DP realised that the deepening of its electoral footprint remained dependent on the NNP's internal factionalism and the erosion of that party's electoral base.

Interrelated issues informed this stance. The NNP's political survival after leaving the GNU was linked to the informal cooperation between the DP and the NNP in the Western Cape from 1997. Using the two levers of survival and cooperation, the DP positioned itself to systematically wear down the NNP's official opposition status. This was not difficult – the NNP's legitimacy was weakening as Afrikaner voters felt marginalised and shifted to the DP. This materialised despite the rebranding of the party as a 'Christian Democrat and non-racial New National Party' (Schulz-Herzenberg, 2005).

The DP improved its performance strikingly from 1994 to 1999, to obtain 9.5 per cent of the national vote, increasing its number of seats in the national assembly from seven to 31. In the Western Cape it received almost 12 per cent of the provincial vote, giving it five seats in the provincial legislature. This showing strengthened the DP's resolve to consolidate its snuffing-out of the NNP and ascend electorally at both the national and provincial levels. The dynamics at play in the Western Cape illustrated this.

The NNP's performance in the 1999 election confirmed its weakening – and it needed a coalition crutch to keep going. It got only 6.9 per cent of the national vote, indicating a crumbling support and signalling a loss of about 13 percentage points compared to its 1994 result. At the provincial level, the NNP still held onto much of its base, though it failed to repeat its outright-majority result of the 1994 elections, managing only 38 per cent of the vote, drawn significantly from the coloured electoral constituency. The ANC's provincial performance of 42 per cent exceeded that of the NNP. The ANC in the provincial legislature had 18 (out of 42) seats, compared to the NNP's 17. The DP had five. The result provided the context for some form of coalition. The DP maintained its stance not to enter into a coalition arrangement with the ANC, and engaging with the NNP was therefore a more expedient choice for the party. This was despite the DP's aggressive election campaign that had undermined the NNP. Expanding on its earlier proposition of establishing a cooperative opposition alliance, the DP and the NNP formed a coalition government in the Western Cape after the 1999 elections (Booysen, 2005: 133), which kept 'the ANC out of power in the Western Cape' (Africa, 2010: 16).

By 2000 the NNP's woes were evident. Seeking to survive, it entered into a formal coalition with the DP and the Federal Alliance to form the DA[3] in mid-2000. Aimed at consolidating the opposition's footprint, the DA boosted the DP-NNP engagement in the province. Collectively, the DA (that is, the DP plus the NNP, along with the minor Federal Alliance) controlled just over 50 per cent of the representation.[4] As Booysen (2011: 297) notes, 'The alliance shielded the NNP in the 2000 local government elections, and also rapidly expanded the standing of the DP through an increase in seats'. Hence, through the formalisation of the DA, the NNP ventured into a post-election coalition agreement that extended its fading electoral relevance.

The alliance between the NNP and the DP soon started faltering. In 2001 tensions between the two spilled over into their coalition. Apart from the dominance of the DP, leadership incompatibility, differences in vision and internal tensions affected the relationship. It was a Cape Town street-renaming scandal that finally broke the camel's back. The DA leadership took an aggressive stance against the NNP-appointed mayor of the metro, Peter Marais, and, being relegated to junior-partner status in the DA, the NNP withdrew from the coalition in 2001 (Jolobe, 2007).

Within the province, the breakdown of the relationship had a direct effect on the governance structure of the provincial government. As

Booysen (2011: 298) highlights in the context of floor-crossing that was used in conjunction with coalition-hopping:

> The NNP's breakaway from the DA in the Western Cape was possible because members were elected in 1999 under the pre-DA, NNP banner. The NNP now flaunted its wares to the ANC, which was keen to use the desperate NNP to capture the Western Cape from the DA, and further expand its presence in Parliament and local government. On the local level, several councils could be captured from the DA.

As a result of the split, the political dynamics in the province underwent yet another shift as a new alliance took shape.

Return of the ANC-NNP partnership of convenience: Provincial realignment

The NNP's swing to the ANC provided the ruling party with the edge it needed to finally take control of the Western Cape. This was supported by floor-crossing legislation (Schulz-Herzenberg, 2005). As much as the ANC was a beneficiary of NNP members filtering into its ranks, so too was the DA (Booysen, 2005). In 2002 the ANC and the NNP entered into a coalition. Through this step, the ANC-NNP coalition wrested control from the DA,[5] allowing the NNP to remain in power. The NNP's pivot away from the DA towards the ANC can be construed as an act of political expediency in the interests of survival (Schulz-Herzenberg, 2005). The NNP's relevance disappearing, the coalition with the ANC provided a lifeline. The floor-crossing legislation of 2002 also facilitated the ANC-NNP coalition by providing members of the NNP with a legitimate opening to defect to the ANC, as well as the DA and other political parties (see Booysen, 2006).

The 2004 national and provincial elections confirmed the decline of the NNP. Winning only 1.7 per cent nationally and 11 per cent in the Western Cape, the party was on the brink of collapse. The ANC's national electoral base had moved beyond the two-thirds level, reaching almost 70 per cent. In the Western Cape, too, the ANC garnered a significant vote share with its performance of 45 per cent. This enabled the ANC, through its alliance with the NNP, to take control of the province. For the NNP, its alliance with the ANC led to it becoming absorbed into the ANC.[6] The NNP was officially dissolved in 2005.

The results of the 2004 election were significant for the province in two ways that were pertinent to coalition politics. First, the ANC managed to take control of the province through its partnership with the NNP. This was further augmented in 2005 during the floor-crossing period, which saw a number of NNP provincial legislature members move to the ANC (Schulz-Herzenberg, 2005). It helped give the ANC an absolute majority in the province. Second, the DA managed to grow its support in the province, with its profile increasing among coloured voters despite the emergence of the 'new kid on the block', the ID led by Patricia de Lille. The 2004 election also showed that the DA's support base had started to resemble a broad church, categorised by Booysen (2005: 143) as 'the old liberals, the unreformed and reactionary old Nats, the reformed Nats that wished to distance themselves from the stigmatised NNP past, and enclaves of new black support coming from the ranks of old Bantustan politics'.

The 2006 local elections: A turning point in the coalition landscape of the metro

The 2006 local government elections proved to be a critical turning point in the DA's political positioning in the Cape Town metro. While the DA won a substantial share of the vote in the metro, it did not have a majority. The party once again was to construct a majority on the basis of coalition formation. It entered into discussions with smaller political parties, including the African Christian Democratic Party (ACDP), which had emerged as a kingmaker, with five other smaller parties. Establishing a bloc of 16 councillors, the group eventually decided to work with the DA through the establishment of a multiparty forum, thereby giving the DA the necessary number of votes it needed to elect Helen Zille as mayor of the metro.

Political developments in the Cape Town metro following the election highlighted the fluidity in maintaining a permanent governance arrangement. It demonstrated the significance of smaller parties while also showing how the two main protagonists, the ANC and the DA, found themselves caught in a political sparring match: each tried to court and leverage its engagement with the smaller political parties by making promises of power-sharing. Negotiations between the ANC and the ID to form a governing partnership in the Cape Town metro in the wake of the 2006 elections reflected the complex nature of coalition arrangements (Van Onselen, 2016).

In January 2007 the DA realised that coalitions are complex arrangements that cannot be sustained by just a 'gentleman's agreement'. The fragility of the multiparty coalition led by the DA after the 2006 local elections was highlighted by the African Muslim Party, which was expelled from the multiparty forum for allegedly conspiring with the ANC. The metro was again being led by an incoherent coalition. The ID was brought into the fold to stabilise metro governance. The DA and the ID jointly delivered a firm council majority. By the time of the 2009 elections, the DA's multiparty municipal coalition had seen several smaller political parties dropped from the partnership. This reorientation of the political dynamics in the metro also helped set the stage for the DA-ID 2010 agreement for a phased merger: ID local councillors held dual membership until the 2011 local elections, and ID MPs and provincial legislatures held dual membership until the 2014 elections.

The DA securing its electoral provincial footprint

The 2009 national and provincial elections were considered by analysts such as Africa (2010: 21) as a defining moment for the DA's electoral dominance in the Western Cape. Internal governance issues exposing competition for political power by factional groups in the ruling ANC saw its election performance decline from 45 per cent in 2004 to 31.5 per cent in 2009 (Africa, 2010: 20). Southall and Daniel (2009: 237) argue that in the period between the 1999 and 2004 elections, the ANC's electoral footprint had grown in the coloured community. This could be attributed to the ANC having in its ranks high-profile community personalities like Ebrahim Rasool, as well as activists and communities linked to the erstwhile United Democratic Front (UDF). Even in working-class communities like Mitchells Plain, the ANC enjoyed a level of confident voter support.

The 2009 shift to the DA, which received 51.2 per cent of the provincial vote, suggests that the new leadership of the ANC under the presidency of Jacob Zuma did not bolster confidence in the electorate; instead, it reinforced a trust deficit in the new ANC president. Africa (2010: 21) notes that the 2005 Zuma rape trial, the corruption case of Schabir Shaik (a close business associate of Zuma), the recall of Thabo Mbeki in 2008 following the ANC Polokwane elective conference, and the exit of Mbeki loyalists to form a new party called the Congress of the People (Cope), were significant push and pull factors in shaping public perceptions of the ANC. While these national issues were critical in shaping public opinion of the ANC, disarray in the party's provincial structures exacerbated existing provincial challenges. The removal of Rasool as premier and his replacement by Lynne Brown fuelled perceptions of distrust in the Zuma leadership. This distrust was exacerbated by what Butler (2009: 70) described as provincial structures in 'complete shambles and the NEC [national executive committee] had to rescue the province after an orgy of defections, expulsions and proliferations of parallel structures'.

In this changing national and provincial political context of the ANC, the DA was able to deepen its electoral footprint in the province. The party's 1999 electoral campaign of 'Fight Back' had been seen as divisive and racially defined against a black-majority party. In 2004 the campaign was softer in tone and exhibited the view that 'South Africans deserve better'; it suggested that the ANC-NNP coalition was not up to the task of being an effective government. The party tried to project that it would bring real change. It used slogans like 'Vote DA for real change'. In 2009 the DA's electoral campaign, under newly elected leader Helen Zille, became more sophisticated. They observed the weakening of the ANC under Zuma, and the slogan of 'One nation, One future' found traction among the electorate in the province. The DA's messaging of 'Vote to win' and 'Stop Zuma' also found resonance among Western Cape voters who were unsure of the meaning of Zuma's leadership for the country and the province. Cope achieved a 7 per cent performance in the Western Cape (higher than the ID). This presented the DA with an option for an informal alliance to bolster its footprint among Mbeki supporters in African townships in the Cape Town metro.

The DA's 2009 victory confirmed the start of its consolidation of its electoral presence in the province. Between 2009 and 2014 it nevertheless faced challenges from branches and public structures aligned with the ANC. The DA was accused of neglecting the poor in vulnerable areas like Gugulethu and Khayelitsha. Lack of service delivery, inhumane conditions in informal areas and prevailing socioeconomic inequalities became battleground issues in areas where protests erupted. The DA was accused of conducting elite politics and neglecting township areas where socioeconomic suffering was endemic. The DA believed that the ANC was stoking the tensions and invoking protests. As Africa (2010: 132) notes, 'The political environment in the province became toxic between 2009 and 2014 and the Western Cape [was] marked by extraordinary levels of distrust and political tension.'

By the time of the 2011 local government elections, the ANC's challenges had continued to deepen. The province's ANC branch structures were wracked with factional politics. The candidate lists were contested, and the ANC offices in the metro were stormed by members who disputed the names on the list (Africa, 2010: 132). The ANC lost 40 wards across the province, while the DA consolidated its electoral presence. This was boosted by the ID becoming fully integrated into the DA in 2010, enhancing the DA's 2011 local election majorities. Patricia de Lille, leader of the ID, was brought into the DA provincial cabinet and later elected mayor of the City of Cape Town. By the time of the 2014 national and provincial elections, the DA had shed the mantle of coalition politics in the province and metro, enjoying an overwhelming electoral victory which gave it the sole mandate to govern. The DA won the 2014 provincial election with close to 60 per cent provincially, and achieved 22 per cent nationally. This trend continued in the 2016 local government elections. The party won a two-thirds majority in the city and 80 wards. It also expanded its presence across the provinces, with coalition arrangements beyond the metro and the provincial government. The ANC lost four councils it had controlled since 2011.[7] The DA concluded deals with small local parties or community organisations, largely from coloured communities that had contested the elections to control the municipal councils in Prince Albert, Laingsburg and Beaufort West, as well as the greater Central Karoo District Municipality. The DA also concluded an agreement with an independent candidate to control Knysna, and entered into a coalition with the Freedom Front Plus (FF+) to rule Hessequa (Phakathi, 2016). In the Kannaland Municipality, which had a long history of controversial and collapsing coalitions, DA and ANC councillors worked together to vote out the Independent Civic Organisation of South Africa (ICOSA), which had won close to 50 per cent of the vote. The DA's coalition partnerships with the Karoo Democratic Force (KDF), the Karoo Gemeenskap Party (KGP) and the Karoo Ontwikkelingsparty, in the Beaufort West, Prince Albert and Laingsburg municipalities, respectively, in 2016 thus helped the DA to gain traction in the Karoo area. The coalitions, however, would not last. In 2020, the DA exited, for example, in Beaufort West, due to tensions over clean government and financial management. The experience showed how coalition arrangements defined through identity politics can be born out of rent-seeking behaviour by parties such as the KGP, which are critical actors at the sub-national level, but use the identity of race as a way to pursue parochial political power.

But in the run-up to the 2019 elections, the DA again had to contend with its 'elite politics' identity and the ANC labelling its governance of the metro and province as racist and lacking transformation. The DA had to deal with ANC allegations that apartheid remained part of the DA's provincial landscape. The Western Cape became an open race, with 26 political parties contesting the provincial election. Both the DA and ANC in the province declined by about 4 percentage points; the smaller parties took the gains. The DA did, however, retain an outright majority of 55.5 per cent. The same broad trend manifested nationally. In general, the DA had campaigned to demonstrate its governance successes, while trying to allay the coloured communities' fears of marginalisation.

FAULTLINES THAT INFORM COALITION FORMATION IN THE WESTERN CAPE

So far this chapter has examined how coalition arrangements unfolded in the Western Cape and Cape Town metro. It will now examine what factors drive coalition formation in the province.

The 'race census' debate

Race and class dimensions underpin the party-political and electoral landscapes, fuelled by South Africa's harsh dynamics of spatial inequalities. The structural and political conditions across the Western Cape are defined by these exact historical inequities. This is not unique to the Western Cape; it reflects the entrenched faultlines of apartheid nationally. The dynamics also inform the formation and robustness of alliances and coalitions in the province. The faultlines undergird much of the argument that voting behaviour unfolds as a race census.

The presumption at one level is that the majority of the coloured vote aligned with the NP was based on the rationale that 'the coloured community [felt] happier with Afrikaner rather than African nationalism' (Johnson, 1996; Africa, 2010: 10). This disaggregation of the voting patterns in the Western Cape was challenged. Scholars like Eldridge and Seekings noted that such a correlation overlooked 'data [that] suggested ... voters' attitudes on a range of issues, not simply their ethnic identity, underlay their voting intentions' (quoted in Africa, 2010: 10). This relates to Habib and Naidu (1999) in their argument about race and ethnicity as primary factors driving the electoral base in the country, and the question whether the symbiotic relationship between race and class has a more synergetic impact on voting behaviour. Desai's (1996) explanation of the role of 'middleman minorities' provides a plausible explanation of voter attraction to the NP.

The 'middleman minorities' argument reflects two significant factors regarding the NP's coalition engagement with the ANC at the national level, and the corresponding effect this created for its electoral footprint in the province. Throughout the protracted Convention for a Democratic South Africa negotiations, the NP's focus was on a consociational form of democracy that allowed for the protection of minority rights, and which included a large section of the public bureaucracy. By accepting the 'sunset clause', the NP gained the opportunity to enter into a pre-election agreement with the ANC, and hence become a junior partner in the GNU. The NP was able therefore to broadly engage in a consociational coalition with the ANC. Following the 1994 election and with the post-election agreement in place, the NP played to the insecurities, interests and rights of minority groups, and used its position in the coalition GNU as the buffer between the ruling ANC and minority groups. Therefore, voting for the NP could be seen by these minority communities as securing 'their intermediate position in the racial hierarchy as constructed by apartheid' (James and Caliguire, 1996: 136). With this in mind, it seems obvious that the NP was able to retain its ideological fit with its traditional base of Afrikaner voters, while it brought other racial minorities into its fold.

In the case of the Western Cape, the deeper issue is about the way in which the race-census outcomes of elections have been used to build coalition arrangements: either to protect political power linked to the opposition, or to leverage power to shift political control away from the ANC as the dominant political actor in South Africa. The province's election landscape suggests that the race-census character of elections aligns with minority fears of being overwhelmed by a racial majority. Party campaigning exploits political conditions and voter anxieties. Coalition formation in these instances, relatively widespread in the Western Cape, becomes a default tactic to develop a model of governance aimed at protecting minority rights under the pretext of an uncertain future in a majoritarian government. The debate on the race-census approach, discussed below, highlights these dynamics that surround coalition politics in the province.

There are two classical schools of thought regarding the interpretation of these dimensions of South Africa's electoral landscape and election outcomes. The first argues that, given the country's historical past, where exclusion and subjugation formed the central tenet of apartheid, and was based on racial identity, race remains the primary factor in determining how the electorate will vote. Analysts like Schlemmer (1999) and Friedman (2005) outlined the foundations of this school, and contend that as much as other economic and social variables are factors in disaggregating voting patterns, the dynamics of race, ethnicity, language and cultural affinities are (and remain) primary drivers of party support. The role of racial identity is seen as critical in shaping the perceptions of the electorate; voters accordingly align to the political party that best represents their racially influenced interests around policy. The second school challenges notions of a race-ethnic-census determination of party choice and election results. Scholars like Habib and Naidu (1999), Taylor and Hoeane (1999), Mattes and Piombo (2001) and Hoeane (2004) interpret voter behaviour from the vantage point of a set of socioeconomic structural conditions that are underpinned by the interplay between race and class identities. Their view is that race informs class, and class informs race. Voting patterns therefore ought to be understood from the way political, economic, social and cultural contexts define multiple identities in communities (Africa, 2010). Habib and Naidu (1999: 190) highlight ambiguities of the race-census debate when they assess the coloured and Indian vote – mindful that the 'coloured vote' determines much of Western Cape party strengths and election outcomes:

> South Africans are seen to vote, not on the basis of their interests and opinions, but rather through the prism of ethnic and racial loyalties. When applied to the Coloured and Indian communities, this racial census theory demarcates electoral behaviour along the African/non-African divide. The Coloured and Indian communities are thus seen to vote for non-African parties because of a racial group loyalty that translates into either a greater cultural affinity with other minority groups, or a fear that an African government would discriminate against them.

Habib and Naidu (1999: 191–194) note that this interpretation contradicts itself.[8] They contend that when class is introduced as 'a variable in the analysis ... the picture of voting patterns [that emerges indicates] significant electoral heterogeneity'. As much as both schools of thought offer insights into the broader characterisation of South Africa's electoral landscape, the interpretations also speak past each other. Africa (2010), in assessing provincial election results in the period 1994–2009 in the Western Cape, notes that both schools of thought are problematic in their assumptions. For Africa (2010: 7), the more nuanced and party-oriented point of departure is:

> While individual decision-making processes are critically important, voters are only one part of the electoral equation; political parties and the choices they offer constitute the other part. This raises concerns about the adequacy of accounts which view election outcomes as primarily determined by the characteristics of the electorate… (B)ehavioural motivations and/or demographic characteristics of the electorate … open up the space for political parties to abscond from their duty to provide voters with adequate information.

Electoral campaigns

The perception of race and class in influencing voter behaviour and identities led political parties to structure their election campaigns in terms of a reactionary response, as opposed to disaggregating the multiple identities the electorate holds at any given time. Political parties targeted those voting communities and groups that were uncertain of their political future under a black-majority government. The NNP's electoral results in the period from 1994 to 2005 were shaped by the view that race politics was more relevant than understanding the way race and class influenced the electoral space.

Similarly, the DP viewed race as a drawcard to express its positioning in the province. While this worked in aligning the NNP and the DP in their coalition formations, it ignored the reasons why the NNP's traditional support base had been shifting towards the DP – among others, the NNP's swing to become a broader political home to a cross-section of minority groups. It was arguably a way for the NNP's traditional supporters to protect their interests and group identity, which could not be guaranteed under the party's lack of cohesion and vulnerable leadership. It suggested that the electorate preferred a stable political centre.

Similarly, the DP/DA's 1999 'Fight Back' slogan or 'Vote DA for real change' played into racial polarising tactics. From 2009 onwards, the DA was able to capitalise on the ANC's changing internal political nature and use its campaigning message to highlight that the DA was more stable, and waiting in the wings to be the next government of the country. Inherent to the complex provincial electoral landscape, therefore, is the way political parties cultivate electoral campaigns.

The campaigns in the Western Cape have often been focused on placating anxieties and fears. In 2009 the ANC used the strategy of appealing to working-class and marginalised coloured communities living on farms, to criticise the DA for not pushing land reform. This appeared ironic, considering that the national policy remained an unresolved question. Therefore it would appear that the notion of a 'coloured vote' is often utilised as an overarching group identity in election campaigning, though it tends to overlook that the salient identity of race is only one part of the spectrum of identities and ideological affiliations that find resonance with the Western Cape's electorate.

Expediency

A further dynamic was that the NNP-DP and DA-NNP coalition partnerships were formed for political expediency. For the NNP it was survival and maintaining its relevance, while for the DP/DA it was establishing a bigger presence electorally. This type of coalition formation represented a hybrid of an electoral coalition (where political parties pool votes through an alliance so that they can obtain an electoral majority) and a coalition governance model (that allows for some form of power-sharing agreement) (Jolobe, 2007: 80). For both the DA and the NNP, entrenching their power positions in the Western Cape became overarching considerations. On the other hand, expediency can have an adverse impact. In the case of the DA-NNP alliance, trying to find alignment despite differences in leadership styles, mismatched policy visions, and the dominance of one partner over the other, led to a revolving-door coalition. The NNP's musical chairs of leaving the GNU, aligning with the DP, entering the DA and then aligning with the ANC, suggested that the NNP was never comfortable in its position as a coalition partner. The instability in the party influenced the way voters perceived its ability to represent their interests. It fostered electoral distrust.

In the case of the DA, though, the assimilated nuances of the dynamics of electoral behaviour should not be overlooked. The nuances include economic exclusion, poverty, inequality or a general lack of improvement in the material status of the poor and the vulnerable. The question becomes how the old patterns combine with new nuances to influence voters to switch loyalties between political parties, especially where coalition political arrangements are formed as a reductionist approach to increasing the political footprint of political parties. The coalitions often highlight the suffering of the indigent and marginalised while playing on the racial identity of the electorate. For the DA, the identity of serving 'elite interests' in the provinces remained a significant issue of contention. As much as the ANC tried to exploit these socioeconomic divisions in the province, it also found itself unable to draw electoral support away from the DA.

A sophisticated electorate

The interplay of political developments between the national and provincial spheres was a further discernible dynamic. Party behaviour, campaign messages and events between elections shaped the voters' perceptions of political parties (Africa, 2010: 25). The range of developments was not lost on Western Cape voters. The electorate comprises active citizens with precise understandings of the actions of political parties. As parties enter coalition agreements, voters often feel disparaged, suspecting that their votes are being used as a means to an end. Consequently, voters use their voting power to punish parties by shifting their vote to another party, or they become apathetic. Loss of confidence in the party follows – a phenomenon that helps explain why the ANC, which had gained control of the province in 2004, lost its provincial grip again when Lynne Brown replaced Ebrahim Rasool as premier. Voters observed and were affected when the ANC's leadership squabbles and factional politics in the provincial and branch structures unfolded, and continued. The perception of trust becomes fundamental to the way the electorate responds to power-sharing arrangements and changes in personalities with which they feel comfortable. For example, by bringing Patricia de Lille into the DA, the party had wanted to gain her coloured support base for the DA.

CONCLUSION

This chapter dissected the way coalition politics unfolded in the Western Cape. It argued that fluid political developments impacted on the way coalition-building evolved. It also noted that as much as race is a significant factor in voting behaviour and hence for the potential to form party coalitions, it is by far not the only salient driver. There are other issues that also influence whether and the way in which coalitions are formed. These include political parties' compulsion to gain or maintain political power, survival, or opposition parties' need to keep the ANC from gaining control in the legislature and the metro of Cape Town. Equally, the opinion of the electorate and internal legitimacy issues within a provincially dominant party (in this case, the DA) may create distrust.

The fluidity of coalition politics in the Western Cape underscores competitive party politics, where the ANC and the DA (and the NNP when it still existed) have been willing to use race as the driver in how they seek out votes. In adjunct actions, minor opposition parties in the province mobilised race and race-based community party identities to gain access to rent-seeking cooperation with the DA. Political parties have parochially defined the coloured community as a homogeneous voting bloc (Africa, 2020) – this voting bloc is numerically central to election outcomes and government institution in the province. However, the political parties have often made sweeping assumptions about voter behaviour, failing to recognise the centrality of their campaign strategies in positing race as a prominent factor in coalition arrangements. Whenever clear majorities lacked, parties have been willing to move beyond ideological differences and engage in coalition arrangements that would bring them power.

REFERENCES

Adam, H. 1994. 'Ethnic vs civic nationalism: South Africa's non-racialism in comparative perspective', *South African Sociological Review*, 7 (1), 15–30.

Africa, C. 2010. 'Party support and voter behaviour in the Western Cape: Trends and patterns since 1994', *Journal of African Elections*, 9 (2), 5–31.

Africa, C. 2015. 'Reducing toxic election campaigns: Negative campaigning and race-based politics in the Western Cape', *Journal of African Elections*, 14 (1), 124–148.

Africa, C. 6 May 2020. 'The myth of the coloured vote unpacked', *SABC News*, https://www.sabcnews.com/sabcnews/the-myth-of-the-coloured-vote-unpacked/, accessed 13 December 2020.

Butler, A. 28 April 2009. 'Several reasons for SA to bask in the post-election glow', *Business Day*.

Booysen, S. 2005. 'The Democratic Alliance: Progress and pitfalls', in Piombo, J. and Nijzink, L. (eds.) *Electoral Politics in South Africa: Assessing the first democratic decade*. New York: Palgrave Macmillan, 129–147.

Booysen, S. 2006. 'The will of the parties versus the will of the people? Defections, elections and alliances in South Africa', *Party Politics*, 12 (6), 751–770.

Booysen, S. 2011. *The African National Congress and the Regeneration of Political Power*. Johannesburg: Wits University Press.

Desai, A. 1996. *Arise Ye Coolies: Apartheid and the Indian, 1960–1995*. Johannesburg: Impact.

Friedman S. 2005. 'A voice for some: South Africa's ten years of democracy', in Piombo, J. and Nijzink, L. (eds.) *Electoral Politics in South Africa: Assessing the first democratic decade*. New York: Palgrave Macmillan, 3–22.

Habib, A. and Naidu, S. 1999. 'Election 99: Was there a "coloured" and "Indian" vote?', *Politikon: South African Journal of Political Studies*, 26 (2), 189–199.

Hoeane, T. 2004. 'Under strain: The racial/ethnic interpretation of South Africa's 2004 election', *Journal of African Elections*, 3 (2), 1–26.

James, W. and Caliguire, D. 1996. 'Conclusion', in James, W., Caliguire, D. and Cullinan, K. (eds.) *Now That We Are Free: Coloured communities in a democratic South Africa*. Cape Town: Institute for Democracy in South Africa.

Jolobe, Z. 2007. 'Things fall apart: Can the centre hold? The state of coalition politics in the Cape Metropolitan Council', in Buhlungu, S., Daniel, J., Southall, R. and Lutchman, J. (eds.) *State of the Nation: South Africa 2007*. Cape Town: HSRC Press, 78–94.

Jolobe, Z. 2018. 'The politics of dominance and survival: Coalition politics in South Africa', in Ngubane, S. (ed.) *Complexities of Coalition Politics in Southern Africa*. Durban: Accord, 73–105.

Johnson, R. W. 1996. 'The 1994 election: Outcome and analysis', in Johnson, R. W. and Schlemmer, L. (eds.) *Launching Democracy in South Africa*. New Haven: Yale University Press.

Mangcu, X. 2003. 'The state of race relations in post-apartheid South Africa', in Daniel, J., Habib, A. and Southall, R. (eds.) *State of the Nation: South Africa 2003–2004*. Cape Town: HSRC Press, 105–137.

Mattes, R. B. and Gouws, A. 1999. 'Race, ethnicity and voting behavior: Lessons from South Africa', in Reynolds, A. and Sisk, T. (eds.) *Elections and Conflict Resolution in Africa*. Washington, D. C.: United States Institute of Peace, 119–142.

Mattes, R. B. and Piombo, J. 2001. 'South Africa's general election of 1999', *Democratization*, 8 (3), 101–128.

Phakathi, B. 12 August 2016. 'DA bags coalition deals in Prince Albert, Laingsburg and Beaufort West', *Business Day*, https://www.businesslive.co.za/bd/politics/2016-08-12-da-bags-coalition-deals-in-prince-albert-laingsburg-and-beaufort-west/, accessed 20 December 2020.

Schlemmer, L. 1999. 'Democracy or democratic hegemony? The future of political pluralism in South Africa', in Giliomee, H. and Simkins, C. (eds.) *The Awkward Embrace: One party domination and democracy*. Cape Town: Tafelberg Publishers, 281–300.

Schulz-Herzenberg, C. 2005. 'The New National Party: The end of the road', in Piombo, J. and Nijzink, L. (eds.) *Electoral Politics in South Africa: Assessing the first democratic decade*. New York: Palgrave Macmillan, 166–186.

Southall, R. and Daniel, J. 2005. 'The state of parties post-election 2004: ANC dominance and opposition enfeeblement', in Daniel, J., Southall, R. and Lutchman, J. (eds.) *State of the Nation: South Africa: 2004–2005*. Cape Town: HSRC Press, 34–57.

Taylor, R. and Hoeane, T. 1999. 'Interpreting the South African Election of June 1999', *Politikon*, 26 (2), 133–144.

Van Onselen, G. 11 July 2016. 'Anatomy of a coalition coup: Are there lessons ahead of the August election?', *Business Live*, https://www.businesslive.co.za/bd/opinion/columnists/2016-07-11-anatomy-of-a-coalition-coup-are-there-lessons-ahead-of-the-august-election/, accessed 10 April 2020.

Welsh, D. 1999. 'The Democratic Party', in Reynolds, A. (ed.) *Election '99 South Africa: From Mandela to Mbeki*. Cape Town: David Philip, 89–100.

FIFTEEN
―――

Power transition in KwaZulu-Natal
Post-1994 coalitions in action

Lukhona Mnguni

Coalition politics have been a prominent feature in KwaZulu-Natal politics since at least 1994, at both the provincial and local government levels. Political power in the province has changed hands in various transitions at both levels since 1994. These transitions were characterised largely by negotiation-related changes and electoral shifts between political parties. In the process, new and small parties split off the bigger ones; some thrived, others stumbled. Some became power brokers in coalition governments. Violence and the threat of violence were part of the backdrop to party politics in much of the period, albeit declining over time.

Political cooperation between two or more parties has existed in KwaZulu-Natal since 1994. Initially, much focus was on the provincial government, with the Inkatha Freedom Party (IFP) and the African National Congress (ANC) sharing power between 1994 and 2006. In the early democracy days the ANC was an underdog in KwaZulu-Natal politics, drawing its support mainly from urban areas, while the

IFP dominated in the vast rural areas. The IFP had led the KwaZulu bantustan ('homeland') since the 1970s, enjoying political monopoly, as other political parties were banned and operated underground. In the homelands period of apartheid South Africa, the IFP played an ambiguous role, collaborating with the regime, while claiming the status of an internal wing of the ANC and its liberation struggle (Makhanya, 2019). In this way, there was a type of alliance between the ANC and the IFP even in those early days. The ANC-IFP disagreements on strategies and tactics in the fight for liberation converted into political competition over black constituencies once the political space opened up in the early 1990s. Much of the contest played out in increased violent confrontation between the two parties, well into the early post-apartheid period. Therefore, while political cooperation and power-sharing after the 1994 transition were part of the strategy for party-political dominance, they also served as an antidote to violence.

This chapter tracks the evolution of coalition politics in KwaZulu-Natal, especially as manifested since 1994. It shows how the ANC emerged from underdog status to become an established and predominant party in the province, and how this new stature subsequently suffered modest decline. The chapter is organised along the lines of a periodisation of the rise and decline of the major party-political coalitions in the province. Political parties continuously enter and exit the timeline. It reviews the history of various coalition arrangements in KwaZulu-Natal, provincially and locally. Unlike other political science literature that focuses on how coalition governments lead to unstable government and policy incoherence, this chapter appraises KwaZulu-Natal coalitions from the viewpoint that they contributed to political stability and tolerance in a province that could have been the bloodbath of South Africa's democracy. The pre-1994 history and violence between the ANC and the IFP are not the subject of focus, as this has been explored extensively in the literature. Here, we focus on the lesser-articulated dimension of the ANC-IFP relationship, coalitions, collaboration and political competition in the democratic era, using empirical evidence from secondary data.

THE BROAD COALITION LANDSCAPE IN KWAZULU-NATAL: THE RISE AND DECLINE OF THE ANC AND THE IFP

The coalition arrangements at a provincial level saw the IFP cooperate with the ANC from 1994 to 2006. The 1994–99 period is characterised as a forced coalition due to national developments – a government of national unity (GNU) that included the IFP. The ANC-IFP coalition government of 1994 was a peculiar one. The political rivalry introduced bitter conflict that led to thousands of deaths (Taylor, 2002; Kaufman, 2017), and the IFP was accused of collaborating with apartheid South Africa against the ANC – effectively alleged to be selling out the liberation struggle. This chapter argues that the active courtship that took place between the ANC and the IFP made it possible in some respects for their coalition to endure beyond 1999 to 2006. As the ANC's dominance took root in the province, the IFP, however, came to distrust the ANC.

The rise of the ANC in KwaZulu-Natal can be attributed to a number of factors, including national transitional developments in the early 1990s, ANC strategy, and the IFP's own decisions and intraparty processes that weakened the party in its rural strongholds in the province. The ANC became more interested and involved in fuelling rifts within the IFP, while positioning itself as an alternative government in the province. In 2011, the focus shifted to local government coalitions as the founding of the National Freedom Party (NFP) – an IFP splinter party – broke the IFP's back in its core constituencies. It paved the way for ANC-NFP coalitions in almost 20 municipalities.

The decline of the IFP unfolded on various fronts. First, the lack of internal party democracy within the IFP became a cause for political fallouts, leading some of its leaders to resign and form splinter parties. The IFP's inability to strategise and reinvigorate the party (Piper, 2009) made it redundant to more voters. Second, the IFP leader, Mangosuthu Buthelezi, moved from his provincial base to represent his party in the national assembly, and as a relatively senior member of the national Cabinet. His departure meant that the IFP would rely on a new leadership core in the province, even if Buthelezi retained a strong hold over IFP operations. Buthelezi also retained vested interests in IFP appointments in provincial government. Third, the coalition government of 1994 saw the appointment of three prominent ANC members, Zweli Mkhize, S'bu Ndebele and Jacob Zuma, to the provincial cabinet as members of the executive council (MECs). They gained visibility for the ANC as they carried out their provincial government responsibilities. It also meant they could use their positions to be seen as providing services, and to build patronage networks and alliances, hence elevating the ANC's competition with the IFP.

The ANC foothold in KwaZulu-Natal spread, enhanced by the rise of Jacob Zuma into national ANC and national government leadership. Provincial and national ANC support in KwaZulu-Natal peaked in the 2009 to 2014 period, when Zuma assumed and established his South African presidency. However, in the 2019 elections, the ANC's newfound dominance suffered a massive 10-percentage-point decline in KwaZulu-Natal. If this trajectory continues in future elections and with the imminent reality that independent candidates will contest seats in the provincial legislature, the chapter concludes that coalition politics in KwaZulu-Natal could be in the offing once more at the provincial level, besides becoming even more articulated in local elections, as seen in recent years.

PERIODISATION OF COALITION AND ALLIANCE FORMATION, MAINTENANCE AND DISSOLUTION

The following periodisation follows the parameters broadly of South Africa's electoral cycles. For the political parties in the province, it was about the contest for political power – and the associated benefits of advancing party stature and access to benefits. In KwaZulu-Natal, besides the general developmental agendas, the promotion of identity and a degree of Zulu nationalism also combined with the representation of traditional authorities and their interests to constitute powerful motivations to gain control over the levers of power.

The formation and operation of a provincial coalition: 1994–99

South Africa's interim constitution of 1993 created the possibility of a GNU under section 88(2), expressing clearly that 'a party holding at least 20 seats in the National Assembly and which has decided to participate in the government of national unity, shall be entitled to be allocated one or more of the Cabinet portfolios in respect of which Ministers referred to in subsection (1)' (Constitution of the Republic of South Africa, 1993). The New National Party (NNP) and the IFP, having accumulated 82 and 43 seats, respectively, in the national assembly, qualified to join the GNU even though the ANC had received a majority (252) of the 400 seats and could form a government on its own. The IFP received ministerial positions, with its leader, Mangosuthu Buthelezi, becoming the first minister of home affairs in democratic South Africa. The ambitions of IFP leaders to be part of the GNU left them duty-bound to accommodate the ANC in KwaZulu-Natal. Provincial cooperation between the two parties followed.

In KwaZulu-Natal, the IFP won 41 of the 81 seats in the provincial legislature, with a 50.32 per cent electoral lead (see Table 15.1). A coalition government with the ANC, which had 26 seats, provided for great political stability in the province (and also meant that opposition to the government had only 14 seats). Despite this rapprochement, the partners continued to view each other as political rivals. This sustained the ANC as an opposition party inside and outside the legislature, regardless of the coalition arrangement. The GNU helped stabilise the KwaZulu-Natal coalition by creating mutual interests for both ANC and IFP national and provincial leaders. It was in the interest of all involved for the coalitions to work. Many efforts were made to sustain and improve relations between the two political parties (Laurence, 1999).

The history of political violence between these parties meant they needed to bury the hatchet and build a political alliance for the benefit of KwaZulu-Natal citizens. However, the violence between them continued, straining their relationship and putting in jeopardy political cooperation. Well-documented events of brutality include the Shobashobane massacre (25 December 1995), the Richmond killings (peaking in 1997/98) and the Nongoma assassinations (1999–2000), indicating difficulty in undoing political violence in KwaZulu-Natal (Taylor, 2002). The party leaders reached a truce by mid-1996 and the 'political leaders declared the political conflict over', even though 'flashpoints' kept presenting themselves, needing to be 'understood in terms of a matrix of integrated issues that [were] rooted in what [was] a systemic problem' (Taylor, 2002: 474). The truce declared by party leaders sent a ceasefire message to constituencies, for their political cooperation to endure. The coalition reinforced the need to broker sustainable peace between the ANC and the IFP.

The 1994 premier of the province, the IFP's Frank Mdlalose, promised when opening the provincial legislature in that year, 'I pledge that in this house and beyond its walls, there is no longer any such animal as a political enemy' (Keller, 1994). This commitment to peace-building was demonstrated by the appointment of three ANC politicians as MECs: Jacob Zuma, Zweli Mkhize and S'bu Ndebele. This arrangement was reminiscent of consociational democracy, a notion that had been explored pre-1994 (given the ethnic and racial tensions prevalent in the later years of apartheid, especially in KwaZulu-Natal; see Lijphart, 1998; Taylor, 2008; Dlamini, 2015). Consociational democracy places emphasis on politics 'of accommodation whereby the leaders of the diverse segments are convinced not only of the desirability of preserving the whole system, but also of the need to find solutions to problems in spite of their ideological and other disagreements' (Southall, 1983: 79).

The overarching desire for accommodative politics led to an agreement between the ANC and the IFP in 1995, whereby 'in Durban [municipality; later renamed eThekwini] the two parties would be represented on a 50-50 basis on the "non-statutory" side in the run-up to the interim council's formation' (Eveleth, 1996). It was another commitment to extend cooperation between the two parties, beyond national and provincial government. It was short-lived, however, as the IFP soon reneged on the agreement. It opted to work with the NNP and the Democratic Party (DP) which secured the mayorship, even though the city was seen as an ANC stronghold. Elements of distrust and calculated cooperation began to characterise the ANC-IFP coalition in KwaZulu-Natal. As evidence of the strained relationship,

Table 15.1: Electoral trends in KwaZulu-Natal illustrating changing dynamics, 1994–2019

Political party	Provincial election results in KwaZulu-Natal											
	1994		1999		2004		2009		2014		2019	
	%	seats	%	seats	%	seats	%	seats	%	seats	%	seats
African Christian Democratic Party (ACDP)	0.67	1	1.81	1	1.78	2	0.68	1	0.44	0	0.48	1
African National Congress (ANC)	32.23	26	39.38	32	46.98	38	62.95	51	64.52	52	54.21	44
African Transformation Movement (ATM)	-	-	-	-	-	-	-	-	-	-	0.49	1
Congress of the People (Cope)	-	-	-	-	-	-	1.29	1	0.16	0	0.14	0
Democratic Party/ Democratic Alliance (DP/DA)	2.15	2	8.16	7	8.35	7	9.15	7	12.76	10	13.90	11
Economic Freedom Fighters (EFF)	-	-	-	-	-	-	-	-	1.85	2	9.71	8
Inkatha Freedom Party (IFP)	50.32	41	41.90	34	36.82	30	22.40	18	10.86	9	16.35	13
Minority Front (MF)	1.34	1	2.93	2	2.61	2	2.05	2	1.02	1	0.52	1
National Freedom Party (NFP)	-	-	-	-	-	-	-	-	7.31	6	1.57	1
National Party/New National Party (NP/NNP)	11.21	9	3.28	3	0.52	0	-	-	-	-	-	-
Pan Africanist Congress (PAC)	0.73	1	0.26	0	0.19	0	0.07	0	0.08	0	0.07	0
United Democratic Movement (UDM)	-	-	1.17	1	0.75	1	0.23	0	0.17	0	0.10	0

Source: Author's compilation, based on IEC, 2019.

the municipal elections in KwaZulu-Natal took place seven months later than in the rest of the country, in June 1996, after being postponed twice (Johnston and Johnson, 1997). The IFP registered losses; it was especially its 1994 white voter support and votes from black township areas that had declined (Johnston and Johnson, 1997).

The ANC, however, surpassed its expectations in Durban and Pietermaritzburg, emerging victorious, and registered victories in other urban areas, including Newcastle, the hometown of the then IFP premier Frank Mdlalose (*The Irish Times*, 1996). This established the ANC as more palatable to urban residents, while the IFP remained dominant in rural areas and small towns across the province. (In some urban areas, the IFP even trailed minority parties such as the Minority Front, the NNP and the DP.) This was unsurprising, as the IFP had been founded to service and sustain institutions of 'self-rule' in the rural areas of the then KwaZulu homeland, endearing itself to traditional leaders and locals alike. Therefore, campaigns and political visibility had an IFP bias in the rural areas, with many of the areas treated at the time as no-go areas for the ANC.

The electioneering behaviour in the 1996 municipal elections contradicted the pronouncement by Mdlalose that the IFP and the ANC would no longer be political enemies. When the stakes were high, the IFP and the ANC supplemented their rhetoric of political cooperation and contested each other vigorously. The 1996 culture and results, however, also did not stop attempts to forge ahead with peace negotiations to achieve better coexistence on the ground across KwaZulu-Natal.

This also led to serious overtures for greater courtship. For example, in December 1997, senior IFP leader Lionel Mtshali attended the ANC's 50th elective conference (Laurence, 1999), where Nelson Mandela was handing over the ANC leadership baton to Thabo Mbeki. Mtshali's attendance was meant to signify reconciliation between the two parties and reflected affirmation at the time of shared history between the IFP and the ANC. In 1998, Thabo Mbeki was invited as a guest of King Zwelithini and Prince Mangosuthu Buthelezi at the commemorative event of the 1838 Battle of Blood River (Laurence, 1999). This gesture signalled that traditional leaders in the province were accepting of the ANC and its leadership. It also meant the concept of 'no-go areas' was diminishing. The messaging was clear – the coalition between the ANC and the IFP at the national and provincial levels was yielding closer and increasing cooperation, and party members of both organisations were encouraged to follow suit.

The ANC's incumbency as the national government with Nelson Mandela's leadership started to resonate with IFP constituencies, winning over parts of the IFP base to the ANC. Also, the ANC MECs serving in the IFP-led KwaZulu-Natal government were using their positions to strategically position the ANC in the province. Narend Singh of the IFP admits to this, saying the party 'realised that ANC MECs were trying to use their positions to take power. They used the largesse afforded them by their provincial ministries to campaign for the ANC. In this, they were supported by their even more cash-flush colleagues in national government' (Joubert, 2018: 115–116). ANC MEC S'bu Ndebele served as MEC for transport and used this position to launch novel initiatives that endeared him to business people and local communities. In 1998, for example, he introduced the Vukuzakhe ('rise up and build yourselves') programme for the development of emerging contractors. He later explained that the intention was to build a 'regulatory framework that goes beyond the generally applied preferential procurement system by setting aside a budget that is reserved for Vukuzakhe contractors'.[1] The ANC MEC was thereby seen as delivering on economic-transformation objectives. Inevitably, the process established a base for 'new money', increasing prospects for funding for the ANC from this new empowerment patronage network.

Concurrently, however, there were debates that compromised the cooperative relationship between the ANC and the IFP, such as the issue of where the provincial capital city should be. The debate, pitting Ulundi (the capital of the KwaZulu government) against Pietermaritzburg (the capital of Natal province) raged for years, with the two cities used alternately. It became a June 1999 election campaign issue (Maharaj, 2001). It contributed to a growing schism between the IFP national leadership and its premier, Mdlalose. The matter was eventually settled in 2004, when the ANC assumed the premiership of the province, with Pietermaritzburg becoming the seat of provincial government.

This first period of coalition government in KwaZulu-Natal (1994–97) also marked important intraparty changes, which affected party strength and standing in relation to competitors. Political disagreements within the IFP began to heighten, leading to the resignation of its premier in 1997. At the centre of the disagreement were the patronage networks of the IFP in the form of illegal casino operators (Mthembu and Eveleth, 1997). Mdlalose, as premier, wanted to shut them down. However, the illegal operators protested to the IFP, and Buthelezi intervened. Buthelezi, by then based in Pretoria as a cabinet member, convened clandestine meetings with trusted allies to assess these IFP rifts. Mdlalose disagreed with attempts to block his policy wishes. Mdlalose was also at odds with his party leadership when, in late 1996, he expressed the desire to be released from his duties as provincial chair of the IFP (Mthembu and Eveleth, 1997). Due to his closeness to Jacob Zuma, one of the ANC members in his provincial cabinet, the IFP saw Mdlalose as a potential threat, as he could cross over to the 'enemy', the ANC. After Mdlalose stepped down from the premiership, the IFP denied that he had been pushed to resign. In 1998 the ANC-led GNU appointed Mdlalose as ambassador to Egypt. In this way, the ANC used this rift to weaken the IFP, sending away an influential leader while also cushioning him from financial loss, clear courtship for his future cooperation. Mdlalose was replaced with Ben Ngubane, who led the provincial government from March 1997 until the 1999 elections.

Attempts to fortify the provincial coalition: 1999–2004

A final constitution was adopted in June 1996. It did not provide for a GNU but the provision that parties of a certain parliamentary strength could claim a limited number of ministerial positions remained in place until 1999. In fact, when the new constitution was adopted, the NNP decided to leave the GNU while the IFP remained from 1999 to 2004 on the basis of ANC outreach rather than constitutional requirement. Ahead of the 1999 national and provincial elections there was much speculation that Thabo Mbeki intended to appoint Buthelezi as his deputy president (Laurence, 1999). Being in national government was beneficial to the IFP's leader, as it meant higher income as well as security – something he had become accustomed to as leader of the KwaZulu homeland. It also visited prestige on Buthelezi, who had been named acting president several times by Mandela (Beck, 2000). For Mbeki, considering Buthelezi as his deputy president indicated his (Mbeki's) willingness to use the IFP-ANC coalition to resolve some of his own political challenges: appointing Buthelezi would mean not appointing the ANC's then deputy president, Jacob Zuma.

Gumede (2007) details how a delegation of ANC leaders from KwaZulu-Natal, led by S'bu Ndebele, visited Mbeki to address this issue. The aim was to convince Mbeki to attach bold terms and conditions to an offer to Buthelezi: they demanded that the IFP relinquish the KwaZulu-Natal position of premier to the ANC, possibly to Ndebele himself. This meant that the ANC did see the IFP as a dependable partner, but at the same time some in the ANC sought to exploit the opportunity for its own benefit. Buthelezi was also visited with a choice: between personal prestige – to a position of power that he coveted, and which guaranteed him a lifetime income – and standing firm to assert his party's independence without compromising the will of the electorate and loyal members. Buthelezi and the IFP were mindful that coalition arrangements may entail that the dominant party eventually swallow or neutralise a coalition partner.

Sceptical of Mbeki's motives, some leaders within the IFP advised Buthelezi to demand the post be upgraded to that of prime minister. They also demanded considerations 'for greater provincial autonomy and more powers for traditional leaders at local government level' (Gumede, 2007: 313), a longstanding campaign point of the IFP first mooted in the Buthelezi Commission of 1982.[2] This presented zero-sum brinkmanship on the part of the IFP, leaving Mbeki with no choice but to abandon the deputy-president idea and retain Buthelezi as minister of home affairs. The coalition between the two parties would continue without the ANC's attempt at what appeared as a negotiated 'coup' on the IFP in KwaZulu-Natal succeeding. Once this had failed, the post-1999 government in KwaZulu-Natal was formed, with the IFP appointing Lionel Mtshali as the premier.

The IFP suffered provincial electoral losses in the 1999 elections, reducing its seats from 41 to 34, while the ANC increased its seats from 26 to 32. This strengthened the ANC's hand for joint governance, and four ANC leaders were appointed into MEC positions – Dumisani Makhaye, Mike Mabuyakhulu, S'bu Ndebele and Zweli Mkhize. Singh of the IFP admitted that 'from 1999 we found it very difficult to work with the ANC' (Joubert, 2018: 115). One of the difficulties was the absence of a coalition agreement for the parties to hold each other accountable and develop a minimum programme of action on common areas of interest. In the absence of an agreement, much was left to the whims of personalities and the politics of ego. As the wheels began to fall off ANC-IFP cooperation in KwaZulu-Natal, the IFP looked at possible cooperation with the DA ahead of the 2000 local government elections (Joubert, 2018). This was an early warning sign that the IFP would not be beholden to the ANC as it sought political survival and growth in KwaZulu-Natal.

However, as power shifted, peaceful coexistence gained traction and the ANC became more confident of its growth in KwaZulu-Natal. The ANC-IFP relationship nevertheless was strained, given the political threat that the ANC posed to the IFP. The IFP feared being emasculated, smothered by the national brand of the ANC that was growing in people's minds, while the IFP was struggling to modernise and extend its political footprint beyond KwaZulu-Natal. The two parties were now separated by only two seats in the legislature, indicating the ANC's emergence as a future government. The ANC's confidence was evident, with some of its leaders being vocal critics of the IFP-led provincial coalition. ANC MEC Dumisani Makhaye, a persistent critic of IFP premier Mtshali, likened Mtshali to 'Adolf Hitler and the devil' (News24, 2003a). Mtshali felt undermined (Joubert, 2018), and in December 2002 fired Mabuyakhulu and Makhaye as MECs. He awarded the positions to two DA members of the provincial parliament, Roger Burrows and Wilson Ngcobo (Khumalo, 2002; Francis, 2011). The provincial cabinet now consisted of six IFP MECs, two from the ANC and two from the DA. Coalition politics in the province had changed gears.

The ANC never adopted a passive stance in its coalition with the IFP, and the parties remained in political competition for control of the province. Compounding the problems of coalition politics was the policy of floor-crossing, permitting public representatives to join or find a new political party and remain in the legislature. In March 2003 the KwaZulu-Natal MEC for education, Gabriel Ndabandaba, defected from the IFP to the ANC, with premier Mtshali claiming he had fired the MEC (Khumalo and Bisetty, 2003). A DA member of the provincial parliament, Omie Singh, had also defected to the ANC, a few days ahead of Ndabandaba. This left the ANC short of just two members to tip the balance of voting in the provincial legislature and wrest control of the province (Khumalo and Bisetty, 2003). The ANC now had 40 seats with its new allies, and the IFP-DA coalition 38 seats. Two other parties in the legislature, the African Christian Democratic Party (ACDP) and the United Democratic Movement (UDM), each had one seat, thus becoming potential kingmakers if a motion of no confidence was to be tabled. Floor-crossing thus strengthened the ANC's position, and it demanded that Mtshali reinstate both Mabuyakhulu and Makhaye in their MEC positions or face a motion of no confidence. The issue led to public spats between the ANC and the IFP, which required intervention by the national leaderships in the form of a meeting between Mbeki and Buthelezi (News24, 2003b). Eventually, Mabuyakhulu and Makhaye were reinstated – an IFP admission that power was tilting in favour of the ANC. For the IFP, the move to replace the duo with DA members had been a signal that the IFP was willing to materially shift its allegiance in KwaZulu-Natal, despite the existing national cooperation between the IFP and the ANC.

Mbeki's relationship with Buthelezi, then minister of home affairs, was also beleaguered by controversy around the same period, especially after Mbeki appointed Billy Masetlha, a former director-general of the South African Secret Service, as director-general for the Department of Home Affairs (Gumede, 2007), to replace Buthelezi's appointee, Albert Mokoena. Buthelezi threatened court action against the appointment of Masetlha, eventually forcing Mbeki to seek a resignation from Masetlha in order to mend relations with Buthelezi. In 2003 the duo ended up in court when Mbeki challenged Buthelezi about a draft immigration bill that the two were divided on. Following the 2004 elections, Mbeki released Buthelezi from his cabinet, and instead attempted to appoint junior IFP members into the national government, a move that led the IFP leadership to withdraw the party's nominated cabinet ministers (Gumede, 2007). Therefore, the greater the fracture at the national level, the higher the stakes became for coalitions in provincial and local government.

In the interim, the IFP-DA alliance was made possible because the two parties shared 'organising principles such as federalism, and specific policy preferences in the areas of HIV/AIDS, education, crime, employment and poverty reduction strategies' (Francis, 2011: 244). This alliance morphed into a 'coalition for change' as the two organisations joined forces for the 2004 elections. For the DA, this campaign alliance meant the party could access once impenetrable areas, further increasing the culture of political competition. The IFP, aware that its predominant regional power status (Tshishonga, 2012) was slipping away, soon realised it would need some agility to survive.

The twilight of the ANC-IFP coalition: 2004–06

By 2004, there was no ANC-IFP cooperation at the national level,[3] leaving KwaZulu-Natal to configure its own arrangements. Effectively, there was no coalition agreement, and no bottom line on what form the cooperation would take in the wake of the ANC superseding the IFP in the province. The ANC-IFP cracks widened. The ANC was flippant in its treatment of the IFP because the latter had co-campaigned with the DA, leaving the ANC to seek the cooperation of smaller parties to form a government, and discard the IFP as a coalition partner. Ahead of the 2004 national and provincial elections, the IFP led a fragile provincial government and attempted to rebrand itself. The party kept communicating that it 'had strengthened its position through its alliance with the DA' (Africa, 2019: 383). But the electorate was not convinced and the IFP's share of the provincial vote declined from 41.9 per cent in 1999 to 36.8 per cent in 2004 (Africa, 2019), losing four seats and remaining with 30. The ANC increased its standing by six seats in the provincial legislature, which meant that it now occupied 38 out of 80 seats. The ANC's success was in part influenced by its new campaign strategy, which moved from rallies to deploying 'high ranking officials in a door-to-door campaign' (Letsholo, 2005: 5). This brought the party closer to people at the community level, especially in rural areas once dominated by the IFP.

Despite the IFP having campaigned with the DA, the ANC's newly elected premier (elected with the help of small parties, especially the Minority Front), S'bu Ndebele, announced a provincial cabinet that featured two IFP members, Celani Mtetwa and Nyanga Ngubane. The IFP requested Ngubane and Mtetwa to withdraw from Ndebele's provincial cabinet, as their appointment was without the 'express approval' of the party (Mashigo, 2004). However, the ANC and the IFP reached out to each other through Ndebele and Musa Zondi, the IFP national spokesperson at the time. After negotiations, three IFP MECs, Blessed Gwala, Nyanga Ngubane and Narend Singh, were appointed to the provincial executive. (Narend Singh resigned soon thereafter following personal scandal.)

Former IFP national chair Ziba Jiyane was another important player in provincial party politics. He left the IFP in 2005 after characterising Buthelezi as 'undemocratic and a dictator' (Terreblanche and Monare, 2005) and established a splinter organisation, the National Democratic Convention (Nadeco). Nadeco managed to recruit the ACDP's KwaZulu-Natal leader, Hawu Mbatha. Jiyane's rise to the national executive council of the IFP in 2004 had been without Buthelezi's blessing, and was seen as a triumph for the youth testing the boundaries within the party (Terreblanche and Monare, 2005). Jiyane was fairly popular within the IFP and out of it. Nadeco's entry into the KwaZulu-Natal political landscape meant that some IFP local councillors defected to Nadeco and were re-elected to municipal councils under the new party in the March 2006 local government elections. The balance of forces in KwaZulu-Natal was affected. Suddenly, some municipalities needed coalitions to form governments (see next section). One such instance involved Ndwedwe local municipality, where the IFP cooperated with the DA and Nadeco against the ANC (Stolley, 2006). It infuriated ANC leaders. This was when Ndebele, also chair of the ANC in the province, fired the two IFP MECs. Ndebele registered his sense of betrayal by the IFP:

> An issue that has never been satisfactorily resolved has been the inability of the IFP to extend the relationship [at provincial government] to the Local Government level... But the relentless action of undermining and distorting the democratic mandate at local government level by the IFP has left me as Premier and leader of the party, that got the majority of the popular vote at

both the provincial and local government elections in 2004 and 2006, with no option (Stolley, 2006).

Moreover, Jiyane was a controversial figure because of his involvement in deals in the KwaZulu-Natal province. According to reports, Jiyane's Masithembe Bus Transport company was awarded a multimillion-rand contract by the ANC provincial government to operate a fleet of buses (Mthembu, 2007). The contract, which had put Jiyane in debt, was halted by the provincial government in May 2007 as punishment for Nadeco's collaboration with the IFP and the DA in the Ndwedwe local municipality. These Jiyane-Nadeco developments demonstrated how the ANC was consolidating its power, squeezing out competitors politically and monetarily from patronage networks.

On the political side of its consolidation of power, the ANC reached out to the Minority Front as its new coalition partner, with Minority Front leader Amichand Rajbansi becoming the MEC for sport and recreation (Khumalo, 2006). The Minority Front, which appeared insignificant with its two seats in the legislature, was a curious partner for the ANC. But the party's mainly Indian constituency was one the ANC wished to access for its political consolidation project in the province. Rajbansi, who was ambitious, made himself indispensable to the ANC, while the ANC pampered and cared for him (see Naidoo, 2011). For Rajbansi, the reward was increased prestige, and access to the higher networks offered by his cooperation with the ANC.

In November 2006 the ANC-IFP provincial coalition ended. The ANC premier fired the remaining two IFP MECs, in the wake of intraparty IFP developments: a split-off and new non-ANC coalitions that were established in local municipalities, following the 2006 local government elections. The demise of the turbulent ANC-IFP coalition of 12 years was in many respects inevitable. Each of the parties had pursued the coalition for clientelism – in which political parties act as patrons and constituencies are viewed as clients – as 'the particularistic allocation of state resources aimed at maximizing a political actor's probability of election' (Indridason, 2005: 440).

The ANC's consolidation of power in KwaZulu-Natal, 2009

The ANC proceeded to grow and officially govern KwaZulu-Natal without requiring coalition partners in 2009, following the national and provincial elections. With the ANC's KwaZulu-Natal kingpin, Jacob Zuma, now leading the party nationally and governing South Africa as national president, the ANC consolidated its provincial power. It amassed 51 seats in the provincial legislature, while the IFP lost 12 seats compared with 2004. Much of these dynamic shifts were attributed to Zuma's popularity and mass appeal across KwaZulu-Natal at the time, with Zuma's play on Zulu nationalism the weapon that spurred the ANC's growth.[4]

In the lead-up to the Polokwane conference that elected him president of the ANC in 2007, Zuma's campaign featured a Zulu identity (for example, '100% Zulu boy'-branded T-shirts). This worked in rallying against what was a perception of 'Xhosanostra' within the ANC – the fact that the ANC leadership was heavily dominated by Xhosa people, given the Eastern Cape being the birthplace of three successive presidents, Oliver Tambo, Nelson Mandela and Thabo Mbeki. After the 2007 ANC election, Zuma effectively used his Zulu identity to break the IFP's political control of KwaZulu-Natal (Twala, 2010), especially appealing to traditional leadership and other regional elites in the province, including taxi bosses. Zuma sought opportunities for the ANC to diffuse its political presence across the province and thus expand the ANC's electoral prospects.

The battle for local government control: The curious case of the National Freedom Party

While the ANC was growing provincially, local government remained tightly contested. In the 2000 local government elections, the IFP controlled eight of the 10 district municipaliwties in the province, and 41 of 62 local municipalities, but by September 2005 it had lost two districts and five municipalities to the ANC (Terreblanche and Monare, 2005). This was due mainly to the IFP splinter organisation, Nadeco, and councillors who used the floor-crossing policy to join the ANC. The ANC was thus beginning to capitalise on internal rifts within the IFP, as part of consolidating power in the province through establishing new coalitions (without the IFP) in some municipalities. But Nadeco was an undependable partner; it also became a one-man show, embroiled in factional battles, and some members returned to the IFP. The IFP launched Operation Buyelekhaya (meaning 'return home') to recruit Nadeco members to reconsider their disillusionment and return to their IFP home. The IFP was not about to give up its dominance in KwaZulu-Natal local government. However, the party was not resolving its internal strife – the predominant source of its political weakness, caused by refusal to move beyond the cultish politics centred on Buthelezi (Piper, 2014).

A second noteworthy fallout within the IFP resulted in its national chair, Veronica Zanele Magwaza-Msibi, leading a splinter organisation that took with it a substantial number of popular IFP leaders. Magwaza-Msibi was an IFP firebrand who had a significant impact on local government in KwaZulu-Natal. She was the mayor of the Zululand District Municipality from 2000 to 2010, earning the respect of her peers and establishing vast networks. The events that led to that split are documented in a judgment delivered by the KwaZulu-Natal High Court in Pietermaritzburg (*Mcoyi and Others v Inkatha Freedom Party, Mgwaza-Msibi v Inkatha Freedom Party*, 2011). The IFP had decided to postpone its 2009 national elective conference. There were reports in the party of support to get Magwaza-Msibi to succeed Buthelezi as party president. In that year she was IFP premier candidate in KwaZulu-Natal, a recognition of her leadership strength. However, in January 2010 the IFP's national leadership took a decision to redeploy Magwaza-Msibi to the provincial legislature, a move her supporters saw as a demotion. A founder of her intra-IFP support structure, The Friends of VZ, said the party wanted to move her 'because they want to make sure that she loses touch with the people at grass roots level' (Mdletshe and Papayya, 2010). The ANC Women's League KwaZulu-Natal chair concurred with the criticisms of the redeployment. The ANC actors promised Magwaza-Msibi a home in the ANC if she opted to leave the IFP.

All indications were that the ANC wanted to exploit the rift in the IFP, and Buthelezi stubbornly refused to address the root cause of the IFP's problems – an absence of internal democracy. The IFP central structure acted to reinforce Buthelezi's will. The founders of The Friends of VZ[5] were investigated for 'divisive behaviour'; it was argued that they were officially propping up a factional structure. On 9 May 2010 the national council resolved unanimously to dismiss them. Magwaza-Msibi disassociated herself from the The Friends of VZ and voted in favour of the resolution, thereby securing time. The Friends of VZ in 2010 had claimed in court that the IFP's leadership was characterised by 'despotism and intolerance of competition', a claim similar to that made by Jiyane in 2005. The ANC once more took advantage of this restive moment within the IFP. In line with the ANC Women's League's statements, ANC leaders expressed their opinions on the IFP's internal power wrangles (Buthelezi, 2010) and strategically aligned themselves with the disgruntled faction within the IFP. With local government elections set for 2011, it was an opportunity to find allies from within the IFP and weaken the IFP.

In August 2010, Buthelezi addressed an extended IFP national council meeting. In his speech he outlined the ANC's role in sowing divisions in the IFP; he cited various ANC leaders remarking, for example, that Buthelezi was undemocratic and a dictator. The IFP national council resolved to institute disciplinary charges against Magwaza-Msibi, accusing her of politically divisive behaviour. This prompted the court challenge from Magwaza-Msibi and her supporters. Two separate court cases heard concurrently would eventually seal the parties' fates. The first case was a matter between the four aggrieved IFP members led by Wiseman Mcoyi, and the IFP, over it being compelled to hold a national conference; the second case was between Zanele Magwaza-Msibi and the IFP, over disciplinary charges put to her by the party (*Mcoyi and Others v Inkatha Freedom Party, Mgwaza-Msibi v Inkatha Freedom Party,* 2011).

Interpreting the crisis, the judge in the Magwaza-Msibi case observed that there was 'an internecine conflict going on in the IFP. The schism is manifest in two rival factions and despite Magwaza-Msibi's protestation the schism is between those of her supporters and what has been described, whether charitably or not, as the "old guard".' This conflict was about a battle 'for mastery of the soul and membership of the IFP and hence the pejorative terms used by one to describe the other'. The court found no compelling reasons to force the IFP to hold a national elective conference and legitimated the decisions of the IFP to expel Mgwaza-Msibi's supporters and to institute disciplinary proceedings against Magwaza-Msibi (*Mcoyi and Others v Inkatha Freedom Party, Mgwaza-Msibi v Inkatha Freedom Party*, 2011).

In early 2011 Magwaza-Msibi announced the formation of the National Freedom Party (NFP), with the intention to contest in the local government elections scheduled for 18 May 2011. She launched the NFP as 'a home to all South Africans, irrespective of their race, colour or creed' (News24, 2011). Buthelezi (2011) described the news as bitter-sweet, calling it an end to a painful chapter that was characterised by 'treachery and deceit, divisiveness and even violence'. Once more, Buthelezi was not taking any responsibility for causing the IFP's political demise.

The rift between the IFP and the NFP turned acrimonious. In fact, interparty violence ensued soon after the formation of the NFP. A tragic scene of brazen violence played out at the Ntuzuma Magistrate's Court precinct in the presence of police. NFP councillor Mzonjani Zulu was allegedly attacked with a spear by Siya Dlamini, an IFP supporter, at which Zulu drew a gun and discharged fatal shots (Madlala, 2012). Zulu had been at the court to support another NFP councillor, Bhungu Gwala, who was accused, along with his sons, of having murdered an IFP councillor. Additional incidents of intraparty violence within the NFP emerged as the stakes got higher following the outcome of the 2011 elections.

Given Magwaza-Msibi's popularity within the IFP and the visible rebellion she had unleashed on the party, it was clear that the NFP would dent the IFP in its core constituencies. The ANC immediately sought to court the NFP, since the future of many a KwaZulu-Natal municipality was suddenly in the balance, were the NFP to succeed. The NFP did succeed, to an extent (see Table 15.2), especially in the 2011 local elections: it chiselled away at IFP support. The NFP amassed 11 per cent of the provincial vote, appealing largely to youth and women disaffected with the IFP but unwilling to vote for the ANC.

The net result was the IFP losing control over 21 municipalities in KwaZulu-Natal (Hickel, 2015), with the majority of them coming under control of an ANC-NFP coalition. The IFP retained only two municipalities with a clear majority, Msinga and Ulundi (Berkowitz, 2016). This unprecedented outcome and the subsequent ANC-NFP coalition arrangements across several municipalities gave rise to suspicion that the NFP had been an ANC project all along.

As kingmakers in various municipalities, some NFP councillors began to quarrel over positions and political cooperation with the ANC. In at least three municipalities – uMlalazi in eShowe, Umtshezi at Estcourt and Imbabazane near Estcourt – signs of rebellion from NFP councillors were visible. NFP councillors in these three municipalities preferred political cooperation with the IFP, a move that elicited threats of expulsion from the NFP leadership, given that they had signed a memorandum of understanding for cooperation with the ANC in all 19 hung municipalities (Miya, 2011). NFP leaders were unwilling to have their allegiance to the ANC betrayed. Then-president Jacob Zuma appointed Magwaza-Msibi as a deputy minister after the 2014 national and provincial elections. The IFP leadership described Magwaza-Msibi as an ANC proxy participating in 'a divide-and-rule strategy intended to consign the IFP to the dustbin of history' (Hickel, 2015: 201).

By 2016 the wheels had come off in the NFP; it had been reduced to a nonentity. Internal power struggles had wreaked havoc. Some party leaders resisted having a national elective conference, an ironic twist, given the NFP's own erstwhile reasons for having exited the IFP. The NFP's declining fortunes were related to Magwaza-Msibi suffering a stroke in late 2014. It removed her from public life for a considerable time; she only reappeared in the national assembly two years later (Makinana, 2016). All along, Zuma nevertheless retained her as deputy minister for science and technology, even with her reduced ability, a clear abidance with their political pact. She resigned as an MP on the eve of the 2019 general elections.

The rebound of the IFP and emergence of other parties, 2015–20

As the NFP floundered, the IFP slowly started to rebound. Berkowitz (2017) traces early signs of the IFP's resurgence:

Table 15.2: Coalition formations in main municipalities where the NFP was present, 2011 and 2016

Political party[i]	Local election coalition formations	
	2011	2016[ii]
UMzinyathi District	ANC-NFP coalition	IFP-led coalition
Zululanda District	NFP-ANC coalition	IFP-led coalition
Okhahlamba	ANC-NFP coalition	ANC
eNdumeni	ANC-NFP coalition	IFP-led coalition
Nquthu[iii]	ANC-NFP coalition	IFP-led coalition
Umvoti	ANC-NFP coalition	ANC
eMadlangeni	ANC-NFP coalition	ANC
Dannhauser	ANC-NFP coalition	ANC
eDumbe	NFP	ANC-led coalition
UPhongolo	ANC-NFP coalition	ANC
AbaQulusi	ANC-NFP coalition	IFP-led coalition
Nongoma	NFP-ANC coalition	IFP
Jozini	ANC-NFP coalition	IFP-led minority
Mtubatuba	ANC-NFP coalition	IFP-led coalition
uMlalazi	ANC-NFP coalition	ANC
Mthonjaneni	ANC-NFP coalition	IFP
Nkandla	ANC-NFP coalition	IFP

[i] Umtshezi and Imbabazane do not appear as they were amalgamated ahead of the 2016 municipal elections.
[ii] Results do not factor in ward by-elections after 2016.
[iii] At Nquthu a coalition government could not be brokered and a by-election was held in May 2017.

Source: IEC and media reports, 2011, 2016.

Between 2011 and 2015 the IFP won a handful of strategically vital by-elections in some of the very municipalities where the ANC-NFP majority was as slim as one seat. In a December 2012 round of by-elections the party won a ward off the NFP in Hlabisa and another off the ANC in Nkandla. In 2015 the IFP repeated the trick with a by-election win in Ntambanana. The party had regressed from control of twenty municipalities to just two in 2011, but by 2015 the IFP's tally was up to five.

An ANC-NFP coalition government in Mtubatuba local municipality was dogged by significant governance problems, leading to its dissolution by the provincial government in 2015. The move was read as a sign that the ANC in the province would not be protecting the NFP at all costs. On the other hand, the ANC might have sensed the NFP was 'careering towards oblivion' (Berkowitz, 2017) and saw a chance to wrest full control of the municipality. The Mtubatuba by-election in May 2015 led to the ANC increasing its seats from 15 to 18, the IFP sustaining its 15 seats, and the NFP dropping from five to two. Three new parties entered the fray with one seat each: the Economic Freedom Fighters (EFF), the Democratic Alliance (DA) and the African Independent Congress (AIC).

The new parties had started entering soon after the 2011 local elections. The EFF did preparatory work for its provincial entrance. EFF leader Julius Malema visited Buthelezi at his Durban offices in January 2014. The strategic meeting was for Malema to apologise for utterances he had made about the IFP when he was president of the ANC Youth League – the EFF knew it would get a hostile reception without this overture. Malema had charged, 'There is no democracy in the IFP … an old man who is refusing to go on retirement even when he is sick wants to die president of the IFP' (Kings, 2014). For the IFP, the EFF presented a possible future coalition partner. There was a clear mutual interest for a united front against the ANC.

Real disappointment was yet to come for the NFP. In 2016 the party was disqualified from participating in the local government elections, bar Nquthu local municipality, following delays and mismanagement over its participation payment to the Electoral Commission. This effectively meant the death of the NFP, leaving space for other parties to compete for its support base.

The 2016 local government elections saw the IFP rebound as it regained control of five municipalities through loose coalitions with the

DA and the EFF in Jozini, Mtubatuba, Abaqulusi (Vryheid), Ndumeni and Nqutu (African News Agency, 2016). The IFP gained a clear advantage over the ANC in two district municipalities, Umzinyathi and Zululand. In a concurrent coalition in the newly formed Estcourt/Loskop municipality (Inkosi Langalibalele local municipality), the Al Jama-ah party decided to go into a coalition with the ANC. The ANC had run out of coalition partners from the pool of stronger opposition parties in KwaZulu-Natal. The IFP went on to govern the two districts with the help of the EFF and the DA as coalition partners. The ANC no longer featured – at least at that time – in the plans of the IFP.

In principle, the DA, the IFP and the EFF decided not to work with the ANC after the 2016 local elections in the province. However, this changed for the IFP in 2019, when the DA fell into disarray, losing its federal leader, Mmusi Maimane, and Johannesburg mayor, Herman Mashaba. With Johannesburg without a mayor, the ANC courted the IFP to support its mayoral candidate, Geoff Makhubo, in possible exchange for support in some KwaZulu-Natal municipalities. The IFP voted for Makhubo, a move that peeved the DA provincial leader in KwaZulu-Natal, who accused the IFP of dishonesty. He said, 'The IFP approached us [KwaZulu-Natal DA], and gave us many reasons why they could not work with the ANC. We then opted in the interest of KwaZulu-Natal to support them [the IFP] and we did not take any position as a mayor, deputy mayor or speaker to show that it was not about us but it was about people' (Hans, 2019). The IFP responded that the grievance of the KwaZulu-Natal DA was misplaced, saying it had acted based on the prevalent dynamics in the City of Johannesburg. IFP national spokesperson Mkhuleko Hlengwa stated that 'at times in the City of Johannesburg we have been undermined, overlooked and isolated, contrary to the dictates of the Cooperation Agreement; but despite these challenges we have pressed on' (Hans, 2019).

It is clear that coalition arrangements in KwaZulu-Natal are in a precarious state, driven by multiple interests that often depend on dynamics beyond the province. Parties will continue to switch allegiances depending on strategic advantages to govern, especially for the ANC and the IFP, as they remain the more dominant players on the local government landscape in the province.

CONCLUSION

The future of coalitions in KwaZulu-Natal remains uncertain, given the shifting and inconsistent party-political interests that drive them. Coalitions are fragile when there is no agreement to which partners can be held. The ANC-IFP coalition was driven largely by unscripted beliefs and expectations: there was no effective point of reference for dispute resolution, hence the reliance on national leaders to mediate when schisms arose. Parties without an agreement tend to chase their own political interests, and to scramble for whatever benefits are available to them, even if it jeopardises the relationship between the parties to the coalition. Yet a coalition agreement that is not legally enforceable is not a panacea in its own right.

The ANC-IFP coalition was weakened when the two parties stopped cooperating at the national level. The focus shifted to KwaZulu-Natal, a province that had opened up to political competition and in which the ANC had been making inroads since 1994. The growth trajectory tilted in the ANC's favour, and the parting of ways with the IFP in 2006 led to greater visibility for the ANC as it dominated the cabinet with the assistance of a relatively small party that posed negligible competition. Holding more MEC positions in the provincial executive also meant increased visibility and patronage networks in the province for the ANC. The IFP, on the other hand, realised that loyalty to its coalition with the ANC could further harm the party, as the provincial coalition had worked much to the IFP's detriment and the ANC's gain. Thus, the IFP turned its focus to local government, consolidating its core constituencies until the founding of the NFP, which broke the IFP's dominance in rural parts of KwaZulu-Natal.

Two splinter organisations, Nadeco and the NFP, altered the growth trajectory of the IFP. However, these splinter organisations have not been sustainable. They too suffered chronic problems of factionalism, intolerance and a lack of internal democracy – the very issues that had driven their founders away from the IFP. The IFP could be on a new political development trajectory, having elected a new president, Velenkosini Hlabisa, in 2019. Only time will tell if it is not too late to entrench a culture of internal democracy, given how its absence has weakened the party over the years, led to splits and fed coalition politics.

In retrospect, the 1994 coalition between the IFP and the ANC in KwaZulu-Natal paved the way for a political truce and serial coalition arrangements between the two parties. Their history of mutual violence meant their coexistence was fragile but conciliatory nevertheless. It was, however, this same coalition that wounded the IFP, as the ANC's popularity in national government crept into constituencies traditionally associated with the IFP. The ANC MECs appointed to the provincial cabinet maximised their positions to access IFP traditional constituencies while planting in the minds of citizens that ANC leaders too were capable of governing. The ANC went through a phase of not needing coalitions in KwaZulu-Natal, except at the local government level. Then it faced a significant decline in the 2019 elections. If this trend continues, a provincial coalition government will once more be in the offing. However, the stability of any future provincial coalition in KwaZulu-Natal will depend significantly on national developments, as this chapter has demonstrated how multi-layered political cooperation creates greater stability for coalition arrangements.

REFERENCES

Africa, C. 2019. 'Do election campaigns matter in South Africa? An examination of fluctuations in support for the ANC, DA, IFP and NNP, 1994–2019', *South African Journal of Political Studies*, 46 (4), 371–389.

African News Agency. 18 August 2016. 'IFP to control five KZN municipalities with DA, EFF help', *The Citizen*, https://citizen.co.za/news/south-africa/1255880/ifp-to-control-five-kzn-municipalities-with-da-eff-help/, accessed 25 May 2020.

Beck, R. 2000. *The History of South Africa*. London: Greenwood Press.

Berkowitz, P. 6 July 2016. 'How much will we (and the ANC) miss the NFP in the 2016 elections?', https://paulberkowitz.co.za/how-much-will-we-and-the-anc-miss-the-nfp-in-the-2016-elections/, accessed 27 May 2020.

Berkowitz, P. 21 May 2017. 'Nquthu by-elections: so many parties fighting so hard for such small spoils', http://paulberkowitz.co.za/category/politics/municipal-analysis/, accessed 27 May 2020.

Buthelezi, M. 22 August 2010. 'The origins of our internal troubles', *Politicsweb*, https://www.politicsweb.co.za/party/the-origins-of-our-internal-troubles--buthelezi, accessed 27 May 2020.

Buthelezi, M. 26 January 2011. 'Zanele Magwaza-Msibi has abandoned the IFP', https://www.ifp.org.za/zanele-magwaza-msibi-abandoned-ifp/, accessed 27 May 2020.

Constitution of the Republic of South Africa, Act No. 200 of 1993.

Dlamini, S. 2015. 'The theory and application of consociational democracy in South Africa: A case study of KwaZulu-Natal'. PhD thesis, University of South Africa.

Electoral Commission (IEC) of South Africa, www.elections.org.za, accessed 20 May 2020.

Eveleth, A. 19 April 1996. 'Real reasons behind ANC's election panic', *Mail & Guardian*, https://mg.co.za/article/1996-04-19-real-reasons-behind-ancs-election-panic/, accessed 25 May 2020.

Francis, S. 2011. *Institutionalizing Elites: Political elite formation and change in KwaZulu-Natal provincial legislature*. Boston: Brill.

Gibson, N. 2011. 'What happened to the "Promised Land"? A Fanonian perspective on post-apartheid South Africa', *Antipode*, 44 (1), 51–73.

Gumede, W. 2007. *Thabo Mbeki and the Battle for the Soul of the ANC*. London: Zed Books.

Hans, B. 10 December 2019. 'DA spits fire over IFP voting for ANC's Joburg mayoral candidate', *IOL*, https://www.iol.co.za/news/politics/da-spits-fire-over-ifp-voting-for-ancs-joburg-mayoral-candidate-38992825, accessed 29 May 2020.

Hickel, J. 2015. *Democracy as Death: The moral order of anti-liberal politics in South Africa*. Los Angeles: University of California Press.

Indridason, I. H. 2005. 'A theory of coalitions and clientelism: Coalition politics in Iceland, 1945–2000', *European Journal of Political Research*, 44, 439–464.

Johnston, A. and Johnson, R. 1997. 'The local elections in KwaZulu-Natal: 26 June 1996', *African Affairs*, 96 (384), 377–398.

Joubert, J. 2018. *Who Will Rule in 2019?* Johannesburg: Jonathan Ball Publishers.

Kaufman, S. 2017. 'South Africa's civil war, 1985–1995', *South African Journal of International Affairs*, 24 (4), 501–521.

Keller, B. 12 May 1994. 'Mandela completes his cabinet, giving Buthelezi a post', *The New York Times*, https://www.nytimes.com/1994/05/12/world/mandela-completes-his-cabinet-giving-buthelezi-a-post.html, accessed 30 May 2020.

Khumalo, S. 6 December 2002. 'Axed KwaZulu-Natal MECs look to IFP', *IOL*, https://www.iol.co.za/news/politics/axed-kwazulu-natal-mecs-look-to-ifp-98429, accessed 25 May 2020.

Khumalo, S. 2 November 2006. 'KZN cabinet gets a shake-up', *IOL*, https://www.iol.co.za/news/politics/kzn-cabinet-gets-a-shake-up-301318, accessed 25 May 2020.

Khumalo, S. and Bisetty, K. 25 March 2003. 'Education minister "couldn't take it anymore"', *IOL*, https://www.iol.co.za/news/politics/education-minister-couldnt-take-it-anymore-103219, accessed 25 May 2020.

Kings, S. 20 January 2014. 'Malema and Buthelezi make friendly', *Mail & Guardian*, https://mg.co.za/article/2014-01-20-malema-and-buthelezi-make-friendly/, accessed 10 June 2020.

Laurence, P. 7 June 1999. 'Attention turns to relationship of ANC and former foes IFP', *The Irish Times*, https://www.irishtimes.com/news/attention-turns-to-relationship-of-anc-and-former-foes-ifp-1.193152, accessed 10 June 2020.

Letsholo, S. 2005. 'How the ANC won the 2004 elections: Perspectives on voting behaviour in South Africa'. EISA Occasional Paper, 31, 1–16.

Lijphart, A. 1998. 'South African democracy: Majoritarian or consociational?', *Democratization*, 5 (4), 144–150.

Madlala, M. 16 October 2012. 'Court shooting: pistol was drawn out of his pants', *IOL*, https://www.iol.co.za/dailynews/news/court-shooting-pistol-was-drawn-out-of-his-pants-1403879, accessed 27 May 2020.

Maharaj, B. 2001. 'A tale of two capitals: Pietermaritzburg versus Ulundi', *South African Geographical Journal*, 83 (3), 198–207.

Makhanya, S. 23 August 2019. 'In conversation with IFP's Prince Mangosuthu Buthelezi – Part 2', *SABC News*, https://www.youtube.com/watch?v=CZwgabQy2zI, accessed 25 May 2020.

Makinana, A. 27 November 2016. 'Two years after her stroke, NFP head is back in the House', *News24*, https://www.news24.com/news24/SouthAfrica/News/two-years-after-her-stroke-nfp-head-is-back-in-the-house-20161126, accessed 27 May 2020.

Mashigo, L. 24 April 2004. 'Premier "not told" of IFP cabinet withdrawals', *IOL*, https://www.iol.co.za/news/politics/premier-not-told-of-ifp-cabinet-withdrawals-211343, accessed 10 June 2020.

Mcoyi and Others v Inkatha Freedom Party, Mgwaza-Msibi v Inkatha Freedom Party (5449/2010, 8622/2010) [2011] ZAKZPHC 1; 2011 (4) SA 298 (KZP) (17 January 2011).

Mdletshe, C. and Papayya, M. 27 January 2010. 'Redeployment sparks anger', *Sowetan Live*, https://www.sowetanlive.co.za/news/2010-01-27-redeployment-sparks-anger/, accessed 25 May 2020.

Miya, S. 6 June 2011. 'Hung municipalities: NFP councillors defy party by voting with IFP', *News24*, https://www.news24.com/news24/archives/witness/Hung-municipalities-NFP-councillors-defy-party-by-voting-with-IFP-20150430, accessed 10 June 2020.

Mthembu, B. 12 June 2007. 'Former Nadeco leader could lose it all', *IOL*, https://www.iol.co.za/news/politics/former-nadeco-leader-could-lose-it-all-361681, accessed 10 June 2020.

Mthembu, E. and Eveleth, A. 31 January 1997. 'How Mdlalose "resigned"',

Mail & Guardian, https://mg.co.za/article/1997-01-31-how-mdlalose-resigned/, accessed 10 June 2020.

Naidoo, Y. 31 December 2011. 'Bengal Tiger was a great survivor of politics', *TimesLIVE*, https://www.timeslive.co.za/politics/2011-12-31-bengal-tiger-was-the-great-survivor-of-politics/, accessed 20 May 2020.

News24. 16 April 2003 (2003a). 'Mtshali makes up with Makhaye', https://www.news24.com/News24/Mtshali-makes-up-with-Makhaye-20030416, accessed 5 June 2020.

News24. 7 April 2003 (2003b). 'Mtshali told to reinstate MECs', https://www.news24.com/News24/Mtshali-told-to-reintstate-MECs-20030407, accessed 10 June 2020.

News24. 25 January 2011. 'IFP breakaway party launched', https://www.news24.com/News24/ifp-breakaway-party-launched-20110125, accessed 25 May 2020.

Piper, L. 2009. 'Inkatha Freedom Party: The elephants' graveyard', in Southall, R. and Daniel, J. (eds.). *Zunami! The South African elections of 2009*. Johannesburg: Jacana Media.

Piper, L. 2014. 'Inkatha Freedom Party: The elephants' graveyard', in Schulz-Herzenberg, C. and Southall, R. (eds.) *Election 2014: The campaigns, results and future prospects*. Johannesburg: Jacana Media, 89–103.

Polity. 2004. 'Ndebele: Launch of provincial Vukuzakhe council', https://www.polity.org.za/article/ndebele-launch-of-provincial-vukuzakhe-council-05042004-2004-04-05, accessed 27 May 2020.

Southall, R. 1983. 'Consociationalism in South Africa: The Buthelezi Commission and beyond', *Journal of Modern African Studies*, 21 (1), 77–112.

Stolley, G. 2 November 2006. 'Ndebele sacks IFP MECs from KZN cabinet', *IOL*, https://www.iol.co.za/news/politics/ndebele-sacks-ifp-mecs-from-kzn-cabinet-301265, accessed 25 May 2020.

Taylor, R. 2002. 'Justice denied: Political violence in KwaZulu-Natal after 1994', *African Affairs,* 101, 473–508.

Taylor, R. 2008. 'Ending apartheid: The relevance of consociationalism', in Ben-Porat, G. (ed.) *The Failure of the Middle East Peace Process?* London: Palgrave Macmillan, 97–110.

Terreblanche, C. and Monare, M. 4 September 2005. 'IFP elects loyalist as new chairperson', *IOL*, https://www.iol.co.za/news/politics/ifp-elects-loyalist-as-new-chairperson-252542, accessed 25 May 2020.

The Irish Times. 29 June 1996. 'ANC sweeps KwaZulu towns', https://www.irishtimes.com/news/anc-sweeps-kwazulu-towns-1.62979, accessed 10 June 2020.

Tshishonga, N. 2012. 'IFP versus NFP – opening new spaces in once-no-go KwaZulu-Natal', in Booysen, S. (ed.) *Local Elections in South Africa*. Bloemfontein: Sun Media, 151–172.

Twala, C. 2010. 'Jacob Zuma's "Zuluness" appeal during the April 2009 elections in South Africa: An attempt to break the IFP's grip on Zulu social and political structures?', *Journal for Contemporary History*, 35 (2), 66–83.

Part V

The way forward: Mechanisms, lessons, futures

OVERALL, THE PICTURE OF COALITION POLITICS in South Africa is not an appealing one. It is one in which party politics rule. Elections that do not deliver an absolute majority to a political party tend to become meaningless as political parties and leaders enter the coalition arena and strike deals – frequently unstable – that do not prioritise citizen and voter interest. Optimal service delivery and sound, stable governance become secondary to the strategic wars the political parties wage to gain the upper hand by means of coalition formation after indecisive elections. Given these cultures and experiences of coalition politics in South Africa, the question arises: what is South Africa's coalitions future? A multitude of variables contribute to this equation – and this section synthesises the most relevant ones. To help order the cacophony, the section unpacks the hierarchy of driving forces, trends, mindsets of political parties, and events. Jointly and in conjunction with the mass of relevant detail that emerges from the chapters, this future-oriented synthesis signals to the coalition practitioner and planner how to direct and steer coalition practices once, or if, they become confirmed as South Africa's new political reality.

SIXTEEN

Political conditions that facilitate coalition formation and workability

Amuzweni Ngoma

Alliances and coalitions have become the mainstay of many democracies globally. Political parties and voters alike accrue experience and lessons on what drives and sustains alliances and coalitions, and the effects they have on policy, governance and society. This volume presents a range of case studies and identifies key phenomena that indicate the functionality and durability of party-political coalitions in their role of public governance. This chapter takes stock of a select set of strategic lessons on coalition politics and practice. It draws on coalition experiences in Africa and Europe, using Africa-to-Europe, Africa-to-Africa and Europe-to-Europe comparisons. To conclude the analysis and lead into the conclusion of the book, it offers theoretically selected cases on coalition practice, focusing on the factors that the discussions in this volume have shown to affect the negotiation and management of governing coalitions.

It uses a comparative case-study approach to illuminate the effects of six such phenomena on the practice of coalition politics: political culture, intraparty dynamics, party leadership, coalition negotiations, coalition agreements and electoral cycles. These are not the only determinants and conditions (see Figure 17.1 in the next chapter), but all are pivotal. Illustrations of how they typically play out in country settings help illuminate their current and future roles in coalition politics in South Africa.

The quality of the coalition experience, politics and practices is taken as the ability to sustain and meet the goals of the coalition. Coalition goals may extend into longer-term joint governance and even the reconstitution of political parties, but is more likely to be term-specific. Fluidity and dissolution are possible, if not probable, which gives rise to multiple opportunities for new coalition negotiation and constitution within a single electoral term. This experience is geared towards party leaders accessing power, indicating the manipulation of the political systems, and superficial institutionalisation of coalition practice as a form of government.

While European countries have longer histories of governing coalitions, party leaders are taking longer periods of time to convene successful coalitions, and record multiple failed takes at negotiation. As the electoral patterns in Europe continue to shift, coalition formation is increasingly characterised by the personal motivation and interest of party leaders rather than party and partisan interests, thereby weakening institutionalised coalition practice. Simultaneously, African countries and their politicians are rapidly gaining experience in the constitution of coalitions, especially minimal coalitions, whether or not these are sustained or meet intended policy and governance goals. The chapter concludes by showing that in both regions, while there are pragmatic differences in histories and drivers of coalition experiences, it is the quality of coalition practice that brings these experiences together.

POLITICAL CULTURE: MAURITIUS AND DENMARK

The prevailing political culture and the processes and mechanisms that guide coalition negotiation are influential factors in the type and quality of coalitions that are formed. Mauritius and Denmark have longstanding histories of coalition formation, and are selected to help review the interfacing of political culture and coalition politics. Both countries present insights into the positive evolution and inimical mutation of coalition politics. The culture of pursuing coalitions as a form of government does not depend on the society in question being homogeneous (Denmark) or heterogeneous (Mauritius) – the culture arises depending on the political parties over time being unable repeatedly to win absolute or outright majorities.

Mauritius

Mauritius is a longstanding African multiparty democracy that has maintained a largely peaceful democratic status since independence in 1968 (Mozaffar, 2005: 263).[1] It has been governed by coalitions – and its first coalition government lasted for 15 years (Kadima and Kasenally, 2006). Pre-electoral alliance formation and governing by coalition are entrenched practices that help define Mauritian political culture. Politicians have upheld coalitions as the central political strategy for 'accommodating ethnic diversity, building consensus and promoting social cohesion' (Kadima, 2014: 13). There is, in effect, long-term political socialisation of the practice of alliances and coalitions in Mauritius.

Owing largely to the country's ethnic and religious plurality, including a delineated social class character that is geographically concentrated, neither one of the two large and, at the time, dominant parties, the Mouvement Militant Mauricien (Mauritian Militant Movement) and the Labour Party, has been able to clinch an absolute electoral majority (Sithanen, 2003; Kadima, 2014). The Militant Socialist Movement, a breakaway party from the Mouvement Militant Mauricien, is the country's third largest party. 'Ethnic politics' are 'an important determinant' of coalition politics, argues Sithanen (2003: 3), and Mauritian political parties navigate the social cleavages using, among other things, pre-electoral alliances as a political strategy to win elections (Kadima, 2014: 13).

The 2019 election changed the balance of power in coalition formation, by giving the Militant Socialist Movement a majority that was sufficient to help it construct a minimal winning coalition without either of the former two dominant parties. The election did not erase the need for coalition formation but rewarded the one party, the Militant Socialist Movement, that had appeared in multiple iterations of Mauritian coalition governments in the course of the preceding three decades. In 1982, 1983, 1987, 1991 and 2000, it was variously in coalition with the Mouvement Militant Mauricien or the Labour Party. The only exceptions were in 1995, and again in 2005, when it became part of an opposition coalition, as the Labour Party and the Mouvement Militant Mauricien formed a coalition, which collapsed in 1998 (Carroll and Carroll, 1999). Thus, the Militant Socialist Movement, once a junior partner in Mauritian coalitions, evolved into the formateur position, forming a ruling coalition with smaller and regionally concentrated political parties. Few other junior coalition parties, particularly in Western European democracies, have managed to achieve such success (Klüver and Spoon, 2020).

Denmark

Denmark, like Mauritius, has had a longstanding culture of coalition formation. Denmark's enduring coalitions are aided by a culture of 'consensus politics' and 'political dialogue' (Madsen, 2015: 10). Political conflict, tension and competition associated with and arising from governing through coalitions is managed through this culture of 'consensus-oriented politics' (Madsen, 2015). Coalition government formation is eased by the fact that Denmark is a highly homogeneous society in which political parties do not mobilise on linguistic, religious or ethnic lines (Christiansen and Klemmensen, 2015: 31).

Fundamental to the understanding of Denmark's ingrained coalition culture is the fact that for over a century Denmark's proportional representation (PR) electoral system contributed in such a way that no single party won an absolute majority (Førde, 2015). The parties compete electorally, but coalesce and cooperate after the elections to govern (Madsen, 2015). Between 1945 and 2015 Denmark had 34 minority governments and four minimum winning coalitions (Bassi, 2016). These coalitions have been constituted relatively smoothly, taking on average 1.8 attempts (unsuccessful and then aborted initiatives) between 1945 and 1995 to constitute either a minority or a minimum winning coalition (Diermeier et al., 2001), illustrating the acceptance of coalition government practice. Yet the sheer number of coalition governments also indicates the inherent instability of coalition governing arrangements, even in an entrenched coalition culture.

Denmark's coalition political culture is sustained by good coalition governance practice, as parties must formulate coalition agreements that have to be approved by their national committees. This builds intraparty support for the coalition and establishes broad-based buy-in and consensus, as the discussion of the agreement is dispersed across all political parties, including sections of society such as the media (Kadima, 2015; Madsen 2015). Nevertheless, interparty policy impasse and intraparty conflict have been important reasons for the collapse of Danish coalitions. For example, the 2014 collapse was incited by disagreement on 'the sale of shares in the government owned national energy company', leading to the Danish Socialistisk Folkeparti (Socialist People's Party), abandoning the coalition with the Socialdemokraterne (Social Democrats) and Radikale Venstre (Social Liberal Party) coalition (Madsen, 2015: 10–11). The failed coalition negotiations after the 2015 elections indicated the shifting dynamic in Danish coalition culture – the Radikale Venstre formed a single-party minority government (Madsen, 2015). While this was unusual for Denmark, it continued to approach governing through established coalition practice, and formulated a coalition agreement *even in the absence of a coalition*. Its government programme was seen as a broad compromise that accommodated the interests of other parties (Pedersen, 2015). It was a symbolic agreement therefore that went unsigned by the other parties, but accommodated the interests of the Danish People's Party by increasing public spending, and those of the Liberal Alliance and Conservatives as it sought to reduce the taxes of Denmark's highest-income earners. In 2019 there was a change of power, and the new tendency of minority government – in this case by the Socialdemokraterne – on the basis of multiparty cooperation continued. It enjoyed a majority due to the confidence-and-supply arrangement with the Radikale Venstre, the Danish Socialistisk Folkeparti and the Enhedslisten – De Rød-Grønne (Red-Green Alliance).

These two cases show how a strong culture of coalition governing, while ingrained over time, also changes in content. Both cases show high levels of acceptance that coalition formation and supplementary cooperation between parties are the unavoidable precondition to forming a government. Yet the need to find alternatives to the set forms of multiparty government persists.

INTRAPARTY DYNAMICS: MOZAMBIQUE AND GERMANY

Intraparty dynamics, as in the politics and practices of political parties, their leaders and members affect coalition practice by (among other things) impacting on a party's ability to be an effective coalition partner (Berkowitz, 2011). Inimical intraparty dynamics, different decision-making regimes and divergent levels of acceptance of the need to compromise can weaken coalition management and stability. The cases of Mozambique and Germany demonstrate the destabilising effect on coalitions of the increasing dynamic of personal interest prevailing over partisan preferences.

Mozambique

In Mozambique opposition alliances have typically been formed to secure parliamentary representation since parties were unable to individually gain enough votes that surpass the PR electoral threshold (Kadima, 2014: 7). Within Mozambique's two-party system, smaller parties tend to coalesce towards either the Frente de Libertação de Moçambique (Frelimo) or the Resistência Nacional Moçambicana (Renamo) as the dominant parties (Nuvunga and Sitoe, 2013). Significantly, while many Mozambican political parties have been able to form such alliances and coalitions when they governed jointly, their ability to sustain these and obtain seats in parliament has been minimal, with only two coalitions managing to serve one or two parliamentary terms (Mulhovo, 2018).

In the country's coalition experience the Renamo-União Electoral (Renamo-UE) coalition is instructive, with Renamo being the 'ultra-dominant' force with 'every aspect of the coalition's strategies and operations' revolving around it (Kadima and Matsimbe, 2006: 160) and dominating the seven smaller alliance partners. Poor intraparty and intra-alliance democracy resulted in the party being accused of centralising coalition decision-making and treating the coalition as an extension of itself, leading to its subsequent collapse (Mulhovo, 2018). While Renamo stands out, hostile intraparty dynamics and practices among Mozambique's smaller parties have equally hampered their ability to constitute viable pre-electoral alliances. For example, weak trust among party members, exacerbated by internal conflict and contestation over party leadership positions, has hindered coalition formation. In the same way that coalition partners that drive individual party agendas weaken stability once a coalition is formed, coalition formation is also weakened by party members and/or leaders who pursue self-interest in coalition negotiation. Germany shares this with Mozambique but is differentiated by electoral timing.

Before parties can begin the typically arduous coalition or alliance negotiations, their ideological and policy positions need to have been agreed upon internally. The preference for positions should have at least been outlined, while the interface between party mechanisms and structures and the coalition should ideally also be detailed. This allows policy and office-seeking parties to maximise beneficial coalition outcomes. Yet coalition experience in Mozambique shows that this is not always the case. For example, party leaders from small political parties participating in electoral pacts that compete against Frelimo and Renamo may abdicate that relationship and declare support for a leading competitor, as happened in the 2009 elections when 'the chair of the Constructive Opposition declared support' to Frelimo (Mulhovo, 2018: 64). Similarly, in the 2014 Mozambican elections the party leader of the Opposition Hand in Hand accepted a Renamo parliamentary position, leaving the pre-electoral pact of small parties. In addition, 'the lack of statutes, lack of registration, lack of resources, mutual accusations of betrayal of the coalition principles among the members, lack of clear ideology and commitments to internal agreements, low trust and an unclear support base' collapsed Mozambique's small party pre-electoral alliances (Mulhovo, 2018: 64).

Germany

Having had 21 minimal-winning coalitions that have run government (Bassi, 2016: 251), Germany has an established history of coalition formation at the federal level and is well known for its coalition stability (Kirchsteiger and Puppe, 1997). Part of this derives from the ability of German political parties to speedily broker governing coalitions.

The 2017 election showed that this is changing (Hornung et al., 2020: 332). Instead of German parties seeking to maximise their respective party's office- and policy-seeking agendas after the 2017 election, coalition formation was hampered by intraparty conflict in which 'individual interests and personal trust rather than partisan unitary programmes were most relevant to the negotiation process and outcome' (Hornung et al., 2020: 332). Instead of the common occurrence in coalition politics of ideological distance from one another and divergent policy preferences collapsing coalition formation, a lack of mutual trust and the interplay of intraparty power games were central to the collapse of the first negotiations between the Christian Democratic Union of Germany/Christian Social Union in Bavaria (CDU/CSU), the Freie Demokratische Partei (Free Democratic Party) and the Grüne (Greens) (Hornung et al., 2020: 340, 341). The intraparty power games were characterised by leadership squabbles as party leaders sought to displace each other and gain leadership prominence. Dynamics such as party factional divisions, internal fragmentation and squabbles consumed and diverted the energy and resources of party members.

While electoral timing and the length of coalition experience distinguish Mozambique and Germany, leadership contestation, the risk of obfuscation and electoral decline that parties may suffer after being a junior coalition partner, especially when the senior partner does not uphold the coalition agreements, and the increasing dynamic of personal interest before partisan preferences, bring these countries' coalition experiences closer together (Hornung et al., 2020). Importantly, the rise of the intraparty dynamic in coalition negotiation erases the ability to closely predict future coalition constellations (Hornung et al., 2020).

PARTY LEADERSHIP: SOUTH AFRICA AND NIGERIA

Party leaders have the power to produce favourable political contexts in which alliances and coalitions form, thrive or disintegrate. The office- and power-seeking political and personal motives of party leaders, along with their leadership styles, have interfaced with interparty competition and intraparty dynamics in ways that have undermined coalition politics and practice, and resulted in the frequent dissolution of old coalitions and uptake of new ones. The motives, roles and personality of party leaders are enduring determinants of the workability of governing coalitions (Kadima, 2014). This section compares two African cases for their richness in demonstrating these factors. Chapter 1 showed that the decline of the power of the African National Congress (ANC) and its growing factionalisation have triggered a widespread appetite but also necessity for coalition formation. In forming pre-electoral alliances, Nigerian party leaders have similarly been driven by the motive of unseating the ruling People's Democratic Party, in addition to desiring to increase their electoral competitiveness and viability (Aliyu, 2018).

South Africa

In South Africa, seeking to take advantage of the steadily shifting balance of power, party leaders of both the Democratic Alliance (DA) and the Economic Freedom Fighters (EFF) as the two largest opposition parties, as well as those from smaller parties, such as the United Democratic Movement (UDM) and the African Christian Democratic Party (ACDP), have deployed coalitions as a political strategy to access power and office or at least the patronage that derives from confidence-and-supply arrangements. The agreements to form coalitions have typically taken place at the national level and between national party leaders, and been devolved to the provincial and local government level, to be led and managed by party leaders in those localities.

Cooperation and consensus-building among party leaders within a coalition has been tenuous, as illustrated by the extreme case of the Nelson Mandela Bay metro (see chapter 13). Nelson Mandela Bay's

DA-led coalition was fragile due to the conflict between metro leaders of the DA and the UDM, Athol Trollip and the late Mongameli Bobani, due to an inability to build consensus. In addition, South Africa's national-level party leaders have at different times acted as centrifugal forces in local government coalitions – also well illustrated in the case of Nelson Mandela Bay. UDM national leader Bantu Holomisa stated that he would not 'jump' every time Trollip reached out to him to express frustration about the conflict (De Kock et al., 2017). On the one hand, the ANC's national leadership tolerated misbehaviour of Nelson Mandela Bay councillors because it effectively destabilised the DA-led coalition. On the other hand, the EFF national leader, Julius Malema, compromised the sustainability of the Nelson Mandela Bay coalition when he announced in national parliament that his party would table a motion of no confidence against Trollip as mayor, due to the DA and EFF ideological differences on land ownership (*News24*, 2018). Malema routinely broke out of his party's cooperative stance with the ANC and the DA alike, seeking to differentiate EFF party identity as it has declared itself to be a 'government in waiting' (*IOL*, 2014). This interparty competition dynamic seeped into all the DA-led coalitions in Nelson Mandela Bay, the City of Johannesburg and the City of Tshwane.

In day-to-day coalition practice and management, South African party leaders, whether in formal coalitions or loose cooperation alliances, have flouted the conditions of their formal or informal coalition agreements, and the committees that seek to address and resolve conflict. For example, the Inkatha Freedom Party's leaders abrogated their agreement with the DA in KwaZulu-Natal and moved into a new coalition with the ANC. In Nelson Mandela Bay, Bobani and Trollip flouted the processes of the committee that was set up to address their conflict. Coalition agreements and conflict-resolution committees point to an emergent practice of coalition governance. Early evidence in South Africa suggests that such mechanisms occasionally, but not necessarily, stabilised coalition practice.

Nigeria

Nigerian parties find it difficult to form and sustain viable alliances and coalitions (Lodge, 2014: 237). In the country's dominant-party system, the ability of opposition parties to successfully form viable pre-electoral alliances has been compromised by weak political parties that are largely structurally defective and operationally fragile (Abba and Babalola, 2017: 131). Party leaders are typically chosen and inserted by party financiers (referred to as 'godfathers') who exert their influence on the party (Abba and Babalola, 2017). Party leaders and financiers are also typically undifferentiated from the party, where the identity of the party is associated with the personality of its leader.

In examining the performance of Nigeria's opposition parties in forming pre-election alliances between 2003 and 2015, Aliyu (2018: 300) found that factors similar to those in South Africa compromised successful alliance formation in Nigeria. He argued that Nigerian parties' decision-making on alliance formation, and the choice of alliance parties, are centralised by a clique of party leaders, and then decentralised to national state and local government branches (Aliyu, 2018: 306). Aliyu averred that the failure of Nigerian parties to form viable alliances is driven by the 'lack of trust among opposition politicians, the inability of party leaders to compromise on office-related side payments and legal regulatory impediments [that] combine to militate against opposition parties' electoral alliance formation'.

Parties and party leaders across the different levels are therefore not unitary, consensus-seeking actors in coalition politics. Their specific actions and motivations to access power affect the workability and sustainability of the alliances and coalitions they form. Certain politician personalities create unstable working coalitions: these leaders understand the inherent risk that minimum winning coalitions carry (Luebbert, 1986, as cited by Kadima, 2014) and thus use this to seek access to power and position.

COALITION NEGOTIATIONS: BELGIUM AND SPAIN

Alliance and coalition formation hinges on successful coalition negotiation. The Belgian negotiation process and the outcomes of the May 2019 federal election offer critical insights into coalition practice. As parties repeatedly disagreed at the negotiations, caretaker coalition governments took the helm, spending months in government in a manner that enabled them to win the respect of the electorate – thereby adding new coalition constellations that could be preferred in future. In comparison, the intricate Spanish negotiations demonstrated the substantial role of the allocation of rewards in the successful constitution of coalitions.

Belgium

After the May 2019 federal elections in Belgium, it took the political parties 493 days and 13 attempts of negotiation to successfully agree on and constitute the Vivaldi coalition government (Kopp, 2020). This was the country's second longest period of coalition negotiations, with the first being the 541 days after the 2010 elections (Kopp, 2020). Between 1950 and 1995, it took Belgium on average a month to negotiate and constitute a federal government (Martin and Vanberg, 2003). It appears, therefore, that as Belgium's political parties repeatedly fail to agree on coalition configurations, the country is losing the knack for swift formation of coalition governments.

In the final attempt to constitute a coalition government in September 2020, Belgium's King Phillipe appointed the chair of Vooruit (Socialist Party Differently) to begin the coalition talks, and Egbert Lachaert, chair of the Open Vlaamse Liberalen en Democraten (Open Flemish Liberals and Democrats), to guide the talks. The two acted as co-preformateurs[2] and brokered the Vivaldi coalition government. This government is meant to operate until 2024 under Prime Minister Alexander De Croo, leader of the Open Vlaamse Liberalen en Democraten, and Deputy Prime Minister Frank Vandenbroucke of the Socialist Democrats (Kopp, 2020). Impetus was given to the negotiations, therefore, by pressure from the king, combined with the need to constitute a government that addressed the challenges wrought by the COVID-19 global pandemic, and the desire to avoid new elections that could deliver right-wing populist Vlaams Belang (Flemish Interest) as the largest party (Kopp, 2020). While the Vivaldi coalition agreed on the distribution of the government budget, the negotiators 'never really started to negotiate on a government programme' (Pilet, 2020: 446).

The negotiations to form the Vivaldi coalition government also demonstrated the ability to constitute an ideologically diverse front – in this instance, a heterogeneous centre-left to centre-right coalition. Vivaldi comprised four political groups and seven political parties: the liberals, made up of the Open Vlaamse Liberalen en Democraten and the Reformist Movement; the social democrats comprising Vooruit and the Parti Socialiste (Socialist Party); the greens, with Groen and Ecolo; and the Christen-Democratisch en Vlaams (Bock, 2020; Kopp, 2020; Pilet, 2020). There was significance in which parties were relegated to the opposition. The top two parties were the regionalist Nieuw-Vlaamse Alliantie (New Flemish Alliance) and the reactionary-right Vlaams Belang (Medeiros et al., 2020; Pilet, 2020). The Nieuw-Vlaamse Alliantie won the most votes in the May 2019 federal election, at 16 per cent and 25 seats in the chamber of representatives. Vlaams Belang followed at 12 per cent and 18 seats. The third largest party was the Parti Socialiste with 9.46 per cent of the votes and 20 seats in the chamber (Pilet, 2020: 443). In tandem with Warwick's (1996) assertion that anti-system, populist or politically extreme parties may be consistently excluded from government formation, Vlaams Belang (the second largest party) did not feature in any of the coalition constellations preferred by the other Belgian political parties (Pilet, 2020). It was also the second instance in which the Nieuw-Vlaamse Alliantie nationalists had an electoral majority but were not part of a governing coalition, as happened in the Wallonian-led 2010/2011 coalition government (Kopp, 2020). It was therefore the exclusion of these parties that required careful navigation and potentially presented Vivaldi with a difficult political situation (Pilet, 2020).

Spain
In addition to the failure to build trust and respect, coalition negotiations can also collapse if parties perceive the rewards as insufficient or incommensurate. Spain's elections in 2019 were a case in point. Initial negotiations, between the Partido Socialista Obrero Español (Socialist Workers' Party) led by Pedro Sánchez and the Unidas Podemos (United We Can) led by Pablo Iglesias, failed in July

2019. The Partido Socialista Obrero Español had taken the lead in the April 2019 elections, winning 123 seats out of the total of 350, with Unidas Podemos getting 42 seats (Zanotti and Rama, 2019). However, Unidas Podemos wielded an upper hand in the coalition negotiations, given that smaller political parties agreed to enter a coalition with the Partido Socialista Obrero Español *if* Unidas Podemos was in it.

Without these, the Partido Socialista Obrero Español was left with Spain's right-wing parties which would not enter a coalition with it (Zanotti and Rama, 2019). Unidas Podemos sought the prime-ministerial role, and the ministries of environment, employment and economics (BBC, 2019). It initially rejected the ministerial-role offerings made by the Partido Socialista Obrero Español, describing them as 'inexistent or empty' (BBC, 2019). Iglesias complained that the posts were 'cosmetic', and that this reflected that the Partido Socialista Obrero Español lacked respect for his party.

On the other hand, the Partido Socialista Obrero Español rejected Unidas Podemos's 'demands for key posts within government', accusing the party of asking to be given 'the government' rather than sharing power (BBC, 2019) through a coalition that allocated posts proportionately or commensurately across the parties. However, the two parties were ultimately able to form Spain's first coalition government in decades.

These two case studies demonstrate the close calibration that is required in coalition negotiations. The aspirations of individual parties and their leaders, along with the balance of powers between parties, interface with one another and also do not remain stable. This means that a coalition government comprises many different moving parts, which need to remain synchronised for the coalition to continue working.

COALITION AGREEMENTS AND COALITION STABILITY: IRELAND AND BOTSWANA

Coalition agreements are known to promote the stability of coalitions. Negotiations in which rigorous, sometimes forceful, disagreement and consensus is forged (Moury and Timmermans, 2013) precede the emergence of coalitions. The absence of trust and high intraparty and intra-cabinet conflict forebode coalition collapse, as well as precarious and tenuous consensus. Just as the formateur roles are important for successful coalition negotiation, pre-electoral and coalition agreements are not only essential tools for formalising the coalition, but also act as an important mechanism of coalition governance. Their ability to serve as effective tools of coalition governance hinges on their capacity to bind all partners *throughout* the government or legislative term (Bowler et al., 2016). Coalition agreements generally also stipulate the measures and mechanisms to be followed in dispute and conflict resolution (Bowler et al., 2016). Dispute and conflict resolution may be done by committees that have broadly or specifically detailed powers for the resolution of conflict (Timmermans, 2006; Bowler et al., 2016).

A coalition agreement is a 'written document containing policy intentions endorsed by the party organisations before government inauguration' (Moury and Timmermans, 2013: 118). Unlike contracts, these agreements 'cannot be enforced by a judge and they are not self-policing' (Timmermans, 2006: 272), referring to the fact that the signing parties cannot enforce all aspects of the agreement. Pre-electoral alliances that are formed to win elections are also governed by formalised agreements, as in the case of Botswana. These agreements specify the terms of cooperation and the distribution of portfolios should the alliance win, as well as governance mechanisms. The governance mechanisms range from what the alliance's communication strategies will be, to codes of conduct and dispute mechanisms.

Ireland

The case of Ireland demonstrates decisions about what goes into a coalition agreement and what is omitted for later discussion and ratification. The Comhaontas Glas (Green Party), Fianna Fáil (Warriors of Ireland) and Fine Gael (United Ireland) parties drafted a 100-plus-page agreement (Davis, 2020). The two larger parties, Fianna Fáil and Fine Gael, had a conflict-ridden history and therefore elected to have a detailed policy and programmatic outline. The content was dominated by details of government programmes for the renewal of the economy and job creation, universal healthcare, housing, education, foreign relations, and the climate and green deals, among other things. It included the broad principles of how the coalition government would function. The agreement was a compromise, representing the sum total of the three parties coming together, yet one in which 'every party doesn't win everything' (BBC, 2020).

Under the functioning of government, the coalition deal details portfolio allocation and distribution between the three parties and 'how ongoing work and potential disagreement will be resolved' (Programme for Government, 2020: 123). Following the sequential bargaining logic of Ecker et al. (2015), the parties agreed upfront on an equal distribution of government ministries between Fine Gael and Fianna Fáil (six each), with Comhaontas Glas receiving three ministerial positions. Less important position allocation was deferred. The taoiseach position (prime minister) would be rotated between Fianna Fáil and Fine Gael, with each getting a half term within the legislative period.

The party leaders not holding the office of the taoiseach would hold the office of the tánaiste (deputy prime minister), with the aim of improving coordination and openness within government (Programme of Government, 2020: 123). A policy and programme implementation unit would be formed under the tánaiste, with the express aim of assisting 'cabinet [and] cabinet committees and conducting oversight of the implementation of government' (Programme of Government, 2020: 123). An assistant secretary would lead and manage the unit, along with other staff members. The assistant secretary would also attend the government forums of secretaries to provide oversight, monitoring and checking the decisions and actions of the selected coalition partner ministers, to ensure that the ministers do not drift from the coalition's agreed government programmes (Timmermans, 2006).

The deal furthermore established a government coordination cabinet committee comprising the three party leaders, who would meet weekly and whenever necessary. The committee had to review the cabinet's agenda and activities, as well as the political priorities and implementation of the programme of government. The deal alluded to a conflict-resolution mechanism, although only in vague terms. Broadly, the parties agreed that no new policy matters would be communicated publicly without having been discussed and agreed on in the coalition. The specific conflict-resolution approach was that parties would 'raise concerns in confidence, as early as possible and in good faith' without bringing in the media (Programme of Government, 2020: 125).

Botswana

In seeking to oust the long-ruling Botswana Democratic Party, Botswana's opposition parties have been forming pre-electoral alliances since 2004 (see Shale, 2007). Pre-election alliance agreements that stipulate the terms of the alliance and the code of conduct of the parties were typically formulated as memoranda of understanding. These opposition parties were capitalising on the early relative electoral successes of the alliances by broadening their agreements into future elections.

For the 2004 elections, three of Botswana's opposition parties, the Bechuanaland People's Party, the Botswana National Front and the Botswana Alliance Movement, formed an election pact to not compete against each other in specific constituencies. The electoral pact was based on a single manifesto, but also ratified through a memorandum of understanding. Botswana uses the first-past-the-post (FPTP) electoral system, and the pact functioned to encourage party members to pool votes and 'vote for whichever of the three parties was standing in their particular constituency' or swop candidates when better success was anticipated (Shale, 2007: 96). While only the Botswana National Front won a seat in those elections, the pact continued and the parties cooperated in the 2005 by-elections (Shale, 2007). The memorandum of understanding also provided for a joint-committee mechanism to monitor and oversee the implementation of the alliances' agreements, as well as the selection of candidates (Shale, 2007). However, the Botswana National Front sought to maintain its party identity, and contravened the alliance's code of conduct, and this collapsed the alliance.

In 2012 and towards the 2014 elections another opposition party pre-electoral alliance emerged, called the Umbrella for Democratic Change. Comprising 'all the various parties and traditions that at one time or another had opposed the Botswana Democratic Party from the left', the Umbrella for Democratic Change was constituted by the Botswana National Front, the Botswana People's Party and the Botswana Movement for Democracy (Brown, 2020: 716). The alliance's party constellation shifted to the Botswana National Front, the Botswana People's Party and the Botswana Congress Party in the run-up to the 2019 elections. This alliance formed despite an interparty trust deficit, reflected by the Botswana Congress Party's mistrust of the Botswana National Front (Brown, 2020).

When the Botswana Democratic Party split and former president Ian Khama moved to the Umbrella for Democratic Change, an Umbrella for Democratic Change alliance victory in the 2019 elections was widely predicted (Brown, 2020). Instead, the Botswana Democratic Party's 2019 election result improved its 2014 performance when Khama had still led it. The Botswana Democratic Party's retention of power was ascribed to, among other things, the ongoing role of the electoral system (Shale, 2007; Poteete, 2012), fragmentation of the party system (Osei-Hwedie, 2001; Shale, 2007), blunders of the opposition party leadership and the Umbrella for Democratic Change's Duma Boko, and the failure of the 'Khama factor' to swing the electorate. Conversely, part of the Botswana Democratic Party's rebound was attributed to the well-calculated actions of its leader, Mokgweetsi Masisi (Brown, 2020). Brown (2020: 719) notes that some Umbrella for Democratic Change alliance members have suggested that with the absence of an 'explicit agreement too much was left uncertain', including 'the role of Ian Khama and the Botswana Patriotic Front'.

In October 2020 opposition parties drafted another memorandum of understanding, with a view to cooperating in the 2024 elections (*Botswana Guardian*, 2020). Excluding the Botswana Movement for Democracy and small parties, the Alliance for Progressives, the Botswana Patriotic Front and the Umbrella for Democratic Change are signatories of the memorandum. The memorandum is reminiscent of the 2005 formative election pact between the Botswana People's Party, Botswana National Front and Botswana Alliance Movement, in which parties agreed that they will not compete against each other in the upcoming local and parliamentary elections taking place between 2020 and 2024 (*Botswana Guardian*, 2020).

As in the case of Ireland, the memorandum of understanding states that the party leaders of Botswana's electoral pact will form a committee that will not only oversee the implementation of the memorandum, but also serve as a platform for the discussion of collaborative election campaigns, and broad interparty collaboration activities (*Botswana Guardian*, 2020). Importantly, though, there is a dearth of research on the agreements that undergird the alliances and coalitions that African political parties form. This may be due to the disintegration of the alliances and coalitions before they can be formalised, or because some of these agreements are not widely publicised.

ELECTORAL TIMING AND CLOSENESS: GERMANY AND BRITAIN

Electoral timing and closeness are factors that promote the disintegration of coalitions. Political parties routinely anticipate electoral liability, especially if they are part of an unpopular government, causing them to abandon the coalition as the next election period draws closer. Their aim is to circumvent 'ruling coalition fragility' (Kadima, 2006: 231). They thereby differentiate themselves, and evade accountability for coalition failures. Based on the data from the 2019 elections in 28 European countries, for the research period 1972 to 2019, Klüver and Spoon (2020) conclude that while there are short-term benefits to joining a coalition government, parties suffer long-term consequences for their participation. This comes as the 'cost of governing' (Van Spange, 2011: 609). The trend across Europe has been that coalition parties, irrespective of size and ideology, lose electoral support in the next elections, especially if they had not held senior executive positions in the coalition government that they joined (Klüver and Spoon, 2020). In contrast, parties in the opposition gained votes.

Germany

The Sozialdemokratische Partei Deutschlands (Social Democratic Party of Germany) is the second largest party in Germany, and has been a junior member of the federal government (in 2013, renewed in 2017), along with the Christlich Demokratische Union Deutschlands

(Christian Democratic Union of Germany) and the Christlich-Soziale Union in Bayern (Christian Social Union in Bavaria) (CDU/CSU), known as the joint faction or The Union. The Sozialdemokratische Partei Deutschlands served as a junior partner to the CDU/CSU in a grand coalition from 1966 to 1969 and from 2005 to 2009, and again since 2013 (after a term in opposition). The Sozialdemokratische Partei Deutschlands then became junior partner in a grand coalition with the CDU/CSU until 2009. This arrangement was renewed after the 2017 federal election. The Sozialdemokratische Partei Deutschlands suffered a relative vote decline in the 2017 elections, after a period back in coalition. This contrasted with the growth in support of the party in 2013, after its period in opposition. Part of the reason for the decline was the policy compromises that junior coalition partners invariably yield to the senior coalition partner in government. The Sozialdemokratische Partei Deutschlands is the second largest party in the bundestag (the German federal parliament), having gained 20.5 per cent of votes cast in the federal election of 2017 (compared with its 25.7 of 2013).

Klüver and Spoon (2019) argue that the reluctance of parties to enter coalitions as junior partners 'can make coalition negotiations a long and hard sell'. By 2019 and with a view to the 2021 elections, the Sozialdemokratische Partei Deutschlands was positioning itself as a more autonomous party, more left-wing than its coalition partners, and with the ability to again become the biggest in the bundestag.

Britain
In contrast to Germany and many other Western European countries, Britain has a low occurrence of coalition formation (Madsen, 2015). Britain has an established two-party system in which the Conservative Party and the Labour Party dominate. This two-party system is largely maintained by a FPTP electoral system (Lodge and Gottfried, 2011; Hughes, 2015). The electoral loss experiences of the Liberal Democrats in the 2010 and 2015 elections nevertheless illustrate vividly the problems of junior coalition partnership, in this instance in the Conservative-Liberal coalition government (Law, 2018). The Labour Party more than the Conservatives has historically cooperated with

the Liberal-Democrats to form a parliamentary majority (Hughes, 2015). However, in the 2010 general elections, which produced a hung parliament, the Conservative Party and Liberal Democrats entered into a coalition that lasted until 2015.

The Liberal Democrats suffered major post-2010 electoral losses, and its support declined in the subsequent local government and general elections (Cutts and Russell, 2015). Nationally, the party lost 15 per cent of its votes and over 4.4 million votes, compared with 2010. The central reason was critical miscalculations about coalition policy choices and support vis-à-vis its 2010 manifesto, mishaps in communicating its identity, and the party's coalition behaviour, including in the run-up to new elections.

In the early stages of the coalition, the Liberal Democrats were not sufficiently vociferous about their policy stances and conceded crucial policy issues. It contradicted its 2010 manifesto, for example, voting to increase fees in a new higher education fee dispensation. The party also reneged on its 2010 manifesto position that no new nuclear power stations would be supported. In the mid-period of the coalition, the party reversed its positive and supportive stance of the coalition; its tone became 'increasingly ... negative and there were clear signs that the party was attempting to differentiate itself from the Conservatives and end its pro-coalition stance' (Cutts and Russell, 2015: 82). Its leader, Nick Clegg, stated that the Liberal Democrats had helped moderate adverse coalition policy stances, such as 'blocking policies from inheritance tax cuts for millionaires to scrapping housing benefit for young people' (Cutts and Russell, 2015: 82). The policy vacillation resulted in voter confusion, about both policy and party identity. The Liberal Democrats were further undermined by the Conservative Party, which directly recruited in the former's constituency. Ultimately, this coalition behaviour cost the Liberal Democrats its third position in the British party-political hierarchy.

Political parties suffer multiple costs when in government, and entering into a coalition threatens party existence. As voters continue to increasingly change their electoral behaviour, coalition fragility as elections draw near will remain a key feature of coalition politics.

CONCLUSION

Where coalitions emerge and dominate, political parties and their actors have demonstrated they can learn and adapt to shifting political contexts. In Mauritius, the ever-changing constellations of government and opposition coalitions may have contributed to democratic consolidation, but is now slowly chipping away at the democratic edifice, raising questions about whether the quality of the Mauritian democracy is waning. Even in this scenario, Mauritius's coalition practice continues to evolve and is producing a rare majority winner in the form of the Militant Socialist Movement.

Second, the Belgian experience of protracted negotiation, along with the other cases, shows a rolling deck in which multiple informateurs and preformateurs attempt to establish a coalition government, which evidences the weakening of the traditional formateur role in successfully convening a coalition. These protracted negotiations bear testimony to the fact that political parties are challenging and rejecting traditional coalition constellations, ironically, in the same way that electorates are shifting partisanship. Unexpected coalition partners are emerging and detailing their expected governmental programmes, and in contexts of trust deficits, they are also seeking to spend as much time reviewing what the other is doing, as in the case of Ireland. And, in a context of rich global coalition practice, including on the African continent, opposition parties in dominant-party systems are taking lessons from other countries on how to wean off a predominant party. Ultimately, the global coalition experience is on a steep learning curve, on which coalition partners perish or thrive; and the quality of coalition politics is being tested and stretched.

REFERENCES

Abba, S. A. and Babalola, D. 2017. 'Contending issues in political parties in Nigeria: The candidate selection process', *Africology: Journal of Pan African Studies*, 11 (1), 118–134.

Aliyu, D. 2018. 'Opposition parties' pre-election alliance failure in Nigeria's Fourth Republic', *Studies in Politics and Society*, 6, 300–316.

Bassi, A. 2016. 'Policy preferences in coalition formation and the stability of minority and surplus governments', *The Journal of Politics*, 79 (1), 250–268.

British Broadcasting Corporation (BBC). 25 July 2019. 'Spain's Pedro Sánchez loses vote to form government', https://www.bbc.com/news/world-europe-49099841, accessed 3 October 2020.

British Broadcasting Corporation (BBC). 15 June 2020. 'Irish government: Deal reached to form coalition', https://www.bbc.com/news/world-europe-53045282, accessed 3 October 2020.

Berkowitz, P. 11 May 2011. 'Shapley values and SA's local coalition politics', *Daily Maverick,* https://www.dailymaverick.co.za/article/2011-05-11-analysis-shapley-values-and-sas-local-coalition-politics/, accessed 7 October 2020.

Botswana Guardian, 5 November 2020. 'It's now or never for opposition', https://www.pressreader.com/botswana/botswana-guardian/20201105/282179358600016, accessed 8 December 2020.

Bowler, S., Brauninger, T., Debus, M. and Indridason, I. H. 2016. 'Let's just agree to disagree: Dispute resolution: Mechanisms in coalition agreements', *Journal of Politics*, 78 (4), 1264–1278.

Bock, P. 7 September 2020. 'Belgium's new government: Why did the "Vivaldi" coalition take so long to form?', *Euronews*, https://services.euronews.com/2020/10/07/belgium-s-new-government-why-did-the-vivaldi-coalition-take-so-long-to-form, accessed 1 December 2020.

Brown, C. 2020. 'Botswana votes 2019: Two-party competition and the Khama factor', *Journal of Southern African Studies*, 46 (4), 703–722.

Carroll, B. W. and Carroll, T. 1999. 'The consolidation of democracy in Mauritius', *Democratization*, 6 (1), 179–197.

Christiansen, F. J. and Klemmensen, R. 2015. 'Danish experiences with coalition governments and coalition governance', in Madsen, H. L. (ed.) *Coalition Building: Finding solutions together.* Denmark: Danish Institute for Parties and Democracy, 26–43.

Cutts, D. and Russell, A. 2015. 'From coalition to catastrophe: The electoral meltdown of the Liberal Democrats', *Britain Votes,* 70–87.

Davis, S. 15 June 2020. 'Rivals Fianna Fáil and Fine Gael reach an agreement to form a government with the Greens', *Euronews*, https://www.euronews.com/2020/06/15/rivals-fianna-fail-and-fine-gael-reach-an-agreement-to-form-a-government-with-the-greens, accessed 1 December 2020.

De Kock, R., Mngxitama-Diko, A. and Capa, S. 24 May 2017. 'Peace deal teeters', *The Herald*.

Diermeier, D., Eraslan, H. and Merlo, A. 2001. 'Coalition governments and comparative constitutional design', *European Economic Review*, 46 (4), 893–907.

Ecker, A., Meyer, T. M. and Müller, W. 2015. 'The distribution of individual positions in coalition governments: A sequential approach', *European Journal of Political Research,* 54, 802–818.

Førde, B. 2015. 'Foreword' in Madsen, H. L. (ed.) *Coalition Building: Finding solutions together*. Denmark: Danish Institute for Parties and Democracy (DIPD), 7.

Hornung, J., Rüsenberg, F., Eckert, N. and Bandelow, C. 2020. 'New insights into coalition negotiations: The case of German government formation', *Negotiation Journal*, 36 (2), 331–352.

Hughes, N. 29 April 2015. 'In a multi-party political environment, the first-past-the-post electoral system may mitigate polarisation', https://blogs.lse.ac.uk/politicsandpolicy/in-a-multi-party-political-environment-the-first-past-the-post-electoral-system-may-mitigate-polarisation/, accessed 28 December 2020.

IOL. 17 May 2014. 'EFF is government in waiting – Mpofu', https://www.iol.co.za/news/politics/eff-is-government-in-waiting-mpofu-1689875, accessed 28 December 2020.

Kadima, D. 2006. 'African party alliances: Comparisons, conclusions and lessons', in Kadima, D. (ed.) *Politics of Party Coalitions in Africa*. Johannesburg: Electoral Institute for Sustainable Democracy in Africa, https://www.eisa.org.za/pub-parties.php, accessed 22 January 2020.

Kadima, D. 2014. 'An introduction to the politics of party alliances and coalitions in socially divided Africa', *Journal of African Elections*, 13 (1), 1–24.

Kadima, D. 2015. 'Lessons learned and good practices', in Madsen, H. L. (ed.) C*oalition Building: Finding solutions together*. Denmark: Danish Institute for Parties and Democracy, 18–23.

Kadima, D. and Kasenally, R. 2006. 'The formation, collapse and revival of political party coalitions in Mauritius: Ethnic logic and calculation at play', in Kadima, D. (ed.) *Politics of Party Coalitions in Africa*. Johannesburg: Electoral Institute for Sustainable Democracy in Africa, https://www.eisa.org.za/pub-parties.php, accessed 30 November 2020.

Kadima, D. and Matsimbe, Z. 2006. 'RENAMO Uniao Electoral: Understanding the longevity and challenges of an opposition party coalition in Mozambique', in Kadima, D. (ed.) *The Politics of Party Coalitions in Africa*. Johannesburg: EISA, 149–178.

Kirchsteiger, G. and Puppe, C. 1997. 'On the formation of political coalitions', *Journal of Institutional and Theoretical Economics*, 153 (2), 293–319.

Klüver, H. and Spoon, J. J. 23 July 2019. 'Across Europe, coalition governments are hurting political parties that join them', *The Washington Post*, https://www.washingtonpost.com/politics/2019/07/23/across-europe-coalition-governments-are-hurting-political-parties-that-join-them/, accessed 30 September 2020.

Klüver, H. and Spoon, J. J. 2020. 'Helping or hurting? How governing as a junior coalition partner influences electoral outcomes', *The Journal of Politics*, 82 (4), 1231–1242.

Kopp, D. 2 October 2020. 'Can Vivaldi keep the country together?', *International Politics and Society,* https://www.ips-journal.eu/interviews/can-vivaldi-keep-the-country-together-4687/, accessed 5 December 2020.

Lodge, T. 2014. 'Some preliminary conclusions on the causes and consequences of political party alliances and coalitions in Africa', *Journal of African Elections,* 13 (1), 234–242.

Lodge, G. and Gottfried, G. 2011. 'Worst of both worlds: Why first past the post no longer works', *Institute for Public Policy Research,* https://www.ippr.org/files/images/media/files/publication/2011/05/Worst%20of%20Both%20Worlds%20Jan2011_1820.pdf, accessed 14 January 2021.

Law, M. 2018. 'When foes become friends and friends become goes: Party political co-operation and the building and sustaining of coalitions'. Background paper. https://za.boell.org/en/2018/07/12/when-foes-become-friends-and-friends-become-foes-party-political-cooperation-and-building accessed 30 May 2020.

Madsen, H. L. 2015. 'Introduction', in Madsen, H. L. (ed.) *Coalition Building: Finding solutions together.* Denmark: Danish Institute for Parties and Democracy, 10–14.

Martin, L. W. and Vanberg, G. 2003. 'Wasting time? The impact of ideology on size and delay in coalition formation', *British Journal of Political Science,* 33, 323–344.

Medeiros, M., Gauvin, J. P. and Chhim, C. 2020. 'Unified voters in a divided society: Ideology and regionalism in Belgium', *Regional & Federal Studies,* https://doi.org/10.1080/13597566.2020.1843021, accessed 30 November 2020.

Moury, C. and Timmermans, A. 2013. 'Inter-party conflict management in coalition governments: Analysing the role of coalition agreements in Belgium, Germany, Italy and the Netherlands', *Politics and Governance,* 1 (2), 117–131.

Mozaffar, S. 2005. 'Negotiating independence in Mauritius', *International Negotiation,* 10, 263–291.

Mulhovo, H. 2018. 'The intricacies and pitfalls of the politics of coalition in Mozambique', in *Complexities of Coalition Politics in Southern Africa.* Monograph Series No. 1/2018. African Dialogue.

Nuvunga, A. and Sitoe, E. 2013. 'Party institutionalisation in Mozambique: The party of the state vs the opposition', *Journal of African Elections,* 12 (1), 109–142.

News24, 4 March 2018. 'We are cutting the throat of whiteness - Julius Malema', https://www.politicsweb.co.za/news-and-analysis/we-are-cutting-the-throat-of-whiteness--julius-mal, accessed 20 March 2018.

Osei-Hwedie, B. Z. 2001. 'The political opposition in Botswana: The politics of factionalism and fragmentation', *Transformation,* 45, 58–77.

Pedersen, H. H. 29 June 2015. 'The Danish single party coalition government',

Party Systems and Governments Observatory, https://whogoverns.eu/the-danish-single-party-coalition-government/, accessed 28 December 2020.

Pilet, J-B. 2020. 'Hard times for governing parties: The 2019 federal elections in Belgium', *West European Politics,* 44 (2), 439–449.

Poteete, A. 2012. 'Electoral competition, factionalism, and persistent dominance in Botswana', *Journal of Modern African Studies,* 50 (1), 75–102.

Programme for Government, 26 October 2020. Department of the Taoiseach. 'Our Shared Future'. https://www.gov.ie/en/publication/7e05d-programme-for-government-our-shared-future/, accessed 5 December 2020.

Shale, V. 2007. 'Opposition party alliances and elections in Botswana, Lesotho and Zambia', *Journal of African Elections,* 6 (1), 98–117.

Sithanen, R. 2003. 'Coalition politics under the tropics: Office seekers, power makers, nation building: A case study of Mauritius'. Paper, Strengthening Democracy through Coalition Building, http://aceproject.org/ero-en/topics/parties-and-candidates/mauritius.pdf, accessed 2 March 2020.

Timmermans, A. 2006. 'Standing apart and sitting together: Enforcing coalition agreements in multiparty systems', *European Journal of Political Research,* 45 (2), 263–283.

Van Spange, J. 2011. 'Keeping the rascals in: Anti-political-establishment parties and their cost of governing in established democracies', *European Journal of Political Research,* 50, 609–635.

Warwick, P. V. 1996. 'Coalition government membership in West European parliamentary democracies', *British Journal of Political Science,* 26 (4), 471–499.

Zanotti, L. and Rama, J. 19 November 2019. 'How Spain's new left-wing coalition fits into Europe's shifting political allegiances', *The Conversation,* https://theconversation.com/how-spains-new-left-wing-coalition-fits-into-europes-shifting-political-allegiances-127144, accessed 14 September 2020.

SEVENTEEN

South Africa's zone of coalition government:
Conflict in unity

SUSAN BOOYSEN

MARRIAGES OF INCONVENIENCE: *The politics of coalitions in South Africa* with its focus on the art, science and desirability of coalitions in South Africa delivers a complex depiction of both the likelihood of increasing realisation of party-political alliances and coalitions in South Africa, and the inherent volatility of coalition government. The practice of coalition politics is a complex instrument of governance, relatively unregulated, and not explicitly anticipated in the constitution and legislative frameworks of the country. Coalitions are furthermore a major instrument used by political parties and their leaders to capture power when electoral outcomes do not favour a single party. Coalitions take shape frequently through opaque negotiations, guided by unspoken expectations of and agreements to payoffs and rules of governance oriented more towards the interests of the political parties and their leaders. Despite these cautions and drawbacks, coalitions are a necessity when electoral verdicts fail to select majority parties in a system of government by electoral majority.

It is a field of South African politics and government that calls for planning, anticipation and management by political leaders. *Marriages of Inconvenience* endeavours, therefore, to unpack and project factors that offer the means to demystify coalitions and enhance democracy and governance practice. The chapters in this volume offer an ample, textured set of factors that affect coalitions in diverse settings, similar to or in contrast with the case of South Africa. The in-depth exploration of international cases and of South Africa helps to set down pointers to both commendable and undesirable coalition outcomes. The causal factors, trends and rich landscape of events that are assessed in the case studies and thematic analyses cover the coalition life-cycle across phases of, broadly, coalition negotiation and formation, operation and maintenance, conflict and dissolution or institutionalisation. It is a circular process that loops back into elections and, likely, coalition renegotiation and reconstitution after a subsequent election.

South Africa has in all probability entered a zone in which the changing party system makes coalition government and governance a fait accompli. As South Africa's hitherto dominant ANC registers uneven performances, the country is likely to embark increasingly on coalition governance practice. Should this not be the case, there will still be a relatively dominant party that retains some fragile outright majorities, but could lean increasingly into the coalition domain at any election. *Marriages of Inconvenience* recognises this South African reality, and seeks to present lessons through comparable scholarly research and analyses of local, broader African and international examples. It aspires to offer knowledge-related tools for South Africa's people, political practitioners and government to take the decisions and effect the actions that will make coalition government stable and conducive to developmental governance, or to change the steps when they fail to maintain sight of the base task of democratic governance. This chapter does not repeat the literature and theory presented in the preceding chapters. It is informed by the preceding expositions, and simply occasionally adds an additional reference. The task of the chapter is to interpret, synthesise and take forward the interpretations and advice from the studies in the previous chapters. It initiates the ordering of a complex set of coalition-related information, applying systems thinking and using the iceberg model of analysis (Kauffman, 1980; Anderson and Johnson, 1997; Kim, 1999). The iceberg is the metaphor for a simple yet systematic depiction of a complex system. The visible tip of the iceberg represents the events and behaviours, in this instance, in coalition politics. These indicators are manifestations of general unfolding trends, just below the surface and not always clearly characterised. The indicators and trends are both anchored in deeper dynamics. The coalitions iceberg in this chapter differentiates between mindsets and, at the foundation, the key drivers of coalition politics.

The rest of this chapter offers an interpretative assessment of factors that impact on party-political coalitions and the governments they operate. It notes the process nature of coalition practice, and the fact that each phase in the process is affected by a hierarchy of influences and causal factors. In this respect, it first outlines the analytical approach. Second, it notes the overall framework in terms of the phases of the life-cycle of coalitions, a factor that all chapters in this volume addresses, directly or through their scoping of coalition trajectories in Africa, and South Africa in particular. It highlights that there is no neat sequencing between the typical phases of formation, operation and maintenance, possible dissolution and renegotiation. Third, the chapter reviews the core drivers of coalition politics in South Africa. In essence, these are identified as the party system, political parties, the electoral system and election results, and the South Africa-specific culture that has evolved and shapes coalition operations. Coalitions as party-political formations interface continuously with governance, and the state of governance infuses coalition practices. The analysis condenses the main content of the driving forces, the trends that unfold on the driving-force base, and the main indicators of coalition practice. This iceberg of coalition-related factors in South Africa operates both across life-cycle phases and within particular phases in the life-cycle of coalitions.

APPROACH TO MAPPING THE MATRIX OF SOUTH AFRICA'S COALITIONS FUTURE

This chapter uses components of a scenarios approach to conclude this study of coalition politics in South Africa. It synthesises the layers of scenario building blocks, and ranks key components, but leaves the composition of alternative futures, and the storylines that accompany them, to the imagination of the reader and practitioner. The emphasis is therefore on establishing the ingredients of contemporary coalition practice and estimating the character of unfolding and future coalition formations and government in South Africa. It draws on lessons and practice from both the global South and North. It collects information about essential drivers, party and leadership mindsets, trends and indicators from the experiences the African continent has delivered. It pairs and compares this evidence with South African conditions from provincial and local coalition practice. It recognises that many uncertainties prevail that will prevent definitive projections of the future (Marren, 2012; Moore and Haran, 2014), in this instance of coalition politics in South Africa. Within this framework of guaranteed uncertainty and instability, the materials collected and analyses assembled for this volume make crucial elements available to the reader while offering a systems framework of ordering the information. The reader, analyst and political practitioner may all reflect on the occurrence of driving forces, trends and indicators in the case at hand, and contemplate the likely trajectories that are to evolve.

The approach is modelled, therefore, on and borrows from those components of scenario-building methodology that identify the complex driving forces, trends and events of the present in an application of the iceberg model of systems thinking. The methodology embraces uncertainties and a range of probabilities, and uses a diversity of data and analysis. It enables the observer, as the future unfolds, to recognise the indicators and signals that point to particular alternative futures. It also equips the strategically minded participant to plan for change, intervene and direct. Briefly, *driving forces* in the case of coalitions may be regarded as the external, long-term accumulated factors that affect coalitions practice in South Africa. The actors do not have immediate and direct control over the driving forces which are linked to the structure of the system. This base, for the case of coalitions in South Africa, includes the political culture that has been shaped around coalition operations in South Africa, legislation, electoral and party systems, policies and institutions. The mindsets of the political parties and their leaders enter as an intermediary layer that has a filtering effect, allowing and enticing some of the key drivers to determine the coalition trends. In this study *trends* are identified as patterns of behaviour or repeated behaviours in the present that may persist into the future. They come with degrees of certainty and uncertainty. The *events* are the concrete, tangible occurrences and behaviours that happen in the terrain of practice. They are often linked to people and organisations. In a deductive logic, the prevalent and important events after repeated occurrences solidify into trends, and trends gain prominence in relation to the forces that prove over time to drive the trends.[1]

LIFE-CYCLES OF COALITIONS AND THE EXPERIENCE OF SOUTH AFRICA

A fundamental part of analysing party-political coalitions, as they are manifested in governance, is to appreciate that coalitions are not permanent institutions. They operate over a life-cycle, comprising in essence negotiation and formation, operation and maintenance, disbandment or dissolution, and possible renegotiation (Figure 17.1). In competitive multiparty political systems, coalition life-cycles are likely to be linked to an electoral cycle. Should party-political minds have converged in the course of the antecedent period of governance, those parties are likely to merge and become a new party-political entity. If not, they will compete as individual parties, hoping to achieve a majority election result, or provide the platform to launch a new round of coalition negotiations. The principle of fixed-term electoral mandates applies as much to a single party as to coalition governments. Yet coalitions' levels of instability and lessened predictability are higher. The coalition's policy programme will be based on negotiation and compromise, and governance itself may be volatile, one of the reasons being that political parties in coalitions use the site of coalition government as both a platform for and an instrument to compete with their coalition partners.

The chapters in this volume offer the material to interpret the life-cycles of coalitions, and in particular governing coalition formations in South Africa. There is a considerable literature on the life-cycle of coalitions, and important contributions are reviewed and adapted in Graeme de Bruyn's chapter. The case-study chapters of Malawi, Kenya and Lesotho, and the South African chapters on the metros of Nelson Mandela Bay, Johannesburg and Tshwane, as well as the provincial governments of KwaZulu-Natal and the Western Cape, all clarify the phases through which coalitions run their course.

The life-cycle specification is part of this chapter's approach to systematise the wealth of information that is available on party-political coalitions in South Africa. The essential phases that are pertinent to the analysis of coalition politics in South Africa are (Figure 17.1):

Negotiation and formation: This is a process between parties, directed by constitutional and legislative frameworks, and influenced by the political culture of coalitions in society. It usually takes place in the aftermath of elections in which no clear winner has emerged. The terms of the agreement, including division of government portfolios, is formalised through some type of coalition agreement. In some cases this remains informal. There may also be complementary

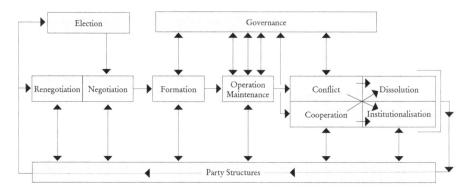

Figure 17.1. Trajectories for coalition life-cycles in South Africa

Source: Author's analysis and interpretations of the literature and chapters in this book.

non-publicised negotiations on coalition payoffs to partners. This phase overlaps with governance.

Operation and maintenance: Interaction between the partners is both party political and governmental. This interface between party politics and governance can be intense and entice disruptions. This phase is fused with governance, and party politics often becomes indistinguishable from governance. Policy convergence between partners, formal coalition agreements and conflict management (the next point) may all facilitate maintenance of the coalition, but none will be a guarantee of coalition success.

Institutionalisation or conflict: In exceptional cases cooperation between partnering coalition parties may evolve into fusion of the parties and the emergence of a new party. Interparty conflict, however, remains more likely. Spontaneous and induced (as part of party strategy) forms of conflict are frequent characteristics of coalition operations. Some coalitions may gain stability and viability through management and, especially, conflict management of relationships between potentially diverse parties. Parties may grow closer and integrate. Alternatively, some parties have intracoalition conflict ingrained in their participation: they want to be seen to be in conflict with their coalition partners.

Dissolution of the coalition: Following escalation of intra-alliance conflict, and the recognised impossibility or undesirability of continuing joint governance, a coalition may formally dissolve. This conflict would have resulted from issues concerning matters of governance at the specific site, policy decisions at another sphere that gave offence, and party structures beyond the site of governance instructing coalition changes.

Renegotiation of the alliance: Political parties may exit an alliance, break the prevailing majority arrangement, and realign with another party to constitute a new coalition. It may be that the dissolution warrants a special election, or movement into a next election if the dissolution had been timed to coincide with the electoral cycle.

Whereas some of the complex undercurrents that affect the phases are already evident from Figure 17.1, both the literature and the studies in this volume show that coalition politics remain anchored in competitive party politics. Party structures and party leadership intervene and direct coalition operations across the phases. The contest between rent-seeking and behaviour driven by policy ideology, mediated by party leaders, is omnipresent. Crispian Olver's chapter analyses the dense interface between politicians and municipal administrations, foregrounding crucial issues concerning rent-seeking trends in coalition politics in South Africa. In the case of the metros of South Africa, the rent-seeking demands that unfold render governance a debilitating experience that ebbs and flows as the different phases take hold.

When political parties in South Africa enter into and operate in coalitions, they have one eye on the electoral cycle. This is a trend the world over, as Heidi Brooks's chapter reveals. Cycle awareness helps parties get out of a coalition when they deem it appropriate and timely. It helps them ascertain when to put distance between themselves and other parties, so as not to carry popular blame for misgovernance, malfeasance or ideological compromise. As the case-study chapters illustrate, this trend is evident in South Africa, albeit with twists. In South Africa's coalition metros, the governing coalitions changed multiple times, and the mere abandonment of one and joining of a new coalition has meant that this type of distance was asserted. For many of the micro-parties, without clear policies, the only 'policy' was to be close to power.

KEY DETERMINANTS, TRENDS AND EVENTS IN SOUTH AFRICA'S EVOLVING COALITION PRACTICE

The objective of this chapter is to bring together a core selection of driving forces, trends and key indicators, which will collectively help inform the understanding and practice of coalitions in South Africa (see Figure 17.2). Many of these variables are applicable to specific phases in the coalition life-cycle, and will impact on either or both the party-political and the governance trajectories. The chapter includes indications of these contexts. All the variables mentioned in this section are dissected in international comparative case studies and thematic contexts in the rest of the book. This section stands on the foundations set down in all of the other chapters of this book.

South Africa's zone of coalition government

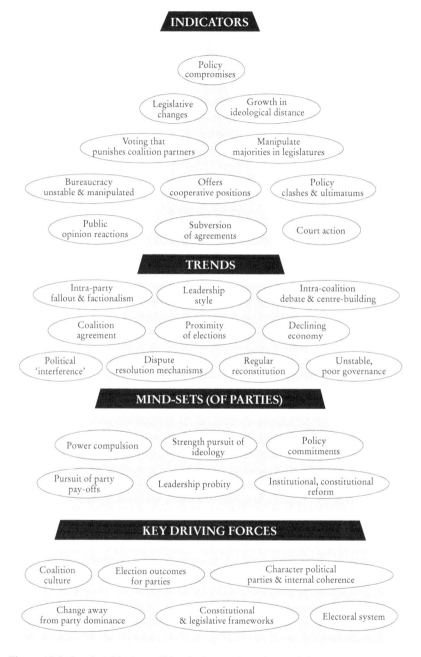

Figure 17.2: South Africa's coalition iceberg – Core factors influencing processes

Source: Author's analysis and interpretations of the literature and chapters in this book.

Key driving forces precipitating and directing coalitions in South Africa

A complex set of key driving forces, or the base structure, undergirds the occurrence and character of coalitions and coalition processes in South Africa. This section highlights the predominant ones.

Change in the dominant-party system

South Africa has until now practised multipartyism in the context of a strongly dominant liberation movement party, the African National Congress (ANC). The ANC has, however, started declining in the electoral stakes. Despite a small trend reversal in 2019, and gaining municipal seats in the 2020–2021 by-elections, it has not recovered unambiguously. The ANC's main redemption by 2020 was the inability of opposition parties to bring compelling offerings to the electorate, as demonstrated in chapter 1. Opposition parties, and especially the main opposition, the Democratic Alliance (DA), remained weak. Voters who are disillusioned or angry with the ANC found other options, like 'protest voting' in the form of voting for small and micro-parties, or abstention instead of voting for an opposition party. The main impact of this change on coalition politics in South Africa has been in the ANC's assertive actions to regain control where it has ceded it, and the party's willingness to use coalition platforms to recover power.

Electoral mandates

Electoral mandates go hand-in-hand with the changing party system, but deserve autonomous mention. It is the electorate in South Africa, as in democratic systems generally, that collectively determines whether any political party will be granted an outright-majority mandate. In democratic South Africa, nationally this has been consistently achieved by the ANC. The Western Cape and KwaZulu-Natal are the provinces that have alternated, and much of the gripping detail of the unfolding coalitions sagas in these two provinces are dissected in the chapters by Sanusha Naidu and Lukhona Mnguni, respectively. In 2019 in Gauteng the ANC came close to ceding its majority. At the local level since 2000, hung councils have necessitated the formation of many local coalition governments, and Mcebisi Ndletyana offers details of

South Africa's 20-plus years of experience with coalition government. Electoral mandates past and future weigh heavily on political parties in coalitions. They calculate the costs or advantages that the liaison may deliver. In order to protect or advance electoral standings, parties (and especially smaller parties) may choose to exit an alliance pre-emptively in the run-up to an election.

Internal politics and policies of the main coalition partners
Opposition parties enter into coalitions usually after an election has confirmed that none of the parties enjoys an outright majority, and hence does not qualify to govern on its own. Such parties are reluctant entrants that realise their dependence on party-partners. It is mostly when parties come together in grand acts of nation-building or reconciliation, or in a quest for an ideological front, that they enter alliances and coalitions voluntarily. In their quest to find numerically suitable partners (strong enough to fill the gap up to a 50 per cent majority), ideologically misfitting partners such as the Economic Freedom Fighters (EFF) and DA have cooperated in the overriding quest at the time to displace the dominant party, the ANC. The EFF later used a demand for national-level DA policy change as publicly stated grounds for exiting. Political parties' dispositions to seek and achieve their parties' policy and ideological goals, or to extract rent for individuals and the party, are major manifestations of internal politics interfacing with governance.

Constitutional and legal frameworks
South Africa is a constitutional democracy, and the constitution sets broad parameters for the formation of government, besides being silent on coalitions generally. The party system – a competitive multiparty democracy (defined in the constitution) – has a direct and multipronged influence on coalition politics, as Khabele Matlosa outlines in the chapter on party and electoral systems in Southern Africa. The electoral system interfaces equally with coalition politics – proportional representation (PR) for national and provincial elections, and mixed proportional with ward-based representation for the local sphere. Coalitions are somewhat more associated with mixed and

PR systems than with first-past-the-post (FPTP), but Matlosa shows that in Southern Africa coalitions occur across the different electoral systems. Proportional systems, especially where they operate without a threshold for parties to be elected (which is the case in South Africa), give more parties the chance to gain representation, and are likely to reduce the chances of an outright majority being won. The chapter by Heidi Brooks presents evidence of how fragmented party systems internationally lead to unstable coalitions. South Africa's earlier use of floor-crossing contributed to highly unstable transitional coalitions.

Evolving coalition culture
Coalition culture in this analysis denotes the practices of frequent use of coalitions by political parties to achieve their objectives of gaining, remaining in or returning to majority power. Part of the culture is that policy and ideology often come second to power gains. The EFF and the African Independent Congress (AIC) have on occasion prioritised policy, but have simultaneously pursued the goals of position elevation and control over government portfolios that may bring rent. The chapters in this book on coalitions in the metropoles illustrate these pursuits in the graphic detail.

Coalitions have also become used in South Africa for small political parties to gain elevation into high municipal positions and executive appointments in national governments. The evolving practice of coalition culture and the mindsets of political power have contributed a major force to South Africa's use of coalitions. These mindsets are distinct from the driving forces yet are also a critical determinant of the coalition practices that will unfold.

These core drivers play their roles mostly in the formation stage of the coalition life-cycle. Party systems and the character of participating political parties may be interpreted as relatively specific to the stages in a coalition's life. Many of these factors – trends and indicators – may also be cross-cutting. They are forceful presences in the maintenance of coalitions, the conflict that arises, and the decisions on whether or not to renegotiate. They also impact substantially on the governance trajectory.

Trends base: Ideology, policy, rent, patronage, power

One of the great coalition debates is whether it is the practice of patronage and quest for clientelism, or the drive for policy maximisation along with ideological convergence, that is essential to coalition formation and operation. This volume confirms the importance of both factors. Figures 17.1 and 17.2 indicate their placement as essential motivating factors. The bulk of the observable trends, or repeat behaviours, in coalition practice in South Africa relate to this base. South Africa's coalition experience has shown that the power-patronage-rent axis often prevails over ideology-policy in coalition contexts across the spheres of government.

The emphasis in coalition politics in South Africa, however, is on co-occurrence. The two variables of ideology-policy and rent-patronage are practically two sides of the same coin in the dynamic of lead parties selecting and bringing in partners into the coalition game.

Negotiable premium placed on policy

The main South African political parties all place a great premium on policy besides their pursuits of the fruits of office. The ANC generally, yet with notable exceptions, has had the benefit of choosing at least partially ideologically compatible coalition partners. In some small-town settings, such considerations were discarded. On occasion, the ANC held power in coalition with the DA. Beyond the mainstream religious and minor left-wing parties, policy agnosticism in South Africa is common. Clientelistic and patronage politics tend to suffice in enlisting these parties to join majority coalitions. As Indridason (2005: 439–464) points out, coalition politics creates a demand for party representatives (or public office-holders) to access the public resources that will be distributed at the discretion of the alliance leaders. While the EFF prominently advances policy advocacy, there is evidence that it settles for dual packages of policy and rent. For example, it ended its DA association in the post-2016 alliances because of policy and race-leadership issues, after it had endeavoured to extract all manner of benefits to the party and its members.

Ideology as a dispensable factor

Sets of recurrent party actions helped to define important trends in this part of interparty coalition practice in South Africa. The EFF, with its ANC Youth League origins, was a likely ANC coalition partner, even if professed policy radicalism was among the EFF's reasons for breaking away from the ANC. As the third biggest and growing party, it had bargaining power, both with the DA[2] and with the ANC. EFF coalition partnerships free the main prospective coalition leaders (the ANC, and also the DA) from negotiating with diverse micro-party clusters. The EFF, however, sought policy undertakings, held ambitions of capturing major municipal positions and/or portfolios and pursued variable rents, even when it remained a modestly supported party (see chapter 1, Table 1.1). The EFF's interest was in building majorities and sharing in the exercise of power, both to illustrate it can govern and to ensure specific forms of patronage for its own constituencies.[3]

The lowly status of policy-ideology in coalitions in South Africa also holds implications for governance stability. Coalitions are more likely to persist if they are between parties with compatible ideologies, or simply if they are broadly in the same range on the ideological spectrum, as Brooks demonstrated in her chapter (see also Casani, 2020). In the 2016 post-election period, the DA metropolitan coalitions comprised the DA, the UDM, the Congress of the People (Cope), the African Christian Democratic Party (ACDP) and the Freedom Front Plus (FF+) – with the support of the EFF in a confidence-and-supply arrangement. Parties to the left of the ANC failed to achieve significant legislative representation. Another trend was, therefore, that the ANC did not have the opportunity to foster high-level inter-left bonds, beyond its Tripartite Alliance.

Patronage apparatuses are king

An important trend was that political parties of all sizes in the South African coalitions game showed that they strive for control of and rent derived from public resources. One of the explanations was that such control could be used to solicit party funding. Another was that, come an election, these parties would be able to claim that they have governed and hence come with experience and knowledge.[4] The choice of coalition partner was determined by political parties' desire for such access, in exchange for these minimal parties filling the numbers gap to make up a minimal coalition. Small parties, such as the Patriotic Alliance (PA) and the AIC, bargained for positions of mayor or deputy mayor, and/or speaker or deputy speaker, in exchange for coalition buy-in, or for a combination of high position and control over portfolios from which they could leverage resources for leaders and parties.

Interparty governing coalitions are inherently about party-political strategy to command government and the state, when or once an individual party is unable to constitute government on its own. The core dynamic is therefore conflict in unity – and it is not surprising that coalition politics is frequently unstable and disruptive. This is in line with practices illustrated by Grant Masterson, using a series of case studies from Africa, as well as Amuzweni Ngoma, when she interprets the culture of coalition formation. There is not necessarily more rent-seeking and corruption when coalitions take over from single-party government, but coalitions are used as a platform that pursues rent, which often amounts to corruption.

Size factor for resource access and the small-party industry
Multiple chapters in this book, along with the literature (see, for example, Chua and Felsenthal, 2006), stress that the size factor often has a greater impact than ideology and policy when it comes to motivations to form coalitions: both minimal and maximal majorities are constructed irrespective of ideological divergence. The exercise of adding up percentages, scouting which parties might be interested in or can be swayed to cooperate in exchange for position and power, has become a central trend in coalition-building in South Africa. The ANC in places lost its outright majority in elections, but required only small-party contributions to reconstitute an outright majority. Clusters of micro-parties availed themselves to help fill the majority deficit.

Almost inevitably, and as Ndletyana documents in this book, minimal coalitions were built in the knowledge that the spoils could then be divided between as few parties as possible (see Chua and Felsenthal, 2006). The trend of the above-weight ambition of South

Africa's small and micro-parties was matched by the willingness of the bigger parties to offer positions of power and influence. This was illustrated by the role of the PA in Nelson Mandela Bay, a one-seat party that occupied the position of mayor, and the UDM, a two-seat party in the same council. Johannesburg, Mogale City, Nelson Mandela Bay and a range of other municipalities illustrated the trend of council majorities being altered by a a single councillor going rogue, without a party officially switching coalition sides.

South Africa's small political parties called some shots on the allocation of top municipal positions. Occasionally they dictated policy nuances and implementation foci – when they had clear policies. Many of the micro-parties on whom majority building depended were community-linked organisations or single-issue parties.

Power and coalitions as a site of struggle
The use of the opportunity to attain, retain or regain political power has been a frequent trend in South Africa's coalition politics. This is important especially for the ANC, which associates control over the institutions of government with affirmation that the struggle over apartheid, and over the legacies of colonialism, continues. Where the ANC lost power, especially in 2016 when it lost outright control of core metropolitan municipalities, and subsequently, there has been an impulse to regain control. This book's case studies of the metropolitan municipalities post-2016, and the studies of KwaZulu-Natal and the Western Cape, all indicate the primacy of the power motive. In the Tshwane metro, in particular, manoeuvres to gain power included collapsing council meetings, getting individual opposition (including DA councillors) to go rogue, mobilising communities to protest against DA councillors, and working with the ANC provincial government to place the metro under administration in the hope that a new election would produce favourable results. Broadly, the large parties have historically sought to manipulate floor-crossing, support small opposition parties and absorb smaller partners to gain or retain power. When opportunities arose, other opposition parties emulated the ANC repertoires.

Coalitions in South African politics have become weaponised

as instruments of contest between the larger political parties. This dynamic operates in conjunction with office-seeking, but concerns party pride and, in the case of the ANC, the impulse to remain the dominant party. In the case of opposition parties, it relates to trying to demonstrate that they can take power from the ANC, frustrate the dominant party, and demonstrate ANC vulnerability to citizens and voters. South Africa's coalition formations are therefore permanently susceptible to destabilisation by party-political opponents and associates. Such practices could be driven by the sheer achievability of renegotiated coalitions attaining power. This trend has been rife in South Africa, especially in cases where opposition alliances, such as the metropolitan ones led by the DA, have pushed the ANC from power. In this context, the ANC has not been a 'good', compliant opposition party, prepared to sit out a five-year term on the opposition benches. It has worked relentlessly to obstruct the governing coalition, for example, in Nelson Mandela Bay and Tshwane, and to alter the line-up of parties that constituted the opposition alliance. Similarly, the DA has not been shy to use this approach in municipalities where the ANC's coalition governments have a precarious hold on power.

South Africa's experience with coalition government to date has revealed a set of trends concerning how the political parties have been using coalitions for multiple purposes that relate to interparty competition – and control over government. These trends are, in the main:

- For bigger parties, to retain power, with the help of smaller partners, to forestall ceding power to growing opposition parties.
- For the bigger parties, to regain power, with the help of smaller partners.
- For smaller parties, to attach themselves to bigger parties and gain elevation into power, despite enjoying minimal electoral support.
- For smaller parties, especially the factional proxy parties, to redistribute power away from Ramaphosa's ANC; in the case of Good, away from the DA; and in the case of the

National Freedom Party (NFP), away from the Inkatha Freedom Party (IFP).
- For smaller parties, to switch coalitions and change government, especially locally.

Intraparty policy and identity choices, plus party leadership in many instances, either facilitated or destabilised interparty coalitions and cooperation, and are therefore confirmed as one of the triggers to coalition formation and dissolution, both in South Africa and internationally, as Brooks also demonstrates in her chapter. The Africa case studies, especially those of Lesotho and Malawi, demonstrate extremities in intraparty dissidence and fallout interfacing with coalition politics.

South African political parties have centralised leadership operations. No South African party permits its provincial leaders, mayors or municipal councillors to negotiate local coalitions without permission from the party's national executive (Gottschalk, 2019). In the case of Johannesburg in 2020, the provincial ANC government, along with senior ANC head-office functionaries, were central in the renegotiation of the Johannesburg coalition, as Makgale's analysis highlights. From Ndletyana's analysis it emerges how several senior ANC leaders negotiated with the national leader of the UDM to get the UDM council representative to help reinstate the ANC in the Nelson Mandela Bay municipality. Court judgments that reversed provincial actions may affect the trend of intersphere interventions. In comparison, De Bruyn's analysis shows how the provincial ANC was drawn into the local coalition sphere.

There is also a broader trend in South Africa and internationally, in using the courts in the battle of the coalitions. On the continent, in the cases of Malawi, one alliance took another to court in a disputed presidential election and won, and in Kenya, coalition leaders, also in presidential elections (which were violence-ridden), ended up in court. South Africa's Constitutional Court became involved in coalition politics when in the mid-2000s the presence of floor-crossing was ruled to contradict PR (and was subsequently eliminated). Motlamelle Kapa's study of the case of Lesotho demonstrates the vast extent to which incessant floor-crossing and associated coalition-hopping destabilise coalition governance. Constitutional and legal reforms may be necessary to regulate and stabilise some aspects of coalition government. However, and as Pierre de Vos points out, the political will of party politicians to vote to self-regulate is in doubt. Furthermore, Nandini Patel's and Gilbert Khadiagala's chapters show that even when regulation exists, politicians circumvent the measures that are designed to constrain the centred and often counterdemocratic ways of operation in coalition politics.

Coalitions and unstable governance
Involvement in coalitions concerns far more than interparty activities – these party-level alliances are formed frequently with the express goal of rising to control government and exercise governance (and gain access to the by-products of being in government). Instability of governance is one of the main trend consequences of fleeting and floating coalitions that the political parties form with a view to optimising power, positions and perks that accrue to parties and individuals. These motivations for coalition formation are subject to change, as are the governance arrangements that take hold. Knowledge that their opportunistic actions in constituting coalition governments will have destabilising effects has not deterred coalition practitioners in South Africa. Had coalitions of instability had more direct electoral consequences, in the sense of extracting, in this instance, vertical accountability, the cooperating parties might display higher levels of responsibility. These trends have meant that in times of coalition manoeuvres, stability and coherence of the governance project were not guaranteed. Besides policies that fluctuated, the bureaucratic structures are subjected to staff turnovers that matched the movements of political principals. Where coalitions rule, functional municipal governance is often at stake, recognising that municipal governance in South Africa generally was already highly dysfunctional (Auditor-General, 2020).

INDICATORS THAT MARK SOUTH AFRICA'S COALITIONS GAME

Interwoven with the major coalition trends in South Africa, a range of indicators of coalition practice has been noted. The indicators comprise concrete, visible events and actions that occur on a regular basis and relate to interparty coalition actions.

The behaviours of political parties and their agents deliver many of these indicators. For example, election results, brought about by parties' actions and their followers' responses, contribute indicators as to whether or not, and what type of, coalitions will be formed. Government in South Africa is constituted through outright majority. In the absence of such a majority, political parties construct majorities – and constitute coalitions, including confidence-and-supply agreements.

The indicators are also manifested in the decisions around policies and payoffs that are made in the formation, maintenance and dissolution of coalitions. Furthermore, the establishment of regulatory frameworks for coalition practice is an indicator of the character of coalitions and whether or not they will be maintained.

Political parties' behaviours to maintain themselves in good standing with the electorate are important indicators of coalition practice. When this fails, parties may try to reinvent themselves (as the ANC set out to do under Ramaphosa, and the DA under Helen Zille), or split and shed the dissenting faction. Once parties split, the descendent parties may be so repulsed by their former host that they join forces with opposition parties, rather than the former host (as was the case with the UDM and Cope in relation to the ANC). Alternatively, the former host could still have centripetal power over the split-offs, and co-operation, possibly even reconciliation, could result. Serial splitting and fractionalisation of the political parties – as evidenced in the multiplicity of parties in South Africa's 2019 national and provincial elections (MISTRA, 2019) – could help predominant parties to rebuff onslaughts because such fractionalisation prevents the congealing of a major, united opposition-party challenge.

Many voter attitudes and orientations can typically be anticipated in the face of certain factors. For example, adverse economic conditions are likely to precipitate incumbent disadvantage, and in societies where economic issues have salience, ideological alliances are more likely – and once such alliances and coalitions are in place, they tend to be more stable. Deep identity cleavages and ideological polarisation in the electorate potentially but not necessarily circumscribe the range of likely alliance and coalitions partners. As a range of chapters indicate, in the unfolding early stages of coalition politics in South Africa, a clear set of rules has not solidified, except for the majority-power trend: as long as the actions build, help retain or reintroduce majority power for aspirant political parties, the parties will justify the means.

The emerging predictabilities, noticeably, are centred on party action – and what is in it for the political parties. Particracy in the time of coalitions frequently rules over electoral democracy and democratic governance.[5] There is far less attention on what coalition formations can, through sound governance, bring to the citizenry of a province or municipality than on using coalitions to get into government and access the fruits of incumbency. Coalition practice in South Africa has shown that party-political manoeuvres to handle coalitions have often paralysed government. Amid such effects of coalitions, many politicians have shown that non-governance is not of great concern to them.

CONCLUSION

At this time of South Africa's experimentation with political coalitions, a multiparty political system has been confirmed as enduring. However, there is simultaneously no indication that the drift towards more intensive coalition politics is fully appreciated across the political spectrum.

In Africa today, the vast majority of the 50-plus states use multiparty political systems, however tenuous some of them may be. Coalitions and electoral alliances between political parties are common. At national and provincial levels, South Africa at the time of the analysis in this book was still largely dominated by one party. Will the country transition to a setting in which electoral politics and processes rule, but electorates do not return a single majority party to power? This volume dissects core elements of coalitions in South Africa, in the context of international comparisons. It strives to discuss lessons as to what works and what does not when it comes to this form of government. South Africa has to accept that, in order to ensure political stability and pursue a better quality of life for all, it should now start mastering the science and art of coalition politics because, either in the short term or over the longer term, coalition politics may become the norm – as in many parts of the world.

It is hoped that this study, with its systematised, detailed and comparative information – and aptly titled *Marriages of Inconvenience* – will help improve judgements in conceptualising, practising and directing future coalition polities in the domains of both government and party politics.

REFERENCES

Anderson, V. and Johnson, L. 1997. *Systems Thinking Basics from Concepts to Causal Loops*. Cambridge: Pegasus Communications, Inc.

Auditor-General. 1 July 2020. 'Auditor-general releases municipal audit results under the theme – "not much to go around, yet not the right hands at the till"', https://www.gov.za/speeches/auditor-general-kimi-makwetu-releases-municipal-audit-results-1-jul-2020-0000#.

Calise, M. 1994. 'The Italian particracy: Beyond president and parliament', *Political Science Quarterly*, 109 (3), 441–460.

Casani, A. 2020. 'Cross-ideological coalitions under authoritarian regimes: Islamist-left collaboration among Morocco's excluded opposition', *Democratization*, 27 (7), 1183–1201.

Chua, V. C. H. and Felsenthal, D. S. 2006. *Coalition Formation Theories Revisited: An empirical investigation of Aumann's hypothesis*. London: LSE Research Online, http://eprints.lse.ac,ul/archove/00000767, accessed 2 November 2020.

Fahey, L. and Randall, R. M. 1999. *Learning from the Future: Competitive foresight scenarios*. London: John Wiley and Sons.

Feltham, L. 18 August 2016. 'Malema says the EFF won't form coalitions, but will support DA in hung metros', *Mail & Guardian*, https://mg.co.za/article/2016-08-17-malema-says-the-eff-wont-form-coalitions-but-will-support-da-in-hung-metros/, accessed 1 February 2020.

Gottschalk, K. 20 December 2019. 'Mutual hatred a big reason coalitions fail in SA', *IOL*, www.iol.co.za/news/opinion/mutual-hatred-a-big-reason-coalitions-fail-in-sa-39547294, accessed 25 October 2020.

Indridason, I. H. 2005. 'A theory of coalitions and clientelism: Coalition politics in Iceland, 1945–2000', *European Journal of Political Research*, 44 (3), 439–464.

Kauffman, D. L. Jr. 1980. *Systems One: An introduction to systems thinking.* Minneapolis: Future Systems Inc., S. A. Carlton.

Kim, D. H. 1999. *Introduction to Systems Thinking*. Cambridge: Pegasus Communications/Leverage Networks.

Mapungubwe Institute for Strategic Reflection (MISTRA). 2019. Booysen, S. (ed.) 'Voting Trends 25 Years into Democracy: Analysis of South Africa's 2019 election'. Special report, MISTRA, Johannesburg.

Marren, P. 19 October 2012. 'Why scenario-based planning beats prediction', Futures Strategy Group, https://www.futuresstrategygroup.com/blog/pmarren/why-scenario-based-planning-beats-prediction, accessed 20 July 2020.

Moore, D. A. and Haran, U. 19 May 2014. 'A simple tool for making better forecasts', *Harvard Business Review,* https://hbr.org/2014/05/a-simple-tool-for-making-better-forecasts, accessed 2 August 2020.

Schwartz, P. 1996. *The Art of the Long View: Paths to strategic insight for yourself and your company.* New York: Random House.

Notes

Preface
1. This contrasts with the scenario studies by Schreiber (2018), which were based on the assumption that South Africa was going to enter this trajectory generally in 2019, and definitely by 2024.

Chapter 1
1. This was contrary to the ambitious thesis proposed by Langfield (2014), which was popular with DA analysts at the time, that opposition parties, despite a ruling party's dominance, could advance by winning significant subnational offices and using this as a springboard to establish a governance record that would persuade voters of the party's ability to govern.
2. Other than in a few European countries, Oyugi (2006) points out that coalition politics and coalition governments have been characterised by instability and frequent break-ups.
3. Author's Turning Points Monitoring Project (The Changing Dynamics of South African Politics), 2005–2021, drawing on personal observation, primary research and media reportage, 2017–2021.
4. See the general discussions on liberation movement instances by Lindberg and Jones (2010), Mac Giollabhuí (2013) and Southall (2005).
5. This is unless that part of the electorate loyal to but disillusioned with the ANC increasingly abstains and withdraws from politics generally, rather than supporting one of the prevailing opposition parties (Booysen, 2021).
6. See, for example, Olver (n.d.).
7. This can be illustrated in a case in Johannesburg involving the EFF and

the DA (amaBhungane, 2018).
8   Although the GNU constituted a wide-front majority, it is interpreted generally in the domain of building national cohesion in a post-conflict situation, rather than a 'grand coalition'.
9   These results were spread out over (especially) two sets of by-elections, both held after the first surge of COVID-19, and were reported by the Electoral Commission, for example, https://www.elections.org.za/content/About-Us/News/Results-of-the-by-elections-held-on-9-December-2020/, accessed 10 December 2020.
10 Floor-crossing remains a potent instrument at some sites internationally, such as the Lesotho national government, where it is used in conjunction with shifting coalitions to change government frequently (see chapter 7).
11 Boucek (2012) provides valuable theoretical perspectives on the relationship between party dominance and chances for increasing corruption, and Hirschman (1970) distinguishes between alternative ways of reacting to deterioration in organisations (including political parties): 'exit', or quitting the party; and 'voice', when members exercise influence for change from within.
12 Breakaways that could hurt the ANC may also happen on opposition momentum and initiative, when an alliance of opposition parties gains appearances of ability to win, and dominant party members defect to it; these processes are illustrated by Beardsworth (2017).
13 The City of Tshwane, placed under administration of the Gauteng provincial government for much of 2020, is an illustration.

Chapter 2
1   These are parties like the DA, the EFF, the IFP, the NFP, the Minority Front, the Congress of the People, the African Christian Democratic Party and Independent Democrats.
2   Author's telephone interview with journalist Jan-Jan Joubert, 21 May 2020.
3   Author's telephone interviews with 'Mandla', ANC official, 12 April 2020; Sipho Kroma, ANC official, 14 April 2020; Tashreeq Truebody, researcher/presenter Radio 786, 1 May 2020; Morné Pietersen, Eden FM manager, 1 May 2020; and Brenda Leonard, Bush Radio station manager, 1 May 2020.
4   Author's telephone interviews with Nghamula Chauke, Capricorn FM presenter/researcher, 27 April 2020; and Jabulani Baloi, Limpopo SABC producer, 20 April 2020.
5   Author's telephone interviews with Edward Njadu, former ANC councillor, 13 May 2020; and Amos Makhendlane, municipal official, 13 May 2020.
6   Ibid.
7   Author's telephone interview with Morné Pietersen, Eden FM manager, 1 May 2020.
8   Ibid.

9. Johannes Mienies is no longer mayor. His party is now in coalition with the ANC, which got the mayoralty. Author's telephone interview with Edward Njadu, former ANC councillor, 13 May 2020.
10. Author's interview with Africa Bondo, journalist at Karabo FM, 28 April 2020.
11. Author's interview with Sello Hlasa, 27 April 2020.
12. Author's telephone interview with Phillip Kganyane, SACP provincial spokesperson, Free State, 18 April 2020.
13. Author's interview with Solly Mapaila, SACP general secretary, 29 April 2020.
14. The ANC has made promises to work on a policy decision to relocate Matatiele back into KwaZulu-Natal, but the promise has never amounted to any significant effort (Komisa, 2018).
15. Meyer had bought clothing for a rugby team, a decision about which the ANC felt it should have been consulted. 'I told Donson,' explained Meyer, 'that I do not have to account to the ANC how I use the fund' (Terreblanche, 2001). Donson was affronted by the defiance. It is not clear if the DA shared the ANC's outrage at how Meyer had used the discretionary fund, but they certainly had a gripe of their own against him.
16. Author's telephone interview with Bennet Joko, 9 April 2020.
17. Bobani died in November 2020, weeks before he would have been a co-accused in a major municipal fraud and corruption case.
18. Author's telephone interview with Myra Linders, 15 May 2020.

Chapter 3

1. Notably, the longstanding failure of consecutive governments in Chile to address socioeconomic concerns and state service provision resulted in a majority referendum vote in October 2020 to rewrite the market-friendly Pinochet-era constitution, long charged by Chileans with maintaining the country's inequalities (Watson, 2020).
2. See also Martin and Vanberg (2008: 513) on how coalition parties are more likely to dedicate time in their parliamentary speeches to issues that divide the coalition the closer they get to elections.

Chapter 4

1. Despite regular elections, Southern Africa risks relapsing into autocratisation, a possibility reinforced by militaristic responses to the coronavirus, with declarations of states of emergency and heavy deployment of security forces in society.
2. A closed party-list, PR system refers to an electoral system in which parties nominate candidates in the form of a list commensurate with the size of the elective seats in the national assembly. Depending on the number of seats won, the parties field candidates to assume seats in the assembly following the list, and the same method applies in replacing MPs.
3. A threshold in this context refers to the proportion of the national vote (often calculated in percentage terms) each party has to garner in order to qualify for a seat in parliament.

Notes

4   Author interview via WhatsApp with Denis Kadima, executive director, Electoral Institute for Sustainable Democracy in Africa, 31 May 2020.
5   Author interview via WhatsApp with Adriano Nuvunga, executive director, Centre for Democracy and Development, Maputo, 14 May 2020.
6   On 11 June 2020, in a case between the New Nation Movement (a minor civil society organisation) and Others, and the president of South Africa, the Constitutional Court of South Africa delivered a judgment declaring some aspects of the Electoral Act of 1998 unconstitutional to the 'extent that it requires that adult citizens may be elected to the National Assembly and Provincial Legislatures only through their political parties' (Constitutional Court of South Africa, 2020: 54–55). The implementation of the judgment was suspended for 24 months to allow parliament time to amend the legislation. In implementing this judgment, the South African parliament may steer the electoral system towards a mixed system, as applied in its local government elections. Thus, South Africa may be poised to join Lesotho and Seychelles in the category of Southern African countries operating with mixed electoral systems at the national level.
7   The outcome of the presidential election held on 23 June 2020 witnessed a crushing defeat of the DPP/UDF alliance and ushered in the Tonse coalition government, led by Lazarus Chakwera of the MCP, as the new president, and Saulos Chilima of the United Transformation Movement as the vice president.
8   Author interview with Augustine Magolowondo, director, Democracy Works Foundation, Lilongwe, 3 June 2020.
9   Author interview via WhatsApp with Sy Mamabolo, chief electoral officer at South Africa's Electoral Commission, 2 June 2020.
10 Author interview with Augustine Magolowondo, Chief of Party for Southern Africa Political Parties Programme, Democracy Works Foundation, Lilongwe, 3 June 2020.
11 Horizontal accountability refers to checks and balances between and among key organs of the state (the executive, the judiciary and the legislature) predicated on the principle of separation of powers. Vertical accountability denotes the level of responsiveness of the state to society's needs and aspirations and the extent to which the latter holds the former accountable.

Chapter 5

1   Malawi's constitutional court upheld an application from opposition parties to nullify Mutharika's presidential elections victory of May 2019. In early 2020 the court ordered that a new presidential vote be held within 150 days. See also chapter 8.
2   The All Progressives Congress won the 2019 elections by a wide margin, the People's Democratic Party was in a modestly strong second position, and the rest of the parties won negligible numbers of seats in the 360-seat house of representatives.
3   The reforms since he became prime minister in April 2018 included freeing many political detainees, including opposition leader Andargachew Tsege,

lifting the state of emergency, agreeing to give disputed territory to Eritrea, with the Eritrean president declaring an end to the war, and reopening the land border with Eritrea.
4. Author's interview with Roukaya Kasenally on Mauritian coalitions and the island's record on corruption and development at the Balalaika Hotel, Sandton, 4 March 2020.
5. Ramgoolam's trial was yet to begin in late 2020.

Chapter 8
1. Malawi does not have a constitutional court as such. However, when the High Court sits with an enhanced quorum it is colloquially referred to as the Constitutional Court; it is still the High Court through sitting with more than one judge.
2. The Mgwirizano coalition comprised the Republican Party (a breakaway from the MCP), the People's Progressive Movement (a new party), the Movement for Genuine Democratic Change and the People's Transformation Party.
3. Section 65 of the constitution reads, 'The Speaker shall declare vacant the seat of any member of the National Assembly who was, at the time of his or her election, a member of one political party represented in the National Assembly other than by that member alone but who has voluntarily ceased to be a member of that party and has joined another political party represented in the National Assembly.'
4. 'Cashgate' was a massive financial scandal involving corruption, looting and theft by many senior government officials. It first came to light in 2013.
5. The injunction was served by the MP for the Zomba Central constituency, Yunus Mussa.
6. The Constitutional Amendment Act, No. 8 of 2001, provides that: 'The Speaker shall declare vacant the seat of any member of the National Assembly who was, at the time of his or her election, a member of one political party represented in the National Assembly other than by that member alone but who has voluntarily ceased to be a member of that party or has joined another political party represented in the National Assembly, or has joined any other political party, or association or organisation whose objectives or activities are political in nature.' This Act therefore extended section 65 to associations or organisations that are political in nature – and this raised concern.

Chapter 9
1. The South African Constitution does not establish a pure system of parliamentary government in the national and provincial spheres, as the head of the executive, once elected by the legislature, ceases to be a member of the legislature. The South African system also provides for a formal election of the head of the national and provincial executives. The

term 'parliamentary government' also does not neatly describe the system at all three levels of government, because the legislative bodies at the provincial and local government level are not referred to as 'parliament'. But for the sake of convenience, the term 'parliamentary government' is used throughout this chapter to refer to the system that applies in all three spheres of government.

2   The DA has on several occasions alleged that some of its councillors voted for the removal of the DA mayor after being paid bribes by members of the governing party. In 2017, it alleged that a bribe was paid to one of its councillors who seemingly voted with the ANC in a motion of no confidence against West Rand Mogale City municipality mayor Michael Holenstein; see *The Citizen* (2017).

3   Unless otherwise stated, the references in this section are from the Constitution of the Republic of South Africa, Act No. 108 of 1996.

4   In *Tlouamma and Others v Mbethe, Speaker of the National Assembly of the Parliament of the Republic of South Africa and Another* (A 3236/15) [2015] ZAWCHC 140; 2016 (1) SA 534 (WCC); [2016] 1 All SA 235 (WCC); 2016 (2) BCLR 242 (WCC) (7 October 2015), the High Court dismissed the application of Agang, a small opposition party, for the removal of the speaker of the national assembly on the grounds that she acted in a biased manner. The judgment was based partly on the fact that the constitution bestows the power to remove the speaker on the national assembly and not on the court. The court did not definitively rule on whether the actions of the speaker were biased against opposition parties.

5   The constitution also provides for the removal of the president through so-called impeachment. Thus, section 89(1) states that the national assembly can remove the president by a resolution adopted with a supporting vote of at least two-thirds of its members, but only on the grounds of a serious violation of the constitution or the law, serious misconduct, or inability to perform the functions of office. This provision is not directly relevant to the arguments on coalitions, as it will not be used when the president or cabinet loses the political support of a majority of the members of the national assembly, but only where wrongdoing or incapacity is present.

6   Unless otherwise indicated in this section, the section references relate to the Municipal Structures Act, No. 117 of 1998.

7   The executive mayoral system is used in every metropolitan council in South Africa, including Johannesburg, Tshwane, Nelson Mandela Bay, Cape Town, eThekwini and Ekurhuleni. It is also used in most large and medium-sized towns. The reason for the popularity of this system is that it bestows more political power on the party or parties that secure a majority in the council. The collective mayoral system is used in only a very few, usually very small, municipalities; see Toxopeüs (2019). eThekwini used to have a collective executive system and then changed to the executive mayoral system.

8   The Supreme Court of Appeal dismissed an appeal of the judgment in

Premier for the Province of Gauteng and Others v Democratic Alliance and Others (2020), thus confirming the High Court approach. At the time of writing it is not known whether an appeal to the Constitutional Court will follow.

9   See *Majola v The President* (48541/2010) [2012] ZAGPJHC 236 (30 October 2012), where the South Gauteng High Court rejected a challenge to the constitutionality of section 57A read with schedule 1A of the Electoral Act, No. 73 of 1998 because of an alleged inconsistency between these provisions and section 19(3)(b) of the constitution; see Wolf (2014) for a critical discussion of the judgment.

10 Thus, there has been considerable controversy about the ANC provincial leadership's alleged 'imposition' of ward councillor candidates on communities; see Nyakombi (2016).

11 In August 2018, the DA relied on section 27 of the Local Government: Municipal Systems Act to try and prevent the removal of the DA mayor. This followed the removal of the speaker of the council by a vote of no confidence, in which one of the DA councillors, Victor Manyati, abstained from the vote, allowing the vote to pass with 60 votes to 59. A tie would have seen the speaker remain in the position; see Gerber (2018).

12 The Constitutional Court had previously found in *Economic Freedom Fighters v Speaker of the National Assembly and Others; Democratic Alliance v Speaker of the National Assembly and Others* (2016: para 83) that the president had failed to uphold, defend and respect the constitution as the supreme law of the land.

13 Pocketbook politics in this context denotes elected representatives enticed by offers of money or other benefits to do or not to do something, such as taking a bribe to support a vote of no confidence.

14 This problem of vote buying can be addressed only if speakers exercise their discretion on when to allow a secret ballot during a vote of no confidence in a more circumspect manner. I would argue that votes of no confidence should be conducted by secret ballot only in the most exceptional cases, when it is clear that the vote is not primarily aimed at collapsing the government or at grabbing power. The Constitutional Court judgment in *United Democratic Movement v Speaker of the National Assembly and Others* (2017) must be read as applying to a situation in which the head of the executive has clearly abused their power or failed to uphold their constitutional obligations – as was the case with former president Jacob Zuma.

15 A confidence-and-supply agreement most commonly refers to a party (or independent members of a legislature) agreeing to support the government in motions of confidence and appropriation or budget votes; they would either vote in favour of a motion, or abstain. More broadly, it also designates an opposition party agreeing that it will not vote against a minority government.

16 The adoption of ordinary legislation in the national assembly requires

Notes

support by a simple majority of the national assembly members, and not a two-thirds majority as is the case with a constitutional amendment. However, any change would depend on whether the governing party would support such a change, a question that is not possible to answer here.

Chapter 10

1. A metropolitan municipality is a single-tier municipality that governs a conurbation, and differs from the rest of the two-tier local government system consisting of local and district municipalities. Metropolitan municipalities are designated as such by the Municipal Demarcation Board in terms of the Municipal Structures Act, No. 17 of 1998, and currently include Cape Town, Johannesburg, Tshwane, Ekurhuleni, eThekwini, Nelson Mandela Bay, Buffalo City and Mangaung.
2. The South African Constitution (1996) defines the powers of municipalities, which include local planning, land management, utility services, community facilities and public health, while the Local Government: Municipal Structures Act, No. 17 of 1998, describes the categories of municipalities and the division of powers between them.
3. 'Municipal manager' is the generic term for the chief executive officer of a municipality, also referred to in metropolitan municipalities as the 'city manager'.
4. Section 82 versus sections 44 and 56 of the Municipal Structures Act.
5. The 2009 assessment was a consolidated national report based on nine provincial reports, compiled following assessments jointly conducted across the country between April and August 2009. The assessments were designed to 'ascertain the root causes of the current state of distress in many of the county's municipalities in order to inform a National Turn-Around Strategy for Local Government' (De Visser and Steytler, 2009).
6. The South African Cities Network study consisted of nine semi-structured interviews with former local government senior managers and mayoral committee members, covering five of the metros (Foster, 2019: 3).
7. 50 percent of the seats in council are allocated to ward councillors elected on a FPTP basis, and the remaining 50 per cent (referred to as 'PR' councillors) are allocated to councillors drawn from lists compiled by political parties. The allocation of seats to political parties is based on a formula designed to ensure that the total number of ward and PR seats occupied by a party in council is in proportion to the total number of ward and PR votes received by each party, excluding the seats occupied by independent candidates.
8. 'Metro' is used throughout this chapter as an abbreviation for 'metropolitan municipality'.
9. It could be that the inclusion of several parties in the coalition contributed to its stability, as no one party could hold the ANC to ransom.

10. Author interview with Lisa Seftel, political admin interface – City of Johannesburg, 1 August 2017; Author interview with Anthony Still, political admin interface – City of Johannesburg, 18 September 2019.
11. Author interview with Anthony Still, political admin interface – City of Johannesburg, 18 September 2019.
12. Ibid.
13. Ibid.
14. The changes were along the lines of the Cape Town organogram, combining utility services into a single department, and amalgamating legal, human-resources and fleet-management functions into corporate services. This created a number of new posts, including chief operating officer, and heads for governance, group audit, group communications and regions.
15. Author interview by phone with Moeketsi Mosola, political admin interface – City of Tshwane, 1 April 2020.
16. Municipalities are required to set up systems for monitoring their performance in terms of section 40 of the Municipal Systems Act, No. 32 of 2000. Key performance areas (KPAs) are categories of organisational performance that correspond to a municipality's strategic priorities. For each KPA there are measurable key performance indicators (KPIs) established, which are monitored against targets.
17. Author interview with Lisa Seftel, political admin interface – City of Johannesburg, 1 August 2017.
18. Author interview by phone with Moeketsi Mosola, political admin interface – City of Tshwane, 1 April 2020.
19. Ibid.
20. Ibid.
21. Ibid.
22. Author interview by phone with Johann Mettler, political admin interface – Nelson Mandela Bay, 27 May 2020.
23. Ibid.
24. Ibid.
25. Ibid.
26. Managers who are directly accountable to the municipal manager, appointed in terms of section 56 of the Municipal Systems Act 32 of 2000.
27. Author interview with Anthony Still, political admin interface – City of Johannesburg, 18 September 2019; Author interview by phone with Johann Mettler, political admin interface – Nelson Mandela Bay, 27 May 2020.
28. Author interview by phone with Johann Mettler, political admin interface – Nelson Mandela Bay, 27 May 2020.
29. Author interview by phone with Moeketsi Mosola, political admin interface – City of Tshwane, 1 April 2020; Author interview with Yondela Silimela, political admin interface – City of Johannesburg, 9 October 2019; Author interview with Anthony Still, political admin interface –

City of Johannesburg, 18 September 2019.
30. The Corridors of Freedom is a transit-oriented urban-development strategy in which high-density mobility corridors link up dispersed development nodes in the City of Johannesburg. It was inaugurated by mayor Parks Tau in 2013.
31. Author interview with Yondela Silimela, political admin interface – City of Johannesburg, 9 October 2019.
32. Author interview by phone with Moeketsi Mosola, political admin interface – City of Tshwane, 1 April 2020.
33. Author interview with Lisa Seftel, political admin interface – City of Johannesburg, 1 August 2017.
34. Author interview with Anthony Still, political admin interface – City of Johannesburg, 18 September 2019.
35. Author interview with Lisa Seftel, political admin interface – City of Johannesburg, 1 August 2017.
36. Ibid.
37. Author interview by phone with Moeketsi Mosola, political admin interface – City of Tshwane, 1 April 2020.
38. Ibid.
39. Author interview by phone with Johann Mettler, political admin interface – Nelson Mandela Bay, 27 May 2020. A municipality's financial year runs from 1 July to 30 June the following year. In terms of the Municipal Finance Management Act, No. 56 of 2003, all municipal income and expenditure must take place in accordance with a budget that has been approved before the start of the financial year in question. Given the public consultation and council approval processes that are stipulated in the Act, a budget has to be tabled to council at least 90 days before the start of the new financial year, and council must consider the budget for adoption at least 30 days before the start of the financial year. Failure to approve a budget before the start of the financial year constitutes grounds for high-level government intervention in the affairs of the municipality.
40. Author interview by phone with Johann Mettler, political admin interface – Nelson Mandela Bay, 27 May 2020.
41. This refers to a material misstatement of information in the financial statements which is sufficiently incorrect as to impair the extent to which the financial statements can be considered as a true and accurate reflection of the affairs of the entity.
42. The consumer collection rate is the percentage of invoiced rates and service charges that are actually collected, i.e. paid by consumers, in a financial year.
43. Author interview by phone with Moeketsi Mosola, political admin interface – City of Tshwane, 1 April 2020.
44. The contract was based on schedule 32 of the Municipal Finance Management Act, allowing the municipality to utilise another state entity's procurement process (in this instance, a contract from the Development

⁴⁵ Bank of Southern Africa).
⁴⁵ Author interview by phone with Johann Mettler, political admin interface – Nelson Mandela Bay, 27 May 2020.
⁴⁶ The biennial Quality of Life survey conducted by the Gauteng City Region Observatory measures the quality of life, socioeconomic circumstances, attitudes to service delivery, psychosocial attitudes, value base and other characteristics of Gauteng. Started in 2009, it allows for statistically significant comparisons of trends over time for the region as a whole, as well as the municipalities within the region. The results of the latest Quality of Life survey V (2018/19) were released in November 2018.
⁴⁷ Targets set for the performance of municipal functions relating to the built environment (e.g., planning approval, building permits or housing delivery).
⁴⁸ The city had 13 service delivery and budget implementation plan targets that were divided as follows: water and sanitation – 3 (0 achieved), energy and electricity – 3 (1 achieved), roads and transport – 3 (1 achieved) and housing and human settlements – 4 (0 achieved) (Maja, 2019: 3).
⁴⁹ Author interview by phone with Moeketsi Mosola, political admin interface – City of Tshwane, 1 April 2020.
⁵⁰ Ibid.
⁵¹ Author interview by phone with Johann Mettler, political admin interface – Nelson Mandela Bay, 27 May 2020.
⁵² Ibid.

Chapter 11
¹ Chapter 9 gives a full exposition of this concept, in essence an agreement to limited, specific acts of support and cooperation.
² The primary research data in this chapter were gathered for a master's thesis presented in partial fulfilment for the Master of Management in Public Policy degree at the Wits School of Governance; see Makgale (2020).
³ Interviews were granted on the condition of anonymity; to ensure anonymity, generic descriptions are used to ascribe the interview data: the political party representatives are referred to as 'councillors' and representatives from administrative bodies as 'senior officials'.
⁴ The policy emphasises that '(t)he DA believes that every South African family should have access to adequate shelter and supports the interpretation of section 26 of the constitution which requires that this right must be "progressively realised".'
⁵ The Alex shutdown began in June 2019, shortly before the national and provincial elections, spurred by dissatisfaction at poor service delivery and overcrowding in the township. Residents were particularly concerned by the alleged corruption that they believed was at the root of their poor living conditions. The ANC at the time was ready to step into the window of opportunity for campaigning (Booysen, 2019).

6   The Red Ants are a South African private security company specialising in removing 'illegal invaders' from properties.
7   In November 2020 evidence was heard at the Zondo Commission that Makhubo had abused his position as MMC for finance at the municipality to solicit huge amounts for the ANC from companies holding contracts with the city. Makhubo was also said to have gained personally (see, for example, Amashabalala and Madisa, 2020).

Chapter 12
1   *Democratic Alliance and Others v Premier for the Province of Gauteng and Others*, 2020: para 88.
2   See Law (2018: 33) regarding non-ideologically aligned political parties that can be successful coalition partners.
3   The Supreme Court of Appeal dismissed the appeal of the judgment; *Premier for the Province of Gauteng and Others v Democratic Alliance and Others* (394/2020) [2020] ZASCA 136 (27 October 2020). It therefore confirmed the High Court ruling.
4   North Gauteng High Court (2020: para 81) stated: 'It is our view that the most direct cause of the Council's inability to conduct its business in council meetings was the continued disruptions of council meetings by ANC and EFF councillors staging walkouts.'
5   North Gauteng High Court (2020: para 21), with the speaker and DA launching court action to set aside the speaker's suspension, stated: 'The MEC, on advice from counsel, rescinded the decision to suspend the Speaker.'
6   The North Gauteng High Court (2020: para 74) argued: 'A decision in terms of section 139(1)(c) is only appropriate if it is likely to ensure the relevant obligation will be fulfilled. [1] Appointing an Administrator is a stop gap option that is meant to pave the way for an election. Furthermore, an election as a result of the dissolution decision may in fact result in many of the same councillors returning to their positions again resulting in a hung Municipal Council. There is no guarantee that a fresh election will resolve the relevant obligation. It is an option more reliant on hope than certainty and as such cannot, objectively, be viewed as capable of resolving the problem at hand.'
7   Supreme Court of Appeal (SCA) of South Africa (2020) includes the synopsis: 'The SCA noted the findings of the high court that (1) the dissolution decision would have the effect of undoing the votes of the residents of Tshwane and force fresh elections, which was extraordinary from a constitutional standpoint.' It added: 'On the facts of this case, it would constitute irreparable harm that the citizens of Tshwane, who had a fundamental constitutional right to be governed by those they had elected, would be denied this right.' The specific words of the North Gauteng High Court (2020) para 106 were: 'The DA seeks final relief in the form of

a mandamus compelling those ANC and EFF councillors, who have failed to attend meetings or walked out of meetings, to attend and remain in attendance at municipal council meetings.'

8   North Gauteng High Court (2020: para 72) stated: 'These observations are the high water-mark of the case for the Gauteng EC. It is common cause that there is no Mayor, Municipal Manager and Mayoral Committee and the last 7 meetings of the Municipal Council were not quorate due to the disruptions arising from the walkouts from Council meetings by ANC and EFF councillors thus paralysing the Municipal Council. In argument it was categorised as the best example of exceptional circumstances justifying the dissolution of the Municipal Council.' Para 80 continued: 'The answering affidavit signed by the Premier sets out in detail that the Gauteng EC was aware of the collapse of Municipal Council meetings as well as the role of ANC and EFF councillors in causing these collapses.'

9   Financial sustainability for the audit years 2014/15 and 2015/16, illustrated in the auditor-general's findings, were unqualified audit opinions, but with unauthorised expenditure in 2015/16 at R2.03 billion (Tshwane Mayoral Committee Report, 2018: 40). Hence, while the post-2016 ANC portrayed the DA-led coalition as inherently corrupt, the auditor-general had adverse findings and noted overexpenditure and financial-sustainability concerns in both the pre- and post-2016 councils.

Chapter 13

1   Author's personal observations during a fieldwork trip in Port Elizabeth, 24–31 July 2016.

2   This collaboration was illustrated in the Constitutional Court case through which parliament was obligated to hold Zuma to account for misspending public funds.

3   Matatiele previously was allocated to KwaZulu-Natal, but had been relocated to the Eastern Cape. The protests that ensued crystallised into a political party.

4   This explains why in the 2019 elections, the Electoral Commission separated the two parties through a draw. As a result, the ANC was placed in the middle of the ballot paper, and the AIC at the bottom; Eyewitness News (2019).

5   A similar agreement was signed by regional leaders of the party, except the FF+, in Port Elizabeth on 23 August 2016.

6   Letter: Executive Mayor Athol Trollip to UDM President Bantu Holomisa, re: Changes to the Mayoral Committee of the Nelson Mandela Metro Council, 16 May 2017.

7   The panel was made up of the FF+'s Anton Alberts, Cope's Farouk Cassim and the ACDP's Jo-Ann Downs. It excluded both the DA and the UDM.

8   Correspondence: UDM President Bantu Holomisa to ACDP President Kenneth Meshoe, Cope President Mosiuoa Lekota, DA Leader Mmusi

Maimane and FF+ Leader Pieter Groenewald, Re: Nelson Mandela Bay Metro Coalition: Democratic Alliance Continued Defiance Re Reinstatement of Cllr M Bobani, 6 June 2007.
9   The officials were Nkosinathi Dolo, Joram Mkosana, Thabo Williams and ndile Tolom; De Kock and Kimberley (2018).
10 About three months later, Kramer was appointed acting chief financial officer, despite lack of experience in senior management: Bobani seemingly did not hold it against Kramer that he had revealed that Bobani had instructed him to lie. The underserved promotion, albeit interim, may have been a reward for Kramer, for attempting to deceive the court on behalf of the mayor. Despite the possible stain on his reputation and charges of perjury, Kramer did not seem to have minded working closely under Bobani.
11 Author interview with Nqaba Bhanga, 9 July 2020, in person in Port Elizabeth.
12 Author interview with Ncediso Captain, 8 July 2020.
13 Letter: DA Lawyers Minde Schapiro & Smith to lawyers for the speaker Kuben Chetty Inc, Re: Suspension of Council Meeting 12 March 2020 and Speaker's Refusal to Accept Delivery of New Request in Terms of section 29 (1) of the Structures Act and Rule 4.2 of the Council's Rules of Order, 18 March 2020; Letter: DA Eastern Cape and caucus leader Nqaba Bhanga to Minister of Cooperative Governance and Traditional Affairs Nkosazana Dlamini-Zuma, Re: Mayoral Vacancy – Nelson

Chapter 14

1   In a diverse racial society, the interests and securities of minority groups are seen as being protected through power-sharing arrangements.
2   In this context the agreement refers to the DP and the NNP entering into an arrangement aimed at strengthening the opposition footprint. The agreement ensured levels of separate identity while also maintaining the existence of the NNP as an electoral actor. (In respect of an alliance, it is an arrangement that is agreed to before an election, whereas a coalition is formed following an election outcome.) The cooperation agreement between the DP and the NNP was a loose formation levelled at ensuring that both political actors maintained traction in the electoral landscape.
3   The formation of the DA was based on the DP forming an alliance of opposition parties that would come together to form a strengthened bloc of parties against the dominance of the ANC.
4   In the metro, the share of the votes was 53.5 per cent and 38 per cent for the DA and the ANC, respectively.
5   Following the NNP's exit from the DA, the DP retained the use of the name 'Democratic Alliance'.
6   This was at the leadership level, and only minimally at the general-membership and follower levels. NNP members and supporters

migrated largely to the DA (Booysen, 2011).
7. These were Cederberg, Matzikama, Cape Agulhas and the Central Karoo District Municipality.
8. This point is further elaborated by Adam (1994) and also disputed by Mattes and Gouws (1999), who note methodological flaws in drawing such correlations in the data.

Chapter 15
1. This was an explanation given by him in 2004 when launching the provincial Vukuzakhe council ahead of the elections of that year; *Polity* (2004).
2. The Buthelezi Commission was set up by Buthelezi as the leader of KwaZulu, giving it a mandate to look into the future of KwaZulu/Natal across the political, economic, administrative dimensions of governance. The commission made recommmendations on the future constitutional and government structuring of arrangements for the then KwaZulu and Natal regions within a reimagined largely consocational configuration of South Africa.
3. President Thabo Mbeki offered two IFP parliamentarians deputy ministerial positions, but this was not acceptable to the IFP.
4. Faced with political woes, as he was embroiled in rape and corruption charges, Zuma used Zulu 'culture' as part of his defence mechanism (Gibson, 2011).
5. They were Wiseman Mcoyi, Nhlanhla Khawula and Sydney Zulu.

Chapter 16
1. The only other African country that has had uninterrupted democratic rule since independence is Botswana.
2. A preformateur is a political title that is given to someone who consults and negotiates on possible coalitions by order of the king. A formateur is the prime ministerial candidate who then constitutes the potential government coalition, which is then voted in or rejected by political parties in parliament. As the Belgian case shows, the formateur is not always from the largest party.

Chapter 17
1. This scenarios logic is informed by multiple readings; see, for example, Schwartz (1996); Fahey and Randall (1999).
2. Mmusi Maimane and Herman Mashaba were erstwhile DA leaders whose presence made it racially acceptable for the EFF to cooperate with the DA. However, both resigned from the DA after being marginalised, subsequent to unsatisfactory DA performance in an election led by Maimane, and Mashaba rebelling against the reasserted power of Helen Zille in the DA.
3. The EFF stressed that its municipal coalitions with the DA were an act of 'cooperation' rather than 'coalition': 'We offer support to the parties for appointing a mayor and deputy mayor, but we don't have an agreement with the parties' (Feltham, 2016). The agreement was a vote-by-vote tactical

alliance. It included then-mayor Mashaba assenting that Johannesburg refuse collection not be outsourced. See chapter 11 for further analysis.
4   Experience in having been in government is used commonly in opposition parties' election campaigns. It is crucial in South Africa's dominant party system for the opposition parties to make it known that they too have a track record of having been in government.
5   For explications of the term, and comparisons as to how political parties can tower over other parliamentary and presidential systems, see Calise (1994).

Index

Note: Locators in *italics* refer to figures. Locators followed by a 't' indicate a table, e.g. 114t refers to the table on page 114. Locators followed by an 'n' and a number refer to an endnote, e.g. 513n2–3 refers to endnotes 2 and 3 on page 513. Only authors quoted in the text are included in the index.

A

ABC (All Basotho Convention)
   coalitions and governance
     111, 112, 184–186, 186t,
     190–191, 194–195, *195*,
     199–202
   electoral performance 188,
     190t–193t
accountability
   coalitions and 23–25, 68, 80,
     85–86
   defined xiii, 503n11
   electoral system and 84, 114t,
     116–117
   leadership and 271, 293
   secret ballot and 254–257
AFORD (Alliance for Democracy, Malawi)
   coalitions and governance
     210, 212–213, 216–218, 217t,
     221, 227–229
   electoral performance 209,
     213t, 214t
Africa, C. 400, 408, 410, 413

African National Congress *see*
   ANC (African National Congress)
AIC (African Independent Congress)
   and the ANC 47, 59–60,
     273–274, 366–367, 512n3–4
   as coalition partner 324, 378,
     380–381, 392, 488, 491
   electoral performance 16t,
     309t, 364t
Alberts, A. 373
Alexandra township 24–25,
   325–326, 510n5, 511n6
Alford, J. 268, 296, 298
Aliyu, D. 461
All Basotho Convention *see* ABC
   (All Basotho Convention)alliances
   defined 183
   electoral 112, 136–137, 497
   opportunistic 80, 139–141,
     149
   types in South Africa 30t
Altman, D. 3, 5, 211
ANC (African National Congress)

Index

and civic organisations 49–58
coalition with NFP 435–439, 440t, 441
coalitions with NP/NNP 28, 399–400, 404–405, 410–411, 414
coalitions with smaller parties 47, 273–274, 367–368
corruption allegations 275, 288–289, 305–306, 307–308, 312, 316, 511n7
and DA 52, 60, 365–366, 377, 409, 492–493, 505n2
and EFF 20, 321, 324, 343–349, 368, 490
electoral performance 16t, 274t, 308, 309t, 311t, 338t, 364t, 425t
internal coalitions and factions 29–33, 406–408, 415
internal rules and regulations 250–251, 257
use of interparty coalitions 20–22, 26–29, 30t, 33–34
vacillating dominance 5–6, 13–15, 17–19, 336, 486
see also Johannesburg, City of; KwaZulu-Natal; Nelson Mandela Bay metropolitan council; Tshwane Metropolitan council
Angola 105t, 107–109, 115t, 117t
Asia 69, 79, 89
Auditor-General of South Africa 271, 277, 281, 285, 293–294, 352, 353
Austria 78, 81, 88–89

B
Backlund, A. 74, 77
Banda, Joyce 215, 220
Basotho National Party *see* BNP (Basotho National Party)
BDP (Botswana Democratic Party) 106, 130t, 131–132, 467–468
Beaufort West municipality 51–53, 409
Belgium 81, 83, 461–463, 472, 514n2
Bellamy, R. 86–87, 88
Bergman, T. 69, 84
Berkowitz, P. 439–441
Bhanga, Nqaba 275, 388, 391–392
'big men' politics xiii, 40, 51–54
BNP (Basotho National Party)
coalitions 111, 184–185, 186t, 195, 199, 200, 201–202
electoral performance 183, 190t–193t
Bobani, Mongameli
allegations of corruption 275, 288, 502n17
and Nelson Mandela Bay metro council 277, 363, 369–375, 382–387, 389, 390
Booysen, S. 316, 403, 404, 405
Botswana
coalitions in 130t, 131–133, 464–465, 467–469
democracy 98, 515n1
electoral system 102–103, 104, 105t, 106, 119
voter trust and participation 114t, 115t, 117t
Botswana Democratic Party (BDP) 106, 130t, 131–132, 467–468
Britain 78, 83, 469, 470–471
Brown, C. 468
Building Bridges Initiative (Kenya) 175–176
Buthelezi, Mangosuthu
and the ANC 423, 428–429, 431
and IFP factionalism 43, 44–45, 421–422, 433, 436–438, 438, 514n2
Butler, A. 407

C
Cape Town Metropolitan Council
ANC-NP/NNP coalitions 399–400, 404–405
coalitions in 397

DP/DA-NP/NNP coalition
  272–273, 400–404, 405–409
  factors influencing coalition
  formation 410–416
Carrubba, C. J. 183, 184
CCM (Chama Cha Mapinduzi,
  Tanzania) 106, 137, 137–139
Cheeseman, N. 98
Chile 75, 77, 85–86, 502n1
*Chilima & Chakwera v Mutharika
  & EC* 104–106, 221, 225
China, People's Republic of 69
Chinsinga, B. 220
civic organisations 42, 48–57, 59,
  409
coalition agreements 82, 83, 85,
  258–262, 294–295, 464–469,
  482–483
    see also Denmark coalition
    negotiations 461–464
Coalition for Unity and Democracy
  (Ethiopia) 142–144
coalitions
  defined xiv, 101, 183, 310
  types in Africa 112–114, 113t,
  133–141, 151, 183–184
  see also iceberg model of
  analysing coalitions; life-cycle
  of coalitions
coalitions in South Africa
  constitutional and legal
  considerations 235–246,
  487–488, 504n1, 505n4,
  506n16
  impact on city finance
  283–287, 286t, 287t, 509n39,
  509n41, 509n42
  impact on corruption
  287–290, 290, 307–308,
  315–316, 490–491
  impact on policy and service
  delivery 281–283, 291–292,
  291, 318–319, 322–323,
  350–352
  landscape of 13–15, 17–25,
  33–35, 39–43, 41t, 58–63,
  273–275, 500n1

life-cycle of 337–340, 481–484,
  482
limiting dysfunctional
  political-administrative
  interface 293–299
limiting role of party leaders
  251–257
and political-administrative
  interface in metros 270–273,
  275–281, 292–293, 507n1,
  507n3
role of party leaders in
  247–257, 353–356, 370,
  392–393, 459–460
types of 30t
ways to stabilise 258–262,
  506n14–15
see also iceberg model of
analysing coalitions
colonialism, impact on
electoral systems 97, 103, 128–133
community organisations 42,
  48–57, 59, 409
confidence-and-supply agreements
  between DA and EFF 273,
  274, 306, 340, 356, 459
  meaning and use of xiv,
  258–262, 506n15
Congress of the People see Cope
  (Congress of the People)
Congress of South African Trade
  Unions (Cosatu) 29, 30t, 32–33
consensus-building in coalitions
  83, 86–91, 107, 464–469
  see also Denmark
consociational democracy xiv, 424
Cope (Congress of the People)
  and ANC 31, 47, 407
  coalitions with DA 308, 336,
  366, 368, 369, 490
  electoral performance 16t, 42,
  309t, 338t, 364t, 425t
Cosatu (Congress of South African
  Trade Unions) 29, 30t, 32–33

Index

D

DA (Democratic Alliance)
    and the ANC 52, 60, 365–366, 377, 409, 492–493, 505n2
    coalition with IFP 430, 432, 441–442
    coalitions with civic organisations 50, 54, 56–57
    coalitions with FF+ 308, 336, 344, 368, 409, 490
    coalitions with smaller parties 21–22, 272–273, 306, 313, 459
    and corruption 24–25, 287, 289, 382
    and EFF alliances 20, 62, 273–275, 289, 314, 340, 514n3
    and EFF policy/ideology issues 282, 316–318, 355, 487
    electoral performance 16t, 273, 274t, 309t, 311t, 338t, 364t, 425t
    growth and governance in the Western Cape 400–404, 405–409, 413–416, 513n2–3
    internal rules and regulations 250
    internal tensions 62–63, 249, 326–327, 514n2
    as main opposition party 6, 27, 486
    see also Democratic Alliance and Others v Premier for the Province of Gauteng and Others; Johannesburg, City of; Nelson Mandela Bay metropolitan council; Tshwane metropolitan council
Daniel, J. 406
Daniels, Marlon 374–375, 377–378, 380, 381, 391
DC (Democratic Congress, Lesotho)
    coalitions and governance 111, 185–186, 186t, 194–195, 195, 197–199, 201–202
    electoral performance 190t–193t
De Kock, R. 370, 371, 372, 374
De Lille, Patricia 49, 249, 405, 408, 416

De Visser, J. 270, 350, 507n5
democracy
    coalitions and consociational 411–424
    and coalitions in South Africa 22–25
    elections and 99–100
    impact of coalitions on 79–89, 90–91
    political parties and 68, 71–76, 497
    see also electoral systems, impact of coalitions on values; Mauritius
Democratic Alliance *see* DA (Democratic Alliance)
Democratic Alliance and Others v Premier for the Province of Gauteng and Others 245–246, 505n8, 511n4–7
Democratic Congress *see* DC (Democratic Congress, Lesotho)
Democratic Party *see* DA (Democratic Alliance)
Democratic Progressive Party (DPP, Malawi) 213–216, 213t, 217t, 220–224, 503n7
Democratic Republic of Congo *see* DRC (Democratic Republic of Congo)
Denmark 452–453, 454–456
dominant party systems
    in Africa 105t, 106, 108, 109–111, 113t, 129–130, 461
    coalitions in 13, 17, 75–76
    defined 102–103
    South Africa and the ANC 26–27, 30t, 34, 478, 486, 487, 493
Donson, Geoffrey 53–54, 60, 502n15
DPP (Democratic Progressive Party, Malawi) 213–216, 213t, 217t, 220–224, 503n7
DRC (Democratic Republic of Congo) 146
    electoral system 105t, 107–110, 112–113, 119

voter participation 115t, 117t

E
Eastern Europe, coalitions in
 71–74, 77–79, 80–84, 452, 469
Economic Freedom Fighters and Others v Speaker of the National Assembly and Another 252–253
EFF (Economic Freedom Fighters)
 and ANC 20, 321, 324, 343–349, 368, 490
 as coalition partner 23, 62, 341, 459–460, 488, 489–490
 and DA 56–58, 273–275, 289, 314, 340, 514n2-3
 and DA policy/ideology issues 282, 316–318, 355, 487
 electoral performance 16t, 274t
 and FF+ 56, 61
 as king/queenmaker 42, 308–310, 319–322, 328
 in KwaZulu-Natal 47, 425t, 441–442
 origin 31
 see also Johannesburg, City of, role of EFF; Nelson Mandela Bay metropolitan council, role of EFF; Tshwane metropolitan council
Ekurhuleni metropolitan council
 coalitions in 273, 274t
 impact of coalitions on city finance 283–287, 286t, 287t, 509n39, 509n41, 509n42
 impact of coalitions on corruption 276, 287–290, *290*
 impact of coalitions on governance and service delivery 278, 291–292, *291*
elections, defined xv, 99
electoral alliances 112, 136–137, 497
electoral cycles and coalitions 469–471
electoral systems
 coalitions and 6, 70, 112–114, 487–488

colonial legacy in Africa 129–133
defined 99–101
impact of coalitions on values 98, 114–120, 114t, 115t, 117t
and party systems 102–111
types in Southern Africa 97, 105t, 113t
EPRDF (Ethiopian People's Revolutionary Democratic Front) 134, 142–145
Eswatini 103, 104, 105t, 106, 115t, 117t
Ethiopia 134, 142–145, 503n3
Evans, P. 268
Eveleth, A. 424

F
FF+ (Freedom Front Plus)
 coalitions with DA 50, 308, 336, 344, 368, 409, 490
 electoral performance 16t, 309t, 338t
 working with other parties 47, 56, 59, 61
floor-crossing
 defined xv, 26
 implications of 115–116
 see also Lesotho, floor-crossing; Malawi; South Africa, floor-crossing
FORD (Forum for the Restoration of Democracy, Kenya) 159t, 161–162, 164
formateur/preformateur xv, 326, 462, 465, 472, 514n2
Foster, K. 271, 272, 294
FPTP (first-past-the-post) systems
 defined xv
 in Kenya 158, 172
 nature of 70, 116, 117, 119, 132
 in Southern Africa 104–106, 105t, 110, 136, 208, 467
 see also Lesotho
Francis, S. 432
Friedman, S. 411–412

G

Gaitho, M. 176
George municipality 48–49
Germany 78, 81, 88–89, 456, 458, 469–470
Geys, B. 184
governance and coalitions 25, 34–35, 495–497
government of national unity (GNU) in South Africa 26, 27, 112, 399–401, 423, 428, 501n8
governments of national unity in Africa 109, 112–113, 157, 169–170, 228
grand (maximal) coalitions xv, 4, 69, 81, 88–89, 112
Gumede, W. 429

H

Habib, A. 412
Hallifax, S. 82, 83, 85
Hans, B. 442
Harris, P. 102, 107
Heywood, A. 183–184
Hickel, J. 439
Hlasa, Sello 55–57
Holomisa, Bantu 31, 371–374
Hornsby, C. 162, 163
Hornung, J. 458

I

Ibenskas, R. 72, 80–81
iceberg model of analysing coalitions
   driving forces in South African coalitions 486–488
   indicators of South African coalition practice 496–497
   the model 479–481, *485*
   trends in South African coalitions 489–495
ICOSA (Independent Civic Organisation of South Africa) 51–54, 60, 409
ID (Independent Democrats) 16t, 42, 49, 52, 405, 406, 408
ideological coherence
   in ANC-led coalitions 18, 367
   in coalitions worldwide 3–4, 68, 76–77, 80–81, 325, 497
   in DA-led coalitions 309, 316–318, 328–329, 346, 355
   in South African coalitions 19–20, 22–23, 60–61, 324, 487, 489–490
IFP (Inkatha Freedom Party)
   alliances with various parties 308, 432, 439–442
   and ANC 27–28, 30t, 419–422, 423–427, 429–434, 443–444
   electoral performance 309t, 311t, 425t, 435, 440–441
   in Government of National Unity 112, 423, 428–429, 514n3
   internal power struggles and splits 43–47, 427–428, 435–439, 440t
   inclusiveness of electoral system 117t, 118, 120
Independent Civic Organisation of South Africa (ICOSA) 51–54, 60, 409
Independent Democrats 16t, 42, 49, 52, 405, 406, 408
India 75, 87
Indian Congress Party 75
Indridason, I. H. 434, 489
informateur *see* formateur
Inkatha Freedom Party *see* IFP (Inkatha Freedom Party)
Institute of Municipal Managers 271, 296–297
International Criminal Court 149, 171–172
Ireland 78, 464–467
Italy 78, 79, 82, 84

J

Jacoby, W. 70, 78, 81, 88
Japan 69, 75–76, 79
Jiyane, Ziba 44–46, 63, 433–434
Johannesburg, City of
   ANC's pursuit of control

322–325
context for coalition formation
  273–274, 274t, 305–306, 308,
  309t, 310–311, 311t
the DA-led coalition 306–307,
  308–309, 312–319, 325–329,
  442
impact of coalitions on city
  finance 283–287, 286t, 287t,
  509n39, 509n41, 509n42
impact of coalitions on
  corruption 287–290, *290*,
  307–308
impact of coalitions on
  governance and service delivery
  24–25, 276, 278–279, 281–283,
  291–293, *291*
role of EFF 319–322
Joko, Bennet 61
Jolobe, Z. 113
Jubilee Alliance/Party (Kenya)
  149–151, 159t, 171–176

K
Kabukuru, W. 171
Kadima, D.
  coalitions 306, 310–311, 318,
    339, 453
  definitions 101, 112, 183
kaMagwaza-Msibi, Veronica
  Zanele 45–46, 436–439
Kannaland municipality 53–54,
  60–61, 409
KANU (Kenya African National
  Union) 159t, 160–166
Kapa, M. A. 188, 310
Karoo Ontwikkelingsparty (KOP)
  54
Kasenally, R. 148
Kaspin, D. 209
Kenya
  coalitions and rent-seeking
    146, 149–151
  coalitions to oppose KANU
    161–166
  ethnic and political context 2,
    7, 157–158, 159t, 160–161, 177

Government of National
  Unity 169, 169–171
Jubilee coalition 171–176
NARC alliance 166, 166–169
Kenya African National Union
  (KANU) 159t, 160–166
Kenyatta, Jomo 159t, 160–161
Kenyatta, Uhuru 149–151, 159t,
  166, 171–176
Kibaki, Mwai 159t, 162, 164,
  165–170
kingmakers
  civic organisations and 'big
    men' as 48–57
  defined xvi
  identity of 24, 42
  see also EFF (Economic
    Freedom Fighters), as king/
    queenmaker
Klaas, B. 98
Klüver, H. 469, 470
Knysna municipality 48–49
KOP (Karoo Ontwikkelingsparty)
  54
Kramer, Karel 384–385, 513n10
Kura, S. 131
KwaZulu-Natal
  ANC-IFP coalition 26,
    27–28, 423–435, 443–444,
    514n3
  context of coalition formation
    40–44, 41t, 419–423, 425t,
    439–442, 440t
  internal tensions in IFP 435–439

L
Laingsburg municipality 41–42,
  54
Latin America, coalitions in
  69–70, 71–73, 75, 77, 85–86, 210
Law, M. 325, 336
LCD (Lesotho Congress for
  Democracy)
  coalitions and governance
    111, 185, 186t, 187–189,
    192–195, *195*, 197
  electoral performance 182,

190t–193t
legislative coalitions 113–114, 183–185
Lekalake, R. 131–132
Lekota, Mosiuoa 'Terror' 43–44
Lesotho
    context of coalition formation 181–183, 186–189, 190t–193t
    electoral/party system 102, 105t, 110–111, 119
    first coalition 189–196, *195*
    floor-crossing 115–116, 190–191, 203, 494–495, 501n10
    second coalition 197–199
    third coalition 199–202
    types of coalitions in 112, 183–186, 186t
    voter trust and participation 114t, 115t, 117t, 118
Lesotho Congress for Democracy *see* LCD (Lesotho Congress for Democracy)
Leys, C. 160
life-cycle of coalitions 337–340, 481–484, 482
Lindberg, S. 99–100
Linders, Myra 62–63
Linz, J. 210
Lungisa, Andile 377, 379, 384, 385, 388–391, 392

M

Mabogwana, Moafrika 341
McKenzie, Gayton 367–368
Mcoyi and Others v Inkatha Freedom Party, Mgwaza-Msibi v Inkatha Freedom Party 436–438
Madagascar 104, 105t, 106, 114t, 115t, 117t
Maepa, Kgosi 347
Mafaya, Buyelwa 381, 385–392
Magashule, Ace 54–56
Magwaza-Msibi, Veronica Zanele 45–46, 436–439
Maile, Lebogang 351
Maimane, Musi 326–327, 336–337, 514n2
Makhubo, Geoff 289, 307, 327, 511n7
Malawi
    changing coalition formations 216–222, 217t
    electoral system and coalitions 104–106, 105t, 112, 119, 207–212, 504n1
    impact of coalitions 226–230
    political context 209–216, 213t, 214t
    triggers for changing coalitions 39–140, 222–225, 311, 503n1, 504n6
    voter trust and participation 114t, 115t, 117t
Malawi Congress Party *see* MCP (Malawi Congress Party)
Malaysia 69, 76, 79, 86
Malema, Julius 378, 441, 460
Maluti-a-Phofung municipality 32
Mangcu, X. 399
Martin, L. W. 83, 85
Mashaba, Herman
    as DA mayor in Johannesburg 276, 319, 323, 325–327, 514n2
    and EFF 274, 278, 283–284, 289, 321–322
Mashoeshoe, M. 277, 281
Matlosa, K. 187, 197
Mauritius
    coalitions in 146–149, 452–454, 472
    electoral/party system 104, 105t, 107, 119
    voter trust and participation 114t, 115t, 117t
    maximal (grand) coalitions xv, 4, 69, 81, 88–89, 112
Mbandazayo, Lungelo 273
Mbeki, Thabo 407, 426, 428–429, 431
MCA (Metsimaholo Civic Association) 55–57
MCP (Malawi Congress Party)
    coalitions and governance

210, 212–213, 217t, 218–220, 224, 227–228
  electoral performance 209, 213t, 214t, 221
  in Tonse alliance 112, 139–140, 221–222, 503n7
MDC-Alliance (Movement for Democratic Change-Alliance, Zimbabwe) 134–136
Mdlalose, Frank 424, 428
Metsimaholo Civic Association (MCA) 55–57
Metsimaholo municipality 54–58
Mettler, Johann (city manager, Nelson Mandela Bay metro) 277, 280, 288–289, 295–296, 380, 383
Meyer, Stefan 60, 502n15
Mgwirizano (Unity) coalition (Malawi) 213, 215, 219, 222–223, 311, 504n2
Mienies, Johannes 54, 502n9
Miguna, M. 169–170
  minimal coalitions 4
  mistrust of political parties 114t, 116–117, 131–132
  Lesotho and 119, 182, 187–188
mixed member proportional electoral systems
  defined xvii
  in Southern Africa 105t, 110–111, 113t, 115t
Moi, Daniel Arap 159t, 160–161, 162–163, 165–166
Mokgabodi, B. 277, 281
Mokgalapa, Stevens 342, 355
Morgenstern, S. 72, 85
Mosola, Moeketsi (city manager, Tshwane metro) 276, 279–280, 284, 287, 295
Moury, C. 83, 84, 465
Movement for Democratic Change-Alliance (MDC-Alliance, Zimbabwe) 34–136
Mozambique
  alliances and coalitions 112, 114, 456–457, 458
  electoral/party system 105t, 107–109, 119
  voter trust and participation 114t, 115t, 117t
Msimanga, Solly 354–356
Mulhovo, H. 457
Müller, W. C. 70, 82, 259, 337–340
multiparty systems
  in Africa 105t, 107, 127, 131, 151, 497
  defined 103
Muluzi, Bakili 212–213, 217, 219–220, 223, 228–229
Mutharika, Arthur Peter 215–216, 221, 223
Mutharika, Bingu Wa 213, 215, 222
Mutua, M. 167–168

N
Nadeco (National Democratic Convention) 44–45, 46, 63, 433–434, 435–436
Naidu, S. 412
Namibia 98, 105t, 107–109, 114t, 115t, 117t, 119
NARC (National Rainbow Coalition, Kenya) 159t, 166, 166–169
National Alliance Party of Kenya 165–166
National Democratic Convention (Nadeco) 44–45, 46, 63, 433–434, 435–436
National Development Party (Kenya) 159t, 164–165
National Freedom Party *see* NFP (National Freedom Party)
National Party *see* NP/NNP (National Party/New National Party)
National Planning Commission 270, 297
National Rainbow Coalition (NARC, Kenya) 159t, 166, 166–169

Ndebele, S'bu 424, 427, 429, 432–434
Ndegwa, S. 161, 165
NDI/Oslo Center 112, 113
Ndii, D. 168
Ndlozi, Mbuyiseni 342, 355
Nelson Mandela Bay metropolitan council
    ANC-led coalition 380–391
    context of coalition formation 273, 274t, 275, 363–368, 364t
    DA-led coalition 63, 368–375, 391–392
    evaluation of coalitions 392–394, 459–460
    impact of coalitions on city finance 283–287, 286t, 287t, 509n39, 509n41, 509n42
    impact of coalitions on corruption 287–290
    impact of coalitions on governance and service delivery 277, 280–282, 291–292
    role of the EFF 62, 375–379, 460
Netherlands 77–78, 81, 83
New Nation Movement NPC and Others v President of the Republic of South Africa and Others 248, 503n6
New National Party *see* NP/NNP (National Party/New National Party)
NFP (National Freedom Party)
    coalition with ANC 435–441, 440t
    formation 44–47
    support for 16t, 42, 421, 425t
Ngqondi, Gift 371
Nigeria 140–141, 146, 459, 460–461, 503n2
no-party systems 103, 105t, 106
Nordlund, P. 101
NP/NNP (National Party/New National Party)
    coalitions with ANC 28, 399–400, 404–405, 410–411, 414
    coalitions with DP/DA 398, 400–404, 413–415, 513n2–3
    electoral support 16t, 425t
    in Government of National Unity 112, 423, 428
Ntaote, B. 196
Nyane, H. 188

O

Odinga, Jaramogi Oginga 159t, 160, 162
Odinga, Raila 159t, 164–172, 174–176
Olver, C. 273
one-party systems
    coalitions in transition from 72, 73–75, 91
    defined 102
    states transitioning from 97–98, 106, 108, 111, 129–130, 151
    opportunistic alliances 80, 139–141, 149
Orange Democratic Movement (Kenya) 159t, 167–169, 170–171
Oudtshoorn municipality 48–49
'oversized' coalitions xvii, 69, 184
Oyugi, W. O. 183, 310, 500n2

P

PA (Patriotic Alliance)
    as coalition partner 47, 59, 491
    role in Nelson Mandela Bay metro 364t, 367–368, 374–375, 377–378, 381, 492
PAC (Pan Africanist Congress) 16t, 60–61, 338t, 425t
Page, M. 140–141
parliamentary systems
    coalitions in 69–70, 235–236, 261
    in South Africa 238–246, 504n1
Party of National Unity (Kenya) 159t, 167–170
party systems
    defined 101
    types in Southern Africa 97–98, 102–103, 105t
Patriotic Alliance *see* PA

(Patriotic Alliance)
Paun, A. 82, 83, 85
People's Republic of China 69
Peters, B. G. 191–192, 268
Peters, R-M. 164
Pierre, J. 191–192
Pilet, J-B. 462–463
plurality/majority systems
    in Africa 103–107, 105t, 114–115, 114t, 115t, 117–118, 117t
    defined xviii
Poland 72, 74, 77
political culture and coalitions 452–456, 488
political fronts 133–136
political parties
    defined 100–101
    intraparty dynamics and coalitions 456–458
    mergers 137–139
    role of leaders in South Africa 247–257, 459–461
    see also mistrust of political parties
political-administrative interface see coalitions in South Africa
PR systems see proportional representation (PR) systems
preformateur/formateur xv, 326, 462, 465, 472, 514n2
presidential systems, coalitions in 69–70, 71–73, 130–131, 210–211, 261
    see also Malawi
Pridham, G. 73, 80, 83–84, 88
Prince, Truman 51–52, 53–54
proportional representation (PR) systems
    coalitions in 70, 87, 454
    defined xviii
    inclusiveness and stability 117t, 118–119
    in Lesotho 187–189
    representation and participation 113t, 114–116, 117
    in South Africa 248, 272, 507n7
    in Southern Africa 105t, 107–110, 487–488, 502n2, 502n3

Q
queenmakers see kingmakers

R
Rajbansi, Amichand 434
Ramaphosa, Cyril 196, 496
Reilly, B. 100–101, 102, 103–104, 107
rent-seeking
    in African coalitions 141, 146–151
    defined xix, 145
    in South African coalitions 19–20, 31, 382–387, 389, 484, 489–491
Renui, J. M. 81
representation, impact of electoral system and coalitions 113t, 114–116, 488
Reynolds, A. 100, 103, 110
right-wing populism in Europe 70, 77–78, 88–89, 462
    see also Germany; Italy
Ruto, William 149, 150–151, 159t, 170–174, 176
Rwanda 146

S
SACP (South African Communist Party) 29, 30t, 32–33, 57–58, 134
SAFTU (South African Federation of Trade Unions), formation 32–33
SALGA (South African Local Government Association) 271, 296–298
Salih, M. 101
Sasolburg see Metsimaholo municipality
Saulos Klause Chilima & Lazarus McCarthy Chakwera v Arthur Peter Mutharika & the Electoral Commission 104–106, 221, 225
Savage, L. 71, 73, 74, 84

Schlemmer, L. 411–412
secret ballot in no-confidence votes 253–257, 258, 506n14
Seftel, Lisa (executive director, Johannesburg transport) 278, 284
Sehnbruch, K. 86
Sejanamane, M. 189–190, 195, 197
Seychelles 105t, 110–111, 115t, 117t
Shale, V. 110, 133, 310, 467
Siavelis, P. M. 86
Singh, Narend 427, 429, 433
single-member pluralities (FPTP) xix, 70, 113t
Slovakia 72, 79, 80, 82–84
South Africa
    electoral/party system 105t, 107–110, 110, 119, 272, 503n6, 507n7
    floor-crossing 33, 115, 248–249, 404–405, 430–431, 494–495
    voter trust and participation 114t, 115t, 117t
    see also coalitions in South Africa
South African Chamber of Commerce and Industry 341
South African Cities Network 271–272, 275, 277, 283, 294
South African Communist Party (SACP) 29, 30t, 32–33, 57–58, 134
South African Federation of Trade Unions (SAFTU) 32–33
South African Local Government Association (SALGA) 271, 296–298
Southall, R. 406, 424
Spain 78–79, 81, 461–462, 463–464
Spoon, J. J. 469, 470
Sridharan, E. 75, 87
Sri Lanka 79, 87
stability of coalitions
    electoral system and 119–120
    factors influencing 4–5, 71–73, 81–84, 90–91, 110, 469–471, 483
    impact of intraparty dynamics and party leadership 85–86, 251, 456–461, 494–495
    in South Africa 17–19, 34–35, 244–246, 258, 292–293, 493
    ways to increase 259–260, 262, 464–469
    see also floor-crossing
Stellenbosch municipality 62–63
Steytler, N. 270, 350, 507n5
Strøm, K. 70, 82, 259
Svasand, L. 220

T
Tanzania
    coalitions 137, 137–139
    electoral system 104, 105t, 106
    voter trust and participation 114t, 115t, 117t
Taylor, R. 424
Teles, F. 353–354
Thabazimbi Residents Association (TRA) 49–50
Throup, D. 162, 163
tiebreakers *see* kingmakers
Tigray People's Liberation Front (Ethiopia) 134, 142
Timmermans, A. 83, 465
Tlouamma and Others v Mbethe, Speaker of the National Assembly of the Parliament of the Republic of South Africa and Another 505n4
TRA (Thabazimbi Residents Association) 49–50
Tripartite Alliance 29, 30t, 32–33, 134
Trollip, Athol 62, 368, 369–374, 378, 460
trust *see* mistrust of political parties
Tshwane metropolitan council
    coalitions in 273–275, 276, 279–280, 292–293, 508n14
    context of coalitions 274t, 336–337, 338t
    impact of ANC-DA wrangling 24–25, 245–246, 262, 333–334
    impact of coalition leadership 353–356

impact of coalitions on city
finance 283–287, 286t, 287t,
509n39, 509n41, 509n42
impact of coalitions on
corruption 287–290, 290
impact of coalitions on
governance and service delivery
281–283, 291–292, 291,
350–353, 510n48, 512n9
involvement of Gauteng High
Court 511n4-7, 512n8
life-cycle of ANC-led coalition
339, 343–350, 350t, 492
life-cycle of DA-led coalition
337–343
significance as metro 335
two-party systems, defined 102

U
UDF (United Democratic Front,
Malawi)
coalitions and governance
212–214, 216, 216–221, 217t,
226–229
electoral performance 209–210,
213t, 214t, 503n7
UDM (United Democratic
Movement)
as coalition partner 30t, 431,
459–460
coalitions in Nelson Mandela
Bay metro 363, 368–375, 492
electoral performance 16t,
309t, 364t, 425t
formation 31
*United Democratic Movement v
Speaker of the National
Assembly and Others* 250,
253–257, 506n14
United Kingdom (UK) 78, 83,
469, 470–471

V
Vanberg, G. 83, 85
Volden, C. 183, 184
voters
influence of race and ethnicity
410, 411–413
participation in elections 19,
115t, 117–118, 172
see also mistrust of political
parties

W
Weber, M. 268, 298
Western Cape
ANC-NNP coalition 26, 28,
30t, 33, 399–401, 404–405
DP/DA coalitions 400–404,
406–409
factors influencing coalition
formation 410–416
origin and nature of coalitions
in 40–42, 41t, 397–398
role of community organisations
48–49, 51–54
Western Europe 69–70, 71–73, 76–79,
80–84, 452, 469
Wolf, T. 172
women, political participation
117t, 118
Wong, C. 76, 86

Y
youth, political participation 19,
118, 172

Z
Zambia 102, 104, 105t, 114t, 115t,
117t
ZANU-PF (Zimbabwe African
National Union-Patriotic Front)
106, 113, 135, 136
Zanzibar 137, 137–139
Zille, Helen 273, 366
Zimbabwe
electoral system 104, 105t,
106, 119
opposing the dominant party
113, 131, 134–136
political participation 114t,
115t, 117t
Zuma, Jacob 255, 367, 407, 422,
435, 506n12, 514n4

Milton Keynes UK
Ingram Content Group UK Ltd.
UKHW010210030124
435363UK00004B/436